The Poetical Works of
JOHN MILTON

OXFORD UNIVERSITY PRESS
AMEN HOUSE, E.C. 4
London Edinburgh Glasgow New York
Toronto Melbourne Capetown Bombay
Calcutta Madras
HUMPHREY MILFORD
PUBLISHER TO THE UNIVERSITY

JOHN MILTON

From an engraving after the painting by Faithorne

The Poetical Works of
JOHN MILTON

Edited after the Original Texts by
H. C. BEECHING

NEW EDITION
with Translations of the Italian, Latin
and Greek Poems from
the Columbia University Edition
and a Reader's Guide by
W. SKEAT

HUMPHREY MILFORD
OXFORD UNIVERSITY PRESS
London New York Toronto

This edition of Milton's Poems was first published in 1904, and reprinted in 1906, 1908, 1910, 1912, 1914, 1916 (twice), 1919, 1922, 1925, 1928, 1930, and 1935. Translations of the Latin, Greek, and Italian poems, and the Reader's Guide were added in 1938, and reprinted in 1941.

PRINTED IN GREAT BRITAIN

O.S.A.

PREFACE.

THIS edition of Milton's Poetry is a reprint, as careful as Editor and Printers have been able to make it, from the earliest printed copies of the several poems. First the 1645 volume of the *Minor Poems* has been printed entire ; then follow in order the poems added in the reissue of 1673 ; the *Paradise Lost*, from the edition of 1667 ; and the *Paradise Regain'd* and *Samson Agonistes* from the edition of 1671.

The most interesting portion of the book must be reckoned the first section of it, which reproduces for the first time the scarce small octavo of 1645. The only reprint of the *Minor Poems* in the old spelling, so far as I know, is the one edited by Mitford, but that followed the edition of 1673, which is comparatively uninteresting since it could not have had Milton's oversight as it passed through the press. We know that it was set up from a copy of the 1645 edition, because it reproduces some pointless eccentricities such as the varying form of the chorus to Psalm cxxxvi ; but while it corrects the *errata* tabulated in that edition it commits many more blunders of its own. It is valuable, however, as the *editio princeps* of ten of the sonnets, and it contains one important alteration in the *Ode on the Nativity*. This and all other alterations will be found noted where they occur. I have not thought it necessary to note mere differences of spelling between the two editions, but a word may find place here upon their general character. Generally it may be said that, where the two editions differ, the later spelling is that now in use. Thus words like *goddess, darkness*, usually written in the first edition with one final *s*, have two, while on the other hand words like *vernall, youthfull*, and monosyllables

Preface.

like *hugg, farr*, lose their double letter. Many monosyllables, e. g. *som, cours, glimps, wher, vers, aw, els, don, ey, ly*, so written in 1645, take on in 1673 an *e* mute, while words like *harpe, windes, onely*, lose it. By a reciprocal change *ayr* and *cipress* become *air* and *cypress*; and the vowels in *daign, vail, neer, beleeve, sheild, boosom, eeven, battail, travailer*, and many other words are similarly modernized. On the other hand there are a few cases where the 1645 edition exhibits the spelling which has succeeded in fixing itself, as *travail* (1673, *travel*) in the sense of labour ; and *rob'd, profane, human, flood* and *bloody, forest, triple, alas, huddling*, are found where the 1673 edition has *roab'd, prophane, humane, floud* and *bloudy, forrest, tripple, alass* and *hudling*. Indeed the spelling in this later edition is not untouched by seventeenth century inconsistency. It retains here and there forms like *shameles, cateres*, (where 1645 reads *cateress*), and occasionally reverts to the older-fashioned spelling of monosyllables without the mute *e*. In the *Epitaph on the Marchioness of Winchester*, it reads—' And *som* flowers and *some* bays.' But undoubtedly the impression on the whole is of a much more modern text.

In the matter of small or capital letters I have followed the old copy, except in one or two places where a personification seemed not plainly enough marked to a modern reader without a capital. Thus in *Il Penseroso*, l. 49, I print *Leasure*, although both editions read *leasure*; and in the *Vacation Exercise*, l. 71, *Times* for *times*. Also where the employment or omission of a capital is plainly due to misprinting, as too frequently in the 1673 edition, I silently make the correction. Examples are, *notes* for *Notes* in Sonnet xvii. l. 13 ; *Anointed* for *anointed* in Psalm ii. l. 12.

In regard to punctuation I have followed the old printers except in obvious misprints, and followed them also, as far as possible, in their distribution of roman and italic type and in the grouping of words and lines in the various titles. To follow them exactly was impossible, as the books are so very different in size.

At this point the candid reader may perhaps ask what advantage is gained by presenting these poems to modern readers in the dress of a bygone age. If the question were put to me I should probably evade it by pointing out that Mr. Frowde is issuing an edition based upon this, in which the spelling is frankly that of to-day. But if the question were pressed, I think a sufficient answer might be found. To begin with, I should point out that even Prof. Masson, who in his excellent edition argues the point and decides in favour of modern spelling, allows that

(vi)

Preface.

'there are peculiarities of Milton's spelling which are really significant, and ought therefore to be noted or preserved.' But who is to determine exactly which words are spelt according to the poet's own instructions, and which according to the printer's whim? It is notorious that in *Paradise Lost* some words were spelt upon a deliberate system, and it may very well happen that in the volume of minor poems which the poet saw through the press in 1645, there were spellings no less systematic. Prof. Masson makes a great point of the fact that Milton's own spelling, exhibited in the autograph manuscript of some of the minor poems preserved in Trinity College, Cambridge, does not correspond with that of the printed copy[1]. This is certainly true, as the reader may see for himself by comparing the passage from the manuscript given in the appendix with the corresponding place in the text. Milton's own spelling revels in redundant *e*'s, while the printer of the 1645 book is very sparing of them. But in cases where the spelling affects the metre, we find that the printed text and Milton's manuscript closely correspond; and it is upon its value in determining the metre, quite as much as its antiquarian interest, that I should base a justification of this reprint. Take, for instance, such a line as the eleventh of *Comus*, which Prof. Masson gives as:—

> Amongst the enthroned gods on sainted seats.

A reader not learned in Miltonic rhythms will certainly read this line:

> Amongst th' enthronèd gods

But the 1645 edition reads:

> Amongst the enthron'd gods

and so does Milton's manuscript. Again, in line 597, Prof. Masson reads:

> It shall be in eternal restless change
> Self-fed and self-consumed. If this fail,
> The pillared firmament is rottenness, &c.

But the 1645 text and Milton's manuscript read *self-consum'd*;

---

[1] This manuscript, invaluable to all students of Milton, has lately been facsimiled under the superintendence of Dr. Aldis Wright, and published at the Cambridge University Press.

Preface.

after which word there is to be understood a metrical pause to mark the violent transition of the thought.

Again in the second line of the *Sonnet to a Nightingale* Prof. Masson has :

> Warblest at eve when all the woods are still

but the early edition, which probably follows Milton's spelling, though in this case we have no manuscript to compare, reads 'Warbl'st.' So the original text of *Samson*, l. 670, has 'temper'st.'

The retention of the old system of punctuation may be less defensible, but I have retained it because it may now and then be of use in determining a point of syntax. The absence of a comma, for example, after the word *hearse* in the 58th line of the *Epitaph on the Marchioness of Winchester*, printed by Prof. Masson thus :—

> And some flowers, and some bays
> For thy hearse. to strew thy ways,

but in the 1645 edition :—

> And som Flowers, and som Bays,
> For thy Hears to strew the ways,

goes to prove that *for* here must be taken as *'fore*.

Of the *Paradise Lost* there were two editions issued during Milton's lifetime, and while the first has been taken as our text, all the variants in the second, not being simple misprints, have been recorded in the notes. In one respect, however, in the distribution of the poem into twelve books instead of ten, it has seemed best, for the sake of practical convenience, to follow the second edition. A word may be allowed here on the famous correction among the *Errata* prefixed to the first edition ; 'Lib. 2. v. 414, for *we* read *wee*.' This correction shows not only that Milton had theories about spelling, but also that he found means, though his sight was gone, to ascertain whether his rules had been carried out by his printer ; and in itself this fact justifies a facsimile reprint. What the principle in the use of the double vowel exactly was (and it is found to affect the other monosyllabic pronouns) it is not so easy to discover, though roughly it is clear the reduplication was intended to mark emphasis. For example, in the speech of the Divine Son after the battle in heaven (vi. 810–817) the pronouns which the voice would naturally emphasize are spelt with the double vowel :

Preface.

> Stand onely and behold
> Gods indignation on these Godless pourd
> By mee; not you but mee they have despis'd,
> Yet envied; against mee is all thir rage,
> Because the Father, t'whom in Heav'n supream
> Kingdom and Power and Glorie appertains,
> Hath honourd me according to his will.
> Therefore to mee thir doom he hath assig'n'd.

In the Son's speech offering himself as Redeemer (iii. 227–249) where the pronoun all through is markedly emphasized, it is printed *mee* the first four times, and afterwards *me*; but it is noticeable that these first four times the emphatic word does not stand in the stressed place of the verse, so that a careless reader might not emphasize it, unless his attention were specially called by some such sign:

> Behold mee then, mee for him, life for life
> I offer, on mee let thine anger fall;
> Account mee man.

In the *Hymn of Creation* (v. 160–209) where *ye* occurs fourteen times, the emphasis and the metrical stress six times out of seven coincide, and the pronoun is spelt *yee*; where it is unemphatic, and in an unstressed place, it is spelt *ye*. Two lines are especially instructive:

> Speak yee who best can tell, ye Sons of light   (l. 160);

and

> Fountains and yee, that warble, as ye flow,
> Melodious murmurs, warbling tune his praise   (l. 195).

In v. 694 it marks, as the voice by its emphasis would mark in reading, a change of subject:

> So spake the false Arch-Angel, and infus'd
> Bad influence into th' unwarie brest
> Of his Associate; *hee* (*i. e.* the associate) together calls, &c.

An examination of other passages, where there is no antithesis, goes to show that the lengthened form of the pronoun is most frequent before a pause (as vii. 95); or at the end of a line (i. 245, 257); or when a foot is inverted (v. 133); or when as object it precedes its verb (v. 612; vii. 747), or as subject follows it (ix. 1109; x. 4). But as we might expect under circumstances where a purist could not correct his own proofs, there are not a few inconsistencies. There does not seem, for example, any special emphasis in the second *we* of the following passage:

> Freely we serve.
> Because *wee* freely love, as in our will
> To love or not; in this we stand or fall   (v. 538).

(ix)

Preface.

On the other hand, in the passage (iii. 41) in which the poet speaks of his own blindness :

> Thus with the Year
> Seasons return, but not to me returns
> Day, &c.

where, if anywhere, we should expect *mee*, we do not find it, though it occurs in the speech eight lines below. It should be added that this differentiation of the pronouns is not found in any printed poem of Milton's before *Paradise Lost*, nor is it found in the Cambridge autograph. In that manuscript the constant forms are *me, wee, yee*. There is one place where there is a difference in the spelling of *she*, and it is just possible that this may not be due to accident. In the first verse of the song in *Arcades*, the MS. reads :

> This, this is *shee* ;

and in the third verse :

> This, this is *she* alone.

This use of the double vowel is found a few times in *Paradise Regain'd*; in ii. 259 and iv. 486, 497 where *mee* begins a line, and in iv. 638 where *hee* is specially emphatic in the concluding lines of the poem. In *Samson Agonistes* it is more frequent (*e. g.* lines 124, 178, 193, 220, 252, 290, 1125). Another word the spelling of which in *Paradise Lost* will be observed to vary is the pronoun *their*, which is spelt sometimes *thir*. The spelling in the Cambridge manuscript is uniformly *thire*, except once when it is *thir*; and where *their* once occurs in the writing of an amanuensis the *e* is struck through. That the difference is not merely a printer's device to accommodate his line may be seen by a comparison of lines 358 and 363 in the First Book, where the shorter word comes in the shorter line. It is probable that the lighter form of the word was intended to be used when it was quite unemphatic. Contrast, for example, in Book iii. l. 59 :

> His own works and *their* works at once to view

with line 113 :

> *Thir* maker and *thir* making and *thir* Fate.

But the use is not consistent, and the form *thir* is not found at all till the 349th line of the First Book. The distinction is kept up in the *Paradise Regain'd* and *Samson Agonistes*, but, if possible, with even less consistency. Such passages, however, as *Paradise Regain'd*, iii. 414–440 ; *Samson Agonistes*, 880–890, are certainly

Preface.

spelt upon a method, and it is noticeable that in the choruses the lighter form is universal.

Paradise Regain'd and *Samson Agonistes* were published in 1671, and no further edition was called for in the remaining three years of the poet's lifetime, so that in the case of these poems there are no new readings to record; and the texts were so carefully revised, that only one fault (*Paradise Regain'd*, ii. 309) was left for correction later. In these and the other poems I have corrected the misprints catalogued in the tables of *Errata*, and I have silently corrected any other unless it might be mistaken for a various reading, when I have called attention to it in a note. Thus I have not recorded such blunders as *Letbian* for *Lesbian* in the 1645 text of *Lycidas*, line 63; or *hallow* for *hollow* in *Paradise Lost*, vi. 484; but I have noted *content* for *concent*, in *At a Solemn Musick*, line 6.

In conclusion I have to offer my sincere thanks to all who have collaborated with me in preparing this Edition; to the Delegates of the Oxford Press for allowing me to undertake it and decorate it with so many facsimiles; to the Controller of the Press for his unfailing courtesy; to the printers and printer's reader for their care and pains. Coming nearer home I cannot but acknowledge the help I have received in looking over proof-sheets from my sister, Mrs. P. A. Barnett, who has ungrudgingly put at the service of this book both time and eyesight. In taking leave of it, I may be permitted to say that it has cost more of both these inestimable treasures than I had anticipated. The last proof reaches me just a year after the first, and the progress of the work has not in the interval been interrupted. *In tenui labor et tenuis gloria.* Nevertheless I cannot be sorry it was undertaken.

H. C. B.

Yattendon Rectory.
November 8, 1899.

CONTENTS.

MISCELLANEOUS POEMS—

	PAGE
ON THE MORNING OF CHRISTS NATIVITY	1
THE HYMN	2
A PARAPHRASE ON PSALM 114	9
PSALM 136	9
THE PASSION	12
ON TIME	14
UPON THE CIRCUMCISION	14
AT A SOLEMN MUSICK	15
AN EPITAPH ON THE MARCHIONESS OF WINCHESTER	16
SONG ON MAY MORNING	18
ON SHAKESPEAR. 1630	18
ON THE UNIVERSITY CARRIER	19
ANOTHER ON THE SAME	19
L'ALLEGRO	20
IL PENSEROSO	24
SONNETS (I–X)	28–32
ARCADES	33
LYCIDAS	37
A MASKE PRESENTED AT LUDLOW CASTLE, 1634	43

POEMS ADDED IN THE 1673 EDITION—

ON THE DEATH OF A FAIR INFANT	76
AT A VACATION EXERCISE	79
THE FIFTH ODE OF HORACE. LIB. I	82
SONNETS (XI–XIX)	82–86
SONNET—On the new forcers of Conscience under the Long Parliament	86
SONNET—On the Lord Gen. Fairfax at the seige of Colchester	87
„ To the Lord Generall Cromwell May 1652	88
„ To Sʳ Henry Vane the younger	88
„ To Mr. Cyriack Skinner upon his Blindness	89

Contents.

	PAGE
PSALMS I–VIII. Done into Verse, 1653	89–96
„ LXXX–LXXXVIII. Done into Metre, 1648 . .	97–110
PASSAGES TRANSLATED IN THE PROSE WRITINGS	111
ADDRESSES TO MILTON	117
ELEGIARUM LIBER	122
SYLVARUM LIBER	143

PARADISE LOST—

Book	I	.	.	.	.	.	.	.	.	.	.	181
„	II	.	.	.	.	.	.	.	.	.	.	201
„	III	.	.	.	.	.	.	.	.	.	.	227
„	IV	.	.	.	.	.	.	.	.	.	.	246
„	V	.	.	.	.	.	.	.	.	.	.	272
„	VI	.	.	.	.	.	.	.	.	.	.	295
„	VII	.	.	.	.	.	.	.	.	.	.	318
„	VIII	.	.	.	.	.	.	.	.	.	.	334
„	IX	.	.	.	.	.	.	.	.	.	.	351
„	X	.	.	.	.	.	.	.	.	.	.	381
„	XI	.	.	.	.	.	.	.	.	.	.	409
„	XII	.	.	.	.	.	.	.	.	.	.	432

PARADISE REGAIN'D—

Book	I	.	.	.	.	.	.	.	.	.	.	451
„	II	.	.	.	.	.	.	.	.	.	.	464
„	III	.	.	.	.	.	.	.	.	.	.	476
„	IV	.	.	.	.	.	.	.	.	.	.	487

SAMSON AGONISTES 503

APPENDIXES—

I (*a*). Specimen of Milton's spelling, from Cambridge autograph
MS. 553
(*b*). Note of a few readings from the same . . . 554
(*c*). Erratum 554

II. TRANSLATIONS OF THE ITALIAN, LATIN, AND GREEK POEMS . 557

A READER'S GUIDE TO MILTON, *by* W. SKEAT . . 607

INDEX OF FIRST LINES 677

POEMS

OF
Mr. *John Milton*,

BOTH
ENGLISH and LATIN,
Compos'd at several times.

Printed by his true Copies.

The S o n g s were set in Musick by
Mr. H E N R Y L A W E S Gentleman of
the K I N G S Chappel, and one
of His M A I E S T I E S
Private Musick.

——*Baccare frontem*
Cingite, ne vati noceat mala lingua futuro,
Virgil, Eclog. 7.

Printed and publish'd according to
ORDER.

LONDON,
Printed by *Ruth Raworth* for *Humphrey Moseley*,
and are to be sold at the signe of the Princes
Arms in S. *Pauls* Church-yard. 1645.

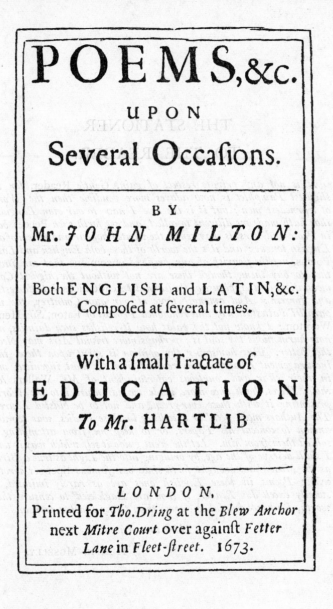

POEMS, &c.

UPON

Several Occasions.

BY

Mr. *JOHN MILTON:*

Both ENGLISH and LATIN, &c.
Composed at several times.

With a small Tractate of

EDUCATION
To Mr. HARTLIB

LONDON,
Printed for *Tho.* Dring at the *Blew Anchor*
next *Mitre Court* over against *Fetter
Lane* in *Fleet-street.* 1673.

THE STATIONER
TO THE READER.

It is not any private respect of gain, Gentle Reader, for the slightest Pamphlet is now adayes more vendible then the Works of learnedest men ; but it is the love I have to our own Language that hath made me diligent to collect, and set forth such Peeces both in Prose and Vers as may renew the wonted honour and esteem of our English tongue : and it's the worth of these both English and Latin Poems, not the flourish of any prefixed encomions that can invite thee to buy them, though these are not without the highest Commendations and Applause of the learnedst Academicks, both domestick and forrein : And amongst those of our own Countrey, the unparallel'd attestation of that renowned Provost of Eaton, Sir Henry Wootton : I know not thy palat how it relishes such dainties, nor how harmonious thy soul is ; perhaps more trivial Airs may please thee better. But howsoever thy opinion is spent upon these, that incouragement I have already received from the most ingenious men in their clear and courteous entertainment of Mr. Wallers late choice Peeces, hath once more made me adventure into the World, presenting it with these ever-green, and not to be blasted Laurels. The Authors more peculiar excellency in these studies, was too well known to conceal his Papers, or to keep me from attempting to sollicit them from him. Let the event guide it self which way it will, I shall deserve of the age, by bringing into the Light as true a Birth, as the Muses have brought forth since our famous Spencer wrote ; whose Poems in these English ones are as rarely imitated, as sweetly excell'd. Reader, if thou art Eagle-eied to censure their worth, I am not fearful to expose them to thy exactest perusal.

Thine to command

HUMPH. MOSELEY.

MISCELLANEOUS POEMS.

On the Morning of CHRISTS Nativity.

Compos'd 1629.

I

THIS is the Month, and this the happy morn
Wherin the Son of Heav'ns eternal King,
Of wedded Maid, and Virgin Mother born,
Our great redemption from above did bring;
For so the holy sages once did sing,
  That he our deadly forfeit should release,
And with his Father work us a perpetual peace.

II

That glorious Form, that Light unsufferable,
And that far-beaming blaze of Majesty,
Wherwith he wont at Heav'ns high Councel-Table,   10
To sit the midst of Trinal Unity,
He laid aside; and here with us to be,
  Forsook the Courts of everlasting Day,
And chose with us a darksom House of mortal Clay.

III

Say Heav'nly Muse, shall not thy sacred vein
Afford a present to the Infant God?
Hast thou no vers, no hymn, or solemn strein,
To welcom him to this his new abode,
Now while the Heav'n by the Suns team untrod,
  Hath took no print of the approching light,   20
And all the spangled host keep watch in squadrons bright?

IV

See how from far upon the Eastern rode
The Star-led Wisards haste with odours sweet,
O run, prevent them with thy humble ode,
And lay it lowly at his blessed feet;
Have thou the honour first, thy Lord to greet,
   And joyn thy voice unto the Angel Quire,
From out his secret Altar toucht with hallow'd fire.

The Hymn.

I

IT was the Winter wilde,
While the Heav'n-born-childe,   30
   All meanly wrapt in the rude manger lies;
Nature in aw to him
Had doff't her gawdy trim,
   With her great Master so to sympathize:
It was no season then for her
To wanton with the Sun her lusty Paramour.

II

Only with speeches fair
She woo's the gentle Air
   To hide her guilty front with innocent Snow,
And on her naked shame,   40
Pollute with sinfull blame,
   The Saintly Vail of Maiden white to throw,
Confounded, that her Makers eyes
Should look so neer upon her foul deformities.

III

But he her fears to cease,
Sent down the meek-eyd Peace,
   She crown'd with Olive green, came softly sliding
Down through the turning sphear
His ready Harbinger,
   With Turtle wing the amorous clouds dividing,   50
And waving wide her mirtle wand,
She strikes a universall Peace through Sea and Land.

  (2)

The Hymn.

IV

No War, or Battails sound
Was heard the World around,
   The idle spear and shield were high up hung;
The hooked Chariot stood
Unstain'd with hostile blood,
   The Trumpet spake not to the armed throng,
And Kings sate still with awfull eye,
As if they surely knew their sovran Lord was by.   60

V

But peacefull was the night
Wherin the Prince of light
   His raign of peace upon the earth began:
The Windes with wonder whist,
Smoothly the waters kist,
   Whispering new joyes to the milde Ocean,
Who now hath quite forgot to rave,
While Birds of Calm sit brooding on the charmed wave.

VI

The Stars with deep amaze
Stand fixt in stedfast gaze,   70
   Bending one way their pretious influence,
And will not take their flight,
For all the morning light,
   Or *Lucifer* that often warn'd them thence;
But in their glimmering Orbs did glow,
Untill their Lord himself bespake, and bid them go.

VII

And though the shady gloom
Had given day her room,
   The Sun himself with-held his wonted speed,
And hid his head for shame,   80
As his inferiour flame,
   The new enlightn'd world no more should need;
He saw a greater Sun appear
Then his bright Throne, or burning Axletree could bear.

VIII

The Shepherds on the Lawn,
Or ere the point of dawn,
   Sate simply chatting in a rustick row;
Full little thought they than,
That the mighty *Pan*
   Was kindly com to live with them below;   90
Perhaps their loves, or els their sheep,
Was all that did their silly thoughts so busie keep.

IX

When such musick sweet
Their hearts and ears did greet,
   As never was by mortall finger strook,
Divinely-warbled voice
Answering the stringed noise,
   As all their souls in blisfull rapture took :
The Air such pleasure loth to lose,
With thousand echo's still prolongs each heav'nly close.

X

Nature that heard such sound   101
Beneath the hollow round
   Of *Cynthia's* seat, the Airy region thrilling,
Now was almost won
To think her part was don,
   And that her raign had here its last fulfilling ;
She knew such harmony alone
Could hold all Heav'n and Earth in happier union.

XI

At last surrounds their sight
A Globe of circular light,   110
   That with long beams the shame-fac't night array'd,
The helmed Cherubim
And sworded Seraphim,
   Are seen in glittering ranks with wings displaid,
Harping in loud and solemn quire,
With unexpressive notes to Heav'ns new-born Heir.

(4)

The Hymn.

XII

Such Musick (as 'tis said)
Before was never made,
   But when of old the sons of morning sung,
While the Creator Great   120
His constellations set,
   And the well-ballanc't world on hinges hung,
And cast the dark foundations deep,
And bid the weltring waves their oozy channel keep.

XIII

Ring out ye Crystall sphears,
Once bless our human ears,
   (If ye have power to touch our senses so)
And let your silver chime
Move in melodious time ;
   And let the Base of Heav'ns deep Organ blow,   130
And with your ninefold harmony
Make up full consort to th'Angelike symphony.

XIV

For if such holy Song
Enwrap our fancy long,
   Time will run back, and fetch the age of gold,
And speckl'd vanity
Will sicken soon and die,
   And leprous sin will melt from earthly mould,
And Hell it self will pass away,
And leave her dolorous mansions to the peering day.   140

XV

Yea Truth, and Justice then
Will down return to men,
   Th'enameld *Arras* of the Rain-bow wearing,
And Mercy set between,
Thron'd in Celestiall sheen,
   With radiant feet the tissued clouds down stearing,
And Heav'n as at som festivall,
Will open wide the Gates of her high Palace Hall.

143-4 Orb'd in a Rain-bow ; and like glories wearing
      Mercy will sit between *1673*

XVI

But wisest Fate sayes no,
This must not yet be so,   150
   The Babe lies yet in smiling Infancy,
That on the bitter cross
Must redeem our loss;
   So both himself and us to glorifie:
Yet first to those ychain'd in sleep,
The wakefull trump of doom must thunder through the deep,

XVII

With such a horrid clang
As on mount *Sinai* rang
   While the red fire, and smouldring clouds out brake:
The aged Earth agast   160
With terrour of that blast,
   Shall from the surface to the center shake,
When at the worlds last session,
The dreadfull Judge in middle Air shall spread his throne.

XVIII

And then at last our bliss
Full and perfect is,
   But now begins; for from this happy day
Th'old Dragon under ground
In straiter limits bound,
   Not half so far casts his usurped sway,   170
And wrath to see his Kingdom fail,
Swindges the scaly Horrour of his foulded tail.

XIX

The Oracles are dumm,
No voice or hideous humm
   Runs through the arched roof in words deceiving.
Apollo from his shrine
Can no more divine,
   With hollow shreik the steep of *Delphos* leaving.
No nightly trance, or breathed spell,
Inspire's the pale-ey'd Priest from the prophetic cell.   180

  (6)

The Hymn.

XX

The lonely mountains o're,
And the resounding shore,
  A voice of weeping heard, and loud lament;
From haunted spring, and dale
Edg'd with poplar pale,
  The parting Genius is with sighing sent,
With flowre-inwov'n tresses torn
The Nimphs in twilight shade of tangled thickets mourn.

XXI

In consecrated Earth,
And on the holy Hearth,   190
  The *Lars*, and *Lemures* moan with midnight plaint,
In Urns, and Altars round,
A drear, and dying sound
  Affrights the *Flamins* at their service quaint;
And the chill Marble seems to sweat,
While each peculiar power forgoes his wonted seat.

XXII

Peor, and *Baalim*,
Forsake their Temples dim,
  With that twise-batter'd god of *Palestine*,
And mooned *Ashtaroth*,   200
Heav'ns Queen and Mother both,
  Now sits not girt with Tapers holy shine,
The Libyc *Hammon* shrinks his horn,
In vain the *Tyrian* Maids their wounded *Thamuz* mourn.

XXIII

And sullen *Moloch* fled,
Hath left in shadows dred,
  His burning Idol all of blackest hue,
In vain with Cymbals ring,
They call the grisly king,
  In dismall dance about the furnace blue;   210
The brutish gods of *Nile* as fast,
Isis and *Orus*, and the Dog *Anubis* hast.

(7)

XXIV

Nor is *Osiris* seen
In *Memphian* Grove, or Green,
    Trampling the unshowr'd Grasse with lowings loud:
Nor can he be at rest
Within his sacred chest,
    Naught but profoundest Hell can be his shroud,
In vain with Timbrel'd Anthems dark
The sable-stoled Sorcerers bear his worshipt Ark.   220

XXV

He feels from *Juda's* Land
The dredded Infants hand,
    The rayes of *Bethlehem* blind his dusky eyn;
Nor all the gods beside,
Longer dare abide,
    Not *Typhon* huge ending in snaky twine:
Our Babe to shew his Godhead true,
Can in his swadling bands controul the damned crew.

XXVI

So when the Sun in bed,
Curtain'd with cloudy red,   230
    Pillows his chin upon an Orient wave,
The flocking shadows pale,
Troop to th'infernall jail,
    Each fetter'd Ghost slips to his severall grave,
And the yellow-skirted *Fayes*,
Fly after the Night-steeds, leaving their Moon-lov'd maze.

XXVII

But see the Virgin blest,
Hath laid her Babe to rest.
    Time is our tedious Song should here have ending,
Heav'ns youngest teemed Star,   240
Hath fixt her polisht Car,
    Her sleeping Lord with Handmaid Lamp attending:
And all about the Courtly Stable,
Bright-harnest Angels sit in order serviceable.

Psalms.

A Paraphrase on *Psalm* 114.

This and the following *Psalm* were don
by the Author at fifteen yeers old.

WHEN the blest seed of *Terah's* faithfull Son,
After long toil their liberty had won,
And past from *Pharian* fields to *Canaan* Land,
Led by the strength of the Almighties hand,
Jehovah's wonders were in *Israel* shown,
His praise and glory was in *Israel* known.
That saw the troubl'd Sea, and shivering fled,
And sought to hide his froth-becurled head
Low in the earth, *Jordans* clear streams recoil,
As a faint host that hath receiv'd the foil.   10
The high, huge-bellied Mountains skip like Rams
Amongst their Ews, the little Hills like Lambs.
Why fled the Ocean? And why skipt the Mountains?
Why turned *Jordan* toward his Crystall Fountains?
Shake earth, and at the presence be agast
Of him that ever was, and ay shall last,
That glassy flouds from rugged rocks can crush,
And make soft rills from fiery flint-stones gush.

Psalm 136.

LET us with a gladsom mind
Praise the Lord, for he is kind,
  For his mercies ay endure,
  Ever faithfull, ever sure.

Let us blaze his Name abroad,
For of gods he is the God;
  For, *&c.*

O let us his praises tell,
That doth the wrathfull tyrants quell.   10
  For, *&c.*

That with his miracles doth make
Amazed Heav'n and Earth to shake.
  For, *&c.*

Psalm 136. 10, 13 That] who *1673*

(9)

That by his wisdom did create
The painted Heav'ns so full of state.
   For, *&c.*   20

That did the solid Earth ordain
To rise above the watry plain.
   For, *&c.*

That by his all-commanding might,
Did fill the new-made world with light.
   For, *&c.*

And caus'd the Golden-tressed Sun,
All the day long his cours to run.
   For, *&c.*   30

The horned Moon to shine by night,
Amongst her spangled sisters bright.
   For, *&c.*

He with his thunder-clasping hand,
Smote the first-born of *Egypt* Land.
   For, *&c.*   40

And in despight of *Pharao* fell,
He brought from thence his *Israel.*
   For, *&c.*

The ruddy waves he cleft in twain,
Of the *Erythræan* main.
   For, *&c.*

The floods stood still like Walls of Glass,
While the Hebrew Bands did pass.
   For, *&c.*   50

But full soon they did devour
The Tawny King with all his power.
   For, *&c.*

His chosen people he did bless
In the wastfull Wildernes.
   For, *&c.*   60

17, 21, 25 That] who *1673*

Psalm 136.

In bloody battail he brought down
Kings of prowess and renown.
   For, *&c.*

He foild bold *Seon* and his host,
That rul'd the *Amorrean* coast.
   For, *&c.*

And large-lim'd *Og* he did subdue,
With all his over hardy crew.
   For, *&c.*   70

And to his Servant *Israel*,
He gave their Land therin to dwell.
   For, *&c.*

He hath with a piteous eye
Beheld us in our misery.
   For, *&c.*   80

And freed us from the slavery
Of the invading enimy.
   For, *&c.*

All living creatures he doth feed,
And with full hand supplies their need.
   For, *&c.*

Let us therfore warble forth
His mighty Majesty and worth.
   For, *&c.*   90

That his mansion hath on high
Above the reach of mortall ey.
    For his mercies ay endure,
    Ever faithfull, ever sure.

Miscellaneous Poems.

The Passion.

I

ERE-while of Musick, and Ethereal mirth,
Wherwith the stage of Ayr and Earth did ring,
And joyous news of heav'nly Infants birth,
My muse with Angels did divide to sing;
But headlong joy is ever on the wing,
    In Wintry solstice like the shortn'd light
Soon swallow'd up in dark and long out-living night.

II

For now to sorrow must I tune my song,
And set my Harpe to notes of saddest wo,
Which on our dearest Lord did sease er'e long,   10
Dangers, and snares, and wrongs, and worse then so,
Which he for us did freely undergo.
    Most perfect *Heroe*, try'd in heaviest plight
Of labours huge and hard, too hard for human wight.

III

He sov'ran Priest stooping his regall head
That dropt with odorous oil down his fair eyes,
Poor fleshly Tabernacle entered,
His starry front low-rooft beneath the skies;
O what a Mask was there, what a disguise!
    Yet more; the stroke of death he must abide,   20
Then lies him meekly down fast by his Brethrens side.

IV

These latter scenes confine my roving vers,
To this Horizon is my *Phoebus* bound,
His Godlike acts, and his temptations fierce,
And former sufferings other where are found;
Loud o're the rest *Cremona's* Trump doth sound;
    Me softer airs befit, and softer strings
Of Lute, or Viol still, more apt for mournful things.

22 latter] latest *1673*

(12)

The Passion.

V

Befriend me night best Patroness of grief,
Over the Pole thy thickest mantle throw,   30
And work my flatter'd fancy to belief,
That Heav'n and Earth are colour'd with my wo;
My sorrows are too dark for day to know:
    The leaves should all be black wheron I write,
And letters where my tears have washt a wannish white.

VI

See see the Chariot, and those rushing wheels,
That whirl'd the Prophet up at *Chebar* flood,
My spirit som transporting *Cherub* feels,
To bear me where the Towers of *Salem* stood,
Once glorious Towers, now sunk in guiltles blood;   40
    There doth my soul in holy vision sit
In pensive trance, and anguish, and ecstatick fit.

VII

Mine eye hath found that sad Sepulchral rock
That was the Casket of Heav'ns richest store,
And here though grief my feeble hands up-lock,
Yet on the softned Quarry would I score
My plaining vers as lively as before;
    For sure so well instructed are my tears,
That they would fitly fall in order'd Characters.

VIII

Or should I thence hurried on viewles wing,   50
Take up a weeping on the Mountains wilde,
The gentle neighbourhood of grove and spring
Would soon unboosom all their Echoes milde,
And I (for grief is easily beguild)
    Might think th'infection of my sorrows loud,
Had got a race of mourners on som pregnant cloud.

This Subject the Author finding to be above the yeers he had,
*   when he wrote it, and nothing satisfi'd with what was*
*   begun, left it unfinisht.*

Miscellaneous Poems.

On Time.

FLY envious *Time*, till thou run out thy race,
Call on the lazy leaden-stepping hours,
Whose speed is but the heavy Plummets pace;
And glut thy self with what thy womb devours,
Which is no more then what is false and vain,
And meerly mortal dross;
So little is our loss,
So little is thy gain.
For when as each thing bad thou hast entomb'd,
And last of all, thy greedy self consum'd,   10
Then long Eternity shall greet our bliss
With an individual kiss;
And Joy shall overtake us as a flood,
When every thing that is sincerely good
And perfectly divine,
With Truth, and Peace, and Love shall ever shine
About the supreme Throne
Of him, t'whose happy-making sight alone,
When once our heav'nly-guided soul shall clime,
Then all this Earthy grosnes quit,   20
Attir'd with Stars, we shall for ever sit,
  Triumphing over Death, and Chance, and thee O Time.

Upon the Circumcision.

YE flaming Powers, and winged Warriours bright,
That erst with Musick, and triumphant song
First heard by happy watchful Shepherds ear,
So sweetly sung your Joy the Clouds along
Through the soft silence of the list'ning night;
Now mourn, and if sad share with us to bear
Your fiery essence can distill no tear,
Burn in your sighs, and borrow
Seas wept from our deep sorrow,
He who with all Heav'ns heraldry whileare   10
Enter'd the world, now bleeds to give us ease;
Alas, how soon our sin
  Sore doth begin
    His Infancy to sease!

At a Solemn Musick.

O more exceeding love or law more just?
Just law indeed, but more exceeding love!
For we by rightfull doom remediles
Were lost in death, till he that dwelt above
High thron'd in secret bliss, for us frail dust
Emptied his glory, ev'n to nakednes;   20
And that great Cov'nant which we still transgress
Intirely satisfi'd,
And the full wrath beside
Of vengeful Justice bore for our excess,
And seals obedience first with wounding smart
This day, but O ere long
Huge pangs and strong
    Will pierce more neer his heart.

At a Solemn Musick.

BLEST pair of *Sirens*, pledges of Heav'ns joy,
Sphear-born harmonious Sisters, Voice, and Vers,
Wed your divine sounds, and mixt power employ
Dead things with inbreath'd sense able to pierce,
And to our high-rais'd phantasie present,
That undisturbed Song of pure content,
Ay sung before the saphire-colour'd throne
To him that sits theron
With Saintly shout, and solemn Jubily,
Where the bright Seraphim in burning row   10
Their loud up-lifted Angel trumpets blow,
And the Cherubick host in thousand quires
Touch their immortal Harps of golden wires,
With those just Spirits that wear victorious Palms,
Hymns devout and holy Psalms
Singing everlastingly;
That we on Earth with undiscording voice
May rightly answer that melodious noise;
As once we did, till disproportion'd sin
Jarr'd against natures chime, and with harsh din   20
Broke the fair musick that all creatures made
To their great Lord, whose love their motion sway'd

6 content] concent *1673*

(15)

In perfect Diapason, whilst they stood
In first obedience, and their state of good.
O may we soon again renew that Song,
And keep in tune with Heav'n, till God ere long
To his celestial consort us unite,
To live with him, and sing in endles morn of light.

An Epitaph on the Marchioness of *Winchester.*

THIS rich Marble doth enterr
The honour'd Wife of *Winchester*,
A Vicounts daughter, an Earls heir,
Besides what her vertues fair
Added to her noble birth,
More then she could own from Earth.
Summers three times eight save one
She had told, alas too soon,
After so short time of breath,
To house with darknes, and with death.　　10
Yet had the number of her days
Bin as compleat as was her praise,
Nature and fate had had no strife
In giving limit to her life.
Her high birth, and her graces sweet,
Quickly found a lover meet;
The Virgin quire for her request
The God that sits at marriage feast;
He at their invoking came
But with a scarce-wel-lighted flame;　　20
And in his Garland as he stood,
Ye might discern a Cipress bud.
Once had the early Matrons run
To greet her of a lovely son,
And now with second hope she goes,
And calls *Lucina* to her throws;
But whether by mischance or blame
Atropos for *Lucina* came;

And with remorsles cruelty,
Spoil'd at once both fruit and tree :   30
The haples Babe before his birth
Had burial, yet not laid in earth,
And the languisht Mothers Womb
Was not long a living Tomb.
So have I seen som tender slip
Sav'd with care from Winters nip,
The pride of her carnation train,
Pluck't up by som unheedy swain,
Who onely thought to crop the flowr
New shot up from vernall showr ;   40
But the fair blossom hangs the head
Side-ways as on a dying bed,
And those Pearls of dew she wears,
Prove to be presaging tears
Which the sad morn had let fall
On her hast'ning funerall.
Gentle Lady may thy grave
Peace and quiet ever have ;
After this thy travail sore
Sweet rest sease thee evermore,   50
That to give the world encrease,
Shortned hast thy own lives lease ;
Here besides the sorrowing
That thy noble House doth bring,
Here be tears of perfect moan
Weept for thee in *Helicon*,
And som Flowers, and som Bays,
For thy Hears to strew the ways,
Sent thee from the banks of *Came*,
Devoted to thy vertuous name ;   60
Whilst thou bright Saint high sit'st in glory,
Next her much like to thee in story,
That fair *Syrian* Shepherdess,
Who after yeers of barrennes,
The highly favour'd *Joseph* bore
To him that serv'd for her before,
And at her next birth much like to thee,
Through pangs fled to felicity,
Far within the boosom bright
Of blazing Majesty and Light,   70

Miscellaneous Poems.

There with thee, new welcom Saint,
Like fortunes may her soul acquaint,
With thee there clad in radiant sheen,
No Marchioness, but now a Queen.

SONG
On *May* morning.

Now the bright morning Star, Dayes harbinger,
Comes dancing from the East, and leads with her
The Flowry *May*, who from her green lap throws
The yellow Cowslip, and the pale Primrose.
    Hail bounteous *May* that dost inspire
    Mirth and youth, and warm desire,
    Woods and Groves, are of thy dressing,
    Hill and Dale, doth boast thy blessing.
Thus we salute thee with our early Song,
And welcom thee, and wish thee long.   10

On *Shakespear.* 1630.

WHAT needs my *Shakespear* for his honour'd Bones,
The labour of an age in piled Stones,
Or that his hallow'd reliques should be hid
Under a Star-ypointing *Pyramid?*
Dear son of memory, great heir of Fame,
What need'st thou such weak witnes of thy name?
Thou in our wonder and astonishment
Hast built thy self a live-long Monument.
For whilst to th'shame of slow-endeavouring art,
Thy easie numbers flow, and that each heart   10
Hath from the leaves of thy unvalu'd Book,
Those Delphick lines with deep impression took,
Then thou our fancy of it self bereaving,
Dost make us Marble with too much conceaving;
And so Sepulcher'd in such pomp dost lie,
That Kings for such a Tomb would wish to die.

On *Shakespear. Reprinted 1632 in the second folio Shakespeare:* Title]
An epitaph on the admirable dramaticke poet W. Shakespeare   1 needs]
neede   6 weak] dull   8 live-long] lasting   10 heart] part   13 it] her

On the University Carrier.

On the University Carrier who
sickn'd in the time of his vacancy, being
forbid to go to *London*, by reason of
the Plague.

HERE lies old· *Hobson*, Death hath broke his girt,
And here alas, hath laid him in the dirt,
Or els the ways being foul, twenty to one,
He's here stuck in a slough, and overthrown.
'Twas such a shifter, that if truth were known,
Death was half glad when he had got him down;
For he had any time this ten yeers full,
Dodg'd with him, betwixt *Cambridge* and the Bull.
And surely, Death could never have prevail'd,
Had not his weekly cours of carriage fail'd;   10
But lately finding him so long at home,
And thinking now his journeys end was come,
And that he had tane up his latest Inne,
In the kind office of a Chamberlin
Shew'd him his room where he must lodge that night,
Pull'd off his Boots, and took away the light:
If any ask for him, it shall be sed,
Hobson has supt, and's newly gon to bed.

Another on the same.

HERE lieth one who did most truly prove,
That he could never die while he could move,
So hung his destiny never to rot
While he might still jogg on, and keep his trot,
Made of sphear-metal, never to decay
Untill his revolution was at stay.
Time numbers motion, yet (without a crime
'Gainst old truth) motion number'd out his time:
And like an Engin mov'd with wheel and waight,
His principles being ceast, he ended strait.   10
Rest that gives all men life, gave him his death,
And too much breathing put him out of breath;

(19)

Nor were it contradiction to affirm
Too long vacation hastned on his term.
Meerly to drive the time away he sickn'd,
Fainted, and died, nor would with Ale be quickn'd;
Nay, quoth he, on his swooning bed out-stretch'd,
If I may not carry, sure Ile ne're be fetch'd,
But vow though the cross Doctors all stood hearers,
For one Carrier put down to make six bearers. 20
Ease was his chief disease, and to judge right,
He di'd for heavines that his Cart went light,
His leasure told him that his time was com,
And lack of load, made his life burdensom,
That even to his last breath (ther be that say't)
As he were prest to death, he cry'd more waight;
But had his doings lasted as they were,
He had bin an immortall Carrier.
Obedient to the Moon he spent his date
In cours reciprocal, and had his fate 30
Linkt to the mutual flowing of the Seas,
Yet (strange to think) his wain was his increase:
His Letters are deliver'd all and gon,
Onely remains this superscription.

L'Allegro.

HENCE loathed Melancholy
Of *Cerberus*, and blackest midnight born,
In *Stygian* Cave forlorn
'Mongst horrid shapes, and shreiks, and sights unholy,
Find out som uncouth cell,
Where brooding darknes spreads his jealous wings,
And the night-Raven sings;
There under *Ebon* shades, and low-brow'd Rocks,
As ragged as thy Locks,
In dark *Cimmerian* desert ever dwell. 10
But com thou Goddes fair and free,
In Heav'n ycleap'd *Euphrosyne*,
And by men, heart-easing Mirth,
Whom lovely *Venus* at a birth
With two sister Graces more
To Ivy-crowned *Bacchus* bore;

L'Allegro.

Or whether (as som Sager sing)
The frolick Wind that breathes the Spring,
Zephir with *Aurora* playing,
As he met her once a Maying,   20
There on Beds of Violets blew,
And fresh-blown Roses washt in dew,
Fill'd her with thee a daughter fair,
So bucksom, blith, and debonair.
Haste thee nymph, and bring with thee
Jest and youthful Jollity,
Quips and Cranks, and wanton Wiles,
Nods, and Becks, and Wreathed Smiles,
Such as hang on *Hebe's* cheek,
And love to live in dimple sleek ;   30
Sport that wrincled Care derides,
And Laughter holding both his sides.
Com, and trip it as ye go
On the light fantastick toe,
And in thy right hand lead with thee,
The Mountain Nymph, sweet Liberty ;
And if I give thee honour due,
Mirth, admit me of thy crue
To live with her, and live with thee,
In unreproved pleasures free ;   40
To hear the Lark begin his flight,
And singing startle the dull night,
From his watch-towre in the skies,
Till the dappled dawn doth rise ;
Then to com in spight of sorrow,
And at my window bid good morrow,
Through the Sweet-Briar, or the Vine,
Or the twisted Eglantine.
While the Cock with lively din,
Scatters the rear of darknes thin,   50
And to the stack, or the Barn dore,
Stoutly struts his Dames before,
Oft list'ning how the Hounds and horn
Chearly rouse the slumbring morn,
From the side of som Hoar Hill,
Through the high wood echoing shrill.

33 ye] you *1673*

(21)

Som time walking not unseen
By Hedge-row Elms, on Hillocks green,
Right against the Eastern gate,
Wher the great Sun begins his state,   60
Rob'd in flames, and Amber light,
The clouds in thousand Liveries dight.
While the Plowman neer at hand,
Whistles ore the Furrow'd Land,
And the Milkmaid singeth blithe,
And the Mower whets his sithe,
And every Shepherd tells his tale
Under the Hawthorn in the dale.
Streit mine eye hath caught new pleasures
Whilst the Lantskip round it measures,   70
Russet Lawns, and Fallows Gray,
Where the nibling flocks do stray,
Mountains on whose barren brest
The labouring clouds do often rest:
Meadows trim with Daisies pide,
Shallow Brooks, and Rivers wide.
Towers, and Battlements it sees
Boosom'd high in tufted Trees,
Wher perhaps som beauty lies,
The Cynosure of neighbouring eyes.   80
Hard by, a Cottage chimney smokes,
From betwixt two aged Okes,
Where *Corydon* and *Thyrsis* met,
Are at their savory dinner set
Of Hearbs, and other Country Messes,
Which the neat-handed *Phillis* dresses;
And then in haste her Bowre she leaves,
With *Thestylis* to bind the Sheaves;
Or if the earlier season lead
To the tann'd Haycock in the Mead,   90
Som times with secure delight
The up-land Hamlets will invite,
When the merry Bells ring round,
And the jocond rebecks sound
To many a youth, and many a maid,
Dancing in the Chequer'd shade;
And young and old com forth to play
On a Sunshine Holyday,

L'Allegro.

Till the live-long day-light fail,
Then to the Spicy Nut-brown Ale,   100
With stories told of many a feat,
How *Faery Mab* the junkets eat,
She was pincht, and pull'd she sed,
And he by Friars Lanthorn led
Tells how the drudging *Goblin* swet,
To ern his Cream-bowle duly set,
When in one night, ere glimps of morn,
His shadowy Flale hath thresh'd the Corn
That ten day-labourers could not end,
Then lies him down the Lubbar Fend.   110
And stretch'd out all the Chimney's length,
Basks at the fire his hairy strength ;
And Crop-full out of dores he flings,
Ere the first Cock his Mattin rings.
Thus don the Tales, to bed they creep,
By whispering Windes soon lull'd asleep.
Towred Cities please us then,
And the busie humm of men,
Where throngs of Knights and Barons bold,
In weeds of Peace high triumphs hold,   120
With store of Ladies, whose bright eies
Rain influence, and judge the prise
Of Wit, or Arms, while both contend
To win her Grace, whom all commend.
There let *Hymen* oft appear
In Saffron robe, with Taper clear,
And pomp, and feast, and revelry,
With mask, and antique Pageantry,
Such sights as youthfull Poets dream
On Summer eeves by haunted stream.   130
Then to the well-trod stage anon,
If *Jonsons* learned Sock be on,
Or sweetest *Shakespear* fancies childe,
Warble his native Wood-notes wilde,
And ever against eating Cares,
Lap me in soft *Lydian* Aires,
Married to immortal verse
Such as the meeting soul may pierce

104 And he by] And by the *1673*

(23)

In notes, with many a winding bout
Of lincked sweetnes long drawn out,   140
With wanton heed, and giddy cunning,
The melting voice through mazes running;
Untwisting all the chains that ty
The hidden soul of harmony.
That *Orpheus* self may heave his head
From golden slumber on a bed
Of heapt *Elysian* flowres, and hear
Such streins as would have won the ear
Of *Pluto*, to have quite set free
His half regain'd *Eurydice*.   150
These delights, if thou canst give,
Mirth with thee, I mean to live.

Il Penseroso.

HENCE vain deluding joyes,
      The brood of folly without father bred,
How little you bested,
      Or fill the fixed mind with all your toyes;
Dwell in som idle brain,
      And fancies fond with gaudy shapes possess,
As thick and numberless
      As the gay motes that people the Sun Beams,
Or likest hovering dreams
      The fickle Pensioners of *Morpheus* train.   10
But hail thou Goddes, sage and holy,
Hail divinest Melancholy,
Whose Saintly visage is too bright
To hit the Sense of human sight;
And therfore to our weaker view,
Ore laid with black staid Wisdoms hue.
Black, but such as in esteem,
Prince *Memnons* sister might beseem,
Or that Starr'd *Ethiope* Queen that strove
To set her beauties praise above   20
The Sea Nymphs, and their powers offended.
Yet thou art higher far descended,

(24)

Il Penseroso.

Thee bright-hair'd *Vesta* long of yore,
To solitary *Saturn* bore;
His daughter she (in *Saturns* raign,
Such mixture was not held a stain)
Oft in glimmering Bowres, and glades
He met her, and in secret shades
Of woody *Ida's* inmost grove,
While yet there was no fear of *Jove.*   30
Com pensive Nun, devout and pure,
Sober, stedfast, and demure,
All in a robe of darkest grain,
Flowing with majestick train,
And sable stole of *Cipres* Lawn,
Over thy decent shoulders drawn.
Com, but keep thy wonted state,
With eev'n step, and musing gate,
And looks commercing with the skies,
Thy rapt soul sitting in thine eyes: 40
There held in holy passion still,
Forget thy self to Marble, till
With a sad Leaden downward cast,
Thou fix them on the earth as fast.
And joyn with thee calm Peace, and Quiet,
Spare Fast, that oft with gods doth diet,
And hears the Muses in a ring,
Ay round about *Joves* Altar sing.
And adde to these retired Leasure,
That in trim Gardens takes his pleasure;   50
But first, and chiefest, with thee bring,
Him that yon soars on golden wing,
Guiding the fiery-wheeled throne,
The Cherub Contemplation,
And the mute Silence hist along,
'Less *Philomel* will daign a Song,
In her sweetest, saddest plight,
Smoothing the rugged brow of night,
While *Cynthia* checks her Dragon yoke,
Gently o're th'accustom'd Oke;   60
Sweet Bird that shunn'st the noise of folly,
Most musicall, most melancholy!
Thee Chauntress oft the Woods among,
I woo to hear thy eeven-Song;

And missing thee, I walk unseen
On the dry smooth-shaven Green,
To behold the wandring Moon,
Riding neer her highest noon,
Like one that had bin led astray
Through the Heav'ns wide pathles way ;　　　70
And oft, as if her head she bow'd,
Stooping through a fleecy cloud.
Oft on a Plat of rising ground,
I hear the far-off *Curfeu* sound,
Over som wide-water'd shoar,
Swinging slow with sullen roar ;
Or if the Ayr will not permit,
Som still removed place will fit,
Where glowing Embers through the room
Teach light to counterfeit a gloom,　　　80
Far from all resort of mirth,
Save the Cricket on the hearth,
Or the Belmans drousie charm,
To bless the dores from nightly harm :
Or let my Lamp at midnight hour,
Be seen in som high lonely Towr,
Where I may oft out-watch the *Bear*,
With thrice great *Hermes*, or unsphear
The spirit of *Plato* to unfold
What Worlds, or what vast Regions hold　　　90
The immortal mind that hath forsook
Her mansion in this fleshly nook :
And of those *Dæmons* that are found
In fire, air, flood, or under ground,
Whose power hath a true consent
With Planet, or with Element.
Som time let Gorgeous Tragedy
In Scepter'd Pall com sweeping by,
Presenting *Thebs*, or *Pelops* line,
Or the tale of *Troy* divine.　　　100
Or what (though rare) of later age,
Ennobled hath the Buskind stage.
But, O sad Virgin, that thy power
Might raise *Musæus* from his bower,
Or bid the soul of *Orpheus* sing
Such notes as warbled to the string,

Drew Iron tears down *Pluto's* cheek,
And made Hell grant what Love did seek.
Or call up him that left half told
The story of *Cambuscan* bold,   110
Of *Camball*, and of *Algarsife*,
And who had *Canace* to wife,
That own'd the vertuous Ring and Glass,
And of the wondrous Hors of Brass,
On which the *Tartar* King did ride ;
And if ought els, great *Bards* beside,
In sage and solemn tunes have sung,
Of Turneys and of Trophies hung ;
Of Forests, and inchantments drear,
Where more is meant then meets the ear. 120
Thus night oft see me in thy pale career,
Till civil-suited Morn appeer,
Not trickt and frounc't as she was wont,
With the Attick Boy to hunt,
But Chercheft in a comly Cloud.
While rocking Winds are Piping loud,
Or usher'd with a shower still,
When the gust hath blown his fill,
Ending on the russling Leaves,
With minute drops from off the Eaves. 130
And when the Sun begins to fling
His flaring beams, me Goddes bring
To arched walks of twilight groves,
And shadows brown that *Sylvan* loves
Of Pine, or monumental Oake,
Where the rude Ax with heaved stroke,
Was never heard the Nymphs to daunt,
Or fright them from their hallow'd haunt.
There in close covert by som Brook,
Where no profaner eye may look,   140
Hide me from Day's garish eie,
While the Bee with Honied thie,
That at her flowry work doth sing,
And the Waters murmuring
With such consort as they keep,
Entice the dewy-feather'd Sleep ;
And let som strange mysterious dream,
Wave at his Wings in Airy stream,

(27)

Of lively portrature display'd,
Softly on my eye-lids laid.   150
And as I wake, sweet musick breath
Above, about, or underneath,
Sent by som spirit to mortals good,
Or th'unseen Genius of the Wood.
But let my due feet never fail,
To walk the studious Cloysters pale,
And love the high embowed Roof,
With antick Pillars massy proof,
And storied Windows richly dight,
Casting a dimm religious light.   160
There let the pealing Organ blow,
To the full voic'd Quire below,
In Service high, and Anthems cleer,
As may with sweetnes, through mine ear,
Dissolve me into extasies,
And bring all Heav'n before mine eyes.
And may at last my weary age
Find out the peacefull hermitage,
The Hairy Gown and Mossy Cell,
Where I may sit and rightly spell   170
Of every Star that Heav'n doth shew,
And every Herb that sips the dew;
Till old experience do attain
To somthing like Prophetic strain.
These pleasures *Melancholy* give,
And I with thee will choose to live.

SONNETS.

I

O Nightingale, that on yon bloomy Spray
    Warbl'st at eeve, when all the Woods are still,
    Thou with fresh hope the Lovers heart dost fill,
    While the jolly hours lead on propitious *May*,
Thy liquid notes that close the eye of Day,
    First heard before the shallow Cuccoo's bill
    Portend success in love; O if *Jove's* will
    Have linkt that amorous power to thy soft lay,

(28)

Now timely sing, ere the rude Bird of Hate
   Foretell my hopeles doom in som Grove ny: 10
   As thou from yeer to yeer hast sung too late
For my relief; yet hadst no reason why,
   Whether the Muse, or Love call thee his mate,
   Both them I serve, and of their train am I.

II

Donna leggiadra il cui bel nome honora
   L'herbosa val di Rheno, e il nobil varco,
   Ben è colui d'ogni valore scarco
   Qual tuo spirto gentil non innamora,
Che dolcemente mostra si di fuora
   De suoi atti soavi giamai parco,
   E i don', che son d'amor saette ed arco,
   La onde l'alta tua virtù s'infiora.
Quando tu vaga parli, o lieta canti
   Che mover possa duro alpestre legno,   10
   Guardi ciascun a gli occhi, ed a gli orecchi
L'entrata, chi di te si truova indegno;
   Gratia sola di sù gli vaglia, inanti
   Che'l disio amoroso al cuor s'invecchi.

III

Qual in colle aspro, al imbrunir di sera
   L'avezza giovinetta pastorella
   Va bagnando l'herbetta strana e bella
   Che mal si spande a disusata spera
Fuor di sua natia alma primavera,
   Cosi Amor meco insù la lingua snella
   Desta il fior novo di strania favella,
   Mentre io di te, vezzosamente altera,
Canto, dal mio buon popol non inteso
   E'l bel Tamigi cangio col bel Arno.   10
   Amor lo volse, ed io a l'altrui peso
Seppi ch' Amor cosa mai volse indarno.
   Deh! foss' il mio cuor lento e'l duro seno
   A chi pianta dal ciel si buon terreno.

(29)

Canzone.

Ridonsi donne e giovani amorosi
M' accostandosi attorno, e perche scrivi,
Perche tu scrivi in lingua ignota e strana
Verseggiando d'amor, e come t'osi?
Dinne, se la tua speme sia mai vana,
E de pensieri lo miglior t' arrivi;
Cosi mi van burlando, altri rivi
Altri lidi t' aspettan, & altre onde
Nelle cui verdi sponde
Spuntati ad hor, ad hor a la tua chioma   10
L'immortal guiderdon d'eterne frondi
Perche alle spalle tue soverchia soma?
*   Canzon dirotti, e tu per me rispondi*
Dice mia Donna, e'l suo dir, è il mio cuore
Questa è lingua di cui si vanta Amore.

IV

Diodati, e te'l dirò con maraviglia,
*   Quel ritroso io ch'amor spreggiar soléa*
*   E de suoi lacci spesso mi ridéa*
*   Gia caddi, ov'huom dabben talhor s'impiglia.*
Ne treccie d'oro, ne guancia vermiglia,
*   M' abbaglian sì, ma sotto nova idea*
*   Pellegrina bellezza che'l cuor bea,*
*   Portamenti alti honesti, e nelle ciglia*
Quel sereno fulgor d' amabil nero,
*   Parole adorne di lingua piu d'una,*   10
*   E'l cantar che di mezzo l'hemispero*
Traviar ben può la faticosa Luna,
*   E degli occhi suoi auventa si gran fuoco*
*   Che l'incerar gli orecchi mi fia poco.*

V

Per certo i bei vostr'occhi Donna mia
*   Esser non puo che non fian lo mio sole*
*   Si mi percuoton forte, come ei suole*
*   Per l'arene di Libia chi s'invia,*

(30)

Sonnets.

Mentre un caldo vapor (ne sentì pria)
  Da quel lato si spinge ove mi duole,
  Che forse amanti nelle lor parole
  Chiaman sospir; io non so che si sia:
Parte rinchiusa, e turbida si cela
  Scosso mi il petto, e poi n'uscendo poco   10
  Quivi d' attorno o s'agghiaccia, o s'ingiela;
Ma quanto a gli occhi giunge a trovar loco
  Tutte le notti a me suol far piovose
  Finche mia Alba rivien colma di rose.

VI

Giovane piano, e semplicetio amante
  Poi che fuggir me stesso in dubbio sono,
  Madonna a voi del mio cuor l'humil dono
  Farò divoto; io certo a prove tante
L'hebbi fedele, intrepido, costante,
  De pensieri leggiadro, accorto, e buono;
  Quando rugge il gran mondo, e scocca il tuono,
  S'arma di se, e d' intero diamante,
Tanto del forse, e d' invidia sicuro,
  Di timori, e speranze al popol use   10
  Quanto d'ingegno, e d' alto valor vago,
E di cetra sonora, e delle muse:
  Sol troverete in tal parte men duro
  Ove amor mise l'insanabil ago.

VII

How soon hath Time the suttle theef of youth,
  Stoln on his wing my three and twentith yeer!
  My hasting dayes flie on with full career,
  But my late spring no bud or blossom shew'th.
Perhaps my semblance might deceive the truth,
  That I to manhood am arriv'd so near,
  And inward ripenes doth much less appear,
  That som more timely-happy spirits indu'th.
Yet be it less or more, or soon or slow,
  It shall be still in strictest measure eev'n,   10
  To that same lot, however mean, or high,
Toward which Time leads me, and the will of Heav'n;
  All is, if I have grace to use it so,
  As ever in my great task Masters eye.

Miscellaneous Poems.

VIII

Captain or Colonel, or Knight in Arms,
   Whose chance on these defenceless dores may sease,
   If ever deed of honour did thee please,
  Guard them, and him within protect from harms,
He can requite thee, for he knows the charms
   That call Fame on such gentle acts as these,
   And he can spred thy Name o're Lands and Seas,
  What ever clime the Suns bright circle warms.
Lift not thy spear against the Muses Bowre,
   The great *Emathian* Conqueror bid spare   10
   The house of *Pindarus*, when Temple and Towre
  Went to the ground: And the repeated air
   Of sad *Electra's* Poet had the power
   To save th' *Athenian* Walls from ruine bare. ·

IX

Lady that in the prime of earliest youth,
   Wisely hath shun'd the broad way and the green,
   And with those few art eminently seen,
  That labour up the Hill of heav'nly Truth,
The better part with *Mary* and with *Ruth*,
   Chosen thou hast, and they that overween,
   And at thy growing vertues fret their spleen,
  No anger find in thee, but pity and ruth.
Thy care is fixt and zealously attends
   To fill thy odorous Lamp with deeds of light,   10
   And Hope that reaps not shame. Therefore be sure
  Thou, when the Bridegroom with his feastfull friends
   Passes to bliss at the mid hour of night,
   Hast gain'd ᵗhy entrance, Virgin wise and pure.

X

Daughter to that good Earl, once President
   Of *Englands* Counsel, and her Treasury,
   Who liv'd in both, unstain'd with gold or fee,
  And left them both, more in himself content,
  Till the sad breaking of that Parlament

VIII. Camb. autograph supplies title, *When the assault was intended to the city*   3 If deed of honour did thee ever please, *1673.*
   IX. 5 with *Ruth*⌉ the *Ruth 1645.*
   X. Camb. autograph supplies title, *To the Lady Margaret Ley.*

(32)

Arcades.

Broke him, as that dishonest victory
At *Chæronéa*, fatal to liberty
Kil'd with report that Old man eloquent,
Though later born, then to have known the dayes
Wherin your Father flourisht, yet by you   10
Madam, me thinks I see him living yet;
So well your words his noble vertues praise,
That all both judge you to relate them true,
And to possess them, Honour'd *Margaret*.

Arcades.

Part of an entertainment presented to the Countess Dowager of *Darby*
at *Harefield*, by som Noble persons of her Family, who appear
on the Scene in pastoral habit, moving toward the
seat of State with this Song.

1. *SONG.*

Look Nymphs, and Shepherds look,
What sudden blaze of majesty
Is that which we from hence descry
Too divine to be mistook:
   This this is she
To whom our vows and wishes bend,
Heer our solemn search hath end.

Fame that her high worth to raise,
Seem'd erst so lavish and profuse,
We may justly now accuse   10
Of detraction from her praise,
   Less then half we find exprest,
   Envy bid conceal the rest.

Mark what radiant state she spreds,
In circle round her shining throne,
Shooting her beams like silver threds,
This this is she alone,
   Sitting like a Goddes bright,
   In the center of her light.

Might she the wise *Latona* be,
Or the towred *Cybele*,   20
Mother of a hunderd gods;
Juno dare's not give her odds;
  Who had thought this clime had held
  A deity so unparalel'd?

As they com forward, the genius of the Wood appears, and
turning toward them, speaks.

Gen. Stay gentle Swains, for though in this disguise,
I see bright honour sparkle through your eyes,
Of famous *Arcady* ye are, and sprung
Of that renowned flood, so often sung,
Divine *Alpheus*, who by secret sluse,   30
Stole under Seas to meet his *Arethuse*;
And ye the breathing Roses of the Wood,
Fair silver-buskind Nymphs as great and good,
I know this quest of yours, and free intent
Was all in honour and devotion ment
To the great Mistres of yon princely shrine,
Whom with low reverence I adore as mine,
And with all helpful service will comply
To further this nights glad solemnity;
And lead ye where ye may more neer behold   40
What shallow-searching *Fame* hath left untold;
Which I full oft amidst these shades alone
Have sate to wonder at, and gaze upon:
For know by lot from *Jove* I am the powr
Of this fair Wood, and live in Oak'n bowr,
To nurse the Saplings tall, and curl the grove
With Ringlets quaint, and wanton windings wove.
And all my Plants I save from nightly ill,
Of noisom winds, and blasting vapours chill.
And from the Boughs brush off the evil dew,   50
And heal the harms of thwarting thunder blew,
Or what the cross dire-looking Planet smites,
Or hurtfull Worm with canker'd venom bites.
When Eev'ning gray doth rise, I fetch my round
Over the mount, and all this hallow'd ground,
And early ere the odorous breath of morn
Awakes the slumbring leaves, or tasseld horn

(34)

Arcades.

Shakes the high thicket, haste I all about,
Number my ranks, and visit every sprout
With puissant words, and murmurs made to bless, 60
But els in deep of night when drowsines
Hath lockt up mortal sense, then listen I
To the celestial *Sirens* harmony,
That sit upon the nine enfolded Sphears,
And sing to those that hold the vital shears,
And turn the Adamantine spindle round,
On which the fate of gods and men is wound.
Such sweet compulsion doth in musick ly,
To lull the daughters of *Necessity*,
And keep unsteddy Nature to her law, 70
And the low world in measur'd motion draw
After the heavenly tune, which none can hear
Of human mould with grosse unpurged ear;
And yet such musick worthiest were to blaze
The peerles height of her immortal praise,
Whose lustre leads us, and for her most fit,
If my inferior hand or voice could hit
Inimitable sounds, yet as we go,
What ere the skill of lesser gods can show,
I will assay, her worth to celebrate, 80
And so attend ye toward her glittering state;
Where ye may all that are of noble stemm
Approach, and kiss her sacred vestures hemm.

2. SONG.

O're the smooth enameld green
Where no print of step hath been,
    Follow me as I sing,
    And touch the warbled string.
Under the shady roof
Of branching Elm Star-proof,
    Follow me, 90
I will bring you where she sits
Clad in splendor as befits
    Her deity.
Such a rural Queen
All *Arcadia* hath not seen.

3. *SONG.*

Nymphs and Shepherds dance no more
 By sandy *Ladons* Lillied banks.
On old *Lycæus* or *Cyllene* hoar,
 Trip no more in twilight ranks,
Though *Erymanth* your loss deplore,
 A better soyl shall give ye thanks.
From the stony *Mænalus*,
Bring your Flocks, and live with us,
Here ye shall have greater grace,
To serve the Lady of this place.
 Though *Syrinx* your *Pans* Mistres were,
 Yet *Syrinx* well might wait on her.
  Such a rural Queen
  All *Arcadia* hath not seen.

100

JUSTA
EDOVARDO KING
naufrago,
ab
Amicis mœrentibus,
amoris
&

μνείας χάειν.

Si rectè calculum ponas, ubique naufragium est.
Pet. Arb.

CANTABRIGIÆ:

Apud *Thomam Buck,* & *Rogerum Daniel,* celeberrimæ
Academiæ typographos. 1638.

Miscellaneous Poems.

Lycidas.

In this Monody the Author bewails a learned Friend, unfortunatly drown'd
in his Passage from *Chester* on the *Irish* Seas, 1637. And by
occasion foretels the ruine of our corrupted Clergy
then in their height.

YET once more, O ye Laurels, and once more
Ye Myrtles brown, with Ivy never-sear,
I com to pluck your Berries harsh and crude,
And with forc'd fingers rude,
Shatter your leaves before the mellowing year.
Bitter constraint, and sad occasion dear,
Compels me to disturb your season due:
For *Lycidas* is dead, dead ere his prime
Young *Lycidas*, and hath not left his peer:
Who would not sing for *Lycidas?* he knew   10
Himself to sing, and build the lofty rhyme.
He must not flote upon his watry bear
Unwept, and welter to the parching wind,
Without the meed of som melodious tear.
  Begin then, Sisters of the sacred well,
That from beneath the seat of *Jove* doth spring,
Begin, and somwhat loudly sweep the string.
Hence with denial vain, and coy excuse,
So may som gentle Muse
With lucky words favour my destin'd Urn,   20
And as he passes turn,
And bid fair peace be to my sable shroud.
For we were nurst upon the self-same hill,
Fed the same flock, by fountain, shade, and rill.
  Together both, ere the high Lawns appear'd
Under the opening eye-lids of the morn,
We drove a field, and both together heard
What time the Gray-fly winds her sultry horn,
Batt'ning our flocks with the fresh dews of night,
Oft till the Star that rose, at Ev'ning, bright   30
Toward Heav'ns descent had slop'd his westering wheel.
Mean while the Rural ditties were not mute,
Temper'd to th'Oaten Flute;
Rough *Satyrs* danc'd, and *Fauns* with clov'n heel,

Lycidas.

From the glad sound would not be absent long,
And old *Damœtas* lov'd to hear our song.

But O the heavy change, now thou art gon,
Now thou art gon, and never must return!
Thee Shepherd, thee the Woods, and desert Caves,
With wilde Thyme and the gadding Vine o'regrown,   40
And all their echoes mourn.
The Willows, and the Hazle Copses green,
Shall now no more be seen,
Fanning their joyous Leaves to thy soft layes.
As killing as the Canker to the Rose,
Or Taint-worm to the weanling Herds that graze,
Or Frost to Flowers, that their gay wardrop wear,
When first the White thorn blows;
Such, *Lycidas*, thy loss to Shepherds ear.

Where were ye Nymphs when the remorseless deep
Clos'd o're the head of your lov'd *Lycidas?*   51
For neither were ye playing on the steep,
Where your old *Bards*, the famous *Druids* ly,
Nor on the shaggy top of *Mona* high,
Nor yet where *Deva* spreads her wisard stream:
Ay me, I fondly dream!
Had ye bin there—for what could that have don?
What could the Muse her self that *Orpheus* bore,
The Muse her self, for her inchanting son
Whom Universal nature did lament,   60
When by the rout that made the hideous roar,
His goary visage down the stream was sent,
Down the swift *Hebrus* to the *Lesbian* shore.

Alas! What boots it with uncessant care
To tend the homely slighted Shepherds trade,
And strictly meditate the thankles Muse,
Were it not better don as others use,
To sport with *Amaryllis* in the shade,
Or with the tangles of *Neæra's* hair?
Fame is the spur that the clear spirit doth raise   70
(That last infirmity of Noble mind)
To scorn delights, and live laborious dayes;
But the fair Guerdon when we hope to find,
And think to burst out into sudden blaze,
Comes the blind *Fury* with th'abhorred shears,
And slits the thin spun life. But not the praise,

Phœbus repli'd, and touch'd my trembling ears;
Fame is no plant that grows on mortal soil,
Nor in the glistering foil
Set off to th'world, nor in broad rumour lies, 80
But lives and spreds aloft by those pure eyes,
And perfet witnes of all judging *Jove*;
As he pronounces lastly on each deed,
Of so much fame in Heav'n expect thy meed.

    O Fountain *Arethuse*, and thou honour'd floud,
Smooth-sliding *Mincius*, crown'd with vocall reeds,
That strain I heard was of a higher mood:
But now my Oate proceeds,
And listens to the Herald of the Sea
That came in *Neptune's* plea, 90
He ask'd the Waves, and ask'd the Fellon winds,
What hard mishap hath doom'd this gentle swain?
And question'd every gust of rugged wings
That blows from off each beaked Promontory,
They knew not of his story,
And sage *Hippotades* their answer brings,
That not a blast was from his dungeon stray'd,
The Ayr was calm, and on the level brine,
Sleek *Panope* with all her sisters play'd.
It was that fatall and perfidious Bark 100
Built in th'eclipse, and rigg'd with curses dark,
That sunk so low that sacred head of thine.

    Next *Camus*, reverend Sire, went footing slow,
His Mantle hairy, and his Bonnet sedge,
Inwrought with figures dim, and on the edge
Like to that sanguine flower inscrib'd with woe.
Ah; Who hath reft (quoth he) my dearest pledge?
Last came, and last did go,
The Pilot of the *Galilean* lake,
Two massy Keyes he bore of metals twain, 110
(The Golden opes, the Iron shuts amain)
He shook his Miter'd locks, and stern bespake,
How well could I have spar'd for thee, young swain,
Anow of such as for their bellies sake,
Creep and intrude, and climb into the fold?
Of other care they little reck'ning make,
Then how to scramble at the shearers feast,
And shove away the worthy bidden guest.

Lycidas.

Blind mouthes! that scarce themselves know how to hold
A Sheep-hook, or have learn'd ought els the least   120
That to the faithfull Herdmans art belongs!
What recks it them? What need they? They are sped;
And when they list, their lean and flashy songs
Grate on their scrannel Pipes of wretched straw,
The hungry Sheep look up, and are not fed,
But swoln with wind, and the rank mist they draw,
Rot inwardly, and foul contagion spread:
Besides what the grim Woolf with privy paw
Daily devours apace, and nothing sed,
But that two-handed engine at the door,   130
Stands ready to smite once, and smite no more.
   Return *Alpheus,* the dread voice is past,
That shrunk thy streams; Return *Sicilian* Muse,
And call the Vales, and bid them hither cast
Their Bels, and Flourets of a thousand hues.
Ye valleys low where the milde whispers use,
Of shades and wanton winds, and gushing brooks,
On whose fresh lap the swart Star sparely looks,
Throw hither all your quaint enameld eyes,
That on the green terf suck the honied showres,   140
And purple all the ground with vernal flowres.
Bring the rathe Primrose that forsaken dies.
The tufted Crow-toe, and pale Gessamine,
The white Pink, and the Pansie freakt with jeat,
The glowing Violet.
The Musk-rose, and the well attir'd Woodbine.
With Cowslips wan that hang the pensive hed,
And every flower that sad embroidery wears:
Bid *Amaranthus* all his beauty shed,
And Daffadillies fill their cups with tears,   150
To strew the Laureat Herse where *Lycid* lies.
For so to interpose a little ease,
Let our frail thoughts dally with false surmise.
Ay me! Whilst thee the shores, and sounding Seas
Wash far away, where ere thy bones are hurld,
Whether beyond the stormy *Hebrides,*
Where thou perhaps under the whelming tide
Visit'st the bottom of the monstrous world;

149 Amaranthus] Amarantus *1673*

Lycidas.

Or whether thou to our moist vows deny'd,
Sleep'st by the fable of *Bellerus* old,   160
Where the great vision of the guarded Mount
Looks toward *Namancos* and *Bayona's* hold;
Look homeward Angel now, and melt with ruth.
And, O ye *Dolphins*, waft the haples youth.

Weep no more, woful Shepherds weep no more,
For *Lycidas* your sorrow is not dead,
Sunk though he be beneath the watry floar,
So sinks the day-star in the Ocean bed,
And yet anon repairs his drooping head,
And tricks his beams, and with new spangled Ore,   170
Flames in the forehead of the morning sky:
So *Lycidas* sunk low, but mounted high,
Through the dear might of him that walk'd the waves
Where other groves, and other streams along,
With *Nectar* pure his oozy Lock's he laves,
And hears the unexpressive nuptiall Song,
In the blest Kingdoms meek of joy and love.
There entertain him all the Saints above,
In solemn troops, and sweet Societies
That sing, and singing in their glory move,   180
And wipe the tears for ever from his eyes.
Now *Lycidas* the Shepherds weep no more;
Hence forth thou art the Genius of the shore,
In thy large recompense, and shalt be good
To all that wander in that perilous flood.

Thus sang the uncouth Swain to th'Okes and rills,
While the still morn went out with Sandals gray,
He touch'd the tender stops of various Quills,
With eager thought warbling his *Dorick* lay:
And now the Sun had stretch'd out all the hills,   190
And now was dropt into the Western bay;
At last he rose, and twitch'd his Mantle blew:
To morrow to fresh Woods, and Pastures new.

A MASKE

PRESENTED

At Ludlow Castle,

1 6 3 4 :

On *Michaelmasse night*, *before the*
RIGHT HONORABLE,

IOHN *Earle of Bridgewater*, *Vicount* BRACKLY,
Lord Præsident *of* WALES, And one of
His MAIESTIES most honorable
Privie Counsell.

Eheu quid volui misero mihi ! floribus austrum
Perditus ————

LONDON

Printed for HUMPHREY ROBINSON,
at the signe of the *Three Pidgeons* in
Pauls Church-yard. 1 6 3 7.

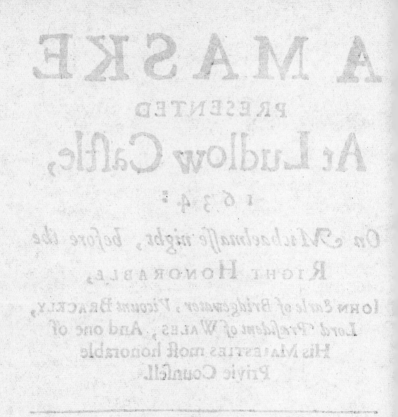

[1] To the Right Honourable, John Lord Vicount Bracly, Son and Heir apparent to the Earl of *Bridgewater*, &c.

MY LORD,

This Poem, *which receiv'd its first occasion of Birth from
your Self, and others of your Noble Family, and much honour
from your own Person in the performance, now returns again
to make a finall Dedication of it self to you. Although not openly
acknowledg'd by the Author, yet it is a legitimate off-spring, so
lovely, and so much desired, that the often Copying of it hath
tir'd my Pen to give my severall friends satisfaction, and brought
me to a necessity of producing it to the publike view ; and now to
offer it up in all rightfull devotion to those fair Hopes, and rare
Endowments of your much-promising Youth, which give a full
assurance, to all that know you, of a future excellence. Live sweet
Lord to be the honour of your Name, and receive this as your own,
from the hands of him, who hath by many favours been long oblig'd
to your most honour'd Parents, and as in this representation your
attendant* Thyrsis, *so now in all reall expression*

> *Your faithfull, and most*
> *humble Servant*
>
> H. LAWES.

[1] The Copy of a Letter writt'n by Sir HENRY WOOTTON, to the Author, upon the following Poem.

From the Colledge, this 13. *of April,* 1638.

SIR,

It was a special favour, when you lately bestowed upon
me here, the first taste of your acquaintance, though no longer
then to make me know that I wanted more time to value it, and

---

[1] Omitted in *1673*.

(45)

to enjoy it rightly; and in truth, if I could then have imagined your farther stay in these parts, which I understood afterwards by Mr. *H.* I would have been bold in our vulgar phrase to mend my draught (for you left me with an extreme thirst) and to have begged your conversation again, joyntly with your said learned Friend, at a poor meal or two, that we might have banded together som good Authors of the antient time: Among which, I observed you to have been familiar.

Since your going, you have charg'd me with new Obligations, both for a very kinde Letter from you dated the sixth of this Month, and for a dainty peece of entertainment which came therwith. Wherin I should much commend the Tragical part, if the Lyrical did not ravish me with a certain Dorique delicacy in your Songs and Odes, wherunto I must plainly confess to have seen yet nothing parallel in our Language: *Ipsa mollities*. But I must not omit to tell you, that I now onely owe you thanks for intimating unto me (how modestly soever) the true Artificer. For the work it self I had view'd som good while before, with singular delight, having receiv'd it from our common Friend Mr. *R.* in the very close of the late *R*'s Poems, Printed at *Oxford*, wherunto it was added (as I now suppose) that the Accessory might help out the Principal, according to the Art of *Stationers*, and to leave the Reader *Con la bocca dolce.*

Now Sir, concerning your travels, wherin I may chalenge a little more priviledge of Discours with you; I suppose you will not blanch *Paris* in your way; therfore I have been bold to trouble you with a few lines to Mr. *M. B.* whom you shall easily find attending the young Lord *S.* as his Governour, and you may surely receive from him good directions for the shaping of your farther journey into *Italy*, where he did reside by my choice som time for the King, after mine own recess from *Venice.*

I should think that your best Line will be thorow the whole length of *France* to *Marseilles*, and thence by Sea to *Genoa*, whence the passage into *Tuscany* is as Diurnal as a *Gravesend* Barge: I hasten as you do to *Florence*, or *Siena*, the rather to tell you a short story from the interest you have given me in your safety.

At *Siena* I was tabled in the House of one *Alberto Scipioni*, an old *Roman* Courtier in dangerous times, having bin Steward to the *Duca di Pagliano*, who with all his Family were strangled, save this onely man that escap'd by foresight of the Tempest: With him I had often much chat of those affairs; Into which he

A Mask.

took pleasure to look back from his Native Harbour; and at my departure toward *Rome* (which had been the center of his experience) I had wonn confidence enough to beg his advice, how I might carry my self securely there, without offence of others, or of mine own conscience. *Signor Arrigo mio* (sayes he) *I pensieri stretti, & il viso sciolto* will go safely over the whole World: Of which *Delphian* Oracle (for so I have found it) your judgement doth need no commentary; and therfore (Sir) I will commit you with it to the best of all securities, Gods dear love, remaining

Your Friend as much at command
as any of longer date,

Henry Wootton.

Postscript.

SIR, *I have expressly sent this my Foot-boy to prevent your departure without som acknowledgement from me of the receipt of your obliging Letter, having myself through som busines, I know not how, neglected the ordinary conveyance. In any part where I shall understand you fixed, I shall be glad, and diligent to entertain you with Home-Novelties; even for som fomentation of our friendship, too soon interrupted in the Cradle.*

The Persons.

The attendant Spirit afterwards in the habit of *Thyrsis*.
Comus with his crew.
The Lady.
1. Brother.
2. Brother.
Sabrina the Nymph.

The cheif persons which presented, were

The Lord *Bracly*,
Mr. *Thomas Egerton* his Brother,
The Lady *Alice Egerton*.

A
MASK

PRESENTED

At LUDLOW-Castle,

1634. &c.

The first Scene discovers a wilde Wood.

The attendant Spirit descends or enters.

BEFORE the starry threshold of *Joves* Court
My mansion is, where those immortal shapes
Of bright aëreal Spirits live insphear'd
In Regions milde of calm and serene Ayr,
Above the smoak and stirr of this dim spot,
Which men call Earth, and with low-thoughted care
Confin'd, and pester'd in this pin-fold here,
Strive to keep up a frail, and Feaverish being
Unmindfull of the crown that Vertue gives
After this mortal change, to her true Servants   10
Amongst the enthron'd gods on Sainted seats.
Yet som there be that by due steps aspire
To lay their just hands on that Golden Key
That ope's the Palace of Eternity:
To such my errand is, and but for such,
I would not soil these pure Ambrosial weeds,
With the rank vapours of this Sin-worn mould.
   But to my task. *Neptune* besides the sway
Of every salt Flood, and each ebbing Stream,
Took in by lot 'twixt high, and neather *Jove*,   20
Imperial rule of all the Sea-girt Iles
That like to rich, and various gemms inlay
The unadorned boosom of the Deep,
Which he to grace his tributary gods

(49)

By course commits to severall government,
And gives them leave to wear their Saphire crowns,
And weild their little tridents, but this Ile
The greatest, and the best of all the main
He quarters to his blu-hair'd deities,
And all this tract that fronts the falling Sun   30
A noble Peer of mickle trust, and power
Has in his charge, with temper'd awe to guide
An old, and haughty Nation proud in Arms :
Where his fair off-spring nurs't in Princely lore,
Are coming to attend their Fathers state,
And new-entrusted Scepter, but their way
Lies through the perplex't paths of this drear Wood,
The nodding horror of whose shady brows
Threats the forlorn and wandring Passinger.
And here their tender age might suffer perill,   40
But that by quick command from Soveran *Jove*
I was dispatcht for their defence, and guard ;
And listen why, for I will tell ye now
What never yet was heard in Tale or Song
From old, or modern Bard in Hall, or Bowr.
  Bacchus that first from out the purple Grape,
Crush't the sweet poyson of mis-used Wine
After the *Tuscan* Mariners transform'd
Coasting the *Tyrrhene* shore, as the winds listed,
On *Circes* Iland fell (who knows not *Circe*   50
The daughter of the Sun ? Whose charmed Cup
Whoever tasted, lost his upright shape,
And downward fell into a groveling Swine)
This Nymph that gaz'd upon his clustring locks,
With Ivy berries wreath'd, and his blithe youth,
Had by him, ere he parted thence, a Son
Much like his Father, but his Mother more,
Whom therfore she brought up and *Comus* nam'd,
Who ripe, and frolick of his full grown age,
Roaving the *Celtick*, and *Iberian* fields,   60
At last betakes him to this ominous Wood,
And in thick shelter of black shades imbowr'd,
Excells his Mother at her mighty Art,
Offring to every weary Travailer,

43 ye] you *1673*

(50)

His orient liquor in a Crystal Glasse,
To quench the drouth of *Phœbus*, which as they taste
(For most do taste through fond intemperate thirst)
Soon as the Potion works, their human count'nance,
Th' express resemblance of the gods, is chang'd
Into som brutish form of Woolf, or Bear,   70
Or Ounce, or Tiger, Hog, or bearded Goat,
All other parts remaining as they were,
And they, so perfect is their misery,
Not once perceive their foul disfigurement,
But boast themselves more comely then before
And all their friends, and native home forget
To roule with pleasure in a sensual stie.
Therfore when any favour'd of high *Jove*,
Chances to pass through this adventrous glade,
Swift as the Sparkle of a glancing Star,   80
I shoot from Heav'n to give him safe convoy,
As now I do: But first I must put off
These my skie robes spun out of *Iris* Wooff,
And take the Weeds and likenes of a Swain,
That to the service of this house belongs,
Who with his soft Pipe, and smooth-dittied Song,
Well knows to still the wilde winds when they roar,
And hush the waving Woods, nor of lesse faith,
And in this office of his Mountain watch,
Likeliest, and neerest to the present ayd   90
Of this occasion. But I hear the tread
Of hatefull steps, I must be viewles now.

Comus *enters with a Charming Rod in one hand, his Glass in the other, with him a rout of Monsters, headed like sundry sorts of wilde Beasts, but otherwise like Men and Women, their Apparel glistring, they com in making a riotous and unruly noise, with Torches in their hands.*

    Comus. The Star that bids the Shepherd fold,
Now the top of Heav'n doth hold,
And the gilded Car of Day,
His glowing Axle doth allay
In the steep *Atlantick* stream,
And the slope Sun his upward beam
Shoots against the dusky Pole,
Pacing toward the other gole   100
Of his Chamber in the East.
Mean while welcom Joy, and Feast,

Midnight shout, and revelry,
Tipsie dance, and Jollity.
Braid your Locks with rosie Twine
Dropping odours, dropping Wine.
Rigor now is gon to bed,
And Advice with scrupulous head,
Strict Age, and sowre Severity,
With their grave Saws in slumber ly.   110
We that are of purer fire
Imitate the Starry Quire,
Who in their nightly watchfull Sphears,
Lead in swift round the Months and Years.
The Sounds, and Seas with all their finny drove
Now to the Moon in wavering Morrice move,
And on the Tawny Sands and Shelves,
Trip the pert Fairies and the dapper Elves;
By dimpled Brook, and Fountain brim,
The Wood-Nymphs deckt with Daisies trim,   120
Their merry wakes and pastimes keep:
What hath night to do with sleep?
Night hath better sweets to prove,
Venus now wakes, and wak'ns Love.
Com let us our rights begin,
'Tis onely day-light that makes Sin
Which these dun shades will ne're report.
Hail Goddesse of Nocturnal sport
Dark vaild *Cotytto*, t' whom the secret flame
Of mid-night Torches burns; mysterious Dame   130
That ne're art call'd, but when the Dragon woom
Of Stygian darknes spets her thickest gloom,
And makes one blot of all the ayr,
Stay thy cloudy Ebon chair,
Wherin thou rid'st with *Hecat*', and befriend
Us thy vow'd Priests, til utmost end
Of all thy dues be done, and none left out,
Ere the blabbing Eastern scout,
The nice Morn on th' *Indian* steep
From her cabin'd loop hole peep,   140
And to the tel-tale Sun discry
Our conceal'd Solemnity.
Com, knit hands, and beat the ground,
In a light fantastick round.

A Mask.

Break off, break off, I feel the different pace,
Of som chast footing neer about this ground.
Run to your shrouds, within these Brakes and Trees,
Our number may affright : Som Virgin sure
(For so I can distinguish by mine Art)
Benighted in these Woods. Now to my charms,   150
And to my wily trains, I shall e're long
Be well stock't with as fair a herd as graz'd
About my Mother *Circe*. Thus I hurl
My dazling Spells into the spungy ayr,
Of power to cheat the eye with blear illusion,
And give it false presentments, lest the place
And my quaint habits breed astonishment,
And put the Damsel to suspicious flight,
Which must not be, for that's against my course ;
I under fair pretence of friendly ends,   160
And well plac't words of glozing courtesie
Baited with reasons not unplausible
Wind me into the easie-hearted man,
And hugg him into snares. When once her eye
Hath met the vertue of this Magick dust,
I shall appear som harmles Villager
Whom thrift keeps up about his Country gear,
But here she comes, I fairly step aside,
And hearken, if I may, her busines here.

The Lady enters.

This way the noise was, if mine ear be true,   170
My best guide now, me thought it was the sound
Of Riot, and ill manag'd Merriment,
Such as the jocond Flute, or gamesom Pipe
Stirs up among the loose unleter'd Hinds,
When for their teeming Flocks, and granges full
In wanton dance they praise the bounteous *Pan*,
And thank the gods amiss. I should be loath
To meet the rudenesse, and swill'd insolence
Of such late Wassailers ; yet O where els
Shall I inform my unacquainted feet   180

167 *omitted* *1673*   168, 9 *order inverted* *1673*
169 If I may, her busines here] If I may her business hear *1673 Errata.*

(53)

In the blind mazes of this tangl'd Wood?
My Brothers when they saw me wearied out
With this long way, resolving here to lodge
Under the spreading favour of these Pines,
Stept as they se'd to the next Thicket side
To bring me Berries, or such cooling fruit
As the kind hospitable Woods provide.
They left me then, when the gray-hooded Eev'n
Like a sad Votarist in Palmers weed
Rose from the hindmost wheels of *Phœbus* wain.   190
But where they are, and why they came not back,
Is now the labour of my thoughts, 'tis likeliest
They had ingag'd their wandring steps too far,
And envious darknes, e're they could return,
Had stole them from me, els O theevish Night
Why shouldst thou, but for som fellonious end,
In thy dark lantern thus close up the Stars,
That nature hung in Heav'n, and fill'd their Lamps
With everlasting oil, to give due light
To the misled and lonely Travailer?   200
This is the place, as well as I may guess,
Whence eev'n now the tumult of loud Mirth
Was rife, and perfet in my list'ning ear,
Yet nought but single darknes do I find.
What might this be? A thousand fantasies
Begin to throng into my memory
Of calling shapes, and beckning shadows dire,
And airy tongues, that syllable mens names
On Sands, and Shoars, and desert Wildernesses.
These thoughts may startle well, but not astound   210
The vertuous mind, that ever walks attended
By a strong siding champion Conscience.——
O welcom pure-ey'd Faith, white-handed Hope,
Thou hovering Angel girt with golden wings,
And thou unblemish't form of Chastity,
I see ye visibly, and now beleeve
That he, the Supreme good, t' whom all things ill
Are but as slavish officers of vengeance,
Would send a glistring Guardian if need were
To keep my life and honour unassail'd.   220
Was I deceiv'd, or did a sable cloud
Turn forth her silver lining on the night?

A Mask.

I did not err, there does a sable cloud
Turn forth her silver lining on the night,
And casts a gleam over this tufted Grove.
I cannot hallow to my Brothers, but
Such noise as I can make to be heard farthest
Ile venter, for my new enliv'nd spirits
Prompt me; and they perhaps are not far off.

. SONG.

 Sweet Echo, sweetest Nymph that liv'st unseen   230
   Within thy airy shell
  By slow Meander's *margent green,*
 And in the violet imbroider'd vale
  Where the love-lorn Nightingale
Nightly to thee her sad Song mourneth well.
Canst thou not tell me of a gentle Pair
  That likest thy Narcissus *are ?*
   O if thou have
  Hid them in som flowry Cave,
   Tell me but where   240
Sweet Queen of Parly, Daughter of the Sphear,
So maist thou be translated to the skies,
And give resounding grace to all Heav'ns Harmonies.

 Com. Can any mortal mixture of Earths mould
Breath such Divine inchanting ravishment ?
Sure somthing holy lodges in that brest,
And with these raptures moves the vocal air
To testifie his hidd'n residence ;
How sweetly did they float upon the wings
Of silence, through the empty-vaulted night   250
At every fall smoothing the Raven doune
Of darknes till it smil'd : I have oft heard
My mother *Circe* with the Sirens three,
Amid'st the flowry-kirtl'd *Naiades*
Culling their Potent hearbs, and balefull drugs,
Who as they sung, would take the prison'd soul,
And lap it in *Elysium, Scylla* wept,
And chid her barking waves into attention,
And fell *Charybdis* murmur'd soft applause :
Yet they in pleasing slumber lull'd the sense,   260
And in sweet madnes rob'd it of it self,

      (55)

But such a sacred, and home-felt delight,
Such sober certainty of waking bliss
I never heard till now. Ile speak to her
And she shall be my Queen. Hail forren wonder
Whom certain these rough shades did never breed
Unlesse the Goddes that in rurall shrine
Dwell'st here with *Pan*, or *Silvan*, by blest Song
Forbidding every bleak unkindly Fog
To touch the prosperous growth of this tall Wood.   270
  La. Nay gentle Shepherd ill is lost that praise
That is addrest to unattending Ears,
Not any boast of skill, but extreme shift
How to regain my sever'd company
Compell'd me to awake the courteous Echo
To give me answer from her mossie Couch.
  Co. What chance good Lady hath bereft you thus?
  La. Dim darknes, and this leavy Labyrinth.
  Co. Could that divide you from neer-ushering guides?
  La. They left me weary on a grassie terf.   280
  Co. By falshood, or discourtesie, or why?
  La. To seek i'th vally som cool friendly Spring.
  Co. And left your fair side all unguarded Lady?
  La. They were but twain, and purpos'd quick return.
  Co. Perhaps fore-stalling night prevented them.
  La. How easie my misfortune is to hit!
  Co. Imports their loss, beside the present need?
  La. No less then if I should my brothers loose.
  Co. Were they of manly prime, or youthful bloom?
  La. As smooth as *Hebe's* their unrazor'd lips.   290
  Co. Two such I saw, what time the labour'd Oxe
In his loose traces from the furrow came,
And the swink't hedger at his Supper sate;
I saw them under a green mantling vine
That crawls along the side of yon small hill,
Plucking ripe clusters from the tender shoots,
Their port was more then human, as they stood;
I took it for a faëry vision
Of som gay creatures of the element
That in the colours of the Rainbow live   300
And play i'th plighted clouds. I was aw-strook,
And as I past, I worshipt: if those you seek
It were a journey like the path to Heav'n,

To help you find them.   *La.* Gentle villager
What readiest way would bring me to that place?
   Co. Due west it rises from this shrubby point.
   La. To find out that, good Shepherd, I suppose,
In such a scant allowance of Star-light,
Would overtask the best Land-Pilots art,
Without the sure guess of well-practiz'd feet,   310
   Co. I know each lane, and every alley green
Dingle, or bushy dell of this wilde Wood,
And every bosky bourn from side to side
My daily walks and ancient neighbourhood,
And if your stray attendance be yet lodg'd,
Or shroud within these limits, I shall know
Ere morrow wake, or the low roosted lark
From her thatch't pallat rowse, if otherwise
I can conduct you Lady to a low
But loyal cottage, where you may be safe   320
Till further quest'.   *La.* Shepherd I take thy word,
And trust thy honest offer'd courtesie,
Which oft is sooner found in lowly sheds
With smoaky rafters, then in tapstry Halls
And Courts of Princes, where it first was nam'd,
And yet is most pretended : In a place
Less warranted then this, or less secure
I cannot be, that I should fear to change it.
Eie me blest Providence, and square my triall
To my proportion'd strength. Shepherd lead on.—— 330

The Two Brothers.

   Eld. Bro. Unmuffle ye faint stars, and thou fair Moon
That wontst to love the travailers benizon,
Stoop thy pale visage through an amber cloud,
And disinherit *Chaos*, that raigns here
In double night of darknes, and of shades ;
Or if your influence be quite damm'd up
With black usurping mists, som gentle taper
Though a rush Candle from the wicker hole
Of som clay habitation visit us
With thy long levell'd rule of streaming light,   340
And thou shalt be our star of *Arcady*,
Or *Tyrian* Cynosure. *2. Bro.* Or if our eyes
Be barr'd that happines, might we but hear

(57)

The folded flocks pen'd in their watled cotes,
Or sound of pastoral reed with oaten stops,
Or whistle from the Lodge, or village cock
Count the night watches to his feathery Dames,
'Twould be som solace yet, som little chearing
In this close dungeon of innumerous bowes.
But O that haples virgin our lost sister   350
Where may she wander now, whether betake her
From the chill dew, amongst rude burrs and thistles?
Perhaps som cold bank is her boulster now
Or 'gainst the rugged bark of som broad Elm
Leans her unpillow'd head fraught with sad fears.
What if in wild amazement, and affright,
Or while we speak within the direfull grasp
Of Savage hunger, or of Savage heat?
    Eld. Bro. Peace brother, be not over-exquisite
To cast the fashion of uncertain evils;   360
For grant they be so, while they rest unknown,
What need a man forestall his date of grief,
And run to meet what he would most avoid?
Or if they be but false alarms of Fear,
How bitter is such self-delusion?
I do not think my sister so to seek,
Or so unprincipl'd in vertues book,
And the sweet peace that goodnes boosoms ever,
As that the single want of light and noise
(Not being in danger, as I trust she is not)   370
Could stir the constant mood of her calm thoughts,
And put them into mis-becoming plight.
Vertue could see to do what vertue would
By her own radiant light, though Sun and Moon
Were in the flat Sea sunk. And Wisdoms self
Oft seeks to sweet retired Solitude,
Where with her best nurse Contemplation
She plumes her feathers, and lets grow her wings
That in the various bussle of resort
Were all to ruffl'd, and somtimes impair'd.   380
He that has light within his own cleer brest
May sit i'th center, and enjoy bright day,
But he that hides a dark soul, and foul thoughts
Benighted walks under the mid-day Sun;
Himself is his own dungeon.

2. *Bro.* Tis most true
That musing meditation most affects
The pensive secrecy of desert cell,
Far from the cheerfull haunt of men, and herds,
And sits as safe as in a Senat house,
For who would rob a Hermit of his Weeds,   390
His few Books, or his Beads, or Maple Dish,
Or do his gray hairs any violence?
But beauty like the fair Hesperian Tree
Laden with blooming gold, had need the guard
Of dragon watch with uninchanted eye,
To save her blossoms, and defend her fruit
From the rash hand of bold Incontinence.
You may as well spred out the unsun'd heaps
Of Misers treasure by an out-laws den,
And tell me it is safe, as bid me hope   400
Danger will wink on Opportunity,
And let a single helpless maiden pass
Uninjur'd in this wilde surrounding wast.
Of night, or lonelines it recks me not,
I fear the dred events that dog them both,
Lest som ill greeting touch attempt the person
Of our unowned sister.
    Eld. Bro. I do not, brother,
Inferr, as if I thought my sisters state
Secure without all doubt, or controversie:
Yet where an equall poise of hope and fear   410
Does arbitrate th'event, my nature is
That I encline to hope, rather then fear,
And gladly banish squint suspicion.
My sister is not so defenceless left
As you imagine, she has a hidden strength
Which you remember not.
    2. *Bro.* What hidden strength,
Unless the strength of Heav'n, if you mean that?
    Eld. Bro. I mean that too, but yet a hidden strength
Which if Heav'n gave it, may be term'd her own:
'Tis chastity, my brother, chastity: 420
She that has that, is clad in compleat steel,
And like a quiver'd Nymph with Arrows keen
May trace huge Forests, and unharbour'd Heaths,
Infamous Hills, and sandy perilous wildes,

Where through the sacred rayes of Chastity,
No savage fierce, Bandite, or mountaneer
Will dare to soyl her Virgin purity,
Yea there, where very desolation dwels
By grots, and caverns shag'd with horrid shades,
She may pass on with unblench't majesty,   430
Be it not don in pride, or in presumption.
Som say no evil thing that walks by night
In fog, or fire, by lake, or moorish fen,
Blew meager Hag, or stubborn unlaid ghost,
That breaks his magick chains at *curfeu* time,
No goblin, or swart faëry of the mine,
Hath hurtfull power o're true virginity.
Do ye beleeve me yet, or shall I call
Antiquity from the old Schools of Greece
To testifie the arms of Chastity?   440
Hence had the huntress *Dian* her dred bow
Fair silver-shafted Queen for ever chaste,
Wherwith she tam'd the brinded lioness
And spotted mountain pard, but set at nought
The frivolous bolt of *Cupid*, gods and men
Fear'd her stern frown, and she was queen oth' Woods.
What was that snaky-headed *Gorgon* sheild
That wise *Minerva* wore, unconquer'd Virgin,
Wherwith she freez'd her foes to congeal'd stone?
But rigid looks of Chast austerity,   450
And noble grace that dash't brute violence
With sudden adoration, and blank aw.
So dear to Heav'n is Saintly chastity,
That when a soul is found sincerely so,
A thousand liveried Angels lacky her,
Driving far off each thing of sin and guilt,
And in cleer dream, and solemn vision
Tell her of things that no gross ear can hear,
Till oft convers with heav'nly habitants
Begin to cast a beam on th'outward shape,   460
The unpolluted temple of the mind,
And turns it by degrees to the souls essence,
Till all be made immortal: but when lust
By unchaste looks, loose gestures, and foul talk,
But most by leud and lavish act of sin,
Lets in defilement to the inward parts,

The soul grows clotted by contagion,
Imbodies, and imbrutes, till she quite loose
The divine property of her first being.
Such are those thick and gloomy shadows damp   470
Oft seen in Charnell vaults, and Sepulchers
Lingering, and sitting by a new made grave,
As loath to leave the body that it lov'd,
And link't it self by carnal sensualty
To a degenerate and degraded state.
    2. Bro. How charming is divine Philosophy!
Not harsh, and crabbed as dull fools suppose,
But musical as is *Apollo's* lute,
And a perpetual feast of nectar'd sweets,
Where no crude surfet raigns. *Eld. Bro.* List, list, I hear
Som far off hallow break the silent Air.   481
    2. Bro. Me thought so too; what should it be?
    Eld. Bro. For certain
Either som one like us night-founder'd here,
Or els som neighbour Wood-man, or at worst,
Som roaving Robber calling to his fellows.
    2. Bro. Heav'n keep my sister, agen agen and neer,
Best draw, and stand upon our guard.
    Eld. Bro. Ile hallow,
If he be friendly he comes well, if not,
Defence is a good cause, and Heav'n be for us.

       The attendant Spirit habited like a Shepherd.

That hallow I should know, what are you? speak;   490
Com not too neer, you fall on iron stakes else.
    Spir. What voice is that, my young Lord? speak agen.
    2. Bro. O brother, 'tis my father Shepherd sure.
    Eld. Bro. Thyrsis? Whose artful strains have oft delaid
The huddling brook to hear his madrigal,
And sweeten'd every muskrose of the dale,
How cam'st thou here good Swain? hath any ram
Slip't from the fold, or young Kid lost his dam,
Or straggling weather the pen't flock forsook?
How couldst thou find this dark sequester'd nook?   500
    Spir. O my lov'd masters heir, and his next joy,
I came not here on such a trivial toy
As a stray'd Ewe, or to pursue the stealth

---

474 sensualty] sensuality *1673*   493 father] *So also 1673 for* father's.

Of pilfering Woolf, not all the fleecy wealth
That doth enrich these Downs, is worth a thought
To this my errand, and the care it brought.
But O my Virgin Lady, where is she?
How chance she is not in your company?
 Eld. Bro. To tell thee sadly Shepherd, without blame,
Or our neglect, we lost her as we came.   510
 Spir. Ay me unhappy then my fears are true.
 Eld. Bro. What fears good *Thyrsis?* Prethee briefly shew.
 Spir. Ile tell ye, 'tis not vain or fabulous,
(Though so esteem'd by shallow ignorance)
What the sage Poëts taught by th' heav'nly Muse,
Storied of old in high immortal vers
Of dire *Chimera's* and inchanted Iles,
And rifted Rocks whose entrance leads to hell,
For such there be, but unbelief is blind.
 Within the navil of this hideous Wood,   520
Immur'd in cypress shades a Sorcerer dwels
Of *Bacchus*, and of *Circe* born, great *Comus*,
Deep skill'd in all his mothers witcheries,
And here to every thirsty wanderer,
By sly enticement gives his banefull cup,
With many murmurs mixt, whose pleasing poison
The visage quite transforms of him that drinks,
And the inglorious likenes of a beast
Fixes instead, unmoulding reasons mintage
Character'd in the face; this have I learn't   530
Tending my flocks hard by i'th hilly crofts,
That brow this bottom glade, whence night by night
He and his monstrous rout are heard to howl
Like stabl'd wolves, or tigers at their prey,
Doing abhorred rites to *Hecate*
In their obscured haunts of inmost bowres.
Yet have they many baits, and guilefull spells
To inveigle and invite th' unwary sense
Of them that pass unweeting by the way.
This evening late by then the chewing flocks   540
Had ta'n their supper on the savoury Herb
Of Knot-grass dew-besprent, and were in fold,
I sate me down to watch upon a bank
With Ivy canopied, and interwove
With flaunting Hony-suckle, and began

A Mask.

Wrapt in a pleasing fit of melancholy
To meditate my rural minstrelsie,
Till fancy had her fill, but ere a close
The wonted roar was up amidst the Woods,
And fill'd the Air with barbarous dissonance,   550
At which I ceas't, and listen'd them a while,
Till an unusuall stop of sudden silence
Gave respit to the drowsie frighted steeds
That draw the litter of close-curtain'd sleep.
At last a soft and solemn breathing sound
Rose like a steam of rich distill'd Perfumes,
And stole upon the Air, that even Silence
Was took e're she was ware, and wish't she might
Deny her nature, and be never more
Still to be so displac't. I was all eare,   560
And took in strains that might create a soul
Under the ribs of Death, but O ere long
Too well I did perceive it was the voice
Of my most honour'd Lady, your dear sister.
Amaz'd I stood, harrow'd with grief and fear,
And O poor hapless Nightingale thought I,
How sweet thou sing'st, how neer the deadly snare!
Then down the Lawns I ran with headlong hast
Through paths, and turnings oft'n trod by day,
Till guided by mine ear I found the place   570
Where that damn'd wisard hid in sly disguise
(For so by certain signes I knew) had met
Already, ere my best speed could prævent,
The aidless innocent Lady his wish't prey,
Who gently ask't if he had seen such two,
Supposing him som neighbour villager;
Longer I durst not stay, but soon I guess't
Ye were the two she mean't, with that I sprung
Into swift flight, till I had found you here,
But furder know I not. *2. Bro.* O night and shades,   580
How are ye joyn'd with hell in triple knot
Against th'unarmed weakness of one Virgin
Alone, and helpless! Is this the confidence
You gave me Brother? *Eld. Bro.* Yes, and keep it still,
Lean on it safely, not a period

547 meditate] meditate upon *1673*   556 steam] stream *1673*
580 furder] further *1673*

(63)

Shall be unsaid for me : against the threats
Of malice or of sorcery, or that power
Which erring men call Chance, this I hold firm,
Vertue may be assail'd, but never hurt,
Surpriz'd by unjust force, but not enthrall'd,   590
Yea even that which mischief meant most harm,
Shall in the happy trial prove most glory.
But evil on it self shall back recoyl,
And mix no more with goodness, when at last
Gather'd like scum, and setl'd to it self
It shall be in eternal restless change
Self-fed, and self-consum'd, if this fail,
The pillar'd firmament is rott'nness,
And earths base built on stubble. But com let's on.
Against th' opposing will and arm of Heav'n   600
May never this just sword be lifted up,
But for that damn'd magician, let him be girt
With all the greisly legions that troop
Under the sooty flag of *Acheron*,
Harpyies and *Hydra's*, or all the monstrous forms
'Twixt *Africa* and *Inde*, Ile find him out,
And force him to restore his purchase back,
Or drag him by the curls, to a foul death,
Curs'd as his life.
    Spir. Alas good ventrous youth,
I love thy courage yet, and bold Emprise,   610
But here thy sword can do thee little stead,
Farr other arms, and other weapons must
Be those that quell the might of hellish charms,
He with his bare wand can unthred thy joynts,
And crumble all thy sinews.
    Eld. Bro. Why prethee Shepherd
How durst thou then thy self approach so neer
As to make this relation?
    Spir. Care and utmost shifts
How to secure the Lady from surprisal,
Brought to my mind a certain Shepherd Lad
Of small regard to see to, yet well skill'd   620
In every vertuous plant and healing herb
That spreds her verdant leaf to th'morning ray,
He lov'd me well, and oft would beg me sing,
Which when I did, he on the tender grass

Would sit, and hearken even to extasie,
And in requitall ope his leather'n scrip,
And shew me simples of a thousand names
Telling their strange and vigorous faculties;
Amongst the rest a small unsightly root,
But of divine effect, he cull'd me out;   630
The leaf was darkish, and had prickles on it,
But in another Countrey, as he said,
Bore a bright golden flowre, but not in this soyl:
Unknown, and like esteem'd, and the dull swayn
Treads on it daily with his clouted shoon,
And yet more med'cinal is it then that *Moly*
That *Hermes* once to wise *Ulysses* gave;
He call'd it *Hæmony*, and gave it me,
And bad me keep it as of sov'ran use
'Gainst all inchantments, mildew blast, or damp   640
Or gastly furies apparition;
I purs't it up, but little reck'ning made,
Till now that this extremity compell'd,
But now I find it true; for by this means
I knew the foul inchanter though disguis'd,
Enter'd the very lime-twigs of his spells,
And yet came off: if you have this about you
(As I will give you when we go) you may
Boldly assault the necromancers hall;
Where if he be, with dauntless hardihood,   650
And brandish't blade rush on him, break his glass,
And shed the lushious liquor on the ground,
But sease his wand, though he and his curst crew
Feirce signe of battail make, and menace high,
Or like the sons of *Vulcan* vomit smoak,
Yet will they soon retire, if he but shrink.
       Eld. Bro. Thyrsis lead on apace, Ile follow thee,
And som good angel bear a sheild before us.

*The Scene changes to a stately Palace, set out with all manner of deliciousness;
soft Musick, Tables spred with all dainties. Comus appears with his rabble,
and the Lady set in an inchanted Chair, to whom he offers his Glass,
which she puts by, and goes about to rise.*

       Comus. Nay Lady sit; if I but wave this wand,
Your nerves are all chain'd up in Alablaster,   660
And you a statue; or as *Daphne* was
Root-bound, that fled *Apollo*.

La. Fool do not boast,
Thou canst not touch the freedom of my minde
With all thy charms, although this corporal rinde
Thou haste immanacl'd, while Heav'n sees good.
    Co. Why are you vext Lady? why do you frown?
Here dwell no frowns, nor anger, from these gates
Sorrow flies farr: See here be all the pleasures
That fancy can beget on youthfull thoughts,
When the fresh blood grows lively, and returns   670
Brisk as the *April* buds in Primrose-season.
And first behold this cordial Julep here
That flames, and dances in his crystal bounds
With spirits of balm, and fragrant Syrops mixt.
Not that *Nepenthes* which the wife of *Thone,*
In *Egypt* gave to *Jove*-born *Helena*
Is of such power to stir up joy as this,
To life so friendly, or so cool to thirst.
Why should you be so cruel to your self,
And to those dainty limms which nature lent   680
For gentle usage, and soft delicacy?
But you invert the cov'nants of her trust,
And harshly deal like an ill borrower
With that which you receiv'd on other terms,
Scorning the unexempt condition
By which all mortal frailty must subsist,
Refreshment after toil, ease after pain,
That have been tir'd all day without repast,
And timely rest have wanted, but fair Virgin
This will restore all soon.
    La. 'Twill not false traitor,   690
'Twill not restore the truth and honesty
That thou hast banish't from thy tongue with lies,
Was this the cottage, and the safe abode
Thou told'st me of? What grim aspects are these,
These oughly-headed Monsters? Mercy guard me!
Hence with thy brew'd inchantments, foul deceiver,
Hast thou betrai'd my credulous innocence
With visor'd falshood, and base forgery,
And wouldst thou seek again to trap me here
With lickerish baits fit to ensnare a brute?   700
Were it a draft for *Juno* when she banquets,
I would not taste thy treasonous offer; none

(66)

But such as are good men can give good things,
And that which is not good, is not delicious
To a well-govern'd and wise appetite.

    Co. O foolishnes of men! that lend their ears
To those budge doctors of the *Stoick* Furr,
And fetch their precepts from the *Cynick* Tub,
Praising the lean and sallow Abstinence.
Wherefore did Nature powre her bounties forth,   710
With such a full and unwithdrawing hand,
Covering the earth with odours, fruits, and flocks,
Thronging the Seas with spawn innumerable,
But all to please, and sate the curious taste?
And set to work millions of spinning Worms,
That in their green shops weave the smooth-hair'd silk
To deck her Sons, and that no corner might
Be vacant of her plenty, in her own loyns
She hutch't th'all-worship't ore, and precious gems
To store her children with; if all the world   720
Should in a pet of temperance feed on Pulse,
Drink the clear stream, and nothing wear but Freize,
Th'all-giver would be unthank't, would be unprais'd,
Not half his riches known, and yet despis'd,
And we should serve him as a grudging master,
As a penurious niggard of his wealth,
And live like Natures bastards, not her sons,
Who would be quite surcharged with her own weight,
And strangl'd with her waste fertility;
Th'earth cumber'd, and the wing'd air dark't with plumes,
The herds would over-multitude their Lords,   731
The Sea o'refraught would swell, and th'unsought diamonds
Would so emblaze the forhead of the Deep,
And so bestudd with Stars, that they below
Would grow inur'd to light, and com at last
To gaze upon the Sun with shameless brows.
List Lady be not coy, and be not cosen'd
With that same vaunted name Virginity,
Beauty is natures coyn, must not be hoorded,
But must be currant, and the good thereof   740
Consists in mutual and partak'n bliss,
Unsavoury in th'injoyment of it self
If you let slip time, like a neglected rose
It withers on the stalk with languish't head.

    (67)

Beauty is natures brag, and must be shown
In courts, at feasts, and high solemnities
Where most may wonder at the workmanship;
It is for homely features to keep home,
They had their name thence; course complexions
And cheeks of sorry grain will serve to ply   750
The sampler, and to teize the huswifes wooll.
What need a vermeil-tinctured lip for that
Love-darting eyes, or tresses like the Morn?
There was another meaning in these gifts,
Think what, and be adviz'd, you are but young yet.
   La. I had not thought to have unlockt my lips
In this unhallow'd air, but that this Jugler
Would think to charm my judgement, as mine eyes,
Obtruding false rules pranckt in reasons garb.
I hate when vice can bolt her arguments,   760
And vertue has no tongue to check her pride:
Impostor do not charge most innocent nature,
As if she would her children should be riotous
With her abundance, she good cateress
Means her provision onely to the good
That live according to her sober laws,
And holy dictate of spare Temperance:
If every just man that now pines with want
Had but a moderate and beseeming share
Of that which lewdly-pamper'd Luxury   770
Now heaps upon som few with vast excess,
Natures full blessings would be well dispenc't
In unsuperfluous eeven proportion,
And she no whit encomber'd with her store,
And then the giver would be better thank't,
His praise due paid, for swinish gluttony
Ne're looks to Heav'n amidst his gorgeous feast,
But with besotted base ingratitude
Cramms, and blasphemes his feeder. Shall I go on?
Or have I said anough? To him that dares   780
Arm his profane tongue with contemptuous words
Against the Sun-clad power of Chastity,
Fain would I somthing say, yet to what end?
Thou hast nor Eare, nor Soul to apprehend
The sublime notion, and high mystery

780 anough] anow *1673*

(68)

That must be utter'd to unfold the sage
And serious doctrine of Virginity,
And thou art worthy that thou shouldst not know
More happiness then this thy present lot.
Enjoy your deer Wit, and gay Rhetorick   790
That hath so well been taught her dazling fence,
Thou art not fit to hear thy self convinc't;
Yet should I try, the uncontrouled worth
Of this pure cause would kindle my rap't spirits
To such a flame of sacred vehemence,
That dumb things would be mov'd to sympathize,
And the brute Earth would lend her nerves, and shake,
Till all thy magick structures rear'd so high,
Were shatter'd into heaps o're thy false head.
    Co. She fables not, I feel that I do fear   800
Her words set off by som superior power;
And though not mortal, yet a cold shuddring dew
Dips me all o're, as when the wrath of *Jove*
Speaks thunder, and the chains of *Erebus*
To som of *Saturns* crew. I must dissemble,
And try her yet more strongly. Com, no more,
This is meer moral babble, and direct
Against the canon laws of our foundation;
I must not suffer this, yet 'tis but the lees
And setlings of a melancholy blood;   810
But this will cure all streight, one sip of this
Will bathe the drooping spirits in delight
Beyond the bliss of dreams. Be wise, and taste.—

*The Brothers rush in with Swords drawn, wrest his Glass out of his hand, and
break it against the ground; his rout make signe of resistance, but are all
driven in; The attendant Spirit comes in.*

    Spir. What, have you let the false enchanter scape?
O ye mistook, ye should have snatcht his wand
And bound him fast; without his rod revers't,
And backward mutters of dissevering power,
We cannot free the Lady that sits here
In stony fetters fixt, and motionless;
Yet stay, be not disturb'd, now I bethink me,   820
Som other means I have which may be us'd,
Which once of *Melibœus* old I learnt
The soothest Shepherd that ere pip't on plains.

  (69)

There is a gentle Nymph not farr from hence,
That with moist curb sways the smooth Severn stream,
Sabrina is her name, a Virgin pure,
Whilom she was the daughter of *Locrine*,
That had the Scepter from his father *Brute*.
The guiltless damsel flying the mad pursuit
Of her enraged stepdam *Guendolen*,   830
Commended her fair innocence to the flood
That stay'd her flight with his cross-flowing course,
The water Nymphs that in the bottom plaid,
Held up their pearled wrists and took her in,
Bearing her straight to aged *Nereus* Hall,
Who piteous of her woes, rear'd her lank head,
And gave her to his daughters to imbathe
In nectar'd lavers strew'd with Asphodil,
And through the porch and inlet of each sense
Dropt in Ambrosial Oils till she reviv'd,   840
And underwent a quick immortal change
Made Goddess of the River; still she retains
Her maid'n gentlenes, and oft at Eeve
Visits the herds along the twilight meadows,
Helping all urchin blasts, and ill luck signes
That the shrewd medling Elfe delights to make,
Which she with pretious viold liquors heals.
For which the Shepherds at their festivals
Carrol her goodnes lowd in rustick layes,
And throw sweet garland wreaths into her stream   850
Of pancies, pinks, and gaudy Daffadils.
And, as the old Swain said, she can unlock
The clasping charm, and thaw the numming spell,
If she be right invok't in warbled Song,
For maid'nhood she loves, and will be swift
To aid a Virgin, such as was her self
In hard besetting need, this will I try
And adde the power of som adjuring verse.

SONG.

Sabrina fair
Listen where thou art sitting   860
Under the glassie, cool, translucent wave,
In twisted braids of Lillies knitting

(70)

A Mask.

The loose train of thy amber-dropping hair,
Listen for dear honour's sake,
Goddess of the silver lake,
Listen and save.

Listen and appear to us
In name of great *Oceanus*,
By the earth-shaking *Neptune's* mace,
And *Tethys* grave majestick pace,   870
By hoary *Nereus* wrincled look,
And the *Carpathian* wisards hook,
By scaly *Tritons* winding shell,
And old sooth-saying *Glaucus* spell,
By *Leucothea's* lovely hands,
And her son that rules the strands,
By *Thetis* tinsel-slipper'd feet,
And the Songs of *Sirens* sweet,
By dead *Parthenope's* dear tomb,
And fair *Ligea's* golden comb,   880
Wherwith she sits on diamond rocks
Sleeking her soft alluring locks,
By all the *Nymphs* that nightly dance
Upon thy streams with wily glance,
Rise, rise, and heave thy rosie head
From thy coral-pav'n bed,
And bridle in thy headlong wave,
Till thou our summons answered have.
Listen and save.

Sabrina *rises, attended by water-Nymphes, and sings.*

By the rushy-fringed bank,   890
Where grows the Willow and the Osier dank,
 My sliding Chariot stayes,
Thick set with Agat, and the azurn sheen
Of Turkis blew, and Emrauld green
 That in the channell strayes,
Whilst from off the waters fleet
Thus I set my printless feet
O're the Cowslips Velvet head,
 That bends not as I tread,
Gentle swain at thy request   900
 I am here.

(71)

Spir. Goddess dear
We implore thy powerful hand
To undo the charmed band
Of true Virgin here distrest,
Through the force, and through the wile
Of unblest inchanter vile.
    Sab. Shepherd 'tis my office best
To help insnared chastity ;
Brightest Lady look on me,   910
Thus I sprinkle on thy brest
Drops that from my fountain pure,
I have kept of pretious cure,
Thrice upon thy fingers tip,
Thrice upon thy rubied lip,
Next this marble venom'd seat
Smear'd with gumms of glutenous heat
I touch with chaste palms moist and cold,
Now the spell hath lost his hold ;
And I must haste ere morning hour   920
To wait in *Amphitrite's* bowr.

Sabrina descends, and the Lady rises out of her seat.

    Spir. Virgin, daughter of *Locrine*
Sprung of old *Anchises* line,
May thy brimmed waves for this
Their full tribute never miss
From a thousand petty rills,
That tumble down the snowy hills :
Summer drouth, or singed air
Never scorch thy tresses fair,
Nor wet *Octobers* torrent flood   930
Thy molten crystal fill with mudd,
May thy billows rowl ashoar
The beryl, and the golden ore,
May thy lofty head be crown'd
With many a tower and terrass round,
And here and there thy banks upon
With Groves of myrrhe, and cinnamon.

Com Lady while Heaven lends us grace,
Let us fly this cursed place,
Lest the Sorcerer us intice   940
With som other new device.

(72)

A Mask.

Not a waste, or needless sound
Till we com to holier ground,
I shall be your faithfull guide
Through this gloomy covert wide,
And not many furlongs thence
Is your Fathers residence,
Where this night are met in state
Many a friend to gratulate
His wish't presence, and beside   950
All the Swains that there abide,
With Jiggs, and rural dance resort,
We shall catch them at their sport,
And our sudden coming there
Will double all their mirth and chere;
Com let us haste, the Stars grow high,
But night sits monarch yet in the mid sky.

The Scene changes, presenting Ludlow *Town and the Presidents Castle,
then com in Countrey-Dancers, after them the attendant Spirit, with the
two Brothers and the Lady.*

SONG.

Spir. *Back Shepherds, back, anough your play,*
Till next Sun-shine holiday,
Here be without duck or nod   960
Other trippings to be trod
Of lighter toes, and such Court guise
As Mercury *did first devise*
With the mincing Dryades
On the Lawns, and on the Leas.

This second Song presents them to their father and mother.

Noble Lord, and Lady bright,
I have brought ye new delight,
Here behold so goodly grown
Three fair branches of your own,
Heav'n hath timely tri'd their youth,   970
Their faith, their patience, and their truth.
And sent them here through hard assays
With a crown of deathless Praise,
To triumph in victorious dance
O're sensual Folly, and Intemperance.

Miscellaneous Poems.

The dances ended, the Spirit Epiloguizes.

Spir. To the Ocean now I fly,
And those happy climes that ly
Where day never shuts his eye,
Up in the broad fields of the sky:
There I suck the liquid ayr   980
All amidst the Gardens fair
Of *Hesperus*, and his daughters three
That sing about the golden tree:
Along the crisped shades and bowres
Revels the spruce and jocond Spring,
The Graces, and the rosie-boosom'd Howres,
Thither all their bounties bring,
That there eternal Summer dwels,
And West winds, with musky wing
About the cedar'n alleys fling   990
Nard, and *Cassia's* balmy smels.
Iris there with humid bow,
Waters the odorous banks that blow
Flowers of more mingled hew
Then her purfl'd scarf can shew,
And drenches with *Elysian* dew
(List mortals, if your ears be true)
Beds of *Hyacinth*, and roses
Where young *Adonis* oft reposes,
Waxing well of his deep wound   1000
In slumber soft, and on the ground
Sadly sits th' *Assyrian* Queen;
But far above in spangled sheen
Celestial *Cupid* her fam'd son advanc't,
Holds his dear *Psyche* sweet intranc't
After her wandring labours long,
Till free consent the gods among
Make her his eternal Bride,
And from her fair unspotted side
Two blissful twins are to be born,   1010
Youth and Joy; so *Jove* hath sworn.
    But now my task is smoothly don,
I can fly, or I can run
Quickly to the green earths end,
Where the bow'd welkin slow doth bend,

(74)

A Mask.

And from thence can soar as soon
To the corners of the Moon.
   Mortals that would follow me,
Love vertue, she alone is free,
She can teach ye how to clime
Higher then the Spheary chime;
Or if Vertue feeble were,
Heav'n it self would stoop to her.

1020

The End.

POEMS ADDED IN THE 1673 EDITION.

Anno aetatis 17.

On the Death of a fair Infant dying of a Cough.

I

O FAIREST flower no sooner blown but blasted,
Soft silken Primrose fading timelesslie,
Summers chief honour if thou hadst out-lasted
Bleak winters force that made thy blossome drie;
For he being amorous on that lovely die
   That did thy cheek envermeil, thought to kiss
But kill'd alas, and then bewayl'd his fatal bliss.

II

For since grim Aquilo his charioter
By boistrous rape th' Athenian damsel got,
He thought it toucht his Deitie full neer,   10
If likewise he some fair one wedded not,
Thereby to wipe away th' infamous blot,
   Of long-uncoupled bed, and childless eld,
Which 'mongst the wanton gods a foul reproach was held.

III

So mounting up in ycie-pearled carr,
Through middle empire of the freezing aire
He wanderd long, till thee he spy'd from farr,
There ended was his quest, there ceast his care.
Down he descended from his Snow-soft chaire,
   But all unwares with his cold-kind embrace   20
Unhous'd thy Virgin Soul from her fair biding place.

On the Death of a fair Infant.

Yet art thou not inglorious in thy fate;
For so *Apollo*, with unweeting hand
Whilome did slay his dearly-loved mate
Young *Hyacinth* born on *Eurotas'* strand,
Young *Hyacinth* the pride of *Spartan* land;
   But then transform'd him to a purple flower
Alack that so to change thee winter had no power.

V

Yet can I not perswade me thou art dead
Or that thy coarse corrupts in earths dark wombe,   30
Or that thy beauties lie in wormie bed,
Hid from the world in a low delved tombe;
Could Heav'n for pittie thee so strictly doom?
   Oh no! for something in thy face did shine
Above mortalitie that shew'd thou wast divine.

Resolve me then oh Soul most surely blest
(If so it be that thou these plaints dost hear)
Tell me bright Spirit where e're thou hoverest
Whether above that high first-moving Spheare
Or in the Elisian fields (if such there were.)   40
   Oh say me true if thou wert mortal wight
And why from us so quickly thou didst take thy flight.

Wert thou some Starr which from the ruin'd roofe
Of shak't Olympus by mischance didst fall;
Which carefull *Jove* in natures true behoofe
Took up, and in fit place did reinstall?
Or did of late earths Sonnes besiege the wall
   Of sheenie Heav'n, and thou some goddess fled
Amongst us here below to hide thy nectar'd head.

VIII

Or wert thou that just Maid who once before   50
Forsook the hated earth, O tell me sooth
And cam'st again to visit us once more?
Or wert thou that sweet smiling Youth!
Or that c[r]own'd Matron sage white-robed Truth?
   Or any other of that heav'nly brood
Let down in clowdie throne to do the world some good.

IX

Or wert thou of the golden-winged hoast,
Who having clad thy self in humane weed,
To earth from thy præfixed seat didst poast,
And after short abode flie back with speed,   60
As if to shew what creatures Heav'n doth breed,
   Thereby to set the hearts of men on fire
To scorn the sordid world, and unto Heav'n aspire.

X

But oh why didst thou not stay here below
To bless us with thy heav'n-lov'd innocence,
To slake his wrath whom sin hath made our foe
To turn Swift-rushing black perdition hence,
Or drive away the slaughtering pestilence,
   To stand 'twixt us and our deserved smart
But thou canst best perform that office where thou art.   70

XI

Then thou the mother of so sweet a child
Her false imagin'd loss cease to lament,
And wisely learn to curb thy sorrows wild;
Think what a present thou to God hast sent,
And render him with patience what he lent;
   This if thou do he will an off-spring give,
That till the worlds last-end shall make thy name to live.

53 Or wert thou] Or wert thou Mercy *conjectured by John Heskin of Ch. Ch. Oxon. from* Ode on Nativity, st. 15.

At a Vacation Exercise.

Anno Aetatis 19. *At a Vacation Exercise in the Colledge, part* Latin, *part* English. *The* Latin *speeches ended, the* English *thus began.*

HAIL native Language, that by sinews weak
Didst move my first endeavouring tongue to speak,
And mad'st imperfect words with childish tripps,
Half unpronounc't, slide through my infant-lipps,
Driving dum silence from the portal dore,
Where he had mutely sate two years before :
Here I salute thee and thy pardon ask,
That now I use thee in my latter task :
Small loss it is that thence can come unto thee,
I know my tongue but little Grace can do thee :   10
Thou needst not be ambitious to be first,
Believe me I have thither packt the worst :
And, if it happen as I did forecast,
The daintest dishes shall be serv'd up last.
I pray thee then deny me not thy aide
For this same small neglect that I have made :
But haste thee strait to do me once a Pleasure,
And from thy wardrope bring thy chiefest treasure ;
Not those new fangled toys, and triming slight
Which takes our late fantasticks with delight,   20
But cull those richest Robes, and gay'st attire
Which deepest Spirits, and choicest Wits desire :
I have some naked thoughts that rove about
And loudly knock to have their passage out ;
And wearie of their place do only stay
Till thou hast deck't them in thy best aray ;
That so they may without suspect or fears
Fly swiftly to this fair Assembly's ears ;
Yet I had rather if I were to chuse,
Thy service in some graver subject use,   30
Such as may make thee search thy coffers round,
Before thou cloath my fancy in fit sound :
Such where the deep transported mind may soare
Above the wheeling poles, and at Heav'ns dore

Look in, and see each blissful Deitie
How he before the thunderous throne doth lie,
Listening to what unshorn *Apollo* sings
To th'touch of golden wires, while *Hebe* brings
Immortal Nectar to her Kingly Sire:
Then passing through the Spherse of watchful fire,   40
And mistie Regions of wide air next under,
And hills of Snow and lofts of piled Thunder,
May tell at length how green-ey'd *Neptune* raves,
In Heav'ns defiance mustering all his waves;
Then sing of secret things that came to pass
When Beldam Nature in her cradle was;
And last of Kings and Queens and *Hero's* old,
Such as the wise *Demodocus* once told
In solemn Songs at King *Alcinous* feast,
While sad *Ulisses* soul and all the rest   50
Are held with his melodious harmonie
In willing chains and sweet captivitie.
But fie my wandring Muse how thou dost stray!
Expectance calls thee now another way,
Thou know'st it must be now thy only bent
To keep in compass of thy Predicament:
Then quick about thy purpos'd business come,
That to the next I may resign my Roome.

Then Ens *is represented as Father of the Prædicaments his ten Sons, whereof the Eldest stood for* Substance *with his Canons, which* Ens *thus speaking, explains.*

Good luck befriend thee Son; for at thy birth
The Faiery Ladies daunc't upon the hearth;   60
Thy drowsie Nurse hath sworn she did them spie
Come tripping to the Room where thou didst lie;
And sweetly singing round about thy Bed
Strew all their blessings on thy sleeping Head.
She heard them give thee this, that thou should'st still
From eyes of mortals walk invisible,
Yet there is something that doth force my fear,
For once it was my dismal hap to hear
A *Sybil* old, bow-bent with crooked age,
That far events full wisely could presage,   70

(80)

At a Vacation Exercise.

And in Times long and dark Prospective Glass
Fore-saw what future dayes should bring to pass,
Your Son, said she, (nor can you it prevent)
Shall subject be to many an Accident.
O're all his Brethren he shall Reign as King,
Yet every one shall make him underling,
And those that cannot live from him asunder
Ungratefully shall strive to keep him under,
In worth and excellence he shall out-go them,
Yet being above them, he shall be below them;   80
From others he shall stand in need of nothing,
Yet on his Brothers shall depend for Cloathing.
To find a Foe it shall not be his hap,
And peace shall lull him in her flowry lap;
Yet shall he live in strife, and at his dore
Devouring war shall never cease to roare;
Yea it shall be his natural property
To harbour those that are at enmity.
What power, what force, what mighty spell, if not
Your learned hands, can loose this Gordian knot?   90

The next Quantity *and* Quality, *spake in Prose, then* Relation *was call'd
by his Name.*

Rivers arise; whether thou be the Son,
Of utmost *Tweed*, or *Oose*, or gulphie *Dun*,
Or *Trent*, who like some earth-born Giant spreads
His thirty Armes along the indented Meads,
Or sullen *Mole* that runneth underneath,
Or *Severn* swift, guilty of Maidens death,
Or Rockie *Avon*, or of Sedgie *Lee*,
Or Coaly *Tine*, or antient hallowed *Dee*,
Or *Humber* loud that keeps the *Scythians* Name,
Or *Medway* smooth, or Royal Towred *Thame*.   100

The rest was Prose.

(81)

Miscellaneous Poems.

The Fifth Ode of Horace. Lib. I.

Quis multa gracilis te puer in Rosa, Rendred almost word for word with-out Rhyme according to the Latin Measure, as near as the Language will permit.

WHAT slender Youth bedew'd with liquid odours
Courts thee on Roses in some pleasant Cave,
    Pyrrha for whom bind'st thou
    In wreaths thy golden Hair,

Plain in thy neatness; O how oft shall he
On Faith and changed Gods complain: and Seas
    Rough with black winds and storms
    Unwonted shall admire:

Who now enjoyes thee credulous, all Gold,
Who always vacant, always amiable   10
    Hopes thee; of flattering gales
    Unmindfull. Hapless they

To whom thou untry'd seem'st fair. Me in my vow'd
Picture the sacred wall declares t' have hung
    My dank and dropping weeds
    To the stern God of Sea.

[The Latin text follows.]

SONNETS.

XI

A Book was writ of late call'd *Tetrachordon*;
    And wov'n close, both matter, form and stile;
    The Subject new: it walk'd the Town a while,
    Numbring good intellects; now seldom por'd on.
Cries the stall-reader, bless us! what a word on
    A title page is this! and some in file
    Stand spelling fals, while one might walk to Mile-
End Green. Why is it harder Sirs then Gordon,
Colkitto, or Macdonnel, or Galasp?
    Those rugged names to our like mouths grow sleek   10
    That would have made *Quintilian* stare and gasp.
Thy age, like ours, O Soul of Sir *John Cheek*,
    Hated not Learning wors then Toad or Asp;
    When thou taught' st *Cambridge*, and King *Edward* Greek.

xi. Camb. Autograph supplies title, *On the Detraction which followed upon my writing certain Treatises.*

(82)

XII.   *On the same.*

I did but prompt the age to quit their cloggs
  By the known rules of antient libertie,
  When strait a barbarous noise environs me
  Of Owles and Cuckoes, Asses, Apes and Doggs.
As when those Hinds that were transform'd to Froggs
  Raild at *Latona's* twin-born progenie
  Which after held the Sun and Moon in fee.
  But this is got by casting Pearl to Hoggs;
That bawle for freedom in their senceless mood,
  And still revolt when truth would set them free.   10
  Licence they mean when they cry libertie;
For who loves that, must first be wise and good;
  But from that mark how far they roave we see
  For all this wast of wealth, and loss of blood.

To Mr. H. Lawes, *on his Aires.*

XIII

Harry whose tuneful and well measur'd Song
  First taught our English Musick how to span
  Words with just note and accent, not to scan
  With *Midas* Ears, committing short and long;
Thy worth and skill exempts thee from the throng,
  With praise enough for Envy to look wan;
  To after age thou shalt be writ the man,
  That with smooth aire couldst humor best our tongue.
Thou honour'st Verse, and Verse must send her wing
  To honour thee, the Priest of *Phœbus* Quire   10
  That tun'st their happiest lines in Hymn, or Story.
Dante shall give Fame leave to set thee higher
  Then his *Casella*, whom he woo'd to sing
  Met in the milder shades of Purgatory.

9 send] lend   *Cambridge Autograph MS.*

XIV

When Faith and Love which parted from thee never,
   Had ripen'd thy just soul to dwell with God,
   Meekly thou didst resign this earthy load
Of Death, call'd Life ; which us from Life doth sever.
Thy Works and Alms and all thy good Endeavour
   Staid not behind, nor in the grave were trod;
   But as Faith pointed with her golden rod,
   Follow'd thee up to joy and bliss for ever.
Love led them on, and Faith who knew them best
   Thy hand-maids, clad them o're with purple beams   10
   And azure wings, that up they flew so drest,
And speak the truth of thee on glorious Theams
   Before the Judge, who thenceforth bid thee rest
   And drink thy fill of pure immortal streams.

On the late Massacher in Piemont.

XV

Avenge O Lord thy slaughter'd Saints, whose bones
   Lie scatter'd on the Alpine mountains cold,
   Ev'n them who kept thy truth so pure of old
   When all our Fathers worship't Stocks and Stones,
Forget not: in thy book record their groanes
   Who were thy Sheep and in their antient Fold
   Slayn by the bloody *Piemontese* that roll'd
   Mother with Infant down the Rocks. Their moans
The Vales redoubl'd to the Hills, and they
   To Heav'n. Their martyr'd blood and ashes sow   10
   O're all th'*Italian* fields where still doth sway
The triple Tyrant: that from these may grow
   A hunder'd-fold, who having learnt thy way
   Early may fly the *Babylonian* wo.

xiv. Camb. Autograph supplies title, *On the Religious Memory of Mrs. Catherine Thomson, my Christian Friend, deceased* 16 *Decemb.* 1646.

Sonnets.

XVI

When I consider how my light is spent,
  E're half my days, in this dark world and wide,
  And that one Talent which is death to hide,
  Lodg'd with me useless, though my Soul more bent
To serve therewith my Maker, and present
  My true account, least he returning chide,
  Doth God exact day-labour, light deny'd,
  I fondly ask ; But patience to prevent
That murmur, soon replies, God doth not need
  Either man's work or his own gifts, who best   10
  Bear his milde yoak, they serve him best, his State
Is Kingly. Thousands at his bidding speed
  And post o're Land and Ocean without rest :
  They also serve who only stand and waite.

XVII

Lawrence of vertuous Father vertuous Son,
  Now that the Fields are dank, and ways are mire,
  Where shall we sometimes meet, and by the fire
  Help wast a sullen day ; what may be won
From the hard Season gaining : time will run
  On smoother, till *Favonius* re-inspire
  The frozen earth ; and cloth in fresh attire
  The Lillie and Rose, that neither sow'd nor spun.
What neat repast shall feast us, light and choice,
  Of Attick tast, with Wine, whence we may rise   10
  To hear the Lute well toucht, or artfull voice
Warble immortal Notes and *Tuskan* Ayre ?
  He who of those delights can judge, and spare
  To interpose them oft, is not unwise.

XVIII

Cyriack, whose Grandsire on the Royal Bench
  Of Brittish *Themis*, with no mean applause
  Pronounc't and in his volumes taught our Lawes,
  Which others at their Barr so often wrench :
To day deep thoughts resolve with me to drench
  In mirth, that after no repenting drawes ;
  Let *Euclid* rest and *Archimedes* pause,

And what the *Swede* intend, and what the *French.*
To measure life, learn thou betimes, and know
    Toward solid good what leads the nearest way;   10
    For other things mild Heav'n a time ordains,
And disapproves that care, though wise in show,
    That with superfluous burden loads the day,
    And when God sends a cheerful hour, refrains.

XIX

Methought I saw my late espoused Saint
    Brought to me like *Alcestis* from the grave,
    Whom *Joves* great Son to her glad Husband gave,
    Rescu'd from death by force though pale and faint.
Mine as whom washt from spot of child-bed taint,
    Purification in the old Law did save,
    And such, as yet once more I trust to have
    Full sight of her in Heaven without restraint,
Came vested all in white, pure as her mind:
    Her face was vail'd, yet to my fancied sight,   10
    Love, sweetness, goodness, in her person shin'd
So clear, as in no face with more delight.
    But O as to embrace me she enclin'd
    I wak'd, she fled, and day brought back my night.

On the new forcers of Conscience under the Long PARLIAMENT.

Because you have thrown of your Prelate Lord,
    And with stiff Vowes renounc'd his Liturgie
    To seise the widdow'd whore Pluralitie
    From them whose sin ye envi'd, not abhor'd,
Dare ye for this adjure the Civill Sword
    To force our Consciences that Christ set free,
    And ride us with a classic Hierarchy
    Taught ye by meer *A. S.* and *Rotherford*?
Men whose Life, Learning, Faith and pure intent
    Would have been held in high esteem with *Paul*   10
    Must now be nam'd and printed Hereticks
By shallow *Edwards* and Scotch what d'ye call:
    But we do hope to find out all your tricks,

Your plots and packing wors then those of *Trent*,
     That so the Parliament
May with their wholsom and preventive Shears
Clip your Phylacteries, though bauk your Ears,
     And succour our just Fears
When they shall read this clearly in your charge
New Presbyter is but *Old Priest* writ Large.   20

The four following sonnets were not published until 1694, and then in a mangled form by Phillips, in his *Life of Milton*; they are here printed from the Cambridge MS., where that to Fairfax is in Milton's autograph.

On the Lord Gen. Fairfax *at the seige of* Colchester.

Fairfax, whose name in armes through Europe rings
 Filling each mouth with envy, or with praise,
 And all her jealous monarchs with amaze,
 And rumors loud, that daunt remotest kings,
Thy firm unshak'n vertue ever brings
 Victory home, though new rebellions raise
 Thir Hydra heads, & the fals North displaies
 Her brok'n league, to impe their serpent wings,
O yet a nobler task awaites thy hand;
 For what can Warr, but endless warr still breed,   10
 Till Truth, & Right from Violence be freed,
And Public Faith cleard from the shamefull brand
 Of Public Fraud. In vain doth Valour bleed
 While Avarice, & Rapine share the land.

Miscellaneous Poems.

To the Lord Generall Cromwell *May* 1652.

On the proposalls of certaine ministers at the Committee for Propagation of the Gospell.

Cromwell, our cheif of men, who through a cloud
   Not of warr onely, but detractions rude,
   Guided by faith & matchless Fortitude
   To peace & truth thy glorious way hast plough'd,
And on the neck of crowned Fortune proud
   Hast reard Gods Trophies, & his work pursu'd,
   While Darwen stream with blood of Scotts imbru'd,
   And *Dunbarr feild* resounds thy praises loud,
And Worsters laureat wreath; yet much remaines
   To conquer still; peace hath her victories   10
   No less renownd then warr, new foes aries
Threatning to bind our soules with secular chaines:
   Helpe us to save free Conscience from the paw
   Of hireling wolves whose Gospell is their maw.

To Sr Henry Vane *the younger.*

Vane, young in yeares, but in sage counsell old,
   Then whome a better Senatour nere held
   The helme of Rome, when gownes not armes repelld
   The feirce Epeirot & the African bold,
Whether to settle peace, or to unfold
   The drift of hollow states, hard to be spelld,
   Then to advise how warr may best, upheld,
   Move by her two maine nerves, Iron & Gold
In all her equipage; besides to know
   Both spirituall powre & civill, what each meanes   10
   What severs each thou 'hast learnt, which few have don.
The bounds of either sword to thee wee ow.
   Therfore on thy firme hand religion leanes
   In peace, & reck'ns thee her eldest son.

(88)

Psalm i.

To Mr. Cyriack Skinner *upon his Blindness.*

Cyriack, this three years day these eys, though clear
  To outward view, of blemish or of spot;
  Bereft of light thir seeing have forgot,
  Nor to thir idle orbs doth sight appear
Of Sun or Moon or Starre throughout the year,
  Or man or woman. Yet I argue not
  Against heavns hand or will, nor bate a jot
  Of heart or hope; but still bear vp and steer
Right onward. What supports me, dost thou ask?
  The conscience, Friend, to have lost them overply'd 10
  In libertyes defence, my noble task,
Of which all Europe talks from side to side.
  This thought might lead me through the world's vain mask
  Content though blind, had I no better guide.

PSAL. I. Done into Verse, 1653.

BLESS'D is the man who hath not walk'd astray
In counsel of the wicked, and ith'way
Of sinners hath not stood, and in the seat
Of scorners hath not sate. But in the great
Jehovahs Law is ever his delight,
And in his Law he studies day and night.
He shall be as a tree which planted grows
By watry streams, and in his season knows
To yield his fruit, and his leaf shall not fall,
And what he takes in hand shall prosper all. 10
Not so the wicked, but as chaff which fann'd
The wind drives, so the wicked shall not stand
In judgment, or abide their tryal then,
Nor sinners in th'assembly of just men.
For the Lord knows th'upright way of the just,
And the way of bad men to ruine must.

(89)

Miscellaneous Poems.

PSAL. II. *Done Aug.* 8. 1653. *Terzetti.*

WHY do the Gentiles tumult, and the Nations
   Muse a vain thing, the Kings of th'earth upstand
   With power, and Princes in their Congregations
Lay deep their plots together through each Land,
   Against the Lord and his Messiah dear.
   Let us break off, say they, by strength of hand
Their bonds, and cast from us, no more to wear,
   Their twisted cords : he who in Heaven doth dwell
   Shall laugh, the Lord shall scoff them, then severe
Speak to them in his wrath, and in his fell   10
   And fierce ire trouble them ; but I saith hee
   Anointed have my King (though ye rebell)
On Sion my holi' hill. A firm decree
   I will declare ; the Lord to me hath say'd
   Thou art my Son I have begotten thee
This day ; ask of me, and the grant is made ;
   As thy possession I on thee bestow
   Th'Heathen, and as thy conquest to be sway'd
Earths utmost bounds : them shalt thou bring full low
   With Iron Scepter bruis'd, and them disperse   20
   Like to a potters vessel shiver'd so.
And now be wise at length ye Kings averse
   Be taught ye Judges of the earth ; with fear
   Jehovah serve, and let your joy converse
With trembling ; kiss the Son least he appear
   In anger and ye perish in the way
   If once his wrath take fire like fuel sere.
Happy all those who have in him their stay.

PSAL. III. Aug. 9. 1653.

When he fled from Absalom.

   LORD how many are my foes
      How many those
   That in arms against me rise
      Many are they

That of my life distrustfully thus say,
No help for him in God there lies.
But thou Lord art my shield my glory,
　　　Thee through my story
　　　Th' exalter of my head I count
　　　　Aloud I cry'd　　　　　　　　　　10
Unto Jehovah, he full soon reply'd
And heard me from his holy mount.
I lay and slept, I wak'd again,
　　　For my sustain
　　　Was the Lord. Of many millions
　　　　The populous rout
I fear not though incamping round about
They pitch against me their Pavillions.
Rise Lord, save me my God for thou
　　　Hast smote ere now　　　　　　20
　　　On the cheek-bone all my foes,
　　　　Of men abhor'd
Hast broke the teeth.　This help was from the Lord;
Thy blessing on thy people flows.

PSAL. IV. *Aug.* 10. 1653.

ANSWER me when I call
God of my righteousness;
In straights and in distress
Thou didst me disinthrall
And set at large; now spare,
　Now pity me, and hear my earnest prai'r.
Great ones how long will ye
My glory have in scorn
How long be thus forborn
Still to love vanity,　　　　　　　　10
To love, to seek, to prize
　Things false and vain and nothing else but lies?
Yet know the Lord hath chose
Chose to himself a part
The good and meek of heart
(For whom to chuse he knows)
Jehovah from on high
　Will hear my voyce what time to him I crie.

(91)

Be aw'd, and do not sin,
Speak to your hearts alone,   20
Upon your beds, each one,
And be at peace within.
Offer the offerings just
    Of righteousness and in Jehovah trust.
Many there be that say
Who yet will shew us good?
Talking like this worlds brood;
But Lord, thus let me pray,
On us lift up the light
    Lift up the favour of thy count'nance bright.   30
Into my heart more joy
And gladness thou hast put
Then when a year of glut
Their stores doth over-cloy
And from their plenteous grounds
    With vast increase their corn and wine abounds.
In peace at once will I
Both lay me down and sleep
For thou alone dost keep
Me safe where ere I lie   40
As in a rocky Cell
    Thou Lord alone in safety mak'st me dwell.

PSAL. V.   Aug. 12. 1653.

JEHOVAH to my words give ear
    My meditation waigh
The voyce of my complaining hear
My King and God for unto thee I pray.
    Jehovah thou my early voyce
        Shalt in the morning hear
    Ith'morning I to thee with choyce
Will rank my Prayers, and watch till thou appear.
    For thou art not a God that takes
        In wickedness delight   10
    Evil with thee no biding makes
Fools or mad men stand not within thy sight.
    All workers of iniquity

Psalm vi.

Thou hat'st; and them unblest
Thou wilt destroy that speak a ly
The bloodi' and guileful man God doth detest.
But I will in thy mercies dear
Thy numerous mercies go
Into thy house; I in thy fear
Will towards thy holy temple worship low.   20
Lord lead me in thy righteousness
Lead me because of those
That do observe if I transgress,
Set thy wayes right before, where my step goes.
For in his faltring mouth unstable
No word is firm or sooth
Their inside, troubles miserable;
An open grave their throat, their tongue they smooth.
God, find them guilty, let them fall
By their own counsels quell'd;   30
Push them in their rebellions all
Still on; for against thee they have rebell'd;
Then all who trust in thee shall bring
Their joy, while thou from blame
Defend'st them, they shall ever sing
And shall triumph in thee, who love thy name.
For thou Jehovah wilt be found
To bless the just man still,
As with a shield thou wilt surround
Him with thy lasting favour and good will.   40

PSAL. VI.   Aug. 13. 1653.

Lord in thine anger do not reprehend me
Nor in thy hot displeasure me correct;
Pity me Lord for I am much deject
Am very weak and faint; heal and amend me,
For all my bones, that even with anguish ake,
Are troubled, yea my soul is troubled sore;
And thou O Lord how long? turn Lord, restore
My soul, O save me for thy goodness sake
For in death no remembrance is of thee;
Who in the grave can celebrate thy praise?   10
Wearied I am with sighing out my dayes,
Nightly my Couch I make a kind of Sea;

(93)

My Bed I water with my tears; mine Eie
  Through grief consumes, is waxen old and dark
Ith' mid'st of all mine enemies that mark.
  Depart all ye that work iniquitie.
Depart from me, for the voice of my weeping
  The Lord hath heard, the Lord hath heard my prai'r
My supplication with acceptance fair
  The Lord will own, and have me in his keeping.   20
Mine enemies shall all be blank and dash't
  With much confusion; then grow red with shame,
They shall return in hast the way they came
  And in a moment shall be quite abash't.

PSAL. VII. Aug. 14. 1653.

Upon the words of Chush *the* Benjamite *against him.*

LORD my God to thee I flie
Save me and secure me under
Thy protection while I crie
Least as a Lion (and no wonder)
He hast to tear my Soul asunder
Tearing and no rescue nigh.

Lord my God if I have thought
Or done this, if wickedness
Be in my hands, if I have wrought
Ill to him that meant me peace,   10
Or to him have render'd less,
And not fre'd my foe for naught;

Let th'enemy pursue my soul
And overtake it, let him tread
My life down to the earth and roul
In the dust my glory dead,
In the dust and there out spread
Lodge it with dishonour foul.

Psalm vii.

Rise Jehovah in thine ire
Rouze thy self amidst the rage   20
Of my foes that urge like fire ;
And wake for me, their furi' asswage ;
Judgment here thou didst ingage
And command which I desire.

So th' assemblies of each Nation
Will surround thee, seeking right,
Thence to thy glorious habitation
Return on high and in their sight.
Jehovah judgeth most upright
All people from the worlds foundation.   30

Judge me Lord, be judge in this
According to my righteousness
And the innocence which is
Upon me : cause at length to cease
Of evil men the wickedness
And their power that do amiss.

But the just establish fast,
Since thou art the just God that tries
Hearts and reins. On God is cast
My defence, and in him lies   40
In him who both just and wise
Saves th' upright of Heart at last.

God is a just Judge and severe,
And God is every day offended ;
If th' unjust will not forbear,
His Sword he whets, his Bow hath bended
Already, and for him intended
The tools of death, that waits him near.

(His arrows purposely made he
For them that persecute.) Behold   50
He travels big with vanitie,
Trouble he hath conceav'd of old
As in a womb, and from that mould
Hath at length brought forth a Lie.

He dig'd a pit, and delv'd it deep,
And fell into the pit he made,
His mischief that due course doth keep.
Turns on his head, and his ill trade
Of violence will undelay'd
Fall on his crown with ruine steep.　　　60

Then will I Jehovah's praise
According to his justice raise
And sing the Name and Deitie
Of Jehovah the most high.

PSAL. VIII. *Aug.* 14. 1653.

O JEHOVAH our Lord how wondrous great
　　And glorious is thy name through all the earth?
So as above the Heavens thy praise to set
　　Out of the tender mouths of latest bearth,

Out of the mouths of babes and sucklings thou
　　Hast founded strength because of all thy foes
To stint th'enemy, and slack th'avengers brow
　　That bends his rage thy providence to oppose.

When I behold thy Heavens, thy Fingers art,
　　The Moon and Starrs which thou so bright hast set, 10
In the pure firmament, then saith my heart,
　　O what is man that thou remembrest yet,

And think'st upon him; or of man begot
　　That him thou visit'st and of him art found;
Scarce to be less then Gods, thou mad'st his lot,
　　With honour and with state thou hast him crown'd.

O're the works of thy hand thou mad'st him Lord,
　　Thou hast put all under his lordly feet,
All Flocks, and Herds, by thy commanding word,
　　All beasts that in the field or forrest meet. 　20

Fowl of the Heavens, and Fish that through the wet
　　Sea-paths in shoals do slide. And know no dearth.
O Jehovah our Lord how wondrous great
　　And glorious is thy name through all the earth.

(96)

Psalm lxxx.

April, 1648.   J. M.

Nine of the Psalms done into Metre, wherein all but what is in a different Character, are the very words of the Text, translated from the Original.

PSAL. LXXX.

1 THOU Shepherd that dost Israel *keep*
   Give ear *in time of need,*
Who leadest like a flock of sheep
   Thy loved Josephs seed,
That sitt'st between the Cherubs *bright*
   Between their wings out-spread
Shine forth, *and from thy cloud give light,*
   And on our foes thy dread.

2 In Ephraims view and Benjamins,
   And in Manasse's sight   10
Awake * thy strength, come, and *be seen*   * *Gnorera.*
   To save us *by thy might.*

3 Turn us again, *thy grace divine*
   To us O God *vouchsafe ;*
Cause thou thy face on us to shine
   And then we shall be safe.

4 Lord God of Hosts, how long wilt thou,
   How long wilt thou declare
Thy *smoking wrath, *and angry brow*   * *Gnashanta.*
   Against thy peoples praire.   20

5 Thou feed'st them with the bread of tears,
   Their bread with tears they eat,
And mak'st them * largely drink the tears   * *Shalish.*
   Wherwith their cheeks are wet.

6 A strife thou mak'st us *and a prey*
   To every neighbour foe,
Among themselves they * laugh, they * play, * *Jilgnagu.*
   And * flouts at us they throw.

7 Return us, *and thy grace divine*,
　　O God of Hosts *vouchsafe*　　　　　　　　30
　Cause thou thy face on us to shine,
　　And then we shall be safe.

8 A Vine from Ægypt thou hast brought,
　　Thy free love made it thine,
　And drov'st out Nations *proud and haut*
　　To plant this *lovely* Vine.

9 Thou did'st prepare for it a place
　　And root it deep and fast
　That it *began to grow apace*,
　　And fill'd the land *at last*.　　　　　　40

10 With her *green* shade *that* cover'd *all*,
　　The Hills were *over-spread*
　Her Bows as *high as* Cedars tall
　　Advanc'd their lofty head.

11 Her branches *on the western side*
　　Down to the Sea she sent,
　And *upward* to that river *wide*
　　Her other branches *went.*

12 Why hast thou laid her Hedges low
　　And brok'n down her Fence,　　　　　　50
　That all may pluck her, as they go,
　　With rudest violence?

13 The *tusked* Boar out of the wood
　　Up turns it by the roots,
　Wild Beasts there brouze, and make their food
　　Her Grapes and tender Shoots.

14 Return now, God of Hosts, look down
　　From Heav'n, thy Seat divine,
　Behold *us, but without a frown*,
　　And visit this *thy* Vine.　　　　　　　60

15 Visit this Vine, which thy right hand
　　Hath set, and planted *long*,
　And the young branch, that for thy self
　　Thou hast made firm and strong.

16 But now it is consum'd with fire,
　　And cut *with Axes* down,
　They perish at thy dreadfull ire,
　　At thy rebuke and frown.

17 Upon the man of thy right hand
　　Let thy *good* hand be *laid*,　　　　　70

Upon the Son of Man, whom thou
　　Strong for thyself hast made.
18 So shall we not go back from thee
　　To wayes of sin and shame,
Quick'n us thou, then *gladly* wee
　　Shall call upon thy Name.
Return us, *and thy grace divine*
　　Lord God of Hosts *voutsafe,*
Cause thou thy face on us to shine,
　　And then we shall be safe.　　　　　80

PSAL. LXXXI.

1 To God our strength sing loud, *and clear,*
　　Sing loud to God *our King,*
To Jacobs God, *that all may hear*
　　Loud acclamations ring.
2 Prepare a Hymn, prepare a Song
　　The Timbrel hither bring
The *cheerfull* Psaltry bring along
　　And Harp *with* pleasant *string.*
3 Blow, *as is wont,* in the new Moon
　　With Trumpets *lofty sound,*　　　　　10
Th' appointed time, the day wheron
　　Our solemn Feast *comes round.*
4 This was a Statute *giv'n of old*
　　For Israel *to observe*
A Law of Jacobs God, *to hola*
　　From whence they might not swerve.
5 This he a Testimony ordain'd
　　In Joseph, *not to change,*
When as he pass'd through Ægypt land;
　　The Tongue I heard, was strange.　　　　20
6 From burden, *and from slavish toyle*
　　I set his shoulder free;
His hands from pots, *and mirie soyle*
　　Deliver'd were *by me.*
7 When trouble did thee sore assaile,
　　On me then didst thou call,

And I to free thee *did not faile,*
   And led thee out of thrall.
I answer'd thee in **thunder deep*   * *Be Sether ragnam.*
   With clouds encompass'd round ;   30
I tri'd thee at the water *steep*
   Of Meriba *renown'd.*

8 Hear O my people, *heark'n well,*
   I testifie to thee
Thou antient flock of Israel,
   If thou wilt list to mee,

9 Through out the land of thy abode
   No alien God shall be
Nor shalt thou to a forein God
   In honour bend thy knee.   40

10 I am the Lord thy God which brought
   Thee out of Ægypt land
Ask large enough, and I, *besought,*
   Will grant thy full demand.

11 And yet my people would not *hear,*
   Nor hearken to my voice ;
And Israel *whom I lov'd so dear*
   Mislik'd me for his choice.

12 Then did I leave them to their will
   And to their wandring mind ;   50
Their own conceits they follow'd still
   Their own devises blind.

13 O that my people would *be wise*
   To serve me *all their daies,*
And O that Israel would *advise*
   To walk my *righteous* waies.

14 Then would I soon bring down their foes
   That now so proudly rise,
And turn my hand against *all those*
   That are their enemies.   60

15 Who hate the Lord should *then be fain*
   To bow to him and bend,
But *they, His people, should remain,*
   Their time should have no end.

16 And he would feed them *from the shock*
   With flower of finest wheat,
And satisfie them from the rock
   With Honey *for their Meat.*

PSAL. LXXXII.

1 GOD in the * great * assembly stands   * *Bagnadath-el.*
    Of Kings and lordly States,
    Among the gods † on both his hands   † *Bekerev.*
    He judges and debates.

2 How long will ye * pervert the right   * *Tishphetu*
    With * judgment false and wrong   *gnavel.*
    Favouring the wicked *by your might,*
    Who thence grow bold and strong?

3 * Regard the * weak and fatherless   * *Shiphtu-dal.*
    * Dispatch the * poor mans cause,   10
    And † raise the man in deep distress
    By † just and equal Lawes.   † *Hatzdiku.*

4 Defend the poor and desolate,
    And rescue from the hands
    Of wicked men the low estate
    Of him *that help demands.*

5 They know not nor will understand,
    In darkness they walk on,
    The Earths foundations all are * mov'd   * *Jimmotu.*
    And * out of order gon.   20

6 I said that ye were Gods, yea all
    The Sons of God most high

7 But ye shall die like men, and fall
    As other Princes *die.*

8 Rise God, * judge thou the earth *in might,*
    This *wicked* earth * redress,   * *Shiphta.*
    For thou art he who shalt by right
    The Nations all possess.

PSAL. LXXXIII.

1 BE not thou silent *now at length*
    O God hold not thy peace,
    Sit not thou still O God of *strength*
    We cry and do not cease.

2 For lo thy *furious* foes *now* * swell
    And * storm outrageously,   * *Jehemajun.*
And they that hate thee *proud and fell*
    Exalt their heads full hie.

3 Against thy people they † contrive   † *Jagnarimu.*
    † Their Plots and Counsels deep,   † *Sod.*   10
* Them to ensnare they chiefly strive   * *Jithjagnatsu gnal.*
    * Whom thou dost hide and keep.   * *Tsephuneca.*

4 Come let us cut them off say they,
    Till they no Nation be
That Israels name for ever may
    Be lost in memory.

5 For they consult † with all their might, † *Lev jaçhdau.*
    And all as one in mind
Themselves against thee they unite
    And in firm union bind.   20

6 The tents of Edom, and the brood
    Of *scornful* Ishmael,
Moab, with them of Hagars blood
    That in the Desert dwell,

7 Gebal and Ammon *there conspire,*
    And *hateful* Amalec,
The Philistims, and they of Tyre
    Whose bounds the Sea doth check.

8 With them *great* Asshur also bands
    And doth confirm the knot,   30
All these have lent their armed hands
    To aid the Sons of Lot.

9 Do to them as to Midian *bold*
    That wasted all the Coast.
To Sisera, and as *is told*
    Thou didst to Jabins *hoast,*
When at the brook of Kishon *old*
    They were repulst and slain,

10 At Endor quite cut off, and rowl'd
    As dung upon the plain.   40

11 As Zeb and Oreb evil sped
    So let their Princes speed
As Zeba, and Zalmunna *bled*
    So let their Princes *bleed.*

12 *For they amidst their pride* have said
    By right now shall we seize

Psalm lxxxiv.

Gods houses, and *will now invade*
    † Their stately Palaces.   † *Neoth Elohim bears both.*

13 My God, oh make them as a wheel
    No quiet let them find,   50
   Giddy and *restless* let *them reel*
    Like stubble from the wind.

14 As *when* an *aged* wood takes fire
    Which on a sudden straies,
   The *greedy* flame runs hier and hier
    Till all the mountains blaze,

15 So with thy whirlwind them pursue,
    And with thy tempest chase ;

16 * And till they * yield thee honour due,   *They seek thy Name.* Heb.
    Lord fill with shame their face.

17 Asham'd and troubl'd let them be,   60
    Troubl'd and sham'd for ever,
   Ever confounded, and so die
    With shame, *and scape it never.*

18 Then shall they know that thou whose name
    Jehova is alone,
   Art the most high, *and thou the same*
    O're all the earth *art one.*

PSAL. LXXXIV.

1 How lovely are thy dwellings fair !
    O Lord of Hoasts, how dear
   The *pleasant* Tabernacles are !
    Where thou do'st dwell so near.

2 My Soul doth long and almost die
    Thy Courts O Lord to see,
   My heart and flesh aloud do crie,
    O living God, for thee.

3 There ev'n the Sparrow *freed from wrong*
    Hath found a house of *rest,*   10
   The Swallow there, to lay her young
    Hath built her *brooding* nest,
   Ev'n *by* thy Altars Lord of Hoasts
    They find their safe abode,
   And home they fly from round the Coasts
    Toward thee, My King, my God.

4 Happy, who in thy house reside
   Where thee they ever praise,
5 Happy, whose strength in thee doth bide,
   And in their hearts thy waies.   20
6 They pass through Baca's *thirstie* Vale,
   That dry and barren ground
As through a fruitfull watry Dale
   Where Springs and Showrs abound.
7 They journey on from strength to strength
   With joy and gladsom cheer
Till all before *our* God *at length*
   In Sion do appear.
8 Lord God of Hoasts hear *now* my praier
   O Jacobs God give ear,   30
9 Thou God our shield look on the face
   Of thy anointed *dear*.
10 For one day in thy Courts *to be*
   Is better, *and more blest*
Then *in the joyes of Vanity*,
   A thousand daies *at best*.
I in the temple of my God
   Had rather keep a dore,
Then dwell in Tents, *and rich abode*
   With Sin *for evermore*.   40
11 For God the Lord both Sun and Shield
   Gives grace and glory *bright*,
No good from them shall be with-held
   Whose waies are just and right.
12 Lord *God* of Hoasts *that raign'st on high,*
   That man is *truly* blest
Who *only* on thee doth relie.
   And in thee only rest.

PSAL. LXXXV.

1 THY Land to favour graciously
   Thou hast not Lord been slack,
Thou hast from *hard* Captivity
   Returned Jacob back.

Psalm lxxxv.

2 Th' iniquity thou didst forgive
   That wrought thy people woe,
And all their Sin, *that did thee grieve*
   Hast hid *where none shall know.*

3 Thine anger all thou hadst remov'd,
   And *calmly* didst return   **10**
From thy †fierce wrath which we had prov'd † Heb. *The*
   Far worse then fire to burn. *burning heat of thy wrath.*

4 God of our saving health and peace,
   Turn us, and us restore,
Thine indignation cause to cease
   Toward us, *and chide no more.*

5 Wilt thou be angry without end,
   For ever angry thus
Wilt thou thy frowning ire extend
   From age to age on us?   **20**

6 Wilt thou not * turn, and *hear our voice* * Heb. *Turn to*
   And us again * revive, *quicken us.*
That so thy people may rejoyce
   By thee preserv'd alive.

7 Cause us to see thy goodness Lord,
   To us thy mercy shew
Thy saving health to us afford
   And life in us renew.

8 *And now* what God the Lord will speak
   I will *go strait and* hear,   **30**
For to his people he speaks peace
   And to his Saints *full dear,*
To his dear Saints he will speak peace,
   But let them never more
Return to folly, *but surcease*
   To trespass as before.

9 Surely to such as do him fear
   Salvation is at hand
And glory shall *ere long appear*
   To dwell within our Land.   **40**

10 Mercy and Truth *that long were miss'd*
   Now *joyfully* are met
Sweet Peace and Righteousness have kiss'd
   And hand in hand are set.

11 Truth from the earth *like to a flowr*
   Shall bud and blossom *then,*

And Justice from her heavenly bowr
  Look down *on mortal men.*
12 The Lord will also then bestow
  Whatever thing is good   50
Our Land shall forth in plenty throw
  Her fruits *to be our food.*
13 Before him Righteousness shall go
  His Royal Harbinger,
Then * will he come, and not be slow   * Heb. *He will*
  His footsteps cannot err.   *set his steps*
                                  to the way.

PSAL. LXXXVI.

1 Thy *gracious* ear, O Lord, encline,
  O hear me *I thee pray,*
For I am poor, and almost pine
  With need, *and sad decay.*
2 Preserve my soul, for † I have trod † Heb. *I am good,*
  Thy waies, and love the just,   *loving, a doer of*
Save thou thy servant O my God   *good and holy*
  Who *still* in thee doth trust.   *things.*
3 Pitty me Lord for daily thee
  I call; 4 O make rejoyce   10
Thy Servants Soul; for Lord to thee
  I lift my soul *and voice,*
5 For thou art good, thou Lord art prone
  To pardon, thou to all
Art full of mercy, thou *alone*
  To them that on thee call.
6 Unto my supplication Lord
  Give ear, and to the crie
Of my *incessant* praiers afford
  Thy hearing graciously.   20
7 I in the day of my distress
  Will call on thee *for aid;*
For thou wilt *grant* me *free access*
  And answer, *what I pray'd.*
8 Like thee among the gods is none
  O Lord, nor any works

Of all that other Gods have done
  Like to thy *glorious* works.
9 The Nations all whom thou hast made
    Shall come, *and all shall frame*
  To bow them low before thee Lord,
    And glorifie thy name.
10 For great thou art, and wonders great
    By thy strong hand are done,
  Thou *in thy everlasting Seat*
    Remainest God alone.
11 Teach me O Lord thy way *most right,*
    I in thy truth will bide,
  To fear thy name my heart unite
    So shall it never slide.
12 Thee will I praise O Lord my God
    Thee honour, and adore
  With my whole heart, and blaze abroad
    Thy name for ever more.
13 For great thy mercy is toward me,
    And thou hast free'd my Soul
  Eev'n from the lowest Hell set free
    From deepest darkness foul.
14 O God the proud against me rise
    And violent men are met
  To seek my life, and in their eyes
    No fear of thee have set.
15 But thou Lord art the God most mild
    Readiest thy grace to shew,
  Slow to be angry, and *art stil'd*
    Most mercifull, most true.
16 O turn to me *thy face at length,*
    And me have mercy on,
  Unto thy servant give thy strength,
    And save thy hand-maids Son.
17 Some sign of good to me afford,
    And let my foes *then* see
  And be asham'd, because thou Lord
    Do'st help and comfort me.

30

40

50

60

Miscellaneous Poems.

PSAL. LXXXVII.

1 AMONG the holy Mountains *high*
    Is his foundation fast,
  There Seated in his Sanctuary,
    His Temple there is plac't.
2 Sions *fair* Gates the Lord loves more
    Then all the dwellings *faire*
  Of Jacobs *Land, though there be store,*
    And all within his care.
3 City of God, most glorious things
    Of thee *abroad* are spoke;   10
4 I mention Egypt, *where proud Kings*
    Did our forefathers yoke,
  I mention Babel to my friends,
    Philistia *full of scorn,*
  And Tyre with Ethiops *utmost ends,*
    Lo this man there was born:
5 But *twise that praise shall in our ear*
    Be said of Sion *last*
  This and this man was born in her,
    High God shall fix her fast.   20
6 The Lord shall write it in a Scrowle
    That ne're shall be out-worn
  When he the Nations doth enrowle
    That this man there was born.
7 Both they who sing, and they who dance
    With sacred Songs are there,
  In thee *fresh brooks, and soft streams glance*
    And all my fountains *clear.*

PSAL. LXXXVIII.

1 LORD God that dost me save and keep,
    All day to thee I cry;
  And all night long, before thee *weep*
    Before thee *prostrate lie.*

(108)

Psalm lxxxviii.

2 Into thy presence let my praier
   With sighs devout ascend
   And to my cries, that *ceaseless are*,
   Thine ear with favour bend.

3 For cloy'd with woes and trouble store
   Surcharg'd my Soul doth lie,   10
   My life *at death's uncherful dore*
   Unto the grave draws nigh.

4 Reck'n'd I am with them that pass
   Down to the *dismal* pit
   I am a * man, but weak alas   * Heb. *A man*
   And for that name unfit.   *without manly*
                                           strength.

5 From life discharg'd and parted quite
   Among the dead *to sleep*,
   And like the slain *in bloody fight*
   That in the grave lie *deep*.   20
   Whom thou rememberest no more,
   Dost never more regard,
   Them from thy hand deliver'd o're
   Deaths hideous house hath barr'd.

6 Thou in the lowest pit *profound*
   Hast set me *all forlorn*,
   Where thickest darkness *hovers round*,
   In horrid deeps *to mourn*.

7 Thy wrath *from which no shelter saves*
   Full sore doth press on me;   30
   * Thou break'st upon me all thy waves,   * *The* Heb.
   * And all thy waves break me.   *bears both.*

8 Thou dost my friends from me estrange,
   And mak'st me odious,
   Me to them odious, *for they change*,
   And I here pent up thus.

9 Through sorrow, and affliction great
   Mine eye grows dim and dead,
   Lord all the day I thee entreat,
   My hands to thee I spread.   40

10 Wilt thou do wonders on the dead,
   Shall the deceas'd arise
   And praise thee *from their loathsom bed*
   With pale and hollow eyes?

11 Shall they thy loving kindness tell
   On whom the grave *hath hold*,

Or they *who* in perdition *dwell*
  Thy faithfulness *unfold?*

12 In darkness can thy mighty *hand*
  Or wondrous acts be known,   50
  Thy justice in the *gloomy* land
  Of *dark* oblivion?

13 But I to thee O Lord do cry
  E're yet my life be spent,
  And *up to thee* my praier *doth hie*
  Each morn, and thee prevent.

14 Why wilt thou Lord my soul forsake,
  And hide thy face from me,

15 That am already bruis'd, and † shake   † Heb. *Prae Con-*
  With terror sent from thee;   *cussione.*   60
  Bruz'd, and afflicted and *so low*
  As ready to expire,
  While I thy terrors undergo
  Astonish'd with thine ire.

16 Thy fierce wrath over me doth flow
  Thy threatnings cut me through.

17 All day they round about me go,
  Like waves they me persue.

18 Lover and friend thou hast remov'd
  And sever'd from me far.   70
  They *fly me now* whom I have lov'd,
  And as in darkness are.

Finis.

Passages from Prose Writings.

A COLLECTION OF PASSAGES TRANS-LATED IN THE PROSE WRITINGS.

[From *Of Reformation in England*, 1641.]

Ah *Constantine*, of how much ill was cause
Not thy Conversion, but those rich demains
That the first wealthy *Pope* receiv'd of thee.

DANTE, Inf. xix. 115.

Founded in chast and humble Poverty,
'Gainst them that rais'd thee dost thou lift thy horn,
Impudent whoore, where hast thou plac'd thy hope?
In thy Adulterers, or thy ill got wealth?
Another *Constantine* comes not in hast.

PETRARCA, Son. 108.

And to be short, at last his guid him brings
Into a goodly valley, where he sees
A mighty mass of things strangely confus'd
Things that on earth were lost or were abus'd.

Then past he to a flowry Mountain green,
Which once smelt sweet, now stinks as odiously;
This was that gift (if you the truth will have)
That *Constantine* to good *Sylvestro* gave.

ARIOSTO, Orl. Fur. xxxiv. 80.

[From *Reason of Church Government*, 1641.]

When I die, let the Earth be roul'd in flames.

(111)

Miscellaneous Poems.

[From *Apology for Smectymnuus*, 1642.]

Laughing to teach the truth
What hinders? as some teachers give to Boys
Junkets and knacks, that they may learne apace.

HORACE, *Sat.* I. 24.

Jesting decides great things
Stronglier, and better oft than earnest can.

Ibid. i. 10. 14.

'Tis you that say it, not I: you do the deeds
And your ungodly deeds find me the words.

SOPHOCLES, *Elec.* 624.

[From *Areopagitica*, 1644.]

This is true Liberty, when free-born Men,
Having to advise the Public, may speak free,
Which he who can, and will, deserv's high praise;
Who neither can nor will, may hold his peace,
What can be juster in a state then this?

EURIPIDES, *Supp.* 438.

[From *Tetrachordon*, 1645.]

Whom do we count a good man, whom but he
Who keeps the laws and statutes of the Senate,
Who judges in great suits and controversies,
Whose witness and opinion wins the cause?
But his own house, and the whole neighbourhood
See his foul inside through his whited skin.

HORACE, *Ep.* i. 16. 40.

[From *The Tenure of Kings and Magistrates*, 1649.]

There can be slaine
No sacrifice to God more acceptable
Than an unjust and wicked king.

SENECA, *Herc. Fur.* 922.

Collection of Passages.

[From *History of Britain*, 1670.]

Brutus *thus addresses* Diana *in the country of* Leogecia.

Goddess of Shades, and Huntress, who at will
Walk'st on the rowling Sphear, and through the deep,
On thy third Reign the Earth look now, and tell
What Land, what Seat of rest thou bidst me seek,
What certain Seat, where I may worship thee
For aye, with Temples vow'd, and Virgin quires.

To whom sleeping before the altar, Diana *in a Vision that night thus
answer'd.*

Brutus far to the West, in th' Ocean wide
Beyond the Realm of *Gaul,* a Land there lies,
Sea-girt it lies, where Giants dwelt of old,
Now void, it fits thy People ; thether bend
Thy course, there shalt thou find a lasting seat,
There to thy Sons another *Troy* shall rise,
And *Kings* be born of thee, whose dredded might
Shall aw the World, and conquer Nations bold.

Joannis Miltoni

LONDINENSIS

POEMATA.

Quorum pleraque · intra
Annum ætatis Vigesimum
Conscripsit.

Nunc primum Edita.

LONDINI,
Typis *R. R.* Prostant ad Insignia Principis,
in Cœmeterio D. *Pauli,* apud *Humphredum*
Moseley. 1645.

HÆC quæ sequuntur de Authore testimonia, tametsi ipse intelligebat non tam de se quam supra se esse dicta, eo quod præclaro ingenio viri, nec non amici ita fere solent laudare, ut omnia suis potius virtutibus, quam veritati congruentia nimis cupide affingant, noluit tamen horum egregiam in se voluntatem non esse notam ; Cum alii præsertim ut id faceret magnopere suaderent. Dum enim nimiæ laudis invidiam totis ab se viribus amolitur, sibique quod plus æquo est non attributum esse mavult, judicium interim hominum cordatorum atque illustrium quin summo sibi honori ducat, negare non potest.

Joannes Baptista Mansus, Marchio Villensis Neapolitanus ad Joannem Miltonium Anglum.

Ut mens, forma, decor, facies, mos, si pietas sic,
  Non Anglus, verùm herclè Angelus ipse fores.

Ad Joannem Miltonem Anglum triplici poeseos laureâ coronandum Græcâ *nimirum,* Latinâ, *atque* Hetruscâ, *Epigramma Joannis Salsilli Romani.*

CEDE Meles, cedat depressa Mincius urna ;
  Sebetus Tassum desinat usque loqui ;
At Thamesis victor cunctis ferat altior undas
  Nam per te Milto par tribus unus erit.

Miscellaneous Poems.

Ad Joannem Miltonum.

GRÆCIA Mæonidem, jactet sibi Roma Maronem,
Anglia Miltonum jactat utrique parem.

Selvaggi.

Al Signor Gio. Miltoni Nobile Inglese.

ODE.

Ergimi all' Etra ò Clio
Perche di stelle intreccierò corona
Non più del Biondo Dio
La Fronde eterna in Pindo, e in Elicona,
Diensi a merto maggior, maggiori i fregi,
A' celeste virtù celesti pregi.

Non puo del tempo edace
Rimaner preda, eterno alto valore
Non puo l' oblio rapace
Furar dalle memorie eccelso onore,   10
Su l' arco di mia cetra un dardo forte
Virtù m' adatti, e ferirò la morte.

Del Ocean profondo
Cinta dagli ampi gorghi Anglia risiede
Separata dal mondo,
Però che il suo valor l' umano eccede:
Questa feconda sà produrre Eroi,
Ch' hanno a ragion del sovruman tra noi.

Alla virtù sbandita
Danno ne i petti lor fido ricetto,   20
Quella gli è sol gradita,
Perche in lei san trovar gioia, e diletto ;
Ridillo tu Giovanni e mostra in tanto
Con tua vera virtù, vero il mio Canto.

Lungi dal Patrio lido
Spinse Zeusi l' industre ardente brama;
Ch' udio d' Helena il grido
Con aurea tromba rimbombar la fama,
E per poterla effigiare al paro
Dalle più belle Idee trasse il priù raro.   30

Cosi l' Ape Ingegnosa
Trae con industria il suo liquor pregiato
Dal giglio e dalla rosa,
E quanti vaghi fiori ornano il prato;
Formano un dolce suon diverse Chorde,
Fan varie voci melodia concorde.

Di bella gloria amante
Milton dal Ciel natio per varie parti
Le peregrine piante
Volgesti a ricercar scienze, ed arti;   40
Del Gallo regnator vedesti i Regni,
E dell' Italia ancor gl' Eroi piu degni.

Fabro quasi divino
Sol virtù rintracciando il tuo pensiero
Vide in ogni confino
Chi di nobil valor calca il sentiero;
L' ottimo dal miglior dopo sceglia
Per fabbricar d' ogni virtu l' Idea.

Quanti nacquero in Flora
O in lei del parlar Tosco appreser l' arte,   50
La cui memoria onora
Il mondo fatta eterna in dotte carte,
Volesti ricercar per tuo tesoro,
E parlasti con lor nell' opre loro.

Nell' altera Babelle
Per te il parlar confuse Giove in vano,
Che per varie favelle
Di se stessa trofeo cadde su'l piano:
Ch' Ode oltr' all Anglia il suo piu degno Idioma
Spagna, Francia, Toscana, e Grecia e Roma.   60

Miscellaneous Poems.

I piu profondi arcani
Ch' occulta la natura e in cielo e in terra
Ch' a Ingegni sovrumani
Troppo avara tal' hor gli chiude, e serra,
Chiaramente conosci, e giungi al fine
Della moral virtude al gran confine.

Non batta il Tempo l' ale,
Fermisi immoto, e in un ferminsi gl' anni,
Che di virtù immortale
Scorron di troppo ingiuriosi a i danni;   70
Che s' opre degne di Poema o storia
Furon gia, l' hai presenti alla memoria.

Dammi tua dolce Cetra
Se vuoi ch' io dica del tuo dolce canto,
Ch' inalzandoti all' Etra
Di farti huomo celeste ottiene il vanto,
Il Tamigi il dirà che gl' è concesso
Per te suo cigno pareggiar Permesso.

Io che in riva del Arno
Tento spiegar tuo merto alto, e preclaro   80
So che fatico indarno,
E ad ammirar, non a lodarlo imparo;
Freno dunque la lingua, e ascolto il core
Che ti prende a lodar con lo stupore.

Del sig. Antonio Francini gentilhuomo Fiorentino.

Joanni Miltoni Londiniensi.

JOANNI MILTONI

LONDINIENSI.

Juveni Patria, virtutibus eximio,

Viro qui multa peregrinatione, studio cuncta orbis terrarum loca perspexit, ut novus Ulysses omnia ubique ab omnibus apprehenderet.

Polyglotto, in cujus ore linguæ jam deperditæ sic reviviscunt, ut idiomata omnia sint in ejus laudibus infacunda; Et jure ea percallet ut admirationes & plausus populorum ab propria sapientia excitatos, intelligat.

Illi, cujus animi dotes corporisque, sensus ad admirationem commovent, & per ipsam motum cuique auferunt; cujus opera ad plausus hortantur, sed vastitate[1] vocem laudatoribus adimunt.

Cui in Memoria totus Orbis: In intellectu Sapientia: in voluntate ardor gloriæ: in ore Eloquentia: Harmonicos celestium Sphærarum sonitus Astronomia Duce audienti; Characteres mirabilium naturæ per quos Dei magnitudo describitur magistra Philosophia legenti; Antiquitatum latebras, vetustatis excidia, eruditionis ambages comite assidua autorum Lectione.

Exquirenti, restauranti, percurrenti.

At cur nitor in arduum?

Illi in cujus virtutibus evulgandis ora Famæ non sufficiant, nec hominum stupor in laudandis satis est, Reverentiæ & amoris ergo hoc ejus meritis debitum admirationis tributum offert Carolus Datus Patricius Florentinus.

Tanto homini servus, tantæ virtutis amator.

---

[1] vastitate] venustate *1673.*

ELEGIARUM

Liber Primus.

Elegia prima ad *Carolum Diodatum.*

TANDEM, chare, tuæ mihi pervenere tabellæ,
  Pertulit & voces nuntia charta tuas,
Pertulit occiduâ Devæ Cestrensis ab orâ
  Vergivium prono quà petit amne salum.
Multùm crede juvat terras aluisse remotas
  Pectus amans nostri, tamque fidele caput,
Quòdque mihi lepidum tellus longinqua sodalem
  Debet, at unde brevi reddere jussa velit.
Me tenet urbs refluâ quam Thamesis alluit undâ,
  Meque nec invitum patria dulcis habet.   10
Jam nec arundiferum mihi cura revisere Camum,
  Nec dudum vetiti me laris angit amor.
Nuda nec arva placent, umbrasque negantia molles,
  Quàm male Phœbicolis convenit ille locus !
Nec duri libet usque minas perferre magistri
  Cæteraque ingenio non subeunda meo.
Si sit hoc exilium patrios adiisse penates,
  Et vacuum curis otia grata sequi,
Non ego vel profugi nomen, sortemve recuso,
  Lætus & exilii conditione fruor.   20
O utinam vates nunquam graviora tulisset
  Ille Tomitano flebilis exul agro ;
Non tunc Jonio quicquam cessisset Homero
  Neve foret victo laus tibi prima Maro.
Tempora nam licet hîc placidis dare libera Musis,
  Et totum rapiunt me mea vita libri.
Excipit hinc fessum sinuosi pompa theatri,
  Et vocat ad plausus garrula scena suos.

Elegia Prima.

Seu catus auditur senior, seu prodigus hæres,
    Seu procus, aut positâ casside miles adest,   30
Sive decennali fœcundus lite patronus
    Detonat inculto barbara verba foro,
Sæpe vafer gnato succurrit servus amanti,
    Et nasum rigidi fallit ubique Patris ;
Sæpe novos illic virgo mirata calores
    Quid sit amor nescit, dum quoque nescit, amat.
Sive cruentatum furiosa Tragœdia sceptrum
    Quassat, & effusis crinibus ora rotat,
Et dolet, & specto, juvat & spectasse dolendo,
    Interdum & lacrymis dulcis amaror inest :   40
Seu puer infelix indelibata reliquit
    Gaudia, & abrupto flendus amore cadit,
Seu ferus è tenebris iterat Styga criminis ultor
    Conscia funereo pectora torre movens,
Seu mæret Pelopeia domus, seu nobilis Ili,
    Aut luit incestos aula Creontis avos.
Sed neque sub tecto semper nec in urbe latemus,
    Irrita nec nobis tempora veris eunt.
Nos quoque lucus habet vicinâ consitus ulmo
    Atque suburbani nobilis umbra loci.   50
Sæpius hic blandas spirantia sydera flammas
    Virgineos videas præteriisse choros.
Ah quoties dignæ stupui miracula formæ
    Quæ possit senium vel reparare Jovis ;
Ah quoties vidi superantia lumina gemmas,
    Atque faces quotquot volvit uterque polus ;
Collaque bis vivi Pelopis quæ brachia vincant,
    Quæque fluit puro nectare tincta via,
Et decus eximium frontis, tremulosque capillos,
    Aurea quæ fallax retia tendit Amor.   60
Pellacesque genas, ad quas hyacinthina sordet
    Purpura, & ipse tui floris, Adoni, rubor.
Cedite laudatæ toties Heroides olim,
    Et quæcunque vagum cepit amica Jovem.
Cedite Achæmeniæ turritâ fronte puellæ,
    Et quot Susa colunt, Memnoniamque Ninon.
Vos etiam Danaæ fasces submittite Nymphæ,
    Et vos Iliacæ, Romuleæque nurus.
Nec Pompeianas Tarpëia Musa columnas
    Jactet, & Ausoniis plena theatra stolis.   70

Miscellaneous Poems.

Gloria Virginibus debetur prima Britannis,
    Extera sat tibi sit fœmina posse sequi.
Tuque urbs Dardaniis Londinum structa colonis
    Turrigerum latè conspicienda caput,
Tu nimium felix intra tua mœnia claudis
    Quicquid formosi pendulus orbis habet.
Non tibi tot cælo scintillant astra sereno
    Endymioneæ turba ministra deæ,
Quot tibi conspicuæ formáque auróque puellæ
    Per medias radiant turba videnda vias. 80
Creditur huc geminis venisse invecta columbis
    Alma pharetrigero milite cincta Venus,
Huic Cnidon, & riguas Simoentis flumine valles,
    Huic Paphon, & roseam posthabitura Cypron.
Ast ego, dum pueri sinit indulgentia cæci,
    Mœnia quàm subitò linquere fausta paro ;
Et vitare procul malefidæ infamia Circes
    Atria, divini Molyos usus ope.
Stat quoque juncosas Cami remeare paludes,
    Atque iterum raucæ murmur adire Scholæ. 90
Interea fidi parvum cape munus amici,
    Paucaque in alternos verba coacta modos.

Elegia secunda, Anno ætatis 17.

In obitum Præconis Academici Cantabrigiensis.

TE, qui conspicuus baculo fulgente solebas
    Palladium toties ore ciere gregem,
Ultima præconum præconem te quoque sæva
    Mors rapit, officio nec favet ipsa suo.
Candidiora licet fuerint tibi tempora plumis
    Sub quibus accipimus delituisse Jovem,
O dignus tamen Hæmonio juvenescere succo,
    Dignus in Æsonios vivere posse dies,
Dignus quem Stygiis medicâ revocaret ab undis
    Arte Coronides, sæpe rogante dea. 10
Tu si jussus eras acies accire togatas,
    Et celer à Phoebo nuntius ire tuo,
Talis in Iliacâ stabat Cyllenius aula
    Alipes, æthereâ missus ab arce Patris.

(124)

Elegia Tertia.

Talis & Eurybates ante ora furentis Achillei
    Rettulit Atridæ jussa severa ducis.
Magna sepulchrorum regina, satelles Averni
    Sæva nimis Musis, Palladi sæva nimis,
Quin illos rapias qui pondus inutile terræ,
    Turba quidem est telis ista petenda tuis.   20
Vestibus hunc igitur pullis Academia luge,
    Et madeant lachrymis nigra feretra tuis.
Fundat & ipsa modos querebunda Elegëia tristes,
    Personet & totis nænia mœsta scholis.

Elegia tertia, Anno ætatis 17.

In obitum Præsulis Wintoniensis.

Mœstus eram, & tacitus nullo comitante sedebam,
    Hærebantque animo tristia plura meo,
Protinus en subiit funestæ cladis Imago
    Fecit in Angliaco quam Libitina solo ;
Dum procerum ingressa est splendentes marmore turres
    Dira sepulchrali mors metuenda face ;
Pulsavitque auro gravidos & jaspide muros,
    Nec metuit satrapum sternere falce greges.
Tunc memini clarique ducis, fratrisque verendi
    Intempestivis ossa cremata rogis.   10
Et memini Heroum quos vidit ad æthera raptos,
    Flevit & amissos Belgia tota duces.
At te præcipuè luxi dignissime præsul,
    Wintoniæque olim gloria magna tuæ ;
Delicui fletu, & tristi sic ore querebar,
    Mors fera Tartareo diva secunda Jovi,
Nonne satis quod sylva tuas persentiat iras,
    Et quod in herbosos jus tibi detur agros,
Quodque afflata tuo marcescant lilia tabo,
    Et crocus, & pulchræ Cypridi sacra rosa,   20
Nec sinis ut semper fluvio contermina quercus
    Miretur lapsus prætereuntis aquæ ?
Et tibi succumbit liquido quæ plurima cœlo
    Evehitur pennis quamlibet augur avis,
Et quæ mille nigris errant animalia sylvis,
    Et quod alunt mutum Proteos antra pecus.

Miscellaneous Poems.

Invida, tanta tibi cum sit concessa potestas,
　Quid juvat humanâ tingere cæde manus?
Nobileque in pectus certas acuisse sagittas,
　Semideamque animam sede fugâsse suâ?   30
Talia dum lacrymans alto sub pectore volvo,
　Roscidus occiduis Hesperus exit aquis,
Et Tartessiaco submerserat æquore currum
　Phœbus, ab eöo littore mensus iter.
Nec mora, membra cavo posui refovenda cubili,
　Condiderant oculos noxque soporque meos.
Cum mihi visus eram lato spatiarier agro,
　Heu nequit ingenium visa referre meum.
Illic puniceâ radiabant omnia luce,
　Ut matutino cum juga sole rubent.   40
Ac veluti cum pandit opes Thaumantia proles,
　Vestitu nituit multicolore solum.
Non dea tam variis ornavit floribus hortos
　Alcinoi, Zephyro Chloris amata levi.
Flumina vernantes lambunt argentea campos,
　Ditior Hesperio flavet arena Tago.
Serpit odoriferas per opes levis aura Favoni,
　Aura sub innumeris humida nata rosis.
Talis in extremis terræ Gangetidis oris
　Luciferi regis fingitur esse domus.   50
Ipse racemiferis dum densas vitibus umbras
　Et pellucentes miror ubique locos,
Ecce mihi subito præsul Wintonius astat,
　Sydereum nitido fulsit in ore jubar;
Vestis ad auratos defluxit candida talos,
　Infula divinum cinxerat alba caput.
Dumque senex tali incedit venerandus amictu,
　Intremuit læto florea terra sono.
Agmina gemmatis plaudunt cælestia pennis,
　Pura triumphali personat æthra tubâ.   60
Quisque novum amplexu comitem cantuque salutat,
　Hosque aliquis placido misit ab ore sonos;
Nate veni, & patrii felix cape gaudia regni,
　Semper ab hinc duro, nate, labore vaca.
Dixit, & aligeræ tetigerunt nablia turmæ,
　At mihi cum tenebris aurea pulsa quies.
Flebam turbatos Cephaleiâ pellice somnos,
　Talia contingant somnia sæpe mihi.

(126)

Elegia Quarta.

Elegia quarta. Anno ætatis 18.

Ad Thomam Junium præceptorem suum apud mercatores Anglicos Hamburgæ agentes Pastoris munere fungentem.

CURRE per immensum subitò mea littera pontum,
　　I, pete Teutonicos læve per æquor agros,
Segnes rumpe moras, & nil, precor, obstet eunti,
　　Et festinantis nil remoretur iter.
Ipse ego Sicanio frænantem carcere ventos
　　Æolon, & virides sollicitabo Deos ;
Cæruleamque suis comitatam Dorida Nymphis,
　　Ut tibi dent placidam per sua regna viam.
At tu, si poteris, celeres tibi sume jugales,
　　Vecta quibus Colchis fugit ab ore viri.　　　　　10
Aut queis Triptolemus Scythicas devenit in oras
　　Gratus Eleusinâ missus ab urbe puer.
Atque ubi Germanas flavere videbis arenas
　　Ditis ad Hamburgæ mœnia flecte gradum,
Dicitur occiso quæ ducere nomen ab Hamâ,
　　Cimbrica quem fertur clava dedisse neci.
Vivit ibi antiquæ clarus pietatis honore
　　Præsul Christicolas pascere doctus oves ;
Ille quidem est animæ plusquam pars altera nostræ,
　　Dimidio vitæ vivere cogor ego.　　　　　20
Hei mihi quot pelagi, quot montes interjecti
　　Me faciunt aliâ parte carere mei !
Charior ille mihi quam tu doctissime Graium
　　Cliniadi, pronepos qui Telamonis erat.
Quámque Stagirites generoso magnus alumno,
　　Quem peperit Libyco Chaonis alma Jovi.
Qualis Amyntorides, qualis Philyrëius Heros
　　Myrmidonum regi, talis & ille mihi.
Primus ego Aonios illo præeunte recessus
　　Lustrabam, & bifidi sacra vireta jugi,　　　　　30
Pieriosque hausi latices, Clioque favente,
　　Castalio sparsi læta ter ora mero.

(127)

Flammeus at signum ter viderat arietis Æthon
    Induxitque auro lanea terga novo,
Bisque novo terram sparsisti Chlori senilem
    Gramine, bisque tuas abstulit Auster opes:
Necdum ejus licuit mihi lumina pascere vultu,
    Aut linguæ dulces aure bibisse sonos.
Vade igitur, cursuque Eurum præverte sonorum,
    Quàm sit opus monitis res docet, ipsa vides.   40
Invenies dulci cum conjuge forte sedentem,
    Mulcentem gremio pignora chara suo,
Forsitan aut veterum prælarga volumina patrum
    Versantem, aut veri biblia sacra Dei.
Cælestive animas saturantem rore tenellas,
    Grande salutiferæ religionis opus.
Utque solet, multam, sit dicere cura salutem,
    Dicere quam decuit, si modo adesset, herum.
Hæc quoque paulum oculos in humum defixa modestos,
    Verba verecundo sis memor ore loqui: 50
Hæc tibi, si teneris vacat inter prælia Musis
    Mittit ab Angliaco littore fida manus.
Accipe sinceram, quamvis sit sera, salutem;
    Fiat & hoc ipso gratior illa tibi.
Sera quidem, sed vera fuit, quam casta recepit
    Icaris a lento Penelopeia viro.
Ast ego quid volui manifestum tollere crimen,
    Ipse quod ex omni parte levare nequit.
Arguitur tardus meritò, noxamque fatetur,
    Et pudet officium deseruisse suum.   60
Tu modò da veniam fasso, veniamque roganti,
    Crimina diminui, quæ patuere, solent.
Non ferus in pavidos rictus diducit hiantes,
    Vulnifico pronos nec rapit ungue leo.
Sæpe sarissiferi crudelia pectora Thracis
    Supplicis ad mœstas delicuere preces.
Extensæque manus avertunt fulminis ictus,
    Placat & iratos hostia parva Deos.
Jamque diu scripsisse tibi fuit impetus illi,
    Neve moras ultra ducere passus Amor.   70
Nam vaga Fama refert, heu nuntia vera malorum!
    In tibi finitimis bella tumere locis.
Teque tuàmque urbem truculento milite cingi,
    Et jam Saxonicos arma parasse duces.

Elegiarum Quarta.

Te circum latè campos populatur Enyo,
    Et sata carne virûm jam cruor arva rigat.
Germanisque suum concessit Thracia Martem,
    Illuc Odrysios Mars pater egit equos.
Perpetuóque comans jam deflorescit oliva,
    Fugit & ærisonam Diva perosa tubam,   80
Fugit io terris, & jam non ultima virgo
    Creditur ad superas justa volasse domos.
Te tamen intereà belli circumsonat horror,
    Vivis & ignoto solus inópsque solo ;
Et, tibi quam patrii non exhibuere penates
    Sede peregrinâ quæris egenus opem.
Patria dura parens, & saxis sævior albis
    Spumea quæ pulsat littoris unda tui,
Siccine te decet innocuos exponere fætus ;
    Siccine in externam ferrea cogis humum,   90
Et sinis ut terris quærant alimenta remotis
    Quos tibi prospiciens miserat ipse Deus,
Et qui læta ferunt de cælo nuntia, quique
    Quæ via post cineres ducat ad astra, docent ?
Digna quidem Stygiis quæ vivas clausa tenebris,
    Æternâque animæ digna perire fame !
Haud aliter vates terræ Thesbitidis olim
    Pressit inassueto devia tesqua pede,
Desertasque Arabum salebras, dum regis Achabi
    Effugit atque tuas, Sidoni dira, manus.   100
Talis & horrisono laceratus membra flagello,
    Paulus ab Æmathiâ pellitur urbe Cilix.
Piscosæque ipsum Gergessæ civis Jesum
    Finibus ingratus jussit abire suis.
At tu sume animos, nec spes cadat anxia curis
    Nec tua concutiat decolor ossa metus.
Sis etenim quamvis fulgentibus obsitus armis,
    Intententque tibi millia tela necem,
At nullis vel inerme latus violabitur armis,
    Deque tuo cuspis nulla cruore bibet.   110
Namque eris ipse Dei radiante sub ægide tutus,
    Ille tibi custos, & pugil ille tibi ;
Ille Sionææ qui tot sub mœnibus arcis
    Assyrios fudit nocte silente viros ;
Inque fugam vertit quos in Samaritidas oras
    Misit ab antiquis prisca Damascus agris,

Terruit & densas pavido cum rege cohortes,
    Aëre dum vacuo buccina clara sonat,
Cornea pulvereum dum verberat ungula campum,
    Currus arenosam dum quatit actus humum,   120
Auditurque hinnitus equorum ad bella ruentûm,
    Et strepitus ferri, murmuraque alta virûm.
Et tu (quod superest miseris) sperare memento,
    Et tua magnanimo pectore vince mala.
Nec dubites quandoque frui melioribus annis,
    Atque iterum patrios posse videre lares.

Elegia quinta, Anno ætatis 20.

In adventum veris.

In se perpetuo Tempus revolubile gyro
    Jam revocat Zephyros vere tepente novos.
Induiturque brevem Tellus reparata juventam,
    Jamque soluta gelu dulce virescit humus.
Fallor? an & nobis redeunt in carmina vires,
    Ingeniumque mihi munere veris adest?
Munere veris adest, iterumque vigescit ab illo
    (Quis putet) atque aliquod jam sibi poscit opus.
Castalis ante oculos, bifidumque cacumen oberrat,
    Et mihi Pyrenen somnia nocte ferunt.   10
Concitaque arcano fervent mihi pectora motu,
    Et furor, & sonitus me sacer intùs agit.
Delius ipse venit, video Penëide lauro
    Implicitos crines, Delius ipse venit.
Jam mihi mens liquidi raptatur in ardua cœli,
    Perque vagas nubes corpore liber eo.
Perque umbras, perque antra feror penetralia vatum,
    Et mihi fana patent interiora Deûm.
Intuiturque animus toto quid agatur Olympo,
    Nec fugiunt oculos Tartara cæca meos.   20
Quid tam grande sonat distento spiritus ore?
    Quid parit hæc rabies, quid sacer iste furor?
Ver mihi, quod dedit ingenium, cantabitur illo;
    Profuerint isto reddita dona modo.

Elegia Quinta.

Jam Philomela tuos foliis adoperta novellis
   Instituis modulos, dum silet omne nemus.
Urbe ego, tu sylvâ simul incipiamus utrique,
   Et simul adventum veris uterque canat.
Veris io rediere vices, celebremus honores
   Veris, & hoc subeat Musa quotannis opus.   30
Jam sol Æthiopas fugiens Tithoniaque arva,
   Flectit ad Arctöas aurea lora plagas.
Est breve noctis iter, brevis est mora noctis opacæ
   Horrida cum tenebris exulat illa suis.
Jamque Lycaonius plaustrum cæleste Boötes
   Non longâ sequitur fessus ut ante viâ,
Nunc etiam solitas circum Jovis atria toto
   Excubias agitant sydera rara polo.
Nam dolus & cædes, & vis cum nocte recessit,
   Neve Giganteum Dii timuere scelus.   40
Forte aliquis scopuli recubans in vertice pastor,
   Roscida cum primo sole rubescit humus,
Hac, ait, hac certè caruisti nocte puellâ
   Phœbe tuâ, celeres quæ retineret equos.
Læta suas repetit sylvas, pharetramque resumit
   Cynthia, Luciferas ut videt alta rotas,
Et tenues ponens radios gaudere videtur
   Officium fieri tam breve fratris ope.
Desere, Phœbus ait, thalamos Aurora seniles,
   Quid juvat effœto procubuisse toro?   50
Te manet Æolides viridi venator in herba,
   Surge, tuos ignes altus Hymettus habet.
Flava verecundo dea crimen in ore fatetur,
   Et matutinos ocyus urget equos.
Exuit invisam Tellus rediviva senectam,
   Et cupit amplexus Phœbe subire tuos;
Et cupit, & digna est, quid enim formosius illâ,
   Pandit ut omniferos luxuriosa sinus,
Atque Arabum spirat messes, & ab ore venusto
   Mitia cum Paphiis fundit amoma rosis.   60
Ecce coronatur sacro frons ardua luco,
   Cingit ut Idæam pinea turris Opim;
Et vario madidos intexit flore capillos,
   Floribus & visa est posse placere suis.

30 quotannis] perennis *1673*

Floribus effusos ut erat redimita capillos
    Tænario placuit diva Sicana Deo.
Aspice Phœbe tibi faciles hortantur amores,
    Mellitasque movent flamina verna preces.
Cinnameâ Zephyrus leve plaudit odorifer alâ,
    Blanditiasque tibi ferre videntur aves.   70
Nec sine dote tuos temeraria quærit amores
    Terra, nec optatos poscit egena toros,
Alma salutiferum medicos tibi gramen in usus
    Præbet, & hinc titulos adjuvat ipsa tuos.
Quòd si te pretium, si te fulgentia tangunt
    Munera, (muneribus sæpe coemptus Amor)
Illa tibi ostentat quascunque sub æquore vasto,
    Et superinjectis montibus abdit opes.
Ah quoties cum tu clivoso fessus Olympo
    In vespertinas præcipitaris aquas,   80
Cur te, inquit, cursu languentem Phœbe diurno
    Hesperiis recipit Cærula mater aquis ?
Quid tibi cum Tethy ? Quid cum Tartesside lymphâ,
    Dia quid immundo perluis ora salo ?
Frigora Phœbe meâ melius captabis in umbrâ,
    Huc ades, ardentes imbue rore comas.
Mollior egelidâ veniet tibi somnus in herbâ,
    Huc ades, & gremio lumina pone meo.
Quáque jaces circum mulcebit lene susurrans
    Aura per humentes corpora fusa rosas.   90
Nec me (crede mihi) terrent Semelëia fata,
    Nec Phäetonteo fumidus axis equo ;
Cum tu Phœbe tuo sapientius uteris igni,
    Huc ades & gremio lumina pone meo.
Sic Tellus lasciva suos suspirat amores ;
    Matris in exemplum cætera turba ruunt.
Nunc etenim toto currit vagus orbe Cupido,
    Languentesque fovet solis ab igne faces.
Insonuere novis lethalia cornua nervis,
    Triste micant ferro tela corusca novo.   100
Jamque vel invictam tentat superasse Dianam,
    Quæque sedet sacro Vesta pudica foco.
Ipsa senescentem reparat Venus annua formam.
    Atque iterum tepido creditur orta mari.
Marmoreas juvenes clamant Hymenæe per urbes,
    Litus io Hymen, & cava saxa sonant.

Elegia Quinta.

Cultior ille venit tunicâque decentior aptâ,
  Puniceum redolet vestis odora crocum.
Egrediturque frequens ad amœni gaudia veris
  Virgineos auro cincta puella sinus.   110
Votum est cuique suum, votum est tamen omnibus unum,
  Ut sibi quem cupiat, det Cytherea virum.
Nunc quoque septenâ modulatur arundine pastor,
  Et sua quæ jungat carmina Phyllis habet.
Navita nocturno placat sua sydera cantu,
  Delphinasque leves ad vada summa vocat.
Jupiter ipse alto cum conjuge ludit Olympo,
  Convocat & famulos ad sua festa Deos.
Nunc etiam Satyri cum sera crepuscula surgunt,
  Pervolitant celeri florea rura choro,   120
Sylvanusque suâ Cyparissi fronde revinctus,
  Semicaperque Deus, semideusque caper.
Quæque sub arboribus Dryades latuere vetustis
  Per juga, per solos expatiantur agros.
Per sata luxuriat fruticetaque Mænalius Pan,
  Vix Cybele mater, vix sibi tuta Ceres,
Atque aliquam cupidus prædatur Oreada Faunus,
  Consulit in trepidos dum sibi Nympha pedes,
Jamque latet, latitansque cupit male tecta videri,
  Et fugit, & fugiens pervelit ipsa capi.   130
Dii quoque non dubitant cælo præponere sylvas,
  Et sua quisque sibi numina lucus habet.
Et sua quisque diu sibi numina lucus habeto,
  Nec vos arboreâ dii precor ite domo.
Te referant miseris te Jupiter aurea terris
  Sæcla, quid ad nimbos aspera tela redis?
Tu saltem lentè rapidos age Phœbe jugales
  Quà potes, & sensim tempora veris eant.
Brumaque productas tardè ferat hispida noctes,
  Ingruat & nostro serior umbra polo.   140

Miscellaneous Poems.

Elegia sexta.

Ad Carolum Diodatum ruri commorantem.

Qui cum idibus Decemb. scripsisset, & sua carmina excusari postulasset si solito minus essent bona, quòd inter lautitias quibus erat ab amicis exceptus, haud satis felicem operam Musis dare se posse affirmabat, hunc habuit responsum.

MITTO tibi sanam non pleno ventre salutem,
    Quâ tu distento forte carere potes.
At tua quid nostram prolectat Musa camœnam,
    Nec sinit optatas posse sequi tenebras ?
Carmine scire velis quàm te redamémque colámque,
    Crede mihi vix hoc carmine scire queas,
Nam neque noster amor modulis includitur arctis,
    Nec venit ad claudos integer ipse pedes.
Quàm bene solennes epulas, hilaremque Decembrim
    Festaque cœlifugam quæ coluere Deum,   10
Deliciasque refers, hyberni gaudia ruris,
    Haustaque per lepidos Gallica musta focos.
Quid quereris refugam vino dapibusque poesin ?
    Carmen amat Bacchum, Carmina Bacchus amat.
Nec puduit Phœbum virides gestasse corymbos,
    Atque hederam lauro præposuisse suæ.
Sæpius Aoniis clamavit collibus Euœ
    Mista Thyonêo turba novena choro.
Naso Corallæis mala carmina misit ab agris :
    Non illic epulæ non sata vitis erat.   20
Quid nisi vina, rosasque racemiferumque Lyæum
    Cantavit brevibus Tëia Musa modis ?
Pindaricosque inflat numeros Teumesius Euan,
    Et redolet sumptum pagina quæque merum.
Dum gravis everso currus crepat axe supinus,
    Et volat Eléo pulvere fuscus eques.
Quadrimoque madens Lyricen Romanus Iaccho
    Dulce canit Glyceran, flavicomamque Chloen.
Jam quoque lauta tibi generoso mensa paratu,
    Mentis alit vires, ingeniumque fovet.   30
Massica fœcundam despumant pocula venam,
    Fundis & ex ipso condita metra cado.

Elegia Sexta.

Addimus his artes, fusumque per intima Phœbum
    Corda, favent uni Bacchus, Apollo, Ceres.
Scilicet haud mirum tam dulcia carmina per te
    Numine composito tres peperisse Deos.
Nunc quoque Thressa tibi cælato barbitos auro
    Insonat argutâ molliter icta manu ;
Auditurque chelys suspensa tapetia circum,
    Virgineos tremulâ quæ regat arte pedes.   40
Illa tuas saltem teneant spectacula Musas,
    Et revocent, quantum crapula pellit iners.
Crede mihi dum psallit ebur, comitataque plectrum
    Implet odoratos festa chorea tholos,
Percipies tacitum per pectora serpere Phœbum,
    Quale repentinus permeat ossa calor,
Perque puellares oculos digitumque sonantem
    Irruet in totos lapsa Thalia sinus.
Namque Elegía levis multorum cura deorum est,
    Et vocat ad numeros quemlibet illa suos ;   50
Liber adest elegis, Eratoque, Ceresque, Venusque,
    Et cum purpureâ matre tenellus Amor.
Talibus inde licent convivia larga poetis,
    Sæpius & veteri commaduisse mero.
At qui bella refert, & adulto sub Jove cælum,
    Heroasque pios, semideosque duces,
Et nunc sancta canit superum consulta deorum,
    Nunc latrata fero regna profunda cane,
Ille quidem parcè Samii pro more magistri
    Vivat, & innocuos præbeat herba cibos ;   60
Stet prope fagineo pellucida lympha catillo,
    Sobriaque è puro pocula fonte bibat.
Additur huic scelerisque vacans, & casta juventus,
    Et rigidi mores, & sine labe manus.
Qualis veste nitens sacrâ, & lustralibus undis
    Surgis ad infensos augur iture Deos.
Hoc ritu vixisse ferunt post rapta sagacem
    Lumina Tiresian, Ogygiumque Linon,
Et lare devoto profugum Calchanta, senemque
    Orpheon edomitis sola per antra feris ;   70
Sic dapis exiguus, sic rivi potor Homerus
    Dulichium vexit per freta longa virum,
Et per monstrificam Perseiæ Phœbados aulam,
    Et vada fœmineis insidiosa sonis,

Perque tuas rex ime domos, ubi sanguine nigro
   Dicitur umbrarum detinuisse greges.
Diis etenim sacer est vates, divûmque sacerdos,
   Spirat & occultum pectus, & ora Jovem.
At tu si quid agam, scitabere (si modò saltem
   Esse putas tanti noscere siquid agam)   80
Paciferum canimus cælesti semine regem,
   Faustaque sacratis sæcula pacta libris,
Vagitumque Dei, & stabulantem paupere tecto
   Qui suprema suo cum patre regna colit.
Stelliparumque polum, modulantesque æthere turmas,
   Et subitò elisos ad sua fana Deos.
Dona quidem dedimus Christi natalibus illa
   Illa sub auroram lux mihi prima tulit.
Te quoque pressa manent patriis meditata cicutis,
   Tu mihi, cui recitem, judicis instar eris.   90

Elegia septima, Anno ætatis undevigesimo.

NONDUM blanda tuas leges Amathusia noram,
   Et Paphio vacuum pectus ab igne fuit.
Sæpe cupidineas, puerilia tela, sagittas,
   Atque tuum sprevi maxime, numen, Amor.
Tu puer imbelles dixi transfige columbas,
   Conveniunt tenero mollia bella duci.
Aut de passeribus tumidos age, parve, triumphos,
   Hæc sunt militiæ digna trophæa tuæ.
In genus humanum quid inania dirigis arma?
   Non valet in fortes ista pharetra viros.   10
Non tulit hoc Cyprius, (neque enim Deus ullus ad iras
   Promptior) & duplici jam ferus igne calet.
Ver erat, & summæ radians per culmina villæ
   Attulerat primam lux tibi Maie diem:
At mihi adhuc refugam quærebant lumina noctem
   Nec matutinum sustinuere jubar.
Astat Amor lecto, pictis Amor impiger alis,
   Prodidit astantem mota pharetra Deum:
Prodidit & facies, & dulce minantis ocelli,
   Et quicquid puero, dignum & Amore fuit.   20

Elegia Septima.

Talis in æterno juvenis Sigeius Olympo
    Miscet amatori pocula plena Jovi;
Aut qui formosas pellexit ad oscula nymphas
    Thiodamantæus Naiade raptus Hylas;
Addideratque iras, sed & has decuisse putares,
    Addideratque truces, nec sine felle minas.
Et miser exemplo sapuisses tutiùs, inquit,
    Nunc mea quid possit dextera testis eris.
Inter & expertos vires numerabere nostras,
    Et faciam vero per tua damna fidem.   30
Ipse ego si nescis strato Pythone superbum
    Edomui Phœbum, cessit & ille mihi;
Et quoties meminit Peneidos, ipse fatetur
    Certiùs & graviùs tela nocere mea.
Me nequit adductum curvare peritiùs arcum,
    Qui post terga solet vincere Parthus eques.
Cydoniusque mihi cedit venator, & ille
    Inscius uxori qui necis author erat.
Est etiam nobis ingens quoque victus Orion,
    Herculeæque manus, Herculeusque comes.   40
Jupiter ipse licet sua fulmina torqueat in me,
    Hærebunt lateri spicula nostra Jovis.
Cætera quæ dubitas meliùs mea tela docebunt,
    Et tua non leviter corda petenda mihi.
Nec te stulte tuæ poterunt defendere Musæ,
    Nec tibi Phœbæus porriget anguis opem.
Dixit, & aurato quatiens mucrone sagittam,
    Evolat in tepidos Cypridos ille sinus.
At mihi risuro tonuit ferus ore minaci,
    Et mihi de puero non metus ullus erat.   50
Et modò quà nostri spatiantur in urbe Quirites
    Et modò villarum proxima rura placent.
Turba frequens, faciéque simillima turba dearum
    Splendida per medias itque reditque vias.
Auctaque luce dies gemino fulgore coruscat,
    Fallor? an & radios hinc quoque Phœbus habet.
Hæc ego non fugi spectacula grata severus,
    Impetus & quò me fert juvenilis, agor.
Lumina luminibus malè providus obvia misi,
    Neve oculos potui continuisse meos.   60
Unam forte aliis supereminuisse notabam,
    Principium nostri lux erat illa mali.

Sic Venus optaret mortalibus ipsa videri,
  Sic regina Deûm conspicienda fuit.
Hanc memor objecit nobis malus ille Cupido,
  Solus & hos nobis texuit antè dolos.
Nec procul ipse vafer latuit, multæque sagittæ,
  Et facis a tergo grande pependit onus.
Nec mora, nunc ciliis hæsit, nunc virginis ori,
  Insilit hinc labiis, insidet inde genis :   70
Et quascunque agilis partes jaculator oberrat,
  Hei mihi, mille locis pectus inerme ferit.
Protinus insoliti subierunt corda furores,
  Uror amans intùs, flammaque totus eram.
Interea misero quæ jam mihi sola placebat,
  Ablata est oculis non reditura meis.
Ast ego progredior tacitè querebundus, & excors,
  Et dubius volui sæpe referre pedem.
Findor, & hæc remanet, sequitur pars altera votum,
  Raptaque tàm subitò gaudia flere juvat.   80
Sic dolet amissum proles Junonia cœlum,
  Inter Lemniacos præcipitata focos.
Talis & abreptum solem respexit, ad Orcum
  Vectus ab attonitis Amphiaraus equis.
Quid faciam infelix, & luctu victus, amores
  Nec licet inceptos ponere, neve sequi.
O utinam spectare semel mihi detur amatos
  Vultus, & coràm tristia verba loqui ;
Forsitan & duro non est adamante creata,
  Forte nec ad nostras surdeat illa preces.   90
Crede mihi nullus sic infeliciter arsit,
  Ponar in exemplo primus & unus ego.
Parce precor teneri cum sis Deus ales amoris,
  Pugnent officio nec tua facta tuo.
Jam tuus O certè est mihi formidabilis arcus,
  Nate deâ, jaculis nec minus igne potens :
Et tua fumabunt nostris altaria donis,
  Solus & in superis tu mihi summus eris.
Deme meos tandem, verùm nec deme furores,
  Nescio cur, miser est suaviter omnis amans :   100
Tu modo da facilis, posthæc mea siqua futura est,
  Cuspis amaturos figat ut una duos.

In Proditionem Bombardicam.

Hæc ego mente olim lævâ, studioque supino
  Nequitiæ posui vana trophæa meæ.
Scilicet abreptum sic me malus impulit error,
  Indocilisque ætas prava magistra fuit.
Donec Socraticos umbrosa Academia rivos
  Præbuit, admissum dedocuitque jugum.
Protinus extinctis ex illo tempore flammis,
  Cincta rigent multo pectora nostra gelu.
Unde suis frigus metuit puer ipse Sagittis,
  Et Diomedéam vim timet ipse Venus.   10

In Proditionem Bombardicam.

Cum simul in regem nuper satrapasque Britannos
  Ausus es infandum perfide Fauxe nefas,
Fallor? an & mitis voluisti ex parte videri,
  Et pensare malâ cum pietate scelus;
Scilicet hos alti missurus ad atria cæli,
  Sulphureo curru flammivolisque rotis.
Qualiter ille feris caput inviolabile Parcis
  Liquit Jördanios turbine raptus agros.

In eandem.

Siccine tentasti cælo donâsse Jäcobum
  Quae septemgemino Bellua monte lates?
Ni meliora tuum poterit dare munera numen,
  Parce precor donis insidiosa tuis.
Ille quidem sine te consortia serus adivit
  Astra, nec inferni pulveris usus ope.
Sic potiùs fœdos in cælum pelle cucullos,
  Et quot habet brutos Roma profana Deos.
Namque hac aut aliâ nisi quemque adjuveris arte,
  Crede mihi cæli vix bene scandet iter.   10

Miscellaneous Poems.

In eandem.

PURGATOREM animæ derisit Jäcobus ignem,
  Et sine quo superûm non adeunda domus.
Frenduit hoc trinâ monstrum Latiale coronâ
  Movit & horrificùm cornua dena minax.
Et nec inultus ait temnes mea sacra Britanne,
  Supplicium spretâ relligione dabis.
Et si stelligeras unquam penetraveris arces,
  Non nisi per flammas triste patebit iter.
O quàm funesto cecinisti proxima vero,
  Verbaque ponderibus vix caritura suis!   10
Nam prope Tartareo sublime rotatus ab igni
  Ibat ad æthereas umbra perusta plagas.

In eandem.

QUEM modò Roma suis devoverat impia diris,
  Et Styge damnarât Tænarioque sinu,
Hunc vice mutatâ jam tollere gestit ad astra,
  Et cupit ad superos evehere usque Deos.

In inventorem Bombardæ.

JAPETIONIDEM laudavit cæca vetustas,
  Qui tulit æthæream solis ab axe facem;
At mihi major erit, qui lurida creditur arma,
  Et trifidum fulmen surripuisse Jovi.

Ad Leonoram Romæ canentem.

ANGELUS unicuique suus (sic credite gentes)
  Obtigit æthereis ales ab ordinibus.
Quid mirum? Leonora tibi si gloria major,
  Nam tua præsentem vox sonat ipsa Deum.

(140)

Ad Leonoram.

Aut Deus, aut vacui certè mens tertia cœli
    Per tua secretò guttura serpit agens;
Serpit agens, facilisque docet mortalia corda
    Sensim immortali assuescere posse sono.
Quòd si cuncta quidem Deus est, per cunctaque fusus,
    In te unâ loquitur, cætera mutus habet.   10

Ad eandem.

ALTERA Torquatum cepit Leonora Poëtam,
    Cujus ab insano cessit amore furens.
Ah miser ille tuo quantò feliciùs ævo
    Perditus, & propter te Leonora foret!
Et te Pieriâ sensisset voce canentem
    Aurea maternæ fila movere lyræ,
Quamvis Dircæo torsisset lumina Pentheo
    Sævior, aut totus desipuisset iners,
Tu tamen errantes cæcâ vertigine sensus
    Voce eadem poteras composuisse tuâ;   10
Et poteras ægro spirans sub corde quietem
    Flexanimo cantu restituisse sibi.

Ad eandem.

CREDULA quid liquidam Sirena Neapoli jactas,
    Claraque Parthenopes fana Achelöiados,
Littoreamque tuâ defunctam Naiada ripâ
    Corpora Chalcidico sacra dedisse rogo?
Illa quidem vivitque, & amœnâ Tibridis undâ
    Mutavit rauci murmura Pausilipi.
Illic Romulidûm studiis ornata secundis,
    Atque homines cantu detinet atque Deos.

Elegiarum Finis.

(141)

Miscellaneous Poems.

[Added in Second Edition, 1673.]

Apologus de Rustico & Hero.

RUSTICUS ex Malo sapidissima poma quotannis
  Legit, & urbano lecta dedit Domino :
Hic incredibili fructûs dulcedine Captus
  Malum ipsam in proprias transtulit areolas.
Hactenus illa ferax, sed longo debilis ævo,
  Mota solo assueto, protinùs aret iners.
Quod tandem ut patuit Domino, spe lusus inani,
  Damnavit celeres in sua damna manus.
Atque ait, Heu quantò satius fuit illa Coloni
  (Parva licet) grato dona tulisse animo !   10
Possem Ego avaritiam frœnare, gulamque voracem :
  Nunc periere mihi & fœtus & ipsa parens.

[From *Defensio pro populo anglicano*, 1651.]

In Salmasii Hundredam.

QUIS expedivit Salmasio suam Hundredam,
Picamque docuit verba nostra conari ?
Magister artis venter, et Jacobei
Centum exulantis viscera marsupii regis.
Quod si dolosi spes refulserit nummi,
Ipse, Antichristi modo qui primatum Papæ
Minatus uno est dissipare sufflatu,
Cantabit ultro Cardinalitium melos.

[From *Defensio secunda*, 1654.]

In Salmasium.

GAUDETE scombri, et quicquid est piscium salo,
Qui frigida hyeme incolitis algentes freta !
Vestrum misertus ille Salmasius Eques
Bonus, amicire nuditatem cogitat ;
Chartæque largus, apparat papyrinos
Vobis cucullos, præferentes Claudii
Insignia, nomenque et decus, Salmasii :
Gestetis ut per omne cetarium forum
Equitis clientes, scriniis mungentium
Cubito virorum, et capsulis, gratissimos.   10

(142)

In obitum Procancellarii medici.

SYLVARUM LIBER.

Anno ætatis 16. In obitum Procancellarii medici.

PARERE fati discite legibus,
Manusque Parcæ jam date supplices,
   Qui pendulum telluris orbem
     Jäpeti colitis nepotes.
Vos si relicto mors vaga Tænaro
Semel vocârit flebilis, heu moræ
   Tentantur incassùm dolique;
     Per tenebras Stygis ire certum est.
Si destinatam pellere dextera
Mortem valeret, non ferus Hercules   10
   Nessi venenatus cruore
     Æmathiâ jacuisset Œtâ.
Nec fraude turpi Palladis invidæ
Vidisset occisum Ilion Hectora, aut
   Quem larva Pelidis peremit
     Ense Locro, Jove lacrymante.
Si triste fatum verba Hecatëia
Fugare possint, Telegoni parens
   Vixisset infamis, potentique
     Ægiali soror usa virgâ.   20
Numenque trinum fallere si queant
Artes medentûm, ignotaque gramina,
   Non gnarus herbarum Machaon
     Eurypyli cecidisset hastâ.
Læsisset & nec te Philyreie
Sagitta echidnæ perlita sanguine,
   Nec tela te fulmenque avitum
     Cæse puer genitricis alvo.
Tuque O alumno major Apolline,
Gentis togatæ cui regimen datum,   30
   Frondosa quem nunc Cirrha luget,
     Et mediis Helicon in undis,

Jam præfuisses Palladio gregi
Lætus, superstes, nec sine gloria,
    Nec puppe lustrasses Charontis
        Horribiles barathri recessus.
At fila rupit Persephone tua
Irata, cum te viderit artibus
    Succoque pollenti tot atris
        Faucibus eripuisse mortis.   40
Colende præses, membra precor tua
Molli quiescant cespite, & ex tuo
    Crescant rosæ, calthæque busto,
        Purpureoque hyacinthus ore.
Sit mite de te judicium Æaci,
Subrideatque Ætnæa Proserpina,
    Interque felices perennis
        Elysio spatiere campo.

In quintum Novembris, Anno ætatis 17.

JAM pius extremâ veniens Jäcobus ab arcto
Teucrigenas populos, latéque patentia regna
Albionum tenuit, jamque inviolabile fœdus
Sceptra Caledoniis conjunxerat Anglica Scotis:
Pacificusque novo felix divesque sedebat
In solio, occultique doli securus & hostis:
Cum ferus ignifluo regnans Acheronte tyrannus,
Eumenidum pater, æthereo vagus exul Olympo,
Forte per immensum terrarum erraverat orbem,
Dinumerans sceleris socios, vernasque fideles,   10
Participes regni post funera mœsta futuros;
Hic tempestates medio ciet aëre diras,
Illic unanimes odium struit inter amicos,
Armat & invictas in mutua viscera gentes;
Regnaque olivifera vertit florentia pace,
Et quoscunque videt puræ virtutis amantes,
Hos cupit adjicere imperio, fraudumque magister
Tentat inaccessum sceleri corrumpere pectus,
Insidiasque locat tacitas, cassesque latentes
Tendit, ut incautos rapiat, seu Caspia Tigris   20
Insequitur trepidam deserta per avia prædam
Nocte sub illuni, & somno nictantibus astris.

Talibus infestat populos Summanus & urbes
Cinctus cæruleæ fumanti turbine flammæ.
Jamque fluentisonis albentia rupibus arva
Apparent, & terra Deo dilecta marino,
Cui nomen dederat quondam Neptunia proles
Amphitryoniaden qui non dubitavit atrocem
Æquore tranato furiali poscere bello,
Ante expugnatæ crudelia sæcula Troiæ.   30

   At simul hanc opibusque & festâ pace beatam
Aspicit, & pingues donis Cerealibus agros,
Quodque magis doluit, venerantem numina veri
Sancta Dei populum, tandem suspiria rupit
Tartareos ignes & luridum olentia sulphur.
Qualia Trinacriâ trux ab Jove clausus in Ætna
Efflat tabifico monstrosus ab ore Tiphœus.
Ignescunt oculi, stridetque adamantinus ordo
Dentis, ut armorum fragor, ictaque cuspide cuspis.
Atque pererrato solum hoc lacrymabile mundo   40
Inveni, dixit, gens hæc mihi sola rebellis,
Contemtrixque jugi, nostrâque potentior arte.
Illa tamen, mea si quicquam tentamina possunt,
Non feret hoc impune diu, non ibit inulta,
Hactenus ; & piceis liquido natat aëre pennis ;
Quà volat, adversi præcursant agmine venti,
Densantur nubes, & crebra tonitrua fulgent.

   Jamque pruinosas velox superaverat alpes,
Et tenet Ausoniæ fines, à parte sinistrâ
Nimbifer Appenninus erat, priscique Sabini,   50
Dextra veneficiis infamis Hetruria, nec non
Te furtiva Tibris Thetidi videt oscula dantem ;
Hinc Mavortigenæ consistit in arce Quirini.
Reddiderant dubiam jam sera crepuscula lucem,
Cum circumgreditur totam Tricoronifer urbem,
Panificosque Deos portat, scapulisque virorum
Evehitur, præeunt summisso poplite reges,
Et mendicantum series longissima fratrum ;
Cereaque in manibus gestant funalia cæci,
Cimmeriis nati in tenebris, vitamque trahentes.   60
Templa dein multis subeunt lucentia tædis
(Vesper erat sacer iste Petro) fremitúsque canentum

Sæpe tholos implet vacuos, & inane locorum.
Qualiter exululat Bromius, Bromiique caterva,
Orgia cantantes in Echionio Aracyntho,
Dum tremit attonitus vitreis Asopus in undis,
Et procul ipse cavâ responsat rupe Cithæron.

His igitur tandem solenni more peractis,
Nox senis amplexus Erebi taciturna reliquit,
Præcipitesque impellit equos stimulante flagello,   70
Captum oculis Typhlonta, Melanchætemque ferocem,
Atque Acherontæo prognatam patre Siopen
Torpidam, & hirsutis horrentem Phrica capillis.
Interea regum domitor, Phlegetontius hæres,
Ingreditur thalamos (neque enim secretus adulter
Producit steriles molli sine pellice noctes)
At vix compositos somnus claudebat ocellos,
Cum niger umbrarum dominus, rectorque silentum,
Prædatorque hominum falsâ sub imagine tectus
Astitit, assumptis micuerunt tempora canis,   80
Barba sinus promissa tegit, cineracea longo
Syrmate verrit humum vestis, pendetque cucullus
Vertice de raso, & ne quicquam desit ad artes,
Cannabeo lumbos constrinxit fune salaces.
Tarda fenestratis figens vestigia calceis.
Talis uti fama est, vastâ Franciscus eremo
Tetra vagabatur solus per lustra ferarum,
Sylvestrique tulit genti pia verba salutis
Impius, atque lupos domuit, Lybicosque leones.

Subdolus at tali Serpens velatus amictu   90
Solvit in has fallax ora execrantia voces;
Dormis nate? Etiamne tuos sopor opprimit artus
Immemor O fidei, pecorumque oblite tuorum,
Dum cathedram venerande tuam, diademaque triplex
Ridet Hyperboreo gens barbara nata sub axe,
Dumque pharetrati spernunt tua jura Britanni;
Surge, age, surge piger, Latius quem Cæsar adorat,
Cui reserata patet convexi janua cæli,
Turgentes animos, & fastus frange procaces,
Sacrilegique sciant, tua quid maledictio possit,   100
Et quid Apostolicæ possit custodia clavis;
Et memor Hesperiæ disjectam ulciscere classem,
Mersaque Iberorum lato vexilla profundo,
Sanctorumque cruci tot corpora fixa probrosæ,

In quintum Novembris.

Thermodoontéa nuper regnante puella.
At tu si tenero mavis torpescere lecto
Crescentesque negas hosti contundere vires,
Tyrrhenum implebit numeroso milite Pontum,
Signaque Aventino ponet fulgentia colle:
Relliquias veterum franget, flammisque cremabit,   110
Sacraque calcabit pedibus tua colla profanis,
Cujus gaudebant soleis dare basia reges.
Nec tamen hunc bellis & aperto Marte lacesses,
Irritus ille labor, tu callidus utere fraude,
Quælibet hæreticis disponere retia fas est;
Jamque ad consilium extremis rex magnus ab oris
Patricios vocat, & procerum de stirpe creatos,
Grandævosque patres trabeâ, canisque verendos;
Hos tu membratim poteris conspergere in auras,
Atque dare in cineres, nitrati pulveris igne   120
Ædibus injecto, quà convenere, sub imis.
Protinus ipse igitur quoscumque habet Anglia fidos
Propositi, factique mone, quisquámne tuorum
Audebit summi non jussa facessere Papæ.
Perculsosque metu subito, casúque stupentes
Invadat vel Gallus atrox, vel sævus Iberus.
Sæcula sic illic tandem Mariana redibunt,
Tuque in belligeros iterum dominaberis Anglos.
Et nequid timeas, divos divasque secundas
Accipe, quotque tuis celebrantur numina fastis.   130
Dixit & adscitos ponens malefidus amictus
Fugit ad infandam, regnum illætabile, Lethen.

    Jam rosea Eoas pandens Tithonia portas
Vestit inauratas redeunti lumine terras;
Mæstaque adhuc nigri deplorans funera nati
Irrigat ambrosiis montana cacumina guttis;
Cum somnos pepulit stellatæ janitor aulæ
Nocturnos visus, & somnia grata revolvens.
    Est locus æternâ septus caligine noctis
Vasta ruinosi quondam fundamina tecti,   140
Nunc torvi spelunca Phoni, Prodotæque bilinguis
Effera quos uno peperit Discordia partu.
Hic inter cæmenta jacent semifractaque saxa,
Ossa inhumata virûm, & trajecta cadavera ferro;

    143 semifractaque] præruptaque *1673*
(147)

Hic Dolus intortis semper sedet ater ocellis,
Jurgiaque, & stimulis armata Calumnia fauces,
Et Furor, atque viæ moriendi mille videntur,
Et Timor, exanguisque locum circumvolat Horror,
Perpetuoque leves per muta silentia Manes
Exululant, tellus & sanguine conscia stagnat.   150
Ipsi etiam pavidi latitant penetralibus antri
Et Phonos, & Prodotes, nulloque sequente per antrum
Antrum horrens, scopulosum, atrum feralibus umbris
Diffugiunt sontes, & retrò lumina vortunt,
Hos pugiles Romæ per sæcula longa fideles
Evocat antistes Babylonius, atque ita fatur.
Finibus occiduis circumfusum incolit æquor
Gens exosa mihi, prudens natura negavit
Indignam penitùs nostro conjungere mundo:
Illuc, sic jubeo, celeri contendite gressu,   160
Tartareoque leves difflentur pulvere in auras
Et rex & pariter satrapæ, scelerata propago
Et quotquot fidei caluere cupidine veræ
Consilii socios adhibete, operisque ministros.
Finierat, rigidi cupidè paruere gemelli.
   Interea longo flectens curvamine cælos
Despicit æthereâ dominus qui fulgurat arce,
Vanaque perversæ ridet conamina turbæ,
Atque sui causam populi volet ipse tueri.
   Esse ferunt spatium, quà distat ab Aside terra   170
Fertilis Europe, & spectat Mareotidas undas;
Hic turris posita est Titanidos ardua Famæ
Ærea, lata, sonans, rutilis vicinior astris
Quàm superimpositum vel Athos vel Pelion Ossæ
Mille fores aditusque patent, totidemque fenestræ,
Amplaque per tenues translucent atria muros;
Excitat hic varios plebs agglomerata susurros;
Qualiter instrepitant circum mulctralia bombis
Agmina muscarum, aut texto per ovilia junco,
Dum Canis æstivum cœli petit ardua culmen   180
Ipsa quidem summâ sedet ultrix matris in arce,
Auribus innumeris cinctum caput eminet olli,
Queis sonitum exiguum trahit, atque levissima captat
Murmura, ab extremis patuli confinibus orbis.
Nec tot Aristoride servator inique juvencæ

149, 150 Manes Exululant,] Manes, Exululat *1673 Errata.*

In quintum Novembris.

Isidos, immiti volvebas lumina vultu,
Lumina non unquam tacito nutantia somno,
Lumina subjectas late spectantia terras.
Istis illa solet loca luce carentia sæpe
Perlustrare, etiam radianti impervia soli.   190
Millenisque loquax auditaque visaque linguis
Cuilibet effundit temeraria, veráque mendax
Nunc minuit, modò confictis sermonibus auget.
Sed tamen a nostro meruisti carmine laudes
Fama, bonum quo non aliud veracius ullum,
Nobis digna cani, nec te memorasse pigebit
Carmine tam longo, servati scilicet Angli
Officiis vaga diva tuis, tibi reddimus æqua.
Te Deus æternos motu qui temperat ignes,
Fulmine præmisso alloquitur, terráque tremente :   200
Fama siles? an te latet impia Papistarum
Conjurata cohors in meque meosque Britannos,
Et nova sceptrigero cædes meditata Jäcobo :
Nec plura, illa statim sensit mandata Tonantis,
Et satis antè fugax stridentes induit alas,
Induit & variis exilia corpora plumis ;
Dextra tubam gestat Temesæo ex ære sonoram.
Nec mora jam pennis cedentes remigat auras,
Atque parum est cursu celeres prævertere nubes,
Jam ventos, jam solis equos post terga reliquit :   210
Et primò Angliacas solito de more per urbes
Ambiguas voces, incertaque murmura spargit,
Mox arguta dolos, & detestabile vulgat
Proditionis opus, nec non facta horrida dictu,
Authoresque addit sceleris, nec garrula cæcis
Insidiis loca structa silet ; stupuere relatis,
Et pariter juvenes, pariter tremuere puellæ,
Effætique senes pariter, tantæque ruinæ
Sensus ad ætatem subitò penetraverat omnem
Attamen interea populi miserescit ab alto   220
Æthereus pater, & crudelibus obstitit ausis
Papicolûm ; capti pœnas raptantur ad acres ;
At pia thura Deo, & grati solvuntur honores ;
Compita læta focis genialibus omnia fumant ;
Turba choros juvenilis agit : Quintoque Novembris
Nulla Dies toto occurrit celebratior anno.

Miscellaneous Poems.

Anno ætatis 17. In obitum Præsulis Eliensis.

ADHUC madentes rore squalebant genæ,
  Et sicca nondum lumina
Adhuc liquentis imbre turgebant salis,
  Quem nuper effudi pius,
Dum mœsta charo justa persolvi rogo
  Wintoniensis præsulis.
Cum centilinguis Fama (proh semper mali
  Cladisque vera nuntia)
Spargit per urbes divitis Britanniæ,
  Populosque Neptuno satos,   10
Cessisse morti, & ferreis sororibus
  Te generis humani decus,
Qui rex sacrorum illâ fuisti in insulâ
  Quæ nomen Anguillæ tenet.
Tunc inquietum pectus irâ protinus
  Ebulliebat fervidâ,
Tumulis potentem sæpe devovens deam:
  Nec vota Naso in Ibida
Concepit alto diriora pectore,
  Graiusque vates parciùs   20
Turpem Lycambis execratus est dolum,
  Sponsamque Neobolen suam.
At ecce diras ipse dum fundo graves,
  Et imprecor neci necem,
Audisse tales videor attonitus sonos
  Leni, sub aurâ, flamine:
Cæcos furores pone, pone vitream
  Bilemque & irritas minas,
Quid temerè violas non nocenda numina,
  Subitoque ad iras percita.   30
Non est, ut arbitraris elusus miser,
  Mors atra Noctis filia,
Erebóve patre creta, sive Erinnye,
  Vastóve nata sub Chao:
Ast illa cælo missa stellato, Dei
  Messes ubique colligit;

(150)

Naturam non pati senium.

Animasque mole carneâ reconditas
In lucem & auras evocat:
Ut cum fugaces excitant Horæ diem
Themidos Jovisque filiæ;   40
Et sempiterni ducit ad vultus patris;
At justa raptat impios
Sub regna furvi luctuosa Tartari,
Sedesque subterraneas
Hanc ut vocantem lætus audivi, citò
Fœdum reliqui carcerem,
Volatilesque faustus inter milites
Ad astra sublimis feror:
Vates ut olim raptus ad cœlum senex
Auriga currus ignei,   50
Non me Boötis terruere lucidi
Sarraca tarda frigore, aut
Formidolosi Scorpionis brachia,
Non ensis Orion tuus.
Prætervolavi fulgidi solis globum,
Longéque sub pedibus deam
Vidi triformem, dum coercebat suos
Frænis dracones aureis.
Erraticorum syderum per ordines,
Per lacteas vehor plagas,   60
Velocitatem sæpe miratus novam,
Donec nitentes ad fores
Ventum est Olympi, & regiam Crystallinam, &
Stratum smaragdis Atrium.
Sed hic tacebo, nam quis effari queat
Oriundus humano patre
Amœnitates illius loci, mihi
Sat est in æternum frui.

Naturam non pati senium.

HEU quàm perpetuis erroribus acta fatiscit
Avia mens hominum, tenebrisque immersa profundis
Œdipodioniam volvit sub pectore noctem!
Quæ vesana suis metiri facta deorum
Audet, & incisas leges adamante perenni

Assimilare suis, nulloque solubile sæclo
Consilium fati perituris alligat horis.
  Ergóne marcescet sulcantibus obsita rugis
Naturæ facies, & rerum publica mater
Omniparum contracta uterum sterilescet ab ævo?   10
Et se fassa senem malè certis passibus ibit
Sidereum tremebunda caput? num tetra vetustas
Annorumque æterna fames, squalorque situsque
Sidera vexabunt? an & insatiabile Tempus
Esuriet Cælum, rapietque in viscera patrem?
Heu, potuitne suas imprudens Jupiter arces
Hoc contra munisse nefas, & Temporis isto
Exemisse malo, gyrosque dedisse perennes?
Ergo erit ut quandoque sono dilapsa tremendo
Convexi tabulata ruant, atque obvius ictu   20
Stridat uterque polus, superâque ut Olympius aulâ
Decidat, horribilisque retectâ Gorgone Pallas.
Qualis in Ægæam proles Junonia Lemnon
Deturbata sacro cecidit de limine cæli.
Tu quoque Phœbe tui casus imitabere nati
Præcipiti curru, subitáque ferere ruinâ
Pronus, & extinctâ fumabit lampade Nereus,
Et dabit attonito feralia sibila ponto.
Tunc etiam aërei divulsis sedibus Hæmi
Dissultabit apex, imoque allisa barathro   30
Terrebunt Stygium dejecta Ceraunia Ditem
In superos quibus usus erat, fraternaque bella.
  At Pater omnipotens fundatis fortius astris
Consuluit rerum summæ, certoque peregit
Pondere fatorum lances, atque ordine summo
Singula perpetuum jussit servare tenorem.
Volvitur hinc lapsu mundi rota prima diurno;
Raptat & ambitos sociâ vertigine cælos.
Tardior haud solito Saturnus, & acer ut olim
Fulmineum rutilat cristatâ casside Mavors.   40
Floridus æternùm Phœbus juvenile coruscat,
Nec fovet effœtas loca per declivia terras
Devexo temone Deus; sed semper amicá
Luce potens eadem currit per signa rotarum,
Surgit odoratis pariter formosus ab Indis
Æthereum pecus albenti qui cogit Olympo
Mane vocans, & serus agens in pascua cæli,

De Idea Platonica.

Temporis & gemino dispertit regna colore.
Fulget, obitque vices alterno Delia cornu,
Cæruleumque ignem paribus complectitur ulnis.   50
Nec variant elementa fidem, solitóque fragore
Lurida perculsas jaculantur fulmina rupes.
Nec per inane furit leviori murmure Corus,
Stringit & armiferos æquali horrore Gelonos
Trux Aquilo, spiratque hyemem, nimbosque volutat.
Utque solet, Siculi diverberat ima Pelori
Rex maris, & raucâ circumstrepit æquora conchâ
Oceani Tubicen, nec vastâ mole minorem
Ægæona ferunt dorso Balearica cete.
Sed neque Terra tibi sæcli vigor ille vetusti   60
Priscus abest, servatque suum Narcissus odorem,
Et puer ille suum tenet & puer ille decorem
Phœbe tuusque & Cypri tuus, nec ditior olim
Terra datum sceleri celavit montibus aurum
Conscia, vel sub aquis gemmas. Sic denique in ævum
Ibit cunctarum series justissima rerum,
Donec flamma orbem populabitur ultima, latè
Circumplexa polos, & vasti culmina cæli ;
Ingentique rogo flagrabit machina mundi.

De Idea Platonica quemadmodum
Aristoteles intellexit.

DICITE sacrorum præsides nemorum deæ,
Tuque O noveni perbeata numinis
Memoria mater, quæque in immenso procul
Antro recumbis otiosa Æternitas,
Monumenta servans, & ratas leges Jovis,
Cælique fastos atque ephemeridas Deûm,
Quis ille primus cujus ex imagine
Natura sollers finxit humanum genus,
Æternus, incorruptus, æquævus polo,
Unusque & universus, exemplar Dei ?   10
Haud ille Palladis gemellus innubæ
Interna proles insidet menti Jovis ;
Sed quamlibet natura sit communior,

Tamen seorsùs extat ad morem unius,
Et, mira, certo stringitur spatio loci;
Seu sempiternus ille syderum comes
Cæli pererrat ordines decemplicis,
Citimúmve terris incolit Lunæ globum:
Sive inter animas corpus adituras sedens
Obliviosas torpet ad Lethes aquas: 20
Sive in remotâ forte terrarum plagâ
Incedit ingens hominis archetypus gigas,
Et diis tremendus erigit celsum caput
Atlante major portitore syderum.
Non cui profundum cæcitas lumen dedit
Dircæus augur vidit hunc alto sinu;
Non hunc silenti nocte Plëiones nepos
Vatum sagaci præpes ostendit choro;
Non hunc sacerdos novit Assyrius, licet
Longos vetusti commemoret atavos Nini,   30
Priscumque Belon, inclytumque Osiridem.
Non ille trino gloriosus nomine
Ter magnus Hermes (ut sit arcani sciens)
Talem reliquit Isidis cultoribus.
At tu perenne ruris Academi decus
(Hæc monstra si tu primus induxti scholis)
Jam jam pöetas urbis exules tuæ
Revocabis, ipse fabulator maximus,
Aut institutor ipse migrabis foras.

Ad Patrem.

NUNC mea Pierios cupiam per pectora fontes
Irriguas torquere vias, totumque per ora
Volvere laxatum gemino de vertice rivum;
Ut tenues oblita sonos audacibus alis
Surgat in officium venerandi Musa parentis.
Hoc utcunque tibi gratum pater optime carmen
Exiguum meditatur opus, nec novimus ipsi
Aptiùs à nobis quæ possint munera donis
Respondere tuis, quamvis nec maxima possint
Respondere tuis, nedum ut par gratia donis   10
Esse queat, vacuis quæ redditur arida verbis.

Ad Patrem.

Sed tamen hæc nostros ostendit pagina census,
Et quod habemus opum chartâ numeravimus istâ,
Quæ mihi sunt nullæ, nisi quas dedit aurea Clio
Quas mihi semoto somni peperere sub antro,
Et nemoris laureta sacri Parnassides umbræ.
  Nec tu vatis opus divinum despice carmen,
Quo nihil æthereos ortus, & semina cæli,
Nil magis humanam commendat origine mentem,
Sancta Promethéæ retinens vestigia flammæ.   20
Carmen amant superi, tremebundaque Tartara carmen
Ima ciere valet, divosque ligare profundos,
Et triplici duros Manes adamante coercet.
Carmine sepositi retegunt arcana futuri
Phœbades, & tremulæ pallentes ora Sibyllæ;
Carmina sacrificus solennes pangit ad aras
Aurea seu sternit motantem cornua taurum;
Seu cùm fata sagax fumantibus abdita fibris
Consulit, & tepidis Parcam scrutatur in extis.
Nos etiam patrium tunc cum repetemus Olympum,   30
Æternæque moræ stabunt immobilis ævi,
Ibimus auratis per cæli templa coronis,
Dulcia suaviloquo sociantes carmina plectro,
Astra quibus, geminique poli convexa sonabunt.
Spiritus & rapidos qui circinat igneus orbes.
Nunc quoque sydereis intercinit ipse choreis
Immortale melos, & inenarrabile carmen;
Torrida dum rutilus compescit sibila serpens,
Demissoque ferox gladio mansuescit Orion;
Stellarum nec sentit onus Maurusius Atlas.   40
Carmina regales epulas ornare solebant,
Cum nondum luxus, vastæque immensa vorago
Nota gulæ, & modico spumabat cœna Lyæo.
Tum de more sedens festa ad convivia vates
Æsculeâ intonsos redimitus ab arbore crines,
Heroumque actus, imitandaque gesta canebat,
Et chaos, & positi latè fundamina mundi,
Reptantesque Deos, & alentes numina glandes,
Et nondum Ætneo quæsitum fulmen ab antro.
Denique quid vocis modulamen inane juvabit,   50
Verborum sensusque vacans, numerique loquacis?
Silvestres decet iste choros, non Orphea cantus,
Qui tenuit fluvios & quercubus addidit aures

Carmine, non citharâ, simulachraque functa canendo
Compulit in lacrymas; habet has à carmine laudes.
   Nec tu perge precor sacras contemnere Musas,
Nec vanas inopesque puta, quarum ipse peritus
Munere, mille sonos numeros componis ad aptos,
Millibus & vocem modulis variare canoram
Doctus, Arionii meritò sis nominis hæres.   60
Nunc tibi quid mirum, si me genuisse poëtam
Contigerit, charo si tam propè sanguine juncti
Cognatas artes, studiumque affine sequamur:
Ipse volens Phœbus se dispertire duobus,
Altera dona mihi, dedit altera dona parenti,
Dividuumque Deum genitorque puerque tenemus.
   Tu tamen ut simules teneras odisse camœnas,
Non odisse reor, neque enim, pater, ire jubebas
Quà via lata patet, quà pronior area lucri,
Certaque condendi fulget spes aurea nummi: 70
Nec rapis ad leges, malè custoditaque gentis
Jura, nec insulsis damnas clamoribus aures.
Sed magis excultam cupiens ditescere mentem,
Me procul urbano strepitu, secessibus altis
Abductum Aoniæ jucunda per otia ripæ
Phœbæo lateri comitem sinis ire beatum.
Officium chari taceo commune parentis,
Me poscunt majora, tuo pater optime sumptu
Cùm mihi Romuleæ patuit facundia linguæ,
Et Latii veneres, & quæ Jovis ora decebant   80
Grandia magniloquis elata vocabula Graiis,
Addere suasisti quos jactat Gallia flores,
Et quam degeneri novus Italus ore loquelam
Fundit, Barbaricos testatus voce tumultus,
Quæque Palæstinus loquitur mysteria vates.
Denique quicquid habet cælum, subjectaque cœlo
Terra parens, terræque & cœlo interfluus aer,
Quicquid & unda tegit, pontique agitabile marmor,
Per te nosse licet, per te, si nosse libebit.
Dimotáque venit spectanda scientia nube,   90
Nudaque conspicuos inclinat ad oscula vultus,
Ni fugisse velim, ni sit libâsse molestum.
   I nunc, confer opes quisquis malesanus avitas
Austriaci gazas, Perüanaque regna præoptas.
Quæ potuit majora pater tribuisse, vel ipse

Jupiter, excepto, donâsset ut omnia, cœlo?
Non potiora dedit, quamvis & tuta fuissent,
Publica qui juveni commisit lumina nato
Atque Hyperionios currus, & fræna diei,
Et circùm undantem radiatâ luce tiaram.   100
Ergo ego jam doctæ pars quamlibet ima catervæ
Victrices hederas inter, laurosque sedebo,
Jamque nec obscurus populo miscebor inerti,
Vitabuntque oculos vestigia nostra profanos.
Este procul vigiles curæ, procul este querelæ,
Invidiæque acies transverso tortilis hirquo,
Sæva nec anguiferos extende Calumnia rictus;
In me triste nihil fædissima turba potestis,
Nec vestri sum juris ego; securaque tutus
Pectora, vipereo gradiar sublimis ab ictu.   110
  At tibi, chare pater, postquam non æqua merenti
Posse referre datur, nec dona rependere factis,
Sit memorâsse satis, repetitaque munera grato
Percensere animo, fidæque reponere menti.
  Et vos, O nostri, juvenilia carmina, lusus,
Si modo perpetuos sperare audebitis annos,
Et domini superesse rogo, lucemque tueri,
Nec spisso rapient oblivia nigra sub Orco,
Forsitan has laudes, decantatumque parentis
Nomen, ad exemplum, sero servabitis ævo.   120

Psalm 114.

Ἰσραὴλ ὅτε παῖδες, ὅτ᾽ ἀγλαὰ φῦλ᾽ Ἰακώβου
Αἰγύπτιον λίπε δῆμον, ἀπεχθέα, βαρβαρόφωνον,
Δὴ τότε μοῦνον ἔην ὅσιον γένος υἷες Ἰούδα·
Ἐν δὲ θεὸς λαοῖσι μέγα κρείων βασίλευεν.
Εἶδε, καὶ ἐντροπάδην φύγαδ᾽ ἐῤῥώησε θάλασσα
Κύματι εἰλυμένη ῥοθίῳ, ὅδ᾽ ἄρ᾽ ἐστυφελίχθη
Ἱρὸς Ἰορδάνης ποτὶ ἀργυροειδέα πηγήν.
Ἐκ δ᾽ ὄρεα σκαρθμοῖσιν ἀπειρέσια κλονέοντο,
Ὡς κριοὶ σφριγόωντες ἐΰτραφερῶ ἐν ἀλωῆ.
Βαιότεραι δ᾽ ἅμα πᾶσαι ἀνασκίρτησαν ἐρίπναι,   10
Οἷα παραὶ σύριγγι φίλῃ ὑπὸ μητέρι ἄρνες.
Τίπτε σύγ᾽ αἰνὰ θάλασσα πέλωρ φύγαδ᾽ ἐῤῥώησας;

Κύματι εἰλυμένη ῥοθίῳ ; τί δ' ἄρ' ἐστυφελίχθης
'Ιρὸς 'Ιορδάνη ποτὶ ἀργυροειδέα πηγὴν ;
Τίπτ' ὄρεα σκαρθμοῖσιν ἀπειρέσια κλονέεσθε
'Ως κριοὶ σφριγόωντες εὔτραφερῷ ἐν ἁλωῇ ;
Βαιοτέραι τί δ' ἀρ' ὑμμὲς ἀνασκιρτῆσατ' ἐρίπναι,
Οἷα παραὶ σύριγγι φίλη ὑπὸ μητέρι ἄρνες,
Σείεο γαῖα τρέουσα θεὸν μεγάλ' ἐκτυπέοντα
Γαῖα, θεὸν τρείουσ' ὕπατον σέβας 'Ισσακίδαο   20
'Ος τε καὶ ἐκ σπιλάδων ποταμοὺς χέε μορμύροντας
Κρήνηντ' ἀέναον πέτρης ἀπὸ δακρυοέσσης.

*Philosophus ad regem quendam qui eum ignotum
& insontem inter reos forte captum inscius
damnaverat* τὴν ἐπὶ θανάτῳ πορευόμενος,
hæc subito misit.

Ω ἄνα εἰ ὀλέσῃς με τὸν ἔννομον, οὐδέ τιν' ἀνδρῶν
Δεινὸν ὅλως δράσαντα, σοφώτατον ἴσθι κάρηνον
Ρηϊδίως ἀφέλοιο, τὸδ' ὕστερον αὖθι νοήσεις,
Μαψ ἀυτως δ' ἀρ' ἔπειτα χρόνῳ μαλα πολλὸν ὀδύρῃ,
Τοιόνδ' ἐκ πόλεως περιώνυμον ἄλκαρ ὀλέσσας.

In Effigiei ejus Sculptorem.

'Αμαθεῖ γεγράφθαι χειρὶ τήνδε μὲν εἰκόνα
Φαίης τάχ' ἂν, πρὸς εἶδος αὐτοφυὲς βλέπων·
Τὸν δ' ἐκτυπωτὸν οὐκ ἐπιγνόντες, φίλοι,
Γελᾶτε φαύλου δυσμίμημα ζωγράφου.

Ad Salsillum poetam Romanum ægrotantem.

SCAZONTES.

O MUSA gressum quæ volens trahis claudum,
Vulcanioque tarda gaudes incessu,
Nec sentis illud in loco minus gratum,

4 Μαψιδίως δ' ἀρ ἔπειτα τεὸν πρὸς θυμὸν ὀδυρῇ   *1673*

Ad Salsillum poetam Romanum.

Quàm cùm decentes flava Dëiope suras
Alternat aureum ante Junonis lectum,
Adesdum & hæc s'is verba pauca Salsillo
Refer, camœna nostra cui tantum est cordi,
Quamque ille magnis prætulit immeritò divis.
Hæc ergo alumnus ille Londini Milto,
Diebus hisce qui suum linquens nidum   10
Polique tractum, (pessimus ubi ventorum,
Insanientis impotensque pulmonis
Pernix anhela sub Jove exercet flabra)
Venit feraces Itali soli ad glebas,
Visum superbâ cognitas urbes famâ
Virosque doctæque indolem juventutis,
Tibi optat idem hic fausta multa Salsille,
Habitumque fesso corpori penitùs sanum ;
Cui nunc profunda bilis infestat renes,
Præcordiisque fixa damnosùm spirat.   20
Nec id pepercit impia quòd tu Romano
Tam cultus ore Lesbium condis melos.
O dulce divûm munus, O salus Hebes
Germana ! Tuque Phœbe morborum terror
Pythone cæso, sive tu magis Pæan
Libenter audis, hic tuus sacerdos est.
Querceta Fauni, vosque rore vinoso
Colles benigni, mitis Euandri sedes,
Siquid salubre vallibus frondet vestris,
Levamen ægro ferte certatim vati.   30
Sic ille charis redditus rursùm Musis
Vicina dulci prata mulcebit cantu.
Ipse inter atros emirabitur lucos
Numa, ubi beatum degit otium æternum,
Suam reclivis semper Ægeriam spectans.
Tumidusque & ipse Tibris hinc delinitus
Spei favebit annuæ colonorum :
Nec in sepulchris ibit obsessum reges
Nimiùm sinistro laxus irruens loro :
Sed fræna melius temperabit undarum,   40
Adusque curvi salsa regna Portumni.

Mansus.

Joannes Baptista Mansus Marchio Villensis vir ingenii laude, tum literarum studio, nec non & bellicâ virtute apud Italos clarus in primis est. Ad quem Torquati Tassi dialogus extat de Amicitia scriptus ; erat enim Tassi amicissimus ; ab quo etiam inter Campaniæ principes celebratur, in illo poemate cui titulus Gerusalemme conquistata, lib. 20.

Fra cavalier magnanimi, è cortesi
Risplende il Manso———

Is authorem Neapoli commorantem summâ benevolentiâ prosecutus est, multaque ei detulit humanitatis officia. Ad hunc itaque hospes ille antequam ab eâ urbe discederet, ut ne ingratum se ostenderet, hoc carmen misit.

Hæc quoque Manse tuæ meditantur carmina laudi
Pierides, tibi Manse choro notissime Phœbi,
Quandoquidem ille alium haud æquo est dignatus honore,
Post Galli cineres, & Mecænatis Hetrusci.
Tu quoque si nostræ tantùm valet aura Camœnæ,
Victrices hederas inter, laurosque sedebis.
Te pridem magno felix concordia Tasso
Junxit, & æternis inscripsit nomina chartis,
Mox tibi dulciloquum non inscia Musa Marinum
Tradidit, ille tuum dici se gaudet alumnum,   10
Dum canit Assyrios divûm prolixus amores ;
Mollis & Ausonias stupefecit carmine nymphas.
Ille itidem moriens tibi soli debita vates
Ossa tibi soli, supremaque vota reliquit.
Nec manes pietas tua chara fefellit amici,
Vidimus arridentem operoso ex ære poetam.
Nec satis hoc visum est in utrumque, & nec pia cessant
Officia in tumulo, cupis integros rapere Orco,
Quà potes, atque avidas Parcarum eludere leges :
Amborum genus, & variâ sub sorte peractam   20
Describis vitam, moresque, & dona Minervæ ;
Æmulus illius Mycalen qui natus ad altam
Rettulit Æolii vitam facundus Homeri.
Ergo ego te Cliûs & magni nomine Phœbi
Manse pater, jubeo longum salvere per ævum
Missus Hyperboreo juvenis peregrinus ab axe.
Nec tu longinquam bonus aspernabere Musam,
Quæ nuper gelidâ vix enutrita sub Arcto

(160)

Imprudens Italas ausa est volitare per urbes.
Nos etiam in nostro modulantes flumine cygnos   30
Credimus obscuras noctis sensisse per umbras,
Quà Thamesis latè puris argenteus urnis
Oceani glaucos perfundit gurgite crines.
Quin & in has quondam pervenit Tityrus oras.
Sed neque nos genus incultum, nec inutile Phœbo,
Quà plaga septeno mundi sulcata Trione
Brumalem patitur longâ sub nocte Boöten.
Nos etiam colimus Phœbum, nos munera Phœbo
Flaventes spicas, & lutea mala canistris,
Halantemque crocum (perhibet nisi vana vetustas)   40
Misimus, & lectas Druidum de gente choreas.
(Gens Druides antiqua sacris operata deorum
Heroum laudes imitandaque gesta canebant)
Hinc quoties festo cingunt altaria cantu
Delo in herbosâ Graiæ de more puellæ
Carminibus lætis memorant Corineïda Loxo,
Fatidicamque Upin, cum flavicomâ Hecaërge
Nuda Caledonio variatas pectora fuco.
Fortunate senex, ergo quacunque per orbem
Torquati decus, & nomen celebrabitur ingens,   50
Claraque perpetui succrescet fama Marini,
Tu quoque in ora frequens venies plausumque virorum,
Et parili carpes iter immortale volatu.
Dicetur tum sponte tuos habitasse penates
Cynthius, & famulas venisse ad limina Musas :
At non sponte domum tamen idem, & regis adivit
Rura Pheretiadæ cælo fugitivus Apollo ;
Ille licet magnum Alciden susceperat hospes ;
Tantùm ubi clamosos placuit vitare bubulcos,
Nobile mansueti cessit Chironis in antrum,   60
Irriguos inter saltus frondosaque tecta
Peneium prope rivum : ibi sæpe sub ilice nigrâ
Ad citharæ strepitum blandâ prece victus amici
Exilii duros lenibat voce labores.
Tum neque ripa suo, barathro nec fixa sub imo,
Saxa stetere loco, nutat Trachinia rupes,
Nec sentit solitas, immania pondera, silvas,
Emotæque suis properant de collibus orni,
Mulcenturque novo maculosi carmine lynces.
Diis dilecte senex, te Jupiter æquus oportet   70

Nascentem, & miti lustrarit lumine Phœbus,
Atlantisque nepos ; neque enim nisi charus ab ortu
Diis superis poterit magno favisse poetae.
Hinc longæva tibi lento sub flore senectus
Vernat, & Æsonios lucratur vivida fusos,
Nondum deciduos servans tibi frontis honores,
Ingeniumque vigens, & adultum mentis acumen.
O mihi si mea sors talem concedat amicum
Phœbæos decorâsse viros qui tam bene norit,
Si quando indigenas revocabo in carmina reges,   80
Arturumque etiam sub terris bella moventem ;
Aut dicam invictæ sociali fœdere mensæ,
Magnanimos Heroas, & (O modo spiritus ad sit)
Frangam Saxonicas Britonum sub Marte phalanges.
Tandem ubi non tacitæ permensus tempora vitæ,
Annorumque satur cineri sua jura relinquam,
Ille mihi lecto madidis astaret ocellis,
Astanti sat erit si dicam sim tibi curæ ;
Ille meos artus liventi morte solutos
Curaret parvâ componi molliter urnâ.   90
Forsitan & nostros ducat de marmore vultus,
Nectens aut Paphiâ myrti aut Parnasside lauri
Fronde comas, at ego securâ pace quiescam.
Tum quoque, si qua fides, si præmia certa bonorum,
Ipse ego cælicolûm semotus in æthera divûm,
Quò labor & mens pura vehunt, atque ignea virtus
Secreti hæc aliquâ mundi de parte videbo
(Quantum fata sinunt) & totâ mente serenùm
Ridens purpureo suffundar lumine vultus
Et simul æthereo plaudam mihi lætus Olympo.   100

Epitaphium Damonis.

EPITAPHIUM
DAMONIS.

Argumentum.

Thyrsis & Damon ejusdem viciniæ Pastores, eadem studia sequuti a
ueritiâ amici erant, ut qui plurimùm. Thyrsis animi causâ profectus peregrè
le obitu Damonis nuncium accepit. Domum postea reversus, & rem ita esse
omperto, se, suamque solitudinem hoc carmine deplorat. Damonis autem
ub personâ hîc intelligitur Carolus Deodatus ex urbe Hetruriæ Luca paterno
;enere oriundus, cætera Anglus ; ingenio, doctrina, clarissimisque cæteris
irtutibus, dum viveret, juvenis egregius.

HIMERIDES nymphæ (nam vos & Daphnin & Hylan,
Et plorata diu meministis fata Bionis)
Dicite Sicelicum Thamesina per oppida carmen :
Quas miser effudit voces, quæ murmura Thyrsis,
Et quibus assiduis exercuit antra querelis,
Fluminaque, fontesque vagos, nemorumque recessus,
Dum sibi præreptum queritur Damona, neque altam
Luctibus exemit noctem loca sola pererrans.
Et jam bis viridi surgebat culmus arista,
Et totidem flavas numerabant horrea messes,   10
Ex quo summa dies tulerat Damona sub umbras,
Nec dum aderat Thyrsis ; pastorem scilicet illum
Dulcis amor Musæ Thusca retinebat in urbe.
Ast ubi mens expleta domum, pecorisque relicti
Cura vocat, simul assuetâ sedítque sub ulmo,
Tum vero amissum tum denique sentit amicum,
Cœpit & immensum sic exonerare dolorem.
  Ite domum impasti, domino jam non vacat, agni.
Hei mihi ! quæ terris, quæ dicam numina cœlo,
Postquam te immiti rapuerunt funere Damon ;   20
Siccine nos linquis, tua sic sine nomine virtus
Ibit, & obscuris numero sociabitur umbris ?
At non ille, animas virgâ qui dividit aureâ,
Ista velit, dignumque tui te ducat in agmen,
Ignavumque procul pecus arceat omne silentum.

Miscellaneous Poems.

Ite domum impasti, domino jam non vacat, agni.
Quicquid erit, certè nisi me lupus antè videbit,
Indeplorato non comminuere sepulchro,
Constabitque tuus tibi honos, longúmque vigebit
Inter pastores : Illi tibi vota secundo   30
Solvere post Daphnin, post Daphnin dicere laudes
Gaudebunt, dum rura Pales, dum Faunus amabit :
Si quid id est, priscamque fidem coluisse, piúmque,
Palladiásque artes, sociúmque habuisse canorum.
    Ite domum impasti, domino jam non vacat, agni.
Hæc tibi certa manent, tibi erunt hæc præmia Damon ;
At mihi quid tandem fiet modò? quis mihi fidus
Hærebit lateri comes, ut tu sæpe solebas
Frigoribus duris, & per loca fœta pruinis,
Aut rapido sub sole, siti morientibus herbis?   40
Sive opus in magnos fuit eminùs ire leones
Aut avidos terrere lupos præsepibus altis ;
Quis fando sopire diem, cantuque solebit?
    Ite domum impasti, domino jam non vacat, agni.
Pectora cui credam? quis me lenire docebit
Mordaces curas, quis longam fallere noctem
Dulcibus alloquiis, grato cùm sibilat igni
Molle pyrum, & nucibus strepitat focus, at malus auster
Miscet cuncta foris, & desuper intonat ulmo.
    Ite domum impasti, domino jam non vacat, agni.   50
Aut æstate, dies medio dum vertitur axe,
Cum Pan æsculeâ somnum capit abditus umbrâ,
Et repetunt sub aquis sibi nota sedilia nymphæ,
Pastoresque latent, stertit sub sepe colonus,
Quis mihi blanditiásque tuas, quis tum mihi risus,
Cecropiosque sales referet, cultosque lepores?
    Ite domum impasti, domino jam non vacat, agni.
At jam solus agros, jam pascua solus oberro,
Sicubi ramosæ densantur vallibus umbræ,
Hic serum expecto, supra caput imber & Eurus   60
Triste sonant, fractæque agitata crepuscula silvæ.
    Ite domum impasti, domino jam non vacat, agni.
Heu quàm culta mihi priùs arva procacibus herbis
Involvuntur, & ipsa situ seges alta fatiscit!
Innuba neglecto marcescit & uva racemo,
Nec myrteta juvant ; ovium quoque tædet, at illæ
Moerent, inque suum convertunt ora magistrum.

(164)

Epitaphium Damonis.

Ite domum impasti, domino jam non vacat, agni.
Tityrus ad corylos vocat, Alphesibœus ad ornos,
Ad salices Ægon, ad flumina pulcher Amyntas,   70
Hîc gelidi fontes, hîc illita gramina musco,
Hîc Zephyri, hîc placidas interstrepit arbutus undas ;
Ista canunt surdo, frutices ego nactus abibam.
Ite domum impasti, domino jam non vacat, agni.
Mopsus ad hæc, nam me redeuntem forte notârat
(Et callebat avium linguas, & sydera Mopsus)
Thyrsi quid hoc ? dixit, quæ te coquit improba bilis ?
Aut te perdit amor, aut te malè fascinat astrum,
Saturni grave sæpe fuit pastoribus astrum,
Intimaque obliquo figit præcordia plumbo.   80
Ite domum impasti, domino jam non vacat, agni.
Mirantur nymphæ, & quid te Thyrsi futurum est ?
Quid tibi vis ? ajunt, non hæc solet esse juventæ
Nubila frons, oculique truces, vultusque severi,
Illa choros, lususque leves, & semper amorem
Jure petit, bis ille miser qui serus amavit.
Ite domum impasti, domino jam non vacat, agni.
Venit Hyas, Dryopéque, & filia Baucidis Ægle
Docta modos, citharæque sciens, sed perdita fastu,
Venit Idumanii Chloris vicina fluenti ;   90
Nil me blanditiæ, nil me solantia verba,
Nil me, si quid adest, movet, aut spes ulla futuri.
Ite domum impasti, domino jam non vacat, agni.
Hei mihi quam similes ludunt per prata juvenci,
Omnes unanimi secum sibi lege sodales,
Nec magis hunc alio quisquam secernit amicum
De grege, sic densi veniunt ad pabula thoes,
Inque vicem hirsuti paribus junguntur onagri ;
Lex eadem pelagi, deserto in littore Proteus
Agmina Phocarum numerat, vilisque volucrum   100
Passer habet semper quicum sit, & omnia circum
Farra libens volitet, serò sua tecta revisens,
Quem si fors letho objecit, seu milvus adunco
Fata tulit rostro, seu stravit arundine fossor,
Protinus ille alium socio petit inde volatu.
Nos durum genus, & diris exercita fatis
Gens homines aliena animis, & pectore discors,
Vix sibi quisque parem de millibus invenit unum,
Aut si sors dederit tandem non aspera votis,

Illum inopina dies quâ non speraveris horâ   110
Surripit, æternum linquens in sæcula damnum.
  Ite domum impasti, domino jam non vacat, agni.
Heu quis me ignotas traxit vagus error in oras
Ite per aëreas rupes, Alpemque nivosam !
Ecquid erat tanti Romam vidisse sepultam ?
Quamvis illa foret, qualem dum viseret olim,
Tityrus ipse suas & oves & rura reliquit ;
Ut te tam dulci possem caruisse sodale,
Possem tot maria alta, tot interponere montes,
Tot sylvas, tot saxa tibi, fluviosque sonantes.   120
Ah certè extremùm licuisset tangere dextram,
Et bene compositos placidè morientis ocellos,
Et dixisse vale, nostri memor ibis ad astra.
  Ite domum impasti, domino jam non vacat, agni.
Quamquam etiam vestri nunquam meminisse pigebit
Pastores Thusci, Musis operata juventus,
Hic Charis, atque Lepos ; & Thuscus tu quoque Damon,
Antiquâ genus unde petis Lucumonis ab urbe.
O ego quantus eram, gelidi cum stratus ad Arni
Murmura, populeumque nemus, quà mollior herba,   130
Carpere nunc violas, nunc summas carpere myrtos,
Et potui Lycidæ certantem audire Menalcam.
Ipse etiam tentare ausus sum, nec puto multùm
Displicui, nam sunt & apud me munera vestra
Fiscellæ, calathique & cerea vincla cicutæ,
Quin & nostra suas docuerunt nomina fagos
Et Datis, & Francinus, erant & vocibus ambo
Et studiis noti, Lydorum sanguinis ambo.
  Ite domum impasti, domino jam non vacat, agni.
Hæc mihi tum læto dictabat roscida luna,   140
Dum solus teneros claudebam cratibus hœdos.
Ah quoties dixi, cùm te cinis ater habebat,
Nunc canit, aut lepori nunc tendit retia Damon,
Vimina nunc texit, varios sibi quod sit in usus ;
Et quæ tum facili sperabam mente futura
Arripui voto levis, & præsentia finxi,
Heus bone numquid agis ? nisi te quid forte retardat
Imus ? & argutâ paulùm recubamus in umbra,
Aut ad aquas Colni, aut ubi jugera Cassibelauni ?
Tu mihi percurres medicos, tua gramina, succos,   150
Helleborúmque, humilésque crocos, foliúmque hyacinthi,

Epitaphium Damonis.

Quasque habet ista palus herbas, artesque medentûm,
Ah pereant herbæ, pereant artesque medentûm
Gramina, postquam ipsi nil profecere magistro.
Ipse etiam, nam nescio quid mihi grande sonabat
Fistula, ab undecimâ jam lux est altera nocte,
Et tum forte novis admôram labra cicutis,
Dissiluere tamen rupta compage, nec ultra
Ferre graves potuere sonos, dubito quoque ne sim
Turgidulus, tamen & referam, vos cedite silvæ.   160
   Ite domum impasti, domino jam non vacat, agni.
Ipse ego Dardanias Rutupina per æquora puppes
Dicam, & Pandrasidos regnum vetus Inogeniæ,
Brennúmque Arviragúmque duces, priscúmque Belinum,
Et tandem Armoricos Britonum sub lege colonos;
Tum gravidam Arturo fatali fraude Jögernen
Mendaces vultus, assumptáque Gorlöis arma,
Merlini dolus. O mihi tum si vita supersit,
Tu procul annosa pendebis fistula pinu
Multùm oblita mihi, aut patriis mutata camœnis   170
Brittonicum strides, quid enim? omnia non licet uni
Non sperâsse uni licet omnia, mi satis ampla
Merces, & mihi grande decus (sim ignotus in ævum
Tum licet, externo penitúsque inglorius orbi)
Si me flava comas legat Usa, & potor Alauni,
Vorticibúsque frequens Abra, & nemus omne Treantæ,
Et Thamesis meus ante omnes, & fusca metallis
Tamara, & extremis me discant Orcades undis.
   Ite domum impasti, domino jam non vacat, agni.
Hæc tibi servabam lentâ sub cortice lauri,   180
Hæc, & plura simul, tum quæ mihi pocula Mansus,
Mansus Chalcidicæ non ultima gloria ripæ
Bina dedit, mirum artis opus, mirandus & ipse,
Et circùm gemino cælaverat argumento:
In medio rubri maris unda, & odoriferum ver
Littora longa Arabum, & sudantes balsama silvæ,
Has inter Phœnix divina avis, unica terris
Cæruleùm fulgens diversicoloribus alis
Auroram vitreis surgentem respicit undis.
Parte alia polus omnipatens, & magnus Olympus;   190
Quis putet? hic quoque Amor, pictæque in nube pharetræ,
Arma corusca faces, & spicula tincta pyropo;
Nec tenues animas, pectúsque ignobile vulgi

(167)

Hinc ferit, at circùm flammantia lumina torquens
Semper in erectum spargit sua tela per orbes
Impiger, & pronos nunquam collimat ad ictus,
Hinc mentes ardere sacræ, formæque deorum.

   Tu quoque in his, nec me fallit spes lubrica Damon,
Tu quoque in his certè es, nam quò tua dulcis abiret
Sanctáque simplicitas, nam quò tua candida virtus?   200
Nec te Lethæo fas quæsivisse sub orco,
Nec tibi conveniunt lacrymæ, nec flebimus ultrà,
Ite procul lacrymæ, purum colit æthera Damon,
Æthera purus habet, pluvium pede reppulit arcum;
Heroúmque animas inter, divósque perennes,
Æthereos haurit latices & gaudia potat
Ore Sacro. Quin tu cœli post jura recepta
Dexter ades, placidúsque fave quicúnque vocaris,
Seu tu noster eris Damon, sive æquior audis
Diodotus, quo te divino nomine cuncti   210
Cœlicolæ nôrint, sylvísque vocabere Damon.
Quòd tibi purpureus pudor, & sine labe juventus
Grata fuit, quòd nulla tori libata voluptas,
En etiam tibi virginei servantur honores;
Ipse caput nitidum cinctus rutilante corona,
Letáque frondentis gestans umbracula palmæ
Æternùm perages immortales hymenæos;
Cantus ubi, choreisque furit lyra mista beatis,
Festa Sionæo bacchantur & Orgia Thyrso.

Finis.

Ad Joannem Rousium.

[Added in Second Edition, 1673.]

Jan. 23. 1646.

Ad *Joannem Rousium* Oxoniensis Academiæ Bibliothecarium.

De libro Poematum amisso, quem ille sibi denuo mitti postulabat, ut cum aliis ostris in Bibliotheca publica reponeret, Ode.

Strophe 1.

GEMELLE cultu simplici gaudens liber,
Fronde licet geminâ,
Munditiéque nitens non operosâ,
Quam manus attulit
Juvenilis olim,
Sedula tamen haud nimii Poetæ;
Dum vagus Ausonias nunc per umbras
Nunc Britannica per vireta lusit
Insons populi, barbitóque devius
Indulsit patrio, mox itidem pectine Daunio   10
Longinquum intonuit melos
Vicinis, & humum vix tetigit pede;

Antistrophe.

Quis te, parve liber, quis te fratribus
Subduxit reliquis dolo?
Cum tu missus ab urbe,
Docto jugiter obsecrante amico,
Illustre tendebas iter
Thamesis ad incunabula
Cærulei patris,
Fontes ubi limpidi   20
Aonidum, thyasusque sacer
Orbi notus per immensos
Temporum lapsus redeunte cœlo,
Celeberque futurus in ævum;

(169)

Miscellaneous Poems.

Strophe 2.

Modò quis deus, aut editus deo
Pristinam gentis miseratus indolem
(Si satis noxas luimus priores
Mollique luxu degener otium)
Tollat nefandos civium tumultus,
Almaque revocet studia sanctus   30
Et relegatas sine sede Musas
Jam penè totis finibus Angligenûm;
Immundasque volucres
Unguibus imminentes
Figat Apollineâ pharetrâ,
Phinéamque abigat pestem procul amne Pegaséo.

Antistrophe.

Quin tu, libelle, nuntii licet malâ
Fide, vel oscitantiâ
Semel erraveris agmine fratrum,
Seu quis te teneat specus,   40
Seu qua te latebra, forsan unde vili
Callo teréris institoris insulsi,
Lætare felix, en iterum tibi
Spes nova fulget posse profundam
Fugere Lethen, vehique Superam
In Jovis aulam remige pennâ;

Strophe 3.

Nam te Roüsius sui
Optat peculî, numeróque justo
Sibi pollicitum queritur abesse,
Rogatque venias ille cujus inclyta   50
Sunt data virûm monumenta curæ:
Téque adytis etiam sacris
Voluit reponi quibus & ipse præsidet
Æternorum operum custos fidelis,
Quæstorque gazæ nobilioris,
Quàm cui præfuit Iön
Clarus Erechtheides
Opulenta dei per templa parentis
Fulvosque tripodas, donaque Delphica
Iön Actæa genitus Creusâ.   60

Ad Joannem Rousium.

Antistrophe.

Ergo tu visere lucos
Musarum ibis amœnos,
Diamque Phœbi rursus ibis in domum
Oxoniâ quam valle colit
Delo posthabitâ,
Bifidóque Parnassi jugo:
Ibis honestus,
Postquam egregiam tu quoque sortem
Nactus abis, dextri prece sollicitatus amici.
Illic legéris inter alta nomina   70
Authorum, Graiæ simul & Latinæ
Antiqua gentis lumina, & verum decus.

Epodos.

Vos tandem haud vacui mei labores,
Quicquid hoc sterile fudit ingenium,
Jam serò placidam sperare jubeo
Perfunctam invidiâ requiem, sedesque beatas
Quas bonus Hermes
Et tutela dabit solers Roüsi,
Quò neque lingua procax vulgi penetrabit, atque longè
Turba legentum prava facesset;   80
At ultimi nepotes,
Et cordatior ætas
Judicia rebus æquiora forsitan
Adhibebit integro sinu.
Tum livore sepulto,
Si quid meremur sana posteritas sciet
Roüsio favente.

Ode tribus constat Strophis, totidémque Antistrophis unâ demum epodo
clausis, quas, tametsi omnes nec versuum numero, nec certis ubique colis
exactè respondeant, ita tamen secuimus, commodè legendi potius, quam ad
antiquos concinendi modos rationem spectantes. Alioquin hoc genus rectiùs
fortasse dici monostrophicum debuerat. Metra partim sunt κατὰ σχέσιν,
partim ἀπολελυμένα. Phaleucia quæ sunt, spondæum tertio loco bis ad-
mittunt, quod idem in secundo loco Catullus ad libitum fecit.

(171)

PARADISE LOST.

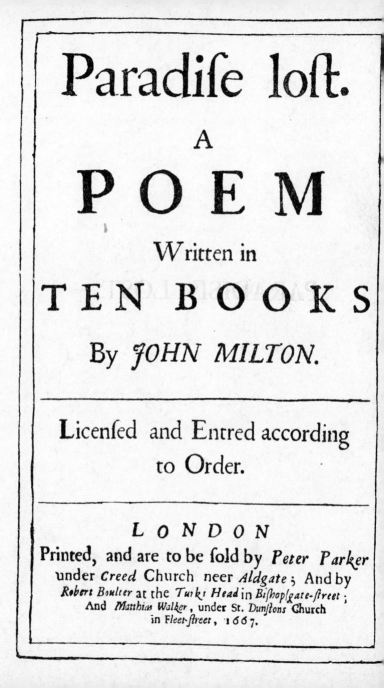

Paradiſe loſt.

A POEM

Written in

TEN BOOKS

By *JOHN MILTON*.

Licenſed and Entred according
to Order.

LONDON
Printed, and are to be ſold by *Peter Parker*
under *Creed* Church neer *Aldgate* ; And by
Robert Boulter at the *Turks Head* in *Biſhopſgate-ſtreet* ;
And *Matthias Walker*, under St. *Dunſtons* Church
in *Fleet-ſtreet*, 1667.

Paradise Lost.

A
POEM
IN
TWELVE BOOKS.

The Author
JOHN MILTON.

The Second Edition
Revised and Augmented by the
same Author.

LONDON,
Printed by *S. Simmons* next door to the
Golden Lion in *Aldersgate-street,* 1674.

IN

Paradisum Amissam

Summi Poetæ

JOHANNIS MILTONI.

Qui legis Amissam Paradisum, grandia magni
   Carmina Miltoni, *quid nisi cuncta legis?*
Res cunctas, & cunctarum primordia rerum,
   Et fata, & fines continet iste liber.
Intima panduntur magni penetralia mundi,
   Scribitur & toto quicquid in Orbe latet.
Terræque, tractusque maris, cælumque profundum
   Sulphureumque Erebi flammivomumque specus.
Quæque colunt terras, Portumque & Tartara cæca,
   Quæque colunt summi lucida regna Poli.
Et quodcunque ullis conclusum est finibus usquam,
   Et sine fine Chaos, & sine fine Deus;
Et sine fine magis, si quid magis est sine fine,
   In Christo erga homines conciliatus amor.
Hæc qui speraret quis crederet esse futurum?
   Et tamen hæc hodie terra Britanna *legit.*
O quantos in bella Duces! quæ protulit arma!
   Quæ canit, et quanta prælia dira tuba.
Cælestes acies! atque in certamine Cælum!
   Et quæ Cælestes pugna deceret agros!
Quantus in ætheriis tollit se Lucifer *armis!*
   Atque ipso graditur vix Michaele *minor!*
Quantis, & quam funestis concurritur iris
   Dum ferus hic stellas protegit, ille rapit!
Dum vulsos Montes ceu Tela reciproca torquent,
   Et non mortali desuper igne pluunt!
Stat dubius cui se parti concedat Olympus,
   Et metuit pugnæ non superesse suæ.

On Paradise Lost.

At simul in cœlis Messiœ insignia fulgent,
  Et currus animes, armaque digna Deo,
Horrendumque rotœ strident, & sœva rotarum
  Erumpunt torvis fulgura luminibus,
Et flammœ vibrant, & vera tonitrua rauco
  Admistis flammis insonuere Polo :
Excidit attonitis mens omnis, & impetus omnis
  Et cassis dextris irrita Tela cadunt.
Ad pœnas fugiunt, & ceu foret Orcus asylum
  Infernis certant condere se tenebris.
Cedite Romani *scriptores, cedite* Graii
  Et quos fama recens vel celebravit anus.
Hœc quicunque leget tantum cecinisse putabit
  Mæonidem *ranas,* Virgilium *culices.*

S. B., M. D.

ON

Paradise Lost.

WHEN I beheld the Poet blind, yet bold,
In slender Book his vast Design unfold,
Messiah Crown'd, Gods Reconcil'd Decree,
Rebelling Angels, the Forbidden Tree,
Heav'n, Hell, Earth, Chaos, All ; the Argument
Held me a while misdoubting his Intent,
That he would ruine (for I saw him strong)
The sacred Truths to Fable and old Song
(So *Sampson* groap'd the Temples Posts in spight)
The World o'rewhelming to revenge his sight.
  Yet as I read, soon growing less severe,
I lik'd his Project, the success did fear ;
Through that wide Field how he his way should find
O're which lame Faith leads Understanding blind ;
Lest he perplex'd the things he would explain,
And what was easie he should render vain.
  Or if a Work so infinite he spann'd,
Jealous I was that some less skilful hand
(Such as disquiet always what is well,
And by ill imitating would excell)
Might hence presume the whole Creations day
To change in Scenes, and show it in a Play.
  Pardon me, Mighty Poet, nor despise
My causeless, yet not impious, surmise.

(178)

On Paradise Lost.

But I am now convinc'd, and none will dare
Within thy Labours to pretend a share.
Thou hast not miss'd one thought that could be fit,
And all that was improper dost omit:
So that no room is here for Writers left,
But to detect their Ignorance or Theft.
    That Majesty which through thy Work doth Reign
Draws the Devout, deterring the Profane.
And things divine thou treatst of in such state
As them preserves, and thee, inviolate.
At once delight and horrour on us seise,
Thou singst with so much gravity and ease;
And above humane flight dost soar aloft
With Plume so strong, so equal, and so soft.
The Bird nam'd from that Paradise you sing
So never flaggs, but always keeps on Wing.
    Where couldst thou words of such a compass find?
Whence furnish such a vast expence of mind?
Just Heav'n thee like *Tiresias* to requite
Rewards with Prophesie thy loss of sight.
    Well mightst thou scorn thy Readers to allure
With tinkling Rhime, of thy own sense secure;
While the *Town-Bayes* writes all the while and spells,
And like a Pack-horse tires without his Bells:
Their Fancies like our Bushy-points appear,
The Poets tag them, we for fashion wear.
I too transported by the Mode offend,
And while I meant to Praise thee must Commend.
Thy Verse created like thy Theme sublime,
In Number, Weight, and Measure, needs not Rhime.

A. M.

In Paradisum Amissam. On Paradise Lost] *Added in the second
edition 1674.*

The Printer to the Reader.

Courteous Reader, there was no Argument at first intended to the Book, but for the satisfaction of many that have desired it, I have procur'd it, and withall a reason of that which stumbled many others, why the Poem Rimes not.

S. Simmons.

The Printer to the Reader] Added in 1668 to the copies then remaining of the first edition, amended in 1669, and omitted in 1670. I have procur'd it, and . . . . not *1669*] is procured *1668*.

THE VERSE.

THE measure is *English* Heroic Verse without Rime, as that of *Homer* in *Greek*, and of *Virgil* in *Latin*; Rime being no necessary Adjunct or true Ornament of Poem or good Verse, in longer Works especially, but the Invention of a barbarous Age, to set off wretched matter and lame Meeter; grac't indeed since by the use of some famous modern Poets, carried away by Custom, but much to thir own vexation, hindrance, and constraint to express many things otherwise, and for the most part worse then else they would have exprest them. Not without cause therefore some both *Italian* and *Spanish* Poets of prime note have rejected Rime both in longer and shorter Works, as have also long since our best *English* Tragedies, as a thing of it self, to all judicious eares, triveal and of no true musical delight; which consists only in apt Numbers, fit quantity of Syllables, and the sense variously drawn out from one Verse into another, not in the jingling sound of like endings, a fault avoyded by the learned Ancients both in Poetry and all good Oratory. This neglect then of Rime so little is to be taken for a defect, though it may seem so perhaps to vulgar Readers, that it rather is to be esteem'd an example set, the first in *English*, of ancient liberty recover'd to Heroic Poem from the troublesom and modern bondage of Rimeing.

The Verse] Added in 1668 to the copies then remaining of the first edition; together with the Argument. In the second edition (1674) the Argument, with the necessary adjustment to the division made in Books vii and x, was distributed through the several books of the poem, as it is here printed.

PARADISE LOST.

BOOK I.

THE ARGUMENT.

THIS first Book proposes first in brief the whole Subject, *Mans disobedience, and the loss thereupon of Paradise wherein he was plac't:* Then touches *the prime cause of his fall, the Serpent, or rather* Satan *in the Serpent; who revolting from God, and drawing to his side many Legions of Angels, was by the command of God driven out of Heaven with all his Crew into the great Deep.* Which action past over, the Poem hasts into the midst of things, presenting *Satan with his Angels now fallen into Hell,* describ'd here, *not in the Center* (for Heaven and Earth may be suppos'd as yet not made, certainly not yet accurst) *but in a place of utter darkness, fitliest call'd* Chaos: *Here* Satan *with his Angels lying on the burning Lake, thunder-struck and astonisht, after a certain space recovers, as from confusion, calls up him who next in Order and Dignity lay by him; they confer of thir miserable fall.* Satan *awakens all his Legions, who lay till then in the same manner confounded; They rise, thir Numbers, array of Battel, thir chief Leaders nam'd, according to the Idols known afterwards in* Canaan *and the Countries adjoyning. To these* Satan *directs his Speech, comforts them with hope yet of regaining Heaven, but tells them lastly of a new World and new kind of Creature to be created, according to an ancient Prophesie or report in Heaven; for that Angels were long before this visible Creation, was the opinion of many ancient Fathers. To find out the truth of this Prophesie, and what to determin thereon he refers to a full Councell. What his Associates thence attempt.* Pandemonium *the Palace of* Satan *rises, suddenly built out of the Deep: The infernal Peers there sit in Counsel.*

OF Mans First Disobedience, and the Fruit
Of that Forbidden Tree, whose mortal tast
Brought Death into the World, and all our woe,
With loss of *Eden,* till one greater Man
Restore us, and regain the blissful Seat,
Sing Heav'nly Muse, that on the secret top
Of *Oreb,* or of *Sinai,* didst inspire
That Shepherd, who first taught the chosen Seed,

In the Beginning how the Heav'ns and Earth
Rose out of *Chaos*: or if *Sion* Hill   10
Delight thee more, and *Siloa's* Brook that flow'd
Fast by the Oracle of God; I thence
Invoke thy aid to my adventrous Song,
That with no middle flight intends to soar
Above th' *Aonian* Mount, while it pursues
Things unattempted yet in Prose or Rhime.
And chiefly Thou O Spirit, that dost prefer
Before all Temples th' upright heart and pure,
Instruct me, for Thou know'st; Thou from the first
Wast present, and with mighty wings outspread   20
Dove-like satst brooding on the vast Abyss
And mad'st it pregnant: What in me is dark
Illumine, what is low raise and support;
That to the highth of this great Argument
I may assert Eternal Providence,
And justifie the wayes of God to men.
   Say first, for Heav'n hides nothing from thy view
Nor the deep Tract of Hell, say first what cause
Mov'd our Grand Parents in that happy State,
Favour'd of Heav'n so highly, to fall off   30
From their Creator, and transgress his Will
For one restraint, Lords of the World besides?
Who first seduc'd them to that fowl revolt?
Th' infernal Serpent; he it was, whose guile
Stird up with Envy and Revenge, deceiv'd
The Mother of Mankinde, what time his Pride
Had cast him out from Heav'n, with all his Host
Of Rebel Angels, by whose aid aspiring
To set himself in Glory above his Peers,
He trusted to have equal'd the most High,   40
If he oppos'd; and with ambitious aim
Against the Throne and Monarchy of God
Rais'd impious War in Heav'n and Battel proud
With vain attempt. Him the Almighty Power
Hurld headlong flaming from th' Ethereal Skie
With hideous ruine and combustion down
To bottomless perdition, there to dwell
In Adamantine Chains and penal Fire,
Who durst defie th' Omnipotent to Arms.
Nine times the Space that measures Day and Night   50

To mortal men, he with his horrid crew
Lay vanquisht, rowling in the fiery Gulfe
Confounded though immortal: But his doom
Reserv'd him to more wrath; for now the thought
Both of lost happiness and lasting pain
Torments him; round he throws his baleful eyes
That witness'd huge affliction and dismay
Mixt with obdurate pride and stedfast hate:
At once as far as Angels kenn he views
The dismal Situation waste and wilde,   60
A Dungeon horrible, on all sides round
As one great Furnace flam'd, yet from those flames
No light, but rather darkness visible
Serv'd only to discover sights of woe,
Regions of sorrow, doleful shades, where peace
And rest can never dwell, hope never comes
That comes to all; but torture without end
Still urges, and a fiery Deluge, fed
With ever-burning Sulphur unconsum'd:
Such place Eternal Justice had prepar'd   70
For those rebellious, here their Prison ordain'd
In utter darkness, and their portion set
As far remov'd from God and light of Heav'n
As from the Center thrice to th' utmost Pole.
O how unlike the place from whence they fell!
There the companions of his fall, o'rewhelm'd
With Floods and Whirlwinds of tempestuous fire,
He soon discerns, and weltring by his side
One next himself in power, and next in crime,
Long after known in *Palestine*, and nam'd   80
Beëlzebub. To whom th' Arch-Enemy,
And thence in Heav'n call'd Satan, with bold words
Breaking the horrid silence thus began.
    If thou beest he; But O how fall'n! how chang'd
From him, who in the happy Realms of Light
Cloth'd with transcendent brightness didst outshine
Myriads though bright: If he whom mutual league,
United thoughts and counsels, equal hope,
And hazard in the Glorious Enterprize,
Joynd with me once, now misery hath joynd   90
In equal ruin: into what Pit thou seest
From what highth fal'n, so much the stronger provd

(183)

He with his Thunder: and till then who knew
The force of those dire Arms? yet not for those
Nor what the Potent Victor in his rage
Can else inflict do I repent or change,
Though chang'd in outward lustre; that fixt mind
And high disdain, from sence of injur'd merit,
That with the mightiest rais'd me to contend,
And to the fierce contention brought along   100
Innumerable force of Spirits arm'd
That durst dislike his reign, and me preferring,
His utmost power with adverse power oppos'd
In dubious Battel on the Plains of Heav'n,
And shook his throne. What though the field be lost?
All is not lost; the unconquerable Will,
And study of revenge, immortal hate,
And courage never to submit or yield:
And what is else not to be overcome?
That Glory never shall his wrath or might   110
Extort from me. To bow and sue for grace
With suppliant knee, and deifie his power
Who from the terrour of this Arm so late
Doubted his Empire, that were low indeed,
That were an ignominy and shame beneath
This downfall; since by Fate the strength of Gods
And this Empyreal substance cannot fail,
Since through experience of this great event
In Arms not worse, in foresight much advanc't,
We may with more successful hope resolve   120
To wage by force or guile eternal Warr
Irreconcileable, to our grand Foe,
Who now triumphs, and in th' excess of joy
Sole reigning holds the Tyranny of Heav'n.

So spake th' Apostate Angel, though in pain,
Vaunting aloud, but rackt with deep despare:
And him thus answer'd soon his bold Compeer.

O Prince, O Chief of many Throned Powers,
That led th' imbattelld Seraphim to Warr
Under thy conduct, and in dreadful deeds   130
Fearless, endanger'd Heav'ns perpetual King;
And put to proof his high Supremacy,
Whether upheld by strength, or Chance, or Fate,
Too well I see and rue the dire event,

That with sad overthrow and foul defeat
Hath lost us Heav'n, and all this mighty Host
In horrible destruction laid thus low,
As far as Gods and Heav'nly Essences
Can perish: for the mind and spirit remains
Invincible, and vigour soon returns,   140
Though all our Glory extinct, and happy state
Here swallow'd up in endless misery.
But what if he our Conquerour, (whom I now
Of force believe Almighty, since no less
Then such could hav orepow'rd such force as ours)
Have left us this our spirit and strength intire
Strongly to suffer and support our pains,
That we may so suffice his vengeful ire,
Or do him mightier service as his thralls
By right of Warr, what e're his business be   150
Here in the heart of Hell to work in Fire,
Or do his Errands in the gloomy Deep;
What can it then avail though yet we feel
Strength undiminisht, or eternal being
To undergo eternal punishment?
Whereto with speedy words th' Arch-fiend reply'd.

    Fall'n Cherube, to be weak is miserable
Doing or Suffering: but of this be sure,
To do ought good never will be our task,
But ever to do ill our sole delight,   160
As being the contrary to his high will
Whom we resist. If then his Providence
Out of our evil seek to bring forth good,
Our labour must be to pervert that end,
And out of good still to find means of evil;
Which oft times may succeed, so as perhaps
Shall grieve him, if I fail not, and disturb
His inmost counsels from their destind aim.
But see the angry Victor hath recall'd
His Ministers of vengeance and pursuit   170
Back to the Gates of Heav'n: The Sulphurous Hail
Shot after us in storm, oreblown hath laid
The fiery Surge, that from the Precipice
Of Heav'n receiv'd us falling, and the Thunder,
Wing'd with red Lightning and impetuous rage,
Perhaps hath spent his shafts, and ceases now

    (185)

To bellow through the vast and boundless Deep.
Let us not slip th' occasion, whether scorn,
Or satiate fury yield it from our Foe.
Seest thou yon dreary Plain, forlorn and wilde,   180
The seat of desolation, voyd of light,
Save what the glimmering of these livid flames
Casts pale and dreadful? Thither let us tend
From off the tossing of these fiery waves,
There rest, if any rest can harbour there,
And reassembling our afflicted Powers,
Consult how we may henceforth most offend
Our Enemy, our own loss how repair,
How overcome this dire Calamity,
What reinforcement we may gain from Hope,   190
If not what resolution from despare.
    Thus Satan talking to his neerest Mate
With Head up-lift above the wave, and Eyes
That sparkling blaz'd, his other Parts besides
Prone on the Flood, extended long and large
Lay floating many a rood, in bulk as huge
As whom the Fables name of monstrous size,
Titanian, or *Earth-born*, that warr'd on *Jove*,
Briarios or *Typhon*, whom the Den
By ancient *Tarsus* held, or that Sea-beast   200
Leviathan, which God of all his works
Created hugest that swim th' Ocean stream:
Him haply slumbring on the *Norway* foam
The Pilot of some small night-founder'd Skiff,
Deeming some Island, oft, as Sea-men tell,
With fixed Anchor in his skaly rind
Moors by his side under the Lee, while Night
Invests the Sea, and wished Morn delayes:
So stretcht out huge in length the Arch-fiend **lay**
Chain'd on the burning Lake, nor ever thence   210
Had ris'n or heav'd his head, but that the will
And high permission of all-ruling Heaven
Left him at large to his own dark designs,
That with reiterated crimes he might
Heap on himself damnation, while he sought
Evil to others, and enrag'd might see
How all his malice serv'd but to bring forth
Infinite goodness, grace and mercy shewn

On Man by him seduc't, but on himself
Treble confusion, wrath and vengeance pour'd.   220
Forthwith upright he rears from off the Pool
His mighty Stature; on each hand the flames
Drivn backward slope their pointing spires, & rowld
In billows, leave i' th' midst a horrid Vale.
Then with expanded wings he stears his flight
Aloft, incumbent on the dusky Air
That felt unusual weight, till on dry Land
He lights, if it were Land that ever burn'd
With solid, as the Lake with liquid fire;
And such appear'd in hue, as when the force   230
Of subterranean wind transports a Hill
Torn from *Pelorus*, or the shatter'd side
Of thundring *Ætna*, whose combustible
And fewel'd entrals thence conceiving Fire,
Sublim'd with Mineral fury, aid the Winds,
And leave a singed bottom all involv'd
With stench and smoak: Such resting found the sole
Of unblest feet. Him followed his next Mate,
Both glorying to have scap't the *Stygian* flood
As Gods, and by their own recover'd strength,   240
Not by the sufferance of supernal Power.
　Is this the Region, this the Soil, the Clime,
Said then the lost Arch Angel, this the seat
That we must change for Heav'n, this mournful gloom
For that celestial light? Be it so, since hee
Who now is Sovran can dispose and bid
What shall be right: fardest from him is best
Whom reason hath equald, force hath made supream
Above his equals. Farewel happy Fields
Where Joy for ever dwells: Hail horrours, hail   250
Infernal world, and thou profoundest Hell
Receive thy new Possessor: One who brings
A mind not to be chang'd by Place or Time.
The mind is its own place, and in it self
Can make a Heav'n of Hell, a Hell of Heav'n.
What matter where, if I be still the same,
And what I should be, all but less then hee
Whom Thunder hath made greater? Here at least
We shall be free; th' Almighty hath not built
Here for his envy, will not drive us hence: 260

Here we may reign secure, and in my choyce
To reign is worth ambition though in Hell:
Better to reign in Hell, then serve in Heav'n.
But wherefore let we then our faithful friends,
Th' associates and copartners of our loss
Lye thus astonisht on th' oblivious Pool,
And call them not to share with us their part
In this unhappy Mansion, or once more
With rallied Arms to try what may be yet
Regained in Heav'n, or what more lost in Hell?   270
    So *Satan* spake, and him *Bëëlzebub*
Thus answer'd. Leader of those Armies bright,
Which but th' Omnipotent none could have foyld,
If once they hear that voyce, their liveliest pledge
Of hope in fears and dangers, heard so oft
In worst extreams, and on the perilous edge
Of battel when it rag'd, in all assaults
Their surest signal, they will soon resume
New courage and revive, though now they lye
Groveling and prostrate on yon Lake of Fire,   280
As we erewhile, astounded and amaz'd,
No wonder, fall'n such a pernicious highth.
    He scarce had ceas't when the superiour Fiend
Was moving toward the shore; his ponderous shield
Ethereal temper, massy, large and round,
Behind him cast; the broad circumference
Hung on his shoulders like the Moon, whose Orb
Through Optic Glass the *Tuscan* Artist views
At Ev'ning from the top of *Fesole,*
Or in *Valdarno,* to descry new Lands,   290
Rivers or Mountains in her spotty Globe.
His Spear, to equal which the tallest Pine
Hewn on *Norwegian* hills, to be the Mast
Of some great Ammiral, were but a wand,
He walkt with to support uneasie steps
Over the burning Marle, not like those steps
On Heavens Azure, and the torrid Clime
Smote on him sore besides, vaulted with Fire;
Nathless he so endur'd, till on the Beach
Of that inflamed Sea, he stood and call'd   300
His Legions, Angel Forms, who lay intrans't
Thick as Autumnal Leaves that strow the Brooks

In *Vallombrosa*, where th' *Etrurian* shades
High overarch't imbowr; or scatterd sedge
Afloat, when with fierce Winds *Orion* arm'd
Hath vext the Red-Sea Coast, whose waves orethrew
Busiris and his *Memphian* Chivalrie,
While with perfidious hatred they pursu'd
The Sojourners of *Goshen*, who beheld
From the safe shore their floating Carkases   310
And broken Chariot Wheels, so thick bestrown
Abject and lost lay these, covering the Flood,
Under amazement of their hideous change.
He call'd so loud, that all the hollow Deep
Of Hell resounded.   Princes, Potentates,
Warriers, the Flowr of Heav'n, once yours, now lost,
If such astonishment as this can sieze
Eternal spirits; or have ye chos'n this place
After the toyl of Battel to repose
Your wearied vertue, for the ease you find   320
To slumber here, as in the Vales of Heav'n?
Or in this abject posture have ye sworn
To adore the Conquerour? who now beholds
Cherube and Seraph rowling in the Flood
With scatter'd Arms and Ensigns, till anon
His swift pursuers from Heav'n Gates discern
Th' advantage, and descending tread us down
Thus drooping, or with linked Thunderbolts
Transfix us to the bottom of this Gulfe.
Awake, arise, or be for ever fall'n.   330
    They heard, and were abasht, and up they sprung
Upon the wing, as when men wont to watch
On duty, sleeping found by whom they dread,
Rouse and bestir themselves ere well awake.
Nor did they not perceave the evil plight
In which they were, or the fierce pains not feel;
Yet to their Generals Voyce they soon obeyd
Innumerable. As when the potent Rod
Of *Amrams* Son in *Egypts* evill day
Wav'd round the Coast, up call'd a pitchy cloud   340
Of *Locusts*, warping on the Eastern Wind,
That ore the Realm of impious *Pharaoh* hung
Like Night, and darken'd all the Land of *Nile*:
So numberless were those bad Angels seen

Hovering on wing under the Cope of Hell
'Twixt upper, nether, and surrounding Fires;
Till, as a signal giv'n, th' uplifted Spear
Of their great Sultan waving to direct
Thir course, in even ballance down they light
On the firm brimstone, and fill all the Plain;   350
A multitude, like which the populous North
Pour'd never from her frozen loyns, to pass
Rhene or the *Danaw*, when her barbarous Sons
Came like a Deluge on the South, and spread
Beneath *Gibraltar* to the *Lybian* sands.
Forthwith from every Squadron and each Band
The Heads and Leaders thither hast where stood
Their great Commander; Godlike shapes and forms
Excelling human, Princely Dignities,
And Powers that earst in Heaven sat on Thrones;   360
Though of their Names in heav'nly Records now
Be no memorial, blotted out and ras'd
By thir Rebellion, from the Books of Life.
Nor had they yet among the Sons of *Eve*
Got them new Names, till wandring ore the Earth,
Through Gods high sufferance for the tryal of man,
By falsities and lyes the greatest part
Of Mankind they corrupted to forsake
God their Creator, and th' invisible
Glory of him, that made them, to transform   370
Oft to the Image of a Brute, adorn'd
With gay Religions full of Pomp and Gold,
And Devils to adore for Deities:
Then were they known to men by various Names,
And various Idols through the Heathen World.
Say, Muse, their Names then known, who first, who last,
Rous'd from the slumber, on that fiery Couch,
At thir great Emperors call, as next in worth
Came singly where he stood on the bare strand,
While the promiscuous croud stood yet aloof?   380
The chief were those who from the Pit of Hell
Roaming to seek their prey on earth, durst fix
Their Seats long after next the Seat of God,
Their Altars by his Altar, Gods ador'd
Among the Nations round, and durst abide
Jehovah thundring out of *Sion*, thron'd

Between the Cherubim; yea, often plac'd
Within his Sanctuary it self their Shrines,
Abominations; and with cursed things
His holy Rites, and solemn Feasts profan'd,   390
And with their darkness durst affront his light.
First *Moloch*, horrid King besmear'd with blood
Of human sacrifice, and parents tears,
Though for the noyse of Drums and Timbrels loud
Their childrens cries unheard, that past through fire
To his grim Idol. Him the *Ammonite*
Worshipt in *Rabba* and her watry Plain,
In *Argob* and in *Basan*, to the stream
Of utmost *Arnon*. Nor content with such
Audacious neighbourhood, the wisest heart   400
Of *Solomon* he led by fraud to build
His Temple right against the Temple of God
On that opprobrious Hill, and made his Grove
The pleasant Vally of *Hinnom*, *Tophet* thence
And black *Gehenna* call'd, the Type of Hell.
Next *Chemos*, th' obscene dread of *Moabs* Sons,
From *Aroer* to *Nebo*, and the wild
Of Southmost *Abarim*; in *Hesebon*
And *Horonaim*, *Seons* Realm, beyond
The flowry Dale of *Sibma* clad with Vines,   410
And *Eleale* to th' *Asphaltick* Pool.
Peor his other Name, when he entic'd
Israel in *Sittim* on their march from *Nile*
To do him wanton rites, which cost them woe.
Yet thence his lustful Orgies he enlarg'd
Even to that Hill of scandal, by the Grove
Of *Moloch* homicide, lust hard by hate;
Till good *Josiah* drove them thence to Hell.
With these came they, who from the bordring flood
Of old *Euphrates* to the Brook that parts   420
Egypt from *Syrian* ground, had general Names
Of *Baalim* and *Ashtaroth*, those male,
These Feminine. For Spirits when they please
Can either Sex assume, or both; so soft
And uncompounded is their Essence pure,
Not ti'd or manacl'd with joynt or limb,
Nor founded on the brittle strength of bones,
Like cumbrous flesh; but in what shape they choose

Dilated or condens't, bright or obscure,
Can execute their aerie purposes,   430
And works of love or enmity fulfill.
For those the Race of *Israel* oft forsook
Their living strength, and unfrequented left
His righteous Altar, bowing lowly down
To bestial Gods; for which their heads as low
Bow'd down in Battel, sunk before the Spear
Of despicable foes.   With these in troop
Came *Astoreth*, whom the *Phœnicians* call'd
Astarte, Queen of Heav'n, with crescent Horns;
To whose bright Image nightly by the Moon   440
Sidonian Virgins paid their Vows and Songs,
In *Sion* also not unsung, where stood
Her Temple on th' offensive Mountain, built
By that uxorious King, whose heart though large,
Beguil'd by fair Idolatresses, fell
To Idols foul.   *Thammuz* came next behind,
Whose annual wound in *Lebanon* allur'd
The *Syrian* Damsels to lament his fate
In amorous dittyes all a Summers day,
While smooth *Adonis* from his native Rock   450
Ran purple to the Sea, suppos'd with blood
Of *Thammuz* yearly wounded: the Love-tale
Infected *Sions* daughters with like heat,
Whose wanton passions in the sacred Porch
Ezekiel saw, when by the Vision led
His eye survay'd the dark Idolatries
Of alienated *Judah*.   Next came one
Who mourn'd in earnest, when the Captive Ark
Maim'd his brute Image, head and hands lopt off
In his own Temple, on the grunsel edge,   460
Where he fell flat, and sham'd his Worshipers:
Dagon his Name, Sea Monster, upward Man
And downward Fish: yet had his Temple high
Rear'd in *Azotus*, dreaded through the Coast
Of *Palestine*, in *Gath* and *Ascalon*,
And *Accaron* and *Gaza's* frontier bounds.
Him follow'd *Rimmon*, whose delightful Seat
Was fair *Damascus*, on the fertil Banks
Of *Abbana* and *Pharphar*, lucid streams.
He also against the house of God was bold: 470

A Leper once he lost and gain'd a King,
Ahaz his sottish Conquerour, whom he drew
Gods Altar to disparage and displace
For one of *Syrian* mode, whereon to burn
His odious offrings, and adore the Gods
Whom he had vanquisht. After these appear'd
A crew who under Names of old Renown,
Osiris, Isis, Orus and their Train
With monstrous shapes and sorceries abus'd
Fanatic *Egypt* and her Priests, to seek   480
Thir wandring Gods disguis'd in brutish forms
Rather then human. Nor did *Israel* scape
Th' infection when their borrow'd Gold compos'd
The Calf in *Oreb* : and the Rebel King
Doubl'd that sin in *Bethel* and in *Dan,*
Lik'ning his Maker to the Grazed Ox,
Jehovah, who in one Night when he pass'd
From *Egypt* marching, equal'd with one stroke
Both her first born and all her bleating Gods.
Belial came last, then whom a Spirit more lewd   490
Fell not from Heaven, or more gross to love
Vice for it self : To him no Temple stood
Or Altar smoak'd ; yet who more oft then hee
In Temples and at Altars, when the Priest
Turns Atheist, as did *Elys* Sons, who fill'd
With lust and violence the house of God.
In Courts and Palaces he also Reigns
And in luxurious Cities, where the noyse
Of riot ascends above thir loftiest Towrs,
And injury and outrage : And when Night   500
Darkens the Streets, then wander forth the Sons
Of *Belial,* flown with insolence and wine.
Witness the Streets of *Sodom,* and that night
In *Gibeah,* when hospitable Dores
Yielded thir Matrons to prevent worse rape.
These were the prime in order and in might ;
The rest were long to tell, though far renown'd,
Th' *Ionian* Gods, of *Javans* Issue held
Gods, yet confest later then Heav'n and Earth
Thir boasted Parents ; *Titan* Heav'ns first born   510

504, 5 hospitable Dores Yielded thir Matrons] the hospitable door Expos'd
Matron *1674*

(193)   H

With his enormous brood, and birthright seis'd
By younger *Saturn*, he from mightier *Jove*
His own and *Rhea's* Son like measure found;
So *Jove* usurping reign'd: these first in *Creet*
And *Ida* known, thence on the Snowy top
Of cold *Olympus* rul'd the middle Air
Thir highest Heav'n; or on the *Delphian* Cliff,
Or in *Dodona*, and through all the bounds
Of *Doric* Land; or who with *Saturn* old
Fled over *Adria* to th' *Hesperian* Fields,   520
And ore the *Celtic* roam'd the utmost Isles.
All these and more came flocking; but with looks
Down cast and damp, yet such wherein appear'd
Obscure som glimps of joy, to have found thir chief
Not in despair, to have found themselves not lost
In loss it self; which on his count'nance cast
Like doubtful hue: but he his wonted pride
Soon recollecting, with high words, that bore
Semblance of worth not substance, gently rais'd
Their fainted courage, and dispel'd their fears.   530
Then strait commands that at the warlike sound
Of Trumpets loud and Clarions be upreard
His mighty Standard; that proud honour claim'd
Azazel as his right, a Cherube tall:
Who forthwith from the glittering Staff unfurld
Th' Imperial Ensign, which full high advanc't
Shon like a Meteor streaming to the Wind
With Gemms and Golden lustre rich imblaz'd,
Seraphic arms and Trophies: all the while
Sonorous mettal blowing Martial sounds: 540
At which the universal Host upsent
A shout that tore Hells Concave, and beyond
Frighted the Reign of *Chaos* and old Night.
All in a moment through the gloom were seen
Ten thousand Banners rise into the Air
With Orient Colours waving: with them rose
A Forrest huge of Spears: and thronging Helms
Appear'd, and serried Shields in thick array
Of depth immeasurable: Anon they move
In perfect *Phalanx* to the *Dorian* mood   550
Of Flutes and soft Recorders; such as rais'd

530 fainted] fa(i)nting *1674*

Paradise Lost.

To highth of noblest temper Hero's old
Arming to Battel, and in stead of rage
Deliberate valour breath'd, firm and unmov'd
With dread of death to flight or foul retreat,
Nor wanting power to mitigate and swage
With solemn touches, troubl'd thoughts, and chase
Anguish and doubt and fear and sorrow and pain
From mortal or immortal minds. Thus they
Breathing united force with fixed thought   560
Mov'd on in silence to soft Pipes that charm'd
Thir painful steps o're the burnt soyle ; and now
Advanc't in view they stand, a horrid Front
Of dreadful length and dazling Arms, in guise
Of Warriers old with order'd Spear and Shield,
Awaiting what command thir mighty Chief
Had to impose : He through the armed Files
Darts his experienc't eye, and soon traverse
The whole Battalion views, thir order due,
Thir visages and stature as of Gods,   570
Thir number last he summs. And now his heart
Distends with pride, and hardning in his strength
Glories : For never since created man,
Met such imbodied force, as nam'd with these
Could merit more then that small infantry
Warr'd on by Cranes : though all the Giant brood
Of *Phlegra* with th' Heroic Race were joyn'd
That fought at *Theb's* and *Ilium*, on each side
Mixt with auxiliar Gods ; and what resounds
In Fable or *Romance* of *Uthers* Son   580
Begirt with *British* and *Armoric* Knights ;
And all who since, Baptiz'd or Infidel
Jousted in *Aspramont* or *Montalban*,
Damasco, or *Marocco*, or *Trebisond*,
Or whom *Biserta* sent from *Afric* shore
When *Charlemain* with all his Peerage fell
By *Fontarabbia*. Thus far these beyond
Compare of mortal prowess, yet observ'd
Thir dread Commander : he above the rest
In shape and gesture proudly eminent   590
Stood like a Towr ; his form had yet not lost
All her Original brightness, nor appear'd
Less then Arch Angel ruind, and th' excess

(195)

Of Glory obscur'd : As when the Sun new ris'n
Looks through the Horizontal misty Air
Shorn of his Beams, or from behind the Moon
In dim Eclips disastrous twilight sheds
On half the Nations, and with fear of change
Perplexes Monarchs. Dark'n'd so, yet shon
Above them all th' Arch Angel : but his face   600
Deep scars of Thunder had intrencht, and care
Sat on his faded cheek. but under Browes
Of dauntless courage, and considerate Pride
Waiting revenge : cruel his eye, but cast
Signs of remorse and passion to behold
The fellows of his crime, the followers rather
(Far other once beheld in bliss) condemn'd
For ever now to have their lot in pain,
Millions of Spirits for his fault amerc't
Of Heav'n, and from Eternal Splendors flung   610
For his revolt, yet faithfull how they stood,
Thir Glory witherd. As when Heavens Fire
Hath scath'd the Forrest Oaks, or Mountain Pines,
With singed top their stately growth though bare
Stands on the blasted Heath. He now prepar'd
To speak ; whereat their doubl'd Ranks they bend
From Wing to Wing, and half enclose him round
With all his Peers : attention held them mute.
Thrice he assayd, and thrice in spite of scorn,
Tears such as Angels weep, burst forth : at last   620
Words interwove with sighs found out their way.

   O Myriads of immortal Spirits, O Powers
Matchless, but with th' Almighty, and that strife
Was not inglorious, though th' event was dire,
As this place testifies, and this dire change
Hateful to utter : but what power of mind
Foreseeing or presaging, from the Depth
Of knowledge past or present, could have fear'd,
How such united force of Gods, how such
As stood like these, could ever know repulse ?   630
For who can yet beleeve, though after loss,
That all these puissant Legions, whose exile
Hath emptied Heav'n, shall faile to re-ascend
Self-rais'd, and repossess their native seat ?
For me, be witness all the Host of Heav'n,

If counsels different, or danger shun'd
By me, have lost our hopes. But he who reigns
Monarch in Heav'n, till then as one secure
Sat on his Throne, upheld by old repute,
Consent or custome, and his Regal State   640
Put forth at full, but still his strength conceal'd,
Which tempted our attempt, and wrought our fall.
Henceforth his might we know, and know our own
So as not either to provoke, or dread
New warr, provok't; our better part remains
To work in close design, by fraud or guile
What force effected not: that he no less
At length from us may find, who overcomes
By force, hath overcome but half his foe.
Space may produce new Worlds; whereof so rife   650
There went a fame in Heav'n that he ere long
Intended to create, and therein plant
A generation, whom his choice regard
Should favour equal to the Sons of Heaven:
Thither, if but to prie, shall be perhaps
Our first eruption, thither or elsewhere:
For this Infernal Pit shall never hold
Cælestial Spirits in Bondage, nor th' Abysse
Long under darkness cover. But these thoughts
Full Counsel must mature: Peace is despaird,   660
For who can think Submission! Warr then, Warr
Open or understood must be resolv'd.
     He spake: and to confirm his words, out-flew
Millions of flaming swords, drawn from the thighs
Of mighty Cherubim; the sudden blaze
Far round illumin'd hell: highly they rag'd
Against the Highest, and fierce with grasped arm's
Clash'd on their sounding shields the din of war,
Hurling defiance toward the vault of Heav'n.
     There stood a Hill not far whose griesly top   670
Belch'd fire and rowling smoak; the rest entire
Shon with a glossie scurff, undoubted sign
That in his womb was hid metallic Ore,
The work of Sulphur. Thither wing'd with speed
A numerous Brigad hasten'd. As when bands
Of Pioners with Spade and Pickaxe arm'd
Forerun the Royal Camp, to trench a Field,

Or cast a Rampart. *Mammon* led them on,
Mammon, the least erected Spirit that fell
From heav'n, for ev'n in heav'n his looks and thoughts 680
Were always downward bent, admiring more
The riches of Heav'ns pavement, trod'n Gold,
Then aught divine or holy else enjoy'd
In vision beatific : by him first
Men also, and by his suggestion taught,
Ransack'd the Center, and with impious hands
Rifl'd the bowels of their mother Earth
For Treasures better hid. Soon had his crew
Op'nd into the Hill a spacious wound
And dig'd out ribs of Gold. Let none admire 690
That riches grow in Hell; that soyle may best
Deserve the pretious bane. And here let those
Who boast in mortal things, and wondring tell
Of *Babel,* and the works of *Memphian* Kings,
Learn how thir greatest Monuments of Fame,
And Strength and Art are easily outdone
By Spirits reprobate, and in an hour
What in an age they with incessant toyle
And hands innumerable scarce perform.
Nigh on the Plain in many cells prepar'd, 700
That underneath had veins of liquid fire
Sluc'd from the Lake, a second multitude
With wondrous Art founded the massie Ore,
Severing each kinde, and scum'd the Bullion dross :
A third as soon had form'd within the ground
A various mould, and from the boyling cells
By strange conveyance fill'd each hollow nook,
As in an Organ from one blast of wind
To many a row of Pipes the sound-board breaths.
Anon out of the earth a Fabrick huge 710
Rose like an Exhalation, with the sound
Of Dulcet Symphonies and voices sweet,
Built like a Temple, where *Pilasters* round
Were set, and Doric pillars overlaid
With Golden Architrave ; nor did there want
Cornice or Freeze, with bossy Sculptures grav'n,
The Roof was fretted Gold. Not *Babilon,*
Nor great *Alcairo* such magnificence

703 founded] found out *1674*

Equal'd in all thir glories, to inshrine
Belus or *Serapis* thir Gods, or seat   720
Thir Kings, when *Ægypt* with *Assyria* strove
In wealth and luxurie. Th' ascending pile
Stood fixt her stately highth, and strait the dores
Op'ning thir brazen foulds discover wide
Within, her ample spaces, o're the smooth
And level pavement: from the arched roof
Pendant by suttle Magic many a row
Of Starry Lamps and blazing Cressets fed
With *Naphtha* and *Asphaltus* yeilded light
As from a sky. The hasty multitude   730
Admiring enter'd, and the work some praise
And some the Architect: his hand was known
In Heav'n by many a Towred structure high,
Where Scepter'd Angels held thir residence,
And sat as Princes, whom the supreme King
Exalted to such power, and gave to rule,
Each in his Herarchie, the Orders bright.
Nor was his name unheard or unador'd
In ancient *Greece* ; and in *Ausonian* land
Men called him *Mulciber* ; and how he fell   740
From Heav'n, they fabl'd, thrown by angry *Jove*
Sheer o're the Chrystal Battlements: from Morn
To Noon he fell, from Noon to dewy Eve,
A Summers day ; and with the setting Sun
Dropt from the Zenith like a falling Star,
On *Lemnos* th' *Ægæan* Ile : thus they relate,
Erring ; for he with this rebellious rout
Fell long before ; nor aught avail'd him now
To have built in Heav'n high Towrs ; nor did he scape
By all his Engins, but was headlong sent   750
With his industrious crew to build in hell.
Mean while the winged Haralds by command
Of Sovran power, with awful Ceremony
And Trumpets sound throughout the Host proclaim
A solemn Councel forthwith to be held
At *Pandæmonium*, the high Capital
Of Satan and his Peers: thir summons call'd
From every Band and squared Regiment
By place or choice the worthiest ; they anon

737 Herarchie] Hierarchie *1674*

With hunderds and with thousands trooping came   760
Attended : all access was throng'd, the Gates
And Porches wide, but chief the spacious Hall
(Though like a cover'd field, where Champions bold
Wont ride in arm'd, and at the Soldans chair
Defi'd the best of *Panim* chivalry
To mortal combat or carreer with Lance)
Thick swarm'd, both on the ground and in the air,
Brusht with the hiss of russling wings. As Bees
In spring time, when the Sun with *Taurus* rides,
Poure forth thir populous youth about the Hive   770
In clusters ; they among fresh dews and flowers
Flie to and fro, or on the smoothed Plank,
The suburb of thir Straw-built Cittadel,
New rub'd with Baume, expatiate and confer
Thir State affairs. So thick the aerie crowd
Swarm'd and were straitn'd ; till the Signal giv'n,
Behold a wonder ! they but now who seemd
In bigness to surpass Earths Giant Sons
Now less then smallest Dwarfs, in narrow room
Throng numberless, like that Pigmean Race   780
Beyond the *Indian* Mount, or Faerie Elves,
Whose midnight Revels, by a Forrest side
Or Fountain some belated Peasant sees,
Or dreams he sees, while over head the Moon
Sits Arbitress, and neerer to the Earth
Wheels her pale course, they on thir mirth & dance
Intent, with jocond Music charm his ear ;
At once with joy and fear his heart rebounds.
Thus incorporeal Spirits to smallest forms
Reduc'd thir shapes immense, and were at large,   790
Though without number still amidst the Hall
Of that infernal Court. But far within
And in thir own dimensions like themselves
The great Seraphic Lords and Cherubim
In close recess and secret conclave sat
A thousand Demy-Gods on golden seat's,
Frequent and full. After short silence then
And summons read, the great consult began.

The End of the First Book.

PARADISE LOST.

BOOK II.

THE ARGUMENT.

The Consultation begun, Satan *debates whether another Battel be to be hazarded for the recovery of Heaven: some advise it, others dissuade: A third proposal is prefer'd, mention'd before by* Satan, *to search the truth of that Prophesie or Tradition in Heaven concerning another world, and another kind of creature equal or not much inferiour to themselves, about this time to be created: Thir doubt who shall be sent on this difficult search:* Satan *thir chief undertakes alone the voyage, is honourd and applauded. The Councel thus ended, the rest betake them several wayes and to several employments, as thir inclinations lead them, to entertain the time till* Satan *return. He passes on his Journey to Hell Gates, finds them shut, and who sat there to guard them, by whom at length they are op'nd, and discover to him the great Gulf between Hell and Heaven; with what difficulty he passes through, directed by* Chaos, *the Power of that place, to the sight of this new World which he sought.*

HIGH on a Throne of Royal State, which far
Outshon the wealth of *Ormus* and of *Ind,*
Or where the gorgeous East with richest hand
Showrs on her Kings *Barbaric* Pearl & Gold,
Satan exalted sat, by merit rais'd
To that bad eminence; and from despair
Thus high uplifted beyond hope, aspires
Beyond thus high, insatiate to pursue
Vain Warr with Heav'n, and by success untaught
His proud imaginations thus displaid.   10
    Powers and Dominions, Deities of Heav'n,
For since no deep within her gulf can hold
Immortal vigor, though opprest and fall'n,
I give not Heav'n for lost. From this descent
Celestial vertues rising, will appear

Argument l. 7 shall] should *1669*

More glorious and more dread then from no fall,
And trust themselves to fear no second fate:
Mee though just right, and the fixt Laws of Heav'n
Did first create your Leader, next, free choice,
With what besides, in Counsel or in Fight, 20
Hath bin achievd of merit, yet this loss
Thus farr at least recover'd, hath much more
Establisht in a safe unenvied Throne
Yielded with full consent. The happier state
In Heav'n, which follows dignity, might draw
Envy from each inferior; but who here
Will envy whom the highest place exposes
Formost to stand against the Thunderers aime
Your bulwark, and condemns to greatest share
Of endless pain? where there is then no good 30
For which to strive, no strife can grow up there
From Faction; for none sure will claim in hell
Precedence, none, whose portion is so small
Of present pain, that with ambitious mind
Will covet more. With this advantage then
To union, and firm Faith, and firm accord,
More then can be in Heav'n, we now return
To claim our just inheritance of old,
Surer to prosper then prosperity
Could have assur'd us; and by what best way, 40
Whether of open Warr or covert guile,
We now debate; who can advise, may speak.

  He ceas'd, and next him *Moloc,* Scepter'd King
Stood up, the strongest and the fiercest Spirit
That fought in Heav'n; now fiercer by despair:
His trust was with th' Eternal to be deem'd
Equal in strength, and rather then be less
Car'd not to be at all; with that care lost
Went all his fear: of God, or Hell, or worse
He reckd not, and these words thereafter spake. 50

  My sentence is for open Warr: Of Wiles,
More unexpert, I boast not: them let those
Contrive who need, or when they need, not now.
For while they sit contriving, shall the rest,
Millions that stand in Arms, and longing wait
The Signal to ascend, sit lingring here
Heav'ns fugitives, and for thir dwelling place

Accept this dark opprobrious Den of shame,
The Prison of his Tyranny who Reigns
By our delay? no, let us rather choose   60
Arm'd with Hell flames and fury all at once
O're Heav'ns high Towrs to force resistless way,
Turning our Tortures into horrid Arms
Against the Torturer; when to meet the noise
Of his Almighty Engin he shall hear
Infernal Thunder, and for Lightning see
Black fire and horror shot with equal rage
Among his Angels; and his Throne it self
Mixt with *Tartarean* Sulphur, and strange fire,
His own invented Torments. But perhaps   70
The way seems difficult and steep to scale
With upright wing against a higher foe.
Let such bethink them, if the sleepy drench
Of that forgetful Lake benumme not still,
That in our proper motion we ascend
Up to our native seat: descent and fall
To us is adverse. Who but felt of late
When the fierce Foe hung on our brok'n Rear
Insulting, and pursu'd us through the Deep,
With what compulsion and laborious flight   80
We sunk thus low? Th' ascent is easie then;
Th' event is fear'd; should we again provoke
Our stronger, some worse way his wrath may find
To our destruction: if there be in Hell
Fear to be worse destroy'd: what can be worse
Then to dwell here, driv'n out from bliss, condemn'd
In this abhorred deep to utter woe;
Where pain of unextinguishable fire
Must exercise us without hope of end
The Vassals of his anger, when the Scourge   90
Inexorably, and the torturing houre
Calls us to Penance? More destroy'd then thus
We should be quite abolisht and expire.
What fear we then? what doubt we to incense
His utmost ire? which to the highth enrag'd,
Will either quite consume us, and reduce
To nothing this essential, happier farr
Then miserable to have eternal being:
Or if our substance be indeed Divine,

And cannot cease to be, we are at worst   100
On this side nothing; and by proof we feel
Our power sufficient to disturb his Heav'n,
And with perpetual inrodes to Allarme,
Though inaccessible, his fatal Throne:
Which if not Victory is yet Revenge.

He ended frowning, and his look denounc'd
Desperate revenge, and Battel dangerous
To less then Gods. On th' other side up rose
Belial, in act more graceful and humane;
A fairer person lost not Heav'n; he seemd   110
For dignity compos'd and high exploit:
But all was false and hollow; though his Tongue
Dropt Manna, and could make the worse appear
The better reason, to perplex and dash
Maturest Counsels: for his thoughts were low;
To vice industrious, but to Nobler deeds
Timorous and slothful: yet he pleas'd the eare,
And with perswasive accent thus began.

I should be much for open Warr, O Peers,
As not behind in hate; if what was urg'd   120
Main reason to perswade immediate Warr,
Did not disswade me most, and seem to cast
Ominous conjecture on the whole success:
When he who most excels in fact of Arms,
In what he counsels and in what excels
Mistrustful, grounds his courage on despair
And utter dissolution, as the scope
Of all his aim, after some dire revenge.
First, what Revenge? the Towrs of Heav'n are fill'd
With Armed watch, that render all access   130
Impregnable; oft on the bordering Deep
Encamp thir Legions, or with obscure wing
Scout farr and wide into the Realm of night,
Scorning surprize. Or could we break our way
By force, and at our heels all Hell should rise
With blackest Insurrection, to confound
Heav'ns purest Light, yet our great Enemie
All incorruptible would on his Throne
Sit unpolluted, and th' Ethereal mould
Incapable of stain would soon expel   140
Her mischief, and purge off the baser fire

Victorious. Thus repuls'd, our final hope
Is flat despair ; we must exasperate
Th' Almighty Victor to spend all his rage,
And that must end us, that must be our cure,
To be no more ; sad cure ; for who would loose,
Though full of pain, this intellectual being,
Those thoughts that wander through Eternity,
To perish rather, swallowd up and lost
In the wide womb of uncreated night,   150
Devoid of sense and motion ? and who knows,
Let this be good, whether our angry Foe
Can give it, or will ever ? how he can
Is doubtful ; that he never will is sure.
Will he, so wise, let loose at once his ire,
Belike through impotence, or unaware,
To give his Enemies thir wish, and end
Them in his anger, whom his anger saves
To punish endless ? wherefore cease we then ?
Say they who counsel Warr, we are decreed,   160
Reserv'd and destin'd to Eternal woe ;
Whatever doing, what can we suffer more,
What can we suffer worse ? is this then worst,
Thus sitting, thus consulting, thus in Arms ?
What when we fled amain, pursu'd and strook
With Heav'ns afflicting Thunder, and besought
The Deep to shelter us ? this Hell then seem'd
A refuge from those wounds : or when we lay
Chain'd on the burning Lake ? that sure was worse.
What if the breath that kindl'd those grim fires   170
Awak'd should blow them into sevenfold rage
And plunge us in the Flames ? or from above
Should intermitted vengeance Arme again
His red right hand to plague us ? what if all
Her stores were op'n'd, and this Firmament
Of Hell should spout her Cataracts of Fire,
Impendent horrors, threatning hideous fall
One day upon our heads ; while we perhaps
Designing or exhorting glorious Warr,
Caught in a fierie Tempest shall be hurl'd   180
Each on his rock transfixt, the sport and prey
Of racking whirlwinds, or for ever sunk
Under yon boyling Ocean, wrapt in Chains ;

There to converse with everlasting groans,
Unrespited, unpitied, unrepreevd,
Ages of hopeless end; this would be worse.
Warr therefore, open or conceal'd, alike
My voice disswades; for what can force or guile
With him, or who deceive his mind, whose eye
Views all things at one view? he from heav'ns highth
All these our motions vain, sees and derides;   191
Not more Almighty to resist our might
Then wise to frustrate all our plots and wiles.
Shall we then live thus vile, the race of Heav'n
Thus trampl'd, thus expell'd to suffer here
Chains and these Torments? better these then worse
By my advice; since fate inevitable
Subdues us, and Omnipotent Decree
The Victors will. To suffer, as to doe,
Our strength is equal, nor the Law unjust   200
That so ordains: this was at first resolv'd,
If we were wise, against so great a foe
Contending, and so doubtful what might fall.
I laugh, when those who at the Spear are bold
And vent'rous, if that fail them, shrink and fear
What yet they know must follow, to endure
Exile, or ignominy, or bonds, or pain,
The sentence of thir Conquerour: This is now
Our doom; which if we can sustain and bear,
Our Supream Foe in time may much remit   210
His anger, and perhaps thus farr remov'd
Not mind us not offending, satisfi'd
With what is punish't; whence these raging fires
Will slack'n, if his breath stir not thir flames.
Our purer essence then will overcome
Thir noxious vapour, or enur'd not feel,
Or chang'd at length, and to the place conformd
In temper and in nature, will receive
Familiar the fierce heat, and void of pain;
This horror will grow milde, this darkness light,   220
Besides what hope the never-ending flight
Of future days may bring, what chance, what change
Worth waiting, since our present lot appeers
For happy though but ill, for ill not worst,
If we procure not to our selves more woe.

Thus *Belial* with words cloath'd in reasons garb
Counsel'd ignoble ease, and peaceful sloath,
Not peace : and after him thus *Mammon* spake.
    Either to disinthrone the King of Heav'n
We warr, if warr be best, or to regain   230
Our own right lost: him to unthrone we then
May hope, when everlasting Fate shall yeild
To fickle Chance, and *Chaos* judge the strife :
The former vain to hope argues as vain
The latter : for what place can be for us
Within Heav'ns bound, unless Heav'ns Lord supream
We overpower? Suppose he should relent
And publish Grace to all, on promise made
Of new Subjection ; with what eyes could we
Stand in his presence humble, and receive   240
Strict Laws impos'd, to celebrate his Throne
With warbl'd Hymns, and to his Godhead sing
Forc't Halleluiahs ; while he Lordly sits
Our envied Sovran, and his Altar breathes
Ambrosial Odours and Ambrosial Flowers,
Our servile offerings. This must be our task
In Heav'n, this our delight ; how wearisom
Eternity so spent in worship paid
To whom we hate. Let us not then pursue
By force impossible, by leave obtain'd   250
Unacceptable, though in Heav'n, our state
Of splendid vassalage, but rather seek
Our own good from our selves, and from our own
Live to our selves, though in this vast recess,
Free, and to none accountable, preferring
Hard liberty before the easie yoke
Of servile Pomp. Our greatness will appear
Then most conspicuous, when great things of small,
Useful of hurtful, prosperous of adverse
We can create, and in what place so e're   260
Thrive under evil, and work ease out of pain
Through labour and endurance. This deep world
Of darkness do we dread? How oft amidst
Thick clouds and dark doth Heav'ns all-ruling Sire
Choose to reside, his Glory unobscur'd,
And with the Majesty of darkness round
Covers his Throne ; from whence deep thunders roar

Must'ring thir rage, and Heav'n resembles Hell?
As he our Darkness, cannot we his Light
Imitate when we please? This Desart soile   270
Wants not her hidden lustre, Gemms and Gold;
Nor want we skill or art, from whence to raise
Magnificence; and what can Heav'n shew more?
Our torments also may in length of time
Become our Elements, these piercing Fires
As soft as now severe, our temper chang'd
Into their temper; which must needs remove
The sensible of pain. All things invite
To peaceful Counsels, and the settl'd State
Of order, how in safety best we may   280
Compose our present evils, with regard
Of what we are and where, dismissing quite
All thoughts of Warr; ye have what I advise.

    He scarce had finisht, when such murmur filld
Th' Assembly, as when hollow Rocks retain
The sound of blustring winds, which all night long
Had rous'd the Sea, now with hoarse cadence lull
Sea-faring men orewatcht, whose Bark by chance
Or Pinnace anchors in a craggy Bay
After the Tempest: Such applause was heard   290
As *Mammon* ended, and his Sentence pleas'd,
Advising peace: for such another Field
They dreaded worse then Hell: so much the fear
Of Thunder and the Sword of *Michael*
Wrought still within them; and no less desire
To found this nether Empire, which might rise
By pollicy, and long process of time,
In emulation opposite to Heav'n.
Which when *Bëèlzebub* perceiv'd, then whom,
Satan except, none higher sat, with grave   300
Aspect he rose, and in his rising seem'd
A Pillar of State; deep on his Front engraven
Deliberation sat and publick care;
And Princely counsel in his face yet shon,
Majestick though in ruin: sage he stood
With *Atlantean* shoulders fit to bear
The weight of mightiest Monarchies; his look
Drew audience and attention still as Night

Or Summers Noon-tide air, while thus he spake.
   Thrones and imperial Powers, off-spring of heav'n,   310
Ethereal Vertues ; or these Titles now
Must we renounce, and changing stile be call'd
Princes of Hell ? for so the popular vote
Inclines, here to continue, and build up here
A growing Empire ; doubtless ; while we dream,
And know not that the King of Heav'n hath doom'd
This place our dungeon, not our safe retreat
Beyond his Potent arm, to live exempt
From Heav'ns high jurisdiction, in new League
Banded against his Throne, but to remaine   320
In strictest bondage, though thus far remov'd,
Under th' inevitable curb, reserv'd
His captive multitude : For he, be sure,
In highth or depth, still first and last will Reign
Sole King, and of his Kingdom loose no part
By our revolt, but over Hell extend
His Empire, and with Iron Scepter rule
Us here, as with his Golden those in Heav'n.
What sit we then projecting Peace and Warr ?
Warr hath determin'd us, and foild with loss   330
Irreparable ; tearms of peace yet none
Voutsaf't or sought ; for what peace will be giv'n
To us enslav'd, but custody severe,
And stripes, and arbitrary punishment
Inflicted ? and what peace can we return,
But to our power hostility and hate,
Untam'd reluctance, and revenge though slow,
Yet ever plotting how the Conquerour least
May reap his conquest, and may least rejoyce
In doing what we most in suffering feel?   340
Nor will occasion want, nor shall we need
With dangerous expedition to invade
Heav'n, whose high walls fear no assault or Siege,
Or ambush from the Deep. What if we find
Some easier enterprize ? There is a place
(If ancient and prophetic fame in Heav'n
Err not) another World, the happy seat
Of som new Race call'd *Man*, about this time
To be created like to us, though less
In power and excellence, but favour'd more   350

   (209)

Of him who rules above; so was his will
Pronounc'd among the Gods, and by an Oath,
That shook Heav'ns whol circumference, confirm'd.
Thither let us bend all our thoughts, to learn
What creatures there inhabit, of what mould,
Or substance, how endu'd, and what thir Power,
And where thir weakness, how attempted best,
By force or suttlety : Though Heav'n be shut,
And Heav'ns high Arbitrator sit secure
In his own strength, this place may lye expos'd   360
The utmost border of his Kingdom, left
To their defence who hold it : here perhaps
Som advantagious act may be achiev'd
By sudden onset, either with Hell fire
To waste his whole Creation, or possess
All as our own, and drive as we were driven,
The punie habitants, or if not drive,
Seduce them to our Party, that thir God
May prove thir foe, and with repenting hand
Abolish his own works. This would surpass   370
Common revenge, and interrupt his joy
In our Confusion, and our Joy upraise
In his disturbance ; when his darling Sons
Hurl'd headlong to partake with us, shall curse
Thir frail Originals, and faded bliss,
Faded so soon. Advise if this be worth
Attempting, or to sit in darkness here
Hatching vain Empires. Thus *Bëelzebub*
Pleaded his devilish Counsel, first devis'd
By *Satan*, and in part propos'd : for whence,   380
But from the Author of all ill could Spring
So deep a malice, to confound the race
Of mankind in one root, and Earth with Hell
To mingle and involve, done all to spite
The great Creatour ? But thir spite still serves
His glory to augment. The bold design
Pleas'd highly those infernal States, and joy
Sparkl'd in all thir eyes ; with full assent
They vote : whereat his speech he thus renews.

    Well have ye judg'd, well ended long debate,   390
Synod of Gods, and like to what ye are,
Great things resolv'd ; which from the lowest deep

Will once more lift us up, in spight of Fate,
Neerer our ancient Seat; perhaps in view
Of those bright confines, whence with neighbouring Arms
And opportune excursion we may chance
Re-enter Heav'n; or else in some milde Zone
Dwell not unvisited of Heav'ns fair Light
Secure, and at the brightning Orient beam
Purge off this gloom; the soft delicious Air,   400
To heal the scarr of these corrosive Fires
Shall breath her balme. But first whom shall we send
In search of this new world, whom shall we find
Sufficient? who shall tempt with wandring feet
The dark unbottom'd infinite Abyss
And through the palpable obscure find out
His uncouth way, or spread his aerie flight
Upborn with indefatigable wings
Over the vast abrupt, ere he arrive
The happy Ile; what strength, what art can then   410
Suffice, or what evasion bear him safe
Through the strict Senteries and Stations thick
Of Angels watching round? Here he had need
All circumspection, and wee now no less
Choice in our suffrage; for on whom we send,
The weight of all and our last hope relies.
    This said, he sat; and expectation held
His look suspence, awaiting who appeer'd
To second, or oppose, or undertake
The perilous attempt; but all sat mute,   420
Pondering the danger with deep thoughts; and each
In others count'nance red his own dismay
Astonisht: none among the choice and prime
Of those Heav'n-warring Champions could be found
So hardie as to proffer or accept
Alone the dreadful voyage; till at last
Satan, whom now transcendent glory rais'd
Above his fellows, with Monarchal pride
Conscious of highest worth, unmov'd thus spake.
    O Progeny of Heav'n, Empyreal Thrones,   430
With reason hath deep silence and demurr
Seis'd us, though undismaid: long is the way
And hard, that out of Hell leads up to Light;

402 breath] misprint for breathe.

Our prison strong, this huge convex of Fire,
Outrageous to devour, immures us round
Ninefold, and gates of burning Adamant
Barr'd over us prohibit all egress.
These past, if any pass, the void profound
Of unessential Night receives him next
Wide gaping, and with utter loss of being   440
Threatens him, plung'd in that abortive gulf.
If thence he scape into what ever world,
Or unknown Region, what remains him less
Then unknown dangers and as hard escape.
But I should ill become this Throne, O Peers,
And this Imperial Sov'ranty, adorn'd
With splendor, arm'd with power, if aught propos'd
And judg'd of public moment, in the shape
Of difficulty or danger could deterre
Me from attempting. Wherefore do I assume   450
These Royalties, and not refuse to Reign,
Refusing to accept as great a share
Of hazard as of honour, due alike
To him who Reigns, and so much to him due
Of hazard more, as he above the rest
High honourd sits? Go therfore mighty powers,
Terror of Heav'n, though fall'n; intend at home,
While here shall be our home, what best may ease
The present misery, and render Hell
More tollerable; if there be cure or charm   460
To respite or deceive, or slack the pain
Of this ill Mansion : intermit no watch
Against a wakeful Foe, while I abroad
Through all the coasts of dark destruction seek
Deliverance for us all : this enterprize
None shall partake with me. Thus saying rose
The Monarch, and prevented all reply,
Prudent, least from his resolution rais'd
Others among the chief might offer now
(Certain to be refus'd) what erst they feard ;   470
And so refus'd might in opinion stand
His rivals, winning cheap the high repute
Which he through hazard huge must earn. But they
Dreaded not more th' adventure then his voice
Forbidding ; and at once with him they rose ;

Thir rising all at once was as the sound
Of Thunder heard remote. Towards him they bend
With awful reverence prone; and as a God
Extoll him equal to the highest in Heav'n:
Nor fail'd they to express how much they prais'd,   480
That for the general safety he despis'd
His own : for neither do the Spirits damn'd
Loose all thir vertue ; least bad men should boast
Thir specious deeds on earth, which glory excites,
Or close ambition varnisht o're with zeal.
Thus they thir doubtful consultations dark
Ended rejoycing in thir matchless Chief:
As when from mountain tops the dusky clouds
Ascending, while the North wind sleeps, o'respread
Heavn's chearful face, the lowring Element   490
Scowls ore the dark'nd lantskip Snow, or showre ;
If chance the radiant Sun with farewell sweet
Extend his ev'ning beam, the fields revive,
The birds thir notes renew, and bleating herds
Attest thir joy, that hill and valley rings.
O shame to men ! Devil with Devil damn'd
Firm concord holds, men onely disagree
Of Creatures rational, though under hope
Of heavenly Grace ; and God proclaiming peace,
Yet live in hatred, enmitie, and strife   500
Among themselves, and levie cruel warres,
Wasting the Earth, each other to destroy :
As if (which might induce us to accord)
Man had not hellish foes anow besides,
That day and night for his destruction waite.
   The *Stygian* Councel thus dissolv'd ; and forth
In order came the grand infernal Peers,
Midst came thir mighty Paramount, and seemd
Alone th' Antagonist of Heav'n, nor less
Then Hells dread Emperour with pomp Supream,   510
And God-like imitated State ; him round
A Globe of fierie Seraphim inclos'd
With bright imblazonrie, and horrent Arms.
Then of thir Session ended they bid cry
With Trumpets regal sound the great result :
Toward the four winds four speedy Cherubim

483 thir] her *1674*

Put to thir mouths the sounding Alchymie
By Haralds voice explain'd : the hollow Abyss
Heard farr and wide, and all the host of Hell
With deafning shout, return'd them loud acclaim.   520
Thence more at ease thir minds and somwhat rais'd
By false presumptuous hope, the ranged powers
Disband, and wandring, each his several way
Pursues, as inclination or sad choice
Leads him perplext, where he may likeliest find
Truce to his restless thoughts, and entertain
The irksome hours, till his great Chief return.
Part on the Plain, or in the Air sublime
Upon the wing, or in swift race contend,
As at th' Olympian Games or *Pythian* fields ;   530
Part curb thir fierie Steeds, or shun the Goal
With rapid wheels, or fronted Brigads form.
As when to warn proud Cities warr appears
Wag'd in the troubl'd Skie, and Armies rush
To Battel in the Clouds, before each Van
Pric forth the Aerie Knights, and couch thir spears
Till thickest Legions close ; with feats of Arms
From either end of Heav'n the welkin burns.
Others with vast *Typhœan* rage more fell
Rend up both Rocks and Hills, and ride the Air   540
In whirlwind ; Hell scarce holds the wilde uproar.
As when *Alcides* from *Oealia* Crown'd
With conquest, felt th' envenom'd robe, and tore
Through pain up by the roots *Thessalian* Pines,
And *Lichas* from the top of *Oeta* threw
Into th' *Euboic* Sea. Others more milde,
Retreated in a silent valley, sing
With notes Angelical to many a Harp
Thir own Heroic deeds and hapless fall
By doom of Battel ; and complain that Fate   550
Free Vertue should enthrall to Force or Chance.
Thir song was partial, but the harmony
(What could it less when Spirits immortal sing ?)
Suspended Hell, and took with ravishment
The thronging audience. In discourse more sweet
(For Eloquence the Soul, Song charms the Sense,)
Others apart sat on a Hill retir'd,

527 his] this *1674*   542 *Oealia*] *Oechalia 1674*

In thoughts more elevate, and reason'd high
Of Providence, Foreknowledge, Will, and Fate,
Fixt Fate, free will, foreknowledge absolute,   560
And found no end, in wandring mazes lost.
Of good and evil much they argu'd then,
Of happiness and final misery,
Passion and Apathie, and glory and shame,
Vain wisdom all, and false Philosophie:
Yet with a pleasing sorcerie could charm
Pain for a while or anguish, and excite
Fallacious hope, or arm th' obdured brest
With stubborn patience as with triple steel.
Another part in Squadrons and gross Bands   570
On bold adventure to discover wide
That dismal World, if any Clime perhaps
Might yeild them easier habitation, bend
Four ways thir flying March, along the Banks
Of four infernal Rivers that disgorge
Into the burning Lake thir baleful streams;
Abhorred *Styx* the flood of deadly hate,
Sad *Acheron* of Sorrow, black and deep;
Cocytus, nam'd of lamentation loud
Heard on the ruful stream; fierce *Phlegeton*   580
Whose waves of torrent fire inflame with rage.
Farr off from these a slow and silent stream,
Lethe the River of Oblivion roules
Her watrie Labyrinth, whereof who drinks,
Forthwith his former state and being forgets,
Forgets both joy and grief, pleasure and pain.
Beyond this flood a frozen Continent
Lies dark and wilde, beat with perpetual storms
Of Whirlwind and dire Hail, which on firm land
Thaws not, but gathers heap, and ruin seems   590
Of ancient pile; all else deep snow and ice,
A gulf profound as that *Serbonian* Bog
Betwixt *Damiata* and mount *Casius* old,
Where Armies whole have sunk: the parching Air
Burns frore, and cold performs th' effect of Fire.
Thither by harpy-footed Furies hail'd,
At certain revolutions all the damn'd
Are brought: and feel by turns the bitter change
Of fierce extreams, extreams by change more fierce,

From Beds of raging Fire to starve in Ice   600
Thir soft Ethereal warmth, and there to pine
Immovable, infixt, and frozen round,
Periods of time, thence hurried back to fire.
They ferry over this *Lethean* Sound
Both to and fro, thir sorrow to augment,
And wish and struggle, as they pass, to reach
The tempting stream, with one small drop to loose
In sweet forgetfulness all pain and woe,
All in one moment, and so neer the brink ;
But fate withstands, and to oppose th' attempt   610
Medusa with *Gorgonian* terror guards
The Ford, and of it self the water flies
All taste of living wight, as once it fled
The lip of *Tantalus.* Thus roving on
In confus'd march forlorn, th' adventrous Bands
With shuddring horror pale, and eyes agast
View'd first thir lamentable lot, and found
No rest : through many a dark and drearie Vaile
They pass'd, and many a Region dolorous,
O're many a Frozen, many a Fierie Alpe,   620
Rocks, Caves, Lakes, Fens, Bogs, Dens, and shades of death,
A Universe of death, which God by curse
Created evil, for evil only good,
Where all life dies, death lives, and nature breeds,
Perverse, all monstrous, all prodigious things,
Abominable, inutterable, and worse
Then Fables yet have feign'd, or fear conceiv'd,
Gorgons and *Hydra's,* and *Chimera's* dire.
    Mean while the Adversary of God and Man,
Satan with thoughts inflam'd of highest design,   630
Puts on swift wings, and toward the Gates of Hell
Explores his solitary flight ; som times
He scours the right hand coast, som times the left,
Now shaves with level wing the Deep, then soares
Up to the fiery concave touring high.
As when farr off at Sea a Fleet descri'd
Hangs in the Clouds, by *Æquinoctial* Winds
Close sailing from *Bengala,* or the Iles
Of *Ternate* and *Tidore,* whence Merchants bring
Thir spicie Drugs : they on the trading Flood   640

631 **toward**] towards *1674*

(216)

Through the wide *Ethiopian* to the Cape
Ply stemming nightly toward the Pole. So seem'd
Farr off the flying Fiend: at last appeer
Hell bounds high reaching to the horrid Roof,
And thrice threefold the Gates; three folds were Brass,
Three Iron, three of Adamantine Rock,
Impenitrable, impal'd with circling fire,
Yet unconsum'd. Before the Gates there sat
On either side a formidable shape;
The one seem'd Woman to the waste, and fair,   650
But ended foul in many a scaly fould
Voluminous and vast, a Serpent arm'd
With mortal sting: about her middle round
A cry of Hell Hounds never ceasing bark'd
With wide *Cerberean* mouths full loud, and rung
A hideous Peal: yet, when they list, would creep,
If aught disturb'd thir noyse, into her woomb,
And kennel there, yet there still bark'd and howl'd
Within unseen. Farr less abhorrd then these
Vex'd *Scylla* bathing in the Sea that parts   660
Calabria from the hoarce *Trinacrian* shore:
Nor uglier follow the Night-Hag, when call'd
In secret, riding through the Air she comes
Lur'd with the smell of infant blood, to dance
With *Lapland* Witches, while the labouring Moon
Eclipses at thir charms. The other shape,
If shape it might be call'd that shape had none
Distinguishable in member, joynt, or limb,
Or substance might be call'd that shadow seem'd,
For each seem'd either; black it stood as Night,   670
Fierce as ten Furies, terrible as Hell,
And shook a dreadful Dart; what seem'd his head
The likeness of a Kingly Crown had on.
Satan was now at hand, and from his seat
The Monster moving onward came as fast,
With horrid strides, Hell trembled as he strode.
Th' undaunted Fiend what this might be admir'd,
Admir'd, not fear'd; God and his Son except,
Created thing naught vallu'd he nor shun'd;
And with disdainful look thus first began.   680
  Whence and what art thou, execrable shape,
That dar'st, though grim and terrible, advance

Thy miscreated Front athwart my way
To yonder Gates? through them I mean to pass,
That be assured, without leave askt of thee:
Retire, or taste thy folly, and learn by proof,
Hell-born, not to contend with Spirits of Heav'n.

   To whom the Goblin full of wrauth reply'd,
Art thou that Traitor Angel, art thou hee,
Who first broke peace in Heav'n and Faith, till then   690
Unbrok'n, and in proud rebellious Arms
Drew after him the third part of Heav'ns Sons
Conjur'd against the highest, for which both Thou
And they outcast from God, are here condemn'd
To waste Eternal daies in woe and pain?
And reck'n'st thou thy self with Spirits of Heav'n,
Hell-doomd, and breath'st defiance here and scorn,
Where I reign King, and to enrage thee more,
Thy King and Lord? Back to thy punishment,
False fugitive, and to thy speed add wings,   700
Least with a whip of Scorpions I pursue
Thy lingring, or with one stroke of this Dart
Strange horror seise thee, and pangs unfelt before.

   So spake the grieslie terrour, and in shape,
So speaking and so threatning, grew ten fold
More dreadful and deform: on th' other side
Incenc't with indignation *Satan* stood
Unterrifi'd, and like a Comet burn'd,
That fires the length of *Ophiucus* huge
In th' Artick Sky, and from his horrid hair   710
Shakes Pestilence and Warr. Each at the Head
Level'd his deadly aime; thir fatall hands
No second stroke intend, and such a frown
Each cast at th' other, as when two black Clouds
With Heav'ns Artillery fraught, come rattling on
Over the *Caspian*, then stand front to front
Hov'ring a space, till Winds the signal blow
To joyn thir dark Encounter in mid air:
So frownd the mighty Combatants, that Hell
Grew darker at thir frown, so matcht they stood;   720
For never but once more was either like
To meet so great a foe: and now great deeds
Had been achiev'd, whereof all Hell had rung,
Had not the Snakie Sorceress that sat

    (218)

Fast by Hell Gate, and kept the fatal Key,
Ris'n, and with hideous outcry rush'd between.

O Father, what intends thy hand, she cry'd,
Against thy only Son? What fury O Son,
Possesses thee to bend that mortal Dart
Against thy Fathers head? and know'st for whom;   730
For him who sits above and laughs the while
At thee ordain'd his drudge, to execute
What e're his wrath, which he calls Justice, bids,
His wrath which one day will destroy ye both.

She spake, and at her words the hellish Pest
Forbore, then these to her *Satan* return'd:

So strange thy outcry, and thy words so strange
Thou interposest, that my sudden hand
Prevented spares to tell thee yet by deeds
What it intends; till first I know of thee,   740
What thing thou art, thus double-form'd, and why
In this infernal Vaile first met thou call'st
Me Father, and that Fantasm call'st my Son?
I know thee not, nor ever saw till now
Sight more detestable then him and thee.

T' whom thus the Portress of Hell Gate reply'd:
Hast thou forgot me then, and do I seem
Now in thine eye so foul, once deemd so fair
In Heav'n, when at th' Assembly, and in sight
Of all the Seraphim with thee combin'd   750
In bold conspiracy against Heav'ns King,
All on a sudden miserable pain
Surpris'd thee, dim thine eyes, and dizzie swumm
In darkness, while thy head flames thick and fast
Threw forth, till on the left side op'ning wide,
Likest to thee in shape and count'nance bright,
Then shining heav'nly fair, a Goddess arm'd
Out of thy head I sprung; amazement seis'd
All th' Host of Heav'n; back they recoild affraid
At first, and call'd me *Sin*, and for a Sign   760
Portentous held me; but familiar grown,
I pleas'd, and with attractive graces won
The most averse, thee chiefly, who full oft
Thy self in me thy perfect image viewing
Becam'st enamour'd, and such joy thou took'st
With me in secret, that my womb conceiv'd

A growing burden. Mean while Warr arose,
And fields were fought in Heav'n; wherein remaind
(For what could else) to our Almighty Foe
Cleer Victory, to our part loss and rout   770
Through all the Empyrean : down they fell
Driv'n headlong from the Pitch of Heaven, down
Into this Deep, and in the general fall
I also; at which time this powerful Key
Into my hand was giv'n, with charge to keep
These Gates for ever shut, which none can pass
Without my op'ning. Pensive here I sat
Alone, but long I sat not, till my womb
Pregnant by thee, and now excessive grown
Prodigious motion felt and rueful throes.   780
At last this odious offspring whom thou seest
Thine own begotten, breaking violent way
Tore through my entrails, that with fear and pain
Distorted, all my nether shape thus grew
Transform'd : but he my inbred enemie
Forth issu'd, brandishing his fatal Dart
Made to destroy : I fled, and cry'd out *Death* ;
Hell trembl'd at the hideous Name, and sigh'd
From all her Caves, and back resounded *Death.*
I fled, but he pursu'd (though more, it seems,   790
Inflam'd with lust then rage) and swifter far,
Me overtook his mother all dismaid,
And in embraces forcible and foule
Ingendring with me, of that rape begot
These yelling Monsters that with ceasless cry
Surround me, as thou sawst, hourly conceiv'd
And hourly born, with sorrow infinite
To me, for when they list into the womb
That bred them they return, and howle and gnaw
My Bowels, their repast ; then bursting forth   800
Afresh with conscious terrours vex me round,
That rest or intermission none I find.
Before mine eyes in opposition sits
Grim *Death* my Son and foe, who sets them on,
And me his Parent would full soon devour
For want of other prey, but that he knows
His end with mine involvd ; and knows that I
Should prove a bitter Morsel, and his bane,

When ever that shall be ; so Fate pronounc'd.
But thou O Father, I forewarn thee, shun   810
His deadly arrow ; neither vainly hope
To be invulnerable in those bright Arms,
Though temper'd heav'nly, for that mortal dint,
Save he who reigns above, none can resist.
    She finish'd, and the suttle Fiend his lore
Soon learnd, now milder, and thus answerd smooth.
Dear Daughter, since thou claim'st me for thy Sire,
And my fair Son here showst me, the dear pledge
Of dalliance had with thee in Heav'n, and joys
Then sweet, now sad to mention, through dire change 820
Befalln us unforeseen, unthought of, know
I come no enemie, but to set free
From out this dark and dismal house of pain,
Both him and thee, and all the heav'nly Host
Of Spirits that in our just pretenses arm'd
Fell with us from on high : from them I go
This uncouth errand sole, and one for all
My self expose, with lonely steps to tread
Th' unfounded deep, & through the void immense
To search with wandring quest a place foretold   830
Should be, and, by concurring signs, ere now
Created vast and round, a place of bliss
In the Pourlieues of Heav'n, and therein plac't
A race of upstart Creatures, to supply
Perhaps our vacant room, though more remov'd,
Least Heav'n surcharg'd with potent multitude
Might hap to move new broiles : Be this or aught
Then this more secret now design'd, I haste
To know, and this once known, shall soon return,
And bring ye to the place where Thou and Death   840
Shall dwell at ease, and up and down unseen
Wing silently the buxom Air, imbalm'd
With odours ; there ye shall be fed and fill'd
Immeasurably, all things shall be your prey.
He ceas'd, for both seemd highly pleasd, and Death
Grinnd horrible a gastly smile, to hear
His famine should be fill'd, and blest his mawe
Destin'd to that good hour : no less rejoyc'd
His mother bad, and thus bespake her Sire.
    The key of this infernal Pit by due,   850

And by command of Heav'ns all-powerful King
I keep, by him forbidden to unlock
These Adamantine Gates; against all force
Death ready stands to interpose his dart,
Fearless to be o'rematcht by living might.
But what ow I to his commands above
Who hates me, and hath hither thrust me down
Into this gloom of *Tartarus* profound,
To sit in hateful Office here confin'd,
Inhabitant of Heav'n, and heav'nlie-born,   860
Here in perpetual agonie and pain,
With terrors and with clamors compasst round
Of mine own brood, that on my bowels feed:
Thou art my Father, thou my Author, thou
My being gav'st me; whom should I obey
But thee, whom follow? thou wilt bring me soon
To that new world of light and bliss, among
The Gods who live at ease, where I shall Reign
At thy right hand voluptuous, as beseems
Thy daughter and thy darling, without end.   870
    Thus saying, from her side the fatal Key,
Sad instrument of all our woe, she took;
And towards the Gate rouling her bestial train,
Forthwith the huge Portcullis high up drew,
Which but her self not all the *Stygian* powers
Could once have mov'd; then in the key-hole turns
Th' intricate wards, and every Bolt and Bar
Of massie Iron or sollid Rock with ease
Unfast'ns: on a sudden op'n flie
With impetuous recoile and jarring sound   880
Th' infernal dores, and on thir hinges grate
Harsh Thunder, that the lowest bottom shook
Of *Erebus*. She op'nd, but to shut
Excel'd her power; the Gates wide op'n stood,
That with extended wings a Bannerd Host
Under spread Ensigns marching might pass through
With Horse and Chariots rankt in loose array;
So wide they stood, and like a Furnace mouth
Cast forth redounding smoak and ruddy flame.
Before thir eyes in sudden view appear   890
The secrets of the hoarie deep, a dark
Illimitable Ocean without bound,

Without dimension, where length, breadth, and highth,
And time and place are lost ; where eldest Night
And *Chaos*, Ancestors of Nature, hold
Eternal *Anarchie*, amidst the noise
Of endless warrs, and by confusion stand.
For hot, cold, moist, and dry, four Champions fierce
Strive here for Maistrie, and to Battel bring
Thir embryon Atoms ; they around the flag   900
Of each his faction, in thir several Clanns,
Light-arm'd or heavy, sharp, smooth, swift or slow,
Swarm populous, unnumber'd as the Sands
Of *Barca* or *Cyrene's* torrid soil,
Levied to side with warring Winds, and poise
Thir lighter wings. To whom these most adhere,
Hee rules a moment ; *Chaos* Umpire sits,
And by decision more imbroiles the fray
By which he Reigns : next him high Arbiter
Chance governs all. Into this wilde Abyss,   910
The Womb of nature and perhaps her Grave,
Of neither Sea, nor Shore, nor Air, nor Fire,
But all these in thir pregnant causes mixt
Confus'dly, and which thus must ever fight,
Unless th' Almighty Maker them ordain
His dark materials to create more Worlds,
Into this wild Abyss the warie fiend
Stood on the brink of Hell and look'd a while,
Pondering his Voyage : for no narrow frith
He had to cross. Nor was his eare less peal'd   920
With noises loud and ruinous (to compare
Great things with small) then when *Bellona* storms,
With all her battering Engines bent to rase
Som Capital City, or less then if this frame
Of Heav'n were falling, and these Elements
In mutinie had from her Axle torn
The stedfast Earth. At last his Sail-broad Vannes
He spreads for flight, and in the surging smoak
Uplifted spurns the ground, thence many a League
As in a cloudy Chair ascending rides   930
Audacious, but that seat soon failing, meets
A vast vacuitie : all unawares
Fluttring his pennons vain plumb down he drops
Ten thousand fadom deep, and to this hour

Down had been falling, had not by ill chance
The strong rebuff of som tumultuous cloud
Instinct with Fire and Nitre hurried him
As many miles aloft : that furie stay'd,
Quencht in a Boggie *Syrtis*, neither Sea,
Nor good dry Land : nigh founderd on he fares,   940
Treading the crude consistence, half on foot,
Half flying ; behoves him now both Oare and Saile.
As when a Gryfon through the Wilderness
With winged course ore Hill or moarie Dale,
Pursues the *Arimaspian*, who by stelth
Had from his wakeful custody purloind
The guarded Gold : So eagerly the fiend
Ore bog or steep, through strait, rough, dense, or rare,
With head, hands, wings, or feet pursues his way,
And swims or sinks, or wades, or creeps, or flyes :   950
At length a universal hubbub wilde
Of stunning sounds and voices all confus'd
Born through the hollow dark assaults his eare
With loudest vehemence : thither he plyes,
Undaunted to meet there what ever power
Or Spirit of the nethermost Abyss
Might in that noise reside, of whom to ask
Which way the neerest coast of darkness lyes
Bordering on light ; when strait behold the Throne
Of *Chaos*, and his dark Pavilion spread   960
Wide on the wasteful Deep ; with him Enthron'd
Sat Sable-vested Night, eldest of things,
The Consort of his Reign ; and by them stood
Orcus and *Ades*, and the dreaded name
Of *Demogorgon* ; Rumor next and Chance,
And Tumult and Confusion all imbroild,
And Discord with a thousand various mouths.
    T' whom *Satan* turning boldly, thus. Ye Powers
And Spirits of this nethermost Abyss,
Chaos and *ancient Night*, I come no Spie,   970
With purpose to explore or to disturb
The secrets of your Realm, but by constraint
Wandring this darksome desart, as my way
Lies through your spacious Empire up to light,
Alone, and without guide, half lost, I seek
What readiest path leads where your gloomie bounds

Confine with Heav'n ; or if som other place
From your Dominion won, th' Ethereal King
Possesses lately, thither to arrive
I travel this profound, direct my course ;   980
Directed, no mean recompence it brings
To your behoof, if I that Region lost,
All usurpation thence expell'd, reduce
To her original darkness and your sway
(Which is my present journey) and once more
Erect the Standerd there of *ancient Night* ;
Yours be th' advantage all, mine the revenge.
    Thus *Satan* ; and him thus the Anarch old
With faultring speech and visage incompos'd
Answer'd. I know thee, stranger, who thou art,   990
That mighty leading Angel, who of late
Made head against Heav'ns King, though overthrown.
I saw and heard, for such a numerous host
Fled not in silence through the frighted deep
With ruin upon ruin, rout on rout,
Confusion worse confounded ; and Heav'n Gates
Pourd out by millions her victorious Bands
Pursuing. I upon my Frontieres here
Keep residence ; if all I can will serve,
That little which is left so to defend   1000
Encroacht on still through our intestine broiles
Weakning the Scepter of old Night : first Hell
Your dungeon stretching far and wide beneath ;
Now lately Heaven and Earth, another World
Hung ore my Realm, link'd in a golden Chain
To that side Heav'n from whence your Legions fell :
If that way be your walk, you have not farr ;
So much the neerer danger ; goe and speed ;
Havock and spoil and ruin are my gain.
    He ceas'd ; and *Satan* staid not to reply,   1010
But glad that now his Sea should find a shore,
With fresh alacritie and force renew'd
Springs upward like a Pyramid of fire
Into the wilde Expanse, and through the shock
Of fighting Elements, on all sides round
Environ'd wins his way ; harder beset
And more endanger'd, then when *Argo* pass'd
Through *Bosporus* betwixt the justling Rocks :

Or when *Ulysses* on the Larbord shunnd
Charybdis, and by th' other whirlpool steard. 1020
So he with difficulty and labour hard
Mov'd on, with difficulty and labour hee;
But hee once past, soon after when man fell,
Strange alteration! Sin and Death amain
Following his track, such was the will of Heav'n,
Pav'd after him a broad and beat'n way
Over the dark Abyss, whose boiling Gulf
Tamely endur'd a Bridge of wondrous length
From Hell continu'd reaching th' utmost Orbe
Of this frail World; by which the Spirits perverse 1030
With easie intercourse pass to and fro
To tempt or punish mortals, except whom
God and good Angels guard by special grace.
But now at last the sacred influence
Of light appears, and from the walls of Heav'n
Shoots farr into the bosom of dim Night
A glimmering dawn; here Nature first begins
Her fardest verge, and *Chaos* to retire
As from her outmost works a brok'n foe
With tumult less and with less hostile din, 1040
That *Satan* with less toil, and now with ease
Wafts on the calmer wave by dubious light
And like a weather-beaten Vessel holds
Gladly the Port, though Shrouds and Tackle torn;
Or in the emptier waste, resembling Air,
Weighs his spread wings, at leasure to behold
Farr off th' Empyreal Heav'n, extended wide
In circuit, undetermind square or round,
With Opal Towrs and Battlements adorn'd
Of living Saphire, once his native Seat; 1050
And fast by hanging in a golden Chain
This pendant world, in bigness as a Starr
Of smallest Magnitude close by the Moon.
Thither full fraught with mischievous revenge,
Accurst, and in a cursed hour he hies.

The End of the Second Book.

PARADISE LOST.

BOOK III.

THE ARGUMENT.

God sitting on his Throne sees Satan *flying towards this world, then newly created; shews him to the Son who sat at his right hand; foretells the success of* Satan *in perverting mankind; clears his own Justice and Wisdom from all imputation, having created Man free and able enough to have withstood his Tempter; yet declares his purpose of grace towards him, in regard he fell not of his own malice, as did* Satan, *but by him seduc't. The Son of God renders praises to his Father for the manifestation of his gracious purpose towards Man; but God again declares, that Grace cannot be extended towards Man without the satisfaction of divine Justice; Man hath offended the majesty of God by aspiring to Godhead, and therefore with all his Progeny devoted to death must dye, unless some one can be found sufficient to answer for his offence, and undergoe his Punishment. The Son of God freely offers himself a Ransome for Man: the Father accepts him, ordains his incarnation, pronounces his exaltation above all Names in Heaven and Earth; commands all the Angels to adore him; they obey, and hymning to their Harps in full Quire, celebrate the Father and the Son. Mean while* Satan *alights upon the bare convex of this Worlds outermost Orb; where wandring he first finds a place since call'd The Lymbo of Vanity; what persons and things fly up thither; thence comes to the Gate of Heaven, describ'd ascending by stairs, and the waters above the Firmament that flow about it: His passage thence to the Orb of the Sun; he finds there* Uriel *the Regent of that Orb, but first changes himself into the shape of a meaner Angel; and pretending a zealous desire to behold the new Creation and Man whom God had plac't here, inquires of him the place of his habitation, and is directed; alights first on Mount Niphates.*

> HAIL holy light, ofspring of Heav'n first-born,
> Or of th' Eternal Coeternal beam
> May I express thee unblam'd? since God is light,
> And never but in unapproached light

Dwelt from Eternitie, dwelt then in thee,
Bright effluence of bright essence increate.
Or hear'st thou rather pure Ethereal stream,
Whose Fountain who shall tell? before the Sun,
Before the Heavens thou wert, and at the voice
Of God, as with a Mantle didst invest   10
The rising world of waters dark and deep,
Won from the void and formless infinite.
Thee I re-visit now with bolder wing,
Escap't the *Stygian* Pool, though long detain'd
In that obscure sojourn, while in my flight
Through utter and through middle darkness borne
With other notes then to th' *Orphean* Lyre
I sung of *Chaos* and *Eternal Night*,
Taught by the heav'nly Muse to venture down
The dark descent, and up to reascend,   20
Though hard and rare: thee I revisit safe,
And feel thy sovran vital Lamp; but thou
Revisit'st not these eyes, that rowle in vain
To find thy piercing ray, and find no dawn;
So thick a drop serene hath quencht thir Orbs,
Or dim suffusion veild. Yet not the more
Cease I to wander where the Muses haunt
Cleer Spring, or shadie Grove, or Sunnie Hill,
Smit with the love of sacred song; but chief
Thee *Sion* and the flowrie Brooks beneath   30
That wash thy hallowd feet, and warbling flow,
Nightly I visit: nor somtimes forget
Those other two equal'd with me in Fate,
So were I equal'd with them in renown,
Blind *Thamyris* and blind *Mæonides*,
And *Tiresias* and *Phineus* Prophets old.
Then feed on thoughts, that voluntarie move
Harmonious numbers; as the wakeful Bird
Sings darkling, and in shadiest Covert hid
Tunes her nocturnal Note. Thus with the Year   40
Seasons return, but not to me returns
Day, or the sweet approach of Ev'n or Morn,
Or sight of vernal bloom, or Summers Rose,
Or flocks, or herds, or human face divine;
But cloud in stead, and ever-during dark
Surrounds me, from the chearful waies of men

Cut off, and for the Book of knowledg fair
Presented with a Universal blanc
Of Natures works to mee expung'd and ras'd,
And wisdome at one entrance quite shut out.   50
So much the rather thou Celestial light
Shine inward, and the mind through all her powers
Irradiate, there plant eyes, all mist from thence
Purge and disperse, that I may see and tell
Of things invisible to mortal sight.
   Now had the Almighty Father from above,
From the pure Empyrean where he sits
High Thron'd above all highth, bent down his eye,
His own works and their works at once to view:
About him all the Sanctities of Heaven   60
Stood thick as Starrs, and from his sight receiv'd
Beatitude past utterance; on his right
The radiant image of his Glory sat,
His onely Son; On Earth he first beheld
Our two first Parents, yet the onely two
Of mankind, in the happie Garden plac't,
Reaping immortal fruits of joy and love,
Uninterrupted joy, unrivald love
In blissful solitude; he then survey'd
Hell and the Gulf between, and *Satan* there   70
Coasting the wall of Heav'n on this side Night
In the dun Air sublime, and ready now
To stoop with wearied wings, and willing feet
On the bare outside of this World, that seem'd
Firm land imbosom'd without Firmament,
Uncertain which, in Ocean or in Air.
Him God beholding from his prospect high,
Wherein past, present, future he beholds,
Thus to his onely Son foreseeing spake.
   Onely begotten Son, seest thou what rage   80
Transports our adversarie, whom no bounds
Prescrib'd, no barrs of Hell, nor all the chains
Heapt on him there, nor yet the main Abyss
Wide interrupt can hold; so bent he seems
On desperat revenge, that shall redound
Upon his own rebellious head. And now
Through all restraint broke loose he wings his way
Not farr off Heav'n, in the Precincts of light,

Directly towards the new created World,
And Man there plac't, with purpose to assay   90
If him by force he can destroy, or worse,
By som false guile pervert ; and shall pervert ;
For man will heark'n to his glozing lyes,
And easily transgress the sole Command,
Sole pledge of his obedience : So will fall
Hee and his faithless Progenie : whose fault?
Whose but his own? ingrate, he had of mee
All he could have ; I made him just and right,
Sufficient to have stood, though free to fall.
Such I created all th' Ethereal Powers   100
And Spirits, both them who stood & them who faild ;
Freely they stood who stood, and fell who fell.
Not free, what proof could they have givn sincere
Of true allegiance, constant Faith or Love,
Where onely what they needs must do, appeard,
Not what they would? what praise could they receive?
What pleasure I from such obedience paid,
When Will and Reason (Reason also is choice)
Useless and vain, of freedom both despoild,
Made passive both, had servd necessitie,   110
Not mee. They therefore as to right belongd,
So were created, nor can justly accuse
Thir maker, or thir making, or thir Fate ;
As if Predestination over-rul'd
Thir will, dispos'd by absolute Decree
Or high foreknowledge ; they themselves decreed
Thir own revolt, not I : if I foreknew,
Foreknowledge had no influence on their fault,
Which had no less prov'd certain unforeknown.
So without least impulse or shadow of Fate,   120
Or aught by me immutablie foreseen,
They trespass, Authors to themselves in all
Both what they judge and what they choose ; for so
I formed them free, and free they must remain,
Till they enthrall themselves : I else must change
Thir nature, and revoke the high Decree
Unchangeable, Eternal, which ordain'd
Thir freedom, they themselves ordain'd thir fall.
The first sort by thir own suggestion fell,
Self-tempted, self-deprav'd : Man falls deceiv'd   130

(230)

By the other first : Man therefore shall find grace,
The other none : in Mercy and Justice both,
Through Heav'n and Earth, so shall my glorie excel,
But Mercy first and last shall brightest shine.
    Thus while God spake, ambrosial fragrance fill'd
All Heav'n, and in the blessed Spirits elect
Sense of new joy ineffable diffus'd :
Beyond compare the Son of God was seen
Most glorious, in him all his Father shon
Substantially express'd, and in his face   140
Divine compassion visibly appeerd,
Love without end, and without measure Grace,
Which uttering thus he to his Father spake.
    O Father, gracious was that word which clos'd
Thy sovran sentence, that Man should find grace ;
For which both Heav'n and Earth shall high extoll
Thy praises, with th' innumerable sound
Of Hymns and sacred Songs, wherewith thy Throne
Encompass'd shall resound thee ever blest.
For should Man finally be lost, should Man   150
Thy creature late so lov'd, thy youngest Son
Fall circumvented thus by fraud, though joynd
With his own folly ? that be from thee farr,
That farr be from thee, Father, who art Judge
Of all things made, and judgest onely right.
Or shall the Adversarie thus obtain
His end, and frustrate thine, shall he fulfill
His malice, and thy goodness bring to naught,
Or proud return though to his heavier doom,
Yet with revenge accomplish't and to Hell   160
Draw after him the whole Race of mankind,
By him corrupted ? or wilt thou thy self
Abolish thy Creation, and unmake,
For him, what for thy glorie thou hast made ?
So should thy goodness and thy greatness both
Be questiond and blaspheam'd without defence.
    To whom the great Creatour thus reply'd.
O Son, in whom my Soul hath chief delight,
Son of my bosom, Son who art alone
My word, my wisdom, and my effectual might,   170
All hast thou spok'n as my thoughts are, all
As my Eternal purpose hath decreed :

Man shall not quite be lost, but sav'd who will,
Yet not of will in him, but grace in me
Freely voutsaft ; once more I will renew
His lapsed powers, though forfeit and enthrall'd
By sin to foul exorbitant desires ;
Upheld by me, yet once more he shall stand
On even ground against his mortal foe,
By me upheld, that he may know how frail   180
His fall'n condition is, and to me ow
All his deliv'rance, and to none but me.
Some I have chosen of peculiar grace
Elect above the rest; so is my will :
The rest shall hear me call, and oft be warnd
Thir sinful state, and to appease betimes
Th' incensed Deitie while offerd grace
Invites ; for I will cleer thir senses dark,
What may suffice, and soft'n stonie hearts
To pray, repent, and bring obedience due.   190
To prayer, repentance, and obedience due,
Though but endevord with sincere intent,
Mine eare shall not be slow, mine eye not shut.
And I will place within them as a guide
My Umpire *Conscience*, whom if they will hear,
Light after light well us'd they shall attain,
And to the end persisting, safe arrive.
This my long sufferance and my day of grace
They who neglect and scorn, shall never taste ;
But hard be hard'nd, blind be blinded more,   200
That they may stumble on, and deeper fall ;
And none but such from mercy I exclude.
But yet all is not don ; Man disobeying,
Disloyal breaks his fealtie, and sinns
Against the high Supremacie of Heav'n,
Affecting God-head, and so loosing all,
To expiate his Treason hath naught left,
But to destruction sacred and devote,
He with his whole posteritie must die,
Die hee or Justice must ; unless for him   210
Som other able, and as willing, pay
The rigid satisfaction, death for death.
Say Heav'nly Powers, where shall we find such love,
Which of ye will be mortal to redeem

Mans mortal crime, and just th' unjust to save,
Dwels in all Heaven charitie so deare?
    He ask'd, but all the Heav'nly Quire stood mute,
And silence was in Heav'n: on mans behalf
Patron or Intercessor none appeerd,
Much less that durst upon his own head draw   220
The deadly forfeiture, and ransom set.
And now without redemption all mankind
Must have bin lost, adjudg'd to Death and Hell
By doom severe, had not the Son of God,
In whom the fulness dwels of love divine,
His dearest mediation thus renewd.
    Father, thy word is past, man shall find grace;
And shall grace not find means, that finds her way,
The speediest of thy winged messengers,
To visit all thy creatures, and to all   230
Comes unprevented, unimplor'd, unsought,
Happie for man, so coming; he her aide
Can never seek, once dead in sins and lost;
Attonement for himself or offering meet,
Indebted and undon, hath none to bring:
Behold mee then, mee for him, life for life
I offer, on mee let thine anger fall;
Account mee man; I for his sake will leave
Thy bosom, and this glorie next to thee
Freely put off, and for him lastly die   240
Well pleas'd, on me let Death wreck all his rage;
Under his gloomie power I shall not long
Lie vanquisht; thou hast givn me to possess
Life in my self for ever, by thee I live,
Though now to Death I yeild, and am his due
All that of me can die, yet that debt paid,
Thou wilt not leave me in the loathsom grave
His prey, nor suffer my unspotted Soule
For ever with corruption there to dwell;
But I shall rise Victorious, and subdue   250
My Vanquisher, spoild of his vanted spoile;
Death his deaths wound shall then receive, & stoop
Inglorious, of his mortall sting disarm'd.
I through the ample Air in Triumph high
Shall lead Hell Captive maugre Hell, and show
The powers of darkness bound. Thou at the sight

Pleas'd, out of Heaven shalt look down and smile,
While by thee rais'd I ruin all my Foes,
Death last, and with his Carcass glut the Grave:
Then with the multitude of my redeemd   260
Shall enter Heaven long absent, and returne,
Father, to see thy face, wherein no cloud
Of anger shall remain, but peace assur'd,
And reconcilement; wrauth shall be no more
Thenceforth, but in thy presence Joy entire.

His words here ended, but his meek aspect
Silent yet spake, and breath'd immortal love
To mortal men, above which only shon
Filial obedience: as a sacrifice
Glad to be offer'd, he attends the will   270
Of his great Father. Admiration seis'd
All Heav'n, what this might mean, & whither tend
Wondring; but soon th' Almighty thus reply'd:
O thou in Heav'n and Earth the only peace
Found out for mankind under wrauth, O thou
My sole complacence! well thou know'st how dear,
To me are all my works, nor Man the least
Though last created, that for him I spare
Thee from my bosom and right hand, to save,
By loosing thee a while, the whole Race lost.   280
Thou therefore whom thou only canst redeeme,
Thir Nature also to thy Nature joyne;
And be thy self Man among men on Earth,
Made flesh, when time shall be, of Virgin seed,
By wondrous birth: Be thou in *Adams* room
The Head of all mankind, though *Adams* Son.
As in him perish all men, so in thee
As from a second root shall be restor'd,
As many as are restor'd, without thee none.
His crime makes guiltie all his Sons, thy merit 290
Imputed shall absolve them who renounce
Thir own both righteous and unrighteous deeds,
And live in thee transplanted, and from thee
Receive new life. So Man, as is most just,
Shall satisfie for Man, be judg'd and die,
And dying rise, and rising with him raise
His Brethren, ransomd with his own dear life.
So Heav'nly love shal outdoo Hellish hate,

(234)

Paradise Lost.

Giving to death, and dying to redeeme,
So dearly to redeem what Hellish hate   300
So easily destroy'd, and still destroyes
In those who, when they may, accept not grace.
Nor shalt thou by descending to assume
Mans Nature, less'n or degrade thine owne.
Because thou hast, though Thron'd in highest bliss
Equal to God, and equally enjoying
God-like fruition, quitted all to save
A World from utter loss, and hast been found
By Merit more then Birthright Son of God,
Found worthiest to be so by being Good,   310
Farr more then Great or High ; because in thee
Love hath abounded more then Glory abounds,
Therefore thy Humiliation shall exalt
With thee thy Manhood also to this Throne ;
Here shalt thou sit incarnate, here shalt Reigne
Both God and Man, Son both of God and Man,
Anointed universal King ; all Power
I give thee, reign for ever, and assume
Thy Merits ; under thee as Head Supream
Thrones, Princedoms, Powers, Dominions I reduce :   320
All knees to thee shall bow, of them that bide
In Heaven, or Earth, or under Earth in Hell ;
When thou attended gloriously from Heav'n
Shalt in the Skie appeer, and from thee send
The summoning Arch-Angels to proclaime
Thy dread Tribunal : forthwith from all Windes
The living, and forthwith the cited dead
Of all past Ages to the general Doom
Shall hast'n, such a peal shall rouse thir sleep.
Then all thy Saints assembl'd, thou shalt judge   330
Bad men and Angels, they arraignd shall sink
Beneath thy Sentence ; Hell, her numbers full,
Thenceforth shall be for ever shut. Mean while
The World shall burn, and from her ashes spring
New Heav'n and Earth, wherein the just shall dwell
And after all thir tribulations long
See golden days, fruitful of golden deeds,
With Joy and Love triumphing, and fair Truth.
Then thou thy regal Scepter shalt lay by,
For regal Scepter then no more shall need,   340

God shall be All in All. But all ye Gods,
Adore him, who to compass all this dies,
Adore the Son, and honour him as mee.
  No sooner had th' Almighty ceas't, but all
The multitude of Angels with a shout
Loud as from numbers without number, sweet
As from blest voices, uttering joy, Heav'n rung
With Jubilee, and loud Hosannas fill'd
Th' eternal Regions : lowly reverent
Towards either Throne they bow, & to the ground   350
With solemn adoration down they cast
Thir Crowns inwove with Amarant and Gold,
Immortal Amarant, a Flour which once
In Paradise, fast by the Tree of Life
Began to bloom, but soon for mans offence
To Heav'n remov'd where first it grew, there grows,
And flours aloft shading the Fount of Life,
And where the river of Bliss through midst of Heavn
Rowls o're *Elisian* Flours her Amber stream ;
With these that never fade the Spirits Elect   360
Bind thir resplendent locks inwreath'd with beams,
Now in loose Garlands thick thrown off, the bright
Pavement that like a Sea of Jasper shon
Impurpl'd with Celestial Roses smil'd.
Then Crown'd again thir gold'n Harps they took,
Harps ever tun'd, that glittering by thir side
Like Quivers hung, and with Præamble sweet
Of charming symphonie they introduce
Thir sacred Song, and waken raptures high ;
No voice exempt, no voice but well could joine   370
Melodious part, such concord is in Heav'n.
  Thee Father first they sung Omnipotent,
Immutable, Immortal, Infinite,
Eternal King ; thee Author of all being,
Fountain of Light, thy self invisible
Amidst the glorious brightness where thou sit'st
Thron'd inaccessible, but when thou shad'st
The full blaze of thy beams, and through a cloud
Drawn round about thee like a radiant Shrine,
Dark with excessive bright thy skirts appeer,   380
Yet dazle Heav'n, that brightest Seraphim
Approach not, but with both wings veil thir eyes.

Thee next they sang of all Creation first,
Begotten Son, Divine Similitude,
In whose conspicuous count'nance, without cloud
Made visible, th' Almighty Father shines,
Whom else no Creature can behold; on thee
Impresst the effulgence of his Glorie abides,
Transfus'd on thee his ample Spirit rests.
Hee Heav'n of Heavens and all the Powers therein   390
By thee created, and by thee threw down
Th' aspiring Dominations: thou that day
Thy Fathers dreadful Thunder didst not spare,
Nor stop thy flaming Chariot wheels, that shook
Heav'ns everlasting Frame, while o're the necks
Thou drov'st of warring Angels disarraid.
Back from pursuit thy Powers with loud acclaime
Thee only extold, Son of thy Fathers might,
To execute fierce vengeance on his foes,
Not so on Man; him through their malice fall'n,   400
Father of Mercie and Grace, thou didst not doome
So strictly, but much more to pitie encline:
No sooner did thy dear and onely Son
Perceive thee purpos'd not to doom frail Man
So strictly, but much more to pitie enclin'd,
He to appease thy wrauth, and end the strife
Of Mercy and Justice in thy face discern'd,
Regardless of the Bliss wherein hee sat
Second to thee, offerd himself to die
For mans offence. O unexampl'd love,   410
Love no where to be found less then Divine!
Hail Son of God, Saviour of Men, thy Name
Shall be the copious matter of my Song
Henceforth, and never shall my Harp thy praise
Forget, nor from thy Fathers praise disjoine.
    Thus they in Heav'n, above the starry Sphear,
Thir happie hours in joy and hymning spent.
Mean while upon the firm opacous Globe
Of this round World, whose first convex divides
The luminous inferior Orbs, enclos'd   420
From *Chaos* and th' inroad of Darkness old,
Satan alighted walks: a Globe farr off
It seem'd, now seems a boundless Continent
Dark, waste, and wild, under the frown of Night

Starless expos'd, and ever-threatning storms
Of *Chaos* blustring round, inclement skie ;
Save on that side which from the wall of Heav'n
Though distant farr som small reflection gaines
Of glimmering air less vext with tempest loud :
Here walk'd the Fiend at large in spacious field.   430
As when a Vultur on *Imaus* bred,
Whose snowie ridge the roving *Tartar* bounds,
Dislodging from a Region scarce of prey
To gorge the flesh of Lambs or yeanling Kids
On Hills where Flocks are fed, flies toward the Springs
Of *Ganges* or *Hydaspes*, *Indian* streams ;
But in his way lights on the barren plaines
Of *Sericana*, where *Chineses* drive
With Sails and Wind thir canie Waggons light :
So on this windie Sea of Land, the Fiend   440
Walk'd up and down alone bent on his prey,
Alone, for other Creature in this place
Living or liveless to be found was none,
None yet, but store hereafter from the earth
Up hither like Aereal vapours flew
Of all things transitorie and vain, when Sin
With vanity had filld the works of men :
Both all things vain, and all who in vain things
Built their fond hopes of Glorie or lasting fame,
Or happiness in this or th' other life ;   450
All who have thir reward on Earth, the fruits
Of painful Superstition and blind Zeal,
Naught seeking but the praise of men, here find
Fit retribution, emptie as thir deeds ;
All th' unaccomplisht works of Natures hand,
Abortive, monstrous, or unkindly mixt,
Dissolvd on earth, fleet hither, and in vain,
Till final dissolution, wander here,
Not in the neighbouring Moon, as some have dreamd ;
Those argent Fields more likely habitants,   460
Translated Saints, or middle Spirits hold
Betwixt th' Angelical and Human kinde :
Hither of ill-joynd Sons and Daughters born
First from the ancient World those Giants came
With many a vain exploit, though then renownd :
The builders next of *Babel* on the Plain

(238)

Of *Sennaar*, and still with vain designe
New *Babels*, had they wherewithall, would build:
Others came single; hee who to be deemd
A God, leap'd fondly into *Ætna* flames   470
Empedocles, and hee who to enjoy
Plato's Elysium, leap'd into the Sea,
Cleombrotus, and many more too long,
Embryos, and Idiots, Eremits and Friers
White, Black and Grey, with all thir trumperie.
Here Pilgrims roam, that stray'd so farr to seek
In *Golgotha* him dead, who lives in Heav'n;
And they who to be sure of Paradise
Dying put on the weeds of *Dominic*,
Or in *Franciscan* think to pass disguis'd;   480
They pass the Planets seven, and pass the fixt,
And that Crystalline Sphear whose ballance weighs
The Trepidation talkt, and that first mov'd;
And now Saint *Peter* at Heav'ns Wicket seems
To wait them with his Keys, and now at foot
Of Heav'ns ascent they lift thir Feet, when loe
A violent cross wind from either Coast
Blows them transverse ten thousand Leagues awry
Into the devious Air; then might ye see
Cowles, Hoods and Habits with thir wearers tost   490
And flutterd into Raggs, then Reliques, Beads,
Indulgences, Dispenses, Pardons, Bulls,
The sport of Winds: all these upwhirld aloft
Fly o're the backside of the World farr off
Into a *Limbo* large and broad, since calld
The Paradise of Fools, to few unknown
Long after, now unpeopl'd, and untrod;
All this dark Globe the Fiend found as he pass'd,
And long he wanderd, till at last a gleame
Of dawning light turnd thither-ward in haste   500
His travell'd steps; farr distant hee descries
Ascending by degrees magnificent
Up to the wall of Heaven a Structure high,
At top whereof, but farr more rich appeerd
The work as of a Kingly Palace Gate
With Frontispice of Diamond and Gold
Imbellisht, thick with sparkling orient **Gemmes**
The Portal shon, inimitable on Earth

By Model, or by shading Pencil drawn.
The Stairs were such as whereon *Jacob* saw   510
Angels ascending and descending, bands
Of Guardians bright, when he from *Esau* fled
To *Padan-Aram* in the field of *Luz,*
Dreaming by night under the open Skie,
And waking cri'd, This is the Gate of Heav'n.
Each Stair mysteriously was meant, nor stood
There alwaies, but drawn up to Heav'n somtimes
Viewless, and underneath a bright Sea flow'd
Of Jasper, or of liquid Pearle, whereon
Who after came from Earth, sayling arriv'd,   520
Wafted by Angels, or flew o're the Lake
Rapt in a Chariot drawn by fiery Steeds.
The Stairs were then let down, whether to dare
The Fiend by easie ascent, or aggravate
His sad exclusion from the dores of Bliss.
Direct against which op'nd from beneath,
Just o're the blissful seat of Paradise,
A passage down to th' Earth, a passage wide,
Wider by farr then that of after-times
Over Mount *Sion,* and, though that were large,   530
Over the *Promis'd Land* to God so dear,
By which, to visit oft those happy Tribes,
On high behests his Angels to and fro
Pass'd frequent, and his eye with choice regard
From *Paneas* the fount of *Jordans* flood
To *Bëersaba,* where the *Holy Land*
Borders on *Ægypt* and the *Arabian* shoare;
So wide the op'ning seemd, where bounds were set
To darkness, such as bound the Ocean wave.
Satan from hence now on the lower stair   540
That scal'd by steps of Gold to Heav'n Gate
Looks down with wonder at the sudden view
Of all this World at once. As when a Scout
Through dark and desart wayes with peril gone
All night; at last by break of chearful dawne
Obtains the brow of some high-climbing Hill,
Which to his eye discovers unaware
The goodly prospect of some forein land
First seen, or some renownd Metropolis
With glistering Spires and Pinnacles adornd,   550

Which now the Rising Sun guilds with his beams.
Such wonder seis'd, though after Heaven seen,
The Spirit maligne, but much more envy seis'd
At sight of all this World beheld so faire.
Round he surveys, and well might, where he stood
So high above the circling Canopie
Of Nights extended shade; from Eastern Point
Of *Libra* to the fleecie Starr that bears
Andromeda farr off *Atlantick* Seas
Beyond th' *Horizon ;* then from Pole to Pole   560
He views in bredth, and without longer pause
Down right into the Worlds first Region throws
His flight precipitant, and windes with ease
Through the pure marble Air his oblique way
Amongst innumerable Starrs, that shon
Stars distant, but nigh hand seemd other Worlds,
Or other Worlds they seemd, or happy Iles,
Like those *Hesperian* Gardens fam'd of old,
Fortunate Fields, and Groves and flourie Vales,
Thrice happy Iles, but who dwelt happy there   570
He stayd not to enquire: above them all
The golden Sun in splendor likest Heaven
Allur'd his eye: Thither his course he bends
Through the calm Firmament; but up or downe
By center, or eccentric, hard to tell,
Or Longitude, where the great Luminarie
Alooff the vulgar Constellations thick,
That from his Lordly eye keep distance due,
Dispenses Light from farr; they as they move
Thir Starry dance in numbers that compute   580
Days, months, and years, towards his all-chearing Lamp
Turn swift their various motions, or are turnd
By his Magnetic beam, that gently warms
The Univers, and to each inward part
With gentle penetration, though unseen,
Shoots invisible vertue even to the deep:
So wondrously was set his Station bright.
There lands the Fiend, a spot like which perhaps
Astronomer in the Sun's lucent Orbe
Through his glaz'd Optic Tube yet never saw.   590
The place he found beyond expression bright,
Compar'd with aught on Earth, Medal or Stone;

Not all parts like, but all alike informd
With radiant light, as glowing Iron with fire ;
If mettal, part seemd Gold, part Silver cleer ;
If stone, Carbuncle most or Chrysolite,
Rubie or Topaz, to the Twelve that shon
In *Aarons* Brestplate, and a stone besides
Imagind rather oft then elsewhere seen,
That stone, or like to that which here below   600
Philosophers in vain so long have sought,
In vain, though by thir powerful Art they binde
Volatil *Hermes*, and call up unbound
In various shapes old *Proteus* from the Sea,
Draind through a Limbec to his Native forme.
What wonder then if fields and regions here
Breathe forth *Elixir* pure, and Rivers run
Potable Gold, when with one vertuous touch
Th' Arch-chimic Sun so farr from us remote
Produces with Terrestrial Humor mixt   610
Here in the dark so many precious things
Of colour glorious and effect so rare ?
Here matter new to gaze the Devil met
Undazl'd, farr and wide his eye commands,
For sight no obstacle found here, nor shade,
But all Sun-shine, as when his Beams at Noon
Culminate from th' *Æquator*, as they now
Shot upward still direct, whence no way round
Shadow from body opaque can fall, and the Aire,
No where so cleer, sharp'nd his visual ray   620
To objects distant farr, whereby he soon
Saw within kenn a glorious Angel stand,
The same whom *John* saw also in the Sun :
His back was turnd, but not his brightness hid ;
Of beaming sunnie Raies, a golden tiar
Circl'd his Head, nor less his Locks behind
Illustrious on his Shoulders fledge with wings
Lay waving round ; on som great charge imploy'd
Hee seemd, or fixt in cogitation deep.
Glad was the Spirit impure ; as now in hope   630
To find who might direct his wandring flight
To Paradise the happie seat of Man,
His journies end and our beginning woe.
But first he casts to change his proper shape,

Which else might work him danger or delay:
And now a stripling Cherube he appeers,
Not of the prime, yet such as in his face
Youth smil'd Celestial, and to every Limb
Sutable grace diffus'd, so well he feignd;
Under a Coronet his flowing haire   640
In curles on either cheek plaid, wings he wore
Of many a coloured plume sprinkl'd with Gold,
His habit fit for speed succinct, and held
Before his decent steps a Silver wand.
He drew not nigh unheard, the Angel bright,
Ere he drew nigh, his radiant visage turnd,
Admonisht by his eare, and strait was known
Th' Arch-Angel *Uriel*, one of the seav'n
Who in God's presence, neerest to his Throne
Stand ready at command, and are his Eyes   650
That run through all the Heav'ns, or down to th' Earth
Bear his swift errands over moist and dry,
O're Sea and Land; him *Satan* thus accostes.
    Uriel, for thou of those seav'n Spirits that stand
In sight of Gods high Throne, gloriously bright,
The first art wont his great authentic will
Interpreter through highest Heav'n to bring,
Where all his Sons thy Embassie attend;
And here art likeliest by supream decree
Like honour to obtain, and as his Eye   660
To visit oft this new Creation round;
Unspeakable desire to see, and know
All these his wondrous works, but chiefly Man,
His chief delight and favour, him for whom
All these his works so wondrous he ordaind,
Hath brought me from the Quires of Cherubim
Alone thus wandring. Brightest Seraph tell
In which of all these shining Orbes hath Man
His fixed seat, or fixed seat hath none,
But all these shining Orbes his choice to dwell;   670
That I may find him, and with secret gaze,
Or open admiration him behold
On whom the great Creator hath bestowd
Worlds, and on whom hath all these graces powrd;
That both in him and all things, as is meet,
The Universal Maker we may praise;

Who justly hath drivn out his Rebell Foes
To deepest Hell, and to repair that loss
Created this new happie Race of Men
To serve him better: wise are all his wayes.   680
    So spake the false dissembler unperceivd;
For neither Man nor Angel can discern
Hypocrisie, the only evil that walks
Invisible, except to God alone,
By his permissive will, through Heav'n and Earth:
And oft though wisdom wake, suspicion sleeps
At wisdoms Gate, and to simplicitie
Resigns her charge, while goodness thinks no ill
Where no ill seems: Which now for once beguil'd
Uriel, though Regent of the Sun, and held   690
The sharpest sighted Spirit of all in Heav'n;
Who to the fraudulent Impostor foule
In his uprightness answer thus returnd.
Faire Angel, thy desire which tends to know
The works of God, thereby to glorifie
The great Work-Maister, leads to no excess
That reaches blame, but rather merits praise
The more it seems excess, that led thee hither
From thy Empyreal Mansion thus alone,
To witness with thine eyes what some perhaps   700
Contented with report heare onely in heav'n:
For wonderful indeed are all his works,
Pleasant to know, and worthiest to be all
Had in remembrance alwayes with delight;
But what created mind can comprehend
Thir number, or the wisdom infinite
That brought them forth, but hid thir causes deep.
I saw when at his Word the formless Mass,
This worlds material mould, came to a heap:
Confusion heard his voice, and wilde uproar   710
Stood rul'd, stood vast infinitude confin'd;
Till at his second bidding darkness fled,
Light shon, and order from disorder sprung:
Swift to thir several Quarters hasted then
The cumbrous Elements, Earth, Flood, Aire, Fire,
And this Ethereal quintessence of Heav'n
Flew upward, spirited with various forms,
That rowld orbicular, and turnd to Starrs
        (244)

Numberless, as thou seest, and how they move ;
Each had his place appointed, each his course,   720
The rest in circuit walles this Universe.
Look downward on that Globe whose hither side
With light from hence, though but reflected, shines ;
That place is Earth the seat of Man, that light
His day, which else as th' other Hemisphere
Night would invade, but there the neighbouring Moon
(So call that opposite fair Starr) her aide
Timely interposes, and her monthly round
Still ending, still renewing through mid Heav'n,
With borrowd light her countenance triform   730
Hence fills and empties to enlighten the Earth,
And in her pale dominion checks the night.
That spot to which I point is *Paradise*,
Adams abode, those loftie shades his Bowre.
Thy way thou canst not miss, me mine requires.
    Thus said, he turnd, and *Satan* bowing low,
As to superior Spirits is wont in Heav'n,
Where honour due and reverence none neglects,
Took leave, and toward the coast of Earth beneath,
Down from th' Ecliptic, sped with hop'd success,   740
Throws his steep flight in many an Aerie wheele,
Nor staid, till on *Niphates* top he lights.

The End of the Third Book.

PARADISE LOST.

BOOK IV.

THE ARGUMENT.

Satan *now in prospect of* Eden, *and nigh the place where he must now attempt the bold enterprize which he undertook alone against God and Man, falls into many doubts with himself, and many passions, fear, envy, and despare; but at length confirms himself in evil, journeys on to Paradise, whose outward prospect and scituation is described, overleaps the bounds, sits in the shape of a Cormorant on the Tree of life, as highest in the Garden to look about him. The Garden describ'd; Satans first sight of* Adam *and* Eve; *his wonder at thir excellent form and happy state, but with resolution to work thir fall; overhears thir discourse, thence gathers that the Tree of knowledge was forbidden them to eat of, under penalty of death; and thereon intends to found his temptation, by seducing them to transgress: then leaves them a while, to know further of thir state by some other means. Mean while* Uriel *descending on a Sun-beam warns* Gabriel, *who had in charge the Gate of Paradise, that some evil spirit had escap'd the Deep, and past at Noon by his Sphere in the shape of a good Angel down to Paradise, discovered after by his furious gestures in the Mount.* Gabriel *promises to find him out ere morning. Night coming on,* Adam *and* Eve *discourse of going to thir rest: thir Bower describ'd; thir Evening worship.* Gabriel *drawing forth his Bands of Night-watch to walk the round of Paradise, appoints two strong Angels to* Adams *Bower, least the evill spirit should be there doing some harm to* Adam *or* Eve *sleeping; there they find him at the ear of* Eve, *tempting her in a dream, and bring him, though unwilling, to* Gabriel; *by whom question'd, he scornfully answers, prepares resistance, but hinder'd by a Sign from Heaven, flies out of Paradise.*

  O FOR that warning voice, which he who saw
Th' *Apocalyps*, heard cry in Heav'n aloud,
Then when the Dragon, put to second rout,
Came furious down to be reveng'd on men,
Wo to the inhabitants on Earth! that now,
While time was, our first Parents had bin warnd
The coming of thir secret foe, and scap'd
Haply so scap'd his mortal snare; for now
Satan, now first inflam'd with rage came down,
The Tempter ere th' Accuser of man-kind,   10
To wreck on innocent frail man his loss
Of that first Battel, and his flight to Hell:
Yet not rejoycing in his speed, though bold,
Far off and fearless, nor with cause to boast,
Begins his dire attempt, which nigh the birth
Now rowling, boiles in his tumultuous brest,
And like a devillish Engine back recoiles
Upon himself; horror and doubt distract
His troubl'd thoughts, and from the bottom stirr
The Hell within him, for within him Hell   20
He brings, and round about him, nor from Hell
One step no more then from himself can fly
By change of place: Now conscience wakes despair
That slumberd, wakes the bitter memorie
Of what he was, what is, and what must be
Worse; of worse deeds worse sufferings must ensue.
Sometimes towards *Eden* which now in his view
Lay pleasant, his grievd look he fixes sad,
Sometimes towards Heav'n and the full-blazing Sun,
Which now sat high in his Meridian Towre: 30
Then much revolving, thus in sighs began.
  O thou that with surpassing Glory crownd,
Look'st from thy sole Dominion like the God
Of this new World; at whose sight all the Starrs
Hide thir diminisht heads; to thee I call,
But with no friendly voice, and add thy name
O Sun, to tell thee how I hate thy beams
That bring to my remembrance from what state
I fell, how glorious once above thy Spheare;
Till Pride and worse Ambition threw me down   40
Warring in Heav'n against Heav'ns matchless King:
Ah wherefore! he deservd no such return

From me, whom he created what I was
In that bright eminence, and with his good
Upbraided none; nor was his service hard.
What could be less then to afford him praise,
The easiest recompence, and pay him thanks,
How due! yet all his good prov'd ill in me,
And wrought but malice; lifted up so high
I sdeind subjection, and thought one step higher   50
Would set me highest, and in a moment quit
The debt immense of endless gratitude,
So burthensome, still paying, still to ow;
Forgetful what from him I still receivd,
And understood not that a grateful mind
By owing owes not, but still pays, at once
Indebted and dischargd; what burden then?
O had his powerful Destiny ordaind
Me some inferiour Angel, I had stood
Then happie; no unbounded hope had rais'd   60
Ambition. Yet why not? som other Power
As great might have aspir'd, and me though mean
Drawn to his part; but other Powers as great
Fell not, but stand unshak'n, from within
Or from without, to all temptations arm'd.
Hadst thou the same free Will and Power to stand?
Thou hadst: whom hast thou then or what to accuse,
But Heav'ns free Love dealt equally to all?
Be then his Love accurst, since love or hate,
To me alike, it deals eternal woe.   70
Nay curs'd be thou; since against his thy will
Chose freely what it now so justly rues.
Me miserable! which way shall I flie
Infinite wrauth, and infinite despaire?
Which way I flie is Hell; my self am Hell;
And in the lowest deep a lower deep
Still threatning to devour me opens wide,
To which the Hell I suffer seems a Heav'n.
O then at last relent: is there no place
Left for Repentance, none for Pardon left?   80
None left but by submission; and that word
Disdain forbids me, and my dread of shame
Among the spirits beneath, whom I seduc'd
With other promises and other vaunts

Then to submit, boasting I could subdue
Th' Omnipotent. Ay me, they little know
How dearly I abide that boast so vaine,
Under what torments inwardly I groane:
While they adore me on the Throne of Hell,
With Diadem and Scepter high advancd   90
The lower still I fall, onely Supream
In miserie; such joy Ambition findes.
But say I could repent and could obtaine
By Act of Grace my former state; how soon
Would highth recal high thoughts, how soon unsay
What feign'd submission swore: ease would recant
Vows made in pain, as violent and void.
For never can true reconcilement grow
Where wounds of deadly hate have peirc'd so deep:
Which would but lead me to a worse relapse,   100
And heavier fall: so should I purchase deare
Short intermission bought with double smart.
This knows my punisher; therefore as farr
From granting hee, as I from begging peace:
All hope excluded thus, behold in stead
Of us out-cast, exil'd, his new delight,
Mankind created, and for him this World.
So farwel Hope, and with Hope farwel Fear,
Farwel Remorse: all Good to me is lost;
Evil be thou my Good; by thee at least   110
Divided Empire with Heav'ns King I hold
By thee, and more then half perhaps will reigne;
As Man ere long, and this new World shall know.
    Thus while he spake, each passion dimm'd his face
Thrice chang'd with pale, ire, envie and despair,
Which marrd his borrow'd visage, and betraid
Him counterfet, if any eye beheld.
For heav'nly mindes from such distempers foule
Are ever cleer. Whereof hee soon aware,
Each perturbation smooth'd with outward calme,   120
Artificer of fraud; and was the first
That practisd falshood under saintly shew,
Deep malice to conceale, couch't with revenge:
Yet not anough had practisd to deceive
Uriel once warnd; whose eye pursu'd him down
The way he went, and on th' *Assyrian* mount

Saw him disfigur'd, more then could befall
Spirit of happie sort : his gestures fierce
He markd and mad demeanour, then alone,
As he suppos'd all unobserv'd, unseen.   130
So on he fares, and to the border comes
Of *Eden*, where delicious Paradise,
Now nearer, Crowns with her enclosure green,
As with a rural mound the champain head
Of a steep wilderness, whose hairie sides
With thicket overgrown, grottesque and wilde,
Access deni'd ; and over head up grew
Insuperable highth of loftiest shade,
Cedar, and Pine, and Firr, and branching Palm
A Silvan Scene, and as the ranks ascend   140
Shade above shade, a woodie Theatre
Of stateliest view. Yet higher then thir tops
The verdurous wall of Paradise up sprung :
Which to our general Sire gave prospect large
Into his neather Empire neighbouring round.
And higher then that wall a circling row
Of goodliest Trees loaden with fairest Fruit,
Blossoms and Fruits at once of golden hue
Appeerd, with gay enameld colours mixt :
On which the Sun more glad impress'd his beams   150
Then in fair Evening Cloud, or humid Bow,
When God hath showrd the earth ; so lovely seemd
That Lantskip : And of pure now purer aire
Meets his approach, and to the heart inspires
Vernal delight and joy, able to drive
All sadness but despair : now gentle gales
Fanning thir odoriferous wings dispense
Native perfumes, and whisper whence they stole
Those balmie spoiles. As when to them who sail
Beyond the *Cape of Hope*, and now are past   160
Mozambic, off at Sea North-East windes blow
Sabean Odours from the spicie shoare
Of *Arabie* the blest, with such delay
Well pleas'd they slack thir course, and many a League
Cheard with the grateful smell old Ocean smiles.
So entertaind those odorous sweets the Fiend
Who came thir bane, though with them better pleas'd
Then *Asmodeus* with the fishie fume,

That drove him, though enamourd, from the Spouse
Of *Tobits* Son, and with a vengeance sent   170
From *Media* post to *Ægypt*, there fast bound.
   Now to th' ascent of that steep savage Hill
Satan had journied on, pensive and slow;
But further way found none, so thick entwin'd,
As one continu'd brake, the undergrowth
Of shrubs and tangling bushes had perplext
All path of Man or Beast that past that way:
One Gate there onely was, and that look'd East
On th' other side: which when th' arch-fellon saw
Due entrance he disdaind, and in contempt,   180
At one slight bound high overleap'd all bound
Of Hill or highest Wall, and sheer within
Lights on his feet. As when a prowling Wolfe,
Whom hunger drives to seek new haunt for prey,
Watching where Shepherds pen thir Flocks at eeve
In hurdl'd Cotes amid the field secure,
Leaps o're the fence with ease into the Fould:
Or as a Thief bent to unhoord the cash
Of some rich Burgher, whose substantial dores,
Cross-barrd and bolted fast, fear no assault,   190
In at the window climbes, or o're the tiles:
So clomb this first grand Thief into Gods Fould:
So since into his Church lewd Hirelings climbe.
Thence up he flew, and on the Tree of Life,
The middle Tree and highest there that grew,
Sat like a Cormorant; yet not true Life
Thereby regaind, but sat devising Death
To them who liv'd; nor on the vertue thought
Of that life-giving Plant, but only us'd
For prospect, what well us'd had bin the pledge   200
Of immortalitie. So little knows
Any, but God alone, to value right
The good before him, but perverts best things
To worst abuse, or to thir meanest use.
Beneath him with new wonder now he views
To all delight of human sense expos'd
In narrow room Natures whole wealth, yea more,
A Heaven on Earth: for blissful Paradise
Of God the Garden was, by him in the East
Of *Eden* planted; *Eden* stretchd her Line   210

From *Auran* Eastward to the Royal Towrs
Of Great *Seleucia*, built by *Grecian* Kings,
Or where the Sons of *Eden* long before
Dwelt in *Telassar:* in this pleasant soile
His farr more pleasant Garden God ordaind;
Out of the fertil ground he caus'd to grow
All Trees of noblest kind for sight, smell, taste;
And all amid them stood the Tree of Life,
High eminent, blooming Ambrosial Fruit
Of vegetable Gold; and next to Life   220
Our Death the Tree of Knowledge grew fast by,
Knowledge of Good bought dear by knowing ill.
Southward through *Eden* went a River large,
Nor chang'd his course, but through the shaggie hill
Pass'd underneath ingulft, for God had thrown
That Mountain as his Garden mould high rais'd
Upon the rapid current, which through veins
Of porous Earth with kindly thirst up drawn,
Rose a fresh Fountain, and with many a rill
Waterd the Garden; thence united fell   230
Down the steep glade, and met the neather Flood,
Which from his darksom passage now appeers,
And now divided into four main Streams,
Runs divers, wandring many a famous Realme
And Country whereof here needs no account,
But rather to tell how, if Art could tell,
How from that Saphire Fount the crisped Brooks,
Rowling on Orient Pearl and sands of Gold,
With mazie error under pendant shades
Ran Nectar, visiting each plant, and fed   240
Flours worthy of Paradise which not nice Art
In Beds and curious Knots, but Nature boon
Powrd forth profuse on Hill and Dale and Plaine,
Both where the morning Sun first warmly smote
The open field, and where the unpierc't shade
Imbround the noontide Bowrs: Thus was this place,
A happy rural seat of various view:
Groves whose rich Trees wept odorous Gumms and Balme,
Others whose fruit burnisht with Golden Rinde
Hung amiable, *Hesperian* Fables true,   250
If true, here onely, and of delicious taste:
Betwixt them Lawns, or level Downs, and Flocks

Grasing the tender herb, were interpos'd,
Or palmie hilloc, or the flourie lap
Of som irriguous Valley spread her store,
Flours of all hue, and without Thorn the Rose:
Another side, umbrageous Grots and Caves
Of coole recess, o're which the mantling Vine
Layes forth her purple Grape, and gently creeps
Luxuriant; mean while murmuring waters fall   260
Down the slope hills, disperst, or in a Lake,
That to the fringed Bank with Myrtle crownd,
Her chrystall mirror holds, unite thir streams.
The Birds thir quire apply; aires, vernal aires,
Breathing the smell of field and grove, attune
The trembling leaves, while Universal *Pan*
Knit with the *Graces* and the *Hours* in dance
Led on th' Eternal Spring. Not that faire field
Of *Enna*, where *Proserpin* gathring flours
Her self a fairer Floure by gloomie *Dis*   270
Was gatherd, which cost *Ceres* all that pain
To seek her through the world; nor that sweet Grove
Of *Daphne* by *Orontes*, and th' inspir'd
Castalian Spring might with this Paradise
Of *Eden* strive; nor that *Nyseian* Ile
Girt with the River *Triton*, where old *Cham*,
Whom Gentiles *Ammon* call and *Libyan Jove*,
Hid *Amalthea* and her Florid Son
Young *Bacchus* from his Stepdame *Rhea's* eye;
Nor where *Abassin* Kings thir issue Guard,   280
Mount *Amara*, though this by som suppos'd
True Paradise under the *Ethiop* Line
By *Nilus* head, enclos'd with shining Rock,
A whole dayes journey high, but wide remote
From this *Assyrian* Garden, where the Fiend
Saw undelighted all delight, all kind
Of living Creatures new to sight and strange:
Two of far nobler shape erect and tall,
Godlike erect, with native Honour clad
In naked Majestie seemd Lords of all,   290
And worthie seemd, for in thir looks Divine
The image of thir glorious Maker shon,
Truth, Wisdome, Sanctitude severe and pure,
Severe, but in true filial freedom plac't;

Whence true autoritie in men; though both
Not equal, as their sex not equal seemd;
For contemplation hee and valour formd,
For softness shee and sweet attractive Grace,
Hee for God only, shee for God in him:
His fair large Front and Eye sublime declar'd   300
Absolute rule; and Hyacinthin Locks
Round from his parted forelock manly hung
Clustring, but not beneath his shoulders broad:
Shee as a vail down to the slender waste
Her unadorned golden tresses wore
Dissheveld, but in wanton ringlets wav'd
As the Vine curles her tendrils, which impli'd
Subjection, but requir'd with gentle sway,
And by her yeilded, by him best receivd,
Yeilded with coy submission, modest pride,   310
And sweet reluctant amorous delay.
Nor those mysterious parts were then conceald,
Then was not guiltie shame, dishonest shame
Of natures works, honor dishonorable,
Sin-bred, how have ye troubl'd all mankind
With shews instead, meer shews of seeming pure,
And banisht from mans life his happiest life,
Simplicitie and spotless innocence.
So passd they naked on, nor shund the sight
Of God or Angel, for they thought no ill: 320
So hand in hand they passd, the lovliest pair
That ever since in loves imbraces met,
Adam the goodliest man of men since born
His Sons, the fairest of her Daughters *Eve.*
Under a tuft of shade that on a green
Stood whispering soft, by a fresh Fountain side
They sat them down, and after no more toil
Of thir sweet Gardning labour then suffic'd
To recommend coole *Zephyr*, and made ease
More easie, wholsom thirst and appetite   330
More grateful, to thir Supper Fruits they fell,
Nectarine Fruits which the compliant boughes
Yeilded them, side-long as they sat recline
On the soft downie Bank damaskt with flours:
The savourie pulp they chew, and in the rinde
Still as they thirsted scoop the brimming stream;

Nor gentle purpose, nor endearing smiles
Wanted, nor youthful dalliance as beseems
Fair couple, linkt in happie nuptial League,
Alone as they. About them frisking playd   340
All Beasts of th' Earth, since wilde, and of all chase
In Wood or Wilderness, Forrest or Den ;
Sporting the Lion rampd, and in his paw
Dandl'd the Kid ; Bears, Tygers, Ounces, Pards
Gambold before them, th' unwieldy Elephant
To make them mirth us'd all his might, and wreathd
His Lithe Proboscis ; close the Serpent sly
Insinuating, wove with Gordian twine
His breaded train, and of his fatal guile
Gave proof unheeded ; others on the grass   350
Coucht, and now fild with pasture gazing sat,
Or Bedward ruminating ; for the Sun
Declin'd was hasting now with prone carreer
To th' Ocean Iles, and in th' ascending Scale
Of Heav'n the Starrs that usher Evening rose :
When *Satan* still in gaze, as first he stood,
Scarce thus at length faild speech recoverd sad.

    O Hell ! what doe mine eyes with grief behold,
Into our room of bliss thus high advanc't
Creatures of other mould, earth-born perhaps,   360
Not Spirits, yet to heav'nly Spirits bright
Little inferior ; whom my thoughts pursue
With wonder, and could love, so lively shines
In them Divine resemblance, and such grace
The hand that formd them on thir shape hath pourd.
Ah gentle pair, yee little think how nigh
Your change approaches, when all these delights
Will vanish and deliver ye to woe,
More woe, the more your taste is now of joy ;
Happie, but for so happie ill secur'd   370
Long to continue, and this high seat your Heav'n
Ill fenc't for Heav'n to keep out such a foe
As now is enterd ; yet no purpos'd foe
To you whom I could pittie thus forlorne
Though I unpittied : League with you I seek,
And mutual amitie so streight, so close,
That I with you must dwell, or you with me
Henceforth ; my dwelling haply may not please

Like this fair Paradise, your sense, yet such
Accept your Makers work; he gave it me,   380
Which I as freely give; Hell shall unfould,
To entertain you two, her widest Gates,
And send forth all her Kings; there will be room,
Not like these narrow limits, to receive
Your numerous ofspring; if no better place,
Thank him who puts me loath to this revenge
On you who wrong me not for him who wrongd.
And should I at your harmless innocence
Melt, as I doe, yet public reason just,
Honour and Empire with revenge enlarg'd,   390
By conquering this new World, compels me now
To do what else though damnd I should abhorre.
   So spake the Fiend, and with necessitie,
The Tyrants plea, excus'd his devilish deeds.
Then from his loftie stand on that high Tree
Down he alights among the sportful Herd
Of those fourfooted kindes, himself now one,
Now other, as thir shape servd best his end
Neerer to view his prey, and unespi'd
To mark what of thir state he more might learn   400
By word or action markt: about them round
A Lion now he stalkes with fierie glare,
Then as a Tiger, who by chance hath spi'd
In some Purlieu two gentle Fawnes at play,
Strait couches close, then rising changes oft
His couchant watch, as one who chose his ground
Whence rushing he might surest seise them both
Grip't in each paw: when *Adam* first of men
To first of women *Eve* thus moving speech,
Turnd him all eare to heare new utterance flow.   410
   Sole partner and sole part of all these joyes,
Dearer thy self then all; needs must the Power
That made us, and for us this ample World
Be infinitly good, and of his good
As liberal and free as infinite,
That rais'd us from the dust and plac't us here
In all this happiness, who at his hand
Have nothing merited, nor can performe
Aught whereof hee hath need, hee who requires
From us no other service then to keep   420

(256)

This one, this easie charge, of all the Trees
In Paradise that beare delicious fruit
So various, not to taste that onely Tree
Of knowledge, planted by the Tree of Life,
So neer grows Death to Life, what ere Death is,
Som dreadful thing no doubt; for well thou knowst
God hath pronounc't it death to taste that Tree,
The only sign of our obedience left
Among so many signes of power and rule
Conferrd upon us, and Dominion giv'n   430
Over all other Creatures that possesse
Earth, Aire, and Sea. Then let us not think hard
One easie prohibition, who enjoy
Free leave so large to all things else, and choice
Unlimited of manifold delights :
But let us ever praise him, and extoll
His bountie, following our delightful task
To prune these growing Plants, & tend these Flours,
Which were it toilsom, yet with thee were sweet.

    To whom thus *Eve* repli'd. O thou for whom   440
And from whom I was formd flesh of thy flesh,
And without whom am to no end, my Guide
And Head, what thou hast said is just and right.
For wee to him indeed all praises owe,
And daily thanks, I chiefly who enjoy
So farr the happier Lot, enjoying thee
Preëminent by so much odds, while thou
Like consort to thy self canst no where find.
That day I oft remember, when from sleep
I first awak't, and found my self repos'd   450
Under a shade on flours, much wondring where
And what I was, whence thither brought, and how.
Not distant far from thence a murmuring sound
Of waters issu'd from a Cave and spread
Into a liquid Plain, then stood unmov'd
Pure as th' expanse of Heav'n; I thither went
With unexperienc't thought, and laid me downe
On the green bank, to look into the cleer
Smooth Lake, that to me seemd another Skie.
As I bent down to look, just opposite,   460
A Shape within the watry gleam appeerd
Bending to look on me, I started back,

It started back, but pleasd I soon returnd,
Pleas'd it returnd as soon with answering looks
Of sympathie and love, there I had fixt
Mine eyes till now, and pin'd with vain desire,
Had not a voice thus warnd me, What thou seest,
What there thou seest fair Creature is thy self,
With thee it came and goes: but follow me,
And I will bring thee where no shadow staies   470
Thy coming, and thy soft imbraces, hee
Whose image thou art, him thou shall enjoy
Inseparablie thine, to him shalt beare
Multitudes like thy self, and thence be call'd
Mother of human Race: what could I doe,
But follow strait, invisibly thus led?
Till I espi'd thee, fair indeed and tall,
Under a Platan, yet methought less faire,
Less winning soft, less amiablie milde,
Then that smooth watry image; back I turnd,   480
Thou following cryd'st aloud, Return fair *Eve*,
Whom fli'st thou? whom thou fli'st, of him thou art,
His flesh, his bone; to give thee being I lent
Out of my side to thee, neerest my heart
Substantial Life, to have thee by my side
Henceforth an individual solace dear;
Part of my Soul I seek thee, and thee claim
My other half: with that thy gentle hand
Seisd mine, I yeilded, and from that time see
How beauty is excelld by manly grace   490
And wisdom, which alone is truly fair.
So spake our general Mother, and with eyes
Of conjugal attraction unreprov'd,
And meek surrender, half imbracing leand
On our first Father, half her swelling Breast
Naked met his under the flowing Gold
Of her loose tresses hid: he in delight
Both of her Beauty and submissive Charms
Smil'd with superior Love, as *Jupiter*
On *Juno* smiles, when he impregns the Clouds   500
That shed *May* Flowers; and press'd her Matron lip
With kisses pure: aside the Devil turnd
For envie, yet with jealous leer maligne
Ey'd them askance, and to himself thus plaind.

Sight hateful, sight tormenting! thus these two
Imparadis't in one anothers arms
The happier *Eden*, shall enjoy thir fill
Of bliss on bliss, while I to Hell am thrust,
Where neither joy nor love, but fierce desire,
Among our other torments not the least,　　　　510
Still unfulfill'd with pain of longing pines;
Yet let me not forget what I have gain'd
From thir own mouths; all is not theirs it seems:
One fatal Tree there stands of Knowledge call'd,
Forbidden them to taste: Knowledge forbidd'n?
Suspicious, reasonless. Why should thir Lord
Envie them that? can it be sin to know,
Can it be death? and do they onely stand
By Ignorance, is that thir happie state,
The proof of thir obedience and thir faith?　　　520
O fair foundation laid whereon to build
Thir ruine! Hence I will excite thir minds
With more desire to know, and to reject
Envious commands, invented with designe
To keep them low whom knowledge might exalt
Equal with Gods; aspiring to be such,
They taste and die: what likelier can ensue?
But first with narrow search I must walk round
This Garden, and no corner leave unspi'd;
A chance but chance may lead where I may meet　　　530
Some wandring Spirit of Heav'n, by Fountain side,
Or in thick shade retir'd, from him to draw
What further would be learnt. Live while ye may,
Yet happie pair; enjoy, till I return,
Short pleasures, for long woes are to succeed.
　　So saying, his proud step he scornful turn'd,
But with sly circumspection, and began
Through wood, through waste, o're hil, o're dale his roam.
Mean while in utmost Longitude, where Heav'n
With Earth and Ocean meets, the setting Sun　　　540
Slowly descended, and with right aspect
Against the eastern Gate of Paradise
Leveld his eevning Rayes: it was a Rock
Of Alablaster, pil'd up to the Clouds,
Conspicuous farr, winding with one ascent
Accessible from Earth, one entrance high;

(259)

The rest was craggie cliff, that overhung
Still as it rose, impossible to climbe.
Betwixt these rockie Pillars *Gabriel* sat
Chief of th' Angelic Guards, awaiting night ;   550
About him exercis'd Heroic Games
Th' unarmed Youth of Heav'n, but nigh at hand
Celestial Armourie, Shields, Helmes, and Speares
Hung high with Diamond flaming, and with Gold.
Thither came *Uriel*, gliding through the Eeven
On a Sun beam, swift as a shooting Starr
In *Autumn* thwarts the night, when vapors fir'd
Impress the Air, and shews the Mariner
From what point of his Compass to beware
Impetuous winds : he thus began in haste.   560
    Gabriel, to thee thy cours by Lot hath giv'n
Charge and strict watch that to this happie place
No evil thing approach or enter in ;
This day at highth of Noon came to my Spheare
A Spirit, zealous, as he seem'd, to know
More of th' Almighties works, and chiefly Man
Gods latest Image : I describ'd his way
Bent all on speed, and markt his Aerie Gate ;
But in the Mount that lies from *Eden* North,
Where he first lighted, soon discernd his looks   570
Alien from Heav'n, with passions foul obscur'd :
Mine eye pursu'd him still, but under shade
Lost sight of him ; one of the banisht crew
I fear, hath ventur'd from the deep, to raise
New troubles ; him thy care must be to find.
    To whom the winged Warriour thus returnd :
Uriel, no wonder if thy perfet sight,
Amid the Suns bright circle where thou sitst,
See farr and wide : in at this Gate none pass
The vigilance here plac't, but such as come   580
Well known from Heav'n ; and since Meridian hour
No Creature thence : if Spirit of other sort,
So minded, have oreleapt these earthie bounds
On purpose, hard thou knowst it to exclude
Spiritual substance with corporeal barr.
But if within the circuit of these walks
In whatsoever shape he lurk, of whom
Thou telst, by morrow dawning I shall know.

So promis'd hee, and *Uriel* to his charge
Returnd on that bright beam, whose point now raisd   590
Bore him slope downward to the Sun now fall'n
Beneath th' *Azores*; whither the prime Orb,
Incredible how swift, had thither rowl'd
Diurnal, or this less volubil Earth
By shorter flight to th' East, had left him there
Arraying with reflected Purple and Gold
The Clouds that on his Western Throne attend:
Now came still Eevning on, and Twilight gray
Had in her sober Liverie all things clad;
Silence accompanied, for Beast and Bird,   600
They to thir grassie Couch, these to thir Nests
Were slunk, all but the wakeful Nightingale;
She all night long her amorous descant sung;
Silence was pleas'd: now glow'd the Firmament
With living Saphirs: *Hesperus* that led
The starrie Host, rode brightest, till the Moon
Rising in clouded Majestie, at length
Apparent Queen unvaild her peerless light,
And o're the dark her Silver Mantle threw.
   When *Adam* thus to *Eve:* Fair Consort, th' hour   610
Of night, and all things now retir'd to rest
Mind us of like repose, since God hath set
Labour and rest, as day and night to men
Successive, and the timely dew of sleep
Now falling with soft slumbrous weight inclines
Our eye-lids; other Creatures all day long
Rove idle unimploid, and less need rest;
Man hath his daily work of body or mind
Appointed, which declares his Dignitie,
And the regard of Heav'n on all his waies;   620
While other Animals unactive range,
And of thir doings God takes no account.
To morrow ere fresh Morning streak the East
With first approach of light, we must be ris'n,
And at our pleasant labour, to reform
Yon flourie Arbors, yonder Allies green,
Our walks at noon, with branches overgrown,
That mock our scant manuring, and require
More hands then ours to lop thir wanton growth:

627 walks] walk 1674

Those Blossoms also, and those dropping Gumms,   630
That lie bestrowne unsightly and unsmooth,
Ask riddance, if we mean to tread with ease;
Mean while, as Nature wills, Night bids us rest.
　　To whom thus *Eve* with perfet beauty adornd.
My Author and Disposer, what thou bidst
Unargu'd I obey; so God ordains,
God is thy Law, thou mine: to know no more
Is womans happiest knowledge and her praise.
With thee conversing I forget all time,
All seasons and thir change, all please alike.   640
Sweet is the breath of morn, her rising sweet,
With charm of earliest Birds; pleasant the Sun
When first on this delightful Land he spreads
His orient Beams, on herb, tree, fruit, and flour,
Glistring with dew; fragrant the fertil earth
After soft showers; and sweet the coming on
Of grateful Eevning milde, then silent Night
With this her solemn Bird and this fair Moon,
And these the Gemms of Heav'n, her starrie train:
But neither breath of Morn when she ascends   650
With charm of earliest Birds, nor rising Sun
On this delightful land, nor herb, fruit, floure,
Glistring with dew, nor fragrance after showers,
Nor grateful Evening mild, nor silent Night
With this her solemn Bird, nor walk by Moon,
Or glittering Starr-light without thee is sweet.
But wherfore all night long shine these, for whom
This glorious sight, when sleep hath shut all eyes?
　　To whom our general Ancestor repli'd.
Daughter of God and Man, accomplisht *Eve*,   660
Those have thir course to finish, round the Earth,
By morrow Eevning, and from Land to Land
In order, though to Nations yet unborn,
Ministring light prepar'd, they set and rise;
Least total darkness should by Night regaine
Her old possession, and extinguish life
In Nature and all things, which these soft fires
Not only enlighten, but with kindly heate
Of various influence foment and warme,
Temper or nourish, or in part shed down   670
Thir stellar vertue on all kinds that grow

　(262)

On Earth, made hereby apter to receive
Perfection from the Suns more potent Ray.
These then, though unbeheld in deep of night,
Shine not in vain, nor think, though men were none,
That heav'n would want spectators, God want praise;
Millions of spiritual Creatures walk the Earth
Unseen, both when we wake, and when we sleep:
All these with ceaseless praise his works behold
Both day and night: how often from the steep   680
Of echoing Hill or Thicket have we heard
Celestial voices to the midnight air,
Sole, or responsive each to others note
Singing thir great Creator: oft in bands
While they keep watch, or nightly rounding walk
With Heav'nly touch of instrumental sounds
In full harmonic number joind, thir songs
Divide the night, and lift our thoughts to Heaven.
    Thus talking hand in hand alone they pass'd
On to thir blissful Bower; it was a place   690
Chos'n by the sovran Planter, when he fram'd
All things to mans delightful use; the roofe
Of thickest covert was inwoven shade
Laurel and Mirtle, and what higher grew
Of firm and fragrant leaf; on either side
Acanthus, and each odorous bushie shrub
Fenc'd up the verdant wall; each beauteous flour,
Iris all hues, Roses, and Gessamin
Rear'd high thir flourisht heads between, and wrought
Mosaic; underfoot the Violet,   700
Crocus, and Hyacinth with rich inlay
Broiderd the ground, more colour'd then with stone
Of costliest Emblem: other Creature here
Beast, Bird, Insect, or Worm durst enter none;
Such was thir awe of man. In shadier Bower
More sacred and sequesterd, though but feignd,
Pan or *Silvanus* never slept, nor Nymph,
Nor *Faunus* haunted. Here in close recess
With Flowers, Garlands, and sweet-smelling Herbs
Espoused *Eve* deckt first her Nuptial Bed,   710
And heav'nly Quires the Hymenæan sung,
What day the genial Angel to our Sire
Brought her in naked beauty more adorn'd

More lovely then *Pandora,* whom the Gods
Endowd with all thir gifts, and O too like
In sad event, when to the unwiser Son
Of *Japhet* brought by *Hermes,* she ensnar'd
Mankind with her faire looks, to be aveng'd
On him who had stole *Joves* authentic fire.

    Thus at thir shadie Lodge arriv'd, both stood,   720
Both turnd, and under op'n Skie ador'd
The God that made both Skie, Air, Earth & Heav'n
Which they beheld, the Moons resplendent Globe
And starrie Pole : Thou also mad'st the Night,
Maker Omnipotent, and thou the Day,
Which we in our appointed work imployd
Have finisht happie in our mutual help
And mutual love, the Crown of all our bliss
Ordain'd by thee, and this delicious place
For us too large, where thy abundance wants   730
Partakers, and uncropt falls to the ground.
But thou hast promis'd from us two a Race
To fill the Earth, who shall with us extoll
Thy goodness infinite, both when we wake,
And when we seek, as now, thy gift of sleep.

    This said unanimous, and other Rites
Observing none, but adoration pure
Which God likes best, into thir inmost bower
Handed they went ; and eas'd the putting off
These troublesom disguises which wee wear,   740
Strait side by side were laid, nor turnd I weene
Adam from his fair Spouse, nor *Eve* the Rites
Mysterious of connubial Love refus'd :
Whatever Hypocrites austerely talk
Of puritie and place and innocence,
Defaming as impure what God declares
Pure, and commands to som, leaves free to all.
Our Maker bids increase, who bids abstain
But our Destroyer, foe to God and Man ?
Haile wedded Love, mysterious Law, true sourse   750
Of human ofspring, sole proprietie,
In Paradise of all things common else.
By thee adulterous lust was driv'n from men
Among the bestial herds to raunge, by thee
Founded in Reason, Loyal, Just, and Pure,

Relations dear, and all the Charities
Of Father, Son, and Brother first were known.
Farr be it, that I should write thee sin or blame,
Or think thee unbefitting holiest place,
Perpetual Fountain of Domestic sweets,   760
Whose Bed is undefil'd and chast pronounc't,
Present, or past, as Saints and Patriarchs us'd.
Here Love his golden shafts imploies, here lights
His constant Lamp, and waves his purple wings,
Reigns here and revels ; not in the bought smile
Of Harlots, loveless, joyless, unindeard,
Casual fruition, nor in Court Amours
Mixt Dance, or wanton Mask, or Midnight Bal,
Or Serenate, which the starv'd Lover sings
To his proud fair, best quitted with disdain.   770
These lulld by Nightingales imbraceing slept,
And on thir naked limbs the flourie roof
Showrd Roses, which the Morn repair'd. Sleep on,
Blest pair ; and O yet happiest if ye seek
No happier state, and know to know no more.
    Now had night measur'd with her shaddowie Cone
Half way up Hill this vast Sublunar Vault,
And from thir Ivorie Port the Cherubim
Forth issuing at th' accustomd hour stood armd
To thir night watches in warlike Parade,   780
When *Gabriel* to his next in power thus spake.
    Uzziel, half these draw off, and coast the South
With strictest watch ; these other wheel the North,
Our circuit meets full West. As flame they part
Half wheeling to the Shield, half to the Spear.
From these, two strong and suttle Spirits he calld
That neer him stood, and gave them thus in charge.
    Ithuriel and *Zephon*, with wingd speed
Search through this Garden, leav unsearcht no nook,
But chiefly where those two fair Creatures Lodge,   790
Now laid perhaps asleep secure of harme.
This Eevning from the Sun's decline arriv'd
Who tells of som infernal Spirit seen
Hitherward bent (who could have thought ?) escap'd
The barrs of Hell, on errand bad no doubt :
Such where ye find, seise fast, and hither bring.
    So saying, on he led his radiant Files,

Daz'ling the Moon; these to the Bower direct
In search of whom they sought: him there they found
Squat like a Toad, close at the eare of *Eve ;*   800
Assaying by his Devilish art to reach
The Organs of her Fancie, and with them forge
Illusions as he list, Phantasms and Dreams,
Or if, inspiring venom, he might taint
Th' animal Spirits that from pure blood arise
Like gentle breaths from Rivers pure, thence raise
At least distemperd, discontented thoughts,
Vain hopes, vain aimes, inordinate desires
Blown up with high conceits ingendring pride.
Him thus intent *Ithuriel* with his Spear   810
Touch'd lightly; for no falshood can endure
Touch of Celestial temper, but returns
Of force to its own likeness : up he starts
Discoverd and surpriz'd. As when a spark
Lights on a heap of nitrous Powder, laid
Fit for the Tun som Magazin to store
Against a rumord Warr, the Smuttie graine
With sudden blaze diffus'd, inflames the Aire :
So started up in his own shape the Fiend.
Back stept those two fair Angels half amaz'd   820
So sudden to behold the grieslie King ;
Yet thus, unmovd with fear, accost him soon.
   Which of those rebell Spirits adjudg'd to Hell
Com'st thou, escap'd thy prison, and transform'd,
Why satst thou like an enemie in waite
Here watching at the head of these that sleep ?
   Know ye not then said *Satan,* filld with scorn
Know ye not me ? ye knew me once no mate
For you, there sitting where ye durst not soare ;
Not to know mee argues your selves unknown,   830
The lowest of your throng ; or if ye know,
Why ask ye, and superfluous begin
Your message, like to end as much in vain ?
To whom thus *Zephon,* answering scorn with scorn.
Think not, revolted Spirit, thy shape the same,
Or undiminisht brightness, to be known
As when thou stoodst in Heav'n upright and pure ;
That Glorie then, when thou no more wast good,
Departed from thee, and thou resembl'st now

(266)

Thy sin and place of doom obscure and foule.   840
But come, for thou, besure, shalt give account
To him who sent us, whose charge is to keep
This place inviolable, and these from harm.
  So spake the Cherube, and his grave rebuke
Severe in youthful beautie, added grace
Invincible : abasht the Devil stood,
And felt how awful goodness is, and saw
Vertue in her shape how lovly, saw, and pin'd
His loss ; but chiefly to find here observd
His lustre visibly impar'd ; yet seemd   850
Undaunted. If I must contend, said he,
Best with the best, the Sender not the sent,
Or all at once ; more glorie will be wonn,
Or less be lost. Thy fear, said *Zephon* bold,
Will save us trial what the least can doe
Single against thee wicked, and thence weak.
  The Fiend repli'd not, overcome with rage ;
But like a proud Steed reind, went hautie on,
Chaumping his iron curb : to strive or flie
He held it vain ; awe from above had quelld   860
His heart, not else dismai'd. Now drew they nigh
The western point, where those half-rounding guards
Just met, & closing stood in squadron joind
Awaiting next command. To whom thir Chief
Gabriel from the Front thus calld aloud.
  O friends, I hear the tread of nimble feet
Hasting this way, and now by glimps discerne
Ithuriel and *Zephon* through the shade,
And with them comes a third of Regal port,
But faded splendor wan ; who by his gate   870
And fierce demeanour seems the Prince of Hell,
Not likely to part hence without contest ;
Stand firm, for in his look defiance lours.
  He scarce had ended, when those two approachd
And brief related whom they brought, wher found,
How busied, in what form and posture coucht.
  To whom with stern regard thus *Gabriel* spake.
Why hast thou, *Satan*, broke the bounds prescrib'd
To thy transgressions, and disturbd the charge
Of others, who approve not to transgress   880
By thy example, but have power and right

(267)

To question thy bold entrance on this place;
Imploi'd it seems to violate sleep, and those
Whose dwelling God hath planted here in bliss?
  To whom thus *Satan* with contemptuous brow.
Gabriel, thou hadst in Heav'n th' esteem of wise,
And such I held thee; but this question askt
Puts me in doubt. Lives ther who loves his pain?
Who would not, finding way, break loose from Hell,
Though thither doomd? Thou wouldst thy self, no doubt, 890
And boldly venture to whatever place
Farthest from pain, where thou mightst hope to change
Torment with ease, & soonest recompence
Dole with delight, which in this place I sought;
To thee no reason; who knowst only good,
But evil hast not tri'd: and wilt object
His will who bound us? let him surer barr
His Iron Gates, if he intends our stay
In that dark durance: thus much what was askt.
The rest is true, they found me where they say;   900
But that implies not violence or harme.
  Thus hee in scorn. The warlike Angel mov'd,
Disdainfully half smiling thus repli'd.
O loss of one in Heav'n to judge of wise,
Since *Satan* fell, whom follie overthrew,
And now returns him from his prison scap't,
Gravely in doubt whether to hold them wise
Or not, who ask what boldness brought him hither
Unlicenc't from his bounds in Hell prescrib'd;
So wise he judges it to fly from pain   910
However, and to scape his punishment.
So judge thou still, presumptuous, till the wrauth,
Which thou incurr'st by flying, meet thy flight
Seavenfold, and scourge that wisdom back to Hell,
Which taught thee yet no better, that no pain
Can equal anger infinite provok't.
But wherefore thou alone? wherefore with thee
Came not all Hell broke loose? is pain to them
Less pain, less to be fled, or thou then they
Less hardie to endure? courageous Chief,   920
The first in flight from pain, had'st thou alleg'd
To thy deserted host this cause of flight,
Thou surely hadst not come sole fugitive.

To which the Fiend thus answerd frowning stern.
Not that I less endure, or shrink from pain,
Insulting Angel, well thou knowst I stood
Thy fiercest, when in Battel to thy aide
The blasting volied Thunder made all speed
And seconded thy else not dreaded Spear.
But still thy words at random, as before,   930
Argue thy inexperience what behooves
From hard assaies and ill successes past
A faithful Leader, not to hazard all
Through wayes of danger by himself untri'd.
I therefore, I alone first undertook
To wing the desolate Abyss, and spie
This new created World, whereof in Hell
Fame is not silent, here in hope to find
Better abode, and my afflicted Powers
To settle here on Earth, or in mid Aire;   940
Though for possession put to try once more
What thou and thy gay Legions dare against;
Whose easier business were to serve thir Lord
High up in Heav'n, with songs to hymne his Throne,
And practis'd distances to cringe, not fight.
    To whom the warriour Angel soon repli'd.
To say and strait unsay, pretending first
Wise to flie pain, professing next the Spie,
Argues no Leader, but a lyar trac't,
Satan, and couldst thou faithful add? O name,   950
O sacred name of faithfulness profan'd!
Faithful to whom? to thy rebellious crew?
Armie of Fiends, fit body to fit head;
Was this your discipline and faith ingag'd,
Your military obedience, to dissolve
Allegeance to th' acknowledg'd Power supream?
And thou sly hypocrite, who now wouldst seem
Patron of liberty, who more then thou
Once fawn'd, and cring'd, and servilly ador'd
Heav'ns awful Monarch? wherefore but in hope   960
To dispossess him, and thy self to reigne?
But mark what I arreede thee now, avant;
Flie thither whence thou fledst: if from this houre
Within these hallowd limits thou appeer,

928 The] Thy *1674*

(269)

Back to th' infernal pit I drag thee chaind,
And Seale thee so, as henceforth not to scorne
The facil gates of hell too slightly barrd.
  So threatn'd hee, but *Satan* to no threats
Gave heed, but waxing more in rage repli'd.
  Then when I am thy captive talk of chaines,   970
Proud limitarie Cherube, but ere then
Farr heavier load thy self expect to feel
From my prevailing arme, though Heavens King
Ride on thy wings, and thou with thy Compeers,
Us'd to the yoak, draw'st his triumphant wheels
In progress through the rode of Heav'n Star-pav'd.
  While thus he spake, th' Angelic Squadron bright
Turnd fierie red, sharpning in mooned hornes
Thir Phalanx, and began to hemm him round
With ported Spears, as thick as when a field   980
Of *Ceres* ripe for harvest waving bends
Her bearded Grove of ears, which way the wind
Swayes them; the careful Plowman doubting stands
Least on the threshing floore his hopeful sheaves
Prove chaff. On th' other side *Satan* allarm'd
Collecting all his might dilated stood,
Like *Teneriff* or *Atlas* unremov'd:
His stature reacht the Skie, and on his Crest
Sat horror Plum'd; nor wanted in his graspe
What seemd both Spear and Shield: now dreadful deeds 990
Might have ensu'd, nor onely Paradise
In this commotion, but the Starrie Cope
Of Heav'n perhaps, or all the Elements
At least had gon to rack, disturbd and torne
With violence of this conflict, had not soon
Th' Eternal to prevent such horrid fray
Hung forth in Heav'n his golden Scales, yet seen
Betwixt *Astrea* and the *Scorpion* signe,
Wherein all things created first he weighd,
The pendulous round Earth with ballanc't Aire   1000
In counterpoise, now ponders all events,
Battels and Realms: in these he put two weights
The sequel each of parting and of fight;
The latter quick up flew, and kickt the beam;
Which *Gabriel* spying, thus bespake the Fiend.
  Satan, I know thy strength, and thou knowst mine,

Neither our own but giv'n; what follie then
To boast what Arms can doe, since thine no more
Then Heav'n permits, nor mine, though doubld now
To trample thee as mire: for proof look up,   1010
And read thy Lot in yon celestial Sign
Where thou art weigh'd, & shown how light, how weak,
If thou resist. The Fiend lookt up and knew
His mounted scale aloft: nor more; but fled
Murmuring, and with him fled the shades of night.

The End of the Fourth Book.

PARADISE LOST.

BOOK V.

THE ARGUMENT.

Morning approach't, Eve relates to Adam her troublesome dream; he likes it not, yet comforts her: They come forth to thir day labours: Their Morning Hymn at the Door of their Bower. God to render Man inexcusable sends Raphael to admonish him of his obedience, of his free estate, of his enemy near at hand; who he is, and why his enemy, and whatever else may avail Adam to know. Raphael comes down to Paradise, his appearance describ'd, his coming discern'd by Adam afar off sitting at the door of his Bower; he goes out to meet him, brings him to his lodge, entertains him with the choycest fruits of Paradise got together by Eve; their discourse at Table: Raphael performs his message, minds Adam of his state and of his enemy; relates at Adams request who that enemy is, and how he came to be so, beginning from his first revolt in Heaven, and the occasion thereof; how he drew his Legions after him to the parts of the North, and there incited them to rebel with him, perswading all but only Abdiel a Seraph, who in Argument diswades and opposes him, then forsakes him.

Now morn her rosie steps in th' Eastern Clime
Advancing, sow'd the Earth with Orient Pearle,
When *Adam* wak't, so customd, for his sleep
Was Aerie light, from pure digestion bred,
And temperat vapors bland, which th' only sound
Of leaves and fuming rills, *Aurora's* fan,
Lightly dispers'd, and the shrill Matin Song
Of Birds on every bough; so much the more
His wonder was to find unwak'nd *Eve*
With Tresses discompos'd, and glowing Cheek,
As through unquiet rest: he on his side

10

Leaning half-rais'd, with looks of cordial Love
Hung over her enamour'd, and beheld
Beautie, which whether waking or asleep,
Shot forth peculiar Graces; then with voice
Milde, as when *Zephyrus* on *Flora* breathes,
Her hand soft touching, whisperd thus. Awake
My fairest, my espous'd, my latest found,
Heav'ns last best gift, my ever new delight,
Awake, the morning shines, and the fresh field   20
Calls us, we lose the prime, to mark how spring
Our tended Plants, how blows the Citron Grove,
What drops the Myrrhe, & what the balmie Reed,
How Nature paints her colours, how the Bee
Sits on the Bloom extracting liquid sweet.
  Such whispering wak'd her, but with startl'd eye
On *Adam*, whom imbracing, thus she spake.
  O Sole in whom my thoughts find all repose,
My Glorie, my Perfection, glad I see
Thy face, and Morn return'd, for I this Night,   30
Such night till this I never pass'd, have dream'd,
If dream'd, not as I oft am wont, of thee,
Works of day pass't, or morrows next designe,
But of offence and trouble, which my mind
Knew never till this irksom night; methought
Close at mine ear one call'd me forth to walk
With gentle voice, I thought it thine; it said,
Why sleepst thou *Eve?* now is the pleasant time,
The cool, the silent, save where silence yields
To the night-warbling Bird, that now awake   40
Tunes sweetest his love-labor'd song; now reignes
Full Orb'd the Moon, and with more pleasing light
Shadowie sets off the face of things; in vain,
If none regard; Heav'n wakes with all his eyes,
Whom to behold but thee, Natures desire,
In whose sight all things joy, with ravishment
Attracted by thy beauty still to gaze.
I rose as at thy call, but found thee not;
To find thee I directed then my walk;
And on, methought, alone I pass'd through ways   50
That brought me on a sudden to the Tree
Of interdicted Knowledge: fair it seem'd,
Much fairer to my Fancie then by day:

(273)

And as I wondring lookt, beside it stood
One shap'd and wing'd like one of those from Heav'n
By us oft seen; his dewie locks distill'd
Ambrosia; on that Tree he also gaz'd;
And O fair Plant, said he, with fruit surcharg'd,
Deigns none to ease thy load and taste thy sweet,
Nor God, nor Man; is Knowledge so despis'd?   60
Or envie, or what reserve forbids to taste?
Forbid who will, none shall from me withhold
Longer thy offerd good, why else set here?
This said he paus'd not, but with ventrous Arme
He pluckt, he tasted; mee damp horror chil'd
At such bold words voucht with a deed so bold:
But he thus overjoy'd, O Fruit Divine,
Sweet of thy self, but much more sweet thus cropt,
Forbidd'n here, it seems, as onely fit
For Gods, yet able to make Gods of Men: 70
And why not Gods of Men, since good, the more
Communicated, more abundant growes,
The Author not impair'd, but honourd more?
Here, happie Creature, fair Angelic *Eve*,
Partake thou also; happie though thou art,
Happier thou mayst be, worthier canst not be:
Taste this, and be henceforth among the Gods
Thy self a Goddess, not to Earth confind,
But somtimes in the Air, as wee, somtimes
Ascend to Heav'n, by merit thine, and see   80
What life the Gods live there, and such live thou.
So saying, he drew nigh, and to me held,
Even to my mouth of that same fruit held part
Which he had pluckt; the pleasant savourie smell
So quick'nd appetite, that I, methought,
Could not but taste. Forthwith up to the Clouds
With him I flew, and underneath beheld
The Earth outstretcht immense, a prospect wide
And various: wondring at my flight and change
To this high exaltation: suddenly   90
My Guide was gon, and I, me thought, sunk down,
And fell asleep; but O how glad I wak'd
To find this but a dream! Thus *Eve* her Night
Related, and thus *Adam* answerd sad.

Best Image of my self and dearer half,

The trouble of thy thoughts this night in sleep
Affects me equally; nor can I like
This uncouth dream, of evil sprung I fear;
Yet evil whence? in thee can harbour none,
Created pure. But know that in the Soule   100
Are many lesser Faculties that serve
Reason as chief; among these Fansie next
Her office holds; of all external things,
Which the five watchful Senses represent,
She forms Imaginations, Aerie shapes,
Which Reason joyning or disjoyning, frames
All what we affirm or what deny, and call
Our knowledge or opinion; then retires
Into her private Cell when Nature rests.
Oft in her absence mimic Fansie wakes   110
To imitate her; but misjoyning shapes,
Wilde work produces oft, and most in dreams,
Ill matching words and deeds long past or late.
Som such resemblances methinks I find
Of our last Eevnings talk, in this thy dream,
But with addition strange; yet be not sad.
Evil into the mind of God or Man
May come and go, so unapprov'd, and leave
No spot or blame behind: Which gives me hope
That what in sleep thou didst abhorr to dream,   120
Waking thou never wilt consent to do:
Be not disheart'nd then, nor cloud those looks
That wont to be more chearful and serene
Then when fair Morning first smiles on the World,
And let us to our fresh imployments rise
Among the Groves, the Fountains, and the Flours
That open now thir choicest bosom'd smells
Reservd from night, and kept for thee in store.
    So cheard he his fair Spouse, and she was cheard,
But silently a gentle tear let fall   130
From either eye, and wip'd them with her haire;
Two other precious drops that ready stood,
Each in thir chrystal sluce, hee ere they fell
Kiss'd as the gracious signs of sweet remorse
And pious awe, that feard to have offended.
    So all was cleard, and to the Field they haste.
But first from under shadie arborous roof,

Soon as they forth were come to open sight
Of day-spring, and the Sun, who scarce up risen
With wheels yet hov'ring o're the Ocean brim,   140
Shot paralel to the earth his dewie ray,
Discovering in wide Lantskip all the East
Of Paradise and *Edens* happie Plains,
Lowly they bow'd adoring, and began
Thir Orisons, each Morning duly paid
In various style, for neither various style
Nor holy rapture wanted they to praise
Thir Maker, in fit strains pronounc't or sung
Unmeditated, such prompt eloquence
Flowd from thir lips, in Prose or numerous Verse,   150
More tuneable then needed Lute or Harp
To add more sweetness, and they thus began.

   These are thy glorious works Parent of good,
Almightie, thine this universal Frame,
Thus wondrous fair; thy self how wondrous then!
Unspeakable, who sitst above these Heavens
To us invisible or dimly seen
In these thy lowest works, yet these declare
Thy goodness beyond thought, and Power Divine:
Speak yee who best can tell, ye Sons of light,   160
Angels, for yee behold him, and with songs
And choral symphonies, Day without Night,
Circle his Throne rejoycing, yee in Heav'n,
On Earth joyn all yee Creatures to extoll
Him first, him last, him midst, and without end.
Fairest of Starrs, last in the train of Night,
If better thou belong not to the dawn,
Sure pledge of day, that crownst the smiling Morn
With thy bright Circlet, praise him in thy Spheare
While day arises, that sweet hour of Prime.   170
Thou Sun, of this great World both Eye and Soule,
Acknowledge him thy Greater, sound his praise
In thy eternal course, both when thou climb'st,
And when high Noon hast gaind, & when thou fallst.
Moon, that now meetst the orient Sun, now fli'st
With the fixt Starrs, fixt in thir Orb that flies,
And yee five other wandring Fires that move
In mystic Dance not without Song, resound
His praise, who out of Darkness call'd up Light.

Aire, and ye Elements the eldest birth   180
Of Natures Womb, that in quaternion run
Perpetual Circle, multiform; and mix
And nourish all things, let your ceasless change
Varie to our great Maker still new praise.
Ye Mists and Exhalations that now rise
From Hill or steaming Lake, duskie or grey,
Till the Sun paint your fleecie skirts with Gold,
In honour to the Worlds great Author rise,
Whether to deck with Clouds the uncolourd skie,
Or wet the thirstie Earth with falling showers,   190
Rising or falling still advance his praise.
His praise ye Winds, that from four Quarters blow,
Breathe soft or loud; and wave your tops, ye Pines,
With every Plant, in sign of Worship wave.
Fountains and yee, that warble, as ye flow,
Melodious murmurs, warbling tune his praise.
Joyn voices all ye living Souls, ye Birds,
That singing up to Heaven Gate ascend,
Bear on your wings and in your notes his praise;
Yee that in Waters glide, and yee that walk   200
The Earth, and stately tread, or lowly creep;
Witness if I be silent, Morn or Eeven,
To Hill, or Valley, Fountain, or fresh shade
Made vocal by my Song, and taught his praise.
Hail universal Lord, be bounteous still
To give us onely good; and if the night
Have gathered aught of evil or conceald,
Disperse it, as now light dispels the dark.
    So pray'd they innocent, and to thir thoughts
Firm peace recoverd soon and wonted calm.   210
On to thir mornings rural work they haste
Among sweet dewes and flours; where any row
Of Fruit-trees overwoodie reachd too farr
Thir pamperd boughes, and needed hands to check
Fruitless imbraces: or they led the Vine
To wed her Elm; she spous'd about him twines
Her mariageable arms, and with her brings
Her dowr th' adopted Clusters, to adorn
His barren leaves. Them thus imploid beheld
With pittie Heav'ns high King, and to him call'd 220
Raphael, the sociable Spirit, that deign'd
      (277)

To travel with *Tobias*, and secur'd
His marriage with the seaventimes-wedded Maid.
　Raphael, said hee, thou hear'st what stir on Earth
Satan from Hell scap't through the darksom Gulf
Hath raisd in Paradise, and how disturbd
This night the human pair, how he designes
In them at once to ruin all mankind.
Go therefore, half this day as friend with friend
Converse with *Adam*, in what Bowre or shade　　230
Thou find'st him from the heat of Noon retir'd,
To respit his day-labour with repast,
Or with repose ; and such discourse bring on,
As may advise him of his happie state,
Happiness in his power left free to will,
Left to his own free Will, his Will though free,
Yet mutable, whence warne him to beware
He swerve not too secure : tell him withall
His danger, and from whom, what enemie
Late falln himself from Heaven, is plotting now　　240
The fall of others from like state of bliss;
By violence, no, for that shall be withstood,
But by deceit and lies ; this let him know,
Least wilfully transgressing he pretend
Surprisal, unadmonisht, unforewarnd.
　So spake th' Eternal Father, and fulfilld
All Justice : nor delaid the winged Saint
After his charge receivd ; but from among
Thousand Celestial Ardors, where he stood
Vaild with his gorgeous wings, up springing light　　250
Flew through the midst of Heav'n ; th' angelic Quires
On each hand parting, to his speed gave way
Through all th' Empyreal road ; till at the Gate
Of Heav'n arriv'd, the gate self-opend wide
On golden Hinges turning, as by work
Divine the sov'ran Architect had fram'd.
From hence, no cloud, or, to obstruct his sight,
Starr interpos'd, however small he sees,
Not unconform to other shining Globes,
Earth and the Gard'n of God, with Cedars crownd　　260
Above all Hills. As when by night the Glass
Of *Galileo*, less assur'd, observes
Imagind Lands and Regions in the Moon :

Or Pilot from amidst the *Cyclades*
Delos or *Samos* first appeering kenns
A cloudy spot.   Down thither prone in flight
He speeds, and through the vast Ethereal Skie
Sailes between worlds & worlds, with steddie wing
Now on the polar windes, then with quick Fann
Winnows the buxom Air; till within soare   270
Of Towring Eagles, to all the Fowles he seems
A *Phœnix*, gaz'd by all, as that sole Bird
When to enshrine his reliques in the Sun's
Bright Temple, to *Ægyptian Theb's* he flies.
At once on th' Eastern cliff of Paradise
He lights, and to his proper shape returns
A Seraph wingd; six wings he wore, to shade
His lineaments Divine ; the pair that clad
Each shoulder broad, came mantling o're his brest
With regal Ornament ; the middle pair   280
Girt like a Starrie Zone his waste, and round
Skirted his loines and thighes with downie Gold
And colours dipt in Heav'n ; the third his feet
Shaddowd from either heele with featherd maile
Skie-tinctur'd grain.   Like *Maia's* son he stood,
And shook his Plumes, that Heav'nly fragrance filld
The circuit wide.   Strait knew him all the Bands
Of Angels under watch ; and to his state,
And to his message high in honour rise ;
For on som message high they guessd him bound.   290
Thir glittering Tents he passd, and now is come
Into the blissful field, through Groves of Myrrhe,
And flouring Odours, Cassia, Nard, and Balme ;
A Wilderness of sweets ; for Nature here
Wantond as in her prime, and plaid at will
Her Virgin Fancies, pouring forth more sweet,
Wilde above rule or art ; enormous bliss.
Him through the spicie Forrest onward com
Adam discernd, as in the dore he sat
Of his coole Bowre, while now the mounted Sun   300
Shot down direct his fervid Raies, to warme
Earths inmost womb, more warmth then *Adam* needs
And *Eve* within, due at her hour prepar'd
For dinner savourie fruits, of taste to please
True appetite, and not disrelish thirst

(279)

Of nectarous draughts between, from milkie stream,
Berrie or Grape: to whom thus *Adam* call'd.
   Haste hither *Eve*, and worth thy sight behold
Eastward among those Trees, what glorious shape
Comes this way moving; seems another Morn   310
Ris'n on mid-noon; som great behest from Heav'n
To us perhaps he brings, and will voutsafe
This day to be our Guest. But goe with speed,
And what thy stores contain, bring forth and poure
Abundance, fit to honour and receive
Our Heav'nly stranger; well we may afford
Our givers thir own gifts, and large bestow
From large bestowd, where Nature multiplies
Her fertil growth, and by disburd'ning grows
More fruitful, which instructs us not to spare.   320
   To whom thus *Eve*. *Adam*, earths hallowd mould,
Of God inspir'd, small store will serve, where store,
All seasons, ripe for use hangs on the stalk;
Save what by frugal storing firmness gains
To nourish, and superfluous moist consumes:
But I will haste and from each bough and break,
Each Plant & juciest Gourd will pluck such choice
To entertain our Angel guest, as hee
Beholding shall confess that here on Earth
God hath dispenst his bounties as in Heav'n.   330
   So saying, with dispatchful looks in haste
She turns, on hospitable thoughts intent
What choice to chuse for delicacie best,
What order, so contriv'd as not to mix
Tastes, not well joynd, inelegant, but bring
Taste after taste upheld with kindliest change,
Bestirs her then, and from each tender stalk
Whatever Earth all-bearing Mother yeilds
In *India* East or West, or middle shoare
In *Pontus* or the *Punic* Coast, or where   340
Alcinous reign'd, fruit of all kindes, in coate,
Rough, or smooth rin'd, or bearded husk, or shell
She gathers, Tribute large, and on the board
Heaps with unsparing hand; for drink the Grape
She crushes, inoffensive moust, and meathes
From many a berrie, and from sweet kernels prest
She tempers dulcet creams, nor these to hold

Wants her fit vessels pure, then strews the ground
With Rose and Odours from the shrub unfum'd.
Mean while our Primitive great Sire, to meet   350
His god-like Guest, walks forth, without more train
Accompani'd then with his own compleat
Perfections, in himself was all his state,
More solemn then the tedious pomp that waits
On Princes, when thir rich Retinue long
Of Horses led, and Grooms besmeard with Gold
Dazles the croud, and sets them all agape.
Neerer his presence *Adam* though not awd,
Yet with submiss approach and reverence meek,
As to a superior Nature, bowing low,   360
    Thus said. Native of Heav'n, for other place
None can then Heav'n such glorious shape contain;
Since by descending from the Thrones above,
Those happie places thou hast deignd a while
To want, and honour these, voutsafe with us
Two onely, who yet by sov'ran gift possess
This spacious ground, in yonder shadie Bowre
To rest, and what the Garden choicest bears
To sit and taste, till this meridian heat
Be over, and the Sun more coole decline.   370
    Whom thus the Angelic Vertue answerd milde.
Adam, I therefore came, nor art thou such
Created, or such place hast here to dwell,
As may not oft invite, though Spirits of Heav'n
To visit thee; lead on then where thy Bowre
Oreshades; for these mid-hours, till Eevning rise
I have at will. So to the Silvan Lodge
They came, that like *Pomona's* Arbour smil'd
With flourets deck't and fragrant smells; but *Eve*
Undeckt, save with her self more lovely fair   380
Then Wood-Nymph, or the fairest Goddess feign'd
Of three that in Mount *Ida* naked strove,
Stood to entertain her guest from Heav'n; no vaile
Shee needed, Vertue-proof, no thought infirme
Alterd her cheek. On whom the Angel *Haile*
Bestowd, the holy salutation us'd
Long after to blest *Marie*, second *Eve*.
    Haile Mother of Mankind, whose fruitful Womb
Shall fill the World more numerous with thy Sons

Then with these various fruits the Trees of God   390
Have heap'd this Table. Rais'd of grassie terf
Thir Table was, and mossie seats had round,
And on her ample Square from side to side
All *Autumn* pil'd, though *Spring* and *Autumn* here
Danc'd hand in hand. A while discourse they hold;
No fear lest Dinner coole; when thus began
Our Authour. Heav'nly stranger, please to taste
These bounties which our Nourisher, from whom
All perfet good unmeasur'd out, descends,
To us for food and for delight hath caus'd   400
The Earth to yeild; unsavourie food perhaps
To spiritual Natures; only this I know,
That one Celestial Father gives to all.

    To whom the Angel. Therefore what he gives
(Whose praise be ever sung) to man in part
Spiritual, may of purest Spirits be found
No ingrateful food: and food alike those pure
Intelligential substances require
As doth your Rational; and both contain
Within them every lower facultie   410
Of sense, whereby they hear, see, smell, touch, taste,
Tasting concoct, digest, assimilate,
And corporeal to incorporeal turn.
For know, whatever was created, needs
To be sustaind and fed; of Elements
The grosser feeds the purer, earth the sea,
Earth and the Sea feed Air, the Air those Fires
Ethereal, and as lowest first the Moon;
Whence in her visage round those spots, unpurg'd
Vapours not yet into her substance turn'd.   420
Nor doth the Moon no nourishment exhale
From her moist Continent to higher Orbes.
The Sun that light imparts to all, receives
From all his alimental recompence
In humid exhalations, and at Even
Sups with the Ocean: though in Heav'n the Trees
Of life ambrosial frutage bear, and vines
Yeild Nectar, though from off the boughs each Morn
We brush mellifluous Dewes, and find the ground
Cover'd with pearly grain: yet God hath here   430
Varied his bounty so with new delights,

As may compare with Heaven; and to taste
Think not I shall be nice. So down they sat,
And to thir viands fell, nor seemingly
The Angel, nor in mist, the common gloss
Of Theologians, but with keen dispatch
Of real hunger, and concoctive heate
To transubstantiate; what redounds, transpires
Through Spirits with ease; nor wonder; if by fire
Of sooty coal the Empiric Alchimist   440
Can turn, or holds it possible to turn
Metals of drossiest Ore to perfet Gold
As from the Mine. Mean while at Table *Eve*
Ministerd naked, and thir flowing cups
With pleasant liquors crown'd : O innocence
Deserving Paradise ! if ever, then,
Then had the Sons of God excuse to have bin
Enamour'd at that sight ; but in those hearts
Love unlibidinous reign'd, nor jealousie
Was understood, the injur'd Lovers Hell.   450
    Thus when with meats & drinks they had suffic'd
Not burd'nd Nature, sudden mind arose
In *Adam*, not to let th' occasion pass
Given him by this great Conference to know
Of things above his World, and of thir being
Who dwell in Heav'n, whose excellence he saw
Transcend his own so farr, whose radiant forms
Divine effulgence, whose high Power so far
Exceeded human, and his wary speech
Thus to th' Empyreal Minister he fram'd.   460
    Inhabitant with God, now know I well
Thy favour, in this honour done to man,
Under whose lowly roof thou hast voutsaf't
To enter, and these earthly fruits to taste,
Food not of Angels, yet accepted so,
As that more willingly thou couldst not seem
At Heav'ns high feasts to have fed : yet what compare ?
    To whom the winged Hierarch repli'd.
O *Adam*, one Almightie is, from whom
All things proceed, and up to him return,   470
If not deprav'd from good, created all
Such to perfection, one first matter all,
Indu'd with various forms, various degrees

Of substance, and in things that live, of life;
But more refin'd, more spiritous, and pure,
As neerer to him plac't or neerer tending
Each in thir several active Sphears assignd,
Till body up to spirit work, in bounds
Proportiond to each kind. So from the root
Springs lighter the green stalk, from thence the leaves   480
More aerie, last the bright consummate floure
Spirits odorous breathes: flours and thir fruit
Mans nourishment, by gradual scale sublim'd
To vital Spirits aspire, to animal,
To intellectual, give both life and sense,
Fansie and understanding, whence the soule
Reason receives, and reason is her being,
Discursive, or Intuitive; discourse
Is oftest yours, the latter most is ours,
Differing but in degree, of kind the same.   490
Wonder not then, what God for you saw good
If I refuse not, but convert, as you,
To proper substance; time may come when men
With Angels may participate, and find
No inconvenient Diet, nor too light Fare:
And from these corporal nutriments perhaps
Your bodies may at last turn all to Spirit,
Improv'd by tract of time, and wingd ascend
Ethereal, as wee, or may at choice
Here or in Heav'nly Paradises dwell;   500
If ye be found obedient, and retain
Unalterably firm his love entire
Whose progenie you are. Mean while enjoy
Your fill what happiness this happie state
Can comprehend, incapable of more.
    To whom the Patriarch of mankind repli'd.
O favourable spirit, propitious guest,
Well hast thou taught the way that might direct
Our knowledge, and the scale of Nature set
From center to circumference, whereon   510
In contemplation of created things
By steps we may ascend to God. But say,
What meant that caution joind, *if ye be found
Obedient?* can wee want obedience then
To him, or possibly his love desert

Who formd us from the dust, and plac'd us here
Full to the utmost measure of what bliss
Human desires can seek or apprehend?
   To whom the Angel. Son of Heav'n and Earth,
Attend: That thou art happie, owe to God;   520
That thou continu'st such, owe to thy self,
That is, to thy obedience; therein stand.
This was that caution giv'n thee; be advis'd.
God made thee perfet, not immutable;
And good he made thee, but to persevere
He left it in thy power, ordaind thy will
By nature free, not over-rul'd by Fate
Inextricable, or strict necessity;
Our voluntarie service he requires,
Not our necessitated, such with him   530
Findes no acceptance, nor can find, for how
Can hearts, not free, be tri'd whether they serve
Willing or no, who will but what they must
By Destinie, and can no other choose?
My self and all th' Angelic Host that stand
In sight of God enthron'd, our happie state
Hold, as you yours, while our obedience holds;
On other surety none; freely we serve
Because wee freely love, as in our will
To love or not; in this we stand or fall: 540
And som are fall'n, to disobedience fall'n,
And so from Heav'n to deepest Hell; O fall
From what high state of bliss into what woe!
   To whom our great Progenitor. Thy words
Attentive, and with more delighted eare
Divine instructer, I have heard, then when
Cherubic Songs by night from neighbouring Hills
Aereal Music send: nor knew I not
To be both will and deed created free;
Yet that we never shall forget to love   550
Our maker, and obey him whose command
Single, is yet so just, my constant thoughts
Assur'd me and still assure: though what thou tellst
Hath past in Heav'n, som doubt within me move,
But more desire to hear, if thou consent,
The full relation, which must needs be strange,
Worthy of Sacred silence to be heard;
   (285)

And we have yet large day, for scarce the Sun
Hath finisht half his journey, and scarce begins
His other half in the great Zone of Heav'n.   560
  Thus *Adam* made request, and *Raphael*
After short pause assenting, thus began.
  High matter thou injoinst me, O prime of men,
Sad task and hard, for how shall I relate
To human sense th' invisible exploits
Of warring Spirits; how without remorse
The ruin of so many glorious once
And perfet while they stood; how last unfould
The secrets of another world, perhaps
Not lawful to reveal? yet for thy good   570
This is dispenc't, and what surmounts the reach
Of human sense, I shall delineate so,
By lik'ning spiritual to corporal forms,
As may express them best, though what if Earth
Be but the shaddow of Heav'n, and things therein
Each to other like, more then on earth is thought?
  As yet this world was not, and *Chaos* wilde
Reignd where these Heav'ns now rowl, where Earth now rests
Upon her Center pois'd, when on a day
(For Time, though in Eternitie, appli'd   580
To motion, measures all things durable
By present, past, and future) on such day
As Heav'ns great Year brings forth, th' Empyreal Host
Of Angels by Imperial summons call'd,
Innumerable before th' Almighties Throne
Forthwith from all the ends of Heav'n appeerd
Under thir Hierarchs in orders bright
Ten thousand thousand Ensignes high advanc'd,
Standards, and Gonfalons twixt Van and Reare
Streame in the Aire, and for distinction serve   590
Of Hierarchies, of Orders, and Degrees;
Or in thir glittering Tissues bear imblaz'd
Holy Memorials, acts of Zeale and Love
Recorded eminent. Thus when in Orbes
Of circuit inexpressible they stood,
Orb within Orb, the Father infinite,
By whom in bliss imbosom'd sat the Son,
A midst as from a flaming Mount, whose top
Brightness had made invisible, thus spake.

Hear all ye Angels, Progenie of Light,
Thrones, Dominations, Princedoms, Vertues, Powers,
Hear my Decree, which unrevok't shall stand.
This day I have begot whom I declare
My onely Son, and on this holy Hill
Him have anointed, whom ye now behold
At my right hand; your Head I him appoint;
And by my Self have sworn to him shall bow
All knees in Heav'n, and shall confess him Lord:
Under his great Vice-gerent Reign abide
United as one individual Soule   610
For ever happie: him who disobeyes
Mee disobeyes, breaks union, and that day
Cast out from God and blessed vision, falls
Into utter darkness, deep ingulft, his place
Ordaind without redemption, without end.
  So spake th' Omnipotent, and with his words
All seemd well pleas'd, all seem'd but were not all.
That day, as other solem dayes, they spent
In song and dance about the sacred Hill,
Mystical dance, which yonder starrie Spheare   620
Of Planets and of fixt in all her Wheeles
Resembles nearest, mazes intricate,
Eccentric, intervolv'd, yet regular
Then most, when most irregular they seem:
And in thir motions harmonie Divine
So smooths her charming tones, that Gods own ear
Listens delighted. Eevning approachd
(For we have also our Eevning and our Morn,
We ours for change delectable, not need)
Forthwith from dance to sweet repast they turn   630
Desirous, all in Circles as they stood,
Tables are set, and on a sudden pil'd
With Angels Food, and rubied Nectar flows:
In Pearl, in Diamond, and massie Gold,
Fruit of delicious Vines, the growth of Heav'n.
They eat, they drink, and with refection sweet

627 Eevning approachd] Eevning now approachd *1674*
636–9 On flours repos'd, and with fresh flourets crownd,
        They eate, they drink, and in communion sweet
        Quaff immortalitie and joy, secure
        Of surfet where full measure onely bounds
        Excess, before th' all bounteous King, who showrd *1674*

Are fill'd before th' all bounteous King, who showrd
With copious hand, rejoycing in thir joy.
Now when ambrosial Night with Clouds exhal'd
From that high mount of God, whence light & shade 640
Spring both, the face of brightest Heav'n had changd
To grateful Twilight (for Night comes not there
In darker veile) and roseat Dews dispos'd
All but the unsleeping eyes of God to rest,
Wide over all the Plain, and wider farr
Then all this globous Earth in Plain outspred,
(Such are the Courts of God) Th' Angelic throng
Disperst in Bands and Files thir Camp extend
By living Streams among the Trees of Life,
Pavilions numberless, and sudden reard,   650
Celestial Tabernacles, where they slept
Fannd with coole Winds, save those who in thir course
Melodious Hymns about the sovran Throne
Alternate all night long : but not so wak'd
Satan, so call him now, his former name
Is heard no more in Heav'n ; he of the first,
If not the first Arch-Angel, great in Power,
In favour and præeminence, yet fraught
With envie against the Son of God, that day
Honourd by his great Father, and proclaimd   660
Messiah King anointed, could not beare
Through pride that sight, and thought himself impaird.
Deep malice thence conceiving & disdain,
Soon as midnight brought on the duskie houre
Friendliest to sleep and silence, he resolv'd
With all his Legions to dislodge, and leave
Unworshipt, unobey'd the Throne supream
Contemptuous, and his next subordinate
Awak'ning, thus to him in secret spake.
      Sleepst thou, Companion dear, what sleep can close   670
Thy eye-lids? and remembrest what Decree
Of yesterday, so late hath past the lips
Of Heav'ns Almightie. Thou to me thy thoughts
Wast wont, I mine to thee was wont to impart ;
Both waking we were one ; how then can now
Thy sleep dissent? new Laws thou seest impos'd ;
New Laws from him who reigns, new minds may
      raise

      (288)

In us who serve, new Counsels, to debate
What doubtful may ensue, more in this place
To utter is not safe. Assemble thou   680
Of all those Myriads which we lead the chief;
Tell them that by command, ere yet dim Night
Her shadowie Cloud withdraws, I am to haste,
And all who under me thir Banners wave,
Homeward with flying march where we possess
The Quarters of the North, there to prepare
Fit entertainment to receive our King
The great *Messiah*, and his new commands,
Who speedily through all the Hierarchies
Intends to pass triumphant, and give Laws.   690
   So spake the false Arch-Angel, and infus'd
Bad influence into th' unwarie brest
Of his Associate; hee together calls,
Or several one by one, the Regent Powers,
Under him Regent, tells, as he was taught,
That the most High commanding, now ere Night,
Now ere dim Night had disincumberd Heav'n,
The great Hierarchal Standard was to move;
Tells the suggested cause, and casts between
Ambiguous words and jealousies, to sound   700
Or taint integritie; but all obey'd
The wonted signal, and superior voice
Of thir great Potentate; for great indeed
His name, and high was his degree in Heav'n;
His count'nance, as the Morning Starr that guides
The starrie flock, allur'd them, and with lyes
Drew after him the third part of Heav'ns Host:
Mean while th' Eternal eye, whose sight discernes
Abstrusest thoughts, from forth his holy Mount
And from within the golden Lamps that burne   710
Nightly before him, saw without thir light
Rebellion rising, saw in whom, how spred
Among the sons of Morn, what multitudes
Were banded to oppose his high Decree;
And smiling to his onely Son thus said.
   Son, thou in whom my glory I behold
In full resplendence, Heir of all my might,
Neerly it now concernes us to be sure
Of our Omnipotence, and with what Arms

We mean to hold what anciently we claim   720
Of Deitie or Empire, such a foe
Is rising, who intends to erect his Throne
Equal to ours, throughout the spacious North;
Nor so content, hath in his thought to trie
In battel, what our Power is, or our right.
Let us advise, and to this hazard draw
With speed what force is left, and all imploy
In our defence, lest unawares we lose
This our high place, our Sanctuarie, our Hill.

    To whom the Son with calm aspect and cleer   730
Light'ning Divine, ineffable, serene,
Made answer. Mightie Father, thou thy foes
Justly hast in derision, and secure
Laugh'st at thir vain designes and tumults vain,
Matter to mee of Glory, whom thir hate
Illustrates, when they see all Regal Power
Giv'n me to quell thir pride, and in event
Know whether I be dextrous to subdue
Thy Rebels, or be found the worst in Heav'n.

    So spake the Son, but *Satan* with his Powers   740
Farr was advanc't on winged speed, an Host
Innumerable as the Starrs of Night,
Or Starrs of Morning, Dew-drops, which the Sun
Impearls on every leaf and every flouer.
Regions they pass'd, the mightie Regencies
Of Seraphim and Potentates and Thrones
In thir triple Degrees, Regions to which
All thy Dominion, *Adam*, is no more
Then what this Garden is to all the Earth,
And all the Sea, from one entire globose   750
Stretcht into Longitude; which having pass'd
At length into the limits of the North
They came, and *Satan* to his Royal seat
High on a Hill, far blazing, as a Mount
Rais'd on a Mount, with Pyramids and Towrs
From Diamond Quarries hew'n, & Rocks of Gold,
The Palace of great *Lucifer*, (so call
That Structure in the Dialect of men
Interpreted) which not long after, hee
Affecting all equality with God,   760
In imitation of that Mount whereon

Messiah was declar'd in sight of Heav'n,
The Mountain of the Congregation call'd ;
For thither he assembl'd all his Train,
Pretending so commanded to consult
About the great reception of thir King,
Thither to come, and with calumnious Art
Of counterfeted truth thus held thir ears.
   Thrones, Dominations, Princedomes, Vertues, Powers,
If these magnific Titles yet remain   770
Not meerly titular, since by Decree
Another now hath to himself ingross't
All Power, and us eclipst under the name
Of King anointed, for whom all this haste
Of midnight march, and hurried meeting here,
This onely to consult how we may best
With what may be devis'd of honours new
Receive him coming to receive from us
Knee-tribute yet unpaid, prostration vile,
Too much to one, but double how endur'd,   780
To one and to his image now proclaim'd?
But what if better counsels might erect
Our minds and teach us to cast off this Yoke?
Will ye submit your necks, and chuse to bend
The supple knee? ye will not, if I trust
To know ye right, or if ye know your selves
Natives and Sons of Heav'n possest before
By none, and if not equal all, yet free,
Equally free; for Orders and Degrees
Jarr not with liberty, but well consist.   790
Who can in reason then or right assume
Monarchie over such as live by right
His equals, if in power and splendor less,
In freedome equal? or can introduce
Law and Edict on us, who without law
Erre not, much less for this to be our Lord,
And look for adoration to th' abuse
Of those Imperial Titles which assert
Our being ordain'd to govern, not to serve?
   Thus farr his bold discourse without controule   800
Had audience, when among the Seraphim
Abdiel, then whom none with more zeale ador'd
The Deitie, and divine commands obei'd,

Stood up, and in a flame of zeale severe
The current of his fury thus oppos'd.

    O argument blasphemous, false and proud!
Words which no eare ever to hear in Heav'n
Expected, least of all from thee, ingrate
In place thy self so high above thy Peeres.
Canst thou with impious obloquie condemne   810
The just Decree of God, pronounc't and sworn,
That to his only Son by right endu'd
With Regal Scepter, every Soule in Heav'n
Shall bend the knee, and in that honour due
Confess him rightful King? unjust thou saist
Flatly unjust, to binde with Laws the free,
And equal over equals to let Reigne,
One over all with unsucceeded power.
Shalt thou give Law to God, shalt thou dispute
With him the points of libertie, who made   820
Thee what thou art, & formd the Pow'rs of Heav'n
Such as he pleasd, and circumscrib'd thir being?
Yet by experience taught we know how good,
And of our good, and of our dignitie
How provident he is, how farr from thought
To make us less, bent rather to exalt
Our happie state under one Head more neer
United. But to grant it thee unjust,
That equal over equals Monarch Reigne:
Thy self though great & glorious dost thou count,   830
Or all Angelic Nature joind in one,
Equal to him begotten Son, by whom
As by his Word the mighty Father made
All things, ev'n thee, and all the Spirits of Heav'n
By him created in thir bright degrees,
Crownd them with Glory, & to thir Glory nam'd
Thrones, Dominations, Princedoms, Vertues, Powers,
Essential Powers, nor by his Reign obscur'd,
But more illustrious made, since he the Head
One of our number thus reduc't becomes,   840
His Laws our Laws, all honour to him done
Returns our own. Cease then this impious rage,
And tempt not these; but hast'n to appease
Th' incensed Father, and th' incensed Son,
While Pardon may be found in time besought.

So spake the fervent Angel, but his zeale
None seconded, as out of season judg'd,
Or singular and rash, whereat rejoic'd
Th' Apostat, and more haughty thus repli'd.
That we were formd then saist thou ? & the work   850
Of secondarie hands, by task transferd
From Father to his Son ? strange point and new !
Doctrin which we would know whence learnt : who saw
When this creation was ? rememberst thou
Thy making, while the Maker gave thee being ?
We know no time when we were not as now ;
Know none before us, self-begot, self-rais'd
By our own quick'ning power, when fatal course
Had circl'd his full Orbe, the birth mature
Of this our native Heav'n, Ethereal Sons.   860
Our puissance is our own, our own right hand
Shall teach us highest deeds, by proof to try
Who is our equal : then thou shalt behold
Whether by supplication we intend
Address, and to begirt th' Almighty Throne
Beseeching or besieging. This report,
These tidings carrie to th' anointed King ;
And fly, ere evil intercept thy flight.

He said, and as the sound of waters deep
Hoarce murmur echo'd to his words applause   870
Through the infinite Host, nor less for that
The flaming Seraph fearless, though alone
Encompass'd round with foes, thus answerd bold.

O alienate from God, O spirit accurst,
Forsak'n of all good ; I see thy fall
Determind, and thy hapless crew involv'd
In this perfidious fraud, contagion spred
Both of thy crime and punishment : henceforth
No more be troubl'd how to quit the yoke
Of Gods *Messiah* : those indulgent Laws   880
Will not now be voutsaf't, other Decrees
Against thee are gon forth without recall ;
That Golden Scepter which thou didst reject
Is now an Iron Rod to bruise and breake
Thy disobedience. Well thou didst advise,
Yet not for thy advise or threats I fly
These wicked Tents devoted, least the wrauth

(293)

Impendent, raging into sudden flame
Distinguish not : for soon expect to feel
His Thunder on thy head, devouring fire.   890
Then who created thee lamenting learne,
When who can uncreate thee thou shalt know.
  So spake the Seraph *Abdiel* faithful found,
Among the faithless, faithful only hee ;
Among innumerable false, unmov'd,
Unshak'n, unseduc'd, unterrifi'd
His Loyaltie he kept, his Love, his Zeale ;
Nor number, nor example with him wrought
To swerve from truth, or change his constant mind
Though single.   From amidst them forth he passd,   900
Long way through hostile scorn, which he susteind
Superior, nor of violence fear'd aught ;
And with retorted scorn his back he turn'd
On those proud Towrs to swift destruction doom'd.

The End of the Fifth Book.

PARADISE LOST.

BOOK VI.

THE ARGUMENT.

Raphael *continues to relate how* Michael *and* Gabriel *were sent forth to Battel against* Satan *and his Angels. The first Fight describ'd:* Satan *and his Powers retire under Night: He calls a Councel, invents devilish Engines, which in the second dayes Fight put* Michael *and his Angels to some disorder; But they at length pulling up Mountains overwhelm'd both the force and Machins of* Satan: *Yet the Tumult not so ending, God on the third day sends* Messiah *his Son, for whom he had reserv'd the glory of that Victory: Hee in the Power of his Father coming to the place, and causing all his Legions to stand still on either side, with his Chariot and Thunder driving into the midst of his Enemies, pursues them unable to resist towards the wall of Heaven; which opening, they leap down with horrour and confusion into the place of punishment prepar'd for them in the Deep:* Messiah *returns with triumph to his Father.*

ALL night the dreadless Angel unpursu'd
Through Heav'ns wide Champain held his way, till Morn,
Wak't by the circling Hours, with rosie hand
Unbarr'd the gates of Light.   There is a Cave
Within the Mount of God, fast by his Throne,
Where light and darkness in perpetual round
Lodge and dislodge by turns, which makes through Heav'n
Grateful vicissitude, like Day and Night;
Light issues forth, and at the other dore
Obsequious darkness enters, till her houre   10
To veile the Heav'n, though darkness there might well
Seem twilight here; and now went forth the Morn
Such as in highest Heav'n, arrayd in Gold

Empyreal, from before her vanisht Night,
Shot through with orient Beams : when all the Plain
Coverd with thick embatteld Squadrons bright,
Chariots and flaming Armes, and fierie Steeds
Reflecting blaze on blaze, first met his view :
Warr he perceav'd, warr in procinct, and found
Already known what he for news had thought   20
To have reported : gladly then he mixt
Among those friendly Powers who him receav'd
With joy and acclamations loud, that one
That of so many Myriads fall'n, yet one
Returnd not lost : On to the sacred hill
They led him high applauded, and present
Before the seat supream ; from whence a voice
From midst a Golden Cloud thus milde was heard.
      Servant of God, well done, well hast thou fought
The better fight, who single hast maintaind   30
Against revolted multitudes the Cause
Of Truth, in word mightier then they in Armes ;
And for the testimonie of Truth hast born
Universal reproach, far worse to beare
Then violence : for this was all thy care
To stand approv'd in sight of God, though Worlds
Judg'd thee perverse : the easier conquest now
Remains thee, aided by this host of friends,
Back on thy foes more glorious to return
Then scornd thou didst depart, and to subdue   40
By force, who reason for thir Law refuse,
Right reason for thir Law, and for thir King
Messiah, who by right of merit Reigns.
Goe *Michael* of Celestial Armies Prince,
And thou in Military prowess next
Gabriel, lead forth to Battel these my Sons
Invincible, lead forth my armed Saints
By Thousands and by Millions rang'd for fight ;
Equal in number to that Godless crew
Rebellious, them with Fire and hostile Arms   50
Fearless assault, and to the brow of Heav'n
Pursuing drive them out from God and bliss,
Into thir place of punishment, the Gulf
Of *Tartarus,* which ready opens wide
His fiery *Chaos* to receave thir fall.

So spake the Sovran voice, and Clouds began
To darken all the Hill, and smoak to rowl
In duskie wreathes, reluctant flames, the signe
Of wrauth awak't: nor with less dread the loud
Ethereal Trumpet from on high gan blow: 60
At which command the Powers Militant,
That stood for Heav'n, in mighty Quadrate joyn'd
Of Union irresistible, mov'd on
In silence thir bright Legions, to the sound
Of instrumental Harmonie that breath'd
Heroic Ardor to advent'rous deeds
Under thir God-like Leaders, in the Cause
Of God and his *Messiah.* On they move
Indissolubly firm ; nor obvious Hill,
Nor streit'ning Vale, nor Wood, nor Stream divides   70
Thir perfet ranks ; for high above the ground
Thir march was, and the passive Air upbore
Thir nimble tread ; as when the total kind
Of Birds in orderly array on wing
Came summond over *Eden* to receive
Thir names of thee ; so over many a tract
Of Heav'n they march'd, and many a Province wide
Tenfold the length of this terrene : at last
Farr in th' Horizon to the North appeer'd
From skirt to skirt a fierie Region, stretcht   80
In battailous aspect, and neerer view
Bristl'd with upright beams innumerable
Of rigid Spears, and Helmets throng'd, and Shields
Various, with boastful Argument portraid,
The banded Powers of *Satan* hasting on
With furious expedition ; for they weend
That self same day by fight, or by surprize
To win the Mount of God, and on his Throne
To set the envier of his State, the proud
Aspirer, but thir thoughts prov'd fond and vain   90
In the mid way : though strange to us it seemd
At first, that Angel should with Angel warr,
And in fierce hosting meet, who wont to meet
So oft in Festivals of joy and love
Unanimous, as sons of one great Sire
Hymning th' Eternal Father : but the shout
Of Battel now began, and rushing sound

Of onset ended soon each milder thought.
High in the midst exalted as a God
Th' Apostat in his Sun-bright Chariot sate   100
Idol of Majestie Divine, enclos'd
With Flaming Cherubim, and golden Shields;
Then lighted from his gorgeous Throne, for now
'Twixt Host and Host but narrow space was left,
A dreadful interval, and Front to Front
Presented stood in terrible array
Of hideous length: before the cloudie Van,
On the rough edge of battel ere it joyn'd,
Satan with vast and haughtie strides advanc't,
Came towring, armd in Adamant and Gold;   110
Abdiel that sight endur'd not, where he stood
Among the mightiest, bent on highest deeds,
And thus his own undaunted heart explores.
    O Heav'n! that such resemblance of the Highest
Should yet remain, where faith and realtie
Remain not; wherefore should not strength & might
There fail where Vertue fails, or weakest prove
Where boldest; though to sight unconquerable?
His puissance, trusting in th' Almightie's aide,
I mean to try, whose Reason I have tri'd   120
Unsound and false; nor is it aught but just,
That he who in debate of Truth hath won,
Should win in Arms, in both disputes alike
Victor; though brutish that contest and foule,
When Reason hath to deal with force, yet so
Most reason is that Reason overcome.
    So pondering, and from his armed Peers
Forth stepping opposite, half way he met
His daring foe, at this prevention more
Incens't, and thus securely him defi'd.   130
    Proud, art thou met? thy hope was to have reacht
The highth of thy aspiring unoppos'd,
The Throne of God unguarded, and his side
Abandond at the terror of thy Power
Or potent tongue; fool, not to think how vain
Against th' Omnipotent to rise in Arms;
Who out of smallest things could without end
Have rais'd incessant Armies to defeat
Thy folly; or with solitarie hand

Reaching beyond all limit, at one blow　　　　140
Unaided could have finisht thee, and whelmd
Thy Legions under darkness ; but thou seest
All are not of thy Train ; there be who Faith
Prefer, and Pietie to God, though then
To thee not visible, when I alone
Seemed in thy World erroneous to dissent
From all : my Sect thou seest, now learn too late
How few somtimes may know, when thousands err.
　　Whom the grand foe with scornful eye askance
Thus answerd. Ill for thee, but in wisht houre　　150
Of my revenge, first sought for thou returnst
From flight, seditious Angel, to receave
Thy merited reward, the first assay
Of this right hand provok't, since first that tongue
Inspir'd with contradiction durst oppose
A third part of the Gods, in Synod met
Thir Deities to assert, who while they feel
Vigour Divine within them, can allow
Omnipotence to none. But well thou comst
Before thy fellows, ambitious to win　　　　160
From me som Plume, that thy success may show
Destruction to the rest : this pause between
(Unanswerd least thou boast) to let thee know ;
At first I thought that Libertie and Heav'n
To heav'nly Soules had bin all one ; but now
I see that most through sloth had rather serve,
Ministring Spirits, trained up in Feast and Song ;
Such hast thou arm'd, the Minstrelsie of Heav'n,
Servilitie with freedom to contend,
As both thir deeds compar'd this day shall prove.　　170
　　To whom in brief thus *Abdiel* stern repli'd.
Apostat still thou errst, nor end wilt find
Of erring, from the path of truth remote :
Unjustly thou deprav'st it with the name
Of *Servitude* to serve whom God ordains,
Or Nature ; God and Nature bid the same,
When he who rules is worthiest, and excells
Them whom he governs. This is servitude,
To serve th' unwise, or him who hath rebelld
Against his worthier, as thine now serve thee,　　180
Thy self not free, but to thy self enthrall'd ;

　　(299)

Yet leudly dar'st our ministring upbraid.
Reign thou in Hell thy Kingdom, let mee serve
In Heav'n God ever blest, and his Divine
Behests obey, worthiest to be obey'd,
Yet Chains in Hell, not Realms expect : mean while
From mee returnd, as erst thou saidst, from flight,
This greeting on thy impious Crest receive.
So saying, a noble stroke he lifted high,
Which hung not, but so swift with tempest fell   190
On the proud Crest of *Satan*, that no sight,
Nor motion of swift thought, less could his Shield
Such ruin intercept : ten paces huge
He back recoild ; the tenth on bended knee
His massie Spear upstaid ; as if on Earth
Winds under ground or waters forcing way
Sidelong, had push't a Mountain from his seat
Half sunk with all his Pines. Amazement seis'd
The Rebel Thrones, but greater rage to see
Thus foil'd thir mightiest, ours joy filld, and shout,   200
Presage of Victorie and fierce desire
Of Battel : whereat *Michael* bid sound
Th' Arch-angel trumpet ; through the vast of Heav'n
It sounded, and the faithful Armies rung
Hosanna to the Highest : nor stood at gaze
The adverse Legions, nor less hideous joyn'd
The horrid shock : now storming furie rose,
And clamour such as heard in Heav'n till now
Was never, Arms on Armour clashing bray'd
Horrible discord, and the madding Wheeles   210
Of brazen Chariots rag'd ; dire was the noise
Of conflict ; over head the dismal hiss
Of fiery Darts in flaming volies flew,
And flying vaulted either Host with fire.
So under fierie Cope together rush'd
Both Battels maine, with ruinous assault
And inextinguishable rage ; all Heav'n
Resounded, and had Earth bin then, all Earth
Had to her Center shook. What wonder ? when
Millions of fierce encountring Angels fought   220
On either side, the least of whom could weild
These Elements, and arm him with the force
Of all thir Regions : how much more of Power

Armie against Armie numberless to raise
Dreadful combustion warring, and disturb,
Though not destroy, thir happie Native seat;
Had not th' Eternal King Omnipotent
From his strong hold of Heav'n high over-rul'd
And limited thir might; though numberd such
As each divided Legion might have seemd　　230
A numerous Host, in strength each armed hand
A Legion; led in fight, yet Leader seemd
Each Warriour single as in Chief, expert
When to advance, or stand, or turn the sway
Of Battel, open when, and when to close
The ridges of grim Warr; no thought of flight,
None of retreat, no unbecoming deed
That argu'd fear; each on himself reli'd,
As onely in his arm the moment lay
Of victorie; deeds of eternal fame　　240
Were don, but infinite: for wide was spred
That Warr and various; somtimes on firm ground
A standing fight, then soaring on main wing
Tormented all the Air; all Air seemd then
Conflicting Fire: long time in eeven scale
The Battel hung; till *Satan,* who that day
Prodigious power had shewn, and met in Armes
No equal, raunging through the dire attack
Of fighting Seraphim confus'd, at length
Saw where the Sword of *Michael* smote, and fell'd　　250
Squadrons at once, with huge two-handed sway
Brandisht aloft the horrid edge came down
Wide wasting; such destruction to withstand
He hasted, and oppos'd the rockie Orb
Of tenfold Adamant, his ample Shield
A vast circumference: At his approach
The great Arch-Angel from his warlike toile
Surceas'd, and glad as hoping here to end
Intestine War in Heav'n, the arch foe subdu'd
Or Captive drag'd in Chains, with hostile frown　　260
And visage all enflam'd first thus began.

　　Author of evil, unknown till thy revolt,
Unnam'd in Heav'n, now plenteous, as thou seest
These Acts of hateful strife, hateful to all,
Though heaviest by just measure on thy self

And thy adherents : how hast thou disturb'd
Heav'ns blessed peace, and into Nature brought
Miserie, uncreated till the crime
Of thy Rebellion ? how hast thou instill'd
Thy malice into thousands, once upright   270
And faithful, now prov'd false. But think not here
To trouble Holy Rest ; Heav'n casts thee out
From all her Confines. Heav'n the seat of bliss
Brooks not the works of violence and Warr.
Hence then, and evil go with thee along
Thy ofspring, to the place of evil, Hell,
Thou and thy wicked crew ; there mingle broiles,
Ere this avenging Sword begin thy doome,
Or som more sudden vengeance wing'd from God
Precipitate thee with augmented paine.   280
   So spake the Prince of Angels ; to whom thus
The Adversarie. Nor think thou with wind
Of airie threats to aw whom yet with deeds
Thou canst not. Hast thou turnd the least of these
To flight, or if to fall, but that they rise
Unvanquisht, easier to transact with mee
That thou shouldst hope, imperious, & with threats
To chase me hence ? erre not that so shall end
The strife which thou call'st evil, but wee style
The strife of Glorie : which we mean to win,   290
Or turn this Heav'n it self into the Hell
Thou fablest, here however to dwell free,
If not to reign : mean while thy utmost force,
And join him nam'd *Almightie* to thy aid,
I flie not, but have sought thee farr and nigh.
   They ended parle, and both addrest for fight
Unspeakable ; for who, though with the tongue
Of Angels, can relate, or to what things
Liken on Earth conspicuous, that may lift
Human imagination to such highth   300
Of Godlike Power : for likest Gods they seemd,
Stood they or mov'd, in stature, motion, arms
Fit to decide the Empire of great Heav'n.
Now wav'd thir fierie Swords, and in the Aire
Made horrid Circles ; two broad Suns thir Shields
Blaz'd opposite, while expectation stood
In horror ; from each hand with speed retir'd

Where erst was thickest fight, th' Angelic throng,
And left large field, unsafe within the wind
Of such commotion, such as to set forth   310
Great things by small, if Natures concord broke,
Among the Constellations warr were sprung,
Two Planets rushing from aspect maligne
Of fiercest opposition in mid Skie,
Should combat, and thir jarring Sphears confound.
Together both with next to Almightie Arme,
Uplifted imminent one stroke they aim'd
That might determine, and not need repeate,
As not of power, at once; nor odds appeerd
In might or swift prevention; but the sword   320
Of *Michael* from the Armorie of God
Was giv'n him temperd so, that neither keen
Nor solid might resist that edge: it met
The sword of *Satan* with steep force to smite
Descending, and in half cut sheere, nor staid,
But with swift wheele reverse, deep entring shar'd
All his right side; then *Satan* first knew pain,
And writh'd him to and fro convolv'd; so sore
The griding sword with discontinuous wound
Pass'd through him, but th' Ethereal substance clos'd 330
Not long divisible, and from the gash
A stream of Nectarous humor issuing flow'd
Sanguin, such as Celestial Spirits may bleed,
And all his Armour staind ere while so bright.
Forthwith on all sides to his aide was run
By Angels many and strong, who interpos'd
Defence, while others bore him on thir Shields
Back to his Chariot; where it stood retir'd
From off the files of warr: there they him laid
Gnashing for anguish and despite and shame   340
To find himself not matchless, and his pride
Humbl'd by such rebuke, so farr beneath
His confidence to equal God in power.
Yet soon he heal'd; for Spirits that live throughout
Vital in every part, not as frail man
In Entrailes, Heart or Head, Liver or Reines,
Cannot but by annihilating die;
Nor in thir liquid texture mortal wound
Receive, no more then can the fluid Aire:

All Heart they live, all Head, all Eye, all Eare,   350
All Intellect, all Sense, and as they please,
They Limb themselves, and colour, shape or size
Assume, as likes them best, condense or rare.
　　Mean while in other parts like deeds deservd
Memorial, where the might of *Gabriel* fought,
And with fierce Ensignes pierc'd the deep array
Of *Moloc* furious King, who him defi'd,
And at his Chariot wheeles to drag him bound
Threatn'd, nor from the Holie One of Heav'n
Refrein'd his tongue blasphemous; but anon   360
Down clov'n to the waste, with shatterd Armes
And uncouth paine fled bellowing. On each wing
Uriel and *Raphael* his vaunting foe,
Though huge, and in a Rock of Diamond Armd,
Vanquish'd *Adramelec*, and *Asmadai*,
Two potent Thrones, that to be less then Gods
Disdain'd, but meaner thoughts learnd in thir flight,
Mangl'd with gastly wounds through Plate and Maile.
Nor stood unmindful *Abdiel* to annoy
The Atheist crew, but with redoubl'd blow   370
Ariel and *Arioc*, and the violence
Of *Ramiel* scorcht and blasted overthrew.
I might relate of thousands, and thir names
Eternize here on Earth; but those elect
Angels contented with thir fame in Heav'n
Seek not the praise of men; the other sort
In might though wondrous and in Acts of Warr,
Nor of Renown less eager, yet by doome
Canceld from Heav'n and sacred memorie,
Nameless in dark oblivion let them dwell.   380
For strength from Truth divided and from Just,
Illaudable, naught merits but dispraise
And ignominie, yet to glorie aspires
Vain glorious, and through infamie seeks fame:
Therfore Eternal silence be thir doome.
　　And now thir mightiest quelld, the battel swerv'd,
With many an inrode gor'd; deformed rout
Enter'd, and foul disorder; all the ground
With shiverd armour strow'n, and on a heap
Chariot and Charioter lay overturnd   390
And fierie foaming Steeds; what stood, recoyld

Orewearied, through the faint Satanic Host
Defensive scarce, or with pale fear surpris'd,
Then first with fear surpris'd and sense of paine
Fled ignominious, to such evil brought
By sinne of disobedience, till that hour
Not liable to fear or flight or paine.
Far otherwise th' inviolable Saints
In Cubic Phalanx firm advanc't entire,
Invulnerable, impenitrably arm'd :   400
Such high advantages thir innocence
Gave them above thir foes, not to have sinnd,
Not to have disobei'd ; in fight they stood
Unwearied, unobnoxious to be pain'd
By wound, though from thir place by violence mov'd.
    Now Night her course began, and over Heav'n
Inducing darkness, grateful truce impos'd,
And silence on the odious dinn of Warr :
Under her Cloudie covert both retir'd,
Victor and Vanquisht : on the foughten field   410
Michael and his Angels prevalent
Encamping, plac'd in Guard thir Watches round,
Cherubic waving fires : on th' other part
Satan with his rebellious disappeerd,
Far in the dark dislodg'd, and void of rest,
His Potentates to Councel call'd by night ;
And in the midst thus undismai'd began.
    O now in danger tri'd, now known in Armes
Not to be overpowerd, Companions deare,
Found worthy not of Libertie alone,   420
Too mean pretense, but what we more affect,
Honour, Dominion, Glorie, and renowne,
Who have sustaind one day in doubtful fight,
(And if one day, why not Eternal dayes ?)
What Heavens Lord had powerfullest to send
Against us from about his Throne, and judg'd
Sufficient to subdue us to his will,
But proves not so : then fallible, it seems,
Of future we may deem him, though till now
Omniscient thought. True is, less firmly arm'd,   430
Some disadvantage we endur'd and paine,
Till now not known, but known as soon contemnd,
Since now we find this our Empyreal forme

Incapable of mortal injurie
Imperishable, and though peirc'd with wound,
Soon closing, and by native vigour heal'd.
Of evil then so small as easie think
The remedie; perhaps more valid Armes,
Weapons more violent, when next we meet,
May serve to better us, and worse our foes,   440
Or equal what between us made the odds,
In Nature none: if other hidden cause
Left them Superiour, while we can preserve
Unhurt our mindes, and understanding sound,
Due search and consultation will disclose.
    He sat; and in th' assembly next upstood
Nisroc, of Principalities the prime;
As one he stood escap't from cruel fight,
Sore toild, his riv'n Armes to havoc hewn,
And cloudie in aspect thus answering spake.   450
Deliverer from new Lords, leader to free
Enjoyment of our right as Gods; yet hard
For Gods, and too unequal work we find
Against unequal armes to fight in paine,
Against unpaind, impassive; from which evil
Ruin must needs ensue; for what availes
Valour or strength, though matchless, quelld with pain
Which all subdues, and makes remiss the hands
Of Mightiest. Sense of pleasure we may well
Spare out of life perhaps, and not repine,   460
But live content, which is the calmest life:
But pain is perfet miserie, the worst
Of evils, and excessive, overturnes
All patience. He who therefore can invent
With what more forcible we may offend
Our yet unwounded Enemies, or arme
Our selves with like defence, to mee deserves
No less then for deliverance what we owe.
    Whereto with look compos'd *Satan* repli'd.
Not uninvented that, which thou aright   470
Beleivst so main to our success, I bring;
Which of us who beholds the bright surface
Of this Ethereous mould whereon we stand,
This continent of spacious Heav'n, adornd
With Plant, Fruit, Flour Ambrosial, Gemms & Gold,

Whose Eye so superficially surveyes
These things, as not to mind from whence they grow
Deep under ground, materials dark and crude,
Of spiritous and fierie spume, till toucht
With Heav'ns ray, and temperd they shoot forth   480
So beauteous, op'ning to the ambient light.
These in thir dark Nativitie the Deep
Shall yeild us, pregnant with infernal flame,
Which into hollow Engins long and round
Thick-rammd, at th' other bore with touch of fire
Dilated and infuriate shall send forth
From far with thundring noise among our foes
Such implements of mischief as shall dash
To pieces, and orewhelm whatever stands
Adverse, that they shall fear we have disarmd   490
The Thunderer of his only dreaded bolt.
Nor long shall be our labour, yet ere dawne,
Effect shall end our wish. Mean while revive ;
Abandon fear ; to strength and counsel joind
Think nothing hard, much less to be despaird.
He ended, and his words thir drooping chere
Enlightn'd, and thir languisht hope reviv'd.
Th' invention all admir'd, and each, how hee
To be th' inventer miss'd, so easie it seemd
Once found, which yet unfound most would have thought
Impossible : yet haply of thy Race   501
In future dayes, if Malice should abound,
Some one intent on mischief, or inspir'd
With dev'lish machination might devise
Like instrument to plague the Sons of men
For sin, on warr and mutual slaughter bent.
Forthwith from Councel to the work they flew,
None arguing stood, innumerable hands
Were ready, in a moment up they turnd
Wide the Celestial soile, and saw beneath   510
Th' originals of Nature in thir crude
Conception ; Sulphurous and Nitrous Foame
They found, they mingl'd, and with suttle Art,
Concocted and adusted they reduc'd
To blackest grain, and into store conveyd :
Part hidd'n veins diggd up (nor hath this Earth
Entrails unlike) of Mineral and Stone,

Whereof to found thir Engins and thir Balls
Of missive ruin; part incentive reed
Provide, pernicious with one touch to fire.   520
So all ere day-spring, under conscious Night
Secret they finish'd, and in order set,
With silent circumspection unespi'd.
Now when fair Morn Orient in Heav'n appeerd
Up rose the Victor Angels, and to Arms
The matin Trumpet Sung: in Arms they stood
Of Golden Panoplie, refulgent Host,
Soon banded; others from the dawning Hills
Lookd round, and Scouts each Coast light-armed scoure,
Each quarter, to descrie the distant foe,   530
Where lodg'd, or whither fled, or if for fight,
In motion or in alt: him soon they met
Under spred Ensignes moving nigh, in slow
But firm Battalion; back with speediest Sail
Zophiel, of Cherubim the swiftest wing,
Came flying, and in mid Aire aloud thus cri'd.
    Arme, Warriours, Arme for fight, the foe at hand,
Whom fled we thought, will save us long pursuit
This day, fear not his flight; so thick a Cloud
He comes, and settl'd in his face I see   540
Sad resolution and secure: let each
His Adamantine coat gird well, and each
Fit well his Helme, gripe fast his orbed Shield,
Born eevn or high, for this day will pour down,
If I conjecture aught, no drizling showr,
But ratling storm of Arrows barbd with fire.
So warnd he them aware themselves, and soon
In order, quit of all impediment;
Instant without disturb they took Allarm,
And onward move Embattelld; when behold   550
Not distant far with heavie pace the Foe
Approaching gross and huge; in hollow Cube
Training his devilish Enginrie, impal'd
On every side with shaddowing Squadrons Deep,
To hide the fraud. At interview both stood
A while, but suddenly at head appeerd
Satan: And thus was heard Commanding loud.
    Vangard, to Right and Left the Front unfould;
That all may see who hate us, how we seek

Peace and composure, and with open brest   560
Stand readie to receive them, if they like
Our overture, and turn not back perverse ;
But that I doubt, however witness Heaven,
Heav'n witness thou anon, while we discharge
Freely our part : yee who appointed stand
Do as you have in charge, and briefly touch
What we propound, and loud that all may hear.
  So scoffing in ambiguous words, he scarce
Had ended ; when to Right and Left the Front
Divided, and to either Flank retir'd.   570
Which to our eyes discoverd new and strange,
A triple-mounted row of Pillars laid
On Wheels (for like to Pillars most they seem'd
Or hollow'd bodies made of Oak or Firr
With branches lopt, in Wood or Mountain fell'd)
Brass, Iron, Stonie mould, had not thir mouthes
With hideous orifice gap't on us wide,
Portending hollow truce ; at each behind
A Seraph stood, and in his hand a Reed
Stood waving tipt with fire ; while we suspense,   580
Collected stood within our thoughts amus'd,
Not long, for sudden all at once thir Reeds
Put forth, and to a narrow vent appli'd
With nicest touch. Immediate in a flame,
But soon obscurd with smoak, all Heav'n appeerd,
From those deep-throated Engins belcht, whose roar
Emboweld with outragious noise the Air,
And all her entrails tore, disgorging foule
Thir devillish glut, chaind Thunderbolts and Hail
Of Iron Globes, which on the Victor Host   590
Level'd, with such impetuous furie smote,
That whom they hit, none on thir feet might stand,
Though standing else as Rocks, but down they fell
By thousands, Angel on Arch-Angel rowl'd ;
The sooner for thir Arms, unarm'd they might
Have easily as Spirits evaded swift
By quick contraction or remove ; but now
Foule dissipation follow'd and forc't rout ;
Nor serv'd it to relax thir serried files.
What should they do ? if on they rusht, repulse   600
Repeated, and indecent overthrow

Doubl'd, would render them yet more despis'd,
And to thir foes a laughter; for in view
Stood rankt of Seraphim another row
In posture to displode thir second tire
Of Thunder: back defeated to return
They worse abhorr'd. *Satan* beheld thir plight,
And to his Mates thus in derision call'd.
  O Friends, why come not on these Victors proud?
Ere while they fierce were coming, and when wee,   610
To entertain them fair with open Front
And Brest, (what could we more?) propounded terms
Of composition, strait they chang'd thir minds,
Flew off, and into strange vagaries fell,
As they would dance, yet for a dance they seemd
Somwhat extravagant and wilde, perhaps
For joy of offerd peace : but I suppose
If our proposals once again were heard
We should compel them to a quick result.
  To whom thus *Belial* in like gamesom mood.   620
Leader, the terms we sent were terms of weight,
Of hard contents, and full of force urg'd home,
Such as we might perceive amus'd them all,
And stumbl'd many, who receives them right,
Had need from head to foot well understand;
Not understood, this gift they have besides,
They shew us when our foes walk not upright.
  So they among themselves in pleasant veine
Stood scoffing, highthn'd in thir thoughts beyond
All doubt of Victorie, eternal might   630
To match with thir inventions they presum'd
So easie, and of his Thunder made a scorn,
And all his Host derided, while they stood
A while in trouble; but they stood not long,
Rage prompted them at length, & found them arms
Against such hellish mischief fit to oppose.
Forthwith (behold the excellence, the power
Which God hath in his mighty Angels plac'd)
Thir Arms away they threw, and to the Hills
(For Earth hath this variety from Heav'n   640
Of pleasure situate in Hill and Dale)
Light as the Lightning glimps they ran, they flew,
From thir foundations loosning to and fro

They pluckt the seated Hills with all thir load,
Rocks, Waters, Woods, and by the shaggie tops
Up lifting bore them in thir hands : Amaze,
Be sure, and terrour seis'd the rebel Host,
When coming towards them so dread they saw
The bottom of the Mountains upward turn'd,
Till on those cursed Engins triple-row   650
They saw them whelmd, and all thir confidence
Under the weight of Mountains buried deep,
Themselves invaded next, and on thir heads
Main Promontories flung, which in the Air
Came shadowing, and opprest whole Legions arm'd,
Thir armor help'd their harm, crush't in and brus'd
Into thir substance pent, which wrought them pain
Implacable, and many a dolorous groan,
Long strugling underneath, ere they could wind
Out of such prison, though Spirits of purest light,   660
Purest at first, now gross by sinning grown.
The rest in imitation to like Armes
Betook them, and the neighbouring Hills uptore ;
So Hills amid the Air encountered Hills
Hurl'd to and fro with jaculation dire,
That under ground they fought in dismal shade ;
Infernal noise ; Warr seem'd a civil Game
To this uproar ; horrid confusion heapt
Upon confusion rose : and now all Heav'n
Had gone to wrack, with ruin overspred,   670
Had not th' Almightie Father where he sits
Shrin'd in his Sanctuarie of Heav'n secure,
Consulting on the sum of things, foreseen
This tumult, and permitted all, advis'd :
That his great purpose he might so fulfill,
To honour his Anointed Son aveng'd
Upon his enemies, and to declare
All power on him transferr'd : whence to his Son
Th' Assessor of his Throne he thus began.
    Effulgence of my Glorie, Son belov'd,   680
Son in whose face invisible is beheld
Visibly, what by Deitie I am,
And in whose hand what by Decree I doe,
Second Omnipotence, two dayes are past,
Two dayes, as we compute the dayes of Heav'n,

Since *Michael* and his Powers went forth to tame
These disobedient; sore hath been thir fight,
As likeliest was, when two such Foes met arm'd;
For to themselves I left them, and thou knowst,
Equal in their Creation they were form'd,   690
Save what sin hath impaird, which yet hath wrought
Insensibly, for I suspend thir doom;
Whence in perpetual fight they needs must last
Endless, and no solution will be found:
Warr wearied hath perform'd what Warr can do,
And to disorder'd rage let loose the reines,
With Mountains as with Weapons arm'd, which makes
Wild work in Heav'n, and dangerous to the maine.
Two dayes are therefore past, the third is thine;
For thee I have ordain'd it, and thus farr   700
Have sufferd, that the Glorie may be thine
Of ending this great Warr, since none but Thou
Can end it. Into thee such Vertue and Grace
Immense I have transfus'd, that all may know
In Heav'n and Hell thy Power above compare,
And this perverse Commotion governd thus,
To manifest thee worthiest to be Heir
Of all things, to be Heir and to be King
By Sacred Unction, thy deserved right.
Go then thou Mightiest in thy Fathers might,   710
Ascend my Chariot, guide the rapid Wheeles
That shake Heav'ns basis, bring forth all my Warr,
My Bow and Thunder, my Almightie Arms
Gird on, and Sword upon thy puissant Thigh;
Pursue these sons of Darkness, drive them out
From all Heav'ns bounds into the utter Deep:
There let them learn, as likes them, to despise
God and *Messiah* his anointed King.
  He said, and on his Son with Rayes direct
Shon full, he all his Father full exprest   720
Ineffably into his face receiv'd,
And thus the filial Godhead answering spake.
  O Father, O Supream of heav'nly Thrones,
First, Highest, Holiest, Best, thou alwayes seekst
To glorifie thy Son, I alwayes thee,
As is most just; this I my Glorie account,
My exaltation, and my whole delight,

That thou in me well pleas'd declarst thy will
Fulfill'd, which to fulfil is all my bliss.
Scepter and Power, thy giving, I assume,   730
And gladlier shall resign, when in the end
Thou shalt be All in All, and I in thee
For ever, and in mee all whom thou lov'st;
But whom thou hat'st, I hate, and can put on
Thy terrors, as I put thy mildness on,
Image of thee in all things; and shall soon,
Armd with thy might, rid heav'n of these rebell'd,
To thir prepar'd ill Mansion driven down
To chains of Darkness, and th' undying Worm,
That from thy just obedience could revolt,   740
Whom to obey is happiness entire.
Then shall thy Saints unmixt, and from th' impure
Farr separate, circling thy holy Mount
Unfained *Halleluiahs* to thee sing,
Hymns of high praise, and I among them chief.
So said, he o're his Scepter bowing, rose
From the right hand of Glorie where he sate,
And the third sacred Morn began to shine
Dawning through Heav'n: forth rush'd with whirl-wind sound
The Chariot of Paternal Deitie,   750
Flashing thick flames, Wheele within Wheele undrawn,
It self instinct with Spirit, but convoyd
By four Cherubic shapes, four Faces each
Had wondrous, as with Starrs thir bodies all
And Wings were set with Eyes, with Eyes the Wheels
Of Beril, and careering Fires between;
Over thir heads a chrystal Firmament,
Whereon a Saphir Throne, inlaid with pure
Amber, and colours of the showrie Arch.
Hee in Celestial Panoplie all armd   760
Of radiant *Urim*, work divinely wrought,
Ascended, at his right hand Victorie
Sate Eagle-wing'd, beside him hung his Bow
And Quiver with three-bolted Thunder stor'd,
And from about him fierce Effusion rowld
Of smoak and bickering flame, and sparkles dire;
Attended with ten thousand thousand Saints,
He onward came, farr off his coming shon,
And twentie thousand (I thir number heard)

Chariots of God, half on each hand were seen: 770
Hee on the wings of Cherub rode sublime
On the Crystallin Skie, in Saphir Thron'd.
Illustrious farr and wide, but by his own
First seen, them unexpected joy surpriz'd,
When the great Ensign of *Messiah* blaz'd
Aloft by Angels born, his Sign in Heav'n:
Under whose Conduct *Michael* soon reduc'd
His Armie, circumfus'd on either Wing,
Under thir Head imbodied all in one.
Before him Power Divine his way prepar'd;   780
At his command the uprooted Hills retir'd
Each to his place, they heard his voice and went
Obsequious, Heav'n his wonted face renewed,
And with fresh Flourets Hill and Valley smil'd.
This saw his hapless Foes, but stood obdur'd,
And to rebellious fight rallied thir Powers
Insensate, hope conceiving from despair.
In heav'nly Spirits could such perverseness dwell?
But to convince the proud what Signs availe,
Or Wonders move th' obdurate to relent?   790
They hard'nd more by what might most reclame,
Grieving to see his Glorie, at the sight
Took envie, and aspiring to his highth,
Stood reimbattell'd fierce, by force or fraud
Weening to prosper, and at length prevaile
Against God and *Messiah*, or to fall
In universal ruin last, and now
To final Battel drew, disdaining flight,
Or faint retreat; when the great Son of God
To all his Host on either hand thus spake.   800
   Stand still in bright array ye Saints, here stand
Ye Angels arm'd, this day from Battel rest;
Faithful hath been your Warfare, and of God
Accepted, fearless in his righteous Cause,
And as ye have receivd, so have ye don
Invincibly: but of this cursed crew
The punishment to other hand belongs,
Vengeance is his, or whose he sole appoints;
Number to this dayes work is not ordain'd
Nor multitude, stand onely and behold   810
Gods indignation on these Godless pourd

By mee; not you but mee they have despis'd,
Yet envied; against mee is all thir rage,
Because the Father, t'whom in Heav'n supream
Kingdom and Power and Glorie appertains,
Hath honourd me according to his will.
Therefore to mee thir doom he hath assig'n'd;
That they may have thir wish, to trie with mee
In Battel which the stronger proves, they all,
Or I alone against them, since by strength   820
They measure all, of other excellence
Not emulous, nor care who them excells;
Nor other strife with them do I voutsafe.
   So spake the Son, and into terrour chang'd
His count'nance too severe to be beheld
And full of wrauth bent on his Enemies.
At once the Four spred out thir Starrie wings
With dreadful shade contiguous, and the Orbes
Of his fierce Chariot rowld, as with the sound
Of torrent Floods, or of a numerous Host.   830
Hee on his impious Foes right onward drove,
Gloomie as Night; under his burning Wheeles
The stedfast Empyrean shook throughout,
All but the Throne it self of God. Full soon
Among them he arriv'd; in his right hand
Grasping ten thousand Thunders, which he sent
Before him, such as in thir Soules infix'd
Plagues; they astonisht all resistance lost,
All courage; down thir idle weapons drop'd;
O're Shields and Helmes, and helmed heads he rode 840
Of Thrones and mighty Seraphim prostrate,
That wish'd the Mountains now might be again
Thrown on them as a shelter from his ire.
Nor less on either side tempestuous fell
His arrows, from the fourfold-visag'd Foure,
Distinct with eyes, and from the living Wheels,
Distinct alike with multitude of eyes,
One Spirit in them rul'd, and every eye
Glar'd lightning, and shot forth pernicious fire
Among th' accurst, that witherd all thir strength, 850
And of thir wonted vigour left them draind,
Exhausted, spiritless, afflicted, fall'n.
Yet half his strength he put not forth, but check'd

His Thunder in mid Volie, for he meant
Not to destroy, but root them out of Heav'n:
The overthrown he rais'd, and as a Heard
Of Goats or timerous flock together throngd
Drove them before him Thunder-struck, pursu'd
With terrors and with furies to the bounds
And Chrystall wall of Heav'n, which op'ning wide,   860
Rowld inward, and a spacious Gap disclos'd
Into the wastful Deep; the monstrous sight
Strook them with horror backward, but far worse
Urg'd them behind; headlong themselvs they threw
Down from the verge of Heav'n, Eternal wrauth
Burnt after them to the bottomless pit.

    Hell heard th' unsufferable noise, Hell saw
Heav'n ruining from Heav'n, and would have fled
Affrighted; but strict Fate had cast too deep
Her dark foundations, and too fast had bound.   870
Nine dayes they fell; confounded *Chaos* roard,
And felt tenfold confusion in thir fall
Through his wilde Anarchie, so huge a rout
Incumberd him with ruin: Hell at last
Yawning receavd them whole, and on them clos'd,
Hell thir fit habitation fraught with fire
Unquenchable, the house of woe and paine.
Disburd'nd Heav'n rejoic'd, and soon repaird
Her mural breach, returning whence it rowld.
Sole Victor from th' expulsion of his Foes   880
Messiah his triumphal Chariot turnd:
To meet him all his Saints, who silent stood
Eye witnesses of his Almightie Acts,
With Jubilie advanc'd; and as they went,
Shaded with branching Palme, each order bright,
Sung Triumph, and him sung Victorious King,
Son, Heire, and Lord, to him Dominion giv'n,
Worthiest to Reign: he celebrated rode
Triumphant through mid Heav'n, into the Courts
And Temple of his mightie Father Thron'd   890
On high; who into Glorie him receav'd,
Where now he sits at the right hand of bliss.

    Thus measuring things in Heav'n by things on Earth
At thy request, and that thou maist beware
By what is past, to thee I have reveal'd

What might have else to human Race bin hid:
The discord which befel, and Warr in Heav'n
Among th' Angelic Powers, and the deep fall
Of those too high aspiring, who rebelld
With *Satan*, hee who envies now thy state,   900
Who now is plotting how he may seduce
Thee also from obedience, that with him
Bereavd of happiness thou maist partake
His punishment, Eternal miserie;
Which would be all his solace and revenge,
As a despite don against the most High,
Thee once to gaine Companion of his woe.
But list'n not to his Temptations, warne
Thy weaker; let it profit thee to have heard
By terrible Example the reward   910
Of disobedience; firm they might have stood,
Yet fell; remember, and fear to transgress.

The End of the Sixth Book.

PARADISE LOST.

BOOK VII.

THE ARGUMENT.

Raphael *at the request of* Adam *relates how and wherefore this world was first created; that God, after the expelling of* Satan *and his Angels out of Heaven, declar'd his pleasure to create another World and other Creatures to dwell therein; sends his Son with Glory and attendance of Angels to perform the work of Creation in six dayes: the Angels celebrate with Hymns the performance thereof, and his reascention into Heaven.*

    DESCEND from Heav'n *Urania*, by that name
If rightly thou art call'd, whose Voice divine
Following, above th' *Olympian* Hill I soare,
Above the flight of *Pegasean* wing.
The meaning, not the Name I call: for thou
Nor of the Muses nine, nor on the top
Of old *Olympus* dwell'st, but Heav'nlie borne,
Before the Hills appeerd, or Fountain flow'd,
Thou with Eternal wisdom didst converse,
Wisdom thy Sister, and with her didst play   10
In presence of th' Almightie Father, pleas'd
With thy Celestial Song. Up led by thee
Into the Heav'n of Heav'ns I have presum'd,
An Earthlie Guest, and drawn Empyreal Aire,
Thy tempring; with like safetie guided down
Return me to my Native Element:
Least from this flying Steed unrein'd, (as once
Bellerophon, though from a lower Clime)
Dismounted, on th' *Aleian* Field I fall

Erroneous, there to wander and forlorne.   20
Half yet remaines unsung, but narrower bound
Within the visible Diurnal Spheare;
Standing on Earth, not rapt above the Pole,
More safe I Sing with mortal voice, unchang'd
To hoarce or mute, though fall'n on evil dayes,
On evil dayes though fall'n, and evil tongues;
In darkness, and with dangers compast round,
And solitude; yet not alone, while thou
Visit'st my slumbers Nightly, or when Morn
Purples the East: still govern thou my Song,   30
Urania, and fit audience find, though few.
But drive farr off the barbarous dissonance
Of *Bacchus* and his Revellers, the Race
Of that wilde Rout that tore the *Thracian* Bard
In *Rhodope*, where Woods and Rocks had Eares
To rapture, till the savage clamor dround
Both Harp and Voice; nor could the Muse defend
Her Son. So fail not thou, who thee implores :
For thou art Heav'nlie, shee an empty dreame.

    Say Goddess, what ensu'd when *Raphael*,   40
The affable Arch-angel, had forewarn'd
Adam by dire example to beware
Apostasie, by what befell in Heaven
To those Apostates, least the like befall
In Paradise to *Adam* or his Race,
Charg'd not to touch the interdicted Tree,
If they transgress, and slight that sole command,
So easily obeyd amid the choice
Of all tasts else to please thir appetite.
Though wandring.   He with his consorted *Eve*   50
The storie heard attentive, and was fill'd
With admiration, and deep Muse to heare
Of things so high and strange, things to thir thought
So unimaginable as hate in Heav'n,
And Warr so neer the Peace of God in bliss
With such confusion: but the evil soon
Driv'n back redounded as a flood on those
From whom it sprung, impossible to mix
With Blessedness.   Whence *Adam* soon repeal'd
The doubts that in his heart arose: and now   60
Led on, yet sinless, with desire to know

     (319)

What neerer might concern him, how this World
Of Heav'n and Earth conspicuous first began,
When, and whereof created, for what cause,
What within *Eden* or without was done
Before his memorie, as one whose drouth
Yet scarce allay'd still eyes the current streame,
Whose liquid murmur heard new thirst excites,
Proceeded thus to ask his Heav'nly Guest.

    Great things, and full of wonder in our eares,   70
Farr differing from this World, thou hast reveal'd
Divine Interpreter, by favour sent
Down from the Empyrean to forewarne
Us timely of what might else have bin our loss,
Unknown, which human knowledg could not reach :
For which to the infinitly Good we owe
Immortal thanks, and his admonishment
Receave with solemne purpose to observe
Immutably his sovran will, the end
Of what we are.   But since thou hast voutsaf't   80
Gently for our instruction to impart
Things above Earthly thought, which yet concernd
Our knowing, as to highest wisdom seemd,
Deign to descend now lower, and relate
What may no less perhaps availe us known,
How first began this Heav'n which we behold
Distant so high, with moving Fires adornd
Innumerable, and this which yeelds or fills
All space, the ambient Aire wide interfus'd
Imbracing round this florid Earth, what cause   90
Mov'd the Creator in his holy Rest
Through all Eternitie so late to build
In *Chaos*, and the work begun, how soon
Absolv'd, if unforbid thou maist unfold
What wee, not to explore the secrets aske
Of his Eternal Empire, but the more
To magnifie his works, the more we know.
And the great Light of Day yet wants to run
Much of his Race though steep, suspens in Heav'n
Held by thy voice, thy potent voice he heares,   100
And longer will delay to heare thee tell
His Generation, and the rising Birth
Of Nature from the unapparent Deep :

Or if the Starr of Eevning and the Moon
Haste to thy audience, Night with her will bring
Silence, and Sleep listning to thee will watch,
Or we can bid his absence, till thy Song
End, and dismiss thee ere the Morning shine.

    Thus *Adam* his illustrious Guest besought:
And thus the Godlike Angel answerd milde.   110
This also thy request with caution askt
Obtaine: though to recount Almightie works
What words or tongue of Seraph can suffice,
Or heart of man suffice to comprehend?
Yet what thou canst attain, which best may serve
To glorifie the Maker, and inferr
Thee also happier, shall not be withheld
Thy hearing, such Commission from above
I have receav'd, to answer thy desire
Of knowledge within bounds ; beyond abstain   120
To ask, nor let thine own inventions hope
Things not reveal'd which th' invisible King,
Onely Omniscient hath supprest in Night,
To none communicable in Earth or Heaven:
Anough is left besides to search and know.
But Knowledge is as food, and needs no less
Her Temperance over Appetite, to know
In measure what the mind may well contain,
Oppresses else with Surfet, and soon turns
Wisdom to Folly, as Nourishment to Winde.   130

    Know then, that after *Lucifer* from Heav'n
(So call him, brighter once amidst the Host
Of Angels, then that Starr the Starrs among)
Fell with his flaming Legions through the Deep
Into his place, and the great Son returnd
Victorious with his Saints, th' Omnipotent
Eternal Father from his Throne beheld
Thir multitude, and to his Son thus spake.

    At least our envious Foe hath fail'd, who thought
All like himself rebellious, by whose aid   140
This inaccessible high strength, the seat
Of Deitie supream, us dispossest,
He trusted to have seis'd, and into fraud
Drew many, whom thir place knows here no more;
Yet farr the greater part have kept, I see,

Thir station, Heav'n yet populous retaines
Number sufficient to possess her Realmes
Though wide, and this high Temple to frequent
With Ministeries due and solemn Rites:
But least his heart exalt him in the harme   150
Already done, to have dispeopl'd Heav'n,
My damage fondly deem'd, I can repaire
That detriment, if such it be to lose
Self-lost, and in a moment will create
Another World, out of one man a Race
Of men innumerable, there to dwell,
Not here, till by degrees of merit rais'd
They open to themselves at length the way
Up hither, under long obedience tri'd,
And Earth be chang'd to Heavn, & Heav'n to Earth, 160
One Kingdom, Joy and Union without end.
Mean while inhabit laxe, ye Powers of Heav'n,
And thou my Word, begotten Son, by thee
This I perform, speak thou, and be it don:
My overshadowing Spirit and might with thee
I send along, ride forth, and bid the Deep
Within appointed bounds be Heav'n and Earth,
Boundless the Deep, because I am who fill
Infinitude, nor vacuous the space.
Though I uncircumscrib'd my self retire,   170
And put not forth my goodness, which is free
To act or not, Necessitie and Chance
Approach not mee, and what I will is Fate.
    So spake th' Almightie, and to what he spake
His Word, the Filial Godhead, gave effect.
Immediate are the Acts of God, more swift
Then time or motion, but to human ears
Cannot without process of speech be told,
So told as earthly notion can receave.
Great triumph and rejoycing was in Heav'n   180
When such was heard declar'd the Almightie's will;
Glorie they sung to the most High, good will
To future men, and in thir dwellings peace:
Glorie to him whose just avenging ire
Had driven out th' ungodly from his sight
And th' habitations of the just; to him
Glorie and praise, whose wisdom had ordain'd

Good out of evil to create, in stead
Of Spirits maligne a better Race to bring
Into thir vacant room, and thence diffuse   190
His good to Worlds and Ages infinite.
So sang the Hierarchies: Mean while the Son
On his great Expedition now appeer'd,
Girt with Omnipotence, with Radiance crown'd
Of Majestie Divine, Sapience and Love
Immense, and all his Father in him shon.
About his Chariot numberless were pour'd
Cherub and Seraph, Potentates and Thrones,
And Vertues, winged Spirits, and Chariots wing'd,
From the Armoury of God, where stand of old   200
Myriads between two brazen Mountains lodg'd
Against a solemn day, harnest at hand,
Celestial Equipage; and now came forth
Spontaneous, for within them Spirit livd,
Attendant on thir Lord: Heav'n op'nd wide
Her ever during Gates, Harmonious sound
On golden Hinges moving, to let forth
The King of Glorie in his powerful Word
And Spirit coming to create new Worlds.
On heav'nly ground they stood, and from the shore   210
They view'd the vast immeasurable Abyss
Outrageous as a Sea, dark, wasteful, wilde,
Up from the bottom turn'd by furious windes
And surging waves, as Mountains to assault
Heav'ns highth, and with the Center mix the Pole.
    Silence, ye troubl'd waves, and thou Deep, peace,
Said then th' Omnific Word, your discord end:
    Nor staid, but on the Wings of Cherubim
Uplifted, in Paternal Glorie rode
Farr into *Chaos*, and the World unborn;   220
For *Chaos* heard his voice: him all his Traine
Follow'd in bright procession to behold
Creation, and the wonders of his might.
Then staid the fervid Wheeles, and in his hand
He took the golden Compasses, prepar'd
In Gods Eternal store, to circumscribe
This Universe, and all created things:
One foot he center'd, and the other turn'd
Round through the vast profunditie obscure,

And said, thus farr extend, thus farr thy ɒounds,   230
This be thy just Circumference, O World.
Thus God the Heav'n created, thus the Earth,
Matter unform'd and void : Darkness profound
Cover'd th' Abyss : but on the watrie calme
His brooding wings the Spirit of God outspred,
And vital vertue infus'd, and vital warmth
Throughout the fluid Mass, but downward purg'd
The black tartareous cold infernal dregs
Adverse to life ; then founded, then conglob'd
Like things to like, the rest to several place   240
Disparted, and between spun out the Air,
And Earth self-ballanc't on her Center hung.
   Let ther be Light, said God, and forthwith Light
Ethereal, first of things, quintessence pure
Sprung from the Deep, and from her Native East
To journie through the airie gloom began,
Sphear'd in a radiant Cloud, for yet the Sun
Was not ; shee in a cloudie Tabernacle
Sojourn'd the while. God saw the Light was good ;
And light from darkness by the Hemisphere   250
Divided : Light the Day, and Darkness Night
He nam'd. Thus was the first Day Eev'n and Morn :
Nor past uncelebrated, nor unsung
By the Celestial Quires, when Orient Light
Exhaling first from Darkness they beheld :
Birth-day of Heav'n and Earth ; with joy and shout
The hollow Universal Orb they fill'd,
And touch't thir Golden Harps, & hymning prais'd
God and his works, Creatour him they sung,
Both when first Eevning was, and when first Morn.   260
   Again, God said, let ther be Firmament
Amid the Waters, and let it divide
The Waters from the Waters : and God made
The Firmament, expanse of liquid, pure,
Transparent, Elemental Air, diffus'd
In circuit to the uttermost convex
Of this great Round : partition firm and sure,
The Waters underneath from those above
Dividing : for as Earth, so hee the World
Built on circumfluous Waters calme, in wide   270
Crystallin Ocean, and the loud misrule

Of *Chaos* farr remov'd, least fierce extreames
Contiguous might distemper the whole frame:
And Heav'n he nam'd the Firmament: So Eev'n
And Morning *Chorus* sung the second Day.
    The Earth was form'd, but in the Womb as yet
Of Waters, Embryon immature involv'd,
Appeer'd not: over all the face of Earth
Main Ocean flow'd, not idle, but with warme
Prolific humour soft'ning all her Globe,   280
Fermented the great Mother to conceave,
Satiate with genial moisture, when God said
Be gather'd now ye Waters under Heav'n
Into one place, and let dry Land appear.
Immediately the Mountains huge appeer
Emergent, and thir broad bare backs upheave
Into the Clouds, thir tops ascend the Skie:
So high as heav'd the tumid Hills, so low
Down sunk a hollow bottom broad and deep,
Capacious bed of Waters: thither they   290
Hasted with glad precipitance, uprowld
As drops on dust conglobing from the drie;
Part rise in crystal Wall, or ridge direct,
For haste; such flight the great command impress'd
On the swift flouds: as Armies at the call
Of Trumpet (for of Armies thou hast heard)
Troop to thir Standard, so the watrie throng,
Wave rowling after Wave, where way they found,
If steep, with torrent rapture, if through Plaine,
Soft-ebbing; nor withstood them Rock or Hill,   300
But they, or under ground, or circuit wide
With Serpent errour wandring, found thir way,
And on the washie Oose deep Channels wore;
Easie, e're God had bid the ground be drie,
All but within those banks, where Rivers now
Stream, and perpetual draw thir humid traine.
The dry Land, Earth, and the great receptacle
Of congregated Waters he call'd Seas:
And saw that it was good, and said, Let th' Earth
Put forth the verdant Grass, Herb yeilding Seed,   310
And Fruit Tree yeilding Fruit after her kind;
Whose Seed is in her self upon the Earth.
He scarce had said, when the bare Earth, till then

Desert and bare, unsightly, unadorn'd,
Brought forth the tender Grass, whose verdure clad
Her Universal Face with pleasant green,
Then Herbs of every leaf, that sudden flour'd
Op'ning thir various colours, and made gay
Her bosom smelling sweet: and these scarce blown,
Forth flourish't thick the clustring Vine, forth crept   320
The smelling Gourd, up stood the cornie Reed
Embattell'd in her field: add the humble Shrub,
And Bush with frizl'd hair implicit: last
Rose as in Dance the stately Trees, and spred
Thir branches hung with copious Fruit: or gemm'd
Thir Blossoms: with high Woods the Hills were crownd,
With tufts the vallies & each fountain side,
With borders long the Rivers. That Earth now
Seemd like to Heav'n, a seat where Gods might dwell,
Or wander with delight, and love to haunt   330
Her sacred shades: though God had yet not rain'd
Upon the Earth, and man to till the ground
None was, but from the Earth a dewie Mist
Went up and waterd all the ground, and each
Plant of the field, which e're it was in the Earth
God made, and every Herb, before it grew
On the green stemm; God saw that it was good:
So Eev'n and Morn recorded the Third Day.
    Again th' Almightie spake: Let there be Lights
High in th' expanse of Heaven to divide   340
The Day from Night; and let them be for Signes,
For Seasons, and for Dayes, and circling Years,
And let them be for Lights as I ordaine
Thir Office in the Firmament of Heav'n
To give Light on the Earth; and it was so.
And God made two great Lights, great for thir use
To Man, the greater to have rule by Day,
The less by Night alterne: and made the Starrs,
And set them in the Firmament of Heav'n
To illuminate the Earth, and rule the Day   350
In thir vicissitude, and rule the Night,
And Light from Darkness to divide. God saw,
Surveying his great Work, that it was good:
For of Celestial Bodies first the Sun
A mightie Spheare he fram'd, unlightsom first,

Though of Ethereal Mould : then form'd the Moon
Globose, and everie magnitude of Starrs,
And sowd with Starrs the Heav'n thick as a field :
Of Light by farr the greater part he took,
Transplanted from her cloudie Shrine, and plac'd   360
In the Suns Orb, made porous to receive
And drink the liquid Light, firm to retaine
Her gather'd beams, great Palace now of Light.
Hither as to thir Fountain other Starrs
Repairing, in thir gold'n Urns draw Light,
And hence the Morning Planet guilds his horns ;
By tincture or reflection they augment
Thir small peculiar, though from human sight
So farr remote, with diminution seen.
First in his East the glorious Lamp was seen,   370
Regent of Day, and all th' Horizon round
Invested with bright Rayes, jocond to run
His Longitude through Heav'ns high rode : the gray
Dawn, and the *Pleiades* before him danc'd
Shedding sweet influence : less bright the Moon,
But opposite in leveld West was set
His mirror with full face borrowing her Light
From him, for other light she needed none
In that aspect, and still that distance keepes
Till night, then in the East her turn she shines,   380
Revolvd on Heav'ns great Axle, and her Reign
With thousand lesser Lights dividual holds,
With thousand thousand Starres, that then appeer'd
Spangling the Hemisphere : then first adornd
With thir bright Luminaries that Set and Rose,
Glad Eevning & glad Morn crownd the fourth day.
     And God said, let the Waters generate
Reptil with Spawn abundant, living Soule :
And let Fowle flie above the Earth, with wings
Displayd on the op'n Firmament of Heav'n.   390
And God created the great Whales, and each
Soul living, each that crept, which plenteously
The waters generated by thir kindes,
And every Bird of wing after his kinde ;
And saw that it was good, and bless'd them, saying,
Be fruitful, multiply, and in the Seas

366 his] her *1674*

And Lakes and running Streams the waters fill;
And let the Fowle be multiply'd on the Earth.
Forthwith the Sounds and Seas, each Creek & Bay
With Frie innumerable swarme, and Shoales   400
Of Fish that with thir Finns & shining Scales
Glide under the green Wave, in Sculles that oft
Bank the mid Sea: part single or with mate
Graze the Sea weed thir pasture, & through Groves
Of Coral stray, or sporting with quick glance
Show to the Sun thir wav'd coats dropt with Gold,
Or in thir Pearlie shells at ease, attend
Moist nutriment, or under Rocks thir food
In jointed Armour watch: on smooth the Seale,
And bended Dolphins play: part huge of bulk   410
Wallowing unweildie, enormous in thir Gate
Tempest the Ocean: there Leviathan
Hugest of living Creatures, on the Deep
Stretcht like a Promontorie sleeps or swimmes,
And seems a moving Land, and at his Gilles
Draws in, and at his Trunck spouts out a Sea.
Mean while the tepid Caves, and Fens and shoares
Thir Brood as numerous hatch, from the Egg that soon
Bursting with kindly rupture forth disclos'd
Thir callow young, but featherd soon and fledge   420
They summ'd thir Penns, and soaring th' air sublime
With clang despis'd the ground, under a cloud
In prospect; there the Eagle and the Stork
On Cliffs and Cedar tops thir Eyries build:
Part loosly wing the Region, part more wise
In common, rang'd in figure wedge thir way,
Intelligent of seasons, and set forth
Thir Aierie Caravan high over Sea's
Flying, and over Lands with mutual wing
Easing thir flight; so stears the prudent Crane   430
Her annual Voiage, born on Windes; the Aire
Floats, as they pass, fann'd with unnumber'd plumes:
From Branch to Branch the smaller Birds with song
Solac'd the Woods, and spred thir painted wings
Till Ev'n, nor then the solemn Nightingal
Ceas'd warbling, but all night tun'd her soft layes:
Others on Silver Lakes and Rivers Bath'd
Thir downie Brest; the Swan with Arched neck

Between her white wings mantling proudly, Rowes
Her state with Oarie feet: yet oft they quit   440
The Dank, and rising on stiff Pennons, towre
The mid Aereal Skie: Others on ground
Walk'd firm; the crested Cock whose clarion sounds
The silent hours, and th' other whose gay Traine
Adorns him, colour'd with the Florid hue
Of Rainbows and Starrie Eyes. The Waters thus
With Fish replenisht, and the Aire with Fowle,
Ev'ning and Morn solemniz'd the Fift day.
   The Sixt, and of Creation last arose
With Eevning Harps and Mattin, when God said,   450
Let th' Earth bring forth Fowle living in her kinde,
Cattel and Creeping things, and Beast of the Earth,
Each in thir kinde. The Earth obey'd, and strait
Op'ning her fertil Woomb teem'd at a Birth
Innumerous living Creatures, perfet formes,
Limb'd and full grown: out of the ground up rose
As from his Laire the wilde Beast where he wonns
In Forrest wilde, in Thicket, Brake, or Den;
Among the Trees in Pairs they rose, they walk'd:
The Cattel in the Fields and Meddowes green: 460
Those rare and solitarie, these in flocks
Pasturing at once, and in broad Herds upsprung.
The grassie Clods now Calv'd, now half appeer'd
The Tawnie Lion, pawing to get free
His hinder parts, then springs as broke from Bonds,
And Rampant shakes his Brinded main; the Ounce,
The Libbard, and the Tyger, as the Moale
Rising, the crumbl'd Earth above them threw
In Hillocks; the swift Stag from under ground
Bore up his branching head: scarse from his mould   470
Behemoth biggest born of Earth upheav'd
His vastness: Fleec't the Flocks and bleating rose,
As Plants: ambiguous between Sea and Land
The River Horse and scalie Crocodile.
At once came forth whatever creeps the ground,
Insect or Worme; those wav'd thir limber fans
For wings, and smallest Lineaments exact
In all the Liveries dect of Summers pride
With spots of Gold and Purple, azure and green:
These as a line thir long dimension drew,   480

Streaking the ground with sinuous trace; not all
Minims of Nature; some of Serpent kinde
Wondrous in length and corpulence involv'd
Thir Snakie foulds, and added wings. First crept
The Parsimonious Emmet, provident
Of future, in small room large heart enclos'd,
Pattern of just equalitie perhaps
Hereafter, join'd in her popular Tribes
Of Commonaltie: swarming next appeer'd
The Femal Bee that feeds her Husband Drone   490
Deliciously, and builds her waxen Cells
With Honey stor'd: the rest are numberless,
And thou thir Natures know'st, and gav'st them Names,
Needless to thee repeated; nor unknown
The Serpent suttl'st Beast of all the field,
Of huge extent somtimes, with brazen Eyes
And hairie Main terrific, though to thee
Not noxious, but obedient at thy call.
Now Heav'n in all her Glorie shon, and rowld
Her motions, as the great first-Movers hand   500
First wheeld thir course; Earth in her rich attire
Consummate lovly smil'd; Aire, Water, Earth,
By Fowl, Fish, Beast, was flown, was swum, was walkt
Frequent; and of the Sixt day yet remain'd;
There wanted yet the Master work, the end
Of all yet don; a Creature who not prone
And Brute as other Creatures, but endu'd
With Sanctitie of Reason, might erect
His Stature, and upright with Front serene
Govern the rest, self-knowing, and from thence   510
Magnanimous to correspond with Heav'n,
But grateful to acknowledge whence his good
Descends, thither with heart and voice and eyes
Directed in Devotion, to adore
And worship God Supream, who made him chief
Of all his works: therefore the Omnipotent
Eternal Father (For where is not hee
Present) thus to his Son audibly spake.
  Let us make now Man in our image, Man
In our similitude, and let them rule   520
Over the Fish and Fowle of Sea and Aire,
Beast of the Field, and over all the Earth,

And every creeping thing that creeps the ground.
This said, he formd thee, *Adam*, thee O Man
Dust of the ground, and in thy nostrils breath'd
The breath of Life; in his own Image hee
Created thee, in the Image of God
Express, and thou becam'st a living Soul.
Male he created thee, but thy consort
Femal for Race; then bless'd Mankinde, and said,   530
Be fruitful, multiplie, and fill the Earth,
Subdue it, and throughout Dominion hold
Over Fish of the Sea, and Fowle of the Aire,
And every living thing that moves on the Earth.
Wherever thus created, for no place
Is yet distinct by name, thence, as thou know'st
He brought thee into this delicious Grove,
This Garden, planted with the Trees of God,
Delectable both to behold and taste;
And freely all thir pleasant fruit for food   540
Gave thee, all sorts are here that all th' Earth yeelds,
Varietie without end; but of the Tree
Which tasted works knowledge of Good and Evil,
Thou mai'st not; in the day thou eat'st, thou di'st;
Death is the penaltie impos'd, beware,
And govern well thy appetite, least sin
Surprise thee, and her black attendant Death.
Here finish'd hee, and all that he had made
View'd, and behold all was entirely good;
So Ev'n and Morn accomplish't the Sixt day: 550
Yet not till the Creator from his work
Desisting, though unwearied, up returnd
Up to the Heav'n of Heav'ns his high abode,
Thence to behold this new created World
Th' addition of his Empire, how it shew'd
In prospect from his Throne, how good, how faire,
Answering his great Idea. Up he rode
Followd with acclamation and the sound
Symphonious of ten thousand Harpes that tun'd
Angelic harmonies: the Earth, the Aire   560
Resounded, (thou remember'st for thou heardst)
The Heav'ns and all the Constellations rung,
The Planets in thir stations list'ning stood,

563 stations] station *1674*

While the bright Pomp ascended jubilant.
Open, ye everlasting Gates, they sung,
Open, ye Heav'ns, your living dores; let in
The great Creator from his work returnd
Magnificent, his Six days work, a World;
Open, and henceforth oft; for God will deigne
To visit oft the dwellings of just Men   570
Delighted, and with frequent intercourse
Thither will send his winged Messengers
On errands of supernal Grace. So sung
The glorious Train ascending: He through Heav'n,
That open'd wide her blazing Portals, led
To Gods Eternal house direct the way,
A broad and ample rode, whose dust is Gold
And pavement Starrs, as Starrs to thee appeer,
Seen in the Galaxie, that Milkie way
Which nightly as a circling Zone thou seest   580
Pouderd with Starrs.   And now on Earth the Seaventh
Eev'ning arose in *Eden*, for the Sun
Was set, and twilight from the East came on,
Forerunning Night; when at the holy mount
Of Heav'ns high-seated top, th' Impereal Throne
Of Godhead, fixt for ever firm and sure,
The Filial Power arriv'd, and sate him down
With his great Father, for he also went
Invisible, yet staid (such priviledge
Hath Omnipresence) and the work ordain'd,   590
Author and end of all things, and from work
Now resting, bless'd and hallowd the Seav'nth day,
As resting on that day from all his work,
But not in silence holy kept; the Harp
Had work and rested not, the solemn Pipe,
And Dulcimer, all Organs of sweet stop,
All sounds on Fret by String or Golden Wire
Temper'd soft Tunings, intermixt with Voice
Choral or Unison; of incense Clouds
Fuming from Golden Censers hid the Mount.   600
Creation and the Six dayes acts they sung,
Great are thy works, *Jehovah*, infinite
Thy power; what thought can measure thee or tongue
Relate thee; greater now in thy return
Then from the Giant Angels; thee that day

Paradise Lost.

Thy Thunders magnifi'd; but to create
Is greater then created to destroy.
Who can impair thee, mighty King, or bound
Thy Empire? easily the proud attempt
Of Spirits apostat and thir Counsels vaine   610
Thou hast repeld, while impiously they thought
Thee to diminish, and from thee withdraw
The number of thy worshippers. Who seekes
To lessen thee, against his purpose serves
To manifest the more thy might: his evil
Thou usest, and from thence creat'st more good.
Witness this new-made World, another Heav'n
From Heaven Gate not farr, founded in view
On the cleer *Hyaline*, the Glassie Sea;
Of amplitude almost immense, with Starr's   620
Numerous, and every Starr perhaps a World
Of destind habitation ; but thou know'st
Thir seasons : among these the seat of men,
Earth with her nether Ocean circumfus'd,
Thir pleasant dwelling place. Thrice happie men,
And sons of men, whom God hath thus advanc't,
Created in his Image, there to dwell
And worship him, and in reward to rule
Over his Works, on Earth, in Sea, or Air,
And multiply a Race of Worshippers   630
Holy and just: thrice happie if they know
Thir happiness, and persevere upright.
    So sung they, and the Empyrean rung,
With *Halleluiahs*: Thus was Sabbath kept.
And thy request think now fulfill'd, that ask'd
How first this World and face of things began,
And what before thy memorie was don
From the beginning, that posteritie
Informd by thee might know; if else thou seek'st
Aught, not surpassing human measure, say.   640

The End of the Seventh Book.

PARADISE LOST.

BOOK VIII.

THE ARGUMENT.

Adam *inquires concerning celestial Motions, is doubtfully answer'd, and exhorted to search rather things more worthy of knowledg:* Adam *assents, and still desirous to detain* Raphael, *relates to him what he remember'd since his own Creation, his placing in Paradise, his talk with God concerning solitude and fit society, his first meeting and Nuptials with* Eve, *his discourse with the Angel thereupon; who after admonitions repeated departs.*

[THE Angel ended, and in *Adams* Eare
So Charming left his voice, that he a while
Thought him still speaking, still stood fixt to hear;
Then as new wak't thus gratefully repli'd.]
What thanks sufficient, or what recompence
Equal have I to render thee, Divine
Hystorian, who thus largely hast allayd
The thirst I had of knowledge, and voutsaf't
This friendly condescention to relate
Things else by me unsearchable, now heard   10
With wonder, but delight, and, as is due,
With glorie attributed to the high
Creator; some thing yet of doubt remaines,
Which onely thy solution can resolve.
When I behold this goodly Frame, this World
Of Heav'n and Earth consisting, and compute,
Thir magnitudes, this Earth a spot, a graine,

1-4 These lines were added in the second edition, (1674), when Book VII was divided into two at line 640. Line 641 had read: 'To whom thus *Adam* gratefully repli'd.'

An Atom, with the Firmament compar'd
And all her numberd Starrs, that seem to rowle
Spaces incomprehensible (for such   20
Thir distance argues and thir swift return
Diurnal) meerly to officiate light
Round this opacous Earth, this punctual spot,
One day and night; in all thir vast survey
Useless besides, reasoning I oft admire,
How Nature wise and frugal could commit
Such disproportions, with superfluous hand
So many nobler Bodies to create,
Greater so manifold to this one use,
For aught appeers, and on thir Orbs impose   30
Such restless revolution day by day
Repeated, while the sedentarie Earth,
That better might with farr less compass move,
Serv'd by more noble then her self, attaines
Her end without least motion, and receaves,
As Tribute such a sumless journey brought
Of incorporeal speed, her warmth and light;
Speed, to describe whose swiftness Number failes.
    So spake our Sire, and by his count'nance seemd
Entring on studious thoughts abstruse, which *Eve*   40
Perceaving where she sat retir'd in sight,
With lowliness Majestic from her seat,
And Grace that won who saw to wish her stay,
Rose, and went forth among her Fruits and Flours,
To visit how they prosper'd, bud and bloom,
Her Nurserie; they at her coming sprung
And toucht by her fair tendance gladlier grew.
Yet went she not, as not with such discourse
Delighted, or not capable her eare
Of what was high: such pleasure she reserv'd,   50
Adam relating, she sole Auditress;
Her Husband the Relater she preferr'd
Before the Angel, and of him to ask
Chose rather: hee, she knew would intermix
Grateful digressions, and solve high dispute
With conjugal Caresses, from his Lip
Not Words alone pleas'd her. O when meet now
Such pairs, in Love and mutual Honour joyn'd?
With Goddess-like demeanour forth she went;

Not unattended, for on her as Queen   60
A pomp of winning Graces waited still,
And from about her shot Darts of desire
Into all Eyes to wish her still in sight.
And *Raphael* now to *Adam's* doubt propos'd
Benevolent and facil thus repli'd.
    To ask or search I blame thee not, for Heav'n
Is as the Book of God before thee set,
Wherein to read his wondrous Works, and learne
His Seasons, Hours, or Days, or Months, or Yeares;
This to attain, whether Heav'n move or Earth,   70
Imports not, if thou reck'n right, the rest
From Man or Angel the great Architect
Did wisely to conceal, and not divulge
His secrets to be scann'd by them who ought
Rather admire; or if they list to try
Conjecture, he his Fabric of the Heav'ns
Hath left to thir disputes, perhaps to move
His laughter at thir quaint Opinions wide
Hereafter, when they come to model Heav'n
And calculate the Starrs, how they will weild   80
The mightie frame, how build, unbuild, contrive
To save appeerances, how gird the Sphear
With Centric and Eccentric scribl'd o're,
Cycle and Epicycle, Orb in Orb:
Alreadie by thy reasoning this I guess,
Who art to lead thy ofspring, and supposest
That Bodies bright and greater should not serve
The less not bright, nor Heav'n such journies run,
Earth sitting still, when she alone receaves
The benefit: consider first, that Great   90
Or Bright inferrs not Excellence: the Earth
Though, in comparison of Heav'n so small,
Nor glistering, may of solid good containe
More plenty then the Sun that barren shines,
Whose vertue on it self workes no effect,
But in the fruitful Earth; there first receavd
His beams, unactive else, thir vigor find.
Yet not to Earth are those bright Luminaries
Officious, but to thee Earths habitant.
And for the Heav'ns wide Circuit, let it speak   100
The Makers high magnificence, who built

So spacious, and his Line stretcht out so farr;
That Man may know he dwells not in his own;
An Edifice too large for him to fill,
Lodg'd in a small partition, and the rest
Ordain'd for uses to his Lord best known.
The swiftness of those Circles attribute,
Though numberless, to his Omnipotence,
That to corporeal substances could adde
Speed almost Spiritual; mee thou thinkst not slow,   110
Who since the Morning hour set out from Heav'n
Where God resides, and ere mid-day arriv'd
In *Eden,* distance inexpressible
By Numbers that have name. But this I urge,
Admitting Motion in the Heav'ns, to shew
Invalid that which thee to doubt it mov'd;
Not that I so affirm, though so it seem
To thee who hast thy dwelling here on Earth.
God to remove his wayes from human sense,
Plac'd Heav'n from Earth so farr, that earthly sight,   120
If it presume, might erre in things too high,
And no advantage gaine. What if the Sun
Be Center to the World, and other Starrs
By his attractive vertue and thir own
Incited, dance about him various rounds?
Thir wandring course now high, now low, then hid,
Progressive, retrograde, or standing still,
In six thou seest, and what if sev'nth to these
The Planet Earth, so stedfast though she seem,
Insensibly three different Motions move?   130
Which else to several Sphears thou must ascribe,
Mov'd contrarie with thwart obliquities,
Or save the Sun his labour, and that swift
Nocturnal and Diurnal rhomb suppos'd,
Invisible else above all Starrs, the Wheele
Of Day and Night; which needs not thy beleefe,
If Earth industrious of her self fetch Day
Travelling East, and with her part averse
From the Suns beam meet Night, her other part
Still luminous by his ray. What if that light   140
Sent from her through the wide transpicuous aire,
To the terrestrial Moon be as a Starr
Enlightning her by Day, as she by Night

This Earth? reciprocal, if Land be there,
Feilds and Inhabitants: Her spots thou seest
As Clouds, and Clouds may rain, and Rain produce
Fruits in her soft'nd Soile, for some to eate
Allotted there; and other Suns perhaps
With thir attendant Moons thou wilt descrie
Communicating Male and Female Light,   150
Which two great Sexes animate the World,
Stor'd in each Orb perhaps with some that live.
For such vast room in Nature unpossest
By living Soule, desert and desolate,
Onely to shine, yet scarce to contribute
Each Orb a glimps of Light, conveyd so farr
Down to this habitable, which returnes
Light back to them, is obvious to dispute.
But whether thus these things, or whether not,
Whether the Sun predominant in Heav'n   160
Rise on the Earth, or Earth rise on the Sun,
Hee from the East his flaming rode begin,
Or Shee from West her silent course advance
With inoffensive pace that spinning sleeps
On her soft Axle, while she paces Eev'n,
And bears thee soft with the smooth Air along,
Sollicit not thy thoughts with matters hid,
Leave them to God above, him serve and feare;
Of other Creatures, as him pleases best,
Wherever plac't, let him dispose: joy thou   170
In what he gives to thee, this Paradise
And thy fair *Eve*: Heav'n is for thee too high
To know what passes there; be lowlie wise:
Think onely what concernes thee and thy being;
Dream not of other Worlds, what Creatures there
Live, in what state, condition or degree,
Contented that thus farr hath been reveal'd
Not of Earth onely but of highest Heav'n.
    To whom thus *Adam* cleerd of doubt, repli'd.
How fully hast thou satisfi'd mee, pure   180
Intelligence of Heav'n, Angel serene,
And freed from intricacies, taught to live,
The easiest way, nor with perplexing thoughts
To interrupt the sweet of Life, from which
God hath bid dwell farr off all anxious cares,

(338)

And not molest us, unless we our selves
Seek them with wandring thoughts, and notions vaine.
But apte the Mind or Fancie is to roave
Uncheckt, and of her roaving is no end;
Till warn'd, or by experience taught, she learn   190
That not to know at large of things remote
From use, obscure and suttle, but to know
That which before us lies in daily life,
Is the prime Wisdom, what is more, is fume,
Or emptiness, or fond impertinence,
And renders us in things that most concerne
Unpractis'd, unprepar'd, and still to seek.
Therefore from this high pitch let us descend
A lower flight, and speak of things at hand
Useful, whence haply mention may arise   200
Of somthing not unseasonable to ask
By sufferance, and thy wonted favour deign'd.
Thee I have heard relating what was don
Ere my remembrance: now hear mee relate
My Storie, which perhaps thou hast not heard;
And Day is yet not spent; till then thou seest
How suttly to detaine thee I devise,
Inviting thee to hear while I relate,
Fond, were it not in hope of thy reply:
For while I sit with thee, I seem in Heav'n,   210
And sweeter thy discourse is to my eare
Then Fruits of Palm-tree pleasantest to thirst
And hunger both, from labour, at the houre
Of sweet repast; they satiate, and soon fill,
Though pleasant, but thy words with Grace Divine
Imbu'd, bring to thir sweetness no satietie.
      To whom thus *Raphael* answer'd heav'nly meek.
Nor are thy lips ungraceful, Sire of men,
Nor tongue ineloquent; for God on thee
Abundantly his gifts hath also pour'd   220
Inward and outward both, his image faire:
Speaking or mute all comliness and grace
Attends thee, and each word, each motion formes
Nor less think wee in Heav'n of thee on Earth
Then of our fellow servant, and inquire
Gladly into the wayes of God with Man:
For God we see hath honour'd thee, and set

(339)

On Man his equal Love : say therefore on ;
For I that Day was absent, as befell,
Bound on a voyage uncouth and obscure,   230
Farr on excursion toward the Gates of Hell ;
Squar'd in full Legion (such command we had)
To see that none thence issu'd forth a spie,
Or enemie, while God was in his work,
Least hee incenst at such eruption bold,
Destruction with Creation might have mixt.
Not that they durst without his leave attempt,
But us he sends upon his high behests
For state, as Sovran King, and to enure
Our prompt obedience. Fast we found, fast shut   240
The dismal Gates, and barricado'd strong ;
But long ere our approaching heard within
Noise, other then the sound of Dance or Song,
Torment, and lowd lament, and furious rage.
Glad we return'd up to the coasts of Light
Ere Sabbath Eev'ning : so we had in charge.
But thy relation now ; for I attend,
Pleas'd with thy words no less then thou with mine.
    So spake the Godlike Power, and thus our Sire.
For Man to tell how human Life began   250
Is hard : for who himself beginning knew ?
Desire with thee still longer to converse
Induc'd me. As new wak't from soundest sleep
Soft on the flourie herb I found me laid
In Balmie Sweat, which with his Beames the Sun
Soon dri'd, and on the reaking moisture fed.
Strait toward Heav'n my wondring Eyes I turnd,
And gaz'd a while the ample Skie, till rais'd
By quick instinctive motion up I sprung,
As thitherward endevoring, and upright   260
Stood on my feet ; about me round I saw
Hill, Dale, and shadie Woods, and sunnie Plaines,
And liquid Lapse of murmuring Streams ; by these,
Creatures that livd, and movd, and walk'd, or flew,
Birds on the branches warbling ; all things smil'd,
With fragrance and with joy my heart oreflow'd.
My self I then perus'd, and Limb by Limb
Survey'd, and sometimes went, and sometimes ran
With supple joints, as lively vigour led :

269 as] and   *1674*

But who I was, or where, or from what cause,   270
Knew not; to speak I tri'd, and forthwith spake,
My Tongue obey'd and readily could name
What e're I saw.   Thou Sun, said I, faire Light,
And thou enlight'nd Earth, so fresh and gay,
Ye Hills and Dales, ye Rivers, Woods, and Plaines
And ye that live and move, fair Creatures, tell,
Tell, if ye saw, how came I thus, how here?
Not of my self; by some great Maker then,
In goodness and in power præeminent;
Tell me, how may I know him, how adore,   280
From whom I have that thus I move and live,
And feel that I am happier then I know.
While thus I call'd, and stray'd I knew not whither,
From where I first drew Aire, and first beheld
This happie Light, when answer none return'd,
On a green shadie Bank profuse of Flours
Pensive I sate me down; there gentle sleep
First found me, and with soft oppression seis'd
My droused sense, untroubl'd, though I thought
I then was passing to my former state   290
Insensible, and forthwith to dissolve:
When suddenly stood at my Head a dream,
Whose inward apparition gently mov'd
My Fancy to believe I yet had being,
And livd: One came, methought, of shape Divine,
And said, thy Mansion wants thee, *Adam*, rise,
First Man, of Men innumerable ordain'd
First Father, call'd by thee I come thy Guide
To the Garden of bliss, thy seat prepar'd.
So saying, by the hand he took me rais'd,   300
And over Fields and Waters, as in Aire
Smooth sliding without step, last led me up
A woodie Mountain; whose high top was plaine,
A Circuit wide, enclos'd, with goodliest Trees
Planted, with Walks, and Bowers, that what I saw
Of Earth before scarce pleasant seemd.   Each Tree
Load'n with fairest Fruit, that hung to the Eye
Tempting, stirr'd in me sudden appetite
To pluck and eate; whereat I wak'd, and found
Before mine Eyes all real, as the dream   310
Had lively shadowd: Here had new begun

My wandring, had not hee who was my Guide
Up hither, from among the Trees appeer'd,
Presence Divine. Rejoycing, but with aw
In adoration at his feet I fell
Submiss: he rear'd me, & Whom thou soughtst I am,
Said mildely, Author of all this thou seest
Above, or round about thee or beneath.
This Paradise I give thee, count it thine
To Till and keep, and of the Fruit to eate: 320
Of every Tree that in the Garden growes
Eate freely with glad heart; fear here no dearth:
But of the Tree whose operation brings
Knowledg of good and ill, which I have set
The Pledge of thy Obedience and thy Faith,
Amid the Garden by the Tree of Life,
Remember what I warne thee, shun to taste,
And shun the bitter consequence: for know,
The day thou eat'st thereof, my sole command
Transgrest, inevitably thou shalt dye;   330
From that day mortal, and this happie State
Shalt loose, expell'd from hence into a World
Of woe and sorrow. Sternly he pronounc'd
The rigid interdiction, which resounds
Yet dreadful in mine eare, though in my choice
Not to incur; but soon his cleer aspect
Return'd and gratious purpose thus renew'd.
Not onely these fair bounds, but all the Earth
To thee and to thy Race I give; as Lords
Possess it, and all things that therein live,   340
Or live in Sea, or Aire, Beast, Fish, and Fowle
In signe whereof each Bird and Beast behold
After thir kindes; I bring them to receave
From thee thir Names, and pay thee fealtie
With low subjection; understand the same
Of Fish within thir watry residence,
Not hither summond, since they cannot change
Thir Element to draw the thinner Aire.
As thus he spake, each Bird and Beast behold
Approaching two and two, These cowring low   350
With blandishment, each Bird stoop'd on his wing.
I nam'd them, as they pass'd, and understood
Thir Nature, with such knowledg God endu'd

My sudden apprehension: but in these
I found not what me thought I wanted still;
And to the Heav'nly vision thus presum'd.

　O by what Name, for thou above all these,
Above mankinde, or aught then mankinde higher,
Surpassest farr my naming, how may I
Adore thee, Author of this Universe,   360
And all this good to man, for whose well being
So amply, and with hands so liberal
Thou hast provided all things: but with mee
I see not who partakes. In solitude
What happiness, who can enjoy alone,
Or all enjoying, what contentment find?
Thus I presumptuous; and the vision bright,
As with a smile more bright'nd, thus repli'd.

　What call'st thou solitude, is not the Earth
With various living creatures, and the Aire   370
Replenisht, and all these at thy command
To come and play before thee, know'st thou not
Thir language and thir wayes, they also know,
And reason not contemptibly; with these
Find pastime, and beare rule; thy Realm is large.
So spake the Universal Lord, and seem'd
So ordering. I with leave of speech implor'd,
And humble deprecation thus repli'd.

　Let not my words offend thee, Heav'nly Power,
My Maker, be propitious while I speak.   380
Hast thou not made me here thy substitute,
And these inferiour farr beneath me set?
Among unequals what societie
Can sort, what harmonie or true delight?
Which must be mutual, in proportion due
Giv'n and receiv'd; but in disparitie
The one intense, the other still remiss
Cannot well suite with either, but soon prove
Tedious alike: Of fellowship I speak
Such as I seek, fit to participate   390
All rational delight, wherein the brute
Cannot be human consort; they rejoyce
Each with thir kinde, Lion with Lioness;
So fitly them in pairs thou hast combin'd;
Much less can Bird with Beast, or Fish with Fowle

(343)

So well converse, nor with the Ox the Ape;
Wors then can Man with Beast, and least of all.
   Whereto th' Almighty answer'd, not displeas'd.
A nice and suttle happiness I see
Thou to thy self proposest, in the choice   400
Of thy Associates, *Adam*, and wilt taste
No pleasure, though in pleasure, solitarie.
What thinkst thou then of mee, and this my State,
Seem I to thee sufficiently possest
Of happiness, or not? who am alone
From all Eternitie, for none I know
Second to mee or like, equal much less.
How have I then with whom to hold converse
Save with the Creatures which I made, and those
To me inferiour, infinite descents   410
Beneath what other Creatures are to thee?
   He ceas'd, I lowly answer'd. To attaine
The highth and depth of thy Eternal wayes
All human thoughts come short, Supream of things;
Thou in thy self art perfet, and in thee
Is no deficience found; not so is Man,
But in degree, the cause of his desire
By conversation with his like to help,
Or solace his defects. No need that thou
Shouldst propagat, already infinite;   420
And through all numbers absolute, though One;
But Man by number is to manifest
His single imperfection, and beget
Like of his like, his Image multipli'd,
In unitie defective, which requires
Collateral love, and deerest amitie.
Thou in thy secresie although alone,
Best with thy self accompanied, seek'st not
Social communication, yet so pleas'd,
Canst raise thy Creature to what highth thou wilt   430
Of Union or Communion, deifi'd;
I by conversing cannot these erect
From prone, nor in thir wayes complacence find.
Thus I embold'nd spake, and freedom us'd
Permissive, and acceptance found, which gain'd
This answer from the gratious voice Divine.
   Thus farr to try thee *Adam*, I was pleas'd,

And finde thee knowing not of Beasts alone,
Which thou hast rightly nam'd, but of thy self,
Expressing well the spirit within thee free,   440
My Image, not imparted to the Brute,
Whose fellowship therefore unmeet for thee
Good reason was thou freely shouldst dislike,
And be so minded still; I, ere thou spak'st,
Knew it not good for Man to be alone,
And no such companie as then thou saw'st
Intended thee, for trial onely brought,
To see how thou could'st judge of fit and meet:
What next I bring shall please thee, be assur'd,
Thy likeness, thy fit help, thy other self,   450
Thy wish, exactly to thy hearts desire.
    Hee ended, or I heard no more, for now
My earthly by his Heav'nly overpowerd,
Which it had long stood under, streind to the highth
In that celestial Colloquie sublime,
As with an object that excels the sense,
Dazl'd and spent, sunk down, and sought repair
Of sleep, which instantly fell on me, call'd
By Nature as in aide, and clos'd mine eyes.
Mine eyes he clos'd, but op'n left the Cell   460
Of Fancie my internal sight, by which
Abstract as in a transe methought I saw,
Though sleeping, where I lay, and saw the shape
Still glorious before whom awake I stood;
Who stooping op'nd my left side, and took
From thence a Rib, with cordial spirits warme,
And Life-blood streaming fresh; wide was the wound,
But suddenly with flesh fill'd up & heal'd:
The Rib he formd and fashond with his hands;
Under his forming hands a Creature grew,   470
Manlike, but different sex, so lovly faire,
That what seemd fair in all the World, seemd now
Mean, or in her summd up, in her containd
And in her looks, which from that time infus'd
Sweetness into my heart, unfelt before,
And into all things from her Aire inspir'd
The spirit of love and amorous delight.
She disappeerd, and left me dark, I wak'd
To find her, or for ever to deplore

Her loss, and other pleasures all abjure: 480
When out of hope, behold her, not farr off,
Such as I saw her in my dream, adornd
With what all Earth or Heaven could bestow
To make her amiable: On she came,
Led by her Heav'nly Maker, though unseen,
And guided by his voice, nor uninformd
Of nuptial Sanctitie and marriage Rites:
Grace was in all her steps, Heav'n in her Eye,
In every gesture dignitie and love.
I overjoyd could not forbear aloud.   490
     This turn hath made amends; thou hast fulfill'd
Thy words, Creator bounteous and benigne,
Giver of all things faire, but fairest this
Of all thy gifts, nor enviest. I now see
Bone of my Bone, Flesh of my Flesh, my Self
Before me; Woman is her Name, of Man
Extracted; for this cause he shall forgoe
Father and Mother, and to his Wife adhere;
And they shall be one Flesh, one Heart, one Soule.
     She heard me thus, and though divinely brought,   500
Yet Innocence and Virgin Modestie,
Her vertue and the conscience of her worth,
That would be woo'd, and not unsought be won,
Not obvious, not obtrusive, but retir'd,
The more desirable, or to say all,
Nature her self, though pure of sinful thought,
Wrought in her so, that seeing me, she turn'd;
I follow'd her, she what was Honour knew,
And with obsequious Majestie approv'd
My pleaded reason. To the Nuptial Bowre   510
I led her blushing like the Morn: all Heav'n,
And happie Constellations on that houre
Shed thir selectest influence; the Earth
Gave sign of gratulation, and each Hill;
Joyous the Birds; fresh Gales and gentle Aires
Whisper'd it to the Woods, and from thir wings
Flung Rose, flung Odours from the spicie Shrub,
Disporting, till the amorous Bird of Night
Sung Spousal, and bid haste the Eevning Starr
On his Hill top, to light the bridal Lamp.   520
Thus I have told thee all my State, and brought

My Storie to the sum of earthly bliss
Which I enjoy, and must confess to find
In all things else delight indeed, but such
As us'd or not, works in the mind no change,
Nor vehement desire, these delicacies
I mean of Taste, Sight, Smell, Herbs, Fruits, & Flours,
Walks, and the melodie of Birds; but here
Farr otherwise, transported I behold,
Transported touch; here passion first I felt, 530
Commotion strange, in all enjoyments else
Superiour and unmov'd, here onely weake
Against the charm of Beauties powerful glance.
Or Nature faild in mee, and left some part
Not proof enough such Object to sustain,
Or from my side subducting, took perhaps
More then enough; at least on her bestow'd
Too much of Ornament, in outward shew
Elaborate, of inward less exact.
For well I understand in the prime end 540
Of Nature her th' inferiour, in the mind
And inward Faculties, which most excell,
In outward also her resembling less
His Image who made both, and less expressing
The character of that Dominion giv'n
O're other Creatures; yet when I approach
Her loveliness, so absolute she seems
And in her self compleat, so well to know
Her own, that what she wills to do or say,
Seems wisest, vertuousest, discreetest, best; 550
All higher knowledge in her presence falls
Degraded, Wisdom in discourse with her
Looses discount'nanc't, and like folly shewes;
Authoritie and Reason on her waite,
As one intended first, not after made
Occasionally; and to consummate all,
Greatness of mind and nobleness thir seat
Build in her loveliest, and create an awe
About her, as a guard Angelic plac't.
To whom the Angel with contracted brow. 560
    Accuse not Nature, she hath don her part;
Do thou but thine, and be not diffident
Of Wisdom, she deserts thee not, if thou

Dismiss not her, when most thou needst her nigh,
By attributing overmuch to things
Less excellent, as thou thy self perceav'st.
For what admir'st thou, what transports thee so,
An outside? fair no doubt, and worthy well
Thy cherishing, thy honouring, and thy love,
Not thy subjection: weigh with her thy self; 570
Then value: Oft times nothing profits more
Then self-esteem, grounded on just and right
Well manag'd; of that skill the more thou know'st,
The more she will acknowledge thee her Head,
And to realities yeild all her shows;
Made so adorn for thy delight the more,
So awful, that with honour thou maist love
Thy mate, who sees when thou art seen least wise.
But if the sense of touch whereby mankind
Is propagated seem such dear delight 580
Beyond all other, think the same voutsaf't
To Cattel and each Beast; which would not be
To them made common & divulg'd, if aught
Therein enjoy'd were worthy to subdue
The Soule of Man, or passion in him move.
What higher in her societie thou findst
Attractive, human, rational, love still;
In loving thou dost well, in passion not,
Wherein true Love consists not; love refines
The thoughts, and heart enlarges, hath his seat 590
In Reason, and is judicious, is the scale
By which to heav'nly Love thou maist ascend,
Not sunk in carnal pleasure, for which cause
Among the Beasts no Mate for thee was found.
To whom thus half abash't *Adam* repli'd.
Neither her out-side formd so fair, nor aught
In procreation common to all kindes
(Though higher of the genial Bed by far,
And with mysterious reverence I deem)
So much delights me, as those graceful acts, 600
Those thousand decencies that daily flow
From all her words and actions, mixt with Love
And sweet compliance, which declare unfeign'd
Union of Mind, or in us both one Soule:
Harmonie to behold in wedded pair

More grateful then harmonious sound to the eare.
Yet these subject not; I to thee disclose
What inward thence I feel, not therefore foild,
Who meet with various objects, from the sense
Variously representing; yet still free   610
Approve the best, and follow what I approve.
To love thou blam'st me not, for love thou saist
Leads up to Heav'n, is both the way and guide;
Bear with me then, if lawful what I ask;
Love not the heav'nly Spirits, and how thir Love
Express they, by looks onely, or do they mix
Irradiance, virtual or immediate touch?
     To whom the Angel with a smile that glow'd
Celestial rosie red, Loves proper hue,
Answer'd. Let it suffice thee that thou know'st   620
Us happie, and without Love no happiness.
Whatever pure thou in the body enjoy'st
(And pure thou wert created) we enjoy
In eminence, and obstacle find none
Of membrane, joynt, or limb, exclusive barrs:
Easier then Air with Air, if Spirits embrace,
Total they mix, Union of Pure with Pure
Desiring; nor restrain'd conveyance need
As Flesh to mix with Flesh, or Soul with Soul.
But I can now no more; the parting Sun   630
Beyond the Earths green Cape and verdant Isles
Hesperean sets, my Signal to depart.
Be strong, live happie, and love, but first of all
Him whom to love is to obey, and keep
His great command; take heed least Passion sway
Thy Judgement to do aught, which else free Will
Would not admit; thine and of all thy Sons
The weal or woe in thee is plac't; beware.
I in thy persevering shall rejoyce,
And all the Blest: stand fast; to stand or fall   640
Free in thine own Arbitrement it lies.
Perfect within, no outward aid require;
And all temptation to transgress repel.
     So saying, he arose; whom *Adam* thus
Follow'd with benediction. Since to part,
Go heavenly Guest, Ethereal Messenger,
Sent from whose sovran goodness I adore.

Gentle to me and affable hath been
Thy condescension, and shall be honour'd ever
With grateful Memorie : thou to mankind   650
Be good and friendly still, and oft return.
  So parted they, the Angel up to Heav'n
From the thick shade, and *Adam* to his Bowre.

The End of the Eighth Book.

PARADISE LOST.

BOOK IX.

THE ARGUMENT.

Satan *having compast the Earth, with meditated guile returns as a mist by Night into Paradise, enters into the Serpent sleeping. Adam and Eve in the Morning go forth to thir labours, which Eve proposes to divide in several places, each labouring apart: Adam consents not, alledging the danger, lest that Enemy, of whom they were forewarn'd, should attempt her found alone: Eve loath to be thought not circumspect or firm enough, urges her going apart, the rather desirous to make tryal of her strength; Adam at last yields: The Serpent finds her alone; his subtle approach, first gazing, then speaking, with much flattery extolling Eve above all other Creatures. Eve wondring to hear the Serpent speak, asks how he attain'd to human speech and such understanding not till now; the Serpent answers, that by tasting of a certain Tree in the Garden he attain'd both to Speech and Reason, till then void of both: Eve requires him to bring her to that Tree, and finds it to be the Tree of Knowledge forbidden: The Serpent now grown bolder, with many wiles and arguments induces her at length to eat; she pleas'd with the taste deliberates awhile whether to impart thereof to Adam or not, at last brings him of the Fruit, relates what persuaded her to eat thereof: Adam at first amaz'd, but perceiving her lost, resolves through vehemence of love to perish with her; and extenuating the trespass, eats also of the Fruit: The effects thereof in them both; they seek to cover thir nakedness; then fall to variance and accusation of one another.*

No more of talk where God or Angel Guest
With Man, as with his Friend, familiar us'd
To sit indulgent, and with him partake
Rural repast, permitting him the while

Venial discourse unblam'd: I now must change
Those Notes to Tragic; foul distrust, and breach
Disloyal on the part of Man, revolt,
And disobedience: On the part of Heav'n
Now alienated, distance and distaste,
Anger and just rebuke, and judgement giv'n,   10
That brought into this World a world of woe,
Sinne and her shadow Death, and Miserie
Deaths Harbinger: Sad task, yet argument
Not less but more Heroic then the wrauth
Of stern *Achilles* on his Foe pursu'd
Thrice Fugitive about *Troy* Wall; or rage
Of *Turnus* for *Lavinia* disespous'd,
Or *Neptun*'s ire or *Juno*'s, that so long
Perplex'd the *Greek* and *Cytherea*'s Son;
If answerable style I can obtaine   20
Of my Celestial Patroness, who deignes
Her nightly visitation unimplor'd,
And dictates to me slumbring, or inspires
Easie my unpremeditated Verse:
Since first this Subject for Heroic Song
Pleas'd me long choosing, and beginning late
Not sedulous by Nature to indite
Warrs, hitherto the onely Argument
Heroic deem'd, chief maistrie to dissect
With long and tedious havoc fabl'd Knights   30
In Battels feign'd; the better fortitude
Of Patience and Heroic Martyrdom
Unsung; or to describe Races and Games,
Or tilting Furniture, emblazon'd Shields,
Impreses quaint, Caparisons and Steeds;
Bases and tinsel Trappings, gorgious Knights
At Joust and Torneament; then marshal'd Feast
Serv'd up in Hall with Sewers, and Seneshals;
The skill of Artifice or Office mean,
Not that which justly gives Heroic name   40
To Person or to Poem. Mee of these
Nor skilld nor studious, higher Argument
Remaines, sufficient of it self to raise
That name, unless an age too late, or cold
Climat, or Years damp my intended wing
Deprest, and much they may, if all be mine,

Paradise Lost.

Not Hers who brings it nightly to my Ear.
   The Sun was sunk, and after him the Starr
Of *Hesperus*, whose Office is to bring
Twilight upon the Earth, short Arbiter   50
Twixt Day and Night, and now from end to end
Nights Hemisphere had veild the Horizon round:
When *Satan* who late fled before the threats
Of *Gabriel* out of *Eden*, now improv'd
In meditated fraud and malice, bent
On mans destruction, maugre what might hap
Of heavier on himself, fearless return'd.
By Night he fled, and at Midnight return'd
From compassing the Earth, cautious of day,
Since *Uriel* Regent of the Sun descri'd   60
His entrance, and forewarnd the Cherubim
That kept thir watch ; thence full of anguish driv'n,
The space of seven continu'd Nights he rode
With darkness, thrice the Equinoctial Line
He circl'd, four times cross'd the Carr of Night
From Pole to Pole, traversing each Colure ;
On the eighth return'd, and on the Coast averse
From entrance or Cherubic Watch, by stealth
Found unsuspected way. There was a place,
Now not, though Sin, not Time, first wraught the change, 70
Where *Tigris* at the foot of Paradise
Into a Gulf shot under ground, till part
Rose up a Fountain by the Tree of Life ;
In with the River sunk, and with it rose
Satan involv'd in rising Mist, then sought
Where to lie hid ; Sea he had searcht and Land
From *Eden* over *Pontus*, and the Poole
Mæotis, up beyond the River *Ob* ;
Downward as farr Antartic ; and in length
West from *Orontes* to the Ocean barr'd   80
At *Darien*, thence to the Land where flowes
Ganges and *Indus:* thus the Orb he roam'd
With narrow search ; and with inspection deep
Consider'd every Creature, which of all
Most opportune might serve his Wiles, and found
The Serpent suttlest Beast of all the Field.
Him after long debate, irresolute
Of thoughts revolv'd, his final sentence chose

Fit Vessel, fittest Imp of fraud, in whom
To enter, and his dark suggestions hide   90
From sharpest sight: for in the wilie Snake,
Whatever sleights none would suspicious mark,
As from his wit and native suttletie
Proceeding, which in other Beasts observ'd
Doubt might beget of Diabolic pow'r
Active within beyond the sense of brute.
Thus he resolv'd, but first from inward griefe
His bursting passion into plaints thus pour'd:
   O Earth, how like to Heav'n, if not preferr'd
More justly, Seat worthier of Gods, as built   100
With second thoughts, reforming what was old!
For what God after better worse would build?
Terrestrial Heav'n, danc't round by other Heav'ns
That shine, yet bear thir bright officious Lamps,
Light above Light, for thee alone, as seems,
In thee concentring all thir precious beams
Of sacred influence: As God in Heav'n
Is Center, yet extends to all, so thou
Centring receav'st from all those Orbs; in thee,
Not in themselves, all thir known vertue appeers   110
Productive in Herb, Plant, and nobler birth
Of Creatures animate with gradual life
Of Growth, Sense, Reason, all summ'd up in Man.
With what delight could I have walk't thee round
If I could joy in aught, sweet interchange
Of Hill and Vallie, Rivers, Woods and Plaines,
Now Land, now Sea, & Shores with Forrest crownd,
Rocks, Dens, and Caves; but I in none of these
Find place or refuge; and the more I see
Pleasures about me, so much more I feel   120
Torment within me, as from the hateful siege
Of contraries; all good to me becomes
Bane, and in Heav'n much worse would be my state.
But neither here seek I, no nor in Heav'n
To dwell, unless by maistring Heav'ns Supreame;
Nor hope to be my self less miserable
By what I seek, but others to make such
As I, though thereby worse to me redound:
For onely in destroying I finde ease
To my relentless thoughts; and him destroyd,   130

Or won to what may work his utter loss,
For whom all this was made, all this will soon
Follow, as to him linkt in weal or woe,
In wo then; that destruction wide may range:
To mee shall be the glorie sole among
The infernal Powers, in one day to have marr'd
What he *Almightie* styl'd, six Nights and Days
Continu'd making, and who knows how long
Before had bin contriving, though perhaps
Not longer then since I in one Night freed   140
From servitude inglorious welnigh half
Th' Angelic Name, and thinner left the throng
Of his adorers: hee to be aveng'd,
And to repair his numbers thus impair'd,
Whether such vertue spent of old now faild
More Angels to Create, if they at least
Are his Created or to spite us more,
Determin'd to advance into our room
A Creature form'd of Earth, and him endow,
Exalted from so base original,   150
With Heav'nly spoils, our spoils; What he decreed
He effected; Man he made, and for him built
Magnificent this World, and Earth his seat,
Him Lord pronounc'd, and, O indignitie!
Subjected to his service Angel wings,
And flaming Ministers to watch and tend
Thir earthie Charge: Of these the vigilance
I dread, and to elude, thus wrapt in mist
Of midnight vapor glide obscure, and prie
In every Bush and Brake, where hap may finde   160
The Serpent sleeping, in whose mazie foulds
To hide me, and the dark intent I bring.
O foul descent! that I who erst contended
With Gods to sit the highest, am now constraind
Into a Beast, and mixt with bestial slime,
This essence to incarnate and imbrute,
That to the hight of Deitie aspir'd;
But what will not Ambition and Revenge
Descend to? who aspires must down as low
As high he soard, obnoxious first or last   170
To basest things. Revenge, at first though sweet,
Bitter ere long back on it self recoiles;

Let it; I reck not, so it light well aim'd,
Since higher I fall short, on him who next
Provokes my envie, this new Favorite
Of Heav'n, this Man of Clay, Son of despite,
Whom us the more to spite his Maker rais'd
From dust: spite then with spite is best repaid.
  So saying, through each Thicket Danck or Drie,
Like a black mist low creeping, he held on   18
His midnight search, where soonest he might finde
The Serpent: him fast sleeping soon he found
In Labyrinth of many a round self-rowld,
His head the midst, well stor'd with suttle wiles:
Not yet in horrid Shade or dismal Den,
Not nocent yet, but on the grassie Herbe
Fearless unfeard he slept: in at his Mouth
The Devil enterd, and his brutal sense,
In heart or head, possessing soon inspir'd
With act intelligential; but his sleep   19
Disturb'd not, waiting close th' approach of Morn.
Now whenas sacred Light began to dawne
In *Eden* on the humid Flours, that breathd
Thir morning Incense, when all things that breath,
From th' Earths great Altar send up silent praise
To the Creator, and his Nostrils fill
With gratefull Smell, forth came the human pair
And joynd thir vocal Worship to the Quire
Of Creatures wanting voice, that done, partake
The season, prime for sweetest Sents and Aires: 20
Then commune how that day they best may ply
Thir growing work: for much thir work outgrew
The hands dispatch of two Gardning so wide.
And *Eve* first to her Husband thus began.
  Adam, well may we labour still to dress
This Garden, still to tend Plant, Herb and Flour.
Our pleasant task enjoyn'd, but till more hands
Aid us, the work under our labour grows,
Luxurious by restraint; what we by day
Lop overgrown, or prune, or prop, or bind,   21
One night or two with wanton growth derides
Tending to wilde. Thou therefore now advise
Or hear what to my mind first thoughts present,

186 not] nor *1674*   213 hear] bear *1674*

Let us divide our labours, thou where choice
Leads thee, or where most needs, whether to wind
The Woodbine round this Arbour, or direct
The clasping Ivie where to climb, while I
In yonder Spring of Roses intermixt
With Myrtle, find what to redress till Noon:
For while so near each other thus all day   220
Our task we choose, what wonder if so near
Looks intervene and smiles, or object new
Casual discourse draw on, which intermits
Our dayes work brought to little, though begun
Early, and th' hour of Supper comes unearn'd.
    To whom mild answer *Adam* thus return'd.
Sole *Eve*, Associate sole, to me beyond
Compare above all living Creatures deare,
Well hast thou motion'd, wel thy thoughts imployd
How we might best fulfill the work which here   230
God hath assign'd us, nor of me shalt pass
Unprais'd : for nothing lovelier can be found
In woman, then to studie houshold good,
And good workes in her Husband to promote.
Yet not so strictly hath our Lord impos'd
Labour, as to debarr us when we need
Refreshment, whether food, or talk between,
Food of the mind, or this sweet intercourse
Of looks and smiles, for smiles from Reason flow,
To brute deni'd, and are of Love the food,   240
Love not the lowest end of human life.
For not to irksom toile, but to delight
He made us, and delight to Reason joyn'd.
These paths and Bowers doubt not but our joynt hands
Will keep from Wilderness with ease, as wide
As we need walk, till younger hands ere long
Assist us : But if much converse perhaps
Thee satiate, to short absence I could yeild.
For solitude somtimes is best societie,
And short retirement urges sweet returne.   250
But other doubt possesses me, least harm
Befall thee sever'd from me ; for thou knowst
What hath bin warn'd us, what malicious Foe
Envying our happiness, and of his own
Despairing, seeks to work us woe and shame

(357)

By sly assault; and somwhere nigh at hand
Watches, no doubt, with greedy hope to find
His wish and best advantage, us asunder,
Hopeless to circumvent us joynd, where each
To other speedie aide might lend at need;   260
Whether his first design be to withdraw
Our fealtie from God, or to disturb
Conjugal Love, then which perhaps no bliss
Enjoy'd by us excites his envie more;
Or this, or worse, leave not the faithful side
That gave thee being, stil shades thee and protects.
The Wife, where danger or dishonour lurks,
Safest and seemliest by her Husband staies,
Who guards her, or with her the worst endures.

To whom the Virgin Majestie of *Eve,*   270
As one who loves, and some unkindness meets,
With sweet austeer composure thus reply'd.

Ofspring of Heav'n and Earth, and all Earths Lord,
That such an Enemie we have, who seeks
Our ruin, both by thee informd I learne,
And from the parting Angel over-heard
As in a shadie nook I stood behind,
Just then returnd at shut of Evening Flours.
But that thou shouldst my firmness therfore doubt
To God or thee, because we have a foe   280
May tempt it, I expected not to hear.
His violence thou fearst not, being such,
As wee, not capable of death or paine,
Can either not receave, or can repell.
His fraud is then thy fear, which plain inferrs
Thy equal fear that my firm Faith and Love
Can by his fraud be shak'n or seduc't;
Thoughts, which how found they harbour in thy brest,
Adam, missthought of her to thee so dear?

To whom with healing words *Adam* reply'd.   290
Daughter of God and Man, immortal *Eve,*
For such thou art, from sin and blame entire:
Not diffident of thee do I dissuade
Thy absence from my sight, but to avoid
Th' attempt it self, intended by our Foe.
For hee who tempts, though in vain, at least asperses
The tempted with dishonour foul, suppos'd

Not incorruptible of Faith, not prooff
Against temptation : thou thy self with scorne
And anger wouldst resent the offer'd wrong,   300
Though ineffectual found : misdeem not then,
If such affront I labour to avert
From thee alone, which on us both at once
The Enemie, though bold, will hardly dare,
Or daring, first on mee th' assault shall light.
Nor thou his malice and false guile contemn ;
Suttle he needs must be, who could seduce
Angels, nor think superfluous others aid.
I from the influence of thy looks receave
Access in every Vertue, in thy sight   310
More wise, more watchful, stronger, if need were
Of outward strength ; while shame, thou looking on,
Shame to be overcome or over-reacht
Would utmost vigor raise, and rais'd unite.
Why shouldst not thou like sense within thee feel
When I am present, and thy trial choose
With me, best witness of thy Vertue tri'd.
     So spake domestick *Adam* in his care
And Matrimonial Love, but *Eve*, who thought
Less attributed to her Faith sincere,   320
Thus her reply with accent sweet renewd.
     If this be our condition, thus to dwell
In narrow circuit strait'nd by a Foe,
Suttle or violent, we not endu'd
Single with like defence, wherever met,
How are we happie, still in fear of harm ?
But harm precedes not sin : onely our Foe
Tempting affronts us with his foul esteem
Of our integritie : his foul esteeme
Sticks no dishonor on our Front, but turns   330
Foul on himself ; then wherfore shund or feard
By us ? who rather double honour gaine
From his surmise prov'd false, finde peace within,
Favour from Heav'n, our witness from th' event.
And what is Faith, Love, Vertue unassaid
Alone, without exterior help sustaind ?
Let us not then suspect our happie State
Left so imperfet by the Maker wise,
As not secure to single or combin'd.

Fraile is our happiness, if this be so,   340
And *Eden* were no *Eden* thus expos'd.
   To whom thus *Adam* fervently repli'd.
O Woman, best are all things as the will
Of God ordain them, his creating hand
Nothing imperfet or deficient left
Of all that he Created, much less Man,
Or ought that might his happie State secure,
Secure from outward force; within himself
The danger lies, yet lies within his power:
Against his will he can receave no harme.   350
But God left free the Will, for what obeyes
Reason, is free, and Reason he made right
But bid her well beware, and still erect,
Least by some faire appeering good surpris'd
She dictate false, and missinforme the Will
To do what God expressly hath forbid.
Not then mistrust, but tender love enjoynes,
That I should mind thee oft, and mind thou me.
Firm we subsist, yet possible to swerve,
Since Reason not impossibly may meet   360
Some specious object by the Foe subornd,
And fall into deception unaware,
Not keeping strictest watch, as she was warnd
Seek not temptation then, which to avoide
Were better, and most likelie if from mee
Thou sever not: Trial will come unsought.
Wouldst thou approve thy constancie, approve
First thy obedience; th' other who can know,
Not seeing thee attempted, who attest?
But if thou think, trial unsought may finde   370
Us both securer then thus warnd thou seemst,
Go; for thy stay, not free, absents thee more;
Go in thy native innocence, relie
On what thou hast of vertue, summon all,
For God towards thee hath done his part, do thine.
   So spake the Patriarch of Mankinde, but *Eve*
Persisted, yet submiss, though last, repli'd.
   With thy permission then, and thus forewarnd
Chiefly by what thy own last reasoning words
Touchd onely, that our trial, when least sought,   380
May finde us both perhaps farr less prepar'd,

The willinger I goe, nor much expect
A Foe so proud will first the weaker seek ;
So bent, the more shall shame him his repulse.
Thus saying, from her Husbands hand her hand
Soft she withdrew, and like a Wood-Nymph light
Oread or *Dryad*, or of *Delia*'s Traine,
Betook her to the Groves, but *Delia*'s self
In gate surpass'd and Goddess-like deport,
Though not as shee with Bow and Quiver armd,   390
But with such Gardning Tools as Art yet rude,
Guiltless of fire had formd, or Angels brought.
To *Pales*, or *Pomona*, thus adornd,
Likest she seemd, *Pomona* when she fled
Vertumnus, or to *Ceres* in her Prime,
Yet Virgin of *Proserpina* from *Jove*.
Her long with ardent look his Eye pursu'd
Delighted, but desiring more her stay.
Oft he to her his charge of quick returne
Repeated, shee to him as oft engag'd   400
To be returnd by Noon amid the Bowre,
And all things in best order to invite
Noontide repast, or Afternoons repose.
O much deceav'd, much failing, hapless *Eve*,
Of thy presum'd return ! event perverse !
Thou never from that houre in Paradise
Foundst either sweet repast, or sound repose ;
Such ambush hid among sweet Flours and Shades
Waited with hellish rancor imminent
To intercept thy way, or send thee back   410
Despoild of Innocence, of Faith, of Bliss.
For now, and since first break of dawne the Fiend.
Meer Serpent in appearance, forth was come,
And on his Quest, where likeliest he might finde
The onely two of Mankinde, but in them
The whole included Race, his purposd prey.
In Bowre and Field he sought, where any tuft
Of Grove or Garden-Plot more pleasant lay,
Thir tendance or Plantation for delight,
By Fountain or by shadie Rivulet   420
He sought them both, but wish'd his hap might find
Eve separate, he wish'd, but not with hope

394 Likest] likeliest *1674*

Of what so seldom chanc'd, when to his wish,
Beyond his hope, *Eve* separate he spies,
Veil'd in a Cloud of Fragrance, where she stood,
Half spi'd, so thick the Roses bushing round
About her glowd, oft stooping to support
Each Flour of slender stalk, whose head though gay
Carnation, Purple, Azure, or spect with Gold,
Hung drooping unsustained, them she upstaies   430
Gently with Mirtle band, mindless the while,
Her self, though fairest unsupported Flour,
From her best prop so farr, and storm so nigh.
Neerer he drew, and many a walk travers'd
Of stateliest Covert, Cedar, Pine, or Palme,
Then voluble and bold, now hid, now seen
Among thick-wov'n Arborets and Flours
Imborderd on each Bank, the hand of *Eve*:
Spot more delicious then those Gardens feign'd
Or of reviv'd *Adonis*, or renownd   440
Alcinous, host of old *Laertes* Son,
Or that, not Mystic, where the Sapient King
Held dalliance with his faire *Egyptian* Spouse.
Much hee the Place admir'd, the Person more.
As one who long in populous City pent,
Where Houses thick and Sewers annoy the Aire,
Forth issuing on a Summers Morn to breathe
Among the pleasant Villages and Farmes
Adjoynd, from each thing met conceaves delight,
The smell of Grain, or tedded Grass, or Kine.   450
Or Dairie, each rural sight, each rural sound ;
If chance with Nymphlike step fair Virgin pass,
What pleasing seemd, for her now pleases more,
She most, and in her looks summs all Delight.
Such Pleasure took the Serpent to behold
This Flourie Plat, the sweet recess of *Eve*
Thus earlie, thus alone ; her Heav'nly forme
Angelic, but more soft, and Feminine,
Her graceful Innocence, her every Aire
Of gesture or lest action overawd   460
His Malice, and with rapine sweet bereav'd
His fierceness of the fierce intent it brought :
That space the Evil one abstracted stood
From his own evil, and for the time remaind

Stupidly good, of enmitie disarm'd,
Of guile, of hate, of envie, of revenge ;
But the hot Hell that alwayes in him burnes,
Though in mid Heav'n, soon ended his delight,
And tortures him now more, the more he sees
Of pleasure not for him ordain'd : then soon   470
Fierce hate he recollects, and all his thoughts
Of mischief, gratulating, thus excites.

    Thoughts, whither have ye led me, with what sweet
Compulsion thus transported to forget
What hither brought us, hate, not love, nor hope
Of Paradise for Hell, hope here to taste
Of pleasure, but all pleasure to destroy,
Save what is in destroying, other joy
To me is lost. Then let me not let pass
Occasion which now smiles, behold alone   480
The Woman, opportune to all attempts,
Her Husband, for I view far round, not nigh,
Whose higher intellectual more I shun,
And strength, of courage hautie, and of limb
Heroic built, though of terrestrial mould,
Foe not informidable, exempt from wound,
I not; so much hath Hell debas'd, and paine
Infeebl'd me, to what I was in Heav'n.
Shee fair, divinely fair, fit Love for Gods,
Not terrible, though terrour be in Love   490
And beautie, not approacht by stronger hate,
Hate stronger, under shew of Love well feign'd,
The way which to her ruin now I tend.

    So spake the Enemie of Mankind, enclos'd
In Serpent, Inmate bad, and toward *Eve*
Address'd his way, not with indented wave,
Prone on the ground, as since, but on his reare,
Circular base of rising foulds, that tour'd
Fould above fould a surging Maze, his Head
Crested aloft, and Carbuncle his Eyes ;   500
With burnisht Neck of verdant Gold, erect
Amidst his circling Spires, that on the grass
Floted redundant : pleasing was his shape,
And lovely, never since of Serpent kind
Lovelier, not those that in *Illyria* chang'd
Hermione and *Cadmus*, or the God

In *Epidaurus*; nor to which transformd
Ammonian Jove, or *Capitoline* was seen,
Hee with *Olympias,* this with her who bore
Scipio the highth of *Rome.* With tract oblique   510
At first, as one who sought access, but feard
To interrupt, side-long he works his way.
As when a Ship by skilful Stearsman wrought
Nigh Rivers mouth or Foreland, where the Wind
Veres oft, as oft so steers, and shifts her Saile;
So varied hee, and of his tortuous Traine
Curld many a wanton wreath in sight of *Eve,*
To lure her Eye; shee busied heard the sound
Of rusling Leaves, but minded not, as us'd
To such disport before her through the Field,   520
From every Beast, more duteous at her call,
Then at *Circean* call the Herd disguis'd.
Hee boulder now, uncall'd before her stood;
But as in gaze admiring: Oft he bowd
His turret Crest, and sleek enamel'd Neck,
Fawning, and lick'd the ground whereon she trod.
His gentle dumb expression turn'd at length
The Eye of *Eve* to mark his play; he glad
Of her attention gaind, with Serpent Tongue
Organic, or impulse of vocal Air,   530
His fraudulent temptation thus began.
    Wonder not, sovran Mistress, if perhaps
Thou canst, who art sole Wonder, much less arm
Thy looks, the Heav'n of mildness, with disdain,
Displeas'd that I approach thee thus, and gaze
Insatiate, I thus single, nor have feard
Thy awful brow, more awful thus retir'd.
Fairest resemblance of thy Maker faire,
Thee all things living gaze on, all things thine
By gift, and thy Celestial Beautie adore   540
With ravishment beheld, there best beheld
Where universally admir'd: but here
In this enclosure wild, these Beasts among,
Beholders rude, and shallow to discerne
Half what in thee is fair, one man except,
Who sees thee? (and what is one?) who shouldst be seen
A Goddess among Gods, ador'd and serv'd
By Angels numberless, thy daily Train.

    So gloz'd the Tempter, and his Proem tun'd;
Into the Heart of *Eve* his words made way,   550
Though at the voice much marveling; at length
Not unamaz'd she thus in answer spake.
What may this mean? Language of Man pronounc't
By Tongue of Brute, and human sense exprest?
The first at lest of these I thought deni'd
To Beasts, whom God on thir Creation-Day
Created mute to all articulat sound;
The latter I demurre, for in thir looks
Much reason, and in thir actions oft appeers.
Thee, Serpent, suttlest beast of all the field   560
I knew, but not with human voice endu'd;
Redouble then this miracle, and say,
How cam'st thou speakable of mute, and how
To me so friendly grown above the rest
Of brutal kind, that daily are in sight?
Say, for such wonder claims attention due.
    To whom the guileful Tempter thus reply'd.
Empress of this fair World, resplendent *Eve*,
Easie to mee it is to tell thee all
What thou commandst and right thou shouldst be obeyd: 570
I was at first as other Beasts that graze
The trodden Herb, of abject thoughts and low,
As was my food, nor aught but food discern'd
Or Sex, and apprehended nothing high:
Till on a day roaving the field, I chanc'd
A goodly Tree farr distant to behold
Loaden with fruit of fairest colours mixt,
Ruddie and Gold: I nearer drew to gaze;
When from the boughes a savorie odour blow'n,
Grateful to appetite, more pleas'd my sense   580
Then smell of sweetest Fenel, or the Teats
Of Ewe or Goat dropping with Milk at Eevn,
Unsuckt of Lamb or Kid, that tend thir play.
To satisfie the sharp desire I had
Of tasting those fair Apples, I resolv'd
Not to deferr; hunger and thirst at once,
Powerful perswaders, quick'nd at the scent
Of that alluring fruit, urg'd me so keene.
About the Mossie Trunk I wound me soon,
For high from ground the branches would require   590

Thy utmost reach or *Adams* : Round the Tree
All other Beasts that saw, with like desire
Longing and envying stood, but could not reach.
Amid the Tree now got, where plentie hung
Tempting so nigh, to pluck and eat my fill
I spar'd not, for such pleasure till that hour
At Feed or Fountain never had I found.
Sated at length, ere long I might perceave
Strange alteration in me, to degree
Of Reason in my inward Powers, and Speech   600
Wanted not long, though to this shape retaind.
Thenceforth to Speculations high or deep
I turnd my thoughts, and with capacious mind
Considerd all things visible in Heav'n,
Or Earth, or Middle, all things fair and good;
But all that fair and good in thy Divine
Semblance, and in thy Beauties heav'nly Ray
United I beheld; no Fair to thine
Equivalent or second, which compel'd
Mee thus, though importune perhaps, to come   610
And gaze, and worship thee of right declar'd
Sovran of Creatures, universal Dame.
  So talk'd the spirited sly Snake ; and *Eve*
Yet more amaz'd unwarie thus reply'd.
  Serpent, thy overpraising leaves in doubt
The vertue of that Fruit, in thee first prov'd :
But say, where grows the Tree, from hence how far?
For many are the Trees of God that grow
In Paradise, and various, yet unknown
To us, in such abundance lies our choice,   620
As leaves a greater store of Fruit untoucht,
Still hanging incorruptible, till men
Grow up to thir provision, and more hands
Help to disburden Nature of her Bearth.
  To whom the wilie Adder, blithe and glad.
Empress, the way is readie, and not long,
Beyond a row of Myrtles, on a Flat,
Fast by a Fountain, one small Thicket past
Of blowing Myrrh and Balme; if thou accept
My conduct, I can bring thee thither soon.   630
  Lead then, said *Eve*. Hee leading swiftly rowld
In tangles, and made intricate seem strait,

Paradise Lost.

To mischief swift. Hope elevates, and joy
Bright'ns his Crest, as when a wandring Fire
Compact of unctuous vapor, which the Night
Condenses, and the cold invirons round,
Kindl'd through agitation to a Flame,
Which oft, they say, some evil Spirit attends,
Hovering and blazing with delusive Light,
Misleads th' amaz'd Night-wanderer from his way   640
To Boggs and Mires, & oft through Pond or Poole,
There swallow'd up and lost, from succour farr.
So glister'd the dire Snake, and into fraud
Led *Eve* our credulous Mother, to the Tree
Of prohibition, root of all our woe;
Which when she saw, thus to her guide she spake.

   Serpent, we might have spar'd our coming hither,
Fruitless to me, though Fruit be here to excess,
The credit of whose vertue rest with thee,
Wondrous indeed, if cause of such effects.   650
But of this Tree we may not taste nor touch;
God so commanded, and left that Command
Sole Daughter of his voice; the rest, we live
Law to our selves, our Reason is our Law.

   To whom the Tempter guilefully repli'd.
Indeed? hath God then said that of the Fruit
Of all these Garden Trees ye shall not eate,
Yet Lords declar'd of all in Earth or Aire?

   To whom thus *Eve* yet sinless. Of the Fruit
Of each Tree in the Garden we may eate,   660
But of the Fruit of this fair Tree amidst
The Garden, God hath said, Ye shall not eate
Thereof, nor shall ye touch it, least ye die.

   She scarse had said, though brief, when now more bold
The Tempter, but with shew of Zeale and Love
To Man, and indignation at his wrong,
New part puts on, and as to passion mov'd,
Fluctuats disturbd, yet comely, and in act
Rais'd, as of som great matter to begin.
As when of old som Orator renound   670
In *Athens* or free *Rome*, where Eloquence
Flourishd, since mute, to som great cause addrest,
Stood in himself collected, while each part,
Motion, each act won audience ere the tongue,

Somtimes in highth began, as no delay
Of Preface brooking through his Zeal of Right.
So standing, moving, or to highth upgrown
The Tempter all impassiond thus began.

O Sacred, Wise, and Wisdom-giving Plant,
Mother of Science, Now I feel thy Power   680
Within me cleere, not onely to discerne
Things in thir Causes, but to trace the wayes
Of highest Agents, deemd however wise.
Queen of this Universe, doe not believe
Those rigid threats of Death; ye shall not Die:
How should ye? by the Fruit? it gives you Life
To Knowledge: By the Threatner? look on mee,
Mee who have touch'd and tasted, yet both live,
And life more perfet have attaind then Fate
Meant mee, by ventring higher then my Lot.   690
Shall that be shut to Man, which to the Beast
Is open? or will God incense his ire
For such a petty Trespass, and not praise
Rather your dauntless vertue, whom the pain
Of Death denounc't, whatever thing Death be,
Deterrd not from atchieving what might leade
To happier life, knowledge of Good and Evil;
Of good, how just? of evil, if what is evil
Be real, why not known, since easier shunnd?
God therefore cannot hurt ye, and be just;   700
Not just, not God; not feard then, nor obeid:
Your feare it self of Death removes the feare.
Why then was this forbid? Why but to awe,
Why but to keep ye low and ignorant,
His worshippers; he knows that in the day
Ye Eate thereof, your Eyes that seem so cleere,
Yet are but dim, shall perfetly be then
Op'nd and cleerd, and ye shall be as Gods,
Knowing both Good and Evil as they know.
That ye should be as Gods, since I as Man,   710
Internal Man, is but proportion meet,
I of brute human, yee of human Gods.
So ye shall die perhaps, by putting off
Human, to put on Gods, death to be wisht,
Though threat'nd, which no worse then this can bring.
And what are Gods that Man may not become

As they, participating God-like food?
The Gods are first, and that advantage use
On our belief, that all from them proceeds;
I question it, for this fair Earth I see,   720
Warm'd by the Sun, producing every kind,
Them nothing: If they all things, who enclos'd
Knowledge of Good and Evil in this Tree,
That whoso eats thereof, forthwith attains
Wisdom without their leave? and wherein lies
Th' offence, that Man should thus attain to know?
What can your knowledge hurt him, or this Tree
Impart against his will if all be his?
Or is it envie, and can envie dwell
In heav'nly brests? these, these and many more   730
Causes import your need of this fair Fruit.
Goddess humane, reach then, and freely taste.

　　He ended, and his words replete with guile
Into her heart too easie entrance won:
Fixt on the Fruit she gaz'd, which to behold
Might tempt alone, and in her ears the sound
Yet rung of his perswasive words, impregn'd
With Reason, to her seeming, and with Truth;
Meanwhile the hour of Noon drew on, and wak'd
An eager appetite, rais'd by the smell   740
So savorie of that Fruit, which with desire,
Inclinable now grown to touch or taste,
Sollicited her longing eye; yet first
Pausing a while, thus to her self she mus'd.

　　Great are thy Vertues, doubtless, best of Fruits,
Though kept from Man, & worthy to be admir'd,
Whose taste, too long forborn, at first assay
Gave elocution to the mute, and taught
The Tongue not made for Speech to speak thy praise:
Thy praise hee also who forbids thy use,   750
Conceales not from us, naming thee the Tree
Of Knowledge, knowledge both of good and evil;
Forbids us then to taste, but his forbidding
Commends thee more, while it inferrs the good
By thee communicated, and our want:
For good unknown, sure is not had, or had
And yet unknown, is as not had at all.
In plain then, what forbids he but to know,

Forbids us good, forbids us to be wise?
Such prohibitions binde not. But if Death 760
Bind us with after-bands, what profits then
Our inward freedom? In the day we eate
Of this fair Fruit, our doom is, we shall die.
How dies the Serpent? hee hath eat'n and lives,
And knows, and speaks, and reasons, and discernes,
Irrational till then. For us alone
Was death invented? or to us deni'd
This intellectual food, for beasts reserv'd?
For Beasts it seems: yet that one Beast which first
Hath tasted, envies not, but brings with joy 770
The good befall'n him, Author unsuspect,
Friendly to man, farr from deceit or guile.
What fear I then, rather what know to feare
Under this ignorance of Good and Evil,
Of God or Death, of Law or Penaltie?
Here grows the Cure of all, this Fruit Divine,
Fair to the Eye, inviting to the Taste,
Of vertue to make wise: what hinders then
To reach, and feed at once both Bodie and Mind?
   So saying, her rash hand in evil hour 780
Forth reaching to the Fruit, she pluck'd, she eat:
Earth felt the wound, and Nature from her seat
Sighing through all her Works gave signs of woe,
That all was lost. Back to the Thicket slunk
The guiltie Serpent, and well might, for *Eve*
Intent now wholly on her taste, naught else
Regarded, such delight till then, as seemd,
In Fruit she never tasted, whether true
Or fansied so, through expectation high
Of knowledg, nor was God-head from her thought. 790
Greedily she ingorg'd without restraint,
And knew not eating Death: Satiate at length,
And hight'nd as with Wine, jocond and boon,
Thus to her self she pleasingly began.
   O Sovran, vertuous, precious of all Trees
In Paradise, of operation blest
To Sapience, hitherto obscur'd, infam'd,
And thy fair Fruit let hang, as to no end
Created; but henceforth my early care,
Not without Song, each Morning, and due praise 800

Shall tend thee, and the fertil burden ease
Of thy full branches offer'd free to all;
Till dieted by thee I grow mature
In knowledge, as the Gods who all things know;
Though others envie what they cannot give;
For had the gift bin theirs, it had not here
Thus grown. Experience, next to thee I owe,
Best guide; not following thee, I had remaind
In ignorance, thou op'nst Wisdoms way,
And giv'st access, though secret she retire.   810
And I perhaps am secret; Heav'n is high,
High and remote to see from thence distinct
Each thing on Earth; and other care perhaps
May have diverted from continual watch
Our great Forbidder, safe with all his Spies
About him. But to *Adam* in what sort
Shall I appeer? shall I to him make known
As yet my change, and give him to partake
Full happiness with mee, or rather not,
But keep the odds of Knowledge in my power   820
Without Copartner? so to add what wants
In Femal Sex, the more to draw his Love,
And render me more equal, and perhaps,
A thing not undesireable, somtime
Superior: for inferior who is free?
This may be well: but what if God have seen
And Death ensue? then I shall be no more,
And *Adam* wedded to another *Eve*,
Shall live with her enjoying, I extinct;
A death to think. Confirm'd then I resolve,   830
Adam shall share with me in bliss or woe:
So dear I love him, that with him all deaths
I could endure, without him live no life.

   So saying, from the Tree her step she turnd,
But first low Reverence don, as to the power
That dwelt within, whose presence had infus'd
Into the plant sciential sap, deriv'd
From Nectar, drink of Gods. *Adam* the while
Waiting desirous her return, had wove
Of choicest Flours a Garland to adorne   840
Her Tresses, and her rural labours crown
As Reapers oft are wont thir Harvest Queen.

Great joy he promis'd to his thoughts, and new
Solace in her return, so long delay'd;
Yet oft his heart, divine of somthing ill,
Misgave him; hee the faultring measure felt;
And forth to meet her went, the way she took
That Morn when first they parted; by the Tree
Of Knowledge he must pass, there he her met,
Scarse from the Tree returning; in her hand   850
A bough of fairest fruit that downie smil'd,
New gatherd, and ambrosial smell diffus'd.
To him she hasted, in her face excuse
Came Prologue, and Apologie to prompt,
Which with bland words at will she thus addrest.

Hast thou not wonderd, *Adam*, at my stay?
Thee I have misst, and thought it long, depriv'd
Thy presence, agonie of love till now
Not felt, nor shall be twice, for never more
Mean I to trie, what rash untri'd I sought,   860
The paine of absence from thy sight. But strange
Hath bin the cause, and wonderful to heare:
This Tree is not as we are told, a Tree
Of danger tasted, nor to evil unknown
Op'ning the way, but of Divine effect
To open Eyes, and make them Gods who taste;
And hath bin tasted such: the Serpent wise,
Or not restraind as wee, or not obeying,
Hath eat'n of the fruit, and is become,
Not dead, as we are threatn'd, but thenceforth   870
Endu'd with human voice and human sense,
Reasoning to admiration, and with mee
Perswasively hath so prevaild, that I
Have also tasted, and have also found
Th' effects to correspond, opener mine Eyes
Dimm erst, dilated Spirits, ampler Heart,
And growing up to Godhead; which for thee
Chiefly I sought, without thee can despise,
For bliss, as thou hast part, to me is bliss,
Tedious, unshar'd with thee, and odious soon.   880
Thou therfore also taste, that equal Lot
May joyne us, equal Joy, as equal Love;
Least thou not tasting, different degree
Disjoyne us, and I then too late renounce

Deitie for thee, when Fate will not permit.
   Thus *Eve* with Countnance blithe her storie told;
But in her Cheek distemper flushing glowd.
On th' other side, *Adam*, soon as he heard
The fatal Trespass done by *Eve*, amaz'd,
Astonied stood and Blank, while horror chill   890
Ran through his veins, and all his joynts relax'd;
From his slack hand the Garland wreath'd for *Eve*
Down drop'd, and all the faded Roses shed:
Speechless he stood and pale, till thus at length
First to himself he inward silence broke.
   O fairest of Creation, last and best
Of all Gods Works, Creature in whom excell'd
Whatever can to sight or thought be formd,
Holy, divine, good, amiable, or sweet!
How art thou lost, how on a sudden lost,   900
Defac't, deflourd, and now to Death devote?
Rather how hast thou yeelded to transgress
The strict forbiddance, how to violate
The sacred Fruit forbidd'n! som cursed fraud
Of Enemie hath beguil'd thee, yet unknown,
And mee with thee hath ruind, for with thee
Certain my resolution is to Die;
How can I live without thee, how forgoe
Thy sweet Converse and Love so dearly joyn'd,
To live again in these wilde Woods forlorn?   910
Should God create another *Eve*, and I
Another Rib afford, yet loss of thee
Would never from my heart; no no, I feel
The Link of Nature draw me: Flesh of Flesh,
Bone of my Bone thou art, and from thy State
Mine never shall be parted, bliss or woe.
   So having said, as one from sad dismay
Recomforted, and after thoughts disturbd
Submitting to what seemd remediless,
Thus in calme mood his Words to *Eve* he turnd.   920
   Bold deed thou hast presum'd, adventrous *Eve*
And peril great provok't, who thus hast dar'd
Had it bin onely coveting to Eye
That sacred Fruit, sacred to abstinence,
Much more to taste it under banne to touch.

        922 hast] hath *1674*

But past who can recall, or don undoe?
Not God Omnipotent, nor Fate, yet so
Perhaps thou shalt not Die, perhaps the Fact
Is not so hainous now, foretasted Fruit,
Profan'd first by the Serpent, by him first   930
Made common and unhallowd ere our taste;
Nor yet on him found deadly, he yet lives,
Lives, as thou saidst, and gaines to live as Man
Higher degree of Life, inducement strong
To us, as likely tasting to attaine
Proportional ascent, which cannot be
But to be Gods, or Angels Demi-gods.
Nor can I think that God, Creator wise,
Though threatning, will in earnest so destroy
Us his prime Creatures, dignifi'd so high,   940
Set over all his Works, which in our Fall,
For us created, needs with us must faile,
Dependent made; so God shall uncreate,
Be frustrate, do, undo, and labour loose,
Not well conceav'd of God, who though his Power
Creation could repeate, yet would be loath
Us to abolish, least the Adversary
Triumph and say; Fickle their State whom God
Most Favors, who can please him long? Mee first
He ruind, now Mankind; whom will he next?   950
Matter of scorne, not to be given the Foe.
However I with thee have fixt my Lot,
Certain to undergoe like doom, if Death
Consort with thee, Death is to mee as Life;
So forcible within my heart I feel
The Bond of Nature draw me to my owne,
My own in thee, for what thou art is mine;
Our State cannot be severd, we are one,
One Flesh; to loose thee were to loose my self.
    So *Adam*, and thus *Eve* to him repli'd.   960
O glorious trial of exceeding Love,
Illustrious evidence, example high!
Ingaging me to emulate, but short
Of thy perfection, how shall I attaine,
Adam, from whose deare side I boast me sprung,
And gladly of our Union heare thee speak,
One Heart, one Soul in both; whereof good prooff

This day affords, declaring thee resolvd,
Rather then Death or aught then Death more dread
Shall separate us, linkt in Love so deare,   970
To undergoe with mee one Guilt, one Crime,
If any be, of tasting this fair Fruit,
Whose vertue, for of good still good proceeds,
Direct, or by occasion hath presented
This happie trial of thy Love, which else
So eminently never had bin known.
Were it I thought Death menac't would ensue
This my attempt, I would sustain alone
The worst, and not perswade thee, rather die
Deserted, then oblige thee with a fact   980
Pernicious to thy Peace, chiefly assur'd
Remarkably so late of thy so true,
So faithful Love unequald; but I feel
Farr otherwise th' event, not Death, but Life
Augmented, op'nd Eyes, new Hopes, new Joyes,
Taste so Divine, that what of sweet before
Hath toucht my sense, flat seems to this, and harsh.
On my experience, *Adam*, freely taste,
And fear of Death deliver to the Windes.

So saying, she embrac'd him, and for joy   990
Tenderly wept, much won that he his Love
Had so enobl'd, as of choice to incurr
Divine displeasure for her sake, or Death.
In recompence (for such compliance bad
Such recompence best merits) from the bough
She gave him of that fair enticing Fruit
With liberal hand : he scrupl'd not to eat
Against his better knowledge, not deceav'd,
But fondly overcome with Femal charm.
Earth trembl'd from her entrails, as again   1000
In pangs, and Nature gave a second groan,
Skie lowr'd, and muttering Thunder, som sad drops
Wept at compleating of the mortal Sin
Original ; while *Adam* took no thought,
Eating his fill, nor *Eve* to iterate
Her former trespass fear'd, the more to soothe
Him with her lov'd societie, that now
As with new Wine intoxicated both
They swim in mirth, and fansie that they feel

Divinitie within them breeding wings 1010
Wherewith to scorn the Earth : but that false Fruit
Farr other operation first displaid,
Carnal desire enflaming, hee on *Eve*
Began to cast lascivious Eyes, she him
As wantonly repaid ; in Lust they burne :
Till *Adam* thus 'gan *Eve* to dalliance move.

    Eve, now I see thou art exact of taste,
And elegant, of Sapience no small part,
Since to each meaning savour we apply,
And Palate call judicious ; I the praise 1020
Yeild thee, so well this day thou hast purvey'd.
Much pleasure we have lost, while we abstain'd
From this delightful Fruit, nor known till now
True relish, tasting ; if such pleasure be
In things to us forbidden, it might be wish'd,
For this one Tree had bin forbidden ten.
But come, so well refresh't, now let us play,
As meet is, after such delicious Fare ;
For never did thy Beautie since the day
I saw thee first and wedded thee, adorn'd 1030
With all perfections, so enflame my sense
With ardor to enjoy thee, fairer now
Than ever, bountie of this vertuous Tree.

    So said he, and forbore not glance or toy
Of amorous intent, well understood
Of *Eve*, whose Eye darted contagious Fire.
Her hand he seis'd, and to a shadie bank,
Thick overhead with verdant roof imbowr'd
He led her nothing loath ; Flours were the Couch,
Pansies, and Violets, and Asphodel, 1040
And Hyacinth, Earths freshest softest lap.
There they thir fill of Love and Loves disport
Took largely, of thir mutual guilt the Seale,
The solace of thir sin, till dewie sleep
Oppress'd them, wearied with thir amorous play.
Soon as the force of that fallacious Fruit,
That with exhilerating vapour bland
About thir spirits had plaid, and inmost powers
Made erre, was now exhal'd, and grosser sleep
Bred of unkindly fumes, with conscious dreams 1050
Encumberd, now had left them, up they rose

As from unrest, and each the other viewing,
Soon found thir Eyes how op'nd, and thir minds
How dark'nd ; innocence, that as a veile
Had shadow'd them from knowing ill, was gon,
Just confidence, and native righteousness,
And honour from about them, naked left
To guiltie shame hee cover'd, but his Robe
Uncover'd more. So rose the *Danite* strong
Herculean Samson from the Harlot-lap   1060
Of *Philistean Dalilah*, and wak'd
Shorn of his strength, They destitute and bare
Of all thir vertue : silent, and in face
Confounded long they sate, as struck'n mute,
Till *Adam*, though not less then *Eve* abasht,
At length gave utterance to these words constraind.

    O *Eve*, in evil hour thou didst give eare
To that false Worm, of whomsoever taught
To counterfet Mans voice, true in our Fall,
False in our promis'd Rising ; since our Eyes   1070
Op'nd we find indeed, and find we know
Both Good and Evil, Good lost, and Evil got,
Bad Fruit of Knowledge, if this be to know,
Which leaves us naked thus, of Honour void,
Of Innocence, of Faith, of Puritie,
Our wonted Ornaments now soild and staind,
And in our Faces evident the signes
Of foul concupiscence ; whence evil store ;
Even shame, the last of evils ; of the first
Be sure then. How shall I behold the face   1080
Henceforth of God or Angel, earst with joy
And rapture so oft beheld ? those heav'nly shapes
Will dazle now this earthly, with thir blaze
Insufferably bright. O might I here
In solitude live savage, in some glade
Obscur'd, where highest Woods impenetrable
To Starr or Sun-light, spread thir umbrage broad,
And brown as Evening : Cover me ye Pines,
Ye Cedars, with innumerable boughs
Hide me, where I may never see them more.   1090
But let us now, as in bad plight, devise
What best may for the present serve to hide
The Parts of each from other, that seem most

        (377)

To shame obnoxious, and unseemliest seen,
Some Tree whose broad smooth Leaves together sowd,
And girded on our loyns, may cover round
Those middle parts, that this new commer, Shame,
There sit not, and reproach us as unclean.
   So counsel'd hee, and both together went
Into the thickest Wood, there soon they chose   1100
The Figtree, not that kind for Fruit renown'd,
But such as at this day to *Indians* known
In *Malabar* or *Decan* spreds her Armes
Braunching so broad and long, that in the ground
The bended Twigs take root, and Daughters grow
About the Mother Tree, a Pillard shade
High overarch't, and echoing Walks between ;
There oft the *Indian* Herdsman shunning heate
Shelters in coole, and tends his pasturing Herds
At Loopholes cut through thickest shade : Those Leaves 1110
They gatherd, broad as *Amazonian* Targe,
And with what skill they had, together sowd,
To gird thir waste, vain Covering if to hide
Thir guilt and dreaded shame ; O how unlike
To that first naked Glorie. Such of late
Columbus found th' *American* so girt
With featherd Cincture, naked else and wilde
Among the Trees on Iles and woodie Shores.
Thus fenc't, and as they thought, thir shame in part
Coverd, but not at rest or ease of Mind,   1120
They sate them down to weep, nor onely Teares
Raind at thir Eyes, but high Winds worse within
Began to rise, high Passions, Anger, Hate,
Mistrust, Suspicion, Discord, and shook sore
Thir inward State of Mind, calme Region once
And full of Peace, now tost and turbulent :
For Understanding rul'd not, and the Will
Heard not her lore, both in subjection now
To sensual Appetite, who from beneathe
Usurping over sovran Reason claimd   1130
Superior sway : From thus distemperd brest,
Adam, estrang'd in look and alterd stile,
Speech intermitted thus to *Eve* renewd.
   Would thou hadst heark'nd to my words, & stai'd
With me, as I besought thee, when that strange

Desire of wandring this unhappie Morn,
I know not whence possessd thee ; we had then
Remaind still happie, not as now, despoild
Of all our good, sham'd, naked, miserable.
Let none henceforth seek needless cause to approve   1140
The Faith they owe ; when earnestly they seek
Such proof, conclude, they then begin to faile.

    To whom soon mov'd with touch of blame thus *Eve*.
What words have past thy Lips, *Adam* severe,
Imput'st thou that to my default, or will
Of wandering, as thou call'st it, which who knows
But might as ill have happ'nd thou being by,
Or to thy self perhaps : hadst thou bin there,
Or here th' attempt, thou could'st not have discernd
Fraud in the Serpent, speaking as he spake ;   1150
No ground of enmitie between us known,
Why hee should mean me ill, or seek to harme.
Was I to have never parted from thy side ?
As good have grown there still a liveless Rib.
Being as I am, why didst not thou the Head
Command me absolutely not to go,
Going into such danger as thou saidst ?
Too facil then thou didst not much gainsay,
Nay, didst permit, approve, and fair dismiss.
Hadst thou bin firm and fixt in thy dissent,   1160
Neither had I transgress'd, nor thou with mee.

    To whom then first incenst *Adam* repli'd.
Is this the Love, is this the recompence
Of mine to thee, ingrateful *Eve*, exprest
Immutable when thou wert lost, not I,
Who might have liv'd and joyd immortal bliss,
Yet willingly chose rather Death with thee :
And am I now upbraided, as the cause
Of thy transgressing ? not enough severe,
It seems, in thy restraint : what could I more ?   1170
I warn'd thee, I admonish'd thee, foretold
The danger, and the lurking Enemie
That lay in wait ; beyond this had bin force,
And force upon free Will hath here no place.
But confidence then bore thee on, secure·
Either to meet no danger, or to finde
Matter of glorious trial ; and perhaps

I also err'd in overmuch admiring
What seemd in thee so perfet, that I thought
No evil durst attempt thee, but I rue   1180
That errour now, which is become my crime,
And thou th' accuser. Thus it shall befall
Him who to worth in Women overtrusting
Lets her Will rule; restraint she will not brook,
And left to her self, if evil thence ensue,
Shee first his weak indulgence will accuse.
  Thus they in mutual accusation spent
The fruitless hours, but neither self-condemning,
And of thir vain contest appeer'd no end.

The End of the Ninth Book.

PARADISE LOST.

BOOK X.

THE ARGUMENT.

Mans *transgression known, the Guardian Angels forsake Paradise, and return up to Heaven to approve thir vigilance, and are approv'd, God declaring that The entrance of* Satan *could not be by them prevented. He sends his Son to judge the Transgressors, who descends and gives Sentence accordingly; then in pity cloaths them both, and reascends.* Sin *and* Death *sitting till then at the Gates of Hell, by wondrous sympathie feeling the success of* Satan *in this new World, and the sin by Man there committed, resolve to sit no longer confin'd in Hell, but to follow* Satan *thir Sire up to the place of Man: To make the way easier from Hell to this World to and fro, they pave a broad Highway or Bridge over* Chaos, *according to the Track that* Satan *first made; then preparing for Earth, they meet him proud of his success returning to Hell; thir mutual gratulation.* Satan *arrives at* Pandemonium, *in full assembly relates with boasting his success against Man; instead of applause is entertained with a general hiss by all his audience, transform'd with himself also suddenly into Serpents, according to his doom giv'n in Paradise; then deluded with a shew of the forbidden Tree springing up before them, they greedily reaching to take of the Fruit, chew dust and bitter ashes. The proceedings of* Sin *and* Death; *God foretels the final Victory of his Son over them, and the renewing of all things; but for the present commands his Angels to make several alterations in the Heavens and Elements.* Adam *more and more perceiving his fall'n condition heavily bewailes, rejects the condolement of* Eve; *she persists and at length appeases him: then to evade the Curse likely to fall on thir Ofspring, proposes to* Adam *violent wayes, which he approves not, but conceiving better hope, puts her in mind of the late Promise made them, that her Seed should be reveng'd on the Serpent, and exhorts her with him to seek Peace of the offended Deity, by repentance and supplication.*

(381)

MEANWHILE the hainous and despightfull act
Of *Satan* done in Paradise, and how
Hee in the Serpent had perverted *Eve,*
Her Husband shee, to taste the fatall fruit,
Was known in Heav'n; for what can scape the Eye
Of God All-seeing, or deceave his Heart
Omniscient, who in all things wise and just,
Hinder'd not *Satan* to attempt the minde
Of Man, with strength entire, and free Will arm'd,
Complete to have discover'd and repulst   10
Whatever wiles of Foe or seeming Friend.
For still they knew, and ought to have still remember'd
The high Injunction not to taste that Fruit,
Whoever tempted; which they not obeying,
Incurr'd, what could they less, the penaltie,
And manifold in sin, deserv'd to fall.
Up into Heav'n from Paradise in hast
Th' Angelic Guards ascended, mute and sad
For Man, for of his state by this they knew,
Much wondring how the suttle Fiend had stoln   20
Entrance unseen. Soon as th' unwelcome news
From Earth arriv'd at Heaven Gate, displeas'd
All were who heard, dim sadness did not spare
That time Celestial visages, yet mixt
With pitie, violated not thir bliss.
About the new-arriv'd, in multitudes
Th' ethereal People ran, to hear and know
How all befell: they towards the Throne Supream
Accountable made haste to make appear
With righteous plea, thir utmost vigilance,   30
And easily approv'd; when the most High
Eternal Father from his secret Cloud,
Amidst in Thunder utter'd thus his voice.
Assembl'd Angels, and ye Powers return'd
From unsuccessful charge, be not dismaid,
Nor troubl'd at these tidings from the Earth,
Which your sincerest care could not prevent,
Foretold so lately what would come to pass,
When first this Tempter cross'd the Gulf from Hell
I told ye then he should prevail and speed   40
On his bad Errand, Man should be seduc't
And flatter'd out of all, believing lies

Against his Maker; no Decree of mine
Concurring to necessitate his Fall,
Or touch with lightest moment of impulse
His free Will, to her own inclining left
In even scale. But fall'n he is, and now
What rests, but that the mortal Sentence pass
On his transgression, Death denounc't that day,
Which he presumes already vain and void,   50
Because not yet inflicted, as he fear'd,
By some immediate stroak; but soon shall find
Forbearance no acquittance ere day end.
Justice shall not return as bountie scorn'd.
But whom send I to judge them? whom but thee
Vicegerent Son, to thee I have transferr'd
All Judgement, whether in Heav'n, or Earth, or Hell.
Easie it may be seen that I intend
Mercie collegue with Justice, sending thee
Mans Friend, his Mediator, his design'd   60
Both Ransom and Redeemer voluntarie,
And destin'd Man himself to judge Man fall'n.
    So spake the Father, and unfoulding bright
Toward the right hand his Glorie, on the Son
Blaz'd forth unclouded Deitie; he full
Resplendent all his Father manifest
Express'd, and thus divinely answer'd milde.
    Father Eternal, thine is to decree,
Mine both in Heav'n and Earth to do thy will
Supream, that thou in mee thy Son belov'd   70
Mayst ever rest well pleas'd. I go to judge
On Earth these thy transgressors, but thou knowst,
Whoever judg'd, the worst on mee must light,
When time shall be, for so I undertook
Before thee; and not repenting, this obtaine
Of right, that I may mitigate thir doom
On me deriv'd, yet I shall temper so
Justice with Mercie, as may illustrate most
Them fully satisfied, and thee appease.
Attendance none shall need, nor Train, where none   80
Are to behold the Judgement, but the judg'd,
Those two; the third best absent is condemn'd,
Convict by flight, and Rebel to all Law

58 may] might *1674*

(383)

Conviction to the Serpent none belongs.
   Thus saying, from his radiant Seat he rose
Of high collateral glorie: him Thrones and Powers,
Princedoms, and Dominations ministrant
Accompanied to Heaven Gate, from whence
Eden and all the Coast in prospect lay.
Down he descended strait; the speed of Gods   90
Time counts not, though with swiftest minutes wing'd.
Now was the Sun in Western cadence low
From Noon, and gentle Aires due at thir hour
To fan the Earth now wak'd, and usher in
The Eevning coole when he from wrauth more coole
Came the mild Judge and Intercessor both
To sentence Man: the voice of God they heard
Now walking in the Garden, by soft windes
Brought to thir Ears, while day declin'd, they heard
And from his presence hid themselves among   100
The thickest Trees, both Man and Wife, till God
Approaching, thus to *Adam* call'd aloud.
   Where art thou *Adam*, wont with joy to meet
My coming seen far off? I miss thee here,
Not pleas'd, thus entertaind with solitude,
Where obvious dutie erewhile appear'd unsaught:
Or come I less conspicuous, or what change
Absents thee, or what chance detains? Come forth.
He came, and with him *Eve*, more loth, though first
To offend, discount'nanc't both, and discompos'd;   110
Love was not in thir looks, either to God
Or to each other, but apparent guilt,
And shame, and perturbation, and despaire,
Anger, and obstinacie, and hate, and guile.
Whence *Adam* faultring long, thus answer'd brief.
   I heard thee in the Garden, and of thy voice
Affraid, being naked, hid my self. To whom
The gracious Judge without revile repli'd.
   My voice thou oft hast heard, and hast not fear'd,
But still rejoyc't, how is it now become   120
So dreadful to thee? that thou art naked, who
Hath told thee? hast thou eaten of the Tree
Whereof I gave thee charge thou shouldst not eat?
   To whom thus *Adam* sore beset repli'd.
O Heav'n! in evil strait this day I stand

Before my Judge, either to undergoe
My self the total Crime, or to accuse
My other self, the partner of my life;
Whose failing, while her Faith to me remaines,
I should conceal, and not expose to blame   130
By my complaint; but strict necessitie
Subdues me, and calamitous constraint,
Least on my head both sin and punishment,
However insupportable, be all
Devolv'd; though should I hold my peace, yet thou
Wouldst easily detect what I conceale.
This Woman whom thou mad'st to be my help,
And gav'st me as thy perfet gift, so good,
So fit, so acceptable, so Divine,
That from her hand I could suspect no ill,   140
And what she did, whatever in it self,
Her doing seem'd to justifie the deed;
Shee gave me of the Tree, and I did eate.
    To whom the sovran Presence thus repli'd.
Was shee thy God, that her thou didst obey
Before his voice, or was shee made thy guide,
Superior, or but equal, that to her
Thou did'st resigne thy Manhood, and the Place
Wherein God set thee above her made of thee,
And for thee, whose perfection farr excell'd   150
Hers in all real dignitie: Adornd
She was indeed, and lovely to attract
Thy Love, not thy Subjection, and her Gifts
Were such as under Government well seem'd,
Unseemly to beare rule, which was thy part
And person, had'st thou known thy self aright.
    So having said, he thus to *Eve* in few:
Say Woman, what is this which thou hast done?
    To whom sad *Eve* with shame nigh overwhelm'd,
Confessing soon, yet not before her Judge   160
Bold or loquacious, thus abasht repli'd.
    The Serpent me beguil'd and I did eate.
    Which when the Lord God heard, without delay
To Judgement he proceeded on th' accus'd
Serpent though brute, unable to transferre
The Guilt on him who made him instrument
Of mischief, and polluted from the end

(385)   o

Of his Creation; justly then accurst,
As vitiated in Nature: more to know
Concern'd not Man (since he no further knew)   170
Nor alter'd his offence; yet God at last
To Satan first in sin his doom apply'd
Though in mysterious terms, judg'd as then best:
And on the Serpent thus his curse let fall.

Because thou hast done this, thou art accurst
Above all Cattel, each Beast of the Field;
Upon thy Belly groveling thou shalt goe,
And dust shalt eat all the days of thy Life.
Between Thee and the Woman I will put
Enmitie, and between thine and her Seed;   180
Her Seed shall bruise thy head, thou bruise his heel.

So spake this Oracle, then verifi'd
When *Jesus* son of *Mary* second *Eve*,
Saw Satan fall like Lightning down from Heav'n,
Prince of the Aire; then rising from his Grave
Spoild Principalities and Powers, triumpht
In open shew, and with ascension bright
Captivity led captive through the Aire,
The Realme it self of Satan long usurpt,
Whom he shall tread at last under our feet;   190
Eevn hee who now foretold his fatal bruise,
And to the Woman thus his Sentence turn'd.

Thy sorrow I will greatly multiplie
By thy Conception; Childern thou shalt bring
In sorrow forth, and to thy Husbands will
Thine shall submit, hee over thee shall rule.

On *Adam* last thus judgement he pronounc'd.
Because thou hast heark'nd to the voice of thy Wife,
And eaten of the Tree concerning which
I charg'd thee, saying: Thou shalt not eate thereof,   200
Curs'd is the ground for thy sake, thou in sorrow
Shalt eate thereof all the days of thy Life;
Thornes also and Thistles it shall bring thee forth
Unbid, and thou shalt eate th' Herb of th' Field,
In the sweat of thy Face shalt thou eate Bread,
Till thou return unto the ground, for thou
Out of the ground wast taken, know thy Birth,
For dust thou art, and shalt to dust returne.

So judg'd he Man, both Judge and Saviour sent,

And th' instant stroke of Death denounc't that day   210
Remov'd farr off; then pittying how they stood
Before him naked to the aire, that now
Must suffer change, disdain'd not to begin
Thenceforth the forme of servant to assume,
As when he wash'd his servants feet, so now
As Father of his Familie he clad
Thir nakedness with Skins of Beasts, or slain,
Or as the Snake with youthful Coate repaid;
And thought not much to cloath his Enemies:
Nor hee thir outward onely with the Skins   220
Of Beasts, but inward nakedness, much more
Opprobrious, with his Robe of righteousness,
Araying cover'd from his Fathers sight.
To him with swift ascent he up return'd,
Into his blissful bosom reassum'd
In glory as of old, to him appeas'd
All, though all-knowing, what had past with Man
Recounted, mixing intercession sweet.
Meanwhile ere thus was sin'd and judg'd on Earth,
Within the Gates of Hell sate Sin and Death,   230
In counterview within the Gates, that now
Stood open wide, belching outrageous flame
Farr into *Chaos*, since the Fiend pass'd through,
Sin opening, who thus now to Death began.
   O Son, why sit we here each other viewing
Idlely, while Satan our great Author thrives
In other Worlds, and happier Seat provides
For us his ofspring deare? It cannot be
But that success attends him; if mishap,
Ere this he had return'd, with fury driv'n   240
By his Avenger, since no place like this
Can fit his punishment, or their revenge.
Methinks I feel new strength within me rise,
Wings growing, and Dominion giv'n me large
Beyond this Deep; whatever drawes me on,
Or sympathie, or som connatural force
Powerful at greatest distance to unite
With secret amity things of like kinde
By secretest conveyance. Thou my Shade
Inseparable must with mee along: 250

241 Avenger] Avengers *1674*

(387)

For Death from Sin no power can separate.
But least the difficultie of passing back
Stay his returne perhaps over this Gulfe
Impassable, impervious, let us try
Adventrous work, yet to thy power and mine
Not unagreeable, to found a path
Over this Maine from Hell to that new World
Where Satan now prevailes, a Monument
Of merit high to all th' infernal Host,
Easing thir passage hence, for intercourse,   260
Or transmigration, as thir lot shall lead.
Nor can I miss the way, so strongly drawn
By this new felt attraction and instinct.
   Whom thus the meager Shadow answerd soon.
Goe whither Fate and inclination strong
Leads thee, I shall not lag behinde, nor erre
The way, thou leading, such a sent I draw
Of carnage, prey innumerable, and taste
The savour of Death from all things there that live:
Nor shall I to the work thou enterprisest   270
Be wanting, but afford thee equal aid.
   So saying, with delight he snuff'd the smell
Of mortal change on Earth. As when a flock
Of ravenous Fowl, though many a League remote,
Against the day of Battel, to a Field,
Where Armies lie encampt, come flying, lur'd
With sent of living Carcasses design'd
For death, the following day, in bloodie fight.
So sented the grim Feature, and upturn'd
His Nostril wide into the murkie Air,   280
Sagacious of his Quarrey from so farr.
Then Both from out Hell Gates into the waste
Wide Anarchie of *Chaos* damp and dark
Flew divers, & with Power (thir Power was great)
Hovering upon the Waters; what they met
Solid or slimie, as in raging Sea
Tost up and down, together crowded drove
From each side shoaling towards the mouth of Hell.
As when two Polar Winds blowing adverse
Upon the *Cronian* Sea, together drive   290
Mountains of Ice, that stop th' imagin'd way
Beyond *Petsora* Eastward, to the rich

Cathaian Coast. The aggregated Soyle
Death with his Mace petrific, cold and dry,
As with a Trident smote, and fix't as firm
As *Delos* floating once; the rest his look
Bound with *Gorgonian* rigor not to move,
And with *Asphaltic* slime; broad as the Gate,
Deep to the Roots of Hell the gather'd beach
They fasten'd, and the Mole immense wraught on   300
Over the foaming deep high Archt, a Bridge
Of length prodigious joyning to the Wall
Immoveable of this now fenceless world
Forfeit to Death; from hence a passage broad,
Smooth, easie, inoffensive down to Hell.
So, if great things to small may be compar'd,
Xerxes, the Libertie of *Greece* to yoke,
From *Susa* his *Memnonian* Palace high
Came to the Sea, and over *Hellespont*
Bridging his way, *Europe* with *Asia* joyn'd,   310
And scourg'd with many a stroak th' indignant waves.
Now had they brought the work by wondrous Art
Pontifical, a ridge of pendent Rock
Over the vext Abyss, following the track
Of *Satan*, to the self same place where hee
First lighted from his Wing, and landed safe
From out of *Chaos* to the outside bare
Of this round World: with Pinns of Adamant
And Chains they made all fast, too fast they made
And durable; and now in little space   320
The Confines met of Empyrean Heav'n
And of this World, and on the left hand Hell
With long reach interpos'd; three sev'ral wayes
In sight, to each of these three places led.
And now thir way to Earth they had descri'd,
To Paradise first tending, when behold
Satan in likeness of an Angel bright
Betwixt the *Centaure* and the *Scorpion* stearing
His *Zenith*, while the Sun in *Aries* rose:
Disguis'd he came, but those his Childern dear   330
Thir Parent soon discern'd, though in disguise.
Hee, after *Eve* seduc't, unminded slunk
Into the Wood fast by, and changing shape
To observe the sequel, saw his guileful act

By *Eve*, though all unweeting, seconded
Upon her Husband, saw thir shame that sought
Vain covertures ; but when he saw descend
The Son of God to judge them, terrifi'd
Hee fled, not hoping to escape, but shun
The present, fearing guiltie what his wrauth   340
Might suddenly inflict ; that past, return'd
By Night, and listning where the hapless Paire
Sate in thir sad discourse, and various plaint,
Thence gatherd his own doom, which understood
Not instant, but of future time. With joy
And tidings fraught, to Hell he now return'd,
And at the brink of *Chaos*, neer the foot
Of this new wondrous Pontifice, unhop't
Met who to meet him came, his Ofspring dear.
Great joy was at thir meeting, and at sight   350
Of that stupendious Bridge his joy encreas'd.
Long hee admiring stood, till Sin, his faire
Inchanting Daughter, thus the silence broke.
     O Parent, these are thy magnific deeds,
Thy Trophies, which thou view'st as not thine own,
Thou art thir Author and prime Architect :
For I no sooner in my Heart divin'd,
My Heart, which by a secret harmonie
Still moves with thine, joyn'd in connexion sweet,
That thou on Earth hadst prosper'd, which thy looks 360
Now also evidence, but straight I felt
Though distant from thee Worlds between, yet felt
That I must after thee with this thy Son ;
Such fatal consequence unites us three :
Hell could no longer hold us in her bounds,
Nor this unvoyageable Gulf obscure
Detain from following thy illustrious track.
Thou hast atchiev'd our libertie, confin'd
Within Hell Gates till now, thou us impow'rd
To fortifie thus farr, and overlay   370
With this portentous Bridge the dark Abyss.
Thine now is all this World, thy vertue hath won
What thy hands builded not, thy Wisdom gain'd
With odds what Warr hath lost, and fully aveng'd
Our foile in Heav'n ; here thou shalt Monarch reign,
There didst not ; there let him still Victor sway,

As Battel hath adjudg'd, from this new World
Retiring, by his own doom alienated,
And henceforth Monarchie with thee divide
Of all things, parted by th' Empyreal bounds,   380
His Quadrature, from thy Orbicular World,
Or trie thee now more dang'rous to his Throne.
    Whom thus the Prince of Darkness answerd glad.
Fair Daughter, and thou Son and Grandchild both,
High proof ye now have giv'n to be the Race
Of *Satan* (for I glorie in the name,
Antagonist of Heav'ns Almightie King)
Amply have merited of me, of all
Th' Infernal Empire, that so neer Heav'ns dore
Triumphal with triumphal act have met,   390
Mine with this glorious Work, & made one Realm
Hell and this World, one Realm, one Continent
Of easie thorough-fare.   Therefore while I
Descend through Darkness, on your Rode with ease
To my associate Powers, them to acquaint
With these successes, and with them rejoyce,
You two this way, among those numerous Orbs
All yours, right down to Paradise descend;
There dwell & Reign in bliss, thence on the Earth
Dominion exercise and in the Aire,   400
Chiefly on Man, sole Lord of all declar'd,
Him first make sure your thrall, and lastly kill.
My Substitutes I send ye, and Create
Plenipotent on Earth, of matchless might
Issuing from mee : on your joynt vigor now
My hold of this new Kingdom all depends,
Through Sin to Death expos'd by my exploit.
If your joynt power prevaile, th' affaires of Hell
No detriment need feare, goe and be strong.
    So saying he dismiss'd them, they with speed   410
Thir course through thickest Constellations held
Spreading thir bane; the blasted Starrs lookt wan,
And Planets, Planet-strook, real Eclips
Then sufferd.   Th' other way *Satan* went down
The Causey to Hell Gate ; on either side
Disparted *Chaos* over built exclaimd,
And with rebounding surge the barrs assaild,

                    397 those] these *1674*

    (391)

That scorn'd his indignation : through the Gate,
Wide open and unguarded, *Satan* pass'd,
And all about found desolate ; for those   420
Appointed to sit there, had left thir charge,
Flown to the upper World ; the rest were all
Farr to the inland retir'd, about the walls
Of *Pandæmonium,* Citie and proud seate
Of *Lucifer,* so by allusion calld,
Of that bright Starr to *Satan* paragond.
There kept thir Watch the Legions, while the Grand
In Council sate, sollicitous what chance
Might intercept thir Emperour sent, so hee
Departing gave command, and they observ'd.   430
As when the *Tartar* from his *Russian* Foe
By *Astracan* over the Snowie Plaines
Retires, or *Bactrian* Sophi from the hornes
Of *Turkish* Crescent, leaves all waste beyond
The Realme of *Aladule,* in his retreate
To *Tauris* or *Casbeen.* So these the late
Heav'n-banisht Host, left desert utmost Hell
Many a dark League, reduc't in careful Watch
Round thir Metropolis, and now expecting
Each hour thir great adventurer from the search   440
Of Forrein Worlds : he through the midst unmarkt,
In shew plebeian Angel militant
Of lowest order, past ; and from the dore
Of that *Plutonian* Hall, invisible
Ascended his high Throne, which under state
Of richest texture spred, at th' upper end
Was plac't in regal lustre. Down a while
He sate, and round about him saw unseen :
At last as from a Cloud his fulgent head
And shape Starr-bright appeer'd, or brighter, clad   450
With what permissive glory since his fall
Was left him, or false glitter : All amaz'd
At that so sudden blaze the *Stygian* throng
Bent thir aspect, and whom they wish'd beheld,
Thir mighty Chief returnd : loud was th' acclaime :
Forth rush'd in haste the great consulting Peers,
Rais'd from thir dark *Divan,* and with like joy
Congratulant approach'd him, who with hand
Silence, and with these words attention won.

Thrones, Dominations, Princedoms, Vertues, Powers, 460
For in possession such, not onely of right,
I call ye and declare ye now, returnd
Successful beyond hope, to lead ye forth
Triumphant out of this infernal Pit
Abominable, accurst, the house of woe,
And Dungeon of our Tyrant: Now possess,
As Lords, a spacious World, to our native Heaven
Little inferiour, by my adventure hard
With peril great atchiev'd. Long were to tell
What I have don, what sufferd, with what paine   470
Voyag'd th' unreal, vast, unbounded deep
Of horrible confusion, over which
By Sin and Death a broad way now is pav'd
To expedite your glorious march; but I
Toild out my uncouth passage, forc't to ride
Th' untractable Abysse, plung'd in the womb
Of unoriginal *Night* and *Chaos* wilde,
That jealous of thir secrets fiercely oppos'd
My journey strange, with clamorous uproare
Protesting Fate supreame; thence how I found   480
The new created World, which fame in Heav'n
Long had foretold, a Fabrick wonderful
Of absolute perfection, therein Man
Plac't in a Paradise, by our exile
Made happie: Him by fraud I have seduc'd
From his Creator, and the more to increase
Your wonder, with an Apple; he thereat
Offended, worth your laughter, hath giv'n up
Both his beloved Man and all his World,
To Sin and Death a prey, and so to us,   490
Without our hazard, labour, or allarme,
To range in, and to dwell, and over Man,
To rule, as over all he should have rul'd.
True is, mee also he hath judg'd, or rather
Mee not, but the brute Serpent in whose shape
Man I deceav'd: that which to mee belongs,
Is enmity, which he will put between
Mee and Mankinde; I am to bruise his heel;
His Seed, when is not set, shall bruise my head:
A World who would not purchase with a bruise,   500
Or much more grievous pain? Ye have th' account

(393)

Of my performance: What remaines, ye Gods,
But up and enter now into full bliss.
  So having said, a while he stood, expecting
Thir universal shout and high applause
To fill his eare, when contrary he hears
On all sides, from innumerable tongues
A dismal universal hiss, the sound
Of public scorn; he wonderd, but not long
Had leasure, wondring at himself now more;   510
His Visage drawn he felt to sharp and spare,
His Armes clung to his Ribs, his Leggs entwining
Each other, till supplanted down he fell
A monstrous Serpent on his Belly prone,
Reluctant, but in vaine, a greater power
Now rul'd him, punisht in the shape he sin'd,
According to his doom: he would have spoke,
But hiss for hiss returnd with forked tongue
To forked tongue, for now were all transform'd
Alike, to Serpents all as accessories   520
To his bold Riot: dreadful was the din
Of hissing through the Hall, thick swarming now
With complicated monsters, head and taile,
Scorpion and Asp, and *Amphisbæna* dire,
Cerastes hornd, *Hydrus*, and *Ellops* drear,
And *Dipsas* (Not so thick swarm'd once the Soil
Bedropt with blood of *Gorgon*, or the Isle
Ophiusa) but still greatest hee the midst,
Now Dragon grown, larger then whom the Sun
Ingenderd in the *Pythian* Vale on slime,   530
Huge *Python*, and his Power no less he seem'd
Above the rest still to retain; they all
Him follow'd issuing forth to th' open Field,
Where all yet left of that revolted Rout
Heav'n-fall'n, in station stood or just array,
Sublime with expectation when to see
In Triumph issuing forth thir glorious Chief;
They saw, but other sight instead, a crowd
Of ugly Serpents; horror on them fell,
And horrid sympathie; for what they saw,   540
They felt themselvs now changing; down thir arms,
Down fell both Spear and Shield, down they as fast,
And the dire hiss renew'd, and the dire form

Catcht by Contagion, like in punishment,
As in thir crime. Thus was th' applause they meant,
Turnd to exploding hiss, triumph to shame
Cast on themselves from thir own mouths. There stood
A Grove hard by, sprung up with this thir change,
His will who reigns above, to aggravate
Thir penance, laden with fair Fruit, like that   550
Which grew in Paradise, the bait of *Eve*
Us'd by the Tempter : on that prospect strange
Thir earnest eyes they fix'd, imagining
For one forbidden Tree a multitude
Now ris'n, to work them furder woe or shame ;
Yet parcht with scalding thurst and hunger fierce,
Though to delude them sent, could not abstain,
But on they rould in heaps, and up the Trees
Climbing, sat thicker than the snakie locks
That curld *Megæra* : greedily they pluck'd   560
The Frutage fair to sight, like that which grew
Neer that bituminous Lake where *Sodom* flam'd ;
This more delusive, not the touch, but taste
Deceav'd ; they fondly thinking to allay
Thir appetite with gust, instead of Fruit
Chewd bitter Ashes, which th' offended taste
With spattering noise rejected : oft they assayd,
Hunger and thirst constraining, drugd as oft,
With hatefullest disrelish writh'd thir jaws
With soot and cinders fill'd ; so oft they fell   570
Into the same illusion, not as Man
Whom they triumph'd once lapst. Thus were they plagu'd
And worn with Famin, long and ceasless hiss,
Till thir lost shape, permitted, they resum'd,
Yearly enjoynd, some say, to undergo
This annual humbling certain number'd days,
To dash thir pride, and joy for Man seduc't.
However some tradition they dispers'd
Among the Heathen of thir purchase got,
And Fabl'd how the Serpent, whom they calld   580
Ophion with *Eurynome*, the wide-
Encroaching *Eve* perhaps, had first the rule
Of high *Olympus*, thence by *Saturn* driv'n
And *Ops*, ere yet *Dictæan Jove* was born.
Mean while in Paradise the hellish pair

Too soon arriv'd, *Sin* there in power before,
Once actual, now in body, and to dwell
Habitual habitant; behind her *Death*
Close following pace for pace, not mounted yet
On his pale Horse: to whom *Sin* thus began.   590
 Second of *Satan* sprung, all conquering *Death*,
What thinkst thou of our Empire now, though earnd
With travail difficult, not better farr
Then stil at Hels dark threshold to have sate watch,
Unnam'd, undreaded, and thy self half starv'd?
 Whom thus the Sin-born Monster answerd soon.
To mee, who with eternal Famin pine,
Alike is Hell, or Paradise, or Heaven,
There best, where most with ravin I may meet;
Which here, though plenteous, all too little seems   600
To stuff this Maw, this vast unhide-bound Corps.
 To whom th' incestuous Mother thus repli'd.
Thou therefore on these Herbs, and Fruits, & Flours
Feed first, on each Beast next, and Fish, and Fowle,
No homely morsels, and whatever thing
The Sithe of Time mowes down, devour unspar'd,
Till I in Man residing through the Race,
His thoughts, his looks, words, actions all infect,
And season him thy last and sweetest prey.
 This said, they both betook them several wayes,   610
Both to destroy, or unimmortal make
All kinds, and for destruction to mature
Sooner or later; which th' Almightie seeing
From his transcendent Seat the Saints among,
To those bright Orders uttered thus his voice.
 See with what heat these Dogs of Hell advance
To waste and havoc yonder World, which I
So fair and good created, and had still
Kept in that state, had not the folly of Man
Let in these wastful Furies, who impute   620
Folly to mee, so doth the Prince of Hell
And his Adherents, that with so much ease
I suffer them to enter and possess
A place so heav'nly, and conniving seem
To gratifie my scornful Enemies,
That laugh, as if transported with some fit
Of Passion, I to them had quitted all,

At random yeilded up to their misrule;
And know not that I call'd and drew them thither
My Hell-hounds, to lick up the draff and filth   630
Which mans polluting Sin with taint hath shed
On what was pure, till cramm'd and gorg'd, nigh burst
With suckt and glutted offal, at one sling
Of thy victorious Arm, well-pleasing Son,
Both *Sin*, and *Death*, and yawning *Grave* at last
Through *Chaos* hurld, obstruct the mouth of Hell
For ever, and seal up his ravenous Jawes.
Then Heav'n and Earth renewd shall be made pure
To sanctitie that shall receive no staine:
Till then the Curse pronounc't on both precedes.   640
    Hee ended, and the heav'nly Audience loud
Sung *Halleluia*, as the sound of Seas,
Through multitude that sung: Just are thy ways,
Righteous are thy Decrees on all thy Works;
Who can extenuate thee ? Next, to the Son,
Destin'd restorer of Mankind, by whom
New Heav'n and Earth shall to the Ages rise,
Or down from Heav'n descend. Such was thir song,
While the Creator calling forth by name
His mightie Angels gave them several charge,   650
As sorted best with present things. The Sun
Had first his precept so to move, so shine,
As might affect the Earth with cold and heat
Scarce tollerable, and from the North to call
Decrepit Winter, from the South to bring
Solstitial summers heat. To the blanc Moone
Her office they prescrib'd, to th' other five
Thir planetarie motions and aspects
In *Sextile*, *Square*, and *Trine*, and *Opposite*,
Of noxious efficacie, and when to joyne   660
In Synod unbenigne, and taught the fixt
Thir influence malignant when to showre,
Which of them rising with the Sun, or falling,
Should prove tempestuous: To the Winds they set
Thir corners, when with bluster to confound
Sea, Aire, and Shoar, the Thunder when to rowle
With terror through the dark Aereal Hall.
Some say he bid his Angels turne ascanse
The Poles of Earth twice ten degrees and more

From the Suns Axle; they with labour push'd   670
Oblique the Centric Globe : Som say the Sun
Was bid turn Reines from th' Equinoctial Rode
Like distant breadth to *Taurus* with the Seav'n
Atlantick Sisters, and the *Spartan* Twins
Up to the *Tropic* Crab ; thence down amaine
By *Leo* and the *Virgin* and the *Scales*,
As deep as *Capricorne*, to bring in change
Of Seasons to each Clime ; else had the Spring
Perpetual smil'd on Earth with vernant Flours,
Equal in Days and Nights, except to those   680
Beyond the Polar Circles ; to them Day
Had unbenighted shon, while the low Sun
To recompence his distance, in thir sight
Had rounded still th' *Horizon*, and not known
Or East or West, which had forbid the Snow
From cold *Estotiland*, and South as farr
Bcneath *Magellan*. At that tasted Fruit
The Sun, as from *Thyestean* Banquet, turn'd
His course intended ; else how had the World
Inhabited, though sinless, more then now,   690
Avoided pinching cold and scorching heate ?
These changes in the Heav'ns, though slow, produc'd
Like change on Sea and Land, sideral blast,
Vapour, and Mist, and Exhalation hot,
Corrupt and Pestilent : Now from the North
Of *Norumbega*, and the *Samoed* shoar
Bursting thir brazen Dungeon, armd with ice
And snow and haile and stormie gust and flaw,
Boreas and *Cœcias* and *Argestes* loud
And *Thrascias* rend the Woods and Seas upturn ;   700
With adverse blast up-turns them from the South
Notus and *Afer* black with thundrous Clouds
From *Serraliona* ; thwart of these as fierce
Forth rush the *Levant* and the *Ponent* Windes
Eurus and *Zephir* with thir lateral noise,
Sirocco, and *Libecchio*. Thus began
Outrage from liveless things ; but Discord first
Daughter of Sin, among th' irrational,
Death introduc'd through fierce antipathie :
Beast now with Beast gan war, & Fowle with Fowle,   710
And Fish with Fish ; to graze the Herb all leaving,

Devourd each other; nor stood much in awe
Of Man, but fled him, or with count'nance grim
Glar'd on him passing: these were from without
The growing miseries, which *Adam* saw
Alreadie in part, though hid in gloomiest shade,
To sorrow abandond, but worse felt within,
And in a troubl'd Sea of passion tost,
Thus to disburd'n sought with sad complaint.

    O miserable of happie! is this the end   720
Of this new glorious World, and mee so late
The Glory of that Glory, who now becom
Accurst of blessed, hide me from the face
Of God, whom to behold was then my highth
Of happiness: yet well, if here would end
The miserie, I deserv'd it, and would beare
My own deservings; but this will not serve;
All that I eate or drink, or shall beget,
Is propagated curse. O voice once heard
Delightfully, *Encrease and multiply*,   730
Now death to heare! for what can I encrease
Or multiplie, but curses on my head?
Who of all Ages to succeed, but feeling
The evil on him brought by me, will curse
My Head, Ill fare our Ancestor impure,
For this we may thank *Adam*; but his thanks
Shall be the execration; so besides
Mine own that bide upon mee, all from mee
Shall with a fierce reflux on mee redound,
On mee as on thir natural center light   740
Heavie, though in thir place. O fleeting joyes
Of Paradise, deare bought with lasting woes!
Did I request thee, Maker, from my Clay
To mould me Man, did I sollicite thee
From darkness to promote me, or here place
In this delicious Garden? as my Will
Concurd not to my being, it were but right
And equal to reduce me to my dust,
Desirous to resigne, and render back
All I receav'd, unable to performe   750
Thy terms too hard, by which I was to hold
The good I sought not. To the loss of that,
Sufficient penaltie, why hast thou added

The sense of endless woes? inexplicable
Thy Justice seems; yet to say truth, too late,
I thus contest; then should have been refusd
Those terms whatever, when they were propos'd:
Thou didst accept them; wilt thou enjoy the good,
Then cavil the conditions? and though God
Made thee without thy leave, what if thy Son   760
Prove disobedient, and reprov'd, retort,
Wherefore didst thou beget me? I sought it not:
Wouldst thou admit for his contempt of thee
That proud excuse? yet him not thy election,
But Natural necessity begot.
God made thee of choice his own, and of his own
To serve him, thy reward was of his grace,
Thy punishment then justly is at his Will.
Be it so, for I submit, his doom is fair,
That dust I am, and shall to dust returne: 770
O welcom hour whenever! why delayes
His hand to execute what his Decree
Fixd on this day? why do I overlive,
Why am I mockt with death, and length'nd out
To deathless pain? how gladly would I meet
Mortalitie my sentence, and be Earth
Insensible, how glad would lay me down
As in my Mothers lap? there I should rest
And sleep secure; his dreadful voice no more
Would Thunder in my ears, no fear of worse   780
To mee and to my ofspring would torment me
With cruel expectation. Yet one doubt
Pursues me still, least all I cannot die,
Least that pure breath of Life, the Spirit of Man
Which God inspir'd, cannot together perish
With this corporeal Clod; then in the Grave,
Or in some other dismal place, who knows
But I shall die a living Death? O thought
Horrid, if true! yet why? it was but breath
Of Life that sinn'd; what dies but what had life   790
And sin? the Bodie properly hath neither.
All of me then shall die: let this appease
The doubt, since humane reach no further knows.
For though the Lord of all be infinite,
Is his wrauth also? be it, man is not so,

But mortal doom'd. How can he exercise
Wrath without end on Man whom Death must end?
Can he make deathless Death? that were to make
Strange contradiction, which to God himself
Impossible is held, as Argument   800
Of weakness, not of Power. Will he draw out,
For angers sake, finite to infinite
In punisht man, to satisfie his rigour
Satisfi'd never; that were to extend
His Sentence beyond dust and Natures Law,
By which all Causes else according still
To the reception of thir matter act,
Not to th' extent of thir own Spheare. But say
That Death be not one stroak, as I suppos'd,
Bereaving sense, but endless miserie   810
From this day onward, which I feel begun
Both in me, and without me, and so last
To perpetuitie; Ay me, that fear
Comes thundring back with dreadful revolution
On my defensless head; both Death and I
Am found Eternal, and incorporate both,
Nor I on my part single, in mee all
Posteritie stands curst: Fair Patrimonie
That I must leave ye, Sons; O were I able
To waste it all my self, and leave ye none!   820
So disinherited how would ye bless
Me now your Curse! Ah, why should all mankind
For one mans fault thus guiltless be condemn'd,
If guiltless? But from mee what can proceed,
But all corrupt, both Mind and Will deprav'd,
Not to do onely, but to will the same
With me; how can they acquitted stand
In sight of God? Him after all Disputes
Forc't I absolve: all my evasions vain
And reasonings, though through Mazes, leads me still   830
But to my own conviction: first and last
On mee, mee onely, as the sourse and spring
Of all corruption, all the blame lights due;
So might the wrauth. Fond wish! couldst thou support
That burden heavier then the Earth to bear,
Then all the World much heavier, though divided

827 they acquitted] they then acquitted *1674*

(401)

With that bad Woman? Thus what thou desir'st,
And what thou fearst, alike destroyes all hope
Of refuge, and concludes thee miserable
Beyond all past example and future,   840
To *Satan* onely like both crime and doom.
O Conscience, into what Abyss of fears
And horrors hast thou driv'n me; out of which
I find no way, from deep to deeper plung'd!
    Thus *Adam* to himself lamented loud
Through the still Night, not now, as ere man fell,
Wholsom and cool, and mild, but with black Air
Accompanied, with damps and dreadful gloom,
Which to his evil Conscience represented
All things with double terror: On the ground   850
Outstretcht he lay, on the cold ground, and oft
Curs'd his Creation, Death as oft accus'd
Of tardie execution, since denounc't
The day of his offence. Why comes not Death,
Said hee, with one thrice acceptable stroke
To end me? Shall Truth fail to keep her word,
Justice Divine not hast'n to be just?
But Death comes not at call, Justice Divine
Mends not her slowest pace for prayers or cries.
O Woods, O Fountains, Hillocks, Dales and Bowrs,   860
With other echo late I taught your Shades
To answer, and resound farr other Song.
Whom thus afflicted when sad *Eve* beheld,
Desolate where she sate, approaching nigh,
Soft words to his fierce passion she assay'd:
But her with stern regard he thus repell'd.
    Out of my sight, thou Serpent, that name best
Befits thee with him leagu'd, thy self as false
And hateful; nothing wants, but that thy shape,
Like his, and colour Serpentine may shew   870
Thy inward fraud, to warn all Creatures from thee
Henceforth; least that too heav'nly form, pretended
To hellish falshood, snare them. But for thee
I had persisted happie, had not thy pride
And wandring vanitie, when lest was safe,
Rejected my forewarning, and disdain'd
Not to be trusted, longing to be seen
Though by the Devil himself, him overweening

To over-reach, but with the Serpent meeting
Fool'd and beguil'd, by him thou, I by thee,   880
To trust thee from my side, imagin'd wise,
Constant, mature, proof against all assaults,
And understood not all was but a shew
Rather then solid vertu, all but a Rib
Crooked by nature, bent, as now appears,
More to the part sinister from me drawn,
Well if thrown out, as supernumerarie
To my just number found. O why did God,
Creator wise, that peopl'd highest Heav'n
With Spirits Masculine, create at last   890
This noveltie on Earth, this fair defect
Of Nature, and not fill the World at once
With Men as Angels without Feminine,
Or find some other way to generate
Mankind? this mischief had not then befall'n,
And more that shall befall, innumerable
Disturbances on Earth through Femal snares,
And straight conjunction with this Sex: for either
He never shall find out fit Mate, but such
As some misfortune brings him, or mistake,   900
Or whom he wishes most shall seldom gain
Through her perverseness, but shall see her gaind
By a farr worse, or if she love, withheld
By Parents, or his happiest choice too late
Shall meet, alreadie linkt and Wedlock-bound
To a fell Adversarie, his hate or shame:
Which infinite calamitie shall cause
To Humane life, and houshold peace confound.

        He added not, and from her turn'd, but *Eve*
Not so repulst, with Tears that ceas'd not flowing,   910
And tresses all disorderd, at his feet
Fell humble, and imbracing them, besaught
His peace, and thus proceeded in her plaint.

        Forsake me not thus, *Adam*, witness Heav'n
What love sincere, and reverence in my heart
I beare thee, and unweeting have offended,
Unhappilie deceav'd; thy suppliant
I beg, and clasp thy knees; bereave me not,
Whereon I live, thy gentle looks, thy aid,
Thy counsel in this uttermost distress,   920

My onely strength and stay: forlorn of thee,
Whither shall I betake me, where subsist?
While yet we live, scarse one short hour perhaps,
Between us two let there be peace, both joyning,
As joyn'd in injuries, one enmitie
Against a Foe by doom express assign'd us,
That cruel Serpent: On me exercise not
Thy hatred for this miserie befall'n,
On me already lost, mee, then thy self
More miserable; both have sin'd, but thou   930
Against God onely, I against God and thee,
And to the place of judgement will return,
There with my cries importune Heaven, that all
The sentence from thy head remov'd may light
On me, sole cause to thee of all this woe,
Mee mee onely just object of his ire.

She ended weeping, and her lowlie plight,
Immoveable till peace obtain'd from fault
Acknowledg'd and deplor'd, in *Adam* wraught
Commiseration; soon his heart relented   940
Towards her, his life so late and sole delight,
Now at his feet submissive in distress,
Creature so faire his reconcilement seeking,
His counsel whom she had displeas'd, his aide;
As one disarm'd, his anger all he lost,
And thus with peaceful words uprais'd her soon.

Unwarie, and too desirous, as before,
So now of what thou knowst not, who desir'st
The punishment all on thy self; alas,
Beare thine own first, ill able to sustaine   950
His full wrauth whose thou feelst as yet lest part,
And my displeasure bearst so ill. If Prayers
Could alter high Decrees, I to that place
Would speed before thee, and be louder heard,
That on my head all might be visited,
Thy frailtie and infirmer Sex forgiv'n,
To me committed and by me expos'd.
But rise, let us no more contend, nor blame
Each other, blam'd enough elsewhere, but strive
In offices of Love, how we may light'n   960
Each others burden in our share of woe;
Since this days Death denounc't, if ought I see,

Will prove no sudden, but a slow-pac't evill,
A long days dying to augment our paine,
And to our Seed (O hapless Seed!) deriv'd.
   To whom thus *Eve*, recovering heart, repli'd.
Adam, by sad experiment I know
How little weight my words with thee can finde,
Found so erroneous, thence by just event
Found so unfortunate; nevertheless,   970
Restor'd by thee, vile as I am, to place
Of new acceptance, hopeful to regaine
Thy Love, the sole contentment of my heart,
Living or dying from thee I will not hide
What thoughts in my unquiet brest are ris'n,
Tending to som relief of our extremes,
Or end, though sharp and sad, yet tolerable,
As in our evils, and of easier choice.
If care of our descent perplex us most,
Which must be born to certain woe, devour'd   980
By Death at last, and miserable it is
To be to others cause of misery,
Our own begotten, and of our Loines to bring
Into this cursed World a woful Race,
That after wretched Life must be at last
Food for so foule a Monster, in thy power
It lies, yet ere Conception to prevent
The Race unblest, to being yet unbegot.
Childless thou art, Childless remaine:
So Death shall be deceav'd his glut, and with us two   990
Be forc'd to satisfie his Rav'nous Maw.
But if thou judge it hard and difficult,
Conversing, looking, loving, to abstain
From Loves due Rites, Nuptial embraces sweet,
And with desire to languish without hope,
Before the present object languishing
With like desire, which would be miserie
And torment less then none of what we dread,
Then both our selves and Seed at once to free
From what we fear for both, let us make short,   1000
Let us seek Death, or hee not found, supply
With our own hands his Office on our selves;
Why stand we longer shivering under feares,
That shew no end but Death, and have the power,

Of many wayes to die the shortest choosing,
Destruction with destruction to destroy.
    She ended heer, or vehement despaire
Broke off the rest; so much of Death her thoughts
Had entertaind, as di'd her Cheeks with pale.
But *Adam* with such counsel nothing sway'd,   1010
To better hopes his more attentive minde
Labouring had rais'd, and thus to *Eve* repli'd.
    Eve, thy contempt of life and pleasure seems
To argue in thee somthing more sublime
And excellent then what thy minde contemnes;
But self-destruction therefore saught, refutes
That excellence thought in thee, and implies,
Not thy contempt, but anguish and regret
For loss of life and pleasure overlov'd.
Or if thou covet death, as utmost end   1020
Of miserie, so thinking to evade
The penaltie pronounc't, doubt not but God
Hath wiselier arm'd his vengeful ire then so
To be forestall'd; much more I fear least Death
So snatcht will not exempt us from the paine
We are by doom to pay; rather such acts
Of contumacie will provoke the highest
To make death in us live: Then let us seek
Som safer resolution, which methinks
I have in view, calling to minde with heed   1030
Part of our Sentence, that thy Seed shall bruise
The Serpents head; piteous amends, unless
Be meant, whom I conjecture, our grand Foe
Satan, who in the Serpent hath contriv'd
Against us this deceit: to crush his head
Would be revenge indeed; which will be lost
By death brought on our selves, or childless days
Resolv'd, as thou proposest; so our Foe
Shall scape his punishment ordain'd, and wee
Instead shall double ours upon our heads.   1040
No more be mention'd then of violence
Against our selves, and wilful barrenness,
That cuts us off from hope, and savours onely
Rancor and pride, impatience and despite,
Reluctance against God and his just yoke
Laid on our Necks. Remember with what mild

And gracious temper he both heard and judg'd
Without wrauth or reviling; wee expected
Immediate dissolution, which we thought
Was meant by Death that day, when lo, to thee   1050
Pains onely in Child-bearing were foretold,
And bringing forth, soon recompenc't with joy,
Fruit of thy Womb: On mee the Curse aslope
Glanc'd on the ground, with labour I must earne
My bread; what harm? Idleness had bin worse;
My labour will sustain me; and least Cold
Or Heat should injure us, his timely care
Hath unbesaught provided, and his hands
Cloath'd us unworthie, pitying while he judg'd;
How much more, if we pray him, will his ear   1060
Be open, and his heart to pitie incline,
And teach us further by what means to shun
Th' inclement Seasons, Rain, Ice, Hail and Snow,
Which now the Skie with various Face begins
To shew us in this Mountain, while the Winds
Blow moist and keen, shattering the graceful locks
Of these fair spreading Trees; which bids us seek
Som better shroud, som better warmth to cherish
Our Limbs benumm'd, ere this diurnal Starr
Leave cold the Night, how we his gather'd beams   1070
Reflected, may with matter sere foment,
Or by collision of two bodies grinde
The Air attrite to Fire, as late the Clouds
Justling or pusht with Winds rude in thir shock
Tine the slant Lightning, whose thwart flame driv'n down
Kindles the gummie bark of Firr or Pine,
And sends a comfortable heat from farr,
Which might supply the Sun: such Fire to use,
And what may else be remedie or cure
To evils which our own misdeeds have wrought,   1080
Hee will instruct us praying, and of Grace
Beseeching him, so as we need not fear
To pass commodiously this life, sustain'd
By him with many comforts, till we end
In dust, our final rest and native home.
What better can we do, then to the place
Repairing where he judg'd us, prostrate fall
Before him reverent, and there confess

Humbly our faults, and pardon beg, with tears
Watering the ground, and with our sighs the Air   1090
Frequenting, sent from hearts contrite, in sign
Of sorrow unfeign'd, and humiliation meek.
Undoubtedly he will relent and turn
From his displeasure; in whose look serene,
When angry most he seem'd and most severe,
What else but favor, grace, and mercie shon?
   So spake our Father penitent, nor *Eve*
Felt less remorse: they forthwith to the place
Repairing where he judg'd them prostrate fell
Before him reverent, and both confess'd   1100
Humbly thir faults, and pardon beg'd, with tears
Watering the ground, and with thir sighs the Air
Frequenting, sent from hearts contrite, in sign
Of sorrow unfeign'd, and humiliation meek.

The End of the Tenth Book.

PARADISE LOST.

BOOK XI.

THE ARGUMENT.

The Son of God presents to his Father the Prayers of our first Parents now repenting, and intercedes for them: God accepts them, but declares that they must no longer abide in Paradise; sends Michael with a Band of Cherubim to dispossess them; but first to reveal to Adam future things: Michaels coming down. Adam shews to Eve certain ominous signs; he discerns Michaels approach, goes out to meet him: the Angel denounces thir departure. Eve's Lamentation. Adam pleads, but submits: The Angel leads him up to a high Hill, sets before him in vision what shall happ'n till the Flood.

THUS they in lowliest plight repentant stood
Praying, for from the Mercie-seat above
Prevenient Grace descending had remov'd
The stonie from thir hearts, and made new flesh
Regenerate grow instead, that sighs now breath'd
Unutterable, which the Spirit of prayer
Inspir'd, and wing'd for Heav'n with speedier flight
Then loudest Oratorie: yet thir port
Not of mean suiters, nor important less
Seem'd thir Petition, then when th' ancient Pair   10
In Fables old, less ancient yet then these,
Deucalion and chaste *Pyrrha* to restore
The Race of Mankind drownd, before the Shrine
Of *Themis* stood devout. To Heav'n thir prayers
Flew up, nor missd the way, by envious windes
Blow'n vagabond or frustrate: in they passd
Dimentionless through Heav'nly dores; then clad

With incense, where the Golden Altar fum'd,
By thir great Intercessor, came in sight
Before the Fathers Throne: Them the glad Son   20
Presenting, thus to intercede began.

    See Father, what first fruits on Earth are sprung
From thy implanted Grace in Man, these Sighs
And Prayers, which in this Golden Censer, mixt
With Incense, I thy Priest before thee bring,
Fruits of more pleasing savour from thy seed
Sow'n with contrition in his heart, then those
Which his own hand manuring all the Trees
Of Paradise could have produc't, ere fall'n
From innocence. Now therefore bend thine eare   30
To supplication, heare his sighs though mute;
Unskilful with what words to pray, let mee
Interpret for him, mee his Advocate
And propitiation, all his works on mee
Good or not good ingraft, my Merit those
Shall perfet, and for these my Death shall pay.
Accept me, and in mee from these receave
The smell of peace toward Mankinde, let him live
Before thee reconcil'd, at least his days
Numberd, though sad, till Death, his doom (which I   40
To mitigate thus plead, not to reverse)
To better life shall yeeld him, where with mee
All my redeemd may dwell in joy and bliss,
Made one with me as I with thee am one.

    To whom the Father, without Cloud, serene.
All thy request for Man, accepted Son,
Obtain, all thy request was my Decree:
But longer in that Paradise to dwell,
The Law I gave to Nature him forbids:
Those pure immortal Elements that know   50
No gross, no unharmoneous mixture foule,
Eject him tainted now, and purge him off
As a distemper, gross to aire as gross,
And mortal food, as may dispose him best
For dissolution wrought by Sin, that first
Distemperd all things, and of incorrupt
Corrupted. I at first with two fair gifts
Created him endowd, with Happiness
And Immortalitie: that fondly lost,

This other serv'd but to eternize woe;
Till I provided Death; so Death becomes
His final remedie, and after Life
Tri'd in sharp tribulation, and refin'd
By Faith and faithful works, to second Life,
Wak't in the renovation of the just,
Resignes him up with Heav'n and Earth renewd.
But let us call to Synod all the Blest
Through Heavn's wide bounds; from them I will not hide
My judgments, how with Mankind I proceed,
As how with peccant Angels late they saw;   70
And in thir state, though firm, stood more confirmd.

    He ended, and the Son gave signal high
To the bright Minister that watch'd, hee blew
His Trumpet, heard in *Oreb* since perhaps
When God descended, and perhaps once more
To sound at general doom. Th' Angelic blast
Filld all the Regions : from thir blissful Bowrs
Of *Amarantin* Shade, Fountain or Spring,
By the waters of Life, where ere they sate
In fellowships of joy : the Sons of Light   80
Hasted, resorting to the Summons high,
And took thir Seats ; till from his Throne supream
Th' Almighty thus pronounc'd his sovran Will.

    O Sons, like one of us Man is become
To know both Good and Evil, since his taste
Of that defended Fruit; but let him boast
His knowledge of Good lost, and Evil got,
Happier, had it suffic'd him to have known
Good by it self, and Evil not at all.
He sorrows now, repents, and prayes contrite,   90
My motions in him, longer then they move,
His heart I know, how variable and vain
Self-left. Least therefore his now bolder hand
Reach also of the Tree of Life, and eat,
And live for ever, dream at least to live
For ever, to remove him I decree,
And send him from the Garden forth to Till
The Ground whence he was taken, fitter soile.
    Michael, this my behest have thou in charge,
Take to thee from among the Cherubim   100
Thy choice of flaming Warriours, least the Fiend

    (411)

Or in behalf of Man, or to invade
Vacant possession som new trouble raise:
Hast thee, and from the Paradise of God
Without remorse drive out the sinful Pair,
From hallowd ground th' unholie, and denounce
To them and to thir Progenie from thence
Perpetual banishment. Yet least they faint
At the sad Sentence rigorously urg'd,
For I behold them soft'nd and with tears   110
Bewailing thir excess, all terror hide.
If patiently thy bidding they obey,
Dismiss them not disconsolate; reveale
To *Adam* what shall come in future dayes,
As I shall thee enlighten, intermix
My Cov'nant in the Womans seed renewd;
So send them forth, though sorrowing, yet in peace:
And on the East side of the Garden place,
Where entrance up from *Eden* easiest climbes,
Cherubic watch, and of a Sword the flame   120
Wide waving, all approach farr off to fright,
And guard all passage to the Tree of Life:
Least Paradise a receptacle prove
To Spirits foule, and all my Trees thir prey,
With whose stol'n Fruit Man once more to delude.
    He ceas'd; and th' Archangelic Power prepar'd
For swift descent, with him the Cohort bright
Of watchful Cherubim; four faces each
Had, like a double *Janus*, all thir shape
Spangl'd with eyes more numerous then those   130
Of *Argus*, and more wakeful then to drouze,
Charm'd with *Arcadian* Pipe, the Pastoral Reed
Of *Hermes*, or his opiate Rod. Mean while
To resalute the World with sacred Light
Leucothea wak'd, and with fresh dews imbalmd
The Earth, when *Adam* and first Matron *Eve*
Had ended now thir Orisons, and found,
Strength added from above, new hope to spring
Out of despaire, joy, but with fear yet linkt;
Which thus to *Eve* his welcome words renewd.   140
    Eve, easily may Faith admit, that all
The good which we enjoy, from Heav'n descends
But that from us ought should ascend to Heav'n

So prevalent as to concerne the mind
Of God high-blest, or to incline his will,
Hard to belief may seem; yet this will Prayer,
Or one short sigh of humane breath, up-borne
Ev'n to the Seat of God. For since I saught
By Prayer th' offended Deitie to appease,
Kneel'd and before him humbl'd all my heart,   150
Methought I saw him placable and mild,
Bending his eare; perswasion in me grew
That I was heard with favour; peace return'd
Home to my brest, and to my memorie
His promise, that thy Seed shall bruise our Foe;
Which then not minded in dismay, yet now
Assures me that the bitterness of death
Is past, and we shall live. Whence Haile to thee
Eve rightly call'd, Mother of all Mankind,
Mother of all things living, since by thee   160
Man is to live, and all things live for Man.

    To whom thus *Eve* with sad demeanour meek.
Ill worthie I such title should belong
To me transgressour, who for thee ordaind
A help, became thy snare; to mee reproach
Rather belongs, distrust and all dispraise:
But infinite in pardon was my Judge,
That I who first brought Death on all, am grac't
The sourse of life; next favourable thou,
Who highly thus to entitle me voutsaf'st,   170
Farr other name deserving. But the Field
To labour calls us now with sweat impos'd,
Though after sleepless Night; for see the Morn,
All unconcern'd with our unrest, begins
Her rosie progress smiling; let us forth,
I never from thy side henceforth to stray,
Wherere our days work lies, though now enjoind
Laborious, till day droop; while here we dwell,
What can be toilsom in these pleasant Walkes?
Here let us live, though in fall'n state, content.   180

    So spake, so wish'd much humbl'd *Eve*, but Fate
Subscrib'd not; Nature first gave Signs, imprest
On Bird, Beast, Aire, Aire suddenly eclips'd
After short blush of Morn; nigh in her sight
The Bird of *Jove*, stoopt from his aerie tour,

(413)

Two Birds of gayest plume before him drove :
Down from a Hill the Beast that reigns in Woods,
First Hunter then, pursu'd a gentle brace,
Goodliest of all the Forrest, Hart and Hinde ;
Direct to th' Eastern Gate was bent thir flight. 190
Adam observ'd, and with his Eye the chase
Pursuing, not unmov'd to *Eve* thus spake.

O *Eve*, some furder change awaits us nigh,
Which Heav'n by these mute signs in Nature shews
Forerunners of his purpose, or to warn
Us haply too secure of our discharge
From penaltie, because from death releast
Some days ; how long, and what till then our life,
Who knows, or more then this, that we are dust,
And thither must return and be no more. 200
Why else this double object in our sight
Of flight pursu'd in th' Air and ore the ground
One way the self-same hour ? why in the East
Darkness ere Dayes mid-course, and Morning light
More orient in yon Western Cloud that draws
O're the blew Firmament a radiant white,
And slow descends, with somthing heav'nly fraught.

He err'd not, for by this the heav'nly Bands
Down from a Skie of Jasper lighted now
In Paradise, and on a Hill made alt, 210
A glorious Apparition, had not doubt
And carnal fear that day dimm'd *Adams* eye.
Not that more glorious, when the Angels met
Jacob in *Mahanaim*, where he saw
The field Pavilion'd with his Guardians bright ;
Nor that which on the flaming Mount appeerd
In *Dothan*, cover'd with a Camp of Fire,
Against the *Syrian* King, who to surprize
One man, Assassin-like had levied Warr,
Warr unproclam'd. The Princely Hierarch 220
In thir bright stand, there left his Powers to seise
Possession of the Garden ; hee alone,
To finde where *Adam* shelterd, took his way,
Not unperceav'd of *Adam*, who to *Eve*,
While the great Visitant approachd, thus spake.

Eve, now expect great tidings, which perhaps
Of us will soon determin, or impose

(414)

New Laws to be observ'd; for I descrie
From yonder blazing Cloud that veils the Hill
One of the heav'nly Host, and by his Gate   230
None of the meanest, some great Potentate
Or of the Thrones above, such Majestie
Invests him coming; yet not terrible,
That I should fear, nor sociably mild,
As *Raphael*, that I should much confide,
But solemn and sublime, whom not to offend,
With reverence I must meet, and thou retire.
He ended; and th' Arch-Angel soon drew nigh,
Not in his shape Celestial, but as Man
Clad to meet Man; over his lucid Armes   240
A militarie Vest of purple flowd
Livelier then *Melibœan*, or the graine
Of *Sarra*, worn by Kings and Hero's old
In time of Truce; *Iris* had dipt the wooff;
His starrie Helme unbuckl'd shew'd him prime
In Manhood where Youth ended; by his side
As in a glistering *Zodiac* hung the Sword,
Satans dire dread, and in his hand the Spear.
Adam bowd low, hee Kingly from his State
Inclin'd not, but his coming thus declar'd.   250
    Adam, Heav'ns high behest no Preface needs:
Sufficient that thy Prayers are heard, and Death,
Then due by sentence when thou didst transgress,
Defeated of his seisure many dayes
Giv'n thee of Grace, wherein thou may'st repent,
And one bad act with many deeds well done
Mayst cover: well may then thy Lord appeas'd
Redeem thee quite from Deaths rapacious claime;
But longer in this Paradise to dwell
Permits not; to remove thee I am come,   260
And send thee from the Garden forth to till
The ground whence thou wast tak'n, fitter Soile.
    He added not, for *Adam* at the newes
Heart-strook with chilling gripe of sorrow stood,
That all his senses bound; *Eve*, who unseen
Yet all had heard, with audible lament
Discover'd soon the place of her retire.
    O unexspected stroke, worse then of Death!
Must I thus leave thee Paradise? thus leave

Thee Native Soile, these happie Walks and Shades,   270
Fit haunt of Gods? where I had hope to spend,
Quiet though sad, the respit of that day
That must be mortal to us both. O flours,
That never will in other Climate grow,
My early visitation, and my last
At Eev'n, which I bred up with tender hand
From the first op'ning bud, and gave ye Names,
Who now shall reare ye to the Sun, or ranke
Your Tribes, and water from th' ambrosial Fount?
Thee lastly nuptial Bowre, by mee adornd   280
With what to sight or smell was sweet; from thee
How shall I part, and whither wander down
Into a lower World, to this obscure
And wilde, how shall we breath in other Aire
Less pure, accustomd to immortal Fruits?
    Whom thus the Angel interrupted milde.
Lament not *Eve*, but patiently resigne
What justly thou hast lost; nor set thy heart,
Thus over fond, on that which is not thine;
Thy going is not lonely, with thee goes   290
Thy Husband, him to follow thou art bound;
Where he abides, think there thy native soile.
    Adam by this from the cold sudden damp
Recovering, and his scatterd spirits returnd,
To *Michael* thus his humble words addressd.
    Celestial, whether among the Thrones, or nam'd
Of them the Highest, for such of shape may seem
Prince above Princes, gently hast thou tould
Thy message, which might else in telling wound,
And in performing end us; what besides   300
Of sorrow and dejection and despair
Our frailtie can sustain, thy tidings bring,
Departure from this happy place, our sweet
Recess, and onely consolation left
Familiar to our eyes, all places else
Inhospitable appeer and desolate,
Nor knowing us nor known: and if by prayer
Incessant I could hope to change the will
Of him who all things can, I would not cease
To wearie him with my assiduous cries: 310
But prayer against his absolute Decree

No more availes then breath against the winde,
Blown stifling back on him that breaths it forth :
Therefore to his great bidding I submit.
This most afflicts me, that departing hence,
As from his face I shall be hid, deprivd
His blessed count'nance ; here I could frequent,
With worship, place by place where he voutsaf'd
Presence Divine, and to my Sons relate ;
On this Mount he appeerd, under this Tree   320
Stood visible, among these Pines his voice
I heard, here with him at this Fountain talk'd :
So many grateful Altars I would reare
Of grassie Terfe, and pile up every Stone
Of lustre from the brook, in memorie,
Or monument to Ages, and thereon
Offer sweet smelling Gumms & Fruits and Flours :
In yonder nether World where shall I seek
His bright appearances, or footstep trace ?
For though I fled him angrie, yet recall'd   330
To life prolongd and promisd Race, I now
Gladly behold though but his utmost skirts
Of glory, and farr off his steps adore.
      To whom thus *Michael* with regard benigne.
Adam, thou know'st Heav'n his, and all the Earth,
Not this Rock onely ; his Omnipresence fills
Land, Sea, and Aire, and every kinde that lives,
Fomented by his virtual power and warmd :
All th' Earth he gave thee to possess and rule,
No despicable gift ; surmise not then   340
His presence to these narrow bounds confin'd
Of Paradise or *Eden* : this had been
Perhaps thy Capital Seate, from whence had spred
All generations, and had hither come
From all the ends of th' Earth, to celebrate
And reverence thee thir great Progenitor.
But this præeminence thou hast lost, brought down
To dwell on eeven ground now with thy Sons :
Yet doubt not but in Vallie and in Plaine
God is as here, and will be found alike   350
Present, and of his presence many a signe
Still following thee, still compassing thee round
With goodness and paternal Love, his Face

Express, and of his steps the track Divine.
Which that thou mayst beleeve, and be confirmd,
Ere thou from hence depart, know I am sent
To shew thee what shall come in future dayes
To thee and to thy Ofspring; good with bad
Expect to hear, supernal Grace contending
With sinfulness of Men; thereby to learn 360
True patience, and to temper joy with fear
And pious sorrow, equally enur'd
By moderation either state to beare,
Prosperous or adverse: so shalt thou lead
Safest thy life, and best prepar'd endure
Thy mortal passage when it comes. Ascend
This Hill; let *Eve* (for I have drencht her eyes)
Here sleep below while thou to foresight wak'st,
As once thou slepst, while Shee to life was formd.

To whom thus *Adam* gratefully repli'd. 370
Ascend, I follow thee, safe Guide, the path
Thou lead'st me, and to the hand of Heav'n submit,
However chast'ning, to the evil turne
My obvious breast, arming to overcom
By suffering, and earne rest from labour won,
If so I may attain. So both ascend
In the Visions of God: It was a Hill
Of Paradise the highest, from whose top
The Hemisphere of Earth in cleerest Ken
Stretcht out to amplest reach of prospect lay. 380
Not higher that Hill nor wider looking round,
Whereon for different cause the Tempter set
Our second *Adam* in the Wilderness,
To shew him all Earths Kingdomes and thir Glory.
His Eye might there command wherever stood
City of old or modern Fame, the Seat
Of mightiest Empire, from the destind Walls
Of *Cambalu*, seat of *Cathaian Can*
And *Samarchand* by *Oxus*, *Temirs* Throne,
To *Paquin* of *Sinæan* Kings, and thence 390
To *Agra* and *Lahor* of great *Mogul*
Down to the golden *Chersonese*, or where
The *Persian* in *Ecbatan* sate, or since
In *Hispahan*, or where the *Russian Ksar*
In *Mosco*, or the Sultan in *Bizance*,

Turchestan-born ; nor could his eye not ken
Th' Empire of *Negus* to his utmost Port
Ercoco and the less Maritine Kings
Mombaza, and *Quiloa,* and *Melind,*
And *Sofala* thought *Ophir,* to the Realme   400
Of *Congo,* and *Angola* fardest South ;
Or thence from *Niger* Flood to *Atlas* Mount
The Kingdoms of *Almansor, Fez* and *Sus,*
Marocco and *Algiers,* and *Tremisen ;*
On *Europe* thence, and where *Rome* was to sway
The World : in Spirit perhaps he also saw
Rich *Mexico* the seat of *Motezume,*
And *Cusco* in *Peru,* the richer seat
Of *Atabalipa,* and yet unspoil'd
Guiana, whose great Citie *Geryons* Sons   410
Call *El Dorado* : but to nobler sights
Michael from *Adams* eyes the Filme remov'd
Which that false Fruit that promis'd clearer sight
Had bred ; then purg'd with Euphrasie and Rue
The visual Nerve, for he had much to see ;
And from the Well of Life three drops instill'd.
So deep the power of these Ingredients pierc'd,
Eevn to the inmost seat of mental sight,
That *Adam* now enforc't to close his eyes,
Sunk down and all his Spirits became intranst :   420
But him the gentle Angel by the hand
Soon rais'd, and his attention thus recall'd.
 Adam, now ope thine eyes, and first behold
Th' effects which thy original crime hath wrought
In some to spring from thee, who never touch'd
Th' excepted Tree, nor with the Snake conspir'd,
Nor sinn'd thy sin, yet from that sin derive
Corruption to bring forth more violent deeds.
 His eyes he op'nd, and beheld a field,
Part arable and tilth, whereon were Sheaves   430
New reapt, the other part sheep-walks and foulds ;
Ith' midst an Altar as the Land-mark stood
Rustic, of grassie sord ; thither anon
A sweatie Reaper from his Tillage brought
First Fruits, the green Eare, and the yellow Sheaf,
Uncull'd, as came to hand ; a Shepherd next
More meek came with the Firstlings of his Flock

Choicest and best; then sacrificing, laid
The Inwards and thir Fat, with Incense strew'd,
On the cleft Wood, and all due Rites perform'd.   440
His Offring soon propitious Fire from Heav'n
Consum'd with nimble glance, and grateful steame;
The others not, for his was not sincere;
Whereat hee inlie rag'd, and as they talk'd,
Smote him into the Midriff with a stone
That beat out life; he fell, and deadly pale
Groand out his Soul with gushing bloud effus'd.
Much at that sight was *Adam* in his heart
Dismai'd, and thus in haste to th' Angel cri'd.

O Teacher, some great mischief hath befall'n   450
To that meek man, who well had sacrific'd;
Is Pietie thus and pure Devotion paid?

T' whom *Michael* thus, hee also mov'd, repli'd.
These two are Brethren, *Adam*, and to come
Out of thy loyns; th' unjust the just hath slain,
For envie that his Brothers Offering found
From Heav'n acceptance; but the bloodie Fact
Will be aveng'd, and th' others Faith approv'd
Loose no reward, though here thou see him die,
Rowling in dust and gore. To which our Sire.   460

Alas, both for the deed and for the cause!
But have I now seen Death? Is this the way
I must return to native dust? O sight
Of terrour, foul and ugly to behold,
Horrid to think, how horrible to feel!

To whom thus *Michael*. Death thou hast seen
In his first shape on man; but many shapes
Of Death, and many are the wayes that lead
To his grim Cave, all dismal; yet to sense
More terrible at th' entrance then within.   470
Some, as thou saw'st, by violent stroke shall die,
By Fire, Flood, Famin, by Intemperance more
In Meats and Drinks, which on the Earth shal bring
Diseases dire, of which a monstrous crew
Before thee shall appear; that thou mayst know
What miserie th' inabstinence of *Eve*
Shall bring on men. Immediately a place
Before his eyes appeard, sad, noysom, dark,
A Lazar-house it seemd, wherein were laid

Numbers of all diseas'd, all maladies   480
Of gastly Spasm, or racking torture, qualmes
Of heart-sick Agonie, all feavorous kinds,
Convulsions, Epilepsies, fierce Catarrhs,
Intestin Stone and Ulcer, Colic pangs,
Dropsies, and Asthma's, and Joint-racking Rheums.
Dire was the tossing, deep the groans, despair
Tended the sick busiest from Couch to Couch;
And over them triumphant Death his Dart
Shook, but delaid to strike, though oft invok't
With vows, as thir chief good, and final hope.   490
Sight so deform what heart of Rock could long
Drie-ey'd behold? *Adam* could not, but wept,
Though not of Woman born; compassion quell'd
His best of Man, and gave him up to tears
A space, till firmer thoughts restraind excess,
And scarce recovering words his plaint renew'd.
   O miserable Mankind, to what fall
Degraded, to what wretched state reserv'd!
Better end heer unborn. Why is life giv'n
To be thus wrested from us? rather why   500
Obtruded on us thus? who if we knew
What we receive, would either not accept
Life offer'd, or soon beg to lay it down,
Glad to be so dismist in peace. Can thus
Th' Image of God in man created once
So goodly and erect, though faultie since,
To such unsightly sufferings be debas't
Under inhuman pains? Why should not Man,
Retaining still Divine similitude
In part, from such deformities be free,   510
And for his Makers Image sake exempt?
   Thir Makers Image, answerd *Michael*, then
Forsook them, when themselves they villifi'd
To serve ungovern'd appetite, and took
His Image whom they serv'd, a brutish vice,
Inductive mainly to the sin of *Eve*.
Therefore so abject is thir punishment,

484 After this line, *1674* adds:
        Dæmoniac Phrenzie, moaping Melancholie
        And Moon struck madness, pining Atrophie,
        Marasmus, and wide wasting Pestilence,

Disfiguring not Gods likeness, but thir own,
Or if his likeness, by themselves defac't
While they pervert pure Natures healthful rules   520
To loathsom sickness, worthily, since they
Gods Image did not reverence in themselves.

    I yeild it just, said *Adam*, and submit.
But is there yet no other way, besides
These painful passages, how we may come
To Death, and mix with our connatural dust?

    There is, said *Michael*, if thou well observe
The rule of not too much, by temperance taught
In what thou eatst and drinkst, seeking from thence
Due nourishment, not gluttonous delight,   530
Till many years over thy head return:
So maist thou live, till like ripe Fruit thou drop
Into thy Mothers lap, or be with ease
Gatherd, not harshly pluckt, for death mature:
This is old age; but then thou must outlive
Thy youth, thy strength, thy beauty, which will change
To withered weak & gray; thy Senses then
Obtuse, all taste of pleasure must forgoe,
To what thou hast, and for the Aire of youth
Hopeful and cheerful, in thy blood will reigne   540
A melancholly damp of cold and dry
To waigh thy spirits down, and last consume
The Balme of Life. To whom our Ancestor.

    Henceforth I flie not Death, nor would prolong
Life much, bent rather how I may be quit
Fairest and easiest of this combrous charge,
Which I must keep till my appointed day
Of rendring up, *Michael* to him repli'd.

    Nor love thy Life, nor hate; but what thou livst
Live well, how long or short permit to Heav'n: 550
And now prepare thee for another sight.

    He lookd and saw a spacious Plaine, whereon
Were Tents of various hue; by some were herds
Of Cattel grazing: others, whence the sound
Of Instruments that made melodious chime
Was heard, of Harp and Organ; and who moovd

---

548 Of rendring up, and patiently attend
My dissolution. *Michael* repli'd. *1674*

Thir stops and chords was seen : his volant touch
Instinct through all proportions low and high
Fled and pursu'd transverse the resonant fugue.
In other part stood one who at the Forge   560
Labouring, two massie clods of Iron and Brass
Had melted (whether found where casual fire
Had wasted woods on Mountain or in Vale,
Down to the veins of Earth, thence gliding hot
To som Caves mouth, or whether washt by stream
From underground) the liquid Ore he dreind
Into fit moulds prepar'd ; from which he formd
First his own Tooles ; then, what might else be wrought
Fusil or grav'n in mettle. After these,
But on the hether side a different sort   570
From the high neighbouring Hills, which was thir Seat,
Down to the Plain descended : by thir guise
Just men they seemd, and all thir study bent
To worship God aright, and know his works
Not hid, nor those things last which might preserve
Freedom and Peace to men : they on the Plain
Long had not walkt, when from the Tents behold
A Beavie of fair Women, richly gay
In Gems and wanton dress ; to the Harp they sung
Soft amorous Ditties, and in dance came on :   580
The Men though grave, ey'd them, and let thir eyes
Rove without rein, till in the amorous Net
Fast caught, they lik'd, and each his liking chose ;
And now of love they treat till th' Eevning Star
Loves Harbinger appeerd ; then all in heat
They light the Nuptial Torch, and bid invoke
Hymen, then first to marriage Rites invok't ;
With Feast and Musick all the Tents resound.
Such happy interview and fair event
Of love & youth not lost, Songs, Garlands, Flours,   590
And charming Symphonies attach'd the heart
Of *Adam*, soon enclin'd to admit delight,
The bent of Nature ; which he thus express'd.
  True opener of mine eyes, prime Angel blest,
Much better seems this Vision, and more hope
Of peaceful dayes portends, then those two past ;
Those were of hate and death, or pain much worse,
Here Nature seems fulfilld in all her ends.

(423)

   To whom thus *Michael.* Judg not what is best
By pleasure, though to Nature seeming meet,   600
Created, as thou art, to nobler end
Holie and pure, conformitie divine.
Those Tents thou sawst so pleasant, were the Tents
Of wickedness, wherein shall dwell his Race
Who slew his Brother; studious they appere
Of Arts that polish Life, Inventers rare,
Unmindful of thir Maker, though his Spirit
Taught them, but they his gifts acknowledg'd none.
Yet they a beauteous ofspring shall beget;
For that fair femal Troop thou sawst, that seemd   610
Of Goddesses, so blithe, so smooth, so gay,
Yet empty of all good wherein consists
Womans domestic honour and chief praise;
Bred onely and completed to the taste
Of lustful appetence, to sing, to dance,
To dress, and troule the Tongue, and roule the Eye.
To these that sober Race of Men, whose lives
Religious titl'd them the Sons of God,
Shall yeild up all thir vertue, all thir fame
Ignobly, to the traines and to the smiles   620
Of these fair Atheists, and now swim in joy,
(Erelong to swim at larg) and laugh; for which
The world erelong a world of tears must weepe.
   To whom thus *Adam* of short joy bereft.
O pittie and shame, that they who to live well
Enterd so faire, should turn aside to tread
Paths indirect, or in the mid way faint!
But still I see the tenor of Mans woe
Holds on the same, from Woman to begin.
   From Mans effeminate slackness it begins,   630
Said th' Angel, who should better hold his place
By wisdome, and superiour gifts receavd.
But now prepare thee for another Scene.
   He lookd and saw wide Territorie spred
Before him, Towns, and rural works between,
Cities of Men with lofty Gates and Towrs,
Concours in Arms, fierce Faces threatning Warr,
Giants of mightie Bone, and bould emprise;
Part wield thir Arms, part courb the foaming Steed,
Single or in Array of Battel rang'd   640

Both Horse and Foot, nor idely mustring stood;
One way a Band select from forage drives
A herd of Beeves, faire Oxen and faire Kine
From a fat Meddow ground; or fleecy Flock,
Ewes and thir bleating Lambs over the Plaine,
Thir Bootie; scarce with Life the Shepherds flye,
But call in aide, which tacks a bloody Fray;
With cruel Tournament the Squadrons joine;
Where Cattel pastur'd late, now scatterd lies
With Carcasses and Arms th' ensanguind Field   650
Deserted: Others to a Citie strong
Lay Siege, encampt; by Batterie, Scale, and Mine,
Assaulting; others from the Wall defend
With Dart and Jav'lin, Stones and sulfurous Fire;
On each hand slaughter and gigantic deeds.
In other part the scepter'd Haralds call
To Council in the Citie Gates: anon
Grey-headed men and grave, with Warriours mixt,
Assemble, and Harangues are heard, but soon
In factious opposition, till at last   660
Of middle Age one rising, eminent
In wise deport, spake much of Right and Wrong,
Of Justice, of Religion, Truth and Peace,
And Judgement from above: him old and young
Exploded, and had seiz'd with violent hands,
Had not a Cloud descending snatch'd him thence
Unseen amid the throng: so violence
Proceeded, and Oppression, and Sword-Law
Through all the Plain, and refuge none was found.
Adam was all in tears, and to his guide   670
Lamenting turnd full sad; O what are these,
Deaths Ministers, not Men, who thus deal Death
Inhumanly to men, and multiply
Ten thousand fould the sin of him who slew
His Brother; for of whom such massacher
Make they but of thir Brethren, men of men?
But who was that Just Man, whom had not Heav'n
Rescu'd, had in his Righteousness bin lost?
     To whom thus *Michael*; These are the product
Of those ill-mated Marriages thou saw'st;   680
Where good with bad were matcht, who of themselves

647 tacks] makes *1674*

(425)

Abhor to joyn; and by imprudence mixt,
Produce prodigious Births of bodie or mind.
Such were these Giants, men of high renown;
For in those dayes Might onely shall be admir'd,
And Valour and Heroic Vertu call'd;
To overcome in Battel, and subdue
Nations, and bring home spoils with infinite
Man-slaughter, shall be held the highest pitch
Of human Glorie, and for Glorie done   690
Of triumph, to be styl'd great Conquerours,
Patrons of Mankind, Gods, and Sons of Gods,
Destroyers rightlier call'd and Plagues of men.
Thus Fame shall be achiev'd, renown on Earth,
And what most merits fame in silence hid.
But hee the seventh from thee, whom thou beheldst
The onely righteous in a World perverse,
And therefore hated, therefore so beset
With Foes for daring single to be just,
And utter odious Truth, that God would come   700
To judge them with his Saints: Him the most High
Rapt in a balmie Cloud with winged Steeds
Did, as thou sawst, receave, to walk with God
High in Salvation and the Climes of bliss,
Exempt from Death; to shew thee what reward
Awaits the good, the rest what punishment;
Which now direct thine eyes and soon behold.
    He look'd, & saw the face of things quite chang'd;
The brazen Throat of Warr had ceast to roar,
All now was turn'd to jollitie and game,   710
To luxurie and riot, feast and dance,
Marrying or prostituting, as befell,
Rape or Adulterie, where passing faire
Allurd them; thence from Cups to civil Broiles.
At length a Reverend Sire among them came,
And of thir doings great dislike declar'd,
And testifi'd against thir wayes; hee oft
Frequented thir Assemblies, whereso met,
Triumphs or Festivals, and to them preachd
Conversion and Repentance, as to Souls   720
In prison under Judgements imminent:
But all in vain: which when he saw, he ceas'd
Contending, and remov'd his Tents farr off;

Then from the Mountain hewing Timber tall,
Began to build a Vessel of huge bulk,
Measur'd by Cubit, length, & breadth, and highth,
Smeard round with Pitch, and in the side a dore
Contriv'd, and of provisions laid in large
For Man and Beast: when loe a wonder strange!
Of everie Beast, and Bird, and Insect small   730
Came seavens, and pairs, and enterd in, as taught
Thir order; last the Sire, and his three Sons
With thir four Wives; and God made fast the dore.
Meanwhile the Southwind rose, & with black wings
Wide hovering, all the Clouds together drove
From under Heav'n; the Hills to their supplie
Vapour, and Exhalation dusk and moist,
Sent up amain; and now the thick'nd Skie
Like a dark Ceeling stood; down rush'd the Rain
Impetuous, and continu'd till the Earth   740
No more was seen; the floating Vessel swum
Uplifted; and secure with beaked prow
Rode tilting o're the Waves, all dwellings else
Flood overwhelmd, and them with all thir pomp
Deep under water rould; Sea cover'd Sea,
Sea without shoar; and in thir Palaces
Where luxurie late reign'd, Sea-monsters whelp'd
And stabl'd; of Mankind, so numerous late,
All left, in one small bottom swum imbark't.
How didst thou grieve then, *Adam*, to behold   750
The end of all thy Ofspring, end so sad,
Depopulation; thee another Floud,
Of tears and sorrow a Floud thee also drown'd,
And sunk thee as thy Sons; till gently reard
By th' Angel, on thy feet thou stoodst at last,
Though comfortless, as when a Father mourns
His Children, all in view destroyd at once;
And scarce to th' Angel utterdst thus thy plaint.
     O Visions ill foreseen! better had I
Liv'd ignorant of future, so had borne   760
My part of evil onely, each dayes lot
Anough to bear; those now, that were dispenst
The burd'n of many Ages, on me light
At once, by my foreknowledge gaining Birth
Abortive, to torment me ere thir being,

(427)

With thought that they must be. Let no man seek
Henceforth to be foretold what shall befall
Him or his Children, evil he may be sure,
Which neither his foreknowing can prevent,
And hee the future evil shall no less   770
In apprehension then in substance feel
Grievous to bear : but that care now is past,
Man is not whom to warne : those few escap't
Famin and anguish will at last consume
Wandring that watrie Desert : I had hope
When violence was ceas't, and Warr on Earth,
All would have then gon well, peace would have crownd
With length of happy days the race of man ;
But I was farr deceav'd ; for now I see
Peace to corrupt no less then Warr to waste.   780
How comes it thus ? unfould, Celestial Guide,
And whether here the Race of man will end.
To whom thus *Michael.* Those whom last thou sawst
In triumph and luxurious wealth, are they
First seen in acts of prowess eminent
And great exploits, but of true vertu void ;
Who having spilt much blood, and don much waste
Subduing Nations, and achievd thereby
Fame in the World, high titles, and rich prey,
Shall change thir course to pleasure, ease, and sloth,   790
Surfet, and lust, till wantonness and pride
Raise out of friendship hostil deeds in Peace.
The conquerd also, and enslav'd by Warr
Shall with thir freedom lost all vertu loose
And feare of God, from whom thir pietie feign'd
In sharp contest of Battel found no aide
Against invaders ; therefore coold in zeale
Thenceforth shall practice how to live secure,
Worldlie or dissolute, on what thir Lords
Shall leave them to enjoy ; for th' Earth shall bear   800
More than anough, that temperance may be tri'd :
So all shall turn degenerate, all deprav'd,
Justice and Temperance, Truth and Faith forgot ;
One Man except, the onely Son of light
In a dark Age, against example good,
Against allurement, custom, and a World
Offended ; fearless of reproach and scorn,

Or violence, hee of thir wicked wayes
Shall them admonish, and before them set
The paths of righteousness, how much more safe,   810
And full of peace, denouncing wrauth to come
On thir impenitence; and shall returne
Of them derided, but of God observd
The one just Man alive; by his command
Shall build a wondrous Ark, as thou beheldst,
To save himself and houshold from amidst
A World devote to universal rack.
No sooner hee with them of Man and Beast
Select for life shall in the Ark be lodg'd,
And shelterd round, but all the Cataracts   820
Of Heav'n set open on the Earth shall powre
Raine day and night, all fountaines of the Deep
Broke up, shall heave the Ocean to usurp
Beyond all bounds, till inundation rise
Above the highest Hills: then shall this Mount
Of Paradise by might of Waves be moovd
Out of his place, pushd by the horned floud,
With all his verdure spoil'd, and Trees adrift
Down the great River to the op'ning Gulf,
And there take root an Iland salt and bare,   830
The haunt of Seales and Orcs, and Sea-mews clang.
To teach thee that God attributes to place
No sanctitie, if none be thither brought
By Men who there frequent, or therein dwell.
And now what further shall ensue, behold.

He lookd, and saw the Ark hull on the floud,
Which now abated, for the Clouds were fled,
Drivn by a keen North-winde, that blowing drie
Wrinkl'd the face of Deluge, as decai'd;
And the cleer Sun on his wide watrie Glass   840
Gaz'd hot, and of the fresh Wave largely drew,
As after thirst, which made thir flowing shrink
From standing lake to tripping ebbe, that stole
With soft foot towards the deep, who now had stopt
His Sluces, as the Heav'n his windows shut.
The Ark no more now flotes, but seems on ground
Fast on the top of som high mountain fixt.
And now the tops of Hills as Rocks appeer;
With clamor thence the rapid Currents drive

Towards the retreating Sea thir furious tyde.   850
Forthwith from out the Arke a Raven flies,
And after him, the surer messenger,
A Dove sent forth once and agen to spie
Green Tree or ground whereon his foot may light;
The second time returning, in his Bill
An Olive leafe he brings, pacific signe:
Anon drie ground appeers, and from his Arke
The ancient Sire descends with all his Train;
Then with uplifted hands, and eyes devout,
Grateful to Heav'n, over his head beholds   860
A dewie Cloud, and in the Cloud a Bow
Conspicuous with three listed colours gay,
Betok'ning peace from God, and Cov'nant new.
Whereat the heart of *Adam* erst so sad
Greatly rejoyc'd, and thus his joy broke forth.

O thou that future things canst represent
As present, Heav'nly instructer, I revive
At this last sight, assur'd that Man shall live
With all the Creatures, and thir seed preserve.
Farr less I now lament for one whole World   870
Of wicked Sons destroyd, then I rejoyce
For one Man found so perfet and so just,
That God voutsafes to raise another World
From him, and all his anger to forget.
But say, what mean those colourd streaks in Heavn,
Distended as the Brow of God appeas'd,
Or serve they as a flourie verge to binde
The fluid skirts of that same watrie Cloud,
Least it again dissolve and showr the Earth?

To whom th' Archangel. Dextrously thou aim'st;   880
So willingly doth God remit his Ire,
Though late repenting him of Man deprav'd,
Griev'd at his heart, when looking down he saw
The whole Earth fill'd with violence, and all flesh
Corrupting each thir way; yet those remoov'd,
Such grace shall one just Man find in his sight,
That he relents, not to blot out mankind,
And makes a Covenant never to destroy
The Earth again by flood, nor let the Sea
Surpass his bounds, nor Rain to drown the World   890

866 that] who *1674*

(430)

With Man therein or Beast; but when he brings
Over the Earth a Cloud, will therein set
His triple-colour'd Bow, whereon to look
And call to mind his Cov'nant: Day and Night,
Seed time and Harvest, Heat and hoary Frost
Shall hold thir course, till fire purge all things new,
Both Heav'n and Earth, wherein the just shall dwell.

The End of the Eleventh Book.

PARADISE LOST.

BOOK XII.

THE ARGUMENT.

The Angel Michael *continues from the Flood to relate what shall succeed; then, in the mention of* Abraham, *comes by degrees to explain, who that Seed of the Woman shall be, which was promised* Adam *and* Eve *in the Fall; his Incarnation, Death, Resurrection, and Ascension; the state of the Church till his second Coming.* Adam *greatly satisfied and recomforted by these Relations and Promises descends the Hill with* Michael; *wakens* Eve, *who all this while had slept, but with gentle dreams compos'd to quietness of mind and submission.* Michael *in either hand leads them out of Paradise, the fiery Sword waving behind them, and the Cherubim taking thir Stations to guard the Place.*

[As one who in his journey bates at Noone,
Though bent on speed, so heer the Archangel paus'd
Betwixt the world destroy'd and world restor'd,
If *Adam* aught perhaps might interpose;
Then with transition sweet new Speech resumes.]
    Thus thou hast seen one World begin and end;
And Man as from a second stock proceed.
Much thou hast yet to see, but I perceave
Thy mortal sight to faile; objects divine
Must needs impaire and wearie human sense: 10
Henceforth what is to com I will relate,
Thou therefore give due audience, and attend.
This second sours of Men, while yet but few,

Argument. The Angel . . . seed] Thence from the Flood relates, and by degrees explains who that seed *1667*.

1–5 These five lines were added in the Second Edition (1674) when the original tenth book was divided into an eleventh and twelfth.

And while the dread of judgement past remains
Fresh in thir mindes, fearing the Deitie,
With some regard to what is just and right
Shall lead thir lives, and multiplie apace,
Labouring the soile, and reaping plenteous crop,
Corn wine and oyle; and from the herd or flock,
Oft sacrificing Bullock, Lamb, or Kid,   20
With large Wine-offerings pour'd, and sacred Feast
Shal spend thir dayes in joy unblam'd, and dwell
Long time in peace by Families and Tribes
Under paternal rule; till one shall rise
Of proud ambitious heart, who not content
With fair equalitie, fraternal state,
Will arrogate Dominion undeserv'd
Over his brethren, and quite dispossess
Concord and law of Nature from the Earth;
Hunting (and Men not Beasts shall be his game)   30
With Warr and hostile snare such as refuse
Subjection to his Empire tyrannous:
A mightie Hunter thence he shall be styl'd
Before the Lord, as in despite of Heav'n,
Or from Heav'n claming second Sovrantie;
And from Rebellion shall derive his name,
Though of Rebellion others he accuse.
Hee with a crew, whom like Ambition joyns
With him or under him to tyrannize,
Marching from *Eden* towards the West, shall finde   40
The Plain, wherein a black bituminous gurge
Boiles out from under ground, the mouth of Hell;
Of Brick, and of that stuff they cast to build
A Citie & Towre, whose top may reach to Heav'n;
And get themselves a name, least far disperst
In foraign Lands thir memorie be lost,
Regardless whether good or evil fame.
But God who oft descends to visit men
Unseen, and through thir habitations walks
To mark thir doings, them beholding soon,   50
Comes down to see thir Citie, ere the Tower
Obstruct Heav'n Towrs, and in derision sets
Upon thir Tongues a various Spirit to rase
Quite out thir Native Language, and instead
To sow a jangling noise of words unknown:

Forthwith a hideous gabble rises loud
Among the Builders ; each to other calls
Not understood, till hoarse, and all in rage,
As mockt they storm ; great laughter was in Heav'n
And looking down, to see the hubbub strange   60
And hear the din ; thus was the building left
Ridiculous, and the work Confusion nam'd.
  Whereto thus *Adam* fatherly displeas'd.
O execrable Son so to aspire
Above his Brethren, to himself assuming
Authoritie usurpt, from God not giv'n :
He gave us onely over Beast, Fish, Fowl
Dominion absolute ; that right we hold
By his donation ; but Man over men
He made not Lord ; such title to himself   70
Reserving, human left from human free.
But this Usurper his encroachment proud
Stayes not on Man ; to God his Tower intends
Siege and defiance : Wretched man ! what food
Will he convey up thither to sustain
Himself and his rash Armie, where thin Aire
Above the Clouds will pine his entrails gross,
And famish him of Breath, if not of Bread ?
  To whom thus *Michael.* Justly thou abhorr'st
That Son, who on the quiet state of men   80
Such trouble brought, affecting to subdue
Rational Libertie ; yet know withall,
Since thy original lapse, true Libertie
Is lost, which alwayes with right Reason dwells
Twinn'd, and from her hath no dividual being :
Reason in man obscur'd, or not obeyd,
Immediately inordinate desires
And upstart Passions catch the Government
From Reason, and to servitude reduce
Man till then free.   Therefore since hee permits   90
Within himself unworthie Powers to reign
Over free Reason, God in Judgement just
Subjects him from without to violent Lords ;
Who oft as undeservedly enthrall
His outward freedom : Tyrannie must be,
Though to the Tyrant thereby no excuse.
Yet somtimes Nations will decline so low

From vertue, which is reason, that no wrong,
But Justice, and some fatal curse annext
Deprives them of thir outward libertie,   100
Thir inward lost: Witness th' irreverent Son
Of him who built the Ark, who for the shame
Don to his Father, heard this heavie curse,
Servant of Servants, on his vitious Race.
Thus will this latter, as the former World,
Still tend from bad to worse, till God at last
Wearied with their iniquities, withdraw
His presence from among them, and avert
His holy Eyes ; resolving from thenceforth
To leave them to thir own polluted wayes;   110
And one peculiar Nation to select
From all the rest, of whom to be invok'd,
A Nation from one faithful man to spring:
Him on this side *Euphrates* yet residing,
Bred up in Idol-worship; O that men
(Canst thou believe ?) should be so stupid grown,
While yet the Patriark liv'd, who scap'd the Flood,
As to forsake the living God, and fall
To worship thir own work in Wood and Stone
For Gods ! yet him God the most High voutsafes   120
To call by Vision from his Fathers house,
His kindred and false Gods, into a Land
Which he will shew him, and from him will raise
A mightie Nation, and upon him showre
His benediction so, that in his Seed
All Nations shall be blest; hee straight obeys,
Not knowing to what Land, yet firm believes:
I see him, but thou canst not, with what Faith
He leaves his Gods, his Friends, and native Soile
Ur of *Chaldæa*, passing now the Ford   130
To *Haran*, after him a cumbrous Train
Of Herds and Flocks, and numerous servitude;
Not wandring poor, but trusting all his wealth
With God, who call'd him, in a land unknown.
Canaan he now attains, I see his Tents
Pitcht about *Sechem*, and the neighbouring Plaine
Of *Moreh* ; there by promise he receaves
Gift to his Progenie of all that Land;
From *Hamath* Northward to the Desert South

(Things by thir names I call, though yet unnam'd)   140
From *Hermon* East to the great Western Sea,
Mount *Hermon*, yonder Sea, each place behold
In prospect, as I point them ; on the shoare
Mount *Carmel* ; here the double-founted stream
Jordan, true limit Eastward ; but his Sons
Shall dwell to *Senir*, that long ridge of Hills.
This ponder, that all Nations of the Earth
Shall in his Seed be blessed ; by that Seed
Is meant thy great deliverer, who shall bruise
The Serpents head ; whereof to thee anon   150
Plainlier shall be reveald. This Patriarch blest,
Whom *faithful Abraham* due time shall call,
A Son, and of his Son a Grand-childe leaves,
Like him in faith, in wisdom, and renown ;
The Grandchilde with twelve Sons increast, departs
From *Canaan*, to a land hereafter call'd
Egypt, divided by the River *Nile* ;
See where it flows, disgorging at seaven mouthes
Into the Sea : to sojourn in that Land
He comes invited by a yonger Son   160
In time of dearth, a Son whose worthy deeds
Raise him to be the second in that Realme
Of *Pharao* : there he dies, and leaves his Race
Growing into a Nation, and now grown
Suspected to a sequent King, who seeks
To stop thir overgrowth, as inmate guests
Too numerous ; whence of guests he makes them slaves
Inhospitably, and kills thir infant Males :
Till by two brethren (those two brethren call
Moses and *Aaron*) sent from God to claime   170
His people from enthralment, they return
With glory and spoile back to thir promis'd Land.
But first the lawless Tyrant, who denies
To know thir God, or message to regard,
Must be compelld by Signes and Judgements dire ;
To blood unshed the Rivers must be turnd,
Frogs, Lice and Flies must all his Palace fill
With loath'd intrusion, and fill all the land ;
His Cattel must of Rot and Murren die,
Botches and blaines must all his flesh imboss,   180
And all his people ; Thunder mixt with Haile,

Haile mixt with fire must rend th' *Egyptian* Skie
And wheel on th' Earth, devouring where it rouls;
What it devours not, Herb, or Fruit, or Graine,
A darksom Cloud of Locusts swarming down
Must eat, and on the ground leave nothing green :
Darkness must overshadow all his bounds,
Palpable darkness, and blot out three dayes ;
Last with one midnight stroke all the first-born
Of *Egypt* must lie dead. Thus with ten wounds   190
This River-dragon tam'd at length submits
To let his sojourners depart, and oft
Humbles his stubborn heart, but still as Ice
More hard'nd after thaw, till in his rage
Pursuing whom he late dismissd, the Sea
Swallows him with his Host, but them lets pass
As on drie land between two christal walls,
Aw'd by the rod of *Moses* so to stand
Divided, till his rescu'd gain thir shoar :
Such wondrous power God to his Saint will lend,   200
Though present in his Angel, who shall goe
Before them in a Cloud, and Pillar of Fire,
By day a Cloud, by night a Pillar of Fire,
To guide them in thir journey, and remove
Behinde them, while th' obdurat King pursues :
All night he will pursue, but his approach
Darkness defends between till morning Watch ;
Then through the Firey Pillar and the Cloud
God looking forth will trouble all his Host
And craze thir Chariot wheels : when by command   210
Moses once more his potent Rod extends
Over the Sea ; the Sea his Rod obeys ;
On thir imbattelld ranks the Waves return,
And overwhelm thir Warr : the Race elect
Safe towards *Canaan* from the shoar advance
Through the wilde Desert, not the readiest way,
Least entring on the *Canaanite* allarmd
Warr terrifie them inexpert, and feare
Return them back to *Egypt*, choosing rather
Inglorious life with servitude ; for life   220
To noble and ignoble is more sweet
Untraind in Armes, where rashness leads not on.

191 This] The *1674*

(437)

This also shall they gain by thir delay
In the wide Wilderness, there they shall found
Thir government, and thir great Senate choose
Through the twelve Tribes, to rule by Laws ordaind:
God from the Mount of *Sinai*, whose gray top
Shall tremble, he descending, will himself
In Thunder Lightning and loud Trumpets sound
Ordaine them Lawes; part such as appertaine   230
To civil Justice, part religious Rites
Of sacrifice, informing them, by types
And shadowes, of that destind Seed to bruise
The Serpent, by what meanes he shall achieve
Mankinds deliverance. But the voice of God
To mortal eare is dreadful; they beseech
That *Moses* might report to them his will,
And terror cease; he grants them thir desire,
Instructed that to God is no access
Without Mediator, whose high Office now   240
Moses in figure beares, to introduce
One greater, of whose day he shall foretell,
And all the Prophets in thir Age, the times
Of great *Messiah* shall sing. Thus Laws and Rites
Establisht, such delight hath God in Men
Obedient to his will, that he voutsafes
Among them to set up his Tabernacle,
The holy One with mortal Men to dwell:
By his prescript a Sanctuary is fram'd
Of Cedar, overlaid with Gold, therein   250
An Ark, and in the Ark his Testimony,
The Records of his Cov'nant, over these
A Mercie-seat of Gold between the wings
Of two bright Cherubim, before him burn
Seaven Lamps as in a Zodiac representing
The Heav'nly fires; over the Tent a Cloud
Shall rest by Day, a fierie gleame by Night,
Save when they journie, and at length they come,
Conducted by his Angel to the Land
Promisd to *Abraham* and his Seed: the rest   260
Were long to tell, how many Battels fought,
How many Kings destroyd, and Kingdoms won,
Or how the Sun shall in mid Heav'n stand still

238 them thir desire] what they besaught *1674*

(438)

A day entire, and Nights due course adjourne,
Mans voice commanding, Sun in *Gibeon* stand,
And thou Moon in the vale of *Aialon*,
Till *Israel* overcome ; so call the third
From *Abraham*, Son of *Isaac*, and from him
His whole descent, who thus shall *Canaan* win.

   Here *Adam* interpos'd. O sent from Heav'n,   270
Enlightner of my darkness, gracious things
Thou hast reveald, those chiefly which concerne
Just *Abraham* and his Seed : now first I finde
Mine eyes true op'ning, and my heart much eas'd,
Erwhile perplext with thoughts what would becom
Of mee and all Mankind ; but now I see
His day, in whom all Nations shall be blest,
Favour unmerited by me, who sought
Forbidd'n knowledge by forbidd'n means.
This yet I apprehend not, why to those   280
Among whom God will deigne to dwell on Earth
So many and so various Laws are giv'n ;
So many Laws argue so many sins
Among them ; how can God with such reside ?

   To whom thus *Michael*. Doubt not but that sin
Will reign among them, as of thee begot ;
And therefore was Law given them to evince
Thir natural pravitie, by stirring up
Sin against Law to fight ; that when they see
Law can discover sin, but not remove,   290
Save by those shadowie expiations weak,
The bloud of Bulls and Goats, they may conclude
Some bloud more precious must be paid for Man,
Just for unjust, that in such righteousness
To them by Faith imputed, they may finde
Justification towards God, and peace
Of Conscience, which the Law by Ceremonies
Cannot appease, nor Man the moral part
Perform, and not performing cannot live.
So Law appears imperfet, and but giv'n   300
With purpose to resign them in full time
Up to a better Cov'nant, disciplin'd
From shadowie Types to Truth, from Flesh to Spirit,
From imposition of strict Laws, to free
Acceptance of large Grace, from servil fear

To filial, works of Law to works of Faith.
And therefore shall not *Moses*, though of God
Highly belov'd, being but the Minister
Of Law, his people into *Canaan* lead;
But *Joshua* whom the Gentiles *Jesus* call,   310
His Name and Office bearing, who shall quell
The adversarie Serpent, and bring back
Through the worlds wilderness long wanderd man
Safe to eternal Paradise of rest.
Meanwhile they in thir earthly *Canaan* plac't
Long time shall dwell and prosper, but when sins
National interrupt thir public peace,
Provoking God to raise them enemies:
From whom as oft he saves them penitent
By Judges first, then under Kings; of whom   320
The second, both for pietie renownd
And puissant deeds, a promise shall receive
Irrevocable, that his Regal Throne
For ever shall endure; the like shall sing
All Prophecie, That of the Royal Stock
Of *David* (so I name this King) shall rise
A Son, the Womans Seed to thee foretold,
Foretold to *Abraham*, as in whom shall trust
All Nations, and to Kings foretold, of Kings
The last, for of his Reign shall be no end.   330
But first a long succession must ensue,
And his next Son for Wealth and Wisdom fam'd,
The clouded Ark of God till then in Tents
Wandring, shall in a glorious Temple enshrine.
Such follow him, as shall be registerd
Part good, part bad, of bad the longer scrowle,
Whose foul Idolatries, and other faults
Heapt to the popular summe, will so incense
God, as to leave them, and expose thir Land,
Thir Citie, his Temple, and his holy Ark   340
With all his sacred things, a scorn and prey
To that proud Citie, whose high Walls thou saw'st
Left in confusion, *Babylon* thence call'd.
There in captivitie he lets them dwell
The space of seventie years, then brings them back,
Remembring mercie, and his Cov'nant sworn
To *David*, stablisht as the dayes of Heav'n.

Returnd from *Babylon* by leave of Kings
Thir Lords, whom God dispos'd, the house of God
They first re-edifie, and for a while   350
In mean estate live moderate, till grown
In wealth and multitude, factious they grow;
But first among the Priests dissension springs,
Men who attend the Altar, and should most
Endeavour Peace: thir strife pollution brings
Upon the Temple it self: at last they seise
The Scepter, and regard not *Davids* Sons,
Then loose it to a stranger, that the true
Anointed King *Messiah* might be born
Barr'd of his right; yet at his Birth a Starr   360
Unseen before in Heav'n proclaims him com,
And guides the Eastern Sages, who enquire
His place, to offer Incense, Myrrh, and Gold;
His place of birth a solemn Angel tells
To simple Shepherds, keeping watch by night;
They gladly thither haste, and by a Quire
Of squadrond Angels hear his Carol sung.
A Virgin is his Mother, but his Sire
The Power of the most High; he shall ascend
The Throne hereditarie, and bound his Reign   370
With earths wide bounds, his glory with the Heav'ns.

He ceas'd, discerning *Adam* with such joy
Surcharg'd, as had like grief bin dew'd in tears,
Without the vent of words, which these he breathd.

   O Prophet of glad tidings, finisher
Of utmost hope! now clear I understand
What oft my steddiest thoughts have searcht in vain,
Why our great expectation should be call'd
The seed of Woman: Virgin Mother, Haile,
High in the love of Heav'n, yet from my Loynes   380
Thou shalt proceed, and from thy Womb the Son
Of God most High; So God with man unites.
Needs must the Serpent now his capital bruise
Expect with mortal paine: say where and when
Thir fight, what stroke shall bruise the Victors heel.

   To whom thus *Michael*. Dream not of thir fight,
As of a Duel, or the local wounds
Of head or heel: not therefore joynes the Son
Manhood to God-head, with more strength to foil

Thy enemie; nor so is overcome   390
Satan, whose fall from Heav'n, a deadlier bruise,
Disabl'd not to give thee thy deaths wound :
Which hee, who comes thy Saviour, shall recure,
Not by destroying *Satan*, but his works
In thee and in thy Seed : nor can this be,
But by fulfilling that which thou didst want,
Obedience to the Law of God, impos'd
On penaltie of death, and suffering death,
The penaltie to thy transgression due,
And due to theirs which out of thine will grow :   400
So onely can high Justice rest appaid.
The Law of God exact he shall fulfill
Both by obedience and by love, though love
Alone fulfill the Law ; thy punishment
He shall endure by coming in the Flesh
To a reproachful life and cursed death,
Proclaming Life to all who shall believe
In his redemption, and that his obedience
Imputed becomes theirs by Faith, his merits
To save them, not thir own, though legal works.   410
For this he shall live hated, be blasphem'd,
Seis'd on by force, judg'd, and to death condemnd
A shameful and accurst, naild to the Cross
By his own Nation, slaine for bringing Life ;
But to the Cross he nailes thy Enemies,
The Law that is against thee, and the sins
Of all mankinde, with him there crucifi'd,
Never to hurt them more who rightly trust
In this his satisfaction ; so he dies,
But soon revives, Death over him no power   420
Shall long usurp; ere the third dawning light
Returne, the Starres of Morn shall see him rise
Out of his grave, fresh as the dawning light,
Thy ransom paid, which Man from death redeems,
His death for Man, as many as offerd Life
Neglect not, and the benefit imbrace
By Faith not void of workes : this God-like act
Annuls thy doom, the death thou shouldst have dy'd,
In sin for ever lost from life ; this act
Shall bruise the head of *Satan*, crush his strength   430
Defeating Sin and Death, his two maine armes,

And fix farr deeper in his head thir stings
Then temporal death shall bruise the Victors heel,
Or theirs whom he redeems, a death like sleep,
A gentle wafting to immortal Life.
Nor after resurrection shall he stay
Longer on Earth then certaine times to appeer
To his Disciples, Men who in his Life
Still follow'd him ; to them shall leave in charge
To teach all nations what of him they learn'd   440
And his Salvation, them who shall beleeve
Baptizing in the profluent streame, the signe
Of washing them from guilt of sin to Life
Pure, and in mind prepar'd, if so befall,
For death, like that which the redeemer dy'd.
All Nations they shall teach ; for from that day
Not onely to the Sons of *Abrahams* Loines
Salvation shall be Preacht, but to the Sons
Of *Abrahams* Faith wherever through the world ;
So in his seed all Nations shall be blest.   450
Then to the Heav'n of Heav'ns he shall ascend
With victory, triumphing through the aire
Over his foes and thine ; there shall surprise
The Serpent, Prince of aire, and drag in Chaines
Through all his realme, & there confounded leave ;
Then enter into glory, and resume
His Seat at Gods right hand, exalted high
Above all names in Heav'n ; and thence shall come,
When this worlds dissolution shall be ripe,
With glory and power to judge both quick & dead   460
To judge th' unfaithful dead, but to reward
His faithful, and receave them into bliss,
Whether in Heav'n or Earth, for then the Earth
Shall all be Paradise, far happier place
Then this of *Eden*, and far happier daies.
   So spake th' Archangel *Michael*, then paus'd,
As at the Worlds great period ; and our Sire
Replete with joy and wonder thus repli'd.
   O goodness infinite, goodness immense !
That all this good of evil shall produce,   470
And evil turn to good ; more wonderful
Then that by which creation first brought forth
Light out of darkness ! full of doubt I stand,

Whether I should repent me now of sin
By mee done and occasiond, or rejoyce
Much more, that much more good thereof shall spring,
To God more glory, more good will to Men
From God, and over wrauth grace shall abound.
But say, if our deliverer up to Heav'n
Must reascend, what will betide the few   480
His faithful, left among th' unfaithful herd,
The enemies of truth; who then shall guide
His people, who defend? will they not deale
Wors with his followers then with him they dealt?
  . Be sure they will, said th' Angel; but from Heav'n
Hee to his own a Comforter will send,
The promise of the Father, who shall dwell
His Spirit within them, and the Law of Faith
Working through love, upon thir hearts shall write,
To guide them in all truth, and also arme   490
With spiritual Armour, able to resist
Satans assaults, and quench his fierie darts,
What Man can do against them, not affraid,
Though to the death, against such cruelties
With inward consolations recompenc't,
And oft supported so as shall amaze
Thir proudest persecuters: for the Spirit
Powrd first on his Apostles, whom he sends
To evangelize the Nations, then on all
Baptiz'd, shall them with wondrous gifts endue   500
To speak all Tongues, and do all Miracles,
As did thir Lord before them. Thus they win
Great numbers of each Nation to receave
With joy the tidings brought from Heav'n: at length
Thir Ministry perform'd, and race well run,
Thir doctrine and thir story written left,
They die; but in thir room, as they forewarne,
Wolves shall succeed for teachers, grievous Wolves,
Who all the sacred mysteries of Heav'n
To thir own vile advantages shall turne   510
Of lucre and ambition, and the truth
With superstitions and traditions taint,
Left onely in those written Records pure,
Though not but by the Spirit understood.
Then shall they seek to avail themselves of names,

Places and titles, and with these to joine
Secular power, though feigning still to act
By spiritual, to themselves appropriating
The Spirit of God, promisd alike and giv'n
To all Beleevers ; and from that pretense,   520
Spiritual Lawes by carnal power shall force
On every conscience ; Laws which none shall finde
Left them inrould, or what the Spirit within
Shall on the heart engrave.   What will they then
But force the Spirit of Grace it self, and binde
His consort Libertie ; what, but unbuild
His living Temples, built by Faith to stand,
Thir own Faith not anothers : for on Earth
Who against Faith and Conscience can be heard
Infallible ? yet many will presume :   530
Whence heavie persecution shall arise
On all who in the worship persevere
Of Spirit and Truth ; the rest, farr greater part,
Will deem in outward Rites and specious formes
Religion satisfi'd ; Truth shall retire
Bestuck with slandrous darts, and works of Faith
Rarely be found : so shall the World goe on,
To good malignant, to bad men benigne,
Under her own waight groaning, till the day
Appeer of respiration to the just,   540
And vengeance to the wicked, at return
Of him so lately promiss'd to thy aid,
The Womans seed, obscurely then foretold,
Now amplier known thy Saviour and thy Lord,
Last in the Clouds from Heav'n to be reveald
In glory of the Father, to dissolve
Satan with his perverted World, then raise
From the conflagrant mass, purg'd and refin'd,
New Heav'ns, new Earth, Ages of endless date
Founded in righteousness and peace and love,   550
To bring forth fruits Joy and eternal Bliss.
    He ended ; and thus *Adam* last reply'd.
How soon hath thy prediction, Seer blest,
Measur'd this transient World, the Race of time,
Till time stand fixt : beyond is all abyss,
Eternitie, whose end no eye can reach.
Greatly instructed I shall hence depart.

(445)

Greatly in peace of thought, and have my fill
Of knowledge, what this vessel can containe;
Beyond which was my folly to aspire. 560
Henceforth I learne, that to obey is best,
And love with feare the onely God, to walk
As in his presence, ever to observe
His providence, and on him sole depend,
Merciful over all his works, with good
Still overcoming evil, and by small
Accomplishing great things, by things deemd weak
Subverting worldly strong, and worldly wise
By simply meek; that suffering for Truths sake
Is fortitude to highest victorie, 570
And to the faithful Death the Gate of Life;
Taught this by his example whom I now
Acknowledge my Redeemer ever blest.

To whom thus also th' Angel last repli'd:
This having learnt, thou hast attained the summe
Of wisdom; hope no higher, though all the Starrs
Thou knewst by name, and all th' ethereal Powers,
All secrets of the deep, all Natures works,
Or works of God in Heav'n, Air, Earth, or Sea,
And all the riches of this World enjoydst, 580
And all the rule, one Empire; onely add
Deeds to thy knowledge answerable, add Faith,
Add Vertue, Patience, Temperance, add Love,
By name to come call'd Charitie, the soul
Of all the rest: then wilt thou not be loath
To leave this Paradise, but shalt possess
A Paradise within thee, happier farr.
Let us descend now therefore from this top
Of Speculation; for the hour precise
Exacts our parting hence; and see the Guards, 590
By mee encampt on yonder Hill, expect
Thir motion, at whose Front a flaming Sword,
In signal of remove, waves fiercely round;
We may no longer stay: go, waken *Eve*;
Her also I with gentle Dreams have calm'd
Portending good, and all her spirits compos'd
To meek submission: thou at season fit
Let her with thee partake what thou hast heard,
Chiefly what may concern her Faith to know,

The great deliverance by her Seed to come   600
(For by the Womans Seed) on all Mankind.
That ye may live, which will be many dayes,
Both in one Faith unanimous though sad,
With cause for evils past, yet much more cheer'd
With meditation on the happie end.

He ended, and they both descend the Hill;
Descended, *Adam* to the Bowre where *Eve*
Lay sleeping ran before, but found her wak't;
And thus with words not sad she him receav'd.

Whence thou returnst, & whither wentst, I know;   610
For God is also in sleep, and Dreams advise,
Which he hath sent propitious, some great good
Presaging, since with sorrow and hearts distress
Wearied I fell asleep: but now lead on;
In mee is no delay; with thee to goe,
Is to stay here; without thee here to stay,
Is to go hence unwilling; thou to mee
Art all things under Heav'n, all places thou,
Who for my wilful crime art banisht hence.
This further consolation yet secure   620
I carry hence; though all by mee is lost,
Such favour I unworthie am voutsaft,
By mee the Promis'd Seed shall all restore.

So spake our Mother *Eve*, and *Adam* heard
Well pleas'd, but answer'd not; for now too nigh
Th' Archangel stood, and from the other Hill
To thir fixt Station, all in bright array
The Cherubim descended; on the ground
Gliding meteorous, as Ev'ning Mist
Ris'n from a River o're the marish glides,   630
And gathers ground fast at the Labourers heel
Homeward returning. High in Front advanc't,
The brandisht Sword of God before them blaz'd
Fierce as a Comet; which with torrid heat,
And vapour as the *Libyan* Air adust,
Began to parch that temperate Clime; whereat
In either hand the hastning Angel caught
Our lingring Parents, and to th' Eastern Gate
Led them direct, and down the Cliff as fast
To the subjected Plaine; then disappeer'd.   640
They looking back, all th' Eastern side beheld

Paradise Lost.

Of Paradise, so late thir happie seat,
Wav'd over by that flaming Brand, the Gate
With dreadful Faces throng'd and fierie Armes :
Som natural tears they drop'd, but wip'd them soon ;
The World was all before them, where to choose
Thir place of rest, and Providence thir guide :
They hand in hand with wandring steps and slow,
Through *Eden* took thir solitarie way.

The End.

PARADISE
REGAIN'D.

A
POEM.

In IV *BOOKS.*

To which is added

SAMSON AGONISTES.

The Author

JOHN MILTON.

LONDON,

Printed by *J. M* for *John Starkey* at the
Mitre in *Fleetstreet,* near *Temple-Bar.*
MDCLXXI.

PARADISE REGAIN'D.

The First Book.

I WHO e're while the happy Garden sung,
By one mans disobedience lost, now sing
Recover'd Paradise to all mankind,
By one mans firm obedience fully tri'd
Through all temptation, and the Tempter foil'd
In all his wiles, defeated and repuls't,
And *Eden* rais'd in the wast Wilderness.
  Thou Spirit who ledst this glorious Eremite
Into the Desert, his Victorious Field
Against the Spiritual Foe, and broughtst him thence   10
By proof the undoubted Son of God, inspire,
As thou art wont, my prompted Song else mute,
And bear through highth or depth of natures bounds
With prosperous wing full summ'd to tell of deeds
Above Heroic, though in secret done,
And unrecorded left through many an Age,
Worthy t' have not remain'd so long unsung.
  Now had the great Proclaimer with a voice
More awful then the sound of Trumpet, cri'd
Repentance, and Heavens Kingdom nigh at hand   20
To all Baptiz'd : to his great Baptism flock'd
With aw the Regions round, and with them came
From *Nazareth* the Son of *Joseph* deem'd
To the flood *Jordan*, came as then obscure,
Unmarkt, unknown ; but him the Baptist soon
Descri'd, divinely warn'd, and witness bore
As to his worthier, and would have resign'd
To him his Heavenly Office, nor was long

His witness unconfirm'd : on him baptiz'd
Heaven open'd, and in likeness of a Dove   30
The Spirit descended, while the Fathers voice
From Heav'n pronounc'd him his beloved Son
That heard the Adversary, who roving still
About the world, at that assembly fam'd
Would not be last, and with the voice divine
Nigh Thunder-struck, th' exalted man, to whom
Such high attest was giv'n, a while survey'd
With wonder, then with envy fraught and rage
Flies to his place, nor rests, but in mid air
To Councel summons all his mighty Peers,   40
Within thick Clouds and dark ten-fold involv'd,
A gloomy Consistory ; and them amidst
With looks agast and sad he thus bespake.
    O ancient Powers of Air and this wide world,
For much more willingly I mention Air,
This our old Conquest, then remember Hell
Our hated habitation ; well ye know
How many Ages, as the years of men,
This Universe we have possest, and rul'd
In manner at our will th' affairs of Earth,   50
Since *Adam* and his facil consort *Eve*
Lost Paradise deceiv'd by me, though since
With dread attending when that fatal wound
Shall be inflicted by the Seed of *Eve*
Upon my head, long the decrees of Heav'n
Delay, for longest time to him is short;
And now too soon for us the circling hours
This dreaded time have compast, wherein we
Must bide the stroak of that long threatn'd wound,
At least if so we can, and by the head   60
Broken be not intended all our power
To be infring'd, our freedom and our being
In this fair Empire won of Earth and Air ;
For this ill news I bring, the Womans seed
Destin'd to this, is late of woman born,
His birth to our just fear gave no small cause,
But his growth now to youths full flowr, displaying
All vertue, grace and wisdom to atchieve
Things highest, greatest, multiplies my fear.
Before him a great Prophet, to proclaim   70

His coming, is sent Harbinger, who all
Invites, and in the Consecrated stream
Pretends to wash off sin, and fit them so
Purified to receive him pure, or rather
To do him honour as their King; all come,
And he himself among them was baptiz'd,
Not thence to be more pure, but to receive
The testimony of Heaven, that who he is
Thenceforth the Nations may not doubt; I saw
The Prophet do him reverence, on him rising   80
Out of the water, Heav'n above the Clouds
Unfold her Crystal Dores, thence on his head
A perfect Dove descend, what e're it meant,
And out of Heav'n the Sov'raign voice I heard,
This is my Son belov'd, in him am pleas'd.
His Mother then is mortal, but his Sire,
He who obtains the Monarchy of Heav'n,
And what will he not do to advance his Son?
His first-begot we know, and sore have felt,
When his fierce thunder drove us to the deep;   90
Who this is we must learn, for man he seems
In all his lineaments, though in his face
The glimpses of his Fathers glory shine.
Ye see our danger on the utmost edge
Of hazard, which admits no long debate,
But must with something sudden be oppos'd,
Not force, but well couch't fraud, well woven snares,
E're in the head of Nations he appear
Their King, their Leader, and Supream on Earth.
I, when no other durst, sole undertook   100
The dismal expedition to find out
And ruine *Adam*, and the exploit perform'd
Successfully; a calmer voyage now
Will waft me; and the way found prosperous once
Induces best to hope of like success.
    He ended, and his words impression left
Of much amazement to th' infernal Crew,
Distracted and surpriz'd with deep dismay
At these sad tidings; but no time was then
For long indulgence to their fears or grief: 110
Unanimous they all commit the care
And management of this main enterprize

To him their great Dictator, whose attempt
At first against mankind so well had thriv'd
In *Adam*'s overthrow, and led thir march
From Hell's deep-vaulted Den to dwell in light,
Regents and Potentates, and Kings, yea gods
Of many a pleasant Realm and Province wide.
So to the Coast of *Jordan* he directs
His easie steps; girded with snaky wiles,   120
Where he might likeliest find this new-declar'd,
This man of men, attested Son of God,
Temptation and all guile on him to try;
So to subvert whom he suspected rais'd
To end his Raign on Earth so long enjoy'd:
But contrary unweeting he fulfill'd
The purpos'd Counsel pre-ordain'd and fixt
Of the most High, who in full frequence bright
Of Angels, thus to *Gabriel* smiling spake.

      Gabriel this day by proof thou shalt behold,   130
Thou and all Angels conversant on Earth
With man or mens affairs, how I begin
To verifie that solemn message late,
On which I sent thee to the Virgin pure
In *Galilee*, that she should bear a Son
Great in Renown, and call'd the Son of God;
Then toldst her doubting how these things could be
To her a Virgin, that on her should come
The Holy Ghost, and the power of the highest
O're-shadow her: this man born and now up-grown,   140
To shew him worthy of his birth divine
And high prediction, henceforth I expose
To Satan; let him tempt and now assay
His utmost subtilty, because he boasts
And vaunts of his great cunning to the throng
Of his Apostasie; he might have learnt
Less over-weening, since he fail'd in *Job*,
Whose constant perseverance overcame
Whate're his cruel malice could invent.
He now shall know I can produce a man   150
Of female Seed, far abler to resist
All his sollicitations, and at length
All his vast force, and drive him back to Hell,
Winning by Conquest what the first man lost

(454)

By fallacy surpriz'd. But first I mean
To exercise him in the Wilderness,
There he shall first lay down the rudiments
Of his great warfare, e're I send him forth
To conquer Sin and Death the two grand foes,
By Humiliation and strong Sufferance :   160
His weakness shall o'recome Satanic strength
And all the world, and mass of sinful flesh ;
That all the Angels and Ætherial Powers,
They now, and men hereafter may discern,
From what consummate vertue I have chose
This perfect Man, by merit call'd my Son,
To earn Salvation for the Sons of men.
    So spake the Eternal Father, and all Heaven
Admiring stood a space, then into Hymns
Burst forth, and in Celestial measures mov'd,   170
Circling the Throne and Singing, while the hand
Sung with the voice, and this the argument.
    Victory and Triumph to the Son of God
Now entring his great duel, not of arms,
But to vanquish by wisdom hellish wiles.
The Father knows the Son ; therefore secure
Ventures his filial Vertue, though untri'd,
Against whate're may tempt, whate're seduce,
Allure, or terrifie, or undermine.
Be frustrate all ye stratagems of Hell,   180
And devilish machinations come to nought.
    So they in Heav'n their Odes and Vigils tun'd :
Mean while the Son of God, who yet some days
Lodg'd in *Bethabara* where *John* baptiz'd,
Musing and much revolving in his brest,
How best the mighty work he might begin
Of Saviour to mankind, and which way first
Publish his God-like office now mature,
One day forth walk'd alone, the Spirit leading ;
And his deep thoughts, the better to converse   190
With solitude, till far from track of men,
Thought following thought, and step by step led on,
He entred now the bordering Desert wild,
And with dark shades and rocks environ'd round,
His holy Meditations thus persu'd.
    O what a multitude of thoughts at once

Awakn'd in me swarm, while I consider
What from within I feel my self, and hear
What from without comes often to my ears,
Ill sorting with my present state compar'd.   200
When I was yet a child, no childish play
To me was pleasing, all my mind was set
Serious to learn and know, and thence to do
What might be publick good; my self I thought
Born to that end, born to promote all truth,
All righteous things : therefore above my years,
The Law of God I read, and found it sweet,
Made it my whole delight, and in it grew
To such perfection, that e're yet my age
Had measur'd twice six years, at our great Feast   210
I went into the Temple, there to hear
The Teachers of our Law, and to propose
What might improve my knowledge or their own;
And was admir'd by all, yet this not all
To which my Spirit aspir'd, victorious deeds
Flam'd in my heart, heroic acts, one while
To rescue *Israel* from the *Roman* yoke,
Thence to subdue and quell o're all the earth
Brute violence and proud Tyrannick pow'r,
Till truth were freed, and equity restor'd :   220
Yet held it more humane, more heavenly first
By winning words to conquer willing hearts,
And make perswasion do the work of fear ;
At least to try, and teach the erring Soul
Not wilfully mis-doing, but unware
Misled : the stubborn only to subdue.
These growing thoughts my Mother soon perceiving
By words at times cast forth inly rejoyc'd,
And said to me apart, high are thy thoughts
O Son, but nourish them and let them soar   230
To what highth sacred vertue and true worth
Can raise them, though above example high;
By matchless Deeds express thy matchless Sire.
For know, thou art no Son of mortal man,
Though men esteem thee low of Parentage,
Thy Father is the Eternal King, who rules
All Heaven and Earth, Angels and Sons of men,
A messenger from God fore-told thy birth

Conceiv'd in me a Virgin, he fore-told
Thou shouldst be great and sit on *David*'s Throne,   240
And of thy Kingdom there should be no end.
At thy Nativity a glorious Quire
Of Angels in the fields of *Bethlehem* sung
To Shepherds watching at their folds by night,
And told them the Messiah now was born,
Where they might see him, and to thee they came;
Directed to the Manger where thou lais't,
For in the Inn was left no better room:
A Star, not seen before in Heaven appearing
Guided the Wise Men thither from the East,   250
To honour thee with Incense, Myrrh, and Gold,
By whose bright course led on they found the place,
Affirming it thy Star new grav'n in Heaven,
By which they knew thee King of *Israel* born.
Just *Simeon* and Prophetic *Anna*, warn'd
By Vision, found thee in the Temple, and spake
Before the Altar and the vested Priest,
Like things of thee to all that present stood.
This having heard, strait I again revolv'd
The Law and Prophets, searching what was writ   260
Concerning the Messiah, to our Scribes
Known partly, and soon found of whom they spake
I am; this chiefly, that my way must lie
Through many a hard assay even to the death,
E're I the promis'd Kingdom can attain,
Or work Redemption for mankind, whose sins
Full weight must be transferr'd upon my head.
Yet neither thus disheartn'd or dismay'd,
The time prefixt I waited, when behold
The Baptist, (of whose birth I oft had heard,   270
Not knew by sight) now come, who was to come
Before Messiah and his way prepare.
I as all others to his Baptism came,
Which I believ'd was from above; but he
Strait knew me, and with loudest voice proclaim'd
Me him (for it was shew'n him so from Heaven)
Me him whose Harbinger he was; and first
Refus'd on me his Baptism to confer,
As much his greater, and was hardly won;
But as I rose out of the laving stream,   280

(457)

Heaven open'd her eternal doors, from whence
The Spirit descended on me like a Dove,
And last the sum of all, my Father's voice,
Audibly heard from Heav'n, pronounc'd me his,
Me his beloved Son, in whom alone
He was well pleas'd; by which I knew the time
Now full, that I no more should live obscure,
But openly begin, as best becomes
The Authority which I deriv'd from Heaven.
And now by some strong motion I am led   290
Into this wilderness, to what intent
I learn not yet, perhaps I need not know;
For what concerns my knowledge God reveals.
   So spake our Morning Star then in his rise,
And looking round on every side beheld
A pathless Desert, dusk with horrid shades;
The way he came not having mark'd, return
Was difficult, by humane steps untrod;
And he still on was led, but with such thoughts
Accompanied of things past and to come   300
Lodg'd in his brest, as well might recommend
Such Solitude before choicest Society.
Full forty days he pass'd, whether on hill
Sometimes, anon in shady vale, each night
Under the covert of some ancient Oak,
Or Cedar, to defend him from the dew,
Or harbour'd in one Cave, is not reveal'd;
Nor tasted humane food, nor hunger felt
Till those days ended, hunger'd then at last
Among wild Beasts: they at his sight grew mild, 310
Nor sleeping him nor waking harm'd, his walk
The fiery Serpent fled, and noxious Worm,
The Lion and fierce Tiger glar'd aloof.
But now an aged man in Rural weeds,
Following, as seem'd, the quest of some stray Ewe,
Or wither'd sticks to gather; which might serve
Against a Winters day when winds blow keen,
To warm him wet return'd from field at Eve,
He saw approach, who first with curious eye
Perus'd him, then with words thus utt'red spake. 320
   Sir, what ill chance hath brought thee to this place
So far from path or road of men, who pass

In Troop or Caravan, for single none
Durst ever, who return'd, and dropt not here
His Carcass, pin'd with hunger and with droughth?
I ask the rather, and the more admire,
For that to me thou seem'st the man, whom late
Our new baptizing Prophet at the Ford
Of *Jordan* honour'd so, and call'd thee Son
Of God; I saw and heard, for we sometimes   330
Who dwell this wild, constrain'd by want, come forth
To Town or Village nigh (nighest is far)
Where ought we hear, and curious are to hear,
What happ'ns new; Fame also finds us out.

    To whom the Son of God. Who brought me hither
Will bring me hence, no other Guide I seek.

    By Miracle he may, reply'd the Swain,
What other way I see not, for we here
Live on tough roots and stubs, to thirst inur'd
More then the Camel, and to drink go far,   340
Men to much misery and hardship born;
But if thou be the Son of God, Command
That out of these hard stones be made thee bread;
So shalt thou save thy self and us relieve
With Food, whereof we wretched seldom taste.

    He ended, and the Son of God reply'd.
Think'st thou such force in Bread? is it not written
(For I discern thee other then thou seem'st)
Man lives not by Bread only, but each Word
Proceeding from the mouth of God; who fed   350
Our Fathers here with Manna; in the Mount
Moses was forty days, nor eat nor drank,
And forty days *Eliah* without food
Wandred this barren waste, the same I now:
Why dost thou then suggest to me distrust,
Knowing who I am, as I know who thou art?

    Whom thus answer'd th' Arch Fiend now undisguis'd.
'Tis true, I am that Spirit unfortunate,
Who leagu'd with millions more in rash revolt
Kept not my happy Station, but was driv'n   360
With them from bliss to the bottomless deep,
Yet to that hideous place not so confin'd
By rigour unconniving, but that oft
Leaving my dolorous Prison I enjoy

Large liberty to round this Globe of Earth,
Or range in th' Air, nor from the Heav'n of Heav'ns
Hath he excluded my resort sometimes.
I came among the Sons of God, when he
Gave up into my hands *Uzzean Job*
To prove him, and illustrate his high worth;   370
And when to all his Angels he propos'd
To draw the proud King *Ahab* into fraud
That he might fall in *Ramoth*, they demurring,
I undertook that office, and the tongues
Of all his flattering Prophets glibb'd with lyes
To his destruction, as I had in charge.
For what he bids I do; though I have lost
Much lustre of my native brightness, lost
To be belov'd of God, I have not lost
To love, at least contemplate and admire   380
What I see excellent in good, or fair,
Or vertuous, I should so have lost all sense.
What can be then less in me then desire
To see thee and approach thee, whom I know
Declar'd the Son of God, to hear attent
Thy wisdom, and behold thy God-like deeds?
Men generally think me much a foe
To all mankind: why should I? they to me
Never did wrong or violence, by them
I lost not what I lost, rather by them   390
I gain'd what I have gain'd, and with them dwell
Copartner in these Regions of the World,
If not disposer; lend them oft my aid,
Oft my advice by presages and signs,
And answers, oracles, portents and dreams,
Whereby they may direct their future life.
Envy they say excites me, thus to gain
Companions of my misery and wo.
At first it may be; but long since with wo
Nearer acquainted, now I feel by proof,   400
That fellowship in pain divides not smart,
Nor lightens aught each mans peculiar load.
Small consolation then, were Man adjoyn'd:
This wounds me most (what can it less) that Man,
Man fall'n shall be restor'd, I never more.
   To whom our Saviour sternly thus reply'd.
      (460)

Paradise Regain'd.

Deservedly thou griev'st, compos'd of lyes
From the beginning, and in lies wilt end ;
Who boast'st release from Hell, and leave to come
Into the Heav'n of Heavens ; thou com'st indeed,   410
As a poor miserable captive thrall,
Comes to the place where he before had sat
Among the Prime in Splendour, now depos'd,
Ejected, emptyed, gaz'd, unpityed, shun'd,
A spectacle of ruin or of scorn
To all the Host of Heaven ; the happy place
Imparts to thee no happiness, no joy,
Rather inflames thy torment, representing
Lost bliss, to thee no more communicable,
So never more in Hell then when in Heaven.   420
But thou art serviceable to Heaven's King.
Wilt thou impute to obedience what thy fear
Extorts, or pleasure to do ill excites ?
What but thy malice mov'd thee to misdeem
Of righteous *Job*, then cruelly to afflict him
With all inflictions, but his patience won ?
The other service was thy chosen task,
To be a lyer in four hundred mouths ;
For lying is thy sustenance, thy food.
Yet thou pretend'st to truth ; all Oracles   430
By thee are giv'n, and what confest more true
Among the Nations ? that hath been thy craft,
By mixing somewhat true to vent more lyes.
But what have been thy answers, what but dark
Ambiguous and with double sense deluding,
Which they who ask'd have seldom understood,
And not well understood as good not known ?
Who ever by consulting at thy shrine
Return'd the wiser, or the more instruct
To flye or follow what concern'd him most,   440
And run not sooner to his fatal snare ?
For God hath justly giv'n the Nations up
To thy Delusions ; justly, since they fell
Idolatrous, but when his purpose is
Among them to declare his Providence
To thee not known, whence hast thou then thy truth,
But from him or his Angels President
In every Province, who themselves disdaining

To approach thy Temples, give thee in command
What to the smallest tittle thou shalt say   450
To thy Adorers; thou with trembling fear,
Or like a Fawning Parasite obey'st;
Then to thy self ascrib'st the truth fore-told.
But this thy glory shall be soon retrench'd;
No more shalt thou by oracling abuse
The Gentiles; henceforth Oracles are ceast,
And thou no more with Pomp and Sacrifice
Shalt be enquir'd at *Delphos* or elsewhere,
At least in vain, for they shall find thee mute.
God hath now sent his living Oracle   460
Into the World, to teach his final will,
And sends his Spirit of Truth henceforth to dwell
In pious Hearts, an inward Oracle
To all truth requisite for men to know.
  So spake our Saviour; but the subtle Fiend,
Though inly stung with anger and disdain,
Dissembl'd, and this answer smooth return'd.
  Sharply thou hast insisted on rebuke,
And urg'd me hard with doings, which not will
But misery hath rested from me; where   470
Easily canst thou find one miserable,
And not inforc'd oft-times to part from truth;
If it may stand him more in stead to lye,
Say and unsay, feign, flatter, or abjure?
But thou art plac't above me, thou art Lord;
From thee I can and must submiss endure
Check or reproof, and glad to scape so quit.
Hard are the ways of truth, and rough to walk,
Smooth on the tongue discourst, pleasing to th' ear,
And tuneable as Silvan Pipe or Song;   480
What wonder then if I delight to hear
Her dictates from thy mouth? most men admire
Vertue, who follow not her lore: permit me
To hear thee when I come (since no man comes)
And talk at least, though I despair to attain.
Thy Father, who is holy, wise and pure,
Suffers the Hypocrite or Atheous Priest
To tread his Sacred Courts, and minister
About his Altar, handling holy things,
Praying or vowing, and vouchsaf'd his voice   490

Paradise Regain'd.

To *Balaam* Reprobate, a Prophet yet
Inspir'd; disdain not such access to me.
  To whom our Saviour with unalter'd brow.
Thy coming hither, though I know thy scope,
I bid not or forbid; do as thou find'st
Permission from above; thou canst not more.
  He added not; and Satan bowing low
His gray dissimulation, disappear'd
Into thin Air diffus'd: for now began
Night with her sullen wing to double-shade   500
The Desert, Fowls in thir clay nests were couch't;
And now wild Beasts came forth the woods to roam.

The End of the First Book.

PARADISE REGAIN'D.

The Second Book.

MEAN while the new-baptiz'd, who yet remain'd
At *Jordan* with the Baptist, and had seen
Him whom they heard so late expresly call'd
Jesus Messiah Son of God declar'd,
And on that high Authority had believ'd,
And with him talkt, and with him lodg'd, I mean
Andrew and *Simon*, famous after known
With others though in Holy Writ not nam'd,
Now missing him thir joy so lately found,
So lately found, and so abruptly gone,   10
Began to doubt, and doubted many days,
And as the days increas'd, increas'd thir doubt:
Sometimes they thought he might be only shewn,
And for a time caught up to God, as once
Moses was in the Mount, and missing long;
And the great *Thisbite* who on fiery wheels
Rode up to Heaven, yet once again to come.
Therefore as those young Prophets then with care
Sought lost *Eliah*, so in each place these
Nigh to *Bethabara*; in *Jerico*   20
The City of Palms, *Ænon*, and *Salem* Old,
Machærus and each Town or City wall'd
On this side the broad lake *Genezaret*,
Or in *Perea*, but return'd in vain.
Then on the bank of *Jordan*, by a Creek:
Where winds with Reeds, and Osiers whisp'ring play
Plain Fishermen, no greater men them call,
Close in a Cottage low together got

Thir unexpected loss and plaints out breath'd.
Alas, from what high hope to what relapse   30
Unlook'd for are we fall'n, our eyes beheld
Messiah certainly now come, so long
Expected of our Fathers ; we have heard
His words, his wisdom full of grace and truth,
Now, now, for sure, deliverance is at hand,
The Kingdom shall to *Israel* be restor'd :
Thus we rejoyc'd, but soon our joy is turn'd
Into perplexity and new amaze :
For whither is he gone, what accident
Hath rapt him from us? will he now retire   40
After appearance, and again prolong
Our expectation?   God of *Israel*,
Send thy Messiah forth, the time is come ;
Behold the Kings of the Earth how they oppress
Thy chosen, to what highth thir pow'r unjust
They have exalted, and behind them cast
All fear of thee, arise and vindicate
Thy Glory, free thy people from thir yoke,
But let us wait ; thus far he hath perform'd,
Sent his Anointed, and to us reveal'd him,   50
By his great Prophet, pointed at and shown,
In publick, and with him we have convers'd ;
Let us be glad of this, and all our fears
Lay on his Providence ; he will not fail
Nor will withdraw him now, nor will recall,
Mock us with his blest sight, then snatch him hence,
Soon we shall see our hope, our joy return.
  Thus they out of their plaints new hope resume
To find whom at the first they found unsought :
But to his Mother *Mary*, when she saw   60
Others return'd from Baptism, not her Son,
Nor left at *Jordan*, tydings of him none ;
Within her brest, though calm ; her brest though pure,
Motherly cares and fears got head, and rais'd
Some troubl'd thoughts, which she in sighs thus clad.
  O what avails me now that honour high
To have conceiv'd of God, or that salute
Hale highly favour'd, among women blest ;
While I to sorrows am no less advanc't,
And fears as eminent, above the lot   70

Of other women, by the birth I bore,
In such a season born when scarce a Shed
Could be obtain'd to shelter him or me
From the bleak air; a Stable was our warmth,
A Manger his, yet soon enforc't to flye
Thence into *Egypt*, till the Murd'rous King
Were dead, who sought his life, and missing fill'd
With Infant blood the streets of *Bethlehem*;
From *Egypt* home return'd, in *Nazareth*
Hath been our dwelling many years, his life   80
Private, unactive, calm, contemplative,
Little suspicious to any King; but now
Full grown to Man, acknowledg'd, as I hear,
By *John* the Baptist, and in publick shown,
Son own'd from Heaven by his Father's voice;
I look't for some great change; to Honour? no,
But trouble, as old *Simeon* plain fore-told,
That to the fall and rising he should be
Of many in *Israel*, and to a sign
Spoken against, that through my very Soul   90
A sword shall pierce, this is my favour'd lot,
My Exaltation to Afflictions high;
Afflicted I may be, it seems, and blest;
I will not argue that, nor will repine.
But where delays he now? some great intent
Conceals him: when twelve years he scarce had seen,
I lost him, but so found, as well I saw
He could not lose himself; but went about
His Father's business; what he meant I mus'd,
Since understand; much more his absence now   100
Thus long to some great purpose he obscures.
But I to wait with patience am inur'd;
My heart hath been a store-house long of things
And sayings laid up, portending strange events.
    Thus *Mary* pondering oft, and oft to mind
Recalling what remarkably had pass'd
Since first her Salutation heard, with thoughts
Meekly compos'd awaited the fulfilling:
The while her Son tracing the Desert wild,
Sole but with holiest Meditations fed,   110
Into himself descended, and at once
All his great work to come before him set;
        (466)

How to begin, how to accomplish best
His end of being on Earth, and mission high:
For Satan with slye preface to return
Had left him vacant, and with speed was gon
Up to the middle Region of thick Air,
Where all his Potentates in Council sate;
There without sign of boast, or sign of joy,
Sollicitous and blank he thus began.   120
    Princes, Heavens antient Sons, Æthereal Thrones,
Demonian Spirits now, from the Element
Each of his reign allotted, rightlier call'd,
Powers of Fire, Air, Water, and Earth beneath,
So may we hold our place and these mild seats
Without new trouble; such an Enemy
Is ris'n to invade us, who no less
Threat'ns then our expulsion down to Hell;
I, as I undertook, and with the vote
Consenting in full frequence was impowr'd,   130
Have found him, view'd him, tasted him, but find
Far other labour to be undergon
Then when I dealt with *Adam* first of Men,
Though *Adam* by his Wives allurement fell,
However to this Man inferior far,
If he be Man by Mothers side at least,
With more then humane gifts from Heav'n adorn'd,
Perfections absolute, Graces divine,
And amplitude of mind to greatest Deeds.
Therefore I am return'd, lest confidence   140
Of my success with *Eve* in Paradise
Deceive ye to perswasion over-sure
Of like succeeding here; I summon all
Rather to be in readiness, with hand
Or counsel to assist; lest I who erst
Thought none my equal, now be over-match'd.
    So spake the old Serpent doubting, and from all
With clamour was assur'd thir utmost aid
At his command; when from amidst them rose
Belial the dissolutest Spirit that fell   150
The sensuallest, and after *Asmodai*
The fleshliest Incubus, and thus advis'd.
    Set women in his eye and in his walk,
Among daughters of men the fairest found;

(467)

Many are in each Region passing fair
As the noon Skie; more like to Goddesses
Then Mortal Creatures, graceful and discreet,
Expert in amorous Arts, enchanting tongues
Perswasive, Virgin majesty with mild
And sweet allay'd, yet terrible to approach,   160
Skill'd to retire, and in retiring draw
Hearts after them tangl'd in Amorous Nets.
Such object hath the power to soft'n and tame
Severest temper, smooth the rugged'st brow,
Enerve, and with voluptuous hope dissolve,
Draw out with credulous desire, and lead
At will the manliest, resolutest brest,
As the Magnetic hardest Iron draws.
Women, when nothing else, beguil'd the heart
Of wisest *Solomon*, and made him build,   170
And made him bow to the Gods of his Wives.
   To whom quick answer Satan thus return'd.
Belial, in much uneven scale thou weigh'st
All others by thy self; because of old
Thou thy self doat'st on womankind, admiring
Thir shape, thir colour, and attractive grace,
None are, thou think'st, but taken with such toys.
Before the Flood thou with thy lusty Crew,
False titl'd Sons of God, roaming the Earth
Cast wanton eyes on the daughters of men,   180
And coupl'd with them, and begot a race.
Have we not seen, or by relation heard,
In Courts and Regal Chambers how thou lurk'st,
In Wood or Grove by mossie Fountain side,
In Valley or Green Meadow to way-lay
Some beauty rare, *Calisto, Clymene,*
Daphne, or *Semele, Antiopa,*
Or *Amymone, Syrinx,* many more
Too long, then lay'st thy scapes on names ador'd,
Apollo, Neptune, Jupiter, or *Pan,*   190
Satyr, or Fawn, or Silvan? But these haunts
Delight not all; among the Sons of Men,
How many have with a smile made small account
Of beauty and her lures, easily scorn'd
All her assaults, on worthier things intent?
Remember that *Pellean* Conquerour,

(468)

A youth, how all the Beauties of the East
He slightly view'd, and slightly over-pass'd;
How hee sirnam'd of *Africa* dismiss'd
In his prime youth the fair *Iberian* maid.   200
For *Solomon* he liv'd at ease, and full
Of honour, wealth, high fare, aim'd not beyond
Higher design then 'to enjoy his State;
Thence to the bait of Women lay expos'd;
But he whom we attempt is wiser far
Then *Solomon*, of more exalted mind,
Made and set wholly on the accomplishment
Of greatest things; what woman will you find,
Though of this Age the wonder and the fame,
On whom his leisure will vouchsafe an eye   210
Of fond desire? or should she confident,
As sitting Queen ador'd on Beauties Throne,
Descend with all her winning charms begirt
To enamour, as the Zone of *Venus* once
Wrought that effect on *Jove*, so Fables tell;
How would one look from his Majestick brow
Seated as on the top of Vertues hill,
Discount'nance her despis'd, and put to rout
All her array; her female pride deject,
Or turn to reverent awe? for Beauty stands   220
In the admiration only of weak minds
Led captive; cease to admire, and all her Plumes
Fall flat and shrink into a trivial toy,
At every sudden slighting quite abasht:
Therefore with manlier objects we must try
His constancy, with such as have more shew
Of worth, of honour, glory, and popular praise;
Rocks whereon greatest men have oftest wreck'd;
Or that which only seems to satisfie
Lawful desires of Nature, not beyond;   230
And now I know he hungers where no food
Is to be found, in the wide Wilderness;
The rest commit to me, I shall let pass
No advantage, and his strength as oft assay.

   He ceas'd, and heard thir grant in loud acclaim;
Then forthwith to him takes a chosen band
Of Spirits likest to himself in guile
To be at hand, and at his beck appear,

If cause were to unfold some active Scene
Of various persons each to know his part;   240
Then to the Desert takes with these his flight;
Where still from shade to shade the Son of God
After forty days fasting had remain'd,
Now hungring first, and to himself thus said.

    Where will this end? four times ten days I have pass'd
Wandring this woody maze, and humane food
Nor tasted, nor had appetite : that Fast
To Vertue I impute not, or count part
Of what I suffer here ; if Nature need not,
Or God support Nature without repast   250
Though needing, what praise is it to endure?
But now I feel I hunger, which declares,
Nature hath need of what she asks ; yet God
Can satisfie that need some other way,
Though hunger still remain: so it remain
Without this bodies wasting, I content me,
And from the sting of Famine fear no harm,
Nor mind it, fed with better thoughts that feed
Mee hungring more to do my Fathers will.

    It was the hour of night, when thus the Son   260
Commun'd in silent walk, then laid him down
Under the hospitable covert nigh
Of Trees thick interwoven ; there he slept,
And dream'd, as appetite is wont to dream,
Of meats and drinks, Natures refreshment sweet ;
Him thought, he by the Brook of *Cherith* stood
And saw the Ravens with thir horny beaks
Food to *Elijah* bringing Even and Morn,
Though ravenous, taught to abstain from what they brought :
He saw the Prophet also how he fled   270
Into the Desert, and how there he slept
Under a Juniper ; then how awakt,
He found his Supper on the coals prepar'd,
And by the Angel was bid rise and eat,
And eat the second time after repose,
The strength whereof suffic'd him forty days,
Sometimes that with *Elijah* he partook,
Or as a guest with *Daniel* at his pulse.
Thus wore out night, and now the Herald Lark
Left his ground-nest, high towring to descry   280

The morns approach, and greet her with his Song:
As lightly from his grassy Couch up rose
Our Saviour, and found all was but a dream,
Fasting he went to sleep, and fasting wak'd.
Up to a hill anon his steps he rear'd,
From whose high top to ken the prospect round,
If Cottage were in view, Sheep-cote or Herd;
But Cottage, Herd or Sheep-cote none he saw,
Only in a bottom saw a pleasant Grove,
With chaunt of tuneful Birds resounding loud;   290
Thither he bent his way, determin'd there
To rest at noon, and entr'd soon the shade
High rooft and walks beneath, and alleys brown
That open'd in the midst a woody Scene,
Natures own work it seem'd (Nature taught Art)
And to a Superstitious eye the haunt
Of Wood-Gods and Wood-Nymphs; he view'd it round,
When suddenly a man before him stood,
Not rustic as before, but seemlier clad,
As one in City, or Court, or Palace bred,   300
And with fair speech these words to him address'd.

With granted leave officious I return,
But much more wonder that the Son of God
In this wild solitude so long should bide
Of all things destitute, and well I know,
Not without hunger. Others of some note,
As story tells, have trod this Wilderness;
The Fugitive Bond-woman with her Son
Out cast *Nebaioth*, yet found he relief
By a providing Angel; all the race   310
Of *Israel* here had famish'd, had not God
Rain'd from Heaven Manna, and that Prophet bold
Native of *Thebez* wandring here was fed
Twice by a voice inviting him to eat.
Of thee these forty days none hath regard,
Forty and more deserted here indeed.

To whom thus Jesus; what conclud'st thou hence?
They all had need, I as thou seest have none.

How hast thou hunger then? Satan reply'd,
Tell me if Food were now before thee set,   320
Would'st thou not eat? Thereafter as I like

309 he] here *1695*

(471)

The giver, answer'd Jesus. Why should that
Cause thy refusal, said the subtle Fiend,
Hast thou not right to all Created things,
Owe not all Creatures by just right to thee
Duty and Service, nor to stay till bid,
But tender all their power? nor mention I
Meats by the Law unclean, or offer'd first
To Idols, those young *Daniel* could refuse;
Nor proffer'd by an Enemy, though who   330
Would scruple that, with want opprest? behold
Nature asham'd, or better to express,
Troubl'd that thou should'st hunger, hath purvey'd
From all the Elements her choicest store
To treat thee as beseems, and as her Lord
With honour, only deign to sit and eat.

He spake no dream, for as his words had end,
Our Saviour lifting up his eyes beheld
In ample space under the broadest shade
A Table richly spred, in regal mode,   340
With dishes pil'd, and meats of noblest sort
And savour, Beasts of chase, or Fowl of game,
In pastry built, or from the spit, or boyl'd,
Gris-amber-steam'd; all Fish from Sea or Shore,
Freshet, or purling Brook, of shell or fin,
And exquisitest name, for which was drain'd
Pontus and *Lucrine* Bay, and *Afric* Coast.
Alas how simple, to these Cates compar'd,
Was that crude Apple that diverted *Eve*!
And at a stately side-board by the wine   350
That fragrant smell diffus'd, in order stood
Tall stripling youths rich clad, of fairer hew
Then *Ganymed* or *Hylas*, distant more
Under the Trees now trip'd, now solemn stood
Nymphs of *Diana*'s train, and *Naiades*
With fruits and flowers from *Amalthea*'s horn,
And Ladies of th' *Hesperides*, that seem'd
Fairer then feign'd of old, or fabl'd since
Of Fairy Damsels met in Forest wide
By Knights of *Logres*, or of *Lyones*,   360
Lancelot or *Pelleas*, or *Pellenore*,
And all the while Harmonious Airs were heard
Of chiming strings, or charming pipes and winds.

(472)

Of gentlest gale *Arabian* odors fann'd
From their soft wings, and *Flora's* earliest smells.
Such was the Splendour, and the Tempter now
His invitation earnestly renew'd.
    What doubts the Son of God to sit and eat?
These are not Fruits forbidden, no interdict
Defends the touching of these viands pure,   370
Thir taste no knowledge works, at least of evil,
But life preserves, destroys life's enemy,
Hunger, with sweet restorative delight.
All these are Spirits of Air, and Woods, and Springs,
Thy gentle Ministers, who come to pay
Thee homage, and acknowledge thee thir Lord:
What doubt'st thou Son of God? sit down and eat.
    To whom thus Jesus temperately reply'd:
Said'st thou not that to all things I had right?
And who withholds my pow'r that right to use?   380
Shall I receive by gift what of my own,
When and where likes me best, I can command?
I can at will, doubt not, assoon as thou,
Command a Table in this Wilderness,
And call swift flights of Angels ministrant
Array'd in Glory on my cup to attend:
Why shouldst thou then obtrude this diligence,
In vain, where no acceptance it can find,
And with my hunger what hast thou to do?
Thy pompous Delicacies I contemn,   390
And count thy specious gifts no gifts but guiles.
    To whom thus answer'd Satan malecontent:
That I have also power to give thou seest,
If of that pow'r I bring thee voluntary
What I might have bestow'd on whom I pleas'd,
And rather opportunely in this place
Chose to impart to thy apparent need,
Why shouldst thou not accept it? but I see
What I can do or offer is suspect;
Of these things others quickly will dispose   400
Whose pains have earn'd the far fet spoil. With that
Both Table and Provision vanish'd quite
With sound of Harpies wings, and Talons heard;
Only the importune Tempter still remain'd,
And with these words his temptation pursu'd.

By hunger, that each other Creature tames,
Thou art not to be harm'd, therefore not mov'd;
Thy temperance invincible besides,
For no allurement yields to appetite,
And all thy heart is set on high designs,   410
High actions: but wherewith to be atchiev'd?
Great acts require great means of enterprise,
Thou art unknown, unfriended, low of birth,
A Carpenter thy Father known, thy self
Bred up in poverty and streights at home;
Lost in a Desert here and hunger-bit:
Which way or from what hope dost thou aspire
To greatness? whence Authority deriv'st,
What Followers, what Retinue canst thou gain,
Or at thy heels the dizzy Multitude,   420
Longer then thou canst feed them on thy cost?
Money brings Honour, Friends, Conquest, and Realms;
What rais'd *Antipater* the *Edomite*,
And his Son *Herod* plac'd on *Juda*'s Throne;
(Thy throne) but gold that got him puissant friends?
Therefore, if at great things thou wouldst arrive,
Get Riches first, get Wealth, and Treasure heap,
Not difficult, if thou hearken to me,
Riches are mine, Fortune is in my hand;
They whom I favour thrive in wealth amain,   430
While Virtue, Valour, Wisdom sit in want.
    To whom thus Jesus patiently reply'd;
Yet Wealth without these three is impotent,
To gain dominion or to keep it gain'd.
Witness those antient Empires of the Earth,
In highth of all thir flowing wealth dissolv'd:
But men endu'd with these have oft attain'd
In lowest poverty to highest deeds;
Gideon and *Jephtha*, and the Shepherd lad,
Whose off-spring on the Throne of *Juda* sat   440
So many Ages, and shall yet regain
That seat, and reign in *Israel* without end.
Among the Heathen, (for throughout the World
To me is not unknown what hath been done
Worthy of Memorial) canst thou not remember
Quintius, Fabricius, Curius, Regulus?
For I esteem those names of men so poor

Who could do mighty things, and could contemn
Riches though offer'd from the hand of Kings.
And what in me seems wanting, but that I   450
May also in this poverty as soon
Accomplish what they did, perhaps and more?
Extol not Riches then, the toyl of Fools
The wise mans cumbrance if not snare, more apt
To slacken Virtue, and abate her edge,
Then prompt her to do aught may merit praise.
What if with like aversion I reject
Riches and Realms; yet not for that a Crown,
Golden in shew, is but a wreath of thorns,
Brings dangers, troubles, cares, and sleepless nights   460
To him who wears the Regal Diadem,
When on his shoulders each mans burden lies;
For therein stands the office of a King,
His Honour, Vertue, Merit and chief Praise,
That for the Publick all this weight he bears.
Yet he who reigns within himself, and rules
Passions, Desires, and Fears, is more a King;
Which every wise and vertuous man attains:
And who attains not, ill aspires to rule
Cities of men, or head-strong Multitudes,   470
Subject himself to Anarchy within,
Or lawless passions in him which he serves.
But to guide Nations in the way of truth
By saving Doctrine, and from errour lead
To know, and knowing worship God aright,
Is yet more Kingly, this attracts the Soul,
Governs the inner man, the nobler part,
That other o're the body only reigns,
And oft by force, which to a generous mind
So reigning can be no sincere delight.   480
Besides to give a Kingdom hath been thought
Greater and nobler done, and to lay down
Far more magnanimous, then to assume.
Riches are needless then, both for themselves,
And for thy reason why they should be sought,
To gain a Scepter, oftest better miss't.

The End of the Second Book.

PARADISE REGAIN'D.

The Third Book.

So spake the Son of God, and Satan stood
A while as mute confounded what to say,
What to reply, confuted and convinc't
Of his weak arguing, and fallacious drift;
At length collecting all his Serpent wiles,
With soothing words renew'd, him thus accosts.
  I see thou know'st what is of use to know,
What best to say canst say, to do canst do;
Thy actions to thy words accord, thy words
To thy large heart give utterance due, thy heart   10
Conteins of good, wise, just, the perfect shape.
Should Kings and Nations from thy mouth consult,
Thy Counsel would be as the Oracle
Urim and *Thummim*, those oraculous gems
On *Aaron*'s breast: or tongue of Seers old
Infallible; or wert thou sought to deeds
That might require th' array of war, thy skill
Of conduct would be such, that all the world
Could not sustain thy Prowess, or subsist
In battel, though against thy few in arms.   20
These God-like Vertues wherefore dost thou hide?
Affecting private life, or more obscure
In savage Wilderness, wherefore deprive
All Earth her wonder at thy acts, thy self
The fame and glory, glory the reward
That sole excites to high attempts the flame
Of most erected Spirits, most temper'd pure
Ætherial, who all pleasures else despise,

Paradise Regain'd.

All treasures and all gain esteem as dross,
And dignities and powers all but the highest?   30
Thy years are ripe, and over-ripe, the Son
Of *Macedonian Philip* had e're these
Won *Asia* and the Throne of *Cyrus* held
At his dispose, young *Scipio* had brought down
The *Carthaginian* pride, young *Pompey* quell'd
The *Pontic* King and in triumph had rode.
Yet years, and to ripe years judgment mature,
Quench not the thirst of glory, but augment.
Great *Julius*, whom now all the world admires,
The more he grew in years, the more inflam'd   40
With glory, wept that he had liv'd so long
Inglorious : but thou yet art not too late.
    To whom our Saviour calmly thus reply'd.
Thou neither dost perswade me to seek wealth
For Empires sake, nor Empire to affect
For glories sake by all thy argument.
For what is glory but the blaze of fame,
The peoples praise, if always praise unmixt?
And what the people but a herd confus'd,
A miscellaneous rabble, who extol   50
Things vulgar, & well weigh'd, scarce worth the praise,
They praise and they admire they know not what;
And know not whom, but as one leads the other;
And what delight to be by such extoll'd,
To live upon thir tongues and be thir talk,
Of whom to be disprais'd were no small praise?
His lot who dares be singularly good.
Th' intelligent among them and the wise
Are few, and glory scarce of few is rais'd.
This is true glory and renown, when God   60
Looking on the Earth, with approbation marks
The just man, and divulges him through Heaven
To all his Angels, who with true applause
Recount his praises; thus he did to *Job*,
When to extend his fame through Heaven & Earth,
As thou to thy reproach mayst well remember,
He ask'd thee, hast thou seen my servant *Job*?
Famous he was in Heaven, on Earth less known;
Where glory is false glory, attributed
To things not glorious, men not worthy of fame.   70

(477)

They err who count it glorious to subdue
By Conquest far and wide, to over-run
Large Countries, and in field great Battels win,
Great Cities by assault : what do these Worthies,
But rob and spoil, burn, slaughter, and enslave
Peaceable Nations, neighbouring, or remote,
Made Captive, yet deserving freedom more
Then those thir Conquerours, who leave behind
Nothing but ruin wheresoe're they rove,
And all the flourishing works of peace destroy,   80
Then swell with pride, and must be titl'd Gods,
Great Benefactors of mankind, Deliverers,
Worship't with Temple, Priest and Sacrifice ;
One is the Son of *Jove*, of *Mars* the other,
Till Conquerour Death discover them scarce men,
Rowling in brutish vices, and deform'd,
Violent or shameful death thir due reward.
But if there be in glory aught of good,
It may by means far different be attain'd
Without ambition, war, or violence ;   90
By deeds of peace, by wisdom eminent,
By patience, temperance ; I mention still
Him whom thy wrongs with Saintly patience born,
Made famous in a Land and times obscure ;
Who names not now with honour patient *Job* ?
Poor *Socrates* (who next more memorable ?)
By what he taught and suffer'd for so doing,
For truths sake suffering death unjust, lives now
Equal in fame to proudest Conquerours.
Yet if for fame and glory aught be done,   100
Aught suffer'd ; if young *African* for fame
His wasted Country freed from *Punic* rage,
The deed becomes unprais'd, the man at least,
And loses, though but verbal, his reward.
Shall I seek glory then, as vain men seek
Oft not deserv'd ? I seek not mine, but his
Who sent me, and thereby witness whence I am.
    To whom the Tempter murmuring thus reply'd.
Think not so slight of glory ; therein least,
Resembling thy great Father : he seeks glory,   110
And for his glory all things made, all things
Orders and governs, nor content in Heaven

(478)

By all his Angels glorifi'd, requires
Glory from men, from all men good or bad,
Wise or unwise, no difference, no exemption ;
Above all Sacrifice, or hallow'd gift
Glory he requires, and glory he 'receives
Promiscuous from all Nations, Jew, or Greek,
Or Barbarous, nor exception hath declar'd ;
From us his foes pronounc't glory he exacts.   120
    To whom our Saviour fervently reply'd.
And reason ; since his word all things produc'd,
Though chiefly not for glory as prime end,
But to shew forth his goodness, and impart
His good communicable to every soul
Freely ; of whom what could he less expect
Then glory and benediction, that is thanks,
The slightest, easiest, readiest recompence
From them who could return him nothing else,
And not returning that would likeliest render   130
Contempt instead, dishonour, obloquy ?
Hard recompence, unsutable return
For so much good, so much beneficence.
But why should man seek glory ? who of his own
Hath nothing, and to whom nothing belongs
But condemnation, ignominy, and shame ?
Who for so many benefits receiv'd
Turn'd recreant to God, ingrate and false,
And so of all true good himself despoil'd,
Yet, sacrilegious, to himself would take   140
That which to God alone of right belongs ;
Yet so much bounty is in God, such grace,
That who advance his glory, not thir own,
Them he himself to glory will advance.
    So spake the Son of God ; and here again
Satan had not to answer, but stood struck
With guilt of his own sin, for he himself
Insatiable of glory had lost all,
Yet of another Plea bethought him soon.
    Of glory as thou wilt, said he, so deem,   150
Worth or not worth the seeking, let it pass :
But to a Kingdom thou art born, ordain'd
To sit upon thy Father *David*'s Throne ;
By Mother's side thy Father, though thy right

(479)

Be now in powerful hands, that will not part
Easily from possession won with arms ;
Judæa now and all the promis'd land
Reduc't a Province under Roman yoke,
Obeys *Tiberius* ; nor is always rul'd
With temperate sway ; oft have they violated   160
The Temple, oft the Law with foul affronts,
Abominations rather, as did once
Antiochus : and think'st thou to regain
Thy right by sitting still or thus retiring?
So did not *Machabeus* : he indeed
Retir'd unto the Desert, but with arms ;
And o're a mighty King so oft prevail'd,
That by strong hand his Family obtain'd,
Though Priests, the Crown, and *David*'s Throne usurp'd,
With *Modin* and her Suburbs once content.   170
If Kingdom move thee not, let move thee Zeal,
And Duty ; Zeal and Duty are not slow ;
But on Occasions forelock watchful wait.
They themselves rather are occasion best,
Zeal of thy Fathers house, Duty to free
Thy Country from her Heathen servitude ;
So shalt thou best fullfil, best verifie
The Prophets old, who sung thy endless raign,
The happier raign the sooner it begins,
Raign then ; what canst thou better do the while?   180
    To whom our Saviour answer thus return'd.
All things are best fullfil'd in thir due time,
And time there is for all things, Truth hath said :
If of my raign Prophetic Writ hath told
That it shall never end, so when begin
The Father in his purpose hath decreed,
He in whose hand all times and seasons roul.
What if he hath decreed that I shall first
Be try'd in humble state, and things adverse,
By tribulations, injuries, insults,   190
Contempts, and scorns, and snares, and violence,
Suffering, abstaining, quietly expecting
Without distrust or doubt, that he may know
What I can suffer, how obey? who best
Can suffer, best can do ; best reign, who first
Well hath obey'd ; just tryal e're I merit

My exaltation without change or end.
But what concerns it thee when I begin
My everlasting Kingdom, why art thou
Sollicitous, what moves thy inquisition?   200
Know'st thou not that my rising is thy fall,
And my promotion will be thy destruction?

   To whom the Tempter inly rackt reply'd.
Let that come when it comes; all hope is lost
Of my reception into grace; what worse?
For where no hope is left, is left no fear;
If there be worse, the expectation more
Of worse torments me then the feeling can.
I would be at the worst; worst is my Port,
My harbour and my ultimate repose,   210
The end I would attain, my final good.
My error was my error, and my crime
My crime; whatever for it self condemn'd,
And will alike be punish'd; whether thou
Raign or raign not; though to that gentle brow
Willingly I could flye, and hope thy raign,
From that placid aspect and meek regard,
Rather then aggravate my evil state,
Would stand between me and thy Fathers ire,
(Whose ire I dread more then the fire of Hell)   220
A shelter and a kind of shading cool
Interposition, as a summers cloud.
If I then to the worst that can be hast,
Why move thy feet so slow to what is best,
Happiest both to thy self and all the world,
That thou who worthiest art should'st be thir King?
Perhaps thou linger'st in deep thoughts detain'd
Of the enterprize so hazardous and high;
No wonder, for though in thee be united
What of perfection can in man be found,   230
Or human nature can receive, consider
Thy life hath yet been private, most part spent
At home, scarce view'd the *Gallilean* Towns,
And once a year *Jerusalem*, few days
Short sojourn; and what thence could'st thou observe?
The world thou hast not seen, much less her glory,
Empires, and Monarchs, and thir radiant Courts,
Best school of best experience, quickest in sight

In all things that to greatest actions lead.
The wisest, unexperienc't, will be ever   240
Timorous and loth, with novice modesty,
(As he who seeking Asses found a Kingdom)
Irresolute, unhardy, unadventrous :
But I will bring thee where thou soon shalt quit
Those rudiments, and see before thine eyes
The Monarchies of the Earth, thir pomp and state,
Sufficient introduction to inform
Thee, of thy self so apt, in regal Arts,
And regal Mysteries ; that thou may'st know
How best their opposition to withstand.   250
    With that (such power was giv'n him then) he took
The Son of God up to a Mountain high.
It was a Mountain at whose verdant feet
A spatious plain out strech't in circuit wide
Lay pleasant ; from his side two rivers flow'd,
Th' one winding, the other strait and left between
Fair Champain with less rivers interveind,
Then meeting joyn'd thir tribute to the Sea :
Fertil of corn the glebe, of oyl and wine,
With herds the pastures throng'd, with flocks the hills, 260
Huge Cities and high towr'd, that well might seem
The seats of mightiest Monarchs, and so large
The Prospect was, that here and there was room
For barren desert fountainless and dry.
To this high mountain top the Tempter brought
Our Saviour, and new train of words began.
    Well have we speeded, and o're hill and dale,
Forest and field, and flood, Temples and Towers
Cut shorter many a league ; here thou behold'st
Assyria and her Empires antient bounds,   270
Araxes and the *Caspian* lake, thence on
As far as *Indus* East, *Euphrates* West,
And oft beyond ; to South the *Persian* Bay,
And inaccessible the *Arabian* drouth :
Here *Ninevee*, of length within her wall
Several days journey, built by *Ninus* old,
Of that first golden Monarchy the seat,
And seat of *Salmanassar*, whose success
Israel in long captivity still mourns ;
There *Babylon* the wonder of all tongues,   280

(482)

As antient, but rebuilt by him who twice
Judah and all thy Father *David*'s house
Led captive, and *Jerusalem* laid waste,
Till *Cyrus* set them free; *Persepolis*
His City there thou seest, and *Bactra* there;
Ecbatana her structure vast there shews,
And *Hecatompylos* her hunderd gates,
There *Susa* by *Choaspes*, amber stream,
The drink of none but Kings; of later fame
Built by *Emathian*, or by *Parthian* hands,   290
The great *Seleucia*, *Nisibis*, and there
Artaxata, *Teredon*, *Tesiphon*,
Turning with easie eye thou may'st behold.
All these the *Parthian*, now some Ages past,
By great *Arsaces* led, who founded first
That Empire, under his dominion holds
From the luxurious Kings of *Antioch* won.
And just in time thou com'st to have a view
Of his great power; for now the *Parthian* King
In *Ctesiphon* hath gather'd all his Host   300
Against the *Scythian*, whose incursions wild
Have wasted *Sogdiana*; to her aid
He marches now in hast; see, though from far,
His thousands, in what martial equipage
They issue forth, Steel Bows, and Shafts their arms
Of equal dread in flight, or in pursuit;
All Horsemen, in which fight they most excel;
See how in warlike muster they appear,
In Rhombs and wedges, and half moons, and wings.

    He look't and saw what numbers numberless   310
The City gates out powr'd, light armed Troops
In coats of Mail and military pride;
In Mail thir horses clad, yet fleet and strong,
Prauncing their riders bore, the flower and choice
Of many Provinces from bound to bound;
From *Arachosia*, from *Candaor* East,
And *Margiana* to the *Hyrcanian* cliffs
Of *Caucasus*, and dark *Iberian* dales,
From *Atropatia* and the neighbouring plains
Of *Adiabene*, *Media*, and the South   320
Of *Susiana* to *Balsara*'s hav'n.
He saw them in thir forms of battell rang'd,

How quick they wheel'd, and flying behind them shot
Sharp sleet of arrowie showers against the face
Of thir pursuers, and overcame by flight;
The field all iron cast a gleaming brown,
Nor wanted clouds of foot, nor on each horn,
Cuirassiers all in steel for standing fight;
Chariots or Elephants endorst with Towers
Of Archers, nor of labouring Pioners   33o
A multitude with Spades and Axes arm'd
To lay hills plain, fell woods, or valleys fill,
Or where plain was raise hill, or over-lay
With bridges rivers proud, as with a yoke;
Mules after these, Camels and Dromedaries,
And Waggons fraught with Utensils of war.
Such forces met not, nor so wide a camp,
When *Agrican* with all his Northern powers
Besieg'd *Albracca*, as Romances tell;
The City of *Gallaphrone*, from thence to win   34o
The fairest of her Sex *Angelica*
His daughter, sought by many Prowest Knights,
Both *Paynim*, and the Peers of *Charlemane*.
Such and so numerous was thir Chivalrie;
At sight whereof the Fiend yet more presum'd,
And to our Saviour thus his words renew'd.
    That thou may'st know I seek not to engage
Thy Vertue, and not every way secure
On no slight grounds thy safety; hear, and mark
To what end I have brought thee hither and shewn   35o
All this fair sight; thy Kingdom though foretold
By Prophet or by Angel, unless thou
Endeavour, as thy Father *David* did,
Thou never shalt obtain; prediction still
In all things, and all men, supposes means,
Without means us'd, what it predicts revokes.
But say thou wer't possess'd of *David*'s Throne
By free consent of all, none opposite,
Samaritan or *Jew*; how could'st thou hope
Long to enjoy it quiet and secure,   36o
Between two such enclosing enemies
Roman and *Parthian*? therefore one of these
Thou must make sure thy own, the *Parthian* first
By my advice, as nearer and of late

Found able by invasion to annoy
Thy country, and captive lead away her Kings
Antigonus, and old *Hyrcanus* bound,
Maugre the *Roman* : it shall be my task
To render thee the *Parthian* at dispose ;
Chuse which thou wilt by conquest or by league   370
By him thou shalt regain, without him not,
That which alone can truly reinstall thee
In *David*'s royal seat, his true Successour,
Deliverance of thy brethren, those ten Tribes
Whose off-spring in his Territory yet serve
In *Habor*, and among the *Medes* dispers't,
Ten Sons of *Jacob*, two of *Joseph* lost
Thus long from *Israel*; serving as of old
Thir Fathers in the land of *Egypt* serv'd,
This offer sets before thee to deliver.   380
These if from servitude thou shalt restore
To thir inheritance, then, nor till then,
Thou on the Throne of *David* in full glory,
From *Egypt* to *Euphrates* and beyond
Shalt raign, and *Rome* or *Cæsar* not need fear.
     To whom our Saviour answer'd thus unmov'd.
Much ostentation vain of fleshly arm,
And fragile arms, much instrument of war
Long in preparing, soon to nothing brought,
Before mine eyes thou hast set ; and in my ear   390
Vented much policy, and projects deep
Of enemies, of aids, battels and leagues,
Plausible to the world, to me worth naught.
Means I must use thou say'st, prediction else
Will unpredict and fail me of the Throne :
My time I told thee, (and that time for thee
Were better farthest off) is not yet come ;
When that comes think not thou to find me slack
On my part aught endeavouring, or to need
Thy politic maxims, or that cumbersome   400
Luggage of war there shewn me, argument
Of human weakness rather then of strength.
My brethren, as thou call'st them ; those Ten Tribes
I must deliver, if I mean to raign
David's true heir, and his full Scepter sway
To just extent over all *Israel*'s Sons ;

     (485)

But whence to thee this zeal, where was it then
For *Israel*, or for *David*, or his Throne,
When thou stood'st up his Tempter to the pride
Of numbring *Israel*, which cost the lives   410
Of threescore and ten thousand *Israelites*
By three days Pestilence? such was thy zeal
To *Israel* then, the same that now to me.
As for those captive Tribes, themselves were they
Who wrought their own captivity, fell off
From God to worship Calves, the Deities
Of *Egypt*, *Baal* next and *Ashtaroth*,
And all the Idolatries of Heathen round,
Besides thir other worse then heathenish crimes;
Nor in the land of their captivity   420
Humbled themselves, or penitent besought
The God of their fore-fathers; but so dy'd
Impenitent, and left a race behind
Like to themselves, distinguishable scarce
From Gentils, but by Circumcision vain,
And God with Idols in their worship joyn'd.
Should I of these the liberty regard,
Who freed, as to their antient Patrimony,
Unhumbl'd, unrepentant, unreform'd,
Headlong would follow; and to thir Gods perhaps   430
Of *Bethel* and of *Dan*? no, let them serve
Thir enemies, who serve Idols with God.
Yet he at length, time to himself best known,
Remembring *Abraham* by some wond'rous call
May bring them back repentant and sincere,
And at their passing cleave the *Assyrian* flood,
While to their native land with joy they hast,
As the Red Sea and *Jordan* once he cleft,
When to the promis'd land thir Fathers pass'd;
To his due time and providence I leave them.   440
  So spake *Israel's* true King, and to the Fiend
Made answer meet, that made void all his wiles.
So fares it when with truth falshood contends.

The End of the Third Book.

PARADISE REGAIN'D.

The Fourth Book.

PERPLEX'D and troubl'd at his bad success
The Tempter stood, nor had what to reply,
Discover'd in his fraud, thrown from his hope,
So oft, and the perswasive Rhetoric
That sleek't his tongue, and won so much on *Eve*,
So little here, nay lost; but *Eve* was *Eve*,
This far his over-match, who self deceiv'd
And rash, before-hand had no better weigh'd
The strength he was to cope with, or his own:
But as a man who had been matchless held   10
In cunning, over-reach't where least he thought,
To salve his credit, and for very spight
Still will be tempting him who foyls him still,
And never cease, though to his shame the more;
Or as a swarm of flies in vintage time,
About the wine-press where sweet moust is powr'd,
Beat off, returns as oft with humming sound;
Or surging waves against a solid rock,
Though all to shivers dash't, the assault renew,
Vain battry, and in froth or bubbles end: 20
So Satan, whom repulse upon repulse
Met ever; and to shameful silence brought,
Yet gives not o're though desperate of success,
And his vain importunity pursues.
He brought our Saviour to the western side
Of that high mountain, whence he might behold
Another plain, long but in bredth not wide;
Wash'd by the Southern Sea, and on the North

(487)

To equal length back'd with a ridge of hills
That screen'd the fruits of the earth and seats of men   30
From cold *Septentrion* blasts, thence in the midst
Divided by a river, of whose banks
On each side an Imperial City stood,
With Towers and Temples proudly elevate
On seven small Hills, with Palaces adorn'd,
Porches and Theatres, Baths, Aqueducts,
Statues and Trophees, and Triumphal Arcs,
Gardens and Groves presented to his eyes,
Above the highth of Mountains interpos'd.
By what strange Parallax or Optic skill   40
Of vision multiplyed through air, or glass
Of Telescope, were curious to enquire:
And now the Tempter thus his silence broke.
    The City which thou seest no other deem
Then great and glorious *Rome*, Queen of the Earth
So far renown'd, and with the spoils enricht
Of Nations; there the Capitol thou seest
Above the rest lifting his stately head
On the *Tarpeian* rock, her Cittadel
Impregnable, and there Mount *Palatine*   50
The Imperial Palace, compass huge, and high
The Structure, skill of noblest Architects,
With gilded battlements, conspicuous far,
Turrets and Terrases, and glittering Spires.
Many a fair Edifice besides, more like
Houses of Gods (so well I have dispos'd
My Aerie Microscope) thou may'st behold
Outside and inside both, pillars and roofs
Carv'd work, the hand of fam'd Artificers
In Cedar, Marble, Ivory or Gold.   60
Thence to the gates cast round thine eye, and see
What conflux issuing forth, or entring in,
Pretors, Proconsuls to thir Provinces
Hasting or on return, in robes of State;
Lictors and rods the ensigns of thir power,
Legions and Cohorts, turmes of horse and wings:
Or Embassies from Regions far remote
In various habits on the *Appian* road,
Or on the *Æmilian*, some from farthest South,
Syene, and where the shadow both way falls,   70

Meroe, Nilotic Isle, and more to West,
The Realm of *Bocchus* to the Black-moor Sea;
From the *Asian* Kings and *Parthian* among these,
From *India* and the golden *Chersoness,*
And utmost *Indian* Isle *Taprobane,*
Dusk faces with white silken Turbants wreath'd:
From *Gallia, Gades,* and the *Brittish* West,
Germans and *Scythians,* and *Sarmatians* North
Beyond *Danubius* to the *Tauric* Pool.
All Nations now to *Rome* obedience pay,　　　　80
To *Rome*'s great Emperour, whose wide domain
In ample Territory, wealth and power,
Civility of Manners, Arts, and Arms,
And long Renown thou justly may'st prefer
Before the *Parthian*; these two Thrones except,
The rest are barbarous, and scarce worth the sight,
Shar'd among petty Kings too far remov'd;
These having shewn thee, I have shewn thee all
The Kingdoms of the world, and all thir glory.
This Emperour hath no Son, and now is old,　　　90
Old, and lascivious, and from *Rome* retir'd
To *Capreæ* an Island small but strong
On the *Campanian* shore, with purpose there
His horrid lusts in private to enjoy,
Committing to a wicked Favourite
All publick cares, and yet of him suspicious,
Hated of all, and hating; with what ease
Indu'd with Regal Vertues as thou art,
Appearing, and beginning noble deeds,
Might'st thou expel this monster from his Throne　　100
Now made a stye, and in his place ascending
A victor people free from servile yoke?
And with my help thou may'st; to me the power
Is given, and by that right I give it thee.
Aim therefore at no less then all the world,
Aim at the highest, without the highest attain'd
Will be for thee no sitting, or not long
On *David*'s Throne, be propheci'd what will.
　　To whom the Son of God unmov'd reply'd.
Nor doth this grandeur and majestic show　　110
Of luxury, though call'd magnificence,
More then of arms before, allure mine eye,
　　(489)

Much less my mind; though thou should'st add to tell
Thir sumptuous gluttonies, and gorgeous feasts
On *Cittron* tables or *Atlantic* stone;
(For I have also heard, perhaps have read)
Their wines of *Setia*, *Cales*, and *Falerne*,
Chios and *Creet*, and how they quaff in Gold,
Crystal and Myrrhine cups imboss'd with Gems
And studs of Pearl, to me should'st tell who thirst   120
And hunger still: then Embassies thou shew'st
From Nations far and nigh; what honour that,
But tedious wast of time to sit and hear
So many hollow complements and lies,
Outlandish flatteries? then proceed'st to talk
Of the Emperour, how easily subdu'd,
How gloriously; I shall, thou say'st, expel
A brutish monster: what if I withal
Expel a Devil who first made him such?
Let his tormenter Conscience find him out,   130
For him I was not sent, nor yet to free
That people victor once, now vile and base,
Deservedly made vassal, who once just,
Frugal, and mild, and temperate, conquer'd well,
But govern ill the Nations under yoke,
Peeling thir Provinces, exhausted all
By lust and rapine; first ambitious grown
Of triumph that insulting vanity;
Then cruel, by thir sports to blood enur'd
Of fighting beasts, and men to beasts expos'd,   140
Luxurious by thir wealth, and greedier still,
And from the daily Scene effeminate.
What wise and valiant man would seek to free
These thus degenerate, by themselves enslav'd,
Or could of inward slaves make outward free?
Know therefore when my season comes to sit
On *David*'s Throne, it shall be like a tree
Spreading and over-shadowing all the Earth,
Or as a stone that shall to pieces dash
All Monarchies besides throughout the world,   150
And of my Kingdom there shall be no end:
Means there shall be to this, but what the means,
Is not for thee to know, nor me to tell.
    To whom the Tempter impudent repli'd.

  (490)

Paradise Regain'd.

I see all offers made by me how slight
Thou valu'st, because offer'd, and reject'st:
Nothing will please the difficult and nice,
Or nothing more then still to contradict:
On the other side know also thou, that I
On what I offer set as high esteem,   160
Nor what I part with mean to give for naught;
All these which in a moment thou behold'st,
The Kingdoms of the world to thee I give;
For giv'n to me, I give to whom I please,
No trifle; yet with this reserve, not else,
On this condition, if thou wilt fall down,
And worship me as thy superior Lord,
Easily done, and hold them all of me;
For what can less so great a gift deserve?
    Whom thus our Saviour answer'd with disdain.   170
I never lik'd thy talk, thy offers less,
Now both abhor, since thou hast dar'd to utter
The abominable terms, impious condition;
But I endure the time, till which expir'd,
Thou hast permission on me. It is written
The first of all Commandments, Thou shalt worship
The Lord thy God, and only him shalt serve;
And dar'st thou to the Son of God propound
To worship thee accurst, now more accurst
For this attempt bolder then that on *Eve*,   180
And more blasphemous? which expect to rue.
The Kingdoms of the world to thee were giv'n,
Permitted rather, and by thee usurp't,
Other donation none thou canst produce:
If given, by whom but by the King of Kings,
God over all supreme? if giv'n to thee,
By thee how fairly is the Giver now
Repaid? But gratitude in thee is lost
Long since. Wert thou so void of fear or shame,
As offer them to me the Son of God,   190
To me my own, on such abhorred pact,
That I fall down and worship thee as God?
Get thee behind me; plain thou now appear'st
That Evil one, Satan for ever damn'd.
    To whom the Fiend with fear abasht reply'd.
Be not so sore offended, Son of God;

Though Sons of God both Angels are and Men,
If I to try whether in higher sort
Then these thou bear'st that title, have propos'd
What both from Men and Angels I receive,   200
Tetrarchs of fire, air, flood, and on the earth
Nations besides from all the quarter'd winds,
God of this world invok't and world beneath;
Who then thou art, whose coming is foretold
To me so fatal, me it most concerns.
The tryal hath indamag'd thee no way,
Rather more honour left and more esteem;
Me naught advantag'd, missing what I aim'd.
Therefore let pass, as they are transitory,
The Kingdoms of this world; I shall no more   210
Advise thee, gain them as thou canst, or not.
And thou thy self seem'st otherwise inclin'd
Then to a worldly Crown, addicted more
To contemplation and profound dispute,
As by that early action may be judg'd,
When slipping from thy Mothers eye thou went'st
Alone into the Temple; there was found
Among the gravest Rabbies disputant
On points and questions fitting *Moses* Chair,
Teaching not taught; the childhood shews the man,   220
As morning shews the day. Be famous then
By wisdom; as thy Empire must extend,
So let extend thy mind o're all the world,
In knowledge, all things in it comprehend,
All knowledge is not couch't in *Moses* Law,
The *Pentateuch* or what the Prophets wrote,
The *Gentiles* also know, and write, and teach
To admiration, led by Natures light;
And with the *Gentiles* much thou must converse,
Ruling them by perswasion as thou mean'st,   230
Without thir learning how wilt thou with them,
Or they with thee hold conversation meet?
How wilt thou reason with them, how refute
Thir Idolisms, Traditions, Paradoxes?
Error by his own arms is best evinc't.
Look once more e're we leave this specular Mount
Westward, much nearer by Southwest, behold
Where on the *Ægean* shore a City stands

Built nobly, pure the air, and light the soil,
Athens the eye of *Greece*, Mother of Arts   240
And Eloquence, native to famous wits
Or hospitable, in her sweet recess,
City or Suburban, studious walks and shades;
See there the Olive Grove of *Academe*,
Plato's retirement, where the *Attic* Bird
Trills her thick-warbl'd notes the summer long,
There flowrie hill *Hymettus* with the sound
Of Bees industrious murmur oft invites
To studious musing; there *Ilissus* rouls
His whispering stream; within the walls then view   250
The schools of antient Sages; his who bred
Great *Alexander* to subdue the world,
Lyceum there, and painted *Stoa* next:
There thou shalt hear and learn the secret power
Of harmony in tones and numbers hit
By voice or hand, and various-measur'd verse,
Æolian charms and *Dorian Lyric* Odes,
And his who gave them breath, but higher sung,
Blind *Melesigenes* thence *Homer* call'd,
Whose Poem *Phœbus* challeng'd for his own.   260
Thence what the lofty grave Tragœdians taught
In *Chorus* or *Iambic*, teachers best
Of moral prudence, with delight receiv'd
In brief sententious precepts, while they treat
Of fate, and chance, and change in human life;
High actions, and high passions best describing:
Thence to the famous Orators repair,
Those antient, whose resistless eloquence
Wielded at will that fierce Democratie,
Shook the Arsenal and fulmin'd over *Greece*,   270
To *Macedon*, and *Artaxerxes* Throne;
To sage Philosophy next lend thine ear,
From Heaven descended to the low-rooft house
Of *Socrates*, see there his Tenement,
Whom well inspir'd the Oracle pronounc'd
Wisest of men; from whose mouth issu'd forth
Mellifluous streams that water'd all the schools
Of Academics old and new, with those
Sirnam'd *Peripatetics*, and the Sect
Epicurean, and the *Stoic* severe;   280

These here revolve, or, as thou lik'st, at home,
Till time mature thee to a Kingdom's waight;
These rules will render thee a King compleat
Within thy self, much more with Empire joyn'd.
 To whom our Saviour sagely thus repli'd.
Think not but that I know these things, or think
I know them not; not therefore am I short
Of knowing what I aught: he who receives
Light from above, from the fountain of light,
No other doctrine needs, though granted true; 290
But these are false, or little else but dreams,
Conjectures, fancies, built on nothing firm.
The first and wisest of them all profess'd
To know this only, that he nothing knew:
The next to fabling fell and smooth conceits,
A third sort doubted all things, though plain sence;
Others in vertue plac'd felicity,
But vertue joyn'd with riches and long life,
In corporal pleasure he, and careless ease,
The Stoic last in Philosophic pride, 300
By him call'd vertue; and his vertuous man,
Wise, perfect in himself, and all possessing
Equal to God, oft shames not to prefer,
As fearing God nor man, contemning all
Wealth, pleasure, pain or torment, death and life,
Which when he lists, he leaves, or boasts he can,
For all his tedious talk is but vain boast,
Or subtle shifts conviction to evade.
Alas what can they teach, and not mislead;
Ignorant of themselves, of God much more, 310
And how the world began, and how man fell
Degraded by himself, on grace depending?
Much of the Soul they talk, but all awrie,
And in themselves seek vertue, and to themselves
All glory arrogate, to God give none,
Rather accuse him under usual names,
Fortune and Fate, as one regardless quite
Of mortal things. Who therefore seeks in these
True wisdom, finds her not, or by delusion
Far worse, her false resemblance only meets, 320
An empty cloud. However many books
Wise men have said are wearisom; who reads

Incessantly, and to his reading brings not
A spirit and judgment equal or superior,
(And what he brings, what needs he elsewhere seek)
Uncertain and unsettl'd still remains,
Deep verst in books and shallow in himself,
Crude or intoxicate, collecting toys,
And trifles for choice matters, worth a spunge;
As Children gathering pibles on the shore.   330
Or if I would delight my private hours
With Music or with Poem, where so soon
As in our native Language can I find
That solace? All our Law and Story strew'd
With Hymns, our Psalms with artful terms inscrib'd,
Our Hebrew Songs and Harps in *Babylon,*
That pleas'd so well our Victors ear, declare
That rather *Greece* from us these Arts deriv'd;
Ill imitated, while they loudest sing
The vices of thir Deities, and thir own   340
In Fable, Hymn, or Song, so personating
Thir Gods ridiculous, and themselves past shame.
Remove their swelling Epithetes thick laid
As varnish on a Harlots cheek, the rest,
Thin sown with aught of profit or delight,
Will far be found unworthy to compare
With *Sion*'s songs, to all true tasts excelling,
Where God is prais'd aright, and Godlike men,
The Holiest of Holies, and his Saints;
Such are from God inspir'd, not such from thee;   350
Unless where moral vertue is express't
By light of Nature not in all quite lost.
Thir Orators thou then extoll'st, as those
The top of Eloquence, Statists indeed,
And lovers of thir Country, as may seem;
But herein to our Prophets far beneath,
As men divinely taught, and better teaching
The solid rules of Civil Government
In thir majestic unaffected stile
Then all the Oratory of *Greece* and *Rome.*   360
In them is plainest taught, and easiest learnt,
What makes a Nation happy, and keeps it so,
What ruins Kingdoms, and lays Cities flat;
These only with our Law best form a King.

So spake the Son of God; but Satan now
Quite at a loss, for all his darts were spent,
Thus to our Saviour with stern brow reply'd.

Since neither wealth, nor honour, arms nor arts,
Kingdom nor Empire pleases thee, nor aught
By me propos'd in life contemplative,   370
Or active, tended on by glory, or fame,
What dost thou in this World? the Wilderness
For thee is fittest place, I found thee there,
And thither will return thee, yet remember
What I foretell thee, soon thou shalt have cause
To wish thou never hadst rejected thus
Nicely or cautiously my offer'd aid,
Which would have set thee in short time with ease
On *David's* Throne; or Throne of all the world,
Now at full age, fulness of time, thy season,   380
When Prophesies of thee are best fullfill'd.
Now contrary, if I read aught in Heaven,
Or Heav'n write aught of Fate, by what the Stars
Voluminous, or single characters,
In thir conjunction met, give me to spell,
Sorrows, and labours, opposition, hate,
Attends thee, scorns, reproaches, injuries,
Violence and stripes, and lastly cruel death,
A Kingdom they portend thee, but what Kingdom,
Real or Allegoric I discern not,   390
Nor when, eternal sure, as without end,
Without beginning; for no date prefixt
Directs me in the Starry Rubric set.

So saying he took (for still he knew his power
Not yet expir'd) and to the Wilderness
Brought back the Son of God, and left him there,
Feigning to disappear. Darkness now rose,
As day-light sunk, and brought in lowring night
Her shadowy off-spring unsubstantial both,
Privation meer of light and absent day.   400
Our Saviour meek and with untroubl'd mind
After his aerie jaunt, though hurried sore,
Hungry and cold betook him to his rest,
Wherever, under some concourse of shades
Whose branching arms thick intertwind might shield
From dews and damps of night his shelter'd head,

But shelter'd slept in vain, for at his head
The Tempter watch'd, and soon with ugly dreams
Disturb'd his sleep; and either Tropic now
'Gan thunder, and both ends of Heav'n, the Clouds   410
From many a horrid rift abortive pour'd
Fierce rain with lightning mixt, water with fire
In ruine reconcil'd: nor slept the winds
Within thir stony caves, but rush'd abroad
From the four hinges of the world, and fell
On the vext Wilderness, whose tallest Pines,
Though rooted deep as high, and sturdiest Oaks
Bow'd thir Stiff necks, loaden with stormy blasts,
Or torn up sheer: ill wast thou shrouded then,
O patient Son of God, yet only stoodst   420
Unshaken; nor yet staid the terror there,
Infernal Ghosts, and Hellish Furies, round
Environ'd thee, some howl'd, some yell'd, some shriek'd,
Some bent at thee thir fiery darts, while thou
Sat'st unappall'd in calm and sinless peace.
Thus pass'd the night so foul till morning fair
Came forth with Pilgrim steps in amice gray;
Who with her radiant finger still'd the roar
Of thunder, chas'd the clouds, and laid the winds,
And grisly Spectres, which the Fiend had rais'd   430
To tempt the Son of God with terrors dire.
And now the Sun with more effectual beams
Had chear'd the face of Earth, and dry'd the wet
From drooping plant, or dropping tree; the birds
Who all things now behold more fresh and green,
After a night of storm so ruinous,
Clear'd up their choicest notes in bush and spray
To gratulate the sweet return of morn;
Nor yet amidst this joy and brightest morn
Was absent, after all his mischief done,   440
The Prince of darkness, glad would also seem
Of this fair change, and to our Saviour came,
Yet with no new device, they all were spent,
Rather by this his last affront resolv'd,
Desperate of better course, to vent his rage,
And mad despight to be so oft repell'd.
Him walking on a Sunny hill he found,
Back'd on the North and West by a thick wood,

(497)

Out of the wood he starts in wonted shape;
And in a careless mood thus to him said.   450
    Fair morning yet betides thee Son of God,
After a dismal night; I heard the rack
As Earth and Skie would mingle; but my self
Was distant; and these flaws, though mortals fear them
As dangerous to the pillard frame of Heaven,
Or to the Earths dark basis underneath,
Are to the main as inconsiderable,
And harmless, if not wholsom, as a sneeze
To mans less universe, and soon are gone;
Yet as being oft times noxious where they light   460
On man, beast, plant, wastful and turbulent,
Like turbulencies in the affairs of men,
Over whose heads they rore, and seem to point,
They oft fore-signifie and threaten ill:
This Tempest at this Desert most was bent;
Of men at thee, for only thou here dwell'st.
Did I not tell thee, if thou didst reject
The perfet season offer'd with my aid
To win thy destin'd seat, but wilt prolong
All to the push of Fate, persue thy way   470
Of gaining *David*'s Throne no man knows when,
For both the when and how is no where told,
Thou shalt be what thou art ordain'd, no doubt;
For Angels have proclaim'd it, but concealing
The time and means: each act is rightliest done,
Not when it must, but when it may be best.
If thou observe not this, be sure to find,
What I foretold thee, many a hard assay
Of dangers, and adversities and pains,
E're thou of *Israel*'s Scepter get fast hold;   480
Whereof this ominous night that clos'd thee round,
So many terrors, voices, prodigies
May warn thee, as a sure fore-going sign.
    So talk'd he, while the Son of God went on
And staid not, but in brief him answer'd thus.
    Mee worse then wet thou find'st not; other harm
Those terrors which thou speak'st of, did me none;
I never fear'd they could, though noising loud
And threatning nigh; what they can do as signs
Betok'ning, or ill boding, I contemn   490

As false portents, not sent from God, but thee;
Who knowing I shall raign past thy preventing,
Obtrud'st thy offer'd aid, that I accepting
At least might seem to hold all power of thee,
Ambitious spirit, and wouldst be thought my God,
And storm'st refus'd, thinking to terrifie
Mee to thy will; desist, thou art discern'd
And toil'st in vain, nor me in vain molest.

To whom the Fiend now swoln with rage reply'd:
Then hear, O Son of *David*, Virgin-born;   500
For Son of God to me is yet in doubt,
Of the Messiah I have heard foretold
By all the Prophets; of thy birth at length
Announc't by *Gabriel* with the first I knew,
And of the Angelic Song in *Bethlehem* field,
On thy birth-night, that sung thee Saviour born.
From that time seldom have I ceas'd to eye
Thy infancy, thy childhood, and thy youth,
Thy manhood last, though yet in private bred;
Till at the Ford of *Jordan* whither all   510
Flock'd to the Baptist, I among the rest,
Though not to be Baptiz'd, by voice from Heav'n
Heard thee pronounc'd the Son of God belov'd.
Thenceforth I thought thee worth my nearer view
And narrower Scrutiny, that I might learn
In what degree or meaning thou art call'd
The Son of God, which bears no single sence;
The Son of God I also am, or was,
And if I was, I am; relation stands;
All men are Sons of God; yet thee I thought   520
In some respect far higher so declar'd.
Therefore I watch'd thy footsteps from that hour,
And follow'd thee still on to this wast wild;
Where by all best conjectures I collect
Thou art to be my fatal enemy.
Good reason then, if I before-hand seek
To understand my Adversary, who
And what he is; his wisdom, power, intent,
By parl, or composition, truce, or league
To win him, or win from him what I can.   530
And opportunity I here have had
To try thee, sift thee, and confess have found thee

Proof against all temptation as a rock
Of Adamant, and as a Center, firm
To the utmost of meer man both wise and good,
Not more; for Honours, Riches, Kingdoms, Glory
Have been before contemn'd, and may agen:
Therefore to know what more thou art then man,
Worth naming Son of God by voice from Heav'n,
Another method I must now begin.   540
    So saying he caught him up, and without wing
Of *Hippogrif* bore through the Air sublime
Over the Wilderness and o're the Plain;
Till underneath them fair *Jerusalem*,
The holy City lifted high her Towers,
And higher yet the glorious Temple rear'd
Her pile, far off appearing like a Mount
Of Alabaster, top't with golden Spires:
There on the highest Pinacle he set
The Son of God; and added thus in scorn: 550
    There stand, if thou wilt stand; to stand upright
Will ask thee skill; I to thy Fathers house
Have brought thee, and highest plac't, highest is best,
Now shew thy Progeny; if not to stand,
Cast thy self down; safely if Son of God:
For it is written, He will give command
Concerning thee to his Angels, in thir hands
They shall up lift thee, lest at any time
Thou chance to dash thy foot against a stone.
    To whom thus Jesus: also it is written,   560
Tempt not the Lord thy God, he said and stood.
But Satan smitten with amazement fell
As when Earths Son *Antæus* (to compare
Small things with greatest) in *Irassa* strove
With *Joves Alcides*, and oft foil'd still rose,
Receiving from his mother Earth new strength,
Fresh from his fall, and fiercer grapple joyn'd,
Throttl'd at length in the Air, expir'd and fell;
So after many a foil the Tempter proud,
Renewing fresh assaults, amidst his pride   570
Fell whence he stood to see his Victor fall.
And as that *Theban* Monster that propos'd
Her riddle, and him, who solv'd it not, devour'd;
That once found out and solv'd, for grief and spight

Cast her self headlong from th' *Ismenian* steep,
So strook with dread and anguish fell the Fiend,
And to his crew, that sat consulting, brought
Joyless triumphals of his hop't success,
Ruin, and desperation, and dismay,
Who durst so proudly tempt the Son of God.   580
So Satan fell and strait a fiery Globe
Of Angels on full sail of wing flew nigh,
Who on their plumy Vans receiv'd him soft
From his uneasie station, and upbore
As on a floating couch through the blithe Air,
Then in a flowry valley set him down
On a green bank, and set before him spred
A table of Celestial Food, Divine,
Ambrosial, Fruits fetcht from the tree of life,
And from the fount of life Ambrosial drink,   590
That soon refresh'd him wearied, and repair'd
What hunger, if aught hunger had impair'd,
Or thirst, and as he fed, Angelic Quires
Sung Heavenly Anthems of his victory
Over temptation, and the Tempter proud.
    True Image of the Father whether thron'd
In the bosom of bliss, and light of light
Conceiving, or remote from Heaven, enshrin'd
In fleshly Tabernacle, and human form,
Wandring the Wilderness, whatever place,   600
Habit, or state, or motion, still expressing
The Son of God, with Godlike force indu'd
Against th' Attempter of thy Fathers Throne,
And Thief of Paradise; him long of old
Thou didst debel, and down from Heav'n cast
With all his Army, now thou hast aveng'd
Supplanted *Adam*, and by vanquishing
Temptation, hast regain'd lost Paradise,
And frustrated the conquest fraudulent:
He never more henceforth will dare set foot   610
In Paradise to tempt; his snares are broke:
For though that seat of earthly bliss be fail'd,
A fairer Paradise is founded now
For *Adam* and his chosen Sons, whom thou
A Saviour art come down to re-install,
Where they shall dwell secure, when time shall be

Of Tempter and Temptation without fear.
But thou, Infernal Serpent, shalt not long
Rule in the Clouds; like an Autumnal Star
Or Lightning thou shalt fall from Heav'n trod down   620
Under his feet: for proof, e're this thou feel'st
Thy wound, yet not thy last and deadliest wound
By this repulse receiv'd, and hold'st in Hell
No triumph; in all her gates *Abaddon* rues
Thy bold attempt; hereafter learn with awe
To dread the Son of God: he all unarm'd
Shall chase thee with the terror of his voice
From thy Demoniac holds, possession foul,
Thee and thy Legions, yelling they shall flye,
And beg to hide them in a herd of Swine,   630
Lest he command them down into the deep
Bound, and to torment sent before thir time.
Hail Son of the most High, heir of both worlds,
Queller of Satan, on thy glorious work
Now enter, and begin to save mankind.

   Thus they the Son of God our Saviour meek
Sung Victor, and from Heavenly Feast refresht
Brought on his way with joy; hee unobserv'd
Home to his Mothers house private return'd.

The End.

SAMSON AGONISTES,

A
DRAMATIC POEM.

The Author
JOHN MILTON.

Ariſtot. Γοet. Cap. 6.

Τεαγωδια μίμησις πεάξεως σπεδαίας, &c.

Tragædia eſt imitatio actionis ſeriæ, &c. *Per miſericordiam &
metum perficiens talium affectuum luſtrationem.*

LONDON,

Printed by *J. M.* for *John Starkey* at the
Mitre in *Fleetſtreet*, near *Temple-Bar.*
MDCLXXI.

I

Of that sort of Dramatic Poem which is call'd Tragedy.

TRAGEDY, as it was antiently compos'd, hath been ever held the gravest, moralest, and most profitable of all other Poems: therefore said by *Aristotle* to be of power by raising pity and fear, or terror, to purge the mind of those and such like passions, that is to temper and reduce them to just measure with a kind of delight, stirr'd up by reading or seeing those passions well imitated. Nor is Nature wanting in her own effects to make good his assertion: for so in Physic things of melancholic hue and quality are us'd against melancholy, sowr against sowr, salt to remove salt humours. Hence Philosophers and other gravest Writers, as *Cicero*, *Plutarch* and others, frequently cite out of Tragic Poets, both to adorn and illustrate thir discourse. The Apostle *Paul* himself thought it not unworthy to insert a verse of *Euripides* into the Text of Holy Scripture, 1 *Cor.* 15. 33. and *Paræus* commenting on the *Revelation*, divides the whole Book as a Tragedy, into Acts distinguisht each by a Chorus of Heavenly Harpings and Song between. Heretofore Men in highest dignity have labour'd not a little to be thought able to compose a Tragedy. Of that honour *Dionysius* the elder was no less ambitious, then before of his attaining to the Tyranny. *Augustus Cæsar* also had begun his *Ajax*, but unable to please his own judgment with what he had begun, left it unfinisht. *Seneca* the Philosopher is by some thought the Author of those Tragedies (at lest the best of them) that go under that name. *Gregory Nazianzen* a Father of the Church, thought it not unbeseeming the sanctity of his person to write a Tragedy, which he entitl'd, *Christ suffering*. This is mention'd to vindicate Tragedy from the small esteem, or rather infamy, which in the account of many it undergoes at this day with other common Interludes; hap'ning through the Poets error of intermixing Comic stuff with Tragic sadness and gravity; or introducing trivial and vulgar persons, which by all judicious hath bin counted absurd; and brought in without discretion, corruptly to gratifie the people. And though antient Tragedy use no Prologue, yet using sometimes, in case of self defence, or explanation, that which *Martial* calls an Epistle; in behalf of this Tragedy coming forth after the antient manner, much different from what among us passes for best, thus much before-hand may be Epistl'd; that *Chorus* is here introduc'd after the Greek manner, not antient only but modern, and still in use among the *Italians*. In the modelling therefore of this Poem, with good reason, the Antients and *Italians* are rather follow'd, as of much more authority and fame. The measure of Verse us'd in the Chorus is of all sorts, call'd by the Greeks *Monostrophic*, or rather *Apolelymenon*, without regard had to *Strophe*, *Antistrophe* or *Epod*, which were a kind of Stanza's fram'd only for the Music, then us'd with the Chorus that sung; not essential to the Poem, and therefore not material; or being divided into Stanza's or Pauses, they may be call'd *Allæostropha*. Division into Act and Scene referring chiefly to the Stage (to which this work never was intended) is here omitted.

It suffices if the whole Drama be found not produc't beyond the fift Act, of the style and uniformitie, and that commonly call'd the Plot, whether intricate or explicit, which is nothing indeed but such œconomy, or disposition of the fable as may stand best with verisimilitude and decorum; they only will best judge who are not unacquainted with *Æschulus*, *Sophocles*, and *Euripides*, the three Tragic Poets unequall'd yet by any, and the best rule to all who endeavour to write Tragedy. The circumscription of time wherein the whole Drama begins and ends, is according to antient rule, and best example, within the space of 24 hours.

The ARGUMENT.

Samson *made Captive, Blind, and now in the Prison at* Gaza, *there to labour as in a common work-house, on a Festival day, in the general cessation from labour, comes forth into the open Air, to a place nigh, somewhat retir'd there to sit a while and bemoan his condition. Where he happens at length to be visited by certain friends and equals of his tribe, which make the Chorus, who seek to comfort him what they can; then by his old Father* Manoa, *who endeavours the like, and withal tells him his purpose to procure his liberty by ransom; lastly, that this Feast was proclaim'd by the* Philistins *as a day of Thanksgiving for thir deliverance from the hands of* Samson, *which yet more troubles him.* Manoa *then departs to prosecute his endeavour with the* Philistian *Lords for* Samson's *redemption; who in the mean while is visited by other persons; and lastly by a publick Officer to require his coming to the Feast before the Lords and People, to play or shew his strength in thir presence; he at first refuses, dismissing the publick Officer with absolute denyal to come; at length perswaded inwardly that this was from God, he yields to go along with him, who came now the second time with great threatnings to fetch him; the Chorus yet remaining on the place,* Manoa *returns full of joyful hope, to procure e're long his Sons deliverance: in the midst of which discourse an* Ebrew *comes in haste confusedly at first; and afterward more distinctly relating the Catastrophe, what* Samson *had done to the* Philistins, *and by accident to himself; wherewith the Tragedy ends.*

The Persons.

Samson.
Manoa *the Father of* Samson.
Dalila *his Wife*.
Harapha *of* Gath.
Publick Officer.
Messenger.
Chorus *of* Danites.

The Scene before the Prison in Gaza.

SAMSON

AGONISTES.

Sams. A LITTLE onward lend thy guiding hand
To these dark steps, a little further on;
For yonder bank hath choice of Sun or shade,
There I am wont to sit, when any chance
Relieves me from my task of servile toyl,
Daily in the common Prison else enjoyn'd me,
Where I a Prisoner chain'd, scarce freely draw
The air imprison'd also, close and damp,
Unwholsom draught: but here I feel amends,
The breath of Heav'n fresh-blowing, pure and sweet,   10
With day-spring born; here leave me to respire.
This day a solemn Feast the people hold
To *Dagon* thir Sea-Idol, and forbid
Laborious works, unwillingly this rest
Thir Superstition yields me; hence with leave
Retiring from the popular noise, I seek
This unfrequented place to find some ease,
Ease to the body some, none to the mind
From restless thoughts, that like a deadly swarm
Of Hornets arm'd, no sooner found alone,   20
But rush upon me thronging, and present
Times past, what once I was, and what am now.
O wherefore was my birth from Heaven foretold
Twice by an Angel, who at last in sight
Of both my Parents all in flames ascended
From off the Altar, where an Off'ring burn'd,
As in a fiery column charioting
His Godlike presence, and from some great act
Or benefit reveal'd to *Abraham*'s race?
Why was my breeding order'd and prescrib'd   30

Samson Agonistes.

As of a person separate to God,
Design'd for great exploits; if I must dye
Betray'd, Captiv'd, and both my Eyes put out,
Made of my Enemies the scorn and gaze;
To grind in Brazen Fetters under task
With this Heav'n-gifted strength? O glorious strength
Put to the labour of a Beast, debas't
Lower then bondslave! Promise was that I
Should *Israel* from *Philistian* yoke deliver;
Ask for this great Deliverer now, and find him   40
Eyeless in *Gaza* at the Mill with slaves,
Himself in bonds under *Philistian* yoke;
Yet stay, let me not rashly call in doubt
Divine Prediction; what if all foretold
Had been fulfilld but through mine own default,
Whom have I to complain of but my self?
Who this high gift of strength committed to me,
In what part lodg'd, how easily bereft me,
Under the Seal of silence could not keep,
But weakly to a woman must reveal it   50
O'recome with importunity and tears.
O impotence of mind, in body strong!
But what is strength without a double share
Of wisdom, vast, unwieldy, burdensom,
Proudly secure, yet liable to fall
By weakest suttleties, not made to rule,
But to subserve where wisdom bears command.
God, when he gave me strength, to shew withal
How slight the gift was, hung it in my Hair.
But peace, I must not quarrel with the will   60
Of highest dispensation, which herein
Happ'ly had ends above my reach to know:
Suffices that to me strength is my bane,
And proves the sourse of all my miseries;
So many, and so huge, that each apart
Would ask a life to wail, but chief of all,
O loss of sight, of thee I most complain!
Blind among enemies, O worse then chains,
Dungeon, or beggery, or decrepit age!
Light the prime work of God to me is extinct,   70
And all her various objects of delight
Annull'd, which might in part my grief have eas'd,

Samson Agonistes.

Inferiour to the vilest now become
Of man or worm; the vilest here excel me,
They creep, yet see, I dark in light expos'd
To daily fraud, contempt, abuse and wrong,
Within doors, or without, still as a fool,
In power of others, never in my own;
Scarce half I seem to live, dead more then half.
O dark, dark, dark, amid the blaze of noon,   80
Irrecoverably dark, total Eclipse
Without all hope of day!
O first created Beam, and thou great Word,
Let there be light, and light was over all;
Why am I thus bereav'd thy prime decree?
The Sun to me is dark
And silent as the Moon,
When she deserts the night
Hid in her vacant interlunar cave.
Since light so necessary is to life,   90
And almost life itself, if it be true
That light is in the Soul,
She all in every part; why was the sight
To such a tender ball as th' eye confin'd?
So obvious and so easie to be quench't,
And not as feeling through all parts diffus'd,
That she might look at will through every pore?
Then had I not been thus exil'd from light;
As in the land of darkness yet in light,
To live a life half dead, a living death,   100
And buried; but O yet more miserable!
My self, my Sepulcher, a moving Grave,
Buried, yet not exempt
By priviledge of death and burial
From worst of other evils, pains and wrongs,
But made hereby obnoxious more
To all the miseries of life,
Life in captivity
Among inhuman foes.
But who are these? for with joint pace I hear   110
The tread of many feet stearing this way;
Perhaps my enemies who come to stare
At my affliction, and perhaps to insult,
Thir daily practice to afflict me more.

Samson Agonistes.

Chor.   This, this is he; softly a while,
Let us not break in upon him;
O change beyond report, thought, or belief!
See how he lies at random, carelessly diffus'd,
With languish't head unprop,
As one past hope, abandon'd   120
And by himself given over;
In slavish habit, ill-fitted weeds
O're worn and soild;
Or do my eyes misrepresent?   Can this be hee,
That Heroic, that Renown'd,
Irresistible *Samson?* whom unarm'd
No strength of man, or fiercest wild beast could withstand;
Who tore the Lion, as the Lion tears the Kid,
Ran on embattelld Armies clad in Iron,
And weaponless himself,   130
Made Arms ridiculous, useless the forgery
Of brazen shield and spear, the hammer'd Cuirass,
Chalybean temper'd steel, and frock of mail
Adamantean Proof;
But safest he who stood aloof,
When insupportably his foot advanc't,
In scorn of thir proud arms and warlike tools,
Spurn'd them to death by Troops.   The bold *Ascalonite*
Fled from his Lion ramp, old Warriors turn'd
Thir plated backs under his heel;   140
Or grovling soild thir crested helmets in the dust.
Then with what trivial weapon came to hand,
The Jaw of a dead Ass, his sword of bone,
A thousand fore-skins fell, the flower of *Palestin*
In *Ramath-lechi* famous to this day:
Then by main force pull'd up, and on his shoulders bore
The Gates of *Azza*, Post, and massie Bar
Up to the Hill by *Hebron*, seat of Giants old,
No journey of a Sabbath day, and loaded so;
Like whom the Gentiles feign to bear up Heav'n.   150
Which shall I first bewail,
Thy Bondage or lost Sight,
Prison within Prison
Inseparably dark?
Thou art become (O worst imprisonment!)
The Dungeon of thy self; thy Soul

Samson Agonistes.

(Which Men enjoying sight oft without cause complain)
Imprison'd now indeed,
In real darkness of the body dwells,
Shut up from outward light   160
To incorporate with gloomy night;
For inward light alas
Puts forth no visual beam.
O mirror of our fickle state,
Since man on earth unparallel'd!
The rarer thy example stands,
By how much from the top of wondrous glory,
Strongest of mortal men,
To lowest pitch of abject fortune thou art fall'n.
For him I reckon not in high estate   170
Whom long descent of birth
Or the sphear of fortune raises;
But thee whose strength, while vertue was her mate
Might have subdu'd the Earth,
Universally crown'd with highest praises.
   Sam.   I hear the sound of words, thir sense the air
Dissolves unjointed e're it reach my ear.
   Chor. Hee speaks, let us draw nigh. Matchless in might,
The glory late of *Israel*, now the grief;
We come thy friends and neighbours not unknown   180
From *Eshtaol* and *Zora*'s fruitful Vale
To visit or bewail thee, or if better,
Counsel or Consolation we may bring,
Salve to thy Sores, apt words have power to swage
The tumors of a troubl'd mind,
And are as Balm to fester'd wounds.
   Sam.   Your coming, Friends, revives me, for I learn
Now of my own experience, not by talk,
How counterfeit a coin they are who friends
Bear in their Superscription (of the most   190
I would be understood) in prosperous days
They swarm, but in adverse withdraw their head
Not to be found, though sought. Yee see, O friends,
How many evils have enclos'd me round;
Yet that which was the worst now least afflicts me,
Blindness, for had I sight, confus'd with shame,
How could I once look up, or heave the head,
Who like a foolish Pilot have shipwrack't,

My Vessel trusted to me from above,
Gloriously rigg'd ; and for a word, a tear,   200
Fool, have divulg'd the secret gift of God
To a deceitful Woman : tell me Friends,
Am I not sung and proverbd for a Fool
In every street, do they not say, how well
Are come upon him his deserts ? yet why ?
Immeasurable strength they might behold
In me, of wisdom nothing more then mean ;
This with the other should, at least, have paird,
These two proportiond ill drove me transverse.

    Chor. Tax not divine disposal, wisest Men   210
Have err'd, and by bad Women been deceiv'd ;
And shall again, pretend they ne're so wise.
Deject not then so overmuch thy self,
Who hast of sorrow thy full load besides ;
Yet truth to say, I oft have heard men wonder
Why thou shouldst wed *Philistian* women rather
Then of thine own Tribe fairer, or as fair,
At least of thy own Nation, and as noble.

    Sam. The first I saw at *Timna*, and she pleas'd
Mee, not my Parents, that I sought to wed,   220
The daughter of an Infidel : they knew not
That what I motion'd was of God ; I knew
From intimate impulse, and therefore urg'd
The Marriage on ; that by occasion hence
I might begin *Israel's* Deliverance,
The work to which I was divinely call'd ;
She proving false, the next I took to Wife
(O that I never had ! fond wish too late)
Was in the Vale of *Sorec*, *Dalila*,
That specious Monster, my accomplisht snare.   230
I thought it lawful from my former act,
And the same end ; still watching to oppress
Israel's oppressours : of what now I suffer
She was not the prime cause, but I my self,
Who vanquisht with a peal of words (O weakness !)
Gave up my fort of silence to a Woman.

    Chor. In seeking just occasion to provoke
The *Philistine*, thy Countries Enemy,
Thou never wast remiss, I bear thee witness :
Yet *Israel* still serves with all his Sons.   240

Samson Agonistes.

Sam.   That fault I take not on me, but transfer
On *Israel*'s Governours, and Heads of Tribes,
Who seeing those great acts which God had done
Singly by me against their Conquerours
Acknowledg'd not, or not at all consider'd
Deliverance offerd : I on th' other side
Us'd no ambition to commend my deeds,
The deeds themselves, though mute, spoke loud the dooer;
But they persisted deaf, and would not seem
To count them things worth notice, till at length   250
Thir Lords the *Philistines* with gather'd powers
Enterd *Judea* seeking mee, who then
Safe to the rock of *Etham* was retir'd,
Not flying, but fore-casting in what place
To set upon them, what advantag'd best ;
Mean while the men of *Judah* to prevent
The harrass of thir Land, beset me round ;
I willingly on some conditions came
Into thir hands, and they as gladly yield me
To the uncircumcis'd a welcom prey,   260
Bound with two cords ; but cords to me were threds
Toucht with the flame : on thir whole Host I flew
Unarm'd, and with a trivial weapon fell'd
Thir choicest youth ; they only liv'd who fled.
Had *Judah* that day join'd, or one whole Tribe,
They had by this possess'd the Towers of *Gath*,
And lorded over them whom now they serve ;
But what more oft in Nations grown corrupt,
And by thir vices brought to servitude,
Then to love Bondage more then Liberty,   270
Bondage with ease then strenuous liberty ;
And to despise, or envy, or suspect
Whom God hath of his special favour rais'd
As thir Deliverer ; if he aught begin,
How frequent to desert him, and at last
To heap ingratitude on worthiest deeds?
   Chor.   Thy words to my remembrance bring
How *Succoth* and the Fort of *Penuel*
Thir great Deliverer contemn'd,
The matchless *Gideon* in pursuit   280
Of *Madian* and her vanquisht Kings :
And how ingrateful *Ephraim*

(515)

Had dealt with *Jephtha*, who by argument,
Not worse then by his shield and spear
Defended *Israel* from the *Ammonite*,
Had not his prowess quell'd thir pride
In that sore battel when so many dy'd
Without Reprieve adjudg'd to death,
For want of well pronouncing *Shibboleth*.

 Sam. Of such examples adde mee to the roul,   290
Mee easily indeed mine may neglect,
But Gods propos'd deliverance not so.

 Chor. Just are the ways of God,
And justifiable to Men ;
Unless there be who think not God at all,
If any be, they walk obscure ;
For of such Doctrine never was there School,
But the heart of the Fool,
And no man therein Doctor but himself.

 Yet more there be who doubt his ways not just,   300
As to his own edicts, found contradicting,
Then give the rains to wandring thought,
Regardless of his glories diminution ;
Till by thir own perplexities involv'd
They ravel more, still less resolv'd,
But never find self-satisfying solution.

 As if they would confine th' interminable,
And tie him to his own prescript,
Who made our Laws to bind us, not himself,
And hath full right to exempt   310
Whom so it pleases him by choice
From National obstriction, without taint
Of sin, or legal debt ;
For with his own Laws he can best dispence.

 He would not else who never wanted means,
Nor in respect of the enemy just cause
To set his people free,
Have prompted this Heroic *Nazarite*,
Against his vow of strictest purity,
To seek in marriage that fallacious Bride,   320
Unclean, unchaste.

 Down Reason then, at least vain reasonings down,
Though Reason here aver
That moral verdit quits her of unclean :

Samson Agonistes.

Unchaste was subsequent, her stain not his.
     But see here comes thy reverend Sire
With careful step, Locks white as doune,
Old *Manoah*: advise
Forthwith how thou oughtst to receive him.
     Sam. Ay me, another inward grief awak't,   330
With mention of that name renews th' assault.
     Man. Brethren and men of *Dan*, for such ye seem,
Though in this uncouth place; if old respect,
As I suppose, towards your once gloried friend,
My Son now Captive, hither hath inform'd
Your younger feet, while mine cast back with age
Came lagging after; say if he be here.
     Chor. As signal now in low dejected state,
As earst in highest, behold him where he lies.
     Man. O miserable change! is this the man,   340
That invincible *Samson*, far renown'd,
The dread of *Israel*'s foes, who with a strength
Equivalent to Angels walk'd thir streets,
None offering fight; who single combatant
Duell'd thir Armies rank't in proud array,
Himself an Army, now unequal match
To save himself against a coward arm'd
At one spears length. O ever failing trust
In mortal strength! and oh what not in man
Deceivable and vain! Nay what thing good   350
Pray'd for, but often proves our woe, our bane?
I pray'd for Children, and thought barrenness
In wedlock a reproach; I gain'd a Son,
And such a Son as all Men hail'd me happy;
Who would be now a Father in my stead?
O wherefore did God grant me my request,
And as a blessing with such pomp adorn'd?
Why are his gifts desirable, to tempt
Our earnest Prayers, then giv'n with solemn hand
As Graces, draw a Scorpions tail behind?   360
For this did the Angel twice descend? for this
Ordain'd thy nurture holy, as of a Plant;
Select, and Sacred, Glorious for a while,
The miracle of men: then in an hour
Ensnar'd, assaulted, overcome, led bound,
Thy Foes derision, Captive, Poor, and Blind

Samson Agonistes.

Into a Dungeon thrust, to work with Slaves?
Alas methinks whom God hath chosen once
To worthiest deeds, if he through frailty err,
He should not so o'rewhelm, and as a thrall   370
Subject him to so foul indignities,
Be it but for honours sake of former deeds.

   Sam. Appoint not heavenly disposition, Father,
Nothing of all these evils hath befall'n me
But justly; I my self have brought them on,
Sole Author I, sole cause: if aught seem vile,
As vile hath been my folly, who have profan'd
The mystery of God giv'n me under pledge
Of vow, and have betray'd it to a woman,
A *Canaanite*, my faithless enemy.   380
This well I knew, nor was at all surpris'd,
But warn'd by oft experience: did not she
Of *Timna* first betray me, and reveal
The secret wrested from me in her highth
Of Nuptial Love profest, carrying it strait
To them who had corrupted her, my Spies,
And Rivals? In this other was there found
More Faith? who also in her prime of love,
Spousal embraces, vitiated with Gold,
Though offer'd only, by the sent conceiv'd   390
Her spurious first-born; Treason against me?
Thrice she assay'd with flattering prayers and sighs,
And amorous reproaches to win from me
My capital secret, in what part my strength
Lay stor'd in what part summ'd, that she might know:
Thrice I deluded her, and turn'd to sport
Her importunity, each time perceiving
How openly, and with what impudence
She purpos'd to betray me, and (which was worse
Then undissembl'd hate) with what contempt   400
She sought to make me Traytor to my self;
Yet the fourth time, when mustring all her wiles,
With blandisht parlies, feminine assaults,
Tongue-batteries, she surceas'd not day nor night
To storm me over-watch't, and wearied out.
At times when men seek most repose and rest,
I yielded, and unlock'd her all my heart,
Who with a grain of manhood well resolv'd

Might easily have shook off all her snares :
But foul effeminacy held me yok't   410
Her Bond-slave ; O indignity, O blot
To Honour and Religion ! servil mind
Rewarded well with servil punishment !
The base degree to which I now am fall'n,
These rags, this grinding, is not yet so base
As was my former servitude, ignoble,
Unmanly, ignominious, infamous,
True slavery, and that blindness worse then this,
That saw not how degeneratly I serv'd.
    Man. I cannot praise thy Marriage choises, Son,   420
Rather approv'd them not ; but thou didst plead
Divine impulsion prompting how thou might'st
Find some occasion to infest our Foes.
I state not that ; this I am sure ; our Foes
Found soon occasion thereby to make thee
Thir Captive, and thir triumph ; thou the sooner
Temptation found'st, or over-potent charms
To violate the sacred trust of silence
Deposited within thee ; which to have kept
Tacit, was in thy power ; true ; and thou bear'st   430
Enough, and more the burden of that fault ;
Bitterly hast thou paid, and still art paying
That rigid score. A worse thing yet remains,
This day the *Philistines* a popular Feast
Here celebrate in *Gaza* ; and proclaim
Great Pomp, and Sacrifice, and Praises loud
To *Dagon*, as their God who hath deliver'd
Thee *Samson* bound and blind into thir hands,
Them out of thine, who slew'st them many a slain.
So *Dagon* shall be magnifi'd, and God,   440
Besides whom is no God, compar'd with Idols,
Disglorifi'd, blasphem'd, and had in scorn
By th' Idolatrous rout amidst thir wine ;
Which to have come to pass by means of thee,
Samson, of all thy sufferings think the heaviest,
Of all reproach the most with shame that ever
Could have befall'n thee and thy Fathers house.
    Sam. Father, I do acknowledge and confess
That I this honour, I this pomp have brought
To *Dagon*, and advanc'd his praises high   450

Among the Heathen round ; to God have brought
Dishonour, obloquie, and op't the mouths
Of Idolists, and Atheists ; have brought scandal
To *Israel*, diffidence of God, and doubt
In feeble hearts, propense anough before
To waver, or fall off and joyn with Idols :
Which is my chief affliction, shame and sorrow,
The anguish of my Soul, that suffers not
Mine eie to harbour sleep, or thoughts to rest.
This only hope relieves me, that the strife   460
With me hath end ; all the contest is now
'Twixt God and *Dagon* ; *Dagon* hath presum'd,
Me overthrown, to enter lists with God,
His Deity comparing and preferring
Before the God of *Abraham*. He, be sure,
Will not connive, or linger, thus provok'd,
But will arise and his great name assert :
Dagon must stoop, and shall e're long receive
Such a discomfit, as shall quite despoil him
Of all these boasted Trophies won on me,   470
And with confusion blank his Worshippers.

    Man. With cause this hope relieves thee, and these words
I as a Prophecy receive : for God,
Nothing more certain, will not long defer
To vindicate the glory of his name
Against all competition, nor will long
Endure it, doubtful whether God be Lord,
Or *Dagon*. But for thee what shall be done ?
Thou must not in the mean while here forgot
Lie in this miserable loathsom plight   480
Neglected. I already have made way
To some *Philistian* Lords, with whom to treat
About thy ransom : well they may by this
Have satisfi'd thir utmost of revenge
By pains and slaveries, worse then death inflicted
On thee, who now no more canst do them harm.

    Sam. Spare that proposal, Father, spare the trouble
Of that sollicitation ; let me here,
As I deserve, pay on my punishment ;
And expiate, if possible, my crime,   490
Shameful garrulity. To have reveal'd
Secrets of men, the secrets of a friend,

How hainous had the fact been, how deserving
Contempt, and scorn of all, to be excluded
All friendship, and avoided as a blab,
The mark of fool set on his front?
But I Gods counsel have not kept, his holy secret
Presumptuously have publish'd, impiously,
Weakly at least, and shamefully: A sin
That Gentiles in thir Parables condemn   500
To thir abyss and horrid pains confin'd.

   Man. Be penitent and for thy fault contrite,
But act not in thy own affliction, Son,
Repent the sin, but if the punishment
Thou canst avoid, self-preservation bids;
Or th' execution leave to high disposal,
And let another hand, not thine, exact
Thy penal forfeit from thy self; perhaps
God will relent, and quit thee all his debt;
Who evermore approves and more accepts   510
(Best pleas'd with humble and filial submission)
Him who imploring mercy sues for life,
Then who self-rigorous chooses death as due;
Which argues over-just, and self-displeas'd
For self-offence, more then for God offended.
Reject not then what offerd means, who knows
But God hath set before us, to return thee
Home to thy countrey and his sacred house,
Where thou mayst bring thy off'rings, to avert
His further ire, with praiers and vows renew'd.   520

   Sam. His pardon I implore; but as for life,
To what end should I seek it? when in strength
All mortals I excell'd, and great in hopes
With youthful courage and magnanimous thoughts
Of birth from Heav'n foretold and high exploits,
Full of divine instinct, after some proof
Of acts indeed heroic, far beyond
The Sons of *Anac*, famous now and blaz'd,
Fearless of danger, like a petty God
I walk'd about admir'd of all and dreaded   530
On hostile ground, none daring my affront.
Then swoll'n with pride into the snare I fell
Of fair fallacious looks, venereal trains,
Softn'd with pleasure and voluptuous life;

Samson Agonistes.

At length to lay my head and hallow'd pledge
Of all my strength in the lascivious lap
Of a deceitful Concubine who shore me
Like a tame Weather, all my precious fleece,
Then turn'd me out ridiculous, despoil'd,
Shav'n, and disarm'd among my enemies.   540

Chor.   Desire of wine and all delicious drinks,
Which many a famous Warriour overturns,
Thou couldst repress, nor did the dancing Rubie
Sparkling, out-pow'rd, the flavor, or the smell,
Or taste that cheers the heart of Gods and men,
Allure thee from the cool Crystalline stream.

Sam.   Where ever fountain or fresh current flow'd
Against the Eastern ray, translucent, pure,
With touch ætherial of Heav'ns fiery rod
I drank, from the clear milkie juice allaying   550
Thirst, and refresht ; nor envy'd them the grape
Whose heads that turbulent liquor fills with fumes.

Chor.   O madness, to think use of strongest wines
And strongest drinks our chief support of health,
When God with these forbid'n made choice to rear
His mighty Champion, strong above compare,
Whose drink was only from the liquid brook.

Sam.   But what avail'd this temperance, not compleat
Against another object more enticing ?
What boots it at one gate to make defence   560
And at another to let in the foe
Effeminatly vanquish't ? by which means,
Now blind, disheartn'd, sham'd, dishonour'd, quell'd,
To what can I be useful, wherein serve
My Nation, and the work from Heav'n impos'd,
But to sit idle on the houshold hearth,
A burdenous drone ; to visitants a gaze,
Or pitied object, these redundant locks
Robustious to no purpose clustring down,
Vain monument of strength ; till length of years   570
And sedentary numness craze my limbs
To a contemptible old age obscure.
Here rather let me drudge and earn my bread,
Till vermin or the draff of servil food
Consume me, and oft-invocated death
Hast'n the welcom end of all my pains.

(522)

Man. Wilt thou then serve the *Philistines* with that gift
Which was expresly giv'n thee to annoy them?
Better at home lie bed-rid, not only idle,
Inglorious, unimploy'd, with age out-worn.   580
But God who caus'd a fountain at thy prayer
From the dry ground to spring, thy thirst to allay
After the brunt of battel, can as easie
Cause light again within thy eies to spring,
Wherewith to serve him better then thou hast;
And I perswade me so; why else this strength
Miraculous yet remaining in those locks?
His might continues in thee not for naught,
Nor shall his wondrous gifts be frustrate thus.

Sam. All otherwise to me my thoughts portend,   590
That these dark orbs no more shall treat with light,
Nor th' other light of life continue long,
But yield to double darkness nigh at hand:
So much I feel my genial spirits droop,
My hopes all flat, nature within me seems
In all her functions weary of herself;
My race of glory run, and race of shame,
And I shall shortly be with them that rest.

Man. Believe not these suggestions which proceed
From anguish of the mind and humours black,   600
That mingle with thy fancy. I however
Must not omit a Fathers timely care
To prosecute the means of thy deliverance
By ransom or how else: mean while be calm,
And healing words from these thy friends admit.

Sam. O that torment should not be confin'd
To the bodies wounds and sores
With maladies innumerable
In heart, head, brest, and reins;
But must secret passage find   610
To th' inmost mind,
There exercise all his fierce accidents,
And on her purest spirits prey,
As on entrails, joints, and limbs,
With answerable pains, but more intense,
Though void of corporal sense.
    My griefs not only pain me
As a lingring disease,

But finding no redress, ferment and rage,
Nor less then wounds immedicable   620
Ranckle, and fester, and gangrene,
To black mortification.
Thoughts my Tormenters arm'd with deadly stings
Mangle my apprehensive tenderest parts,
Exasperate, exulcerate, and raise
Dire inflammation which no cooling herb
Or medcinal liquor can asswage,
Nor breath of Vernal Air from snowy *Alp*.
Sleep hath forsook and giv'n me o're
To deaths benumming Opium as my only cure.   630
Thence faintings, swounings of despair,
And sense of Heav'ns desertion.
   I was his nursling once and choice delight,
His destin'd from the womb,
Promisd by Heavenly message twice descending.
Under his special eie
Abstemious I grew up and thriv'd amain ;
He led me on to mightiest deeds
Above the nerve of mortal arm
Against the uncircumcis'd, our enemies.   640
But now hath cast me off as never known,
And to those cruel enemies,
Whom I by his appointment had provok't,
Left me all helpless with th' irreparable loss
Of sight, reserv'd alive to be repeated
The subject of thir cruelty, or scorn.
Nor am I in the list of them that hope ;
Hopeless are all my evils, all remediless ;
This one prayer yet remains, might I be heard,
No long petition, speedy death,   650
The close of all my miseries, and the balm.
   Chor. Many are the sayings of the wise
In antient and in modern books enroll'd ;
Extolling Patience as the truest fortitude ;
And to the bearing well of all calamities,
All chances incident to mans frail life
Consolatories writ
With studied argument, and much perswasion sought
Lenient of grief and anxious thought,
But with th' afflicted in his pangs thir sound   660

Samson Agonistes.

Little prevails, or rather seems a tune,
Harsh, and of dissonant mood from his complaint,
Unless he feel within
Some sourse of consolation from above;
Secret refreshings, that repair his strength,
And fainting spirits uphold.
    God of our Fathers, what is man!
That thou towards him with hand so various,
Or might I say contrarious,
Temperst thy providence through his short course,   670
Not evenly, as thou rul'st
The Angelic orders and inferiour creatures mute,
Irrational and brute.
Nor do I name of men the common rout,
That wandring loose about
Grow up and perish, as the summer flie,
Heads without name no more rememberd,
But such as thou hast solemnly elected,
With gifts and graces eminently adorn'd
To some great work, thy glory,   680
And peoples safety, which in part they effect:
Yet toward these thus dignifi'd, thou oft
Amidst thir highth of noon,
Changest thy countenance, and thy hand with no regard
Of highest favours past
From thee on them, or them to thee of service.
    Nor only dost degrade them, or remit
To life obscur'd, which were a fair dismission,
But throw'st them lower then thou didst exalt them high,
Unseemly falls in human eie,   690
Too grievous for the trespass or omission,
Oft leav'st them to the hostile sword
Of Heathen and prophane, thir carkasses
To dogs and fowls a prey, or else captiv'd:
Or to the unjust tribunals, under change of times,
And condemnation of the ingrateful multitude.
If these they scape, perhaps in poverty
With sickness and disease thou bow'st them down,
Painful diseases and deform'd,
In crude old age;   700
Though not disordinate, yet causless suffring
The punishment of dissolute days, in fine,

(525)

Just or unjust, alike seem miserable,
For oft alike, both come to evil end.
  So deal not with this once thy glorious **Champion**,
The Image of thy strength, and mighty minister.
What do I beg? how hast thou dealt already?
Behold him in this state calamitous, and turn
His labours, for thou canst, to peaceful end.
  But who is this, what thing of Sea or Land?   710
Femal of sex it seems,
That so bedeckt, ornate, and gay,
Comes this way sailing
Like a stately Ship
Of *Tarsus*, bound for th' Isles
Of *Javan* or *Gadier*
With all her bravery on, and tackle trim,
Sails fill'd, and streamers waving,
Courted by all the winds that hold them play,
An Amber sent of odorous perfume   720
Her harbinger, a damsel train behind;
Some rich *Philistian* Matron she may seem,
And now at nearer view, no other certain
Than *Dalila* thy wife.
  Sam. My Wife, my Traytress, let her not come near me.
  Cho. Yet on she moves, now stands & eies thee fixt,
About t' have spoke, but now, with head declin'd
Like a fair flower surcharg'd with dew, she weeps
And words addrest seem into tears dissolv'd,
Wetting the borders of her silk'n veil: 730
But now again she makes address to speak.
  Dal. With doubtful feet and wavering resolution
I came, still dreading thy displeasure, *Samson*,
Which to have merited, without excuse,
I cannot but acknowledge; yet if tears
May expiate (though the fact more evil drew
In the perverse event then I foresaw)
My penance hath not slack'n'd, though my pardon
No way assur'd. But conjugal affection
Prevailing over fear, and timerous doubt   740
Hath led me on desirous to behold
Once more thy face, and know of thy estate.
If aught in my ability may serve
To light'n what thou suffer'st, and appease
  (526)

Thy mind with what amends is in my power,
Though late, yet in some part to recompense
My rash but more unfortunate misdeed.
   Sam. Out, out *Hyæna*; these are thy wonted arts,
And arts of every woman false like thee,
To break all faith, all vows, deceive, betray,   750
Then as repentant to submit, beseech,
And reconcilement move with feign'd remorse,
Confess, and promise wonders in her change,
Not truly penitent, but chief to try
Her husband, how far urg'd his patience bears,
His vertue or weakness which way to assail:
Then with more cautious and instructed skill
Again transgresses, and again submits;
That wisest and best men full oft beguil'd
With goodness principl'd not to reject   760
The penitent, but ever to forgive,
Are drawn to wear out miserable days,
Entangl'd with a poysnous bosom snake,
If not by quick destruction soon cut off
As I by thee, to Ages an example.
   Dal. Yet hear me *Samson*; not that I endeavour
To lessen or extenuate my offence,
But that on th' other side if it be weigh'd
By it self, with aggravations not surcharg'd,
Or else with just allowance counterpois'd   770
I may, if possible, thy pardon find
The easier towards me, or thy hatred less.
First granting, as I do, it was a weakness
In me, but incident to all our sex,
Curiosity, inquisitive, importune
Of secrets, then with like infirmity
To publish them, both common female faults:
Was it not weakness also to make known
For importunity, that is for naught,
Wherein consisted all thy strength and safety?   780
To what I did thou shewdst me first the way.
But I to enemies reveal'd, and should not.
Nor shouldst thou have trusted that to womans frailty
E're I to thee, thou to thy self wast cruel.
Let weakness then with weakness come to parl
So near related, or the same of kind,

Thine forgive mine; that men may censure thine
The gentler, if severely thou exact not
More strength from me, then in thy self was found.
And what if Love, which thou interpret'st hate,   790
The jealousie of Love, powerful of sway
In human hearts, nor less in mine towards thee,
Caus'd what I did? I saw thee mutable
Of fancy, feard lest one day thou wouldst leave me
As her at *Timna*, sought by all means therefore
How to endear, and hold thee to me firmest:
No better way I saw then by importuning
To learn thy secrets, get into my power
Thy key of strength and safety: thou wilt say,
Why then reveal'd? I was assur'd by those   800
Who tempted me, that nothing was design'd
Against thee but safe custody, and hold:
That made for me, I knew that liberty
Would draw thee forth to perilous enterprises,
While I at home sate full of cares and fears
Wailing thy absence in my widow'd bed;
Here I should still enjoy thee day and night
Mine and Loves prisoner, not the *Philistines*,
Whole to my self, unhazarded abroad,
Fearless at home of partners in my love.   810
These reasons in Loves law have past for good,
Though fond and reasonless to some perhaps:
And Love hath oft, well meaning, wrought much wo,
Yet always pity or pardon hath obtain'd.
Be not unlike all others, not austere
As thou art strong, inflexible as steel.
If thou in strength all mortals dost exceed,
In uncompassionate anger do not so.
   Sam. How cunningly the sorceress displays
Her own transgressions, to upbraid me mine!   820
That malice not repentance brought thee hither,
By this appears: I gave, thou say'st, th' example,
I led the way; bitter reproach, but true,
I to my self was false e're thou to me,
Such pardon therefore as I give my folly,
Take to thy wicked deed: which when thou seest
Impartial, self-severe, inexorable,
Thou wilt renounce thy seeking, and much rather

Confess it feign'd, weakness is thy excuse,
And I believe it, weakness to resist 830
Philistian gold: if weakness may excuse,
What Murtherer, what Traytor, Parricide,
Incestuous, Sacrilegious, but may plead it?
All wickedness is weakness: that plea therefore
With God or Man will gain thee no remission.
But Love constrain'd thee; call it furious rage
To satisfie thy lust: Love seeks to have Love;
My love how couldst thou hope, who tookst the way
To raise in me inexpiable hate,
Knowing, as needs I must, by thee betray'd? 840
In vain thou striv'st to cover shame with shame,
Or by evasions thy crime uncoverst more.

    Dal. Since thou determinst weakness for no plea
In man or woman, though to thy own condemning,
Hear what assaults I had, what snares besides,
What sieges girt me round, e're I consented;
Which might have aw'd the best resolv'd of men,
The constantest to have yielded without blame.
It was not gold, as to my charge thou lay'st,
That wrought with me: thou know'st the Magistrates 850
And Princes of my countrey came in person,
Sollicited, commanded, threatn'd, urg'd,
Adjur'd by all the bonds of civil Duty
And of Religion, press'd how just it was,
How honourable, how glorious to entrap
A common enemy, who had destroy'd
Such numbers of our Nation: and the Priest
Was not behind, but ever at my ear,
Preaching how meritorious with the gods
It would be to ensnare an irreligious 860
Dishonourer of *Dagon*: what had I
To oppose against such powerful arguments?
Only my love of thee held long debate;
And combated in silence all these reasons
With hard contest: at length that grounded maxim
So rife and celebrated in the mouths
Of wisest men; that to the public good
Private respects must yield; with grave authority
Took full possession of me and prevail'd;
Vertue, as I thought, truth, duty so enjoyning. 870

Sam. I thought where all thy circling wiles would end;
In feign'd Religion, smooth hypocrisie.
But had thy love, still odiously pretended,
Bin, as it ought, sincere, it would have taught thee
Far other reasonings, brought forth other deeds.
I before all the daughters of my Tribe
And of my Nation chose thee from among
My enemies, lov'd thee, as too well thou knew'st,
Too well, unbosom'd all my secrets to thee,
Not out of levity, but over-powr'd   880
By thy request, who could deny thee nothing;
Yet now am judg'd an enemy. Why then
Didst thou at first receive me for thy husband?
Then, as since then, thy countries foe profest:
Being once a wife, for me thou wast to leave
Parents and countrey; nor was I their subject,
Nor under their protection but my own,
Thou mine, not theirs: if aught against my life
Thy countrey sought of thee, it sought unjustly,
Against the law of nature, law of nations,   890
No more thy countrey, but an impious crew
Of men conspiring to uphold thir state
By worse than hostile deeds, violating the ends
For which our countrey is a name so dear;
Not therefore to be obey'd. But zeal mov'd thee;
To please thy gods thou didst it; gods unable
To acquit themselves and prosecute their foes
But by ungodly deeds, the contradiction
Of their own deity, Gods cannot be:
Less therefore to be pleas'd, obey'd, or fear'd,   900
These false pretexts and varnish'd colours failing,
Bare in thy guilt how foul must thou appear?
    Dal. In argument with men a woman ever
Goes by the worse, whatever be her cause.
    Sam. For want of words no doubt, or lack of breath,
Witness when I was worried with thy peals.
    Dal. I was a fool, too rash, and quite mistaken
In what I thought would have succeeded best.
Let me obtain forgiveness of thee, *Samson*,
Afford me place to shew what recompence   910
Towards thee I intend for what I have misdone,
Misguided: only what remains past cure

Samson Agonistes.

Bear not too sensibly, nor still insist
To afflict thy self in vain: though sight be lost,
Life yet hath many solaces, enjoy'd
Where other senses want not their delights
At home in leisure and domestic ease,
Exempt from many a care and chance to which
Eye-sight exposes daily men abroad.
I to the Lords will intercede, not doubting   920
Thir favourable ear, that I may fetch thee
From forth this loathsom prison-house, to abide
With me, where my redoubl'd love and care
With nursing diligence, to me glad office,
May ever tend about thee to old age
With all things grateful chear'd, and so suppli'd,
That what by me thou hast lost thou least shalt miss.
   Sam. No, no, of my condition take no care;
It fits not; thou and I long since are twain;
Nor think me so unwary or accurst   930
To bring my feet again into the snare
Where once I have been caught; I know thy trains
Though dearly to my cost, thy ginns, and toyls;
Thy fair enchanted cup, and warbling charms
No more on me have power, their force is null'd,
So much of Adders wisdom I have learn't
To fence my ear against thy sorceries.
If in my flower of youth and strength, when all men
Lov'd, honour'd, fear'd me, thou alone could hate me
Thy Husband, slight me, sell me, and forgo me;   940
How wouldst thou use me now, blind, and thereby
Deceiveable, in most things as a child
Helpless, thence easily contemn'd, and scorn'd,
And last neglected? How wouldst thou insult
When I must live uxorious to thy will
In perfet thraldom, how again betray me,
Bearing my words and doings to the Lords
To gloss upon, and censuring, frown or smile?
This Gaol I count the house of Liberty
To thine whose doors my feet shall never enter.   950
   Dal. Let me approach at least, and touch thy hand.
   Sam. Not for thy life, lest fierce remembrance wake
My sudden rage to tear thee joint by joint.
At distance I forgive thee, go with that;

Bewail thy falshood, and the pious works
It hath brought forth to make thee memorable
Among illustrious women, faithful wives :
Cherish thy hast'n'd widowhood with the gold
Of Matrimonial treason : so farewel.
    Dal. I see thou art implacable, more deaf   960
To prayers, then winds and seas, yet winds to seas
Are reconcil'd at length, and Sea to Shore :
Thy anger, unappeasable, still rages,
Eternal tempest never to be calm'd.
Why do I humble thus my self, and suing
For peace, reap nothing but repulse and hate ?
Bid go with evil omen and the brand
Of infamy upon my name denounc't ?
To mix with thy concernments I desist
Henceforth, nor too much disapprove my own.   970
Fame if not double-fac't is double-mouth'd,
And with contrary blast proclaims most deeds,
On both his wings, one black, th' other white,
Bears greatest names in his wild aerie flight.
My name perhaps among the Circumcis'd
In *Dan*, in *Judah*, and the bordering Tribes,
To all posterity may stand defam'd,
With malediction mention'd, and the blot
Of falshood most unconjugal traduc't.
But in my countrey where I most desire,   980
In *Ecron, Gaza, Asdod*, and in *Gath*
I shall be nam'd among the famousest
Of Women, sung at solemn festivals,
Living and dead recorded, who to save
Her countrey from a fierce destroyer, chose
Above the faith of wedlock-bands, my tomb
With odours visited and annual flowers.
Not less renown'd then in Mount *Ephraim*,
Jael, who with inhospitable guile
Smote *Sisera* sleeping through the Temples nail'd.   990
Nor shall I count it hainous to enjoy
The public marks of honour and reward
Conferr'd upon me, for the piety
Which to my countrey I was judg'd to have shewn.
At this who ever envies or repines
I leave him to his lot, and like my own.

Samson Agonistes.

Chor. She's gone, a manifest Serpent by her sting
Discover'd in the end, till now conceal'd.
    Sam. So let her go, God sent her to debase me,
And aggravate my folly who committed   1000
To such a viper his most sacred trust
Of secresie, my safety, and my life.
    Chor. Yet beauty, though injurious, hath strange power,
After offence returning, to regain
Love once possest, nor can be easily
Repuls't, without much inward passion felt
And secret sting of amorous remorse.
    Sam. Love-quarrels oft in pleasing concord end,
Not wedlock-trechery endangering life.
    Chor. It is not vertue, wisdom, valour, wit,   1010
Strength, comliness of shape, or amplest merit
That womans love can win or long inherit;
But what it is, hard is to say,
Harder to hit,
(Which way soever men refer it)
Much like thy riddle, *Samson*, in one day
Or seven, though one should musing sit;
    If any of these or all, the *Timnian* bride
Had not so soon preferr'd
Thy Paranymph, worthless to thee compar'd,   1020
Successour in thy bed,
Nor both so loosly disally'd
Thir nuptials, nor this last so trecherously
Had shorn the fatal harvest of thy head.
Is it for that such outward ornament
Was lavish't on thir Sex, that inward gifts
Were left for hast unfinish't, judgment scant,
Capacity not rais'd to apprehend
Or value what is best
In choice, but oftest to affect the wrong?   1030
Or was too much of self-love mixt,
Of constancy no root infixt,
That either they love nothing, or not long?
    What e're it be, to wisest men and best
Seeming at first all heavenly under virgin veil,
Soft, modest, meek, demure,
Once join'd, the contrary she proves, a thorn
Intestin, far within defensive arms

(533)

A cleaving mischief, in his way to vertue
Adverse and turbulent, or by her charms   1040
Draws him awry enslav'd
With dotage, and his sense deprav'd
To folly and shameful deeds which ruin ends.
What Pilot so expert but needs must wreck
Embarqu'd with such a Stears-mate at the Helm?
    Favour'd of Heav'n who finds
One vertuous rarely found,
That in domestic good combines:
Happy that house! his way to peace is smooth:
But vertue which breaks through all opposition,   1050
And all temptation can remove,
Most shines and most is acceptable above.
    Therefore Gods universal Law
Gave to the man despotic power
Over his female in due awe,
Nor from that right to part an hour,
Smile she or lowre:
So shall he least confusion draw
On his whole life, not sway'd
By female usurpation, nor dismay'd.   1060
    But had we best retire, I see a storm?
    Sam. Fair days have oft contracted wind and rain.
    Chor. But this another kind of tempest brings.
    Sam. Be less abstruse, my riddling days are past.
    Chor. Look now for no inchanting voice, nor fear
The bait of honied words; a rougher tongue
Draws hitherward, I know him by his stride,
The Giant *Harapha* of *Gath*, his look
Haughty as is his pile high-built and proud.
Comes he in peace? what wind hath blown him hither
I less conjecture then when first I saw   1071
The sumptuous *Dalila* floating this way:
His habit carries peace, his brow defiance.
    Sam. Or peace or not, alike to me he comes.
    Chor. His fraught we soon shall know, he now arrives.
    Har. I come not *Samson*, to condole thy chance,
As these perhaps, yet wish it had not been,
Though for no friendly intent. I am of *Gath*,
Men call me *Harapha*, of stock renown'd
As *Og* or *Anak* and the *Emims* old   1080

That *Kiriathaim* held, thou knowst me now
If thou at all art known. Much I have heard
Of thy prodigious might and feats perform'd
Incredible to me, in this displeas'd,
That I was never present on the place
Of those encounters, where we might have tri'd
Each others force in camp or listed field :
And now am come to see of whom such noise
Hath walk'd about, and each limb to survey,
If thy appearance answer loud report.   1090
   Sam. The way to know were not to see but taste.
   Har. Dost thou already single me; I thought
Gives and the Mill had tam'd thee? O that fortune
Had brought me to the field where thou art fam'd
To have wrought such wonders with an Asses Jaw;
I should have forc'd thee soon with other arms,
Or left thy carkass where the Ass lay thrown :
So had the glory of Prowess been recover'd
To *Palestine*, won by a *Philistine*
From the unforeskinn'd race, of whom thou bear'st   1100
The highest name for valiant Acts, that honour
Certain to have won by mortal duel from thee,
I lose, prevented by thy eyes put out.
   Sam. Boast not of what thou wouldst have done, but do
What then thou would'st, thou seest it in thy hand.
   Har. To combat with a blind man I disdain,
And thou hast need much washing to be toucht.
   Sam. Such usage as your honourable Lords
Afford me assassinated and betray'd,
Who durst not with thir whole united powers   1110
In fight withstand me single and unarm'd,
Nor in the house with chamber Ambushes
Close-banded durst attaque me, no not sleeping,
Till they had hir'd a woman with their gold
Breaking her Marriage Faith to circumvent me.
Therefore without feign'd shifts let be assign'd
Some narrow place enclos'd, where sight may give thee,
Or rather flight, no great advantage on me ;
Then put on all thy gorgeous arms, thy Helmet
And Brigandine of brass, thy broad Habergeon,   1120
Vant-brass and Greves, and Gauntlet, add thy Spear
A Weavers beam, and seven-times-folded shield,

I only with an Oak'n staff will meet thee,
And raise such out-cries on thy clatter'd Iron,
Which long shall not with-hold mee from thy head,
That in a little time while breath remains thee,
Thou oft shalt wish thy self at *Gath* to boast
Again in safety what thou wouldst have done
To *Samson*, but shalt never see *Gath* more.

Har. Thou durst not thus disparage glorious arms 1130
Which greatest Heroes have in battel worn,
Thir ornament and safety, had not spells
And black enchantments, some Magicians Art
Arm'd thee or charm'd thee strong, which thou from Heaven
Feigndst at thy birth was giv'n thee in thy hair,
Where strength can least abide, though all thy hairs
Were bristles rang'd like those that ridge the back
Of chaf't wild Boars, or ruffl'd Porcupines.

Sam. I know no Spells, use no forbidden Arts;
My trust is in the living God who gave me 1140
At my Nativity this strength, diffus'd
No less through all my sinews, joints and bones,
Then thine, while I preserv'd these locks unshorn,
The pledge of my unviolated vow.
For proof hereof, if *Dagon* be thy god,
Go to his Temple, invocate his aid
With solemnest devotion, spread before him
How highly it concerns his glory now
To frustrate and dissolve these Magic spells,
Which I to be the power of *Israel's* God 1150
Avow, and challenge *Dagon* to the test,
Offering to combat thee his Champion bold,
With th' utmost of his Godhead seconded:
Then thou shalt see, or rather to thy sorrow
Soon feel, whose God is strongest, thine or mine.

Har. Presume not on thy God, what e're he be,
Thee he regards not, owns not, hath cut off
Quite from his people, and delivered up
Into thy Enemies hand, permitted them
To put out both thine eyes, and fetter'd send thee 1160
Into the common Prison, there to grind
Among the Slaves and Asses thy comrades,
As good for nothing else, no better service
With those thy boyst'rous locks, no worthy match

Samson Agonistes.

For valour to assail, nor by the sword
Of noble Warriour, so to stain his honour,
But by the Barbers razor best subdu'd.

 Sam. All these indignities, for such they are
From thine, these evils I deserve and more,
Acknowledge them from God inflicted on me   1170
Justly, yet despair not of his final pardon
Whose ear is ever open; and his eye
Gracious to re-admit the suppliant;
In confidence whereof I once again
Defie thee to the trial of mortal fight,
By combat to decide whose god is God,
Thine or whom I with *Israel*'s Sons adore.

 Har. Fair honour that thou dost thy God, in trusting
He will accept thee to defend his cause,
A Murtherer, a Revolter, and a Robber.   1180

 Sam. Tongue-doubtie Giant, how dost thou prove me these?

 Har. Is not thy Nation subject to our Lords?
Thir Magistrates confest it, when they took thee
As a League-breaker and deliver'd bound
Into our hands: for hadst thou not committed
Notorious murder on those thirty men
At *Askalon*, who never did thee harm,
Then like a Robber stripdst them of thir robes?
The *Philistines*, when thou hadst broke the league,
Went up with armed powers thee only seeking,   1190
To others did no violence nor spoil.

 Sam. Among the Daughters of the *Philistines*
I chose a Wife, which argu'd me no foe;
And in your City held my Nuptial Feast:
But your ill-meaning Politician Lords,
Under pretence of Bridal friends and guests,
Appointed to await me thirty spies,
Who threatning cruel death constrain'd the bride
To wring from me and tell to them my secret,
That solv'd the riddle which I had propos'd.   1200
When I perceiv'd all set on enmity,
As on my enemies, where ever chanc'd,
I us'd hostility, and took thir spoil
To pay my underminers in thir coin.
My Nation was subjected to your Lords.
It was the force of Conquest; force with force

Is well ejected when the Conquer'd can.
But I a private person, whom my Countrey
As a league-breaker gave up, bound, presum'd
Single Rebellion and did Hostile Acts.   1210
I was no private but a person rais'd
With strength sufficient and command from Heav'n
To free my Countrey; if their servile minds
Me their Deliverer sent would not receive,
But to thir Masters gave me up for nought,
Th' unworthier they; whence to this day they serve.
I was to do my part from Heav'n assign'd,
And had perform'd it if my known offence
Had not disabl'd me, not all your force:
These shifts refuted, answer thy appellant.   1220
Though by his blindness maim'd for high attempts,
Who now defies thee thrice to single fight,
As a petty enterprise of small enforce.
    Har. With thee a Man condemn'd, a Slave enrol'd,
Due by the Law to capital punishment?
To fight with thee no man of arms will deign.
    Sam. Cam'st thou for this, vain boaster, to survey me,
To descant on my strength, and give thy verdit?
Come nearer, part not hence so slight inform'd;
But take good heed my hand survey not thee.   1230
    Har. O *Baal-zebub*! can my ears unus'd
Hear these dishonours, and not render death?
    Sam. No man with-holds thee, nothing from thy hand
Fear I incurable; bring up thy van,
My heels are fetter'd, but my fist is free.
    Har. This insolence other kind of answer fits.
    Sam. Go baffl'd coward, lest I run upon thee,
Though in these chains, bulk without spirit vast,
And with one buffet lay thy structure low,
Or swing thee in the Air, then dash thee down   1240
To the hazard of thy brains and shatter'd sides.
    Har. By *Astaroth* e're long thou shalt lament
These braveries in Irons loaden on thee.
    Chor. His Giantship is gone somewhat crestfall'n,
Stalking with less unconsci'nable strides,
And lower looks, but in a sultrie chafe.
    Sam. I dread him not, nor all his Giant-brood,
Though Fame divulge him Father of five Sons

All of Gigantic size, *Goliah* chief.

    Chor. He will directly to the Lords, I fear,   1250
And with malitious counsel stir them up
Some way or other yet further to afflict thee.

    Sam. He must allege some cause, and offer'd fight
Will not dare mention, lest a question rise
Whether he durst accept the offer or not,
And that he durst not plain enough appear'd.
Much more affliction then already felt
They cannot well impose, nor I sustain;
If they intend advantage of my labours
The work of many hands, which earns my keeping   1260
With no small profit daily to my owners.
But come what will, my deadliest foe will prove
My speediest friend, by death to rid me hence,
The worst that he can give, to me the best.
Yet so it may fall out, because thir end
Is hate, not help to me, it may with mine
Draw thir own ruin who attempt the deed.

    Chor. Oh how comely it is and how reviving
To the Spirits of just men long opprest!
When God into the hands of thir deliverer   1270
Puts invincible might
To quell the mighty of the Earth, th' oppressour,
The brute and boist'rous force of violent men
Hardy and industrious to support
Tyrannic power, but raging to pursue
The righteous and all such as honour Truth;
He all thir Ammunition
And feats of War defeats
With plain Heroic magnitude of mind
And celestial vigour arm'd,   1280
Thir Armories and Magazins contemns,
Renders them useless, while
With winged expedition
Swift as the lightning glance he executes
His errand on the wicked, who surpris'd
Lose thir defence distracted and amaz'd.

    But patience is more oft the exercise
Of Saints, the trial of thir fortitude,
Making them each his own Deliverer,
And Victor over all   1290

    (539)

That tyrannie or fortune can inflict,
Either of these is in thy lot,
Samson, with might endu'd
Above the Sons of men; but sight bereav'd
May chance to number thee with those
Whom Patience finally must crown.
This Idols day hath bin to thee no day of rest,
   Labouring thy mind
More then the working day thy hands,
And yet perhaps more trouble is behind.   1300
For I descry this way
Some other tending, in his hand
A Scepter or quaint staff he bears,
Comes on amain, speed in his look.
By his habit I discern him now
A Public Officer, and now at hand.
His message will be short and voluble.
   Off. *Ebrews*, the Pris'ner *Samson* here I seek.
   Chor. His manacles remark him, there he sits.
   Off. *Samson*, to thee our Lords thus bid me say;   1310
This day to *Dagon* is a solemn Feast,
With Sacrifices, Triumph, Pomp, and Games;
Thy strength they know surpassing human rate,
And now some public proof thereof require
To honour this great Feast, and great Assembly;
Rise therefore with all speed and come along,
Where I will see thee heartn'd and fresh clad
To appear as fits before th' illustrious Lords.
   Sam. Thou knowst I am an *Ebrew*, therefore tell them,
Our Law forbids at thir Religious Rites   1320
My presence; for that cause I cannot come.
   Off. This answer, be assur'd, will not content them.
   Sam. Have they not Sword-players, and ev'ry sort
Of Gymnic Artists, Wrestlers, Riders, Runners,
Juglers and Dancers, Antics, Mummers, Mimics,
But they must pick me out with shackles tir'd,
And over-labour'd at thir publick Mill,
To make them sport with blind activity?
Do they not seek occasion of new quarrels
On my refusal to distress me more,   1330
Or make a game of my calamities?
Return the way thou cam'st, I will not come.

Samson Agonistes.

Off.   Regard thy self, this will offend them highly.

Sam.   My self? my conscience and internal peace.
Can they think me so broken, so debas'd
With corporal servitude, that my mind ever
Will condescend to such absurd commands?
Although thir drudge, to be thir fool or jester,
And in my midst of sorrow and heart-grief
To shew them feats, and play before thir god,   1340
The worst of all indignities, yet on me
Joyn'd with extream contempt? I will not come.

Off.   My message was impos'd on me with speed,
Brooks no delay: is this thy resolution?

Sam.   So take it with what speed thy message needs.

Off.   I am sorry what this stoutness will produce.

Sam.   Perhaps thou shalt have cause to sorrow indeed.

Chor.   Consider, *Samson*; matters now are strain'd
Up to the highth, whether to hold or break;
He's gone, and who knows how he may report   1350
Thy words by adding fuel to the flame?
Expect another message more imperious,
More Lordly thund'ring then thou well wilt bear.

Sam.   Shall I abuse this Consecrated gift
Of strength, again returning with my hair
After my great transgression, so requite
Favour renew'd, and add a greater sin
By prostituting holy things to Idols;
A *Nazarite* in place abominable
Vaunting my strength in honour to thir *Dagon*?   1360
Besides, how vile, contemptible, ridiculous,
What act more execrably unclean, prophane?

Chor.   Yet with this strength thou serv'st the *Philistines*,
Idolatrous, uncircumcis'd, unclean.

Sam.   Not in thir Idol-worship, but by labour
Honest and lawful to deserve my food
Of those who have me in thir civil power.

Chor.   Where the heart joins not, outward acts defile not.

Sam.   Where outward force constrains, the sentence holds;
But who constrains me to the Temple of *Dagon*,   1370
Not dragging? the *Philistian* Lords command.
Commands are no constraints. If I obey them,
I do it freely; venturing to displease
God for the fear of Man, and Man prefer,

Set God behind: which in his jealousie
Shall never, unrepented, find forgiveness.
Yet that he may dispense with me or thee
Present in Temples at Idolatrous Rites
For some important cause, thou needst not doubt.

    Chor. How thou wilt here come off surmounts my reach.

    Sam. Be of good courage, I begin to feel   1381
Some rouzing motions in me which dispose
To something extraordinary my thoughts.
I with this Messenger will go along,
Nothing to do, be sure, that may dishonour
Our Law, or stain my vow of *Nazarite.*
If there be aught of presage in the mind,
This day will be remarkable in my life
By some great act, or of my days the last.

    Chor. In time thou hast resolv'd, the man returns. 1390

    Off. *Samson*, this second message from our Lords
To thee I am bid say. Art thou our Slave,
Our Captive, at the public Mill our drudge,
And dar'st thou at our sending and command
Dispute thy coming? come without delay;
Or we shall find such Engines to assail
And hamper thee, as thou shalt come of force,
Though thou wert firmlier fastn'd then a rock.

    Sam. I could be well content to try thir Art,
Which to no few of them would prove pernicious.   1400
Yet knowing thir advantages too many,
Because they shall not trail me through thir streets
Like a wild Beast, I am content to go.
Masters commands come with a power resistless
To such as owe them absolute subjection;
And for a life who will not change his purpose?
(So mutable are all the ways of men)
Yet this be sure, in nothing to comply
Scandalous or forbidden in our Law.

    Off. I praise thy resolution, doff these links: 1410
By this compliance thou wilt win the Lords
To favour, and perhaps to set thee free.

    Sam. Brethren farewel, your company along
I will not wish, lest it perhaps offend them
To see me girt with Friends; and how the sight
Of me as of a common Enemy,

Samson Agonistes.

So dreaded once, may now exasperate them
I know not.   Lords are Lordliest in thir wine;
And the well-feasted Priest then soonest fir'd
With zeal, if aught Religion seem concern'd: 1420
No less the people on thir Holy-days
Impetuous, insolent, unquenchable;
Happ'n what may, of me expect to hear
Nothing dishonourable, impure, unworthy
Our God, our Law, my Nation, or my self,
The last of me or no I cannot warrant.
    Chor.   Go, and the Holy One
Of *Israel* be thy guide
To what may serve his glory best, & spread his name
Great among the Heathen round: 1430
Send thee the Angel of thy Birth, to stand
Fast by thy side, who from thy Fathers field
Rode up in flames after his message told
Of thy conception, and be now a shield
Of fire; that Spirit that first rusht on thee
In the camp of *Dan*
Be efficacious in thee now at need.
For never was from Heaven imparted
Measure of strength so great to mortal seed,
As in thy wond'rous actions hath been seen.   1440
But wherefore comes old *Manoa* in such hast
With youthful steps? much livelier than e're while
He seems: supposing here to find his Son,
Or of him bringing to us some glad news?
    Man.   Peace with you brethren; my inducement hither
Was not at present here to find my Son,
By order of the Lords new parted hence
To come and play before them at thir Feast.
I heard all as I came, the City rings
And numbers thither flock, I had no will,   1450
Lest I should see him forc't to things unseemly.
But that which moved my coming now, was chiefly
To give ye part with me what hope I have
With good success to work his liberty.
    Chor.   That hope would much rejoyce us to partake
With thee; say reverend Sire, we thirst to hear.
    Man.   I have attempted one by one the Lords
Either at home, or through the high street passing,

With supplication prone and Fathers tears
To accept of ransom for my Son thir pris'ner,   1460
Some much averse I found and wondrous harsh,
Contemptuous, proud, set on revenge and spite;
That part most reverenc'd *Dagon* and his Priests,
Others more moderate seeming, but thir aim
Private reward, for which both God and State
They easily would set to sale, a third
More generous far and civil, who confess'd
They had anough reveng'd, having reduc't
Thir foe to misery beneath thir fears,
The rest was magnanimity to remit,   1470
If some convenient ransom were propos'd.
What noise or shout was that? it tore the Skie.

   Chor. Doubtless the people shouting to behold
Thir once great dread, captive, & blind before them,
Or at some proof of strength before them shown.

   Man. His ransom, if my whole inheritance
May compass it, shall willingly be paid
And numberd down: much rather I shall chuse
To live the poorest in my Tribe, then richest,
And he in that calamitous prison left.   1480
No, I am fixt not to part hence without him.
For his redemption all my Patrimony,
If need be, I am ready to forgo
And quit: not wanting him, I shall want nothing.

   Chor. Fathers are wont to lay up for thir Sons,
Thou for thy Son art bent to lay out all;
Sons wont to nurse thir Parents in old age,
Thou in old age car'st how to nurse thy Son,
Made older then thy age through eye-sight lost.

   Man. It shall be my delight to tend his eyes,   1490
And view him sitting in the house, enobl'd
With all those high exploits by him atchiev'd,
And on his shoulders waving down those locks,
That of a Nation arm'd the strength contain'd:
And I perswade me God had not permitted
His strength again to grow up with his hair
Garrison'd round about him like a Camp
Of faithful Souldiery, were not his purpose
To use him further yet in some great service,
Not to sit idle with so great a gift   1500

Useless, and thence ridiculous about him.
And since his strength with eye-sight was not lost,
God will restore him eye-sight to his strength.

    Chor. Thy hopes are not ill founded nor seem vain
Of his delivery, and thy joy thereon
Conceiv'd, agreeable to a Fathers love,
In both which we, as next participate.

    Man. I know your friendly minds and—O what noise !
Mercy of Heav'n what hideous noise was that !
Horribly loud unlike the former shout.   1510

    Chor. Noise call you it or universal groan
As if the whole inhabitation perish'd,
Blood, death, and deathful deeds are in that noise,
Ruin, destruction at the utmost point.

    Man. Of ruin indeed methought I heard the noise,
Oh it continues, they have slain my Son.

    Chor. Thy Son is rather slaying them, that outcry
From slaughter of one foe could not ascend.

    Man. Some dismal accident it needs must be ;
What shall we do, stay here or run and see ?   1520

    Chor. Best keep together here, lest running thither
We unawares run into dangers mouth.
This evil on the *Philistines* is fall'n,
From whom could else a general cry be heard ?
The sufferers then will scarce molest us here,
From other hands we need not much to fear.
What if his eye-sight (for to *Israels* God
Nothing is hard) by miracle restor'd,
He now be dealing dole among his foes,
And over heaps of slaughter'd walk his way ?   1530

    Man. That were a joy presumptuous to be thought.

    Chor. Yet God hath wrought things as incredible
For his people of old ; what hinders now ?

    Man. He can I know, but doubt to think he will ;
Yet Hope would fain subscribe, and tempts Belief.
A little stay will bring some notice hither.

    Chor. Of good or bad so great, of bad the sooner ;
For evil news rides post, while good news baits.
And to our wish I see one hither speeding,
An *Ebrew*, as I guess, and of our Tribe.   1540

    Mess. O whither shall I run, or which way flie
The sight of this so horrid spectacle

Which earst my eyes beheld and yet behold ;
For dire imagination still persues me.
But providence or instinct of nature seems,
Or reason though disturb'd, and scarse consulted
To have guided me aright, I know not how,
To thee first reverend *Manoa*, and to these
My Countreymen, whom here I knew remaining,
As at some distance from the place of horrour,   1550
So in the sad event too much concern'd.

    Man. The accident was loud, & here before thee
With rueful cry, yet what it was we hear not,
No Preface needs, thou seest we long to know.

    Mess. It would burst forth, but I recover breath
And sense distract, to know well what I utter.

    Man. Tell us the sum, the circumstance defer.

    Mess. *Gaza* yet stands, but all her Sons are fall'n,
All in a moment overwhelm'd and fall'n.

    Man. Sad, but thou knowst to *Israelites* not saddest 1560
The desolation of a Hostile City.

    Mess. Feed on that first, there may in grief be surfet.

    Man. Relate by whom. *Mess.* By *Samson.*

       Man. That still lessens
The sorrow, and converts it nigh to joy.

    Mess. Ah *Manoa* I refrain, too suddenly
To utter what will come at last too soon ;
Lest evil tidings with too rude irruption
Hitting thy aged ear should pierce too deep.

    Man. Suspense in news is torture, speak them out.

    Mess. Then take the worst in brief, *Samson* is dead. 1570

    Man. The worst indeed, O all my hope's defeated
To free him hence ! but death who sets all free
Hath paid his ransom now and full discharge.
What windy joy this day had I conceiv'd
Hopeful of his Delivery, which now proves
Abortive as the first-born bloom of spring
Nipt with the lagging rear of winters frost.
Yet e're I give the rains to grief, say first,
How dy'd he ? death to life is crown or shame.
All by him fell thou say'st, by whom fell he,   1580
What glorious hand gave *Samson* his deaths wound ?

    Mess. Unwounded of his enemies he fell.

    Man. Wearied with slaughter then or how ? explain.

Samson Agonistes.

Mess. By his own hands. *Man.* Self-violence? what cause
Brought him so soon at variance with himself
Among his foes? *Mess.* Inevitable cause
At once both to destroy and be destroy'd;
The Edifice where all were met to see him
Upon thir heads and on his own he pull'd.
  Man. O lastly over-strong against thy self!   1590
A dreadful way thou took'st to thy revenge.
More than anough we know; but while things yet
Are in confusion, give us if thou canst,
Eye-witness of what first or last was done,
Relation more particular and distinct.
  Mess. Occasions drew me early to this City,
And as the gates I enter'd with Sun-rise,
The morning Trumpets Festival proclaim'd
Through each high street: little I had dispatch't
When all abroad was rumour'd that this day   1600
Samson should be brought forth to shew the people
Proof of his mighty strength in feats and games;
I sorrow'd at his captive state, but minded
Not to be absent at that spectacle.
The building was a spacious Theatre
Half round on two main Pillars vaulted high,
With seats where all the Lords and each degree
Of sort, might sit in order to behold,
The other side was op'n, where the throng
On banks and scaffolds under Skie might stand;   1610
I among these aloof obscurely stood.
The Feast and noon grew high, and Sacrifice
Had fill'd thir hearts with mirth, high chear, & wine,
When to thir sports they turn'd. Immediately
Was *Samson* as a public servant brought,
In thir state Livery clad; before him Pipes
And Timbrels, on each side went armed guards,
Both horse and foot before him and behind
Archers, and Slingers, Cataphracts and Spears.
At sight of him the people with a shout   1620
Rifted the Air clamouring thir god with praise,
Who had made thir dreadful enemy thir thrall.
He patient but undaunted where they led him,
Came to the place, and what was set before him
Which without help of eye, might be assay'd,

(547)

To heave, pull, draw, or break, he still perform'd
All with incredible, stupendious force,
None daring to appear Antagonist.
At length for intermission sake they led him
Between the pillars; he his guide requested   1630
(For so from such as nearer stood we heard)
As over-tir'd to let him lean a while
With both his arms on those two massie Pillars
That to the arched roof gave main support.
He unsuspitious led him; which when *Samson*
Felt in his arms, with head a while enclin'd,
And eyes fast fixt he stood, as one who pray'd,
Or some great matter in his mind revolv'd.
At last with head erect thus cryed aloud,
Hitherto, Lords, what your commands impos'd   1640
I have perform'd, as reason was, obeying,
Not without wonder or delight beheld.
Now of my own accord such other tryal
I mean to shew you of my strength, yet greater;
As with amaze shall strike all who behold.
This utter'd, straining all his nerves he bow'd,
As with the force of winds and waters pent,
When Mountains tremble, those two massie Pillars
With horrible convulsion to and fro,
He tugg'd, he shook, till down they came and drew 1650
The whole roof after them, with burst of thunder
Upon the heads of all who sate beneath,
Lords, Ladies, Captains, Councellors, or Priests,
Thir choice nobility and flower, not only
Of this but each *Philistian* City round
Met from all parts to solemnize this Feast.
Samson with these immixt, inevitably
Pulld down the same destruction on himself;
The vulgar only scap'd who stood without.
    Chor. O dearly-bought revenge, yet glorious!   1660
Living or dying thou hast fulfill'd
The work for which thou wast foretold
To *Israel,* and now ly'st victorious
Among thy slain self-kill'd
Not willingly, but tangl'd in the fold
Of dire necessity, whose law in death conjoin'd
Thee with thy slaughter'd foes in number more

Then all thy life had slain before.
    Semichor. While thir hearts were jocund and sublime,
Drunk with Idolatry, drunk with Wine,   1670
And fat regorg'd of Bulls and Goats,
Chaunting thir Idol, and preferring
Before our living Dread who dwells
In *Silo* his bright Sanctuary:
Among them he a spirit of phrenzie sent,
Who hurt thir minds,
And urg'd them on with mad desire
To call in hast for thir destroyer;
They only set on sport and play
Unweetingly importun'd   1680
Thir own destruction to come speedy upon them.
So fond are mortal men
Fall'n into wrath divine,
As thir own ruin on themselves to invite,
Insensate left, or to sense reprobate,
And with blindness internal struck.
    Semichor. But he though blind of sight,
Despis'd and thought extinguish't quite,
With inward eyes illuminated
His fierie vertue rouz'd   1690
From under ashes into sudden flame,
And as an ev'ning Dragon came,
Assailant on the perched roosts,
And nests in order rang'd
Of tame villatic Fowl; but as an Eagle
His cloudless thunder bolted on thir heads.
So vertue giv'n for lost,
Deprest, and overthrown, as seem'd,
Like that self-begott'n bird
In the *Arabian* woods embost,   1700
That no second knows nor third,
And lay e're while a Holocaust,
From out her ashie womb now teem'd
Revives, reflourishes, then vigorous most
When most unactive deem'd,
And though her body die, her fame survives,
A secular bird ages of lives.
    Man. Come, come, no time for lamentation now,
Nor much more cause, *Samson* hath quit himself

Like *Samson*, and heroicly hath finish'd   1710
A life Heroic, on his Enemies
Fully reveng'd, hath left them years of mourning,
And lamentation to the Sons of *Caphtor*
Through all *Philistian* bounds. To *Israel*
Honour hath left, and freedom, let but them
Find courage to lay hold on this occasion,
To himself and Fathers house eternal fame;
And which is best and happiest yet, all this
With God not parted from him, as was feard,
But favouring and assisting to the end.   1720
Nothing is here for tears, nothing to wail
Or knock the breast, no weakness, no contempt,
Dispraise, or blame, nothing but well and fair,
And what may quiet us in a death so noble.
Let us go find the body where it lies
Sok't in his enemies blood, and from the stream
With lavers pure and cleansing herbs wash off
The clotted gore. I with what speed the while
(*Gaza* is not in plight to say us nay)
Will send for all my kindred, all my friends   1730
To fetch him hence and solemnly attend
With silent obsequie and funeral train
Home to his Fathers house: there will I build him
A Monument, and plant it round with shade
Of Laurel ever green, and branching Palm,
With all his Trophies hung, and Acts enroll'd
In copious Legend, or sweet Lyric Song.
Thither shall all the valiant youth resort,
And from his memory inflame thir breasts
To matchless valour, and adventures high: 1740
The Virgins also shall on feastful days
Visit his Tomb with flowers, only bewailing
His lot unfortunate in nuptial choice,
From whence captivity and loss of eyes.
    Chor.   All is best, though we oft doubt,
What th' unsearchable dispose
Of highest wisdom brings about,
And ever best found in the close.
Oft he seems to hide his face,
But unexpectedly returns   1750
And to his faithful Champion hath in place

Samson Agonistes.

Bore witness gloriously; whence *Gaza* mourns
And all that band them to resist
His uncontroulable intent,
His servants he with new acquist
Of true experience from this great event
With peace and consolation hath dismist,
And calm of mind all passion spent.

The End.

APPENDIX I.

(a)

Specimen of Milton's spelling, from the Cambridge autograph manuscript.

On Time

set on a clock case

Fly envious Time till thou run out thy race
call on the lazie leaden-stepping howres
whose speed is but the heavie plummets pace
& glut thy selfe wth what thy womb devoures
wch is no more then what is false & vaine
& meerly mortall drosse
so little is our losse
so little is thy gaine
for when as each thing bad thou hast entomb'd
& last of all thy greedie selfe consum'd
then long Æternity shall greet our blisse
wth an individuall kisse
and Joy shall overtake us as a flood
when every thing y^t is sincerely good
& pfectly divine
with Truth, & Peace, & Love shall ever shine
about the supreme throne
of him t' whose happy-making sight alone
when once our heav'nly-guided soule shall clime
then all this earthie grossnesse quit
attir'd wth starres wee shall for ever sit
Triumphing over Death, & Chance, & thee O Time.

Appendix I.

(*b*)

Note of a few readings in the same manuscript.

AT A SOLEMN MUSICK.

line 6. *content*. Manuscript reads *concent* as does the Second Edition ; so that *content* is probably a misprint.

ARCADES.

line 22. *hunderd*. Milton's own spelling here is *hundred*. But in the *Errata* to *Paradise Lost* (i. 760) he corrects *hundred* to *hunderd*.

LYCIDAS.

line 64. *uncessant*. Manuscript reads *incessant,* so that *uncessant* is probably a misprint; though that spelling is retained in the Second Edition.

line 82. *perfet*. So in *A Maske*, line 203. In both these places the manuscript has *perfect*, as elsewhere where the word occurs. In the *Solemn Music*, line 23, where the First Edition reads *perfect*, the second reads *perfet*.

A MASK.

lines 168, 169. Manuscript reads—
>*but heere she comes I fairly step aside*
>*& hearken, if I may, her buisnesse heere.*

line 474. *sensualty*. Manuscript also reads *sensualtie,* as the metre requires.

line 493. *father*. Manuscript reads *father's*.

line 553. *drowsie frighted*. Manuscript reads *drowsie flighted*.

line 743. In the manuscript, which reads—
>*If you let slip time like an neglected rose*

a circle has been drawn round the *an,* but probably not by Milton.

(*c*)

Paradise Lost, vii. 451. Bentley's emendation of *soul* for *fowl* should have been noted at the foot of the page. See Genesis i. 30 A. V. margin.

APPENDIX II

Translations of the Italian, Latin, and Greek Poems

From the
Columbia University
Press Edition of
Milton's Works

CONTENTS

		PAGE
Translations from Italian Sonnets	. . . . . .	557
Testimonia		559
Elegy the First, to Charles Diodati		562
Elegy the Second, On the Death of the Beadle of the University of Cambridge	. . . .	564
Elegy the Third, On the Death of the Bishop of Winchester	.	565
Elegy the Fourth, To Thomas Young, his Teacher . .	.	567
Elegy the Fifth, On the Coming of Spring	.	569
Elegy the Sixth, to Charles Diodati, the While He Tarried in the Country	. . . .	573
Elegy the Seventh		575
On the Gunpowder Plot		577
On the Same		577
On the Same		578
On the Same		578
On the Discoverer of Gunpowder		578
To Leonora, as She Sings at Rome		578
To the Same		579
To the Same		579
A Fable about a Countryman and His Master . . .		579
On Salmasius's Hundred		580
On Salmasius		580
A Book of Sylvae :		
I. On the Death of the Vice-Chancellor, a Physician .	.	580
II. On the Fifth of November	.	581
III. On the Death of the Bishop of Ely	.	586
IV. That Nature Submits Not to the Decay of Old Age	.	588
V. On the Platonic Idea, as Aristotle Understood It .	.	589
VI. To my Father	.	590
Psalm CXIV [Greek]	.	593
A king who condemned a philosopher to death [Greek]	.	593
On the Man who Engraved Milton's Likeness [Greek]	.	594
VII. Scazons to Salsilli, a Roman Poet, as He Lay Ill .	.	594
VIII. Manso	.	595
IX. Damon's Epitaph	.	597
X. To John Rouse, Librarian of the University of Oxford	.	603

Translations from Italian Sonnets.

By ARTHUR LIVINGSTON.

(See pp. 29-31.)

[The line numbers in square brackets refer to the originals.]

II

Beauteous lady, whose fair name honoureth the grassy vale and the noble gorge of the Reno, lightened of all burden of worth must be he who is not enamoured of thy gentle spirit :

Which sweetly revealeth itself in ever bounteous dispensations of its graciousness and of those charms—the shafts and the bow of Love—which engarland thine exalted virtue.

When, beautiful, thou speakest, or, in mood of happiness, singest in such guise that the hardest and wildest oak is moved to feeling, one must guard the gateways to ear and eye ;

For if a man be unworthy of thy favour, may the grace of Heaven alone avail him, before love of thee hath aged in his heart.

III

At eventide, on the rugged mountain slope, the practised shepherd girl carefully watereth the tender, beauteous flower exotical, so loath to grow in that high altitude far from the warm vale where it first sprouted.

So, Love, in my case, on my nimble tongue nurseth the first bud of a strange speech that I, deserting Thames for Arno, may sing of thee, winsomely haughty one, in words uncomprehended of my own good people.

Such the behest of Love—and from the fate of others I have learned that Love never yet hath bidden in vain :

Oh, would that my heart were less fertile, my breast more stony, toward one who findeth such fecund soil for the seed she soweth from Heaven !

Canzone

Swains and maidens—all liege to Love—crowd laughingly about me : ' Why, oh why, dost thou write of thy love in a strange and unknown tongue ? How darest thou ? Tell us ' (so they chaff me) ' as thou hopest some day to win thy love and to attain the greatest of thy desires. Other shores, other waters, the banks of another stream, await thee—a fertile soil whereon an immortal guerdon of never-withering green is even now sprouting for thy brow ! Why, then, a burden too heavy for thy shoulders ? '

To thee, my song, will I tell my secret—and do thou make answer for me : my lady saith—and her words are my law—that this is the language Love boasteth as his own !

(557)

Appendix II.

IV

Diodati—and I tell thee in amazement at myself—that same scornful I, who have always shown contempt for Love and have been wont to ridicule his wiles, have fallen into that trap which ensnareth on occasion the best of men.

Not golden tresses nor rosy cheeks have thus dazzled my eyes, but rather a fascinating Beauty exemplifying an Idea unknown, which filleth the heart with beatitude—a bearing fraught with virtue's dignity, the winning sparkle of clear black eyes, a speech adorned with divers languages, and a song such as to send the Moon astray as she followeth her laborious course in the high heavens; fain would I wax my ears against it, but the fire that darteth from her eyes maketh such remedy of little avail.

V

Assuredly, my lady, thy beautiful eyes can be nought else but a Sun to me. They beat upon me as he doth upon the wayfarer through the sands of Lybia:

And from that part of my body wherein dwelleth my woe there rusheth a hot vapor, the like whereof I have never known—in lovers' parlance 'twould perchance be called a sigh, though truly I know not what it be!

Part of it compressed and turbulent hideth in my heaving breast: then a little of it, escaping, doth cool and freeze, thereabout:

But such of it as findeth its way to mine eyes, doth make all my nights of rain until my Dawn returneth, her arms filled with roses.

VI

Ingenuous youth and guileless lover I, certain I cannot be of being ever other than I am. Devotedly, therefore, my Lady, I make thee humble gift of my heart.

That heart, as I can vow after tests innumerable, I have found faithful, fearless, steadfast—in all its thoughts, kindly, tactful, genial. In the face of the roar and thunder of the great world, it girdeth itself with the impenetrable adamant of self confidence as safe from the doubts and envies, the fears and hopes, of the vulgar, as it is enamoured of talent and noble worth, of poetry and the Muses.

One weakness in it wilt thou find; the spot wherein Love hath implanted his incurable dart!

Appendix II.

Translations of the Latin and Greek Poems.

By CHARLES KNAPP.

[TESTIMONIA.]

[Latin on p. 117.]

Here follow *testimonia* with respect to the author. He was perfectly well aware, himself, that they were uttered not so much *about* him as *over* him, because men of preeminent ability, who are one's friends as well, have a habit of phrasing their eulogies in such a way that they conjure up, eagerly, what, from beginning to end, befits their own merits rather than the truth. Yet the author was unwilling that the kindly feeling entertained for him by the writers of these *testimonia* should not be known, especially since others were very earnestly urging him to make them generally known. For, while he is seeking with might and main to fend off from himself the odium that excessive praise begets, and prefers that he should not be credited with more than is his due, he can not, in the meantime, deny that he sees a signal honour to himself in the favourable judgement of men of intellect reinforced by high distinction.

Giovanni Battista Manso, Marquis of Villa, of Naples, to John Milton, Englishman.

[Latin on p. 117.]

If your piety matched your intellect, your figure, your grace and charm, your bearing, your manners, you would be, not an *Angle*, but, in very deed and truth, an *Angel*.

An Epigram, by Giovanni Salsilli, a Roman, on John Milton, who deserves a coronal fashioned of the triple laurel of poesy—Greek, Latin, and Italian.

[Latin on p. 117.]

Yield, Meles, yield; let Mincius, too, lowering his urn, yield; let Sebetus cease to have Tasso forever on his tongue. But let the Thames, victor now, sweep on with billows o'ertopping those of every other stream, for, thanks to you, Milton, he will be, in his single self, full match for the other three.

(559)

Appendix II.

Selvaggi to John Milton.

[Latin on p. 118.]

Let Greece boast, if she will, of Mæonia's son, let Rome boast to herself of Maro! England boasts of Milton, in his one self full match for the other two combined.

ODE.

To John Milton Esquire Gentleman, of England.

[Italian on p. 118.]

Lift me to Heaven on high, O Clio, for of stars shall I make the crown! Not here the foliage, eternal on Pindus and on Helicon, of the fair-haired God! For greatest merit be greatest guerdon due, for godlike virtue, empyreal recompense!

Exalted worth eternal cannot fall prey to the tooth of Time! Rapacious Oblivion cannot rob Memory of supernal Glory! Virtue fit a worthy dart to the bow of my lyre, and Death will I strike to death!

Girt by the vast eddies of the deep Ocean, sits Anglia, severed from the world, because her qualities excel the qualities of all the rest: Potency of her fertile womb it is to bring forth heroes, whom rightfully we deem as more than men!

In their hearts Virtue, elsewhere banished, finds secure repose, of them alone beloved because in her alone can they find joy and pleasure. This shalt thou again make manifest, O Milton! To thee the proof of my song, through thy certain virtue!

Zeuxis an ardent diligence drove far from the shores of his native land; for he heard the golden horn of Fame shouting Helen's glory; and worthily to make her effigy he sought the Rarest among the fairest Ideas.

From rose, from lily, from all the comely flowers that adorn the lea, the artful bee laboriously doth suck his priceless sweet. So doth tuneful music flow from varied strings, concordant melody from voices multiple.

So, enamoured of beauteous Fame, thou didst turn thy wandering feet, O Milton, away from thy native skies, in quest of Sciences and Arts. The realms of the conquering Gaul thou didst behold, and of Italy the most worthy Heroes.

Artisan of Godlike craft, thy Thought, aspiring to virtue alone, surveyed in journeyings afar all such as tread the paths of true nobility. Of the best among the better thou didst make choice to fashion the Idea compendious of all the virtues.

(560)

Appendix II.

All those of Flora [Florence]—whether her own sons or masters through her of the Tuscan tongue—whose memory eternalized in learned pages doth honour to mankind, thou didst frequent for thine own treasuring, communing with them in their works.

Vainly for thee did Jove confuse the tongues in proudly exalted Babel, whereof she fell prostrate to the plain, vanquished of herself. For from thy lips not only England, but Spain, France, Tuscany, Greece, Rome, hear each her noblest speech.

The deepest secrets which Nature hides in Heaven or on Earth, too often covetously concealing them to superhuman Minds, thou hast fully mastered, to reach at last the great boundaries of moral [mortal ?] wisdom.

Let Time cease to beat his wings ! Let him arrest his flight ! At one should halt those years which pass—with fell discourtesy, alas—to the wrong of immortal virtue ! For if meritorious poem or history was e'er begot, thou hast it ever present in thy memory.

But if I must sing of thy sweet song, which exalts thee to the skies and vaunts thereby thy divination, thine own lyre must I have. Through thee, its swan, may Thames proclaim equality with Permessus !

Vainly I, on Arno, strive to expound thy great and effulgent merit ; for sooner than power to praise comes compulsion to admire. A bridle therefore for my tongue, that I may hearken to my heart, which, fraught with stupor, intones thy praise.

By Antonio Francini, Esquire, Gentleman of Florence.

TO JOHN MILTON

OF LONDON.

[Latin on p. 121.]

A young man distinguished by the land of his birth and by his personal merits,

To a man who, through his journeys to foreign lands, has viewed with care full many a place, by his studies has viewed every place the wide world o'er, to the end that, a modern Ulysses, he may apprehend from every people, everywhere, all that each has to offer ;
*   to a polyglot, master of many tongues, on whose lips languages already wholly dead live again with such vigour and might that every speech, when it is employed to praise him, loses its power of utterance —he is, himself, thorough master of them all, so that he understands the expressions of admiration and approval called forth from the peoples by his peculiar wisdom;*

(561)

Appendix II.

to a man whose endowments of mind and body move the senses to admiration, and yet through that very admiration rob every man of power to move, whose masterpieces urge all men to applause, yet by their grace, their charm rob of voice all them that would fain applaud;

to a man in whose memory the wide, wide world is lodged, in whose intellect wisdom, in whose affections an ardent passion for glory, in whose mouth eloquence, who, with astronomy as his guide, hears the harmonious strains of the heavenly spheres, with philosophy as his teacher reads and interprets the true meaning of those marvels of nature by which the greatness of God is portrayed, who, with never-ceasing reading of these authors as his comrade, probes the hidden mysteries of bygone days, restores what the lapse of the ages has laid low, and traverses the intricacies of learning—

but wherefore do I strive 'gainst the steeps?

to him, in the publishing of whose merits the tongues of Rumour herself would prove too few, whose merits are not eulogized as they deserve even by the spellbound admiration of the world, to him, by way of reverence and affection, this tribute of admiration, the just meed of his merits, is offered by

Charles Dati, a Patrician of Florence, offered to this great man by his humble servant, passionate lover of merit so outstanding.

First Book of
ELEGIES.

Elegy the First, to *Charles Diodati.*

[Latin on p. 122.]

At last, dear friend, your letter has come to my hand, and its sheets, serving as messenger, have brought your voice to my ears, aye, brought it from afar, from the western bank of the Dee, by Chester, where the Dee with down-darting waters makes for the Vergivian [Irish] main. Much believe me, much does it pleasure me that lands remote have nurtured a heart so full of love for me, a soul so loyal, and that a quarter of the world far off owes me a charming comrade, a quarter far off, yes, but minded at command to deliver him soon to me.

I am detained in the city that the Thames laves with its refluent waters; possessed am I, though not against my will, by the charming city of my birth. Not now am I concerned to revisit the reedy Cam, nor am I harrowed now by love of my Lares there, this long time denied me. I find no pleasure in fields that are naked and that refuse soft shade; how ill-adapted is such a place to the worshippers of

(562)

Appendix II.

] Phœbus! I am not minded to bear unceasingly the threats of an unbending teacher, and all the other trials that are not to be met by a nature such as mine. If it be exile for a man to visit his home, his father's house, and, free of all anxieties, to pursue the delights of leisure, then I refuse not the name of exile, nor if you will, the *lot* of] exile; nay, right merrily I enjoy the terms imposed by 'exile'. Would to heaven the bard had ne'er borne heavier lot, that famous bard who was exile in Tomis's borders: he had not then yielded aught to Ionia's son, Homer's self, and you, Maro, had been outdone, and the first meed of praise would not now be yours! [I enjoy my] 'exile'], for I am privileged now to give, here, hours free of all else to the calm Muses, and my books—my true life—sweep me off with them, mastering me utterly. Presently, when I am weary grown, the splendour of the rounded theatre welcomes me, and summons me to sound its plaudits, whether I am listening to some canny ancient, or •] to a spendthrift heir, or a suitor is on the boards, or a soldier, with his casque now laid aside, or if some lawyer, grown rich through a suit ten years prolonged, thunders out in an uncouth court out-landish words, or if some roguish slave comes to the aid of a love-struck son, and at every turn tricks the nose of the lad's unbending 5] father. Oft-times, there, a maiden, marvelling at new fires, knows not what love is, yet, while she knows not, loves. Mayhap Tragedy, distraught, shakes her blood-dyed staff, her locks the while flung loose, her eyes rolling wildly. It pains me, and yet I look, and find pleasure in looking though it pains me. Sometimes there is a sweet ə] bitterness in the tears I shed, if some hapless lad leaves joys un-tasted, and falls in death, fit subject thus for tears, through the rend-ing of his love, or if some merciless avenger of crime, issuing from the darkness, traverses again the Styx, and with his funeral brand affrights conscience-stricken souls, or if sorrow o'erwhelms the house 5] of Pelops, or the lordly house of Ilium, or if Creon's court makes atonement for incestuous forebears.

Yet I hide not always 'neath a roof or within the city, nor do the hours of spring slip by void of all profit for me. A grove, too, claims me, a grove thick grown with elms, near the city, and the glorious ɔ] shade of some spot not remote from the town. There o'er and o'er one may see troops of maidens pass, stars, these, that breathe forth alluring fires. Ah, how oft have I gazed, spellbound, on some marvellous form, form fit to have power to renew the ravages of age, 5] even in Jupiter's self! Ah, how oft have I seen eyes that outdid jewels and the fires that either pole keeps in revolution, and necks that surpassed [in whiteness] the [ivory] arms of Pelops, twice alive, and that streaming Way which is steeped in nectar undilute! How oft have I seen peerless beauty of brow, and dancing tresses, the ɔ] golden nets that Cupid, prince of tricksters, spreads, and seductive cheeks—matched with such cheeks the hyacinth's crimson beauty, even the blushing hues of your own flower, Adonis, seem dull and tarnished. Yield, ye heroic maidens, once lauded so oft, yield, too, every maid that e'er enthralled wide-wandering Jove! Yield, ye maids of Achæmenia, maids with foreheads turret-crowned! Yield, all ye maids that dwell in Susa, and in Memnon's Nineveh! Yield, ye, too, nymphs of Greece, lower your *fasces*, yield ye, maids of Ilium, and daughters of Romulus! Let not now the Tarpeian Muse boast of Pompey's Columns, or of the theatres crowded with Ausonian stoles! 'Tis to the maids of Britain that first glory [in beauty] is due! Count it enough, women of other lands, that you can follow them [in beauty]. You, London, city reared by Dardan settlers, made conspicuous far and wide by your towered head, blessed, all too blessed, you enclose within your walls whatever beauty the pendent earth possesses. The stars that flash for you in the unclouded skies—the host that serves Endymion's goddess—number not so many as the maids who, resplendent with beauty of person and with gold, flash radiant on all eyes throughout your streets. Men believe the tale that Venus, Giver of Life, made her way to this city, riding in a car drawn by twin doves, guarded by her quiver-bearing warriors, because she was minded to set below this city Cnidus, and the vales bedewed by Simoïs's stream, Paphos, too, and Cyprus, land of roses.

Yet, while the indulgent kindness of the blind lad permits, I am making ready to leave, with all suddenness, these walls, and, employing the aid of *moly*, plant divine, to evade in a place far distant the ill-famed halls of deceptive Circe. I am resolved, also, to make my way back to the reedy marshes of the Cam, and again to face the uproar of the noisy School.

Meanwhile, take this gift, humble, yes, but sent by a loyal friend, a word or two forced into elegiac measures.

Elegy the Second, Written in His Seventeenth Year.

On the Death of the Beadle of the University of Cambridge.

[Latin on p. 124.]

Once, made conspicuous by your shining mace, you were wont, o'er and o'er, to summon with your Beadle's voice the flock of Pallas: but now Death, the last of Beadles, Death that knows no mercy, is sweeping you, too, away, Beadle though you are, and is showing no favour, herself, to her own office. Granted that your temples were whiter than the plumes 'neath which, so story says, Jove hid, yet you were worthy to be made young again by Thessalian potions, worthy to have power to live on till you reached the years of Æson, worthy to be recalled from the waves of Styx itself by Coronis' son, through his skill as healer, at the oft-repeated prayer of the goddess. Whenever

Appendix II.

you were bidden to summon the gown-clad lines, and to go as swift messenger from *your* Apollo, you looked as the wing-footed god of Cyllene looked when he stood in the Trojan court, sent thither from his father's citadel high in the skies, or as Eurybates looked when, standing before the face of Achilles o'erwhelmed by rage, he brought to him the austere commands of Atreus's son, captain of the host. O Death, mighty Queen of Sepulchres, servant of Avernus, all too cruel to the Muses, too cruel to Pallas, why should you not rather sweep away some useless encumberer of the earth? Such an one should be the target of your shafts, whose like exists in throngs!

Mourn therefore this man, Academe; robed in dark-hued vestments mourn for him, and let his black bier be drenched with your tears. Let plaintive Elegy, herself, pour forth sorrow-stricken strains, and let the mournful chant ring and ring all through our Schools.

Elegy the Third, Written in His Seventeenth Year.

On the Death of the Bishop of Winchester.

[Latin on p. 125.]

Sorrow-stricken was I; I was sitting, voiceless, with no comrade by my side, and many griefs were lodged deep in my soul. Forthwith there rose before my mind a picture of the deadly carnage wrought on England's soil by Libitina, the while accursed Death, to be dreaded by all men for her sepulchral torch, strode within the towered palaces of the great, palaces agleam with marble, and knocked at walls heavy with jasper and with gold, and feared not with her scythe to lay level with the ground the hosts of mighty satraps.

Then I bethought me of a glorious Prince, and of his brother [in arms], a man deserving of all reverence, and of their bodies burned by funeral pyres built before their appointed times; I bethought me, too, of the heroes whom Belgia saw caught up swiftly to the high skies, Belgia, that through all her borders wept for captains lost. But I grieved for you before all others most worthy Bishop, once the crowning glory of the Winchester you loved; I was melted by my tears, and with sorrowing lips voiced thus my plaints:

'Death, merciless Death, goddess second in power only to Tartarean Jove himself, is it not enough that the woods feel to their sorrow your wild rages, and that authority is granted to you over the fields and their green garb, and that the lilies wither and die when they feel the corruption of your breath, and the crocus likewise, and the rose sacred to the lovely goddess of Cyprus, and that you suffer not the oak to be forever near neighbour of the stream, forever marvelling at the smoothly-gliding progress of the passing water? Before you the birds bow, the birds that, in such hosts, ride on their pinions in the liquid sky, aye they bow before you, augurs though they are. Before you bow, too, the thousand creatures that wander where they will in the black forests, and the voiceless flocks that the grottoes of Proteus nurture. Seeing that power so mighty has been granted to you, why, envious Death, why does it pleasure you to dye your hands with the blood of mortals slain, to sharpen your unerring missiles against a noble breast, and to drive from its duly appointed seat the soul that is fully half a god?'

While I, bathed in tears, was turning over such thoughts within the deeps of my soul, Hesperus, dew-besprent, issued from the Western waters, and Phœbus had plunged his car 'neath Tartessus's levels, having measured to the full his journey from the strand that lies beneath the Dawn. Without delay, on my hollow couch I stretched out my limbs, that they might be refreshed; mine eyes had been buried in sleep profound, when I fancied that I was strolling in a spacious field. Ah me! My powers of mind are unequal to telling the tale of the things I saw.

There everything was radiant with crimson light, as when the mountain ranges blush with the early morning sun, and the earth shone there resplendent with raiment of a thousand hues, as when Thaumas's daughter spreads out her riches. Not so varied were the flowers wherewith a goddess, Chloris, beloved of gentle Zephyrus, decked the Gardens of Alcinoüs. Silver-hued were the streams that lapped the verdant plains; yellow was the sand, richer than the sands of the Tagus, in the Hesperian land. Through the rich, fragrance-bearing leafage glided the light gales of Favonius, the dewy gales born 'neath roses uncountable. Such a place is, in men's fancy, the palace of the regal dawn star, in far-off borders, in the land of the Ganges.

While I was marvelling at the close-set shadows cast by the cluster-bearing vines, and at the radiant spaces all about me, lo, of a sudden near me stood the Bishop of Winchester. A radiance as of the stars gleamed in his shining face. White was the robe that streamed down to his golden ankles, white the fillet that had wreathed his sainted head. While the aged [Bishop] moved onward, a reverend figure, so gloriously robed, the flower-strewn earth was all aquiver with joyous sounds; heaven's hosts beat out strains with their jewelled wings, and the air, pure and undefiled, rang with notes of an exultant trump. Each [member of the heavenly choirs] greeted with embraces and with songs his new comrade, and one sent forth from calm and peaceful lips these sounds:

'Draw near, my son; in gladness garner the joys of your Father's kingdom; henceforth always, my son, be free from rugged toil.' This said, the winged squadrons touched their harps. But for me with the passing of the darkness golden rest was routed: I was weeping at the clouding of my slumbers by the mistress of Cephalus.

May such dreams ever my good fortune be.

Appendix II.

Elegy the Fourth, Written in His Eighteenth Year.

To Thomas Young, His Teacher, Serving Now as Chaplain Among the English Merchants Resident in Hamburg.

[Latin on p. 127.]

Speed with all haste, letter of mine, across the illimitable main. Go! o'er its smooth levels make for Germany's borders. Rend asunder all sluggard delays! Let nothing, I pray, block your way as you go. Make haste, let naught delay your progress. I myself will weary Æolus, who bridles the winds in his Sicanian prison, and the green gods, and Doris, too, azure-hued, attended by her nymphs, praying them to grant you a quiet pathway through their realms.

If you can, take to yourself those swift yoke-creatures that drew the car in which Medea fled from the face of her consort, or those by whose aid to Scythia's borders Triptolemus made his way, the charming lad sent from the city of Eleusis.

When you shall see the sands of Germany gleam yellow, deflect your steps to the walls of rich Hamburg, the city that, so story tells us, derives its name from Hama, who, men say, was done to death by a Cimbrian club. There dwells a priest renowned, honoured from days of old for piety, well trained to feed the sheep that follow Christ. He, verily, is more than the half of my life; I live, perforce, with but half a life. Ah me! How many widespread seas, how many mountains interposed coerce me to forego the very half of my self! Dearer to me is he than were you, most learned of the Greeks, to Clinias's son, who was of Telamon's line, and dearer than the mighty Stagirite to his high-born pupil, whom the gracious maid of Chaonia bore as son to Lybian Jove. What Amyntor's son, what Philyra's hero-son were to the king of the Myrmidons, that was this priest to me. He led the way for me, when first I traversed Aonia's retreats and the holy greensward of the twice-cleft ridge, [he led the way for me] when I drank Pieria's waters, and, favoured by Clio, I thrice sprinkled my happy lips with Castalia's wine. But flaming Æthon thrice saw the Sign of the Ram, and thrice clothed with new gold the fleecy back of the Ram, and twice you, Chloris, sprinkled the age-worn earth with new verdure, and twice Auster stole away your riches: yet it was not my privilege to feast mine eyes on his face, or to drink in with mine ears the sweet strains of his voice.

Go, therefore, and with your speed outstrip the thundering Eurus. How much need there is of my admonitions the situation itself teaches, as you see. You will find him sitting, mayhap, with his charming wife, as he fondles in his arms the dear pledges of their love, or as, perchance, he turns this way and that the massive scrolls of the Fathers of old, or the Holy Books of the one true God, or as he feeds with the dew of heaven souls yet weak, yet delicate—wondrous work of religion, bringer of health and salvation. As is men's wont, be concerned to convey to him hearty greetings, such as it were meet and right for your master to convey, if only he were there himself. Fixing modest eyes for a moment on the ground, speak, without fail, to him, with reverent lips, this message too:

'These words—if there is leisure, amid battles, for the Muses—these words a loyal hand sends to you from England's shore. Accept a greeting heartfelt, however late it be; let it, by its very lateness, be to you all the more welcome. Late, yes, but genuine was the greeting that chaste Penelope, daughter of Icarius, received from her laggard lord. But oh, why was *I* minded to seek to purge away guilt, guilt clear to all men's eyes, which he himself is utterly unable to extenuate? He is convicted laggard, rightly convicted, too, and he himself admits his guilt, and is full of shame that he was traitor to his friendly office, his duty. Do you only grant forgiveness to him, now that he has confessed, and is begging for forgiveness: sins ever are made less when they lie open wide to view. A wild beast draws not wide asunder his gaping jaws against panic-stricken victims, nor does a lion drag with wound-dealing claws those who lie prone. The cruel hearts of the lance-bearing Thracians have many a time melted at the sorrow-burdened prayer of suppliants: outstretched hands divert the lightning's strokes, and angry gods are soothed by a tiny victim offered in sacrifice.

'For a long, long time his impulse has been to salute you, and Love has suffered him not to prolong delays, for wide-ranging Rumour tells a story—ah, Rumour, messenger all too truthful of evils!—a story that in places which are your neighbours wars are swelling, that you and your city are girt with grim soldiery, and that the Saxon captains have now made ready their arms. Round about you Enyo is ravaging far and wide the plains, and already blood is watering the tilth-lands sown with the flesh of men. Thrace has surrendered her beloved Mars to the Germans; thither Mars has driven his Odrysian steeds. The olive, [heretofore] ever full-tressed, is losing now its bloom; fled, too, is the goddess that loathed the battle trump with its brazen clangor, gone is she, lo! from the earth—not *now* the last to leave, the righteous maiden [Astraea]: she has flown, men believe, to the dwellings high in the skies. Round you, nevertheless, resounds meanwhile the horrid din of war: you live alone, poor, in an unfamiliar land, and in your need are seeking in a foreign home the sustenance which the Penates of your fathers gave you not. Land of our fathers, hard, unyielding mother, more savage than the white rocks that are lashed by the foaming billows of your sea-strand, is it seemly for you *thus*, *thus* to expose your children who have done no harm, is it *thus* that, with heart of iron, you force them into a foreign land, and suffer those whom God himself, taking thought for you, sent, who bring you glad tidings from the skies, who teach you what way, when men are dust, leads them to the stars, do you suffer them,

I ask, to seek their sustenance in lands far off, remote? Worthy indeed, then, are you to live pent in by Stygian darkness, worthy to perish by the never-ending hunger of the soul. Even so the prophet of the Tishbite land once on a time trod with unaccustomed feet wild wastes, where there were no paths, trod, too, rough stretches of Araby's deserts, the while he fled from the hands of King Ahab, and from your hands, too, accursed woman of Sidon. In such wise, too, fared Paul of Cilicia, when, his limbs mangled by the whistling scourge, he was driven from Emathia's city, and Jesus himself was bidden by the ungrateful citizenry of Gergessa, land of fishermen, to make off from their borders.

'But take you heart and courage : let not your hopes perish, crushed by anxieties, and let not fear, robbing you of your colour, shatter your frame. For, though you are overwhelmed by flashing arms, and though a thousand missiles threaten you with a violent death, yet no weapon will outrage *your* side, undefended by armour though it be, and no spear point will drink of your blood. For you yourself will be kept safe under the flashing ægis of God ; He will keep watch and ward over you, He will be your champion, He, who, under the walls of Zion's fortress, in a single, stilly night laid low so many Assyrians, and turned to flight the men that olden Damascus had sent from her ancient tilth-lands against Samaria's borders, who filled with fright the close-crowding battalions, and their cowering king as well, while through the empty air rang the clanging trump, while horny hoofs lashed the plain to dust, while the chariots driven at full speed shook the sandy ground, and there were heard the neighing of steeds as they dashed to war and the clank of iron and the deep-throated war-cries of men. Remember to hope—so much at least is left for the unfortunate—and by the high spirit of your heart master your ills ; doubt not that soon or late you will enjoy brighter years, and that you will have it in your power once again to see the Lares of your fathers.'

Elegy the Fifth, Written in His Twentieth Year.

On the Coming of Spring.

[Latin on p. 130.]

Time, that rolls back upon itself in never-ending circuit, is already, since the spring is gaining in warmth, calling back the new Zephyrs, Earth, made anew, is clothing herself with a short-lived youth, and, at last, the ground, set free from the frost and the ice, is growing charmingly green. Am I beguiling myself? or is strength coming back into my songs also, and have I, thanks to the bounty of spring, inspiration at my call? *Is* inspiration here, by the gift of spring, and is it again winning vigour from the spring—who would think it?—, and demanding now for itself some achievement, some creation? Castalia's waters dance before mine eyes, and the twice-cleft peak, and at night dreams bring to me Pirene. My soul is deeply stirred, is all aglow with mysterious impulses, the madness of inspiration and holy sounds stir me to my deeps within. The god of Delos himself is coming— I see his locks twined with Peneüs's laurel—, yes, the god of Delos is coming himself. Now my mind is whirled up to the heavenly steeps, and, freed from my body, I move 'mid the roving clouds; through the shades I go, moving through grottoes, the penetralia of the bards: the fanes of the gods are open wide for me, wide to their innermost depths; my soul gazes intently on whatever is done in all Olympus's length and breadth, nor do the blind deeps of Tartarus escape mine eyes.

What lofty strains is my soul sounding forth through my parted lips? What is being born of this madness, this holy frenzy? The spring, the spring that gave me inspiration shall be the theme of that inspiration's songs; thus the gifts of spring will be repaid to her and will bring her profit.

At last, Philomela, enveloped in new-born leaves, you are beginning your tuneful strains, while the wood everywhere is soundless: let us twain begin together, in the city I, you in the woodland; let us two, each in his own part, chant the coming of the spring. The spring-time—sing ho!—is come again in its due turn: let us honour the spring-time, and sound forth her praises; let this be the task essayed by the never-dying Muse! Already the Sun, as he flees from the Æthiopians and from Tithonus's tilth-lands, turns toward the northern regions his golden reins. Short, now, is the journey of the night, short is the tarrying of the dark night; shuddering night and her darkness are going forth to exile. Lycaonian Boötes now no longer, as in other days, follows the Wain through the skies, in a long journey, till he tires; widely sundered now, too, are the stars that throughout the skies are wont to keep their vigil about the halls of Jove. For, with the passing of the night, Guile, and Carnage, and Violence have withdrawn, and the gods have ceased to fear the crimes of the Giants. Mayhap some shepherd, as he lies back on the peak of a crag, when with the first ray of the sun the ground, dew-besprent, grows ruddy, cries, 'This night, this night at least you lacked, Phœbus, a maid of your own choice to hold back your swift steeds.' With rejoicing Cynthia seeks again her beloved forests, and takes up once more her quiver, when, [still] high [in the skies], she sees the wheels that bring the light of day, and, putting off her rays, now dimmed, she is, as all may see, glad that her own task is being made so short by her brother's aid. 'Quit,' cries Phœbus, 'quit, Aurora, the aged couch of Tithonus: wherein does it pleasure you to lie on that outworn couch? For you a hunter is waiting, Æolus's son, on the green sward; rise! Your flame, your loved one Hymettus possesses.' The golden-tressed goddess in her blushing face admits her guilt, and with greater speed presses forward the steeds of early morning.

Appendix II.

Earth, made full of life again, puts off loathèd age, and longs, Phœbus, to enter your enfolding arms. Aye, she longs [to enter them], and deserves [such bliss], too for what is more gloriously lovely than Earth, when, in full luxuriance, she opens wide her bosom, mother of all things, and breathes forth the harvests of Araby, and from her lovely lips pours forth the balmy balsam and the roses of Paphos? Lo, her towering brow is garlanded with a holy grove, even as a turret of pines girdles Ops [Cybele], goddess of Ida ; her tresses, dew-besprent, she intertwines with flowers of divers hues, knowing that by her own flowers *she* could please, even as the Sicanian goddess, when her streaming tresses had been bound with flowers, pleased the god of Tænarum. Look, Apollo, look ! Loves, complaisant, are making appeal, and spring-time gales are setting in train honeyed entreaties ; fragrant Zephyrus beats lightly with his cinnamon-scented wings, and the birds are seen to bring blandishments to you. Not rash is Earth : not without a dowry does she seek your love, nor poverty-burdened does she demand the couch she craves ; no, as giver of life, she proffers you health-giving herbs for healing uses, and thereby, herself, adds to your distinctions, your fair titles. But if rich offerings, if gleaming gifts touch your heart (by gifts o'er and o'er love has been bought in rich measure), she parades before your eyes whatsoever treasures she hides away 'neath the illimitable deeps, and under the superimposed mountains. Ah, how often, when utterly wearied by the steep way up Olympus, you are flinging yourself headlong into the evening waters, how often [then] Earth cries, 'Why, when you are utterly exhausted by your day-long course, why is it the sea-hued mother that welcomes you with the Western waters? What have *you* to do with Tethys ? What with the waters of Tartessus? Why do *you* lave your holy face with impure brine ? Coolness, Phœbus, you will court more pleasantly in the shade that *I* shall offer: come hither, hither to me ; steep your blazing locks in the dew. Softer will be the sleep that will come to you on the cool grass : come hither, come to me, and lay your bright rays [i.e. your radiant head] on my bosom. Where you lie, the gales, whispering softly round about us, will soothe our bodies as they recline at ease on the dewy roses. For me—believe my words—Semele's fate has no terrors, nor the car set smoking by Phaëthon's steeds. Using, Phœbus, your fires more wisely now [than you did in Phaëthon's day], come to me, and lay your bright rays on my bosom.'

Thus the wanton Earth breathes forth her passion, and all the array of creatures everywhere rushes to follow Mother Earth's example. Verily, in the spring-time days Cupid speeds where he lists through all the length and breadth of the world, and from the fires of the sun warms anew his failing torches. The death-dealing horns [of his bow] twang with new strings, his flashing shafts are balefully agleam with new steel. And now he is straining with all his might to conquer one [heretofore] unconquered, even Diana's self, aye, and the Vestal that in her purity sits by the holy hearth. Venus herself renews, year by year, her aging form, and again, so men believe, rises from the warm sea. Through marble cities young men cry, loudly, *Hymenæus* ! The sea-strand and the caverned crags sound forth *Io Hymen* ! Hymenæus comes, richly garbed, comeliness itself, in his tunic well fitted ; his fragrant vestments are redolent of the crimson crocus. In hosts the maids, their virgin bosoms wreathed with gold, go out to garner the joys of the lovely springtime. Each has her own peculiar vow, her own prayer, yet have they all the selfsame prayer ; every one asks that Cytherea shall give to her the mate she craves. Now too the shepherd attunes his strains on his pipe of seven reeds, and Phyllis has a song of her own to join to his. By night the sailor seeks with song to placate his stars, and calls the light dolphins to the surface of the waters. Jupiter himself frolics with his consort on towering Olympus, and to his merrymaking calls his attendant gods. Now the Satyrs, too, when the late twilight rises, fly in swift companies across the flowering countryside, and Sylvanus, crowned with his favourite leaves, leaves of cypress, Sylvanus, the god that is half goat, the goat that is half god. The Dryads that [before] hid 'neath the aged trees now rove over the mountain ridges, across the lonely fields. Through grain field and through coverts Pan runs riot : Cybele, Mother Cybele, and Ceres, too, scarce find safety for themselves. Faunus, all eagerness, would fain make some Oread his prey. But the nymph takes thought for herself by trusting to her trembling feet, and presently she hides, and yet, though sbe hides, covering herself none too well, she is eager to be seen : she flies, yet, as she flies, she would fain have herself be caught. The gods, too, hesitate not to set the woods before the skies : every grove has for itself its own peculiar deities.

And long, long may every grove have for itself its own peculiar deities : go not forth, ye gods, I pray, from your tree-clad homes ! May ages of gold bring you back again, Jupiter, to lands steeped in wretchedness. Why do you return to the clouds your merciless armory ? Do you, at least, Phœbus, drive slowly, as slowly as you may, your speeding yoke-steeds, and let the hours of spring pass but slowly, with progress scarce visible. Let it be late when rough, shaggy winter shall bring to us its nights protracted, and let the shadows assail, later than is their wont, our skies.

Appendix II.

Elegy the Sixth.

To Charles Diodati, the While He Tarried in the Country.

[Latin on p. 134.]

When Diodati had written, on the Ides of December, asking that, if his verses should be less good than usual, their shortcomings should be forgiven, because, so he affirmed, amid the splendid entertainments wherewith he had been greeted by his friends he had not been able to give to the Muses auspicious services, he had this answer.

With a stomach anything but full, I send you a prayer for sound health, of which, perhaps, you, with your stomach stretched to its uttermost, may be in sore need. But why does *your* Muse seek to lure forth *mine*? Why does your Muse not suffer mine to court the obscurity she craves? Should you wish to know through verses of mine how warmly I love you, how dearly I cherish you, *that*, believe me, you could scarce learn through this present song, for my love is not hemmed within close-gripping measures, nor does it come whole and sound to feet that are lame [the elegiac distich].

How well you report the solemn feasts, and the merry, merry December, and the festal celebrations which greeted the God that quitted the skies, the delights and the joys of the countryside in the winter days, and the Gallic must, drained beside the charming hearth! Why do you make lament that poetry is a runaway, banished by wine and splendid feasts? Song loves Bacchus, Bacchus loves songs. Apollo shrank not from wearing the green clusters of ivy berries, aye, shrank not from setting the ivy above his own laurel. Again and yet again on the Aonian Hills the ninefold throng, mingling with the Thyonean troop, has cried aloud, *Euoe!* The songs that Naso sent from the lands of the Coralli [near Tomis] were poor songs, no rich feasts were there, the vine had not been planted there. Of what save wines, and roses, and cluster-bearing Lyæus did the Teian Muse sing in her short measures? Teumesian Euan [Boeotian Bacchus] inspired Pindar's numbers; Pindar's every page is redolent of the wine-cups he had drained, while the heavy chariot, its axle crushed, crashes overturned, and the horseman flies by, swart with the dust of Elis. The lyrist of Rome was drenched with the four-year-old wine as he sang sweetly of Glycera and of Chloë, maid of the golden tresses. In your case, too, the rich table by its generous array nurtures the powers of your mind, and fosters your inspiration. Massic cups foam over with a rich flood of song, and from the very wine jar you pour forth the metres bottled therein. To these blessings we add artistry, and Phœbus diffused throughout the innermost deeps of your soul: you, Bacchus, Apollo, Ceres favour as they favour no one else. It is no wonder, then, that through you three gods, their powers divine co-ordinated, brought to birth songs so sweet. Now

Appendix II.

the Thracian lyre, too, with its fretted gold, sounds for you, touched softly by an artist hand. Amid the hanging tapestries is heard the lyre that with its skilful dancing measures guides the feet of the [maidens. Let sights so glorious detain *your* Muse at least, and let them call back whatever inspiration enervating indulgence in wine drives away. Believe me, while the ivory shall send forth its strains, and the holiday-making throng of dancers, keeping time to the *plec-trum*, shall fill the vaulted, perfumed chambers, you will know full well that Phœbus is making his way, voicelessly, through your heart, [e'en as some sudden glow of warmth makes its way through your very marrow; and through the maidens' eyes, and through their fingers as they sound forth their strains, Thalia will glide swiftly into your bosom, and master it utterly. For light-footed Elegy is the concern of many a god; she calls to her numbers whatsoever god she will. [Bacchus aids elegies: so, too, Erato aids them, and Ceres, and Venus, and dainty, dainty Cupid, by his rosy mother's side. For such poets generous feasts are matters of privilege, and it is theirs again and yet again to drench themselves with old, old wine. But if a poet sings of wars, of Heaven controlled by a Jove full grown, of [duty-doing heroes, of captains that are half gods, if he sings now the holy counsels of the gods above, now the realms deep below wherein howls a savage hound, let him live a simple, frugal life, after the fashion of the teacher who came from Samos, let herbs offer him food [that works no harm, let pellucid water stand near him, in a tiny cup of beechen wood, and let him drink only sober draughts from a pure spring. On such a poet are imposed, too, a youth free of crime, pure and chaste, and a character unyielding, and a name without taint; such an one must be as *you* are, augur, as, resplendent with holy vest- [ments and with lustral waters, you rise, minded to go forth to face the angry gods. In this way, story says, wise Tiresias lived, after the light had been swept away from him, and Ogygian Linus, and Calchas, exiled from his hearth, a hearth doomed to destruction, and aged Orpheus, in the lonely grots, after he had tamed the wild beasts. [So Homer, sparing of food, and a drinker of water, ferried the Duli-chian across the long straits, through the monster-making court of Persa's daughter, child of Phœbus, and the shallows made treacherous by women's songs, aye; through your house, too, king of the world below; when, so men say, with black blood he held fast the com- [panies of the shades. For the bard is sacred to the gods, he is priest of the gods; the secret deeps of his soul, and his very lips alike breathe forth Jove.

If you shall seek to learn what *I* am doing (if only you think it worth your while to seek to know what I am doing), I am hymning [the King of Heavenly Seed, Bringer of Peace, and the blessed genera-tions covenanted by the holy books, and the infant cry of God, and the stabling under a poor roof of Him who with his Father cherishes the realms on high, and of the star-begetting skies, of the companies attuning their strains in the high heavens, and of the [heathen] gods, [

of a sudden crushed, at their own fanes. This song I offered as gift on the birthday of Christ; the first light, as the dawn drew near, gave me this song.

For you other strains too are waiting, strains oft practised, strains struck out from my native country's reeds: you shall serve as the] critic to whom I shall recite them.

Elegy the Seventh, Written in His Nineteenth Year.

[Latin on p. 136.]

I did not yet know your ordinances, seductive Amathusia, and my breast was still empty of Paphian fire. O'er and o'er I spurned Cupid's shafts, as darts of a mere boy, I spurned your power divine,] O mighty Cupid. ' Go, boy,' said I, ' pierce doves, that know naught of fighting—only unmanly wars befit an unmanly captain—or else, tiny lad, lead a proud triumph over sparrows: such trophies are worthy of warfare such as yours. Why guide your idle missiles] 'gainst the sons of men? Not one jot of strength has *your* quiver against sturdy heroes.' The lad of Cyprus brooked not my words— no other god is more prompt to anger—, and so this savage [god] was hot now with double fires.

It was the spring-time, and the light, shining o'er the roof-trees of the houses, had brought to you, May-month, your first day. But] mine eyes were seeking still the vanishing night, and brooked not the early morning brightness. Lo, Love stood at my bed, tireless Love, with spangled wings. The rattling of his quiver betrayed the god as he stood beside me; his face, too, betrayed him, and his lovely eyes •] with their sweet threats, and whatever else was worthy of a lad, worthy e'en of Love. Such is the lad of Sigeum, as, on everlasting Olympus, he mixes the brimming goblets for amorous Jove, or the lad who lured the lovely nymphs to his kisses, Thiodamas's son, Hylas, stolen by a Naiad. He had added wrath—and yet this, too,] one would have thought, became him—and he had added wild threats, full of gall and bitterness. Thus then he spoke: 'Wretch, you had grown wise [in matters of love] more safely through [others'] example: now, you will testify yourself to the power of my right arm. You will be numbered among men who have tried and tested my strength; by] your sufferings I shall fashion credence for the truth. It was I my-self, yes I, that, if you know it not, tamed to the full Phœbus, even when he was exulting in the Python's overthrow, to me even that glorious [god] yielded; as oft as he recalls Peneüs's daughter, he confesses, himself, that *my* darts work surer and deadlier havoc.] Not more skilfully than I can the Parthian horseman draw home and bend his bow, the horseman whose wont it is to win his fight [by shooting his darts] behind his back. The Cydonian hunter, too,

(575)

yields to me ; so, too, did he who, all unwilling, was cause to his wife of a violent death. Mighty Orion, too, was o'ermastered by me, and Hercules's hands, and Hercules's comrade, too. Let Jupiter himself [try to whirl his thunderbolts 'gainst me : my darts will be lodged [first] in the side of Jove. Whatever else you doubt, my shafts will teach you better [than words], and your own heart, to be assailed by me with no light stroke. Fool, fool, neither will the Muses you love [have power to defend you, nor will Phœbus's snake proffer you aid.'

So he spake. Then, brandishing his arrow with the golden tip, he flew away, into the warm bosom of Cypris. But savagely, with threatening lips, he thundered against me, whose one thought was of laughter, and who had no fear of the lad. [.

Sometimes I found delight in the parts of the city where our citizens promenade, sometimes in the neighbouring country-side adjoining country houses. Crowds close compacted, crowds like in faces to goddesses, moved in brilliance to and fro through the midst of the streets and the roads. And so the day flashed bright, glorified [. by a double brightness. Am I beguiling myself? or has Phœbus rays won from this source too? Not grimly did I flee visions so charming ; no, I let myself be driven whithersoever youthful impulse bore me. Lacking all prescience, I sent my glances to meet their glances, nor could I withhold my eyes. One by chance I marked, [(towering [in beauty] over others : that radiance was the beginning of all my woe. So might Venus have wished herself to look to mortals, such the beauty in which the Queen of the Gods herself should have been seen. This lass Cupid, sly rogue, remembering, flung across [(my path : single-handed, he had, before, to my hurt woven these wiles. Hard by, too, the sly rogue was in hiding ; many a shaft, and a huge load of torches hung from his back. Without delay, he clung now to the maiden's eyelids, now to her face, then settled on her lips, [: then was seated on her cheeks : whatever part the agile archer traverses, thence—ah me !—in a thousand places he smites my defenceless breast. Straightway unwonted frenzies entered my heart : I burned within with love, aye, all my being was afire.

Meanwhile, the lass who, alone of lasses, pleased now my tortured [7 soul, was withdrawn from my gaze, ne'er again to return to mine eyes. But I went onward, voicelessly complaining, empty of wit, and, often, irresolute, I was minded to retrace my steps. I am cleft asunder : one half of me tarries behind, the other follows my heart's desire ; I find pleasure in weeping for the joys so suddenly wrested [8 from me. So Juno's son wept for his lost heaven, after he was flung downward, among the hearths of Lemnos. So Amphiaraüs, when he was carried to Orcus by his panic-stricken steeds, looked back at the sun that had been wrested [from his eyes]. What am I to do, a poor [8 unfortunate, by grief o'ermastered? I am not privileged either to lay aside the love I have welcomed, or to pursue it. O may it be vouchsafed to me to look once again on her beloved face, and in her presence to speak words, if only words of sadness ! Mayhap she was

] not fashioned of unyielding adamant, mayhap she would not be deaf to my prayers. Believe me, no other man has e'er burned thus haplessly : I shall be set down as a pattern [of love's woes], yes, I first and alone. Spare me, Cupid, I pray, since you are the winged god of soft love. Let not your deeds be at odds with your gracious office.
] Now, now at least, your bow is full of terrors for me, O child of a goddess, child not less potent by your fires than by your darts. Your altars shall smoke with my gifts, you shall be for me very god, god supreme among the powers above. Take away, at last, my frenzies
] —no, take them not away. I know not why, but the lover, every lover, is so sweetly wretched. Only be gracious, and grant that if, in days to come, any lass is destined to be mine, a single shaft-point shall pierce two hearts destined to love.

All this once on a time, with warped and twisted mind, and with all true zeal laid prostrate I wrote, setting up idle trophies of my worthlessness. So utterly, forsooth, mischievous error wrenched me astray, and drove me onward, and my untaught youth proved but
] misguided teacher, until the shades of Academe proffered to me the Socratic streams, and untaught me, [and loosed] the yoke I had let fall [upon my neck]. Straightway, from that moment, the fires were quenched, my heart has been unyielding, belted with deep ice. Hence the lad fears the cold for his beloved shafts, and Venus herself dreads
] might that matches the might of Diomedes.

On the Gunpowder Plot.

[Latin on p. 139.]

When, traitor Fawkes, you ventured, lately, your sin, godless, unutterable, at once against England's king and Britain's satraps, do I beguile myself ? or did you wish to be accounted in part mild and gentle, and to balance your crime by an evil piety ? No doubt you were minded to send them to the halls of high heaven, in a sulphurous chariot, with wheels of flying flame, even as he whose head the merciless Parcæ had no power to outrage left the Jordan's fields when he was swept away by the whirlwind.

On the Same.

[Latin on p. 139.]

Was it thus you essayed to present [King] James to the skies, you monster skulking on the seven mountains ? Unless your might divine shall have power to bestow better gifts, be more sparing, I pray you,
] traitorous monster, of your gifts. *He* indeed, without your aid, took his way, late, to the friendly stars, making no use of your hellish powder. So drive, rather, to the skies loathsome cowls, and as many

insensate gods as Rome profane possesses, for, unless you aid each of them by such craft, or by some other, he will hardly—believe me— climb easily up the road to the skies.

On the Same.

[Latin on p. 140.]

James [our King] derided the fires that purge the soul, without whose aid the house of them that dwell above is not to be approached! This made the Latin monster, with its triple crown, gnash its teeth, and caused its ten horns to shake with threats horrific. And it cried, 'Not unpunished shall you hold cheap my sacred rites, [son of Britain; you will pay the penalty for spurning religion, and, if ever you shall penetrate the star-bearing heights, it is only through flame that the road, a road burdened with sorrow, will lie open.' O how close to the deadly truth were the words of your prophecy, words that scarce were to lack their due and proper weight, for he [well nigh made his way, wheeled high by Tartarean fire, a shade utterly consumed by flames, to the lofty reaches of the skies.

On the Same.

[Latin on p. 140.]

Him whom but lately godless Rome had doomed by her dire curses, and had condemned to the Styx and the Tænarian gulf, him now Rome, changing utterly her role, is keen to raise aloft to the skies, and she is eager to exalt him, aye, even to the gods on high.

On the Discoverer of Gunpowder.

[Latin on p. 140.]

Japetus's son was praised by the blinded men of old, because he brought from the car of the sun the heavenly torch: but to me *he* will be a greater man who, as the world believes, filched from Jove his ghastly weapons, and his trident thunderbolt.

To Leonora, as She Sings at Rome.

[Latin on p. 140.]

An angel each man—such be your belief, ye peoples—has as his lot, a winged angel from the heavenly ranks. Wherein, then, is it strange, if you, Leonora, have [even] greater glory, since your voice itself sounds forth a god, a very present god? God, or, at least, the Third Intelligence of emptied heaven [i.e. the Third Intelligence, [

Appendix II.

quitting heaven], makes its way unseen through your throat, aye, makes its way, and graciously teaches mortal hearts the power to ⬤] grow accustomed insensibly to sounds immortal. But, if all things are God, and God is transfused through all, yet it is in you alone that He speaks: to all else that He possesses He vouchsafes no voice.

To the Same.

[Latin on p. 141.]

The other Leonora captured Torquato, the poet; for mad love of her he surrendered, of reason reft. Ah, poor unhappy man, how much more blessedly had he been destroyed in *your* times, Leonora,] and because of *you*, had he been aware that, as you sang with Pierian voice, you set in motion the golden strings of your mother's lyre! Though he had twisted his eyes more savagely than Dircæan Pentheus, or though he had, through all his being, lost wit and strength,] yet you, likewise, by your voice could have composed his senses, wandering, blindly reeling, and you, breathing peace through his lovesick heart, could by your soul-swaying strains, have restored him to himself.

To the Same.

[Latin on p. 141.]

Why, Naples, all too credulous, do you boast of the liquid-voiced Siren, and of the glorious fanes of Parthenope, daughter of Acheloüs? Why do you boast that you consigned to a Chalcidian [Neapolitan] funeral-pyre a Naiad of the sea-shore [Parthenope] that ended her] days on your strand? She *lives*, now: she has exchanged the roar of booming Posilipo for the lovely billows of the Tiber. There, graced by the favouring enthusiasm of the sons of Romulus, she holds fast, by her singing, mortal men, aye, and gods, alike.

A Fable about a Countryman and His Master.

[Latin on p. 142.]

A countryman gathered, yearly, from an apple tree the most savoury apples, and gave the apples, thus picked, to his master in the city. The latter, enthralled by the incredible sweetness of the fruit, transferred the tree itself to his own gardens. The tree, always] richly bearing up to that day, yet weakened by long years, straightway withered, now that it had been moved from its wonted soil, and gave up its life. When this was clear at last to the master, deceived by foolish hope, he cursed his hands so swift to work their own loss. Thus he spake: 'Alas, how much better had it been to accept with] grateful heart those gifts of my tenant, small though they were?

(579)

Appendix II.

I could have bridled my greed, and my all-consuming gullet: as it is, the fruit of the tree and the tree itself are both alike now lost to me.'

The End of the Elegies.

On Salmasius's Hundred.

[Latin on p. 142.]

Translated by SAMUEL LEE WOLFF

'WHO provided' Salmasius with his *Hundred*,
And taught the magpie to attempt our words?
His Master of Arts was his 'guts', and Jacobuses
One *Hundred*, the guts of the exiled king's money-bag.
'For if the hope of treacherous coin shall gleam',
The very man who but now threatened to puff away
With a single breath the Primacy of the Pope as Antichrist
Will of his own accord 'sing a tune' to praise a Cardinal.

On Salmasius.

[Latin on p. 142.]

Translated by GEORGE BURNETT

REJOICE ye herrings, and ye fish beside,
That, the winter chill, in cold friths abide ;
For the good Salmasius, that piteous knight,
Of paper liberal, saddens at your plight ;
Your nakedness to clothe, he'll frocks prepare,
The insignia, name, and honours that shall bear
Of Claude Saumaize ; that through the fishy mart,
You all may wear your paper liveries smart,
As clients of the knight ; a prize to those,
Who on their tunic's sleeve do wipe their nose.

A BOOK OF SYLVAE

[Poems in Various Metres.]

I.

On the Death of the Vice-Chancellor, a Physician.

Written in His Sixteenth Year.

[Latin on p. 143.]

Learn to obey the laws of Fate, and raise, at last, your hands in suppliance to the Parcæ, [all] ye that dwell on the pendent orb [of

Appendix II.

earth], ye children's children of Iapetus! If Death, that goes where
] she lists, if Death, leaving Tænarum, shall call you—once—with her
tearful voice, ah! in vain are delays essayed and guiles and wiles: it
is irrevocably ordained *then* that you must go across the darkness of
the Styx. If right arm had power to drive away death, once ap-
] pointed, then Hercules, [else] untameable, had not, poisoned by the
blood of Nessus, fallen in death on Emathian Oeta, nor would Ilium
have seen Hector slain through the shameful guile of spiteful Pallas,
] or him [Sarpedon] whom the phantom of Peleus's son [Patroclus]
slew with his Locrian blade, the while Jove himself shed tears. If
Hecate's magic words had power to put doleful Fate to flight, the
mother of Telegonus would have lived on, in infamy; so too [Medea],
] the sister of Aigialius [Absyrtus], would have lived on by the use of
her all-powerful wand. And if the arts of the healers and herbs
unknown had power to beguile the three goddesses, Machaon, well
versed in herbs, would not have fallen by the spear of Eurypylus, nor
] would you, son of Philyra, have been wounded by the arrow that was
smeared with the Hydra's blood, nor would your grandsire's missiles
and his lightning bolt have slain you [Æsculapius], lad cut from your
mother's womb.

You, too, Vice-Chancellor, yes, you, greater than your fosterling
] Apollo, to whom was assigned control over the gown-clad troup, for
whom at this present leaf-embowered Cirrha is mourning, and Helicon, too, in the midst of his waters, you would be yet alive, happy,
presiding, not without joy, over Pallas's flock, and you would not, in
] Charon's skiff, have visited the grim deeps of the [Tartarean] pit.
But Persephone snapped your thread, angered because she saw that
by your arts and by your all-powerful potions you had wrested so
] many from the black jaws of Death. Master, worthy to be cherished,
may your limbs, I pray, rest quiet 'neath the soft turf, and from the
place of your burial may roses grow, and marigolds, and the crimson-
] faced hyacinth. Mild be Æacus's judgement on you, and may
Ætnæan Proserpina smile upon you; may you stroll in endless life
amid the blessed in the Elysian plains.

II.

On the Fifth of November.

Written in His Seventeenth Year

[Latin on p. 144.]

At last, good [King] James was come from the uttermost North,
and held in his sway the Teucrian-born peoples, and the wide-spreading domains of Albion's folk, and at last an inviolable treaty had
joined the sceptre of England to the Scots of Caledonia, and James,
bringer of peace, blessed, rich, was seated on his new throne, without

concern for secret guile and wile, or [open] foe of his country. At this very time the merciless tyrant that is monarch in fire-flowing Acheron, the father of the Eumenides, roving exile from skyey Olympus, had idly wandered, as it chanced, o'er the illimitable compass of the lands, counting over his allies in crime, his faithful slaves, [to slavery born, destined to be, after sad deaths, sharers in his realm. Here he stirs up tempests accursed in mid-air, there he fashions hatred 'twixt friends whose hearts beat before, ever, as one ; he arms invincible peoples against each other's vitals, and overturns kingdoms that bloom with olive-bearing peace. Whomsoever he [sees loving virtue undefiled, these, every one, he is keen to subject to his sovereignty, and, master of guile in many forms, he seeks with might and main to corrupt the soul inaccessible [as yet] to sin ; he lays plots that make no sound, stretches nets that lie concealed, to lay swift hold on those that take not due heed, as the Caspian tigress [follows her panic-stricken prey through the trackless wastes, 'neath a moonless sky, when the stars are winking with slumber. In such [ways] Summanus assails peoples and cities, wrapped [himself] in a smoking whirlwind of dark flame.

Presently, the lands that are white with wave-resounding cliffs [appear, and the land that is beloved by the god of the sea, to which in olden days Neptune's son [Albion] had given its name, Neptune's son who hesitated not, crossing the seas, to challenge Amphitryon's fierce son to frenzied battle, before the cruel ages that saw the storming of Troy.   [

Soon as he sees this land, blessed with riches and with holiday peace, and its fields fat with the bounties of Ceres, and—a sight that grieved him more sorely still—a people reverencing the holy powers of the true God, at last he bursts forth sighs that reek of Tartarean fires and of lurid sulphur, sighs such as the grim creature, penned by [Jove within Trinacrian Ætna, monstrous Typhœus, breathes forth from his corruption-working mouth. Afire are his eyes, and the adamantine array of his teeth grinds and clashes loudly, as the crash of weapons and spear struck by spear. And then he spake :

'Though I have roamed the wide world o'er, this is the one and only lamentable sight mine eyes have found ; this is the one and only [race that fights against me, that makes light of my yoke, that is mightier than [all] my craft. Yet, if my efforts have aught of power, this race shall not long act thus with impunity, it shall not long go unscathed.'

So far [he spake], and then with his pitch-black wings swims in the [limpid air. Wheresoe'er he flies, confronting [opposing] winds rush before him in serried array, clouds are thickly massed, and lightning flashes gleam in close succession.

Presently, in his swift progress he had flown beyond the frosty Alps, and had reached the borders of Ausonia. On his left were the Apennines, cloud-bearing, and the age-old Sabines, on his right [Etruria, infamous for its sorceries. You too he sees, Tiber, as you give furtive kisses to Thetis. Presently, he alighted on the heights of Quirinus, offspring of Mars. By this time the late twilight had made the light doubtful, at the hour when the Bearer of the Triple Crown makes the rounds of the City, everywhere, and, upborne on the shoulders of men, carries with him the gods wrought of bread. Princes with bowed knees go before him, and a long, long train of begging brothers, bearing in their hands waxen tapers—blind [all], born [all] in Cimmerian darkness, and dragging out existence [there]. Then they enter churches agleam with hosts of torches—it was the evening that is sacred to Peter—, and the uproar of the chanters time and again filled the empty, vaulted chambers, and the void spaces, with such noise as [is heard] when Bromius howls, and Bromius's squadrons, as they chant their orgiastic hymns on Echionian Aracynthus, the while Æsopus quivers, o'erwhelmed, in his glassy billows, and Cithæron himself, far, far away, answers with his crannied cliffs.

When these rites had at length been carried to their end in wonted fashion, Night voicelessly quitted the embraces of aged Erebus, and with her goading scourge drove with headlong speed her steeds—Typhlon, of blinded eyes, savage Melanchætes, Siope, daughter of an Acherontean sire, and Phrix, a shuddering figure with her shaggy mane.

Meanwhile, the Tamer of Kings, Phlegethon's heir [the Pope], entered his bridal chambers (for this stealthy adulterer drags out no sterile nights without a wanton mistress) : but scarce were his eyes composed and closing in sleep when the sable lord of the shades, ruler of the silent folk, who preys on the sons of men, 'neath a misleading guise stood by his side. His temples gleamed with the white locks he had assumed ; a long beard covered his breast ; ashen-hued vestments swept the ground with a long train ; a cowl hung from his shaven crown ; and, that no single thing might be lacking to complete his clever devisings, he bound his lustful loins with a rope of hemp, and his slow-moving feet he fastened in latticed shoes [sandals fastened with straps]. Such a figure, so rumour says, was Francis, as he wandered alone, in the vast desert, amid the loathsome haunts of wild beasts, and to the woodland folk bore godly words of salvation, a godless creature himself, and tamed the wolves and the lions of Libya !

Draped in such raiment, the crafty serpent unstops his lips to utter words like these :

'Do you sleep, my son ? Does slumber deep still o'erwhelm your limbs ? Oh, unmindful of the faith, and forgetful of your flocks ! the while your chair, that all should reverence, and your triple diadem are laughed to scorn by a barbarous people, born 'neath the Hyperborean heavens, the while your rights are spurned by the quiver-bearing Britons ! Rise, speed you ! Rise, sluggard, to whom the Latin Caesar [the Emperor of Germany] makes obeisance ; for you the door of the vaulted skies lies open wide. Break their swollen

spirits, and break their insolent arrogance, and let these sacrilegious
sinners know what power is vested in your curse, what power is [
vested in the custody of the Apostle's key. With mind that recalls
all, avenge Hesperia's fleets [the Armada], scattered wide, and the
Iberians' standards whelmed 'neath the far-flung deep, and the many,
many bodies of your saints fastened on the shameful cross, while the
Thermodontean Maiden lately was their queen. But, if you prefer to [
lie torpid, on your soft, luxurious couch, and refuse to beat to earth the
growing might of your foe, he will fill the Tyrrhenian Sea with his
numerous soldiery, and fix fast his gleaming standards on the Aven-
tine Hill; he will break to pieces what is left of things that are old, [
and burn them with flames, and trample with godless feet your holy
neck—though, once, kings joyed to give kisses to your sandals. And
yet assail him not in wars and in open strife: vain is such toil: as
master of guile make use of trickery; righteous is it to set whatever
nets you will to snare heretics. At this moment their mighty king is [
summoning to council his patricians from his uttermost borders, is
summoning men born of the stock of princes, and aged sires, to be
reverenced for their cloaks and their hoary locks: these, all these
you will have power to scatter limb from limb in the air, by flinging
the fire of nitrous powder 'neath the foundations of the structure [
wherein they are convened. Forthwith, therefore, advise of the plan
proposed and of the deed whatsoever of the faithful England still contains: will any one of your sons venture not to carry out the orders
of the sovereign Pope? When they are sore-stricken by sudden [
panic and amazed at the catastrophe, let the merciless Gaul invade
them, the savage Iberian. So the days of Mary will come back in
that land at last, and you will be lord and master once again over the
warlike Angles. That you may not have one fear, mark that the gods
and goddesses all are favourable, as many powers divine as are [
worshipped on your holy days.'

So spake the traitor, and then, laying off the robes he had assumed,
he fled to his unspeakable, joyless realm, the land of Lethe.

By this time, rosy Tithonia, opening wide the gates of the Dawn,
was clothing the gilded earth with returning light, and, lamenting [
still the mournful death of her swart son [Memnon], she was
besprinkling the mountain-tops with ambrosial drops, when he
who guards the doors of the starry court banished slumbers,
and rolled away the charming visions, the charming dreams of the
night.

There is a place hedged about with the never-ending darkness of
night, once the giant foundations of a building now in ruins, now the [
grot of Murder grim, and of two-tongued Treachery, children two
that at one birth savage Discord mothered. Here amid heaps of
rubble and jagged boulders lie, unburied, bones of men, and corpses
pierced by steel; here sits Guile, black as night, with twisted eyes, [
and Wordy Quarrels, and Calumny, armed with fangs; one sees
Frenzy here, a thousand highways to dying, and Panic Fear; blood-

less Horror flies about the spot, and ceaselessly, through the voiceless
silences, the unsubstantial Manes howl; the earth howls, and, witness
] of all, stands in pools of blood. In the penetralia of the grot skulk,
panic-stricken, Murder himself and Treachery, and, though no one
follows them through the grot, the horrendous cavern, craggy, black
with shades of death, they fly this way and that, these guilty creatures,
] twisting back their eyes. Such were the champions of Rome, loyal
through long, long ages, that the Babylonish priest calls forth for
service, and thus he speaks:

'By the sea that pours round the western limits [of the world]
dwells a nation that I loathe; for its unworthiness prescient Nature
refused to join it closely to our world. Thither—such is my bidding
] —hasten with swift steps, and let them be blown asunder by Tartarean dust into the light air, the king and his satraps alike, a crime-
stained brood; and take with you as sharers in your plan and as
helpers in your work as many as have glowed with passion for the
true faith.'

] So he ended. Eagerly the merciless twain obeyed.

Meantime, the Lord who bends the heavens in a long, long sweep
looks down, the Lord that sends his lightnings from the citadel of
the skies, and he smiles at the idle essays of the perverse crew, and
will be minded himself to keep safe the cause of his own people.

] There is an expanse, men say, where fertile Europe is parted from
the Asian land: that expanse looks towards the waters of Lake
Mæotis. Here is set up the high tower of Rumour, daughter of the
Titaness [Earth], a tower made of bronze, spacious, loud-echoing,
nearer to the ruddy stars than Athos or Pelion is when piled on Ossa.
] It has a thousand doorways, a thousand approaches that stand wide
open, and as many windows, and through the thin walls gleam the
spacious halls within. A rabble rout, gathered here, rouses varied
whisperings, like the noises made by the swarms of flies when they
buzz about the milking-pails, or in the sheep-cotes of rushes inter-
] woven, when the Dog-Star is seeking the heights of heaven, the peak
of the skies in the summer days. Rumour herself is seated at the very
top of her fortress, Rumour, avenger of her mother [Earth]. Conspicuous is her head, girt with uncountable ears, by which she draws
[to herself] every sound, however slight, and catches the lightest
murmur, from the uttermost confines of the wide-spreading earth.
] Not so many were the eyes that you, Arestor's son, unrighteous
warder of the heifer that was known in after days as Isis, kept rolling
in your face that knew no gentleness, eyes that never nodded in
voiceless sleep, eyes that looked down on the lands spread out, far
and wide, beneath. With these eyes Rumour is wont, often, to
] traverse places that lack the light, impenetrable even to the glittering
sun, and, speaking ceaselessly with a thousand tongues, this reckless
creature pours forth to any one she will what she has seen, what she
has heard; skilled in lies, she now makes less the truth, now magni-
fies it by tales of her own imagining.

Appendix II.

But none the less you have earned praises from my song, Rumour, for one good deed, than which there never was a deed more full of [truth ; you are worthy to be sung by me, nor shall I e'er regret that I mentioned you in a strain so long, for, in sooth, it was by your gracious offices, wide-roving goddess, that we English were saved, and render therefore to you your just dues. To you, God, who controls the ever-moving fires, sending before him his lightning-bolt, spake thus, the while the earth trembled: 'Rumour, are you voice- [less, silent ? or is that godless company of Papists unseen by you, that company which has conspired 'gainst me, 'gainst my Britons, and see you naught of the murder, unprecedented, planned 'gainst sceptre-bearing James ?'

So much He said : no more. But she forthwith understood the injunctions of the Lord of the Thunder, and, though she was full swift of flight before, she puts on, now, whistling wings, and clothes [her light body with divers plumes : her right hand carries a sounding trump of Temesæan [i.e. Bruttian, Italian] bronze. Without delay, with her wings she oars her way through the yielding breezes. It contents her not to outstrip in her speed the swift clouds : behind her she leaves now the winds, now the steeds of the sun, and first, in her [wonted manner, through the cities of England she scatters utterances of double meaning, and vague murmurings ; presently, in ringing tones she makes common property the wiles and the accursed work of betrayal, and deeds full of horror in the [mere] telling ; she adds the authors of the crime, nor, in her prattling, does she hold her peace [about the places that had been equipped with unseen treachery. All were confounded by the tales she told ; young men, young maidens alike were a-tremble, in equal measure old men, by years outworn ; understanding of such grievous ruin had, of a sudden, penetrated every age.

But, nevertheless, meanwhile the Father in the skies from the [heights above pities his people, and so he blocked the cruel daring of them that reverence the Pope. They are captured, and are whirled off to heart-rending punishment. But gifts of pious incense and grateful honours are rendered unto God ; the happy cross-roads smoke, everywhere, with genial fires ; youths in throngs set the dances in [train ; and so in all the year's length no day occurs more richly celebrated than the Fifth of November.

III.

On the Death of the Bishop of Ely.

Written in His Seventeenth Year.

[Latin on p. 150.]

My cheeks were still wet, still stained with the dew, and mine eyes were not yet dry. They were swollen with the rain of the melting

brine [of tears], that, lately, out of my affection, I poured forth, while
to the mournful funeral pyre of the Bishop of Ely I paid in full the
rites that were his due, when Rumour of the hundred tongues—ah,
ever messenger all too truthful of disaster!—scattered through the
cities of rich Britain, and through the peoples born of Neptune's seed,
the tale that you had yielded to Death and to the iron-hearted Sisters,
you, the glory of the human race, king of holy men in that isle which
possesses the name of Anguilla [Ely]. Then my unquiet breast
seethed straightway with hot wrath, dooming to the tomb o'er and
o'er the mighty goddess [Death]. Not more dire were the curses
that Ovid conceived in the deeps of his soul against Ibis; with more
restraint the Grecian bard cursed the loathly guilt of Lycambes, and
of Neobule, too, his promised bride. But see! while I was pouring
forth, myself, weighty curses, and praying death on the head of
Death, methought I heard, in deep amazement, such sounds as these,
[borne] by a gentle breath,' neath the gale: 'Fling off your blind
frenzies: fling off your gleaming bile, and your vain threats. Why do
you blindly essay to outrage powers divine no man should injure,
powers stirred of a sudden to wild bursts of rage? Death is not, as
you, poor, deluded mortal, fancy, the swarthy daughter of Night, nor
was she born of Erebus as sire, or of Erinys as mother within illimitable chaos. Rather does she, dispatched from the starry skies,
everywhere gather the harvests of God; souls hidden under a mass
of flesh she calls out into the light, and into the air, even as the
swiftly-fleeting Hours, daughters of Themis and of Jove, rouse the
day; such souls Death leads to the face of the Everlasting Father.
But the godless she justly whirls within the sorrow-burdened realms
of dusky Tartarus, and to seats beneath the earth. When to my joy
I heard Death calling, swiftly I left my loathsome prison, and amid
winged soldiers I was borne in blessedness high upward to the stars,
even as, in far-off days, the aged prophet was caught up, driver of
a chariot of fire, to the skies. Not affrighted was I by the Wain of
gleaming Boötes, a wain made slow by cold, or by the arms of the
appalling Scorpion, or even by your blade, Orion. I flew past the
ball of the gleaming sun, and I saw, far, far below my feet, the glowing goddess, triple-bodied [Diana, as Luna], the while she was with
golden reins seeking to check her dragon team. Through the ranks
of the wandering stars I was borne, and through the Milky stretches,
marvelling oft at my new-found swiftness, until we came to the
shining portals of Olympus, and to the palace of crystal, and the halls
paved with emeralds. But here I will hold my peace, for who, if born
of human sire, would have the strength to set forth in full the loveliness of that place? *I* count it enough to enjoy that place for ever.'

Appendix II.

IV.

That Nature Submits Not to the Decay of Old Age.

[Latin on p. 151.]

Ah me! by what never-ending errors man's wandering mind is driven, driven till it faints, exhausted! O'erwhelmed in darkness deep it rolls within itself night, the night of [blinded] Œdipus. Mad, insane, man's mind dares to measure the deeds of the gods by its own, and ventures to liken to its own the laws graven deep on ada- [a mant that lives for ever; the designs of Fate, not to be loosed by any lapse of time, man links with his own hours, hours that are fore-doomed to die!

Shall, then, the face of Nature, o'ergrown with furrowing wrinkles, wither, and shall the common mother of all things, her all-producing womb contracted, grow barren through the lapse of years? Shall [1 she, confessing herself age-worn, move with uncertain steps, her starry head all a-tremble? Shall the loathsome lapse of time and the never-ending hunger of the years, and squalor, and mouldy decay harry the stars? And shall insatiable Time [Kronos] devour the skies, and whirl his own sire into his vitals? Ah me! Was Jove improvident, [1 unforeseeing? Could he not have fortified his own heights 'gainst such sin as this, have exempted them from the dire evil wrought by Time? Could he not have given them revolutions without end? It will come to pass, then, that some day, slipping asunder with awful crash, the floors of the vaulted heavens shall rush down apace, and each pole, [2 fronting the stroke, shall roar, and that the Olympian will fall from his court on high, and Pallas, too, will fall a figure dread, with her Gorgon uncovered, aye, will fall even as Juno's son, routed from the sacred threshold of the skies, fell down on Ægean Lemnos. You too, Phœbus, with chariot rushing down headlong, will imitate the fall of [2 your own son [Phaëthon], and you will be borne downward in sudden crash, and by your quenched torch Nereus will be set smoking, and he will give forth from his bewildered main hissings fraught with death. Then, too, Hæmus's foundations will be torn asunder, its top-most peak will split in twain, and the Ceraunian Heights, dashed [3 down now into the deepest pit [of Tartarus], will hurl downward, affrighted now, Stygian Dis, and the mountains that, in other days, were used now against the gods in heaven above, now in fratricidal wars.

No! No! The Father Omnipotent, setting the stars on strong foundations, has taken thought for the sum total of things, and with weights inerrant has poised in perfect balance the scales of the Fates, [3 and has bidden each thing in all the mighty array to keep unceasingly the tenor of its way. This is why the 'First Wheel of the Universe' [the *Primum Mobile*] rolls on with diurnal movement, and sweeps the encircled skies along with the whirling course wherein they share.

Appendix II.

Saturn is no slower than was his wont, and Mars, fiery still as in
0] olden, far-off days, Mars of the crested helm, glows still as with the
lightning's gleam. Phœbus is ceaselessly agleam with youth, nor
does this god, deflecting his chariot along downward slopes of the
skies, seek to warm lands exhausted, but always, powerful with
friendly light, he speeds along the self-same marks left by his chariot
wheels. With beauty matching that of other days there rises from
45] the Indians' fragrant lands the star [Lucifer] that, calling them in
the early morn, closes the files of the heavenly flocks in whitening
Olympus, and [at evening] drives them again to the pasture-lands of
the skies, parting the realms of Time with colours twain. Delia, too,
shines on, and with alternate horns [i.e. with waxing and waning
horns] discharges her changing, varying, roles, and with arms match-
50] ing those of old she embraces the cerulean fire. Nor do the elements
show shifting faith, but with their wonted crash the lurid lightning-
bolts smite and shatter the cliffs. With no gentler roar Caurus rages
furiously through the void; with equal horror the wild Aquilo touches
55] the armour-bearing Geloni, breathing winter upon them, and rolling
the clouds. As has been his wont, the King of the Deep lashes
asunder the foundations of Sicilian Pelorus; with his booming shell
the Ocean's trumpeter blares round the levels of the deep, and
Ægæon, as the Balearic whales bear him on their backs, is no smaller
60] than the giant bulk [that was his always]. But neither do you, Earth,
lack that old-time vigour of a far-off age. The Narcissus, too, keeps
its own peculiar fragrance. This lad keeps his own peculiar beauty;
so, too, Phœbus, does that lad of yours [Hyacinthus], so, too, Cypris,
does yours [Adonis]. Nor was the Earth richer in days of old when
she guiltily buried in her mountains the gold destined to work crime,
or hid the jewels 'neath her waters.

65] So, in a word, the righteous series of all things will go on into endless time, until the final fires shall lay waste the wide compass of the
lands, embracing the poles, and the peaks of the vast skies at their
highest, and the enginery of the universe shall burn on a giant pyre.

V.

On the Platonic Idea, as Aristotle Understood It.

[Latin on p. 153.]

Tell, ye goddesses that preside o'er the holy woods, tell, Memory,
most blessed mother of the goddesses nine, tell, Eternity, who dost
recline at ease in thy far-off grot, keeping safe the memorials of the
[5] past and the established ordinances of Jove, the calendar of the skies,
and the record-books of the gods, tell me, I pray, who that first man
was according to whose likeness cunning nature moulded all the sons
of men, a man eternal he, stranger to decay, one in age with the
[10] heavens, single and yet universal, the pattern used by God. He

surely is not lodged in the brain of Jove, a child kept ever concealed therein, twin brother of Pallas, maid alway unwed. Though his nature is a nature shared by many, yet it exists apart, by itself, after the fashion of a being unique, and—strange to say—is fastened in a definite expanse of space. Mayhap, as never-dying comrade of the [15 stars he wanders through the tenfold array of heaven, or dwells in the ball of the moon, nearest [of the heavenly bodies] to earth, or, per-chance, seated amid souls that are destined to enter bodies, he is torpid, void of all life, at the forgetful waters of Lethe, or, mayhap, in [20 some far-off expanse of earth he strides on as mighty giant, this arche-type of man, and raises high his towering head, a figure to be dreaded by gods, a figure taller than Atlas himself, bearer of the stars. No! No! The Dircæan augur, whose very blindness gave him boundless [25 light, never in his bosom's deeps saw *that* man; Pleïone's winged grandson [Hermes, or Hermes Trismegistus] ne'er in the stilly night showed him to the keen-minded company of the seers. The Assyrian priest knows him not, though he tells the long tale of Ninus's forebears, [30 and names Belos, of far-off days, and famous Osiris. Nor did Hermes, the thrice great, the glorious seer with the triple name, skilled though he is in secrets, bequeath mention of that man to the worshippers of Isis.

But [Plato], everlasting glory of the groves of Academe, if *you* were [35 pioneer in bringing such monsters into the Schools, forthwith, forth-with call back again the poets, exiles from your State, since you your-self are greatest of all tellers of fables, or else go forth, yourself, founder of the State therefrom.

VI.

To My Father.

[Latin on p. 154.]

I would fain have the Pierian springs divert, at this instant, their watercourses through my breast; I would fain have the stream loosed from the twin peaks and roll, in all its fulness, o'er my lips, to the end that, forgetting all humble strains, my Muse may rise on daring pinions to discharge her loving service to my father, a father [5] worthy of all reverence. Be its welcome what it may, it is for you, worthy father, that my Muse is toiling o'er this slender achievement. I know not what gifts *from* me can make more fitting answer to your gifts *to* me, though not even the greatest gifts can make answer unto [10] yours: far less can the gratitude that is rendered through empty words, barren gratitude, be a match for gifts [substantial]. Yet, after all, this page sets forth my rating: all that I have of wealth I have counted out on the sheet that is before you, and yet that wealth is naught save what golden Clio has given me, what slumbers have

5] begotten for me within some grot sequestered, and the laurel-thickets
in the holy wood, shady dells on Parnassus.

Do not *you* look down on song divine, creation of the bard, for
naught graces more finely than does song his heavenly source, his
heavenly seed, his mind mortal in origin, for song still keeps holy
10] traces of Prometheus's fire. The gods above love song, and song has
power to rouse the quaking depths of Tartarus, to bind fast the gods
of the deeps below; song restrains with triple adamant the unfeeling
Manes. By song the secrets of the far-distant future are revealed by
15] the daughters of Phœbus, and by quivering Sibyls, pale of lips. The
sacrificer composes [builds] songs at the holy altars, whether he lays
low the bull as it tosses its gilded horns, or, keen of mind, consults
the fates hidden away within the smoking entrails, or in the *exta*,
still warm, searches for [the will of] destiny. So I too, when I shall
20] revisit my native Olympus, and time shall stand immovable, endlessly
delayed, I too shall go, wearing a golden crown, through the realms
of the skies, wedding sweet strains to the soft-sounding *plectrum*: at
those strains the stars and the vaults of the twin poles will ring. At
35] this instant too the fiery spirit that flies round and round 'mid the swiftly
whirling orbs is singing, himself, amid the starry choirs, singing a never-
dying melody, a song beyond all describing, while the ruddy Serpent
checks his hot hissings, and savage Orion, with sword now lowered,
40] turns gentle, and Maurusian Atlas no longer feels his burden.

Songs were wont, in olden days, to adorn the rich feasts of kings,
when luxury, and the limitless abyss of the bottomless gullet were yet
unknown, and the banquet tables foamed only with modest wines.
45] In those days, the bard, seated in accord with custom at the holiday
feast, his unshorn locks bound with leaves from the oak-tree, used to
sing of the achievements of heroes, exploits worthy of imitation, and
the foundations, laid broad and wide, of the world, and of gods
creeping, and of acorns that formed food for gods, and of the lightning-bolt not yet sought from Ætna's grot. In brief, what pleasure
50] will there be in music well attuned if it is empty of voice, empty of
words and of their meanings, and of numbers that talk? Such strains
befit the woodland choirs, not Orpheus, who by his songs held fast the
streams, and added ears to the oaks by his songs, not by his lyre,
and by his singing compelled to tears the shades that were done with
55] life: it is from his *song* that he has these praises.

Persist not, I pray you, to hold cheap the holy Muses, nor think
them idle, poor, for through their bounty you yourself skilfully compose a thousand strains to measures fit, and, since you have been
trained to vary your tuneful voice by a thousand modulations, you
60] would of right be heir of Arion's fame. Wherein is it strange if it
has fallen to your lot to sire me, a poet, if we [you and I], knit so
closely together by dear ties of blood, should pursue arts of one
blood, and kindred studies? Phœbus, wishing to divide himself
65] between us twain, gave one half of his gifts to me, the other half to
my father, and so we, father and son, possess the god in shares.

Appendix II.

Though you pretend that you loathe the dainty Muses, none the less you loathe them not, methinks, for, father, you did not bid me go where a highway lies open wide and broad, where the ground slopes more straightly to gain, and the golden hope of storing away money [7 shines with steady lustre. You are not now dragging me off to the laws, the ill-guarded statutes of our nation, nor are you condemning my ears to the tasteless clamours [of the laws.] But, eager to enrich yet more my mind, you drew me away from the din and the uproar [7 of the city, into seclusions deep, and you suffered me to go amid the delightful leisure of the Aonian stream, a blessed comrade at Apollo's side.

I hold my peace about the service rendered by every father to dear son : on *me* larger demands are made. When, at your expense, best of fathers, the eloquence of Romulus's tongue was opened wide to me, and all its Latin graces, when there lay open to me the exalted [8 words of the Greeks, masters of a noble tongue, words that become the great mouth of Jove himself, you urged me to add the flowers [of language] whereof Gaul boasts, and the talk that the newer Italian pours forth from his degenerate lips, bearing witness by his utterance to barbarian uprisings ; you urged me to learn, too, the mysteries that the seers and the prophets of Palestine speak forth. In a word, [8₅ whatever is contained within the sky, in mother Earth, spread out beneath the skies, or in the air that streams 'twixt earth and sky, whatever the waters cover and the heaving marble of the sea, all this, thanks to you, it is my privilege to know, thanks to you, if it shall be my pleasure to know it. Nay, more, sweeping the clouds apart, [9c Science comes, to be viewed, and, naked, she inclines her bright face to my kisses, unless I should wish to flee, unless I should find it burdensome to taste her kisses.

Go to, now, match your wealth [with mine], whoso'er, unsound of mind, makes his first choice the age-old treasures of Austria, and of the kingdoms of Peru. What greater wealth could have been given [95 by a father, even, if you will, by Jove himself, though he had given all the world, the sky alone excepted ? No choicer gifts, e'en had they been safe, gave he who entrusted to his youthful son the light that is common property of all mankind, and Hyperion's chariot, and the reins of the day, and the tiara undulating with radiant light. [10 Therefore, since I am already a part, albeit the lowliest, of the learned [poetic] throng, I shall sit amid the victors' crowns of ivy and of laurel ; no more now shall I mingle, a figure obscure, with the witless populace, but my footsteps will avoid eyes profane. Keep yourselves far away, wakeful Cares, keep yourselves far away, Com- [10 plaints, and the eye of Envy with its crooked leer. Stretch not wide, merciless Calumny, your snake-bearing jaws. Most loathsome crew, *you* possess naught of baneful power against me, nor am I in *your* control. Safe, with breast secure, I shall stride on, uplifted high from [11 your viper blows.

But for you, father dear, since the power is not vouchsafed me to

(592)

Appendix II.

make just return to your deserts, or to balance your gifts by my achievements, let it be enough that I have made mention of them, that with grateful heart I am telling the tale of your gifts, and am storing them away in a loyal mind.

And now, verses of mine, song of my youth, my sport and frolic, if only you shall venture to hope for never-ceasing years, and to outlive your master's funeral pyre, and then to gaze on the light, and if black forgetfulness shall not whirl you 'neath crowded Orcus, perhaps you will jealously guard these praises, and my father's name, thus lauded in song, guarding them, I mean, to serve as an example for a time far distant.

Psalm CXIV.

[Greek on p. 157.]

When the children of Israel, when the glorious tribes of Jacob left the land of Egypt, a land hateful, of barbarous speech, in that day the sons of Judah were the one holy race, and among its peoples God was king, a king of great might. The sea saw it, and humbly, coiled up in its roaring waters, gave strength to the fugitive, and the holy Jordan was flung violently back towards its silvery fountains. The giant mountains tossed themselves about, and leaped this way and that, even as rams, full of vigour, in a nourishing vineyard. Likewise, all the smaller crags skipped, even as lambs, at the sound of the syrinx, 'neath their loving mothers. Why did you, dread sea, coiled up in your roaring waters, so marvellously give strength to the fugitive? Why were you flung back, holy Jordan, toward your silvery fountains? Why, giant mountains, did ye toss yourselves about, and leap this way and that, even as rams, full of vigour, in a nourishing vineyard? Why, ye smaller crags, did ye skip, even as lambs at the sound of the syrinx 'neath their loving mothers? Shake yourself, Earth, tremble in fear before the Lord as he makes a mighty noise, shake, Earth, fearing the Lord, the loftiest majesty of the son of Isaac, of God who, even from the crags by the sea, poured forth the roaring rivers, and from the dripping rock an ever-flowing fountain.

[Greek on p. 158.]

A king, finding by chance, among men deeply guilty, a philosopher, whom he did not know at all, and who was wholly innocent, condemned the philosopher to death. As the philosopher was going along the road to death, he suddenly sent these verses to the king.

Sir king, if you shall slay me, a man that abides by the law, that has done naught that is dire to any one, easily, mark you, would you destroy a life full wise, but afterwards you will realize what you have done, and then, all in vain, will you lament to your own soul, because you destroyed out of your city such a far-famed bulwark of defence.

[Greek on p. 158.]

On the Man Who Had Engraved Milton's Likeness.

This likeness you would, perchance, say had been graven by an unskilful man, were you to look at the genuine shape and appearance [i.e. its original]. But since, good friends, you know not him whose face is modelled here, you laugh at this misfit imitation by a worthless sculptor.

VII.

Scazons to Salsilli, a Roman Poet, as He Lay Ill.

[Latin on p. 158.]

O Muse, who of choice dost trail a limping foot, and, slow of progress, dost take joy in the gait of Vulcan, and dost think such gait no less charming in its due season than when golden-tressed Deïope moves her comely ankles, now one, now other, before the golden couch of Juno, stand by me, I pray, and bear, if you will, these few words to Salsilli, who takes my Muse so warmly to his heart, preferring her—undeservedly—to the truly mighty poets. These verses that fostering [of yours] at London, Milton, sends to him, Milton, who, in these latter days, quitting his proper nest, and his own expanse of heaven, where the worst of winds, all powerless to control its mad lungs, swiftly plies panting blasts 'neath the skies, came to the fruitful glebe of Italy's soil, to see its cities, known by proud report, its lordly men, and the fine natures of its learned youth; he prays for you full many a blessing, Salsilli, and a state, a habit wholly sound for your exhausted body. At this present, overflowing bile assails your reins, and, firmly lodged within your frame, breathes ruin. Nor did the impious bile spare you for all that you, a man of culture true, mould Lesbian song with your Roman lips.

O sweet gift of the gods, Health, sister of Hebe, O Apollo, terror of diseases, ever since you slew the Python, or if thou hearest with more pleasure *Pæan*, this man is true priest of yours. O oaken groves of Faunus, and hills of Rome, generous with the dew of the grape, gracious seat of Evander, if aught that brings health sends forth leaves within your vales, in eager rivalry bear it as relief for your sore-stricken bard. This done, he, restored again to the dear Muses, will soothe the neighbouring meads with sweet song. Numa himself will marvel, with all his mind, amid the dark groves, where he lives a life of leisure, blessed, never-dying, gazing ever, with head flung back, on his beloved Egeria, and the Tiber too, though he is in

Appendix II.

flood, soothed by him, will favour year by year the hopes of the tillers of the soil. No more will he speed on to assail kings in their tombs, rushing against them, unrestrained, with his left rein too slack, but rather will he control more skilfully the reins of his billows, through all his course to the briny realms of winding Portumnus.

VIII.

Manso.

[Latin on p. 160.]

Giovanni Battista Manso, Marquis of Villa, is a man pre-eminently famous among the Italians, for intellectual merit, devotion to literature, and for warlike prowess as well. It was to him that Torquato Tasso addressed his Dialogue on Friendship, a dialogue still extant, for he was a close friend of Tasso. Tasso mentions him with high praise among the princes of Italy, in the poem entitled Gerusalemme Conquistata, *Book* 20.

> Amongst knights magnanimous and courteous
> Manso shines—

When the author was tarrying in Naples, Manso attended him with unbounded goodwill, and bestowed upon him many kindly services, born of his true humanity. To him, therefore, the sojourner, before he left the city, sent this poem, that he might show himself not ungrateful.

These songs, too, the daughters of Pieria are preparing with all care to sound your praises, Manso, yes, are preparing for you, Manso, well known to the choir of Phœbus, forasmuch as he has deemed no other worthy of equal honour, since the day when Gallus and Etruscan Mæcenas were turned to ashes. You too, if the breath of my song has power so great, shall have a seat among the victors' crowns of ivy and of laurel.

You long, long ago a blessed harmony of hearts joined with mighty Tasso, and so inscribed your names on scrolls that never fade. Presently, the discerning Muse gave to your care sweet-speaking Marini ; he joyed to be called your fosterling the while he sang, at length, the Assyrian loves of the gods [in a poem about Adonis], and, gentle poet that he was, by his song held in amaze the nymphs of Ausonia. Likewise, as he lay dying, the body that he owed to you he bequeathed to you, yes to you alone, and he bequeathed to you his final wishes. Nor did your loving devotion deceive the Manes of your friend : our eyes have seen the poet smiling on us from the bronze so carefully wrought. Nor did you count this enough to do for each ; your devoted offices cease not at the tomb. You are keen to wrest them, incorrupt, from Orcus, in so far as you have power, and to cheat the hungry laws of the Parcæ : hence the lineage of

each you are portraying, and the life led by him amid varying
fortunes, his character, and Minerva's gifts to him ; rival are you of
him [Herodotus] who, born by high Mycale, with eloquent voice
chronicled the life of Æolian Homer. Therefore, in the names of
Clio and of mighty Phœbus, I dispatch to you, father Manso, my
best wishes for your health through the long, long years, I, a youth
from a foreign land, sent from the Hyperborean quarter of the world.
Since you are so gracious, you will not spurn a Muse that comes
from afar, a Muse that, though nurtured but hardly 'neath the cold
Bear, unthinkingly dared, recently, a flight through the cities of
Italy. I too, I am persuaded, have heard through the dark shadows
of the night the swans as they attuned their strains in my own river,
where the silvery Thames, bright-urned, wide-spreading stream,
drenches his grey tresses with the swirling waters of ocean. Nay,
nay, once on a time there came to these shores [of Italy] Tityrus
[Chaucer].

But we English are not a race uncultured, or useless to Phœbus, in
that region of the world which, furrowed by the Wain with its sevenfold team, submits to wintry Boötes during the long nights. We too
cherish Phœbus, we have sent gifts to Phœbus, yellow ears of grain,
and golden apples in baskets, and fragrant crocus (unless the tale is
idle that ancient days record) ; we sent too choirs chosen from the
race of the Druids. The Druids, a time-honoured race, busied with
the holy rites of the gods, were wont to sing the praises of the heroes,
and their achievements worthy of imitation. This is why, whenever
the maidens of Greece, after their custom, on Delos's sward circle the
altars with their festal strains, in gladsome songs make mention of
Loxo, daughter of Corineus, and of Upis, voice of the Fates, and
Hecaërge, too, of the golden tresses, whose breasts were stained with
the Caledonian dye.

Fortunate elder ! So, then, wherever through the compass of the
lands the glory of Torquato and his mighty name shall be heralded,
and the fame of immortal Marini shall grow with fresh brightness,
you too will come again and yet again to the lips of men and into
their plaudits, and with flight matching theirs you will press swiftly
along an imperishable way. Men will say that in those days [the
days of Tasso, Marini, Manso] of his own will the Lord of Cynthus
dwelt in your house, and that the Muses came as servants to your
portals. Yet it was not of his own will that this self-same Apollo
drew near to the house, to the farm-lands of the King, son of Pheres,
what time Phœbus was a fugitive from the skies, though the king had,
as host, welcomed mighty Alcides. One relief had Apollo, only one :
when it pleased him to avoid the clamorous ploughmen, he withdrew
to the famous grot of the gentle Chiron, amid the well-watered vales
and leafy shelters, hard by the streams of Peneüs : there often, under
the dark ilex, induced by the coaxing entreaties of his friend, to the
strains of the lute, he soothed with his voice the hard labours of his
exile. Then the banks stayed not in their appointed places, nor did

the boulders, formerly firmly fixed within the deeps of the Tartarean pit, stay in theirs; the Trachinian cliff nodded, and felt no longer its wonted forests, a giant burden; the mountain ashes, dislodged, hastened down from their hills, and the spotted lynxes were soothed by strains ne'er heard before.

Elder beloved of the gods! It must be that Jupiter and Phœbus and the kindly grandson of Atlas all alike with kindly eyes surveyed you at your birth, for, unless he shall be from his first hours dear to the gods above, a man will ne'er have power to befriend a mighty poet. This is why *your* old age keeps green amid clinging flowers, and by its vigorous life gains for itself the spindles of Æson, preserving for you the graces of your brow, graces not yet fallen, the vigour of your intellect, and the full-grown keenness of your wit. O, may my lot vouchsafe to me a friend so fine, one who knows so well how to honour the men of Phœbus, true men, if ever I shall bring back to my songs the kings of my native land, and Arthur, who set wars in train even 'neath the earth [i.e. in Fairyland], or shall tell of the high-hearted heroes bound together as comrades at that peerless table, and—O, may the spirit come to my aid—I shall break to pieces Saxon phalanxes under the might of Britons' warring. At last when, having measured to the full the span of a life not voiceless, a man full of years, I shall leave to the ashes their rights, that friend would stand, with streaming eyes, beside my bier: it will be enough if I shall say to him, as he stands there, ‘Let me be your concern’. My limbs, relaxed by black death, he would take pains to have bestowed softly, gently, in a tiny urn; mayhap he will carve my features out of marble, wreathing my locks with leafage of Parnassus's laurel; and so I shall rest in undisturbed peace. Then, too, if there is aught of good faith, of loyalty, anywhere, if there are sure rewards for good men, I myself, withdrawn to the ether of the gods that dwell in the skies, in some place to which toil and a clean heart and their own flaming manhood bear good men, from some corner of a world apart I shall see, so far as the Fates permit, all that happens here [i.e. in this world below], and, with all my soul smiling calmly, I shall have a crimson flush upon my face, and at the same time, full of joy, I shall applaud myself in skyey Olympus.

IX.

DAMON'S EPITAPH.

[Latin on p. 163.]

Argument.

Thyrsis and Damon, shepherds of the same neighbourhood, devoted to the same pursuits, were friends from boyhood up, friends as close as e'er men were. Thyrsis, while on a journey for pleasure's sake, received, in foreign lands, a message telling of his friend's death.

Appendix II.

Later, after his return home, when he found that the message was true, he bemoaned himself and his loneliness.

In this poem, by 'Damon' is meant Charles Diodati, descended on his father's side from the Etruscan city of Lucca. In all things else he was an Englishman, a youth, the while he lived, pre-eminent in intellect, in learning, and in all the other brightest and fairest virtues.

Nymphs of Himera—ye keep in mind Daphnis and Hylas both, and the fates of Bion, long, long lamented—sing a strain truly Sicilian through the cities by the Thames, the cries that, in his woe, Thyrsis poured forth, the ceaseless plainings wherewith he harried the grots, and the wide-ranging rivers, and the retreats within the woods, while he made lament that Damon had been wrested from him before his time. Nor did he exempt from his griefs the deeps of the night, as he wandered o'er lonely places. Twice already the stalk was rising high with the green ears of grain, and the granaries were counting as many golden harvests, since his last day had borne Damon away within the shades, and Thyrsis was not yet by his side! for that shepherd the sweet love of the Muse was keeping in a Tuscan city. But when Thyrsis's mind, filled full, and concern for the flock he had left behind called him home, then, verily, soon as he had sat him down 'neath the accustomed elm, he was conscious that his friend was lost, and he began thus to disburden his limitless pain.

> *Go home, unpastured, my lambs:*
> *Your master has no leisure now.*

Woe is me! What powers divine shall I name on earth, what in heaven, since they have swept you off, Damon, by a merciless death? Is it thus, thus, that you leave me? Is merit such as yours to pass thus, nameless, and to be joined with a host of obscure shades? But he that with his golden wand parts the souls would not wish *that*; no, he would guide you to a host worthy of yourself, and would fend far off from you all the worthless herd of the voiceless [dead].

> *Go home, unpastured, my lambs:*
> *Your master has no leisure now.*

Whate'er shall come, one thing is sure: unless a wolf shall see me first, you, Damon, will not be crushed in an unlamented tomb, but your honours will be firmly fixed, firm set for you, and will long have vigorous life among the shepherds. To you, as second only to Daphnis, the shepherds will joy to pay their vows, they will joy to sing of you, as second only to Daphnis, as long as Pales, as long as Faunus shall love the country-side, if it counts for aught to have cherished faith like the faith of olden days, to have cherished righteousness, and the arts of Pallas, and to have had as comrade a man of song.

> *Go home, unpastured, my lambs:*
> *Your master has no leisure now.*

Appendix II.

These sure rewards await you, Damon, they will be yours for aye. But what of me? What loyal comrade will cling to my side, as you were wont oft to do, in the days of unrelenting cold, in places pregnant with frosts, or under the devouring sun, when the plants were dying of thirst, or when there was need to face in hand to hand encounter the monstrous lions, or to frighten the hungry wolves away from the high folds? Who will make it his habit with talking and with song to lay the day to rest?

> *Go home, unpastured, my lambs:*
> *Your master has no leisure now.*

To whom shall I entrust my soul? Who will teach me to lighten consuming cares, who to beguile the long nights with sweet converse, when the mellow pears shall be set hissing by the cheery fire, and the hearth shall crackle with the nuts, the while the evil South Wind confounds all the world outdoors, and thunders down through the elm?

> *Go home, unpastured, my lambs:*
> *Your master has no leisure now.*

Or, in the summer-time, when the day is revolving in mid heaven, when Pan, hidden away in the shade of the oak, courts slumber, and the nymphs seek again their familiar seats 'neath the waters, and the shepherds hide, the farmer snores under the hedge, who will renew for me your blandishments, your laughter, your sallies of Cecropian wit, and your cultured graces?

> *Go home, unpastured, my lambs:*
> *Your master has no leisure now.*

But now, alone, I wander through the fields, alone o'er the meadows, wherever the shadows cast by the branches are close set in the vales. There I wait the evening: over my head the rain and Eurus make mournful sounds, and the rending forests toss in the evening twilight.

> *Go home, unpastured, my lambs:*
> *Your master has no leisure now.*

Ah me! How deeply my tilth-lands, once so well tilled, are clothed now with insolent herbage! The towering grain gapes open with mildew. The grapes, unwedded, are withering, their clusters neglected, and the myrtle-groves pleasure me not. I am weary even of the sheep, and they are turning their eyes in deepest sorrow on their master.

> *Go home, unpastured, my lambs:*
> *Your master has no leisure now.*

Tityrus is calling me to the hazels, Alphesibœus to the mountain ashes, Ægon to the willows, lovely Amyntas to the streams: 'Here are cool springs, here are grasses o'er-spread with moss, here Zephyrs, here the arbutus murmurs amid the quiet waters.' All this they sang to one that was deaf; finding a covert, I went away from them,

> *Go home, unpastured, my lambs:*
> *Your master has no leisure now.*

Appendix II.

To all this Mopsus, when as it chanced, he saw me returning—skilled in the tongues of birds and in the stars was Mopsus—added words of his own : ' Thyrsis, what means this ? What shameless spleen torments you ? Either passion is slaying you, or some star is vexing you with baneful spell. Saturn's star has oft rested heavy on shepherds, and with glancing strokes of his leaden shaft has pierced their hearts to the utmost deeps.'

> *Go home, unpastured, my lambs :*
> *Your master has no leisure now.*

The nymphs are crying in wonder, 'What will become of you, Thyrsis? What mean you? not the wont of youth are this clouded brow, these wild eyes, such stern set features. Her search is—rightly—ever for dancing troops, and light frolics, and for love. Twice wretched is he who loves late.'

> *Go home, unpastured, my lambs :*
> *Your master has no leisure now.*

Hyas is come, and Dryope, and Ægle, daughter of Baucis, trained in measures, and mistress of the lyre, but by pride consumed ; Chloris, too, is come, near neighbour of the Idumanian Stream [the River Chelmer, in Essex]. But their blandishments move me not, their comforting words move me not, naught moves me, if it is at hand, no hope of the future moves me.

> *Go home, unpastured, my lambs :*
> *Your master has no leisure now.*

Woe is me ! How alike are the bullocks that frolic over the meadows ! Of one heart are they, one with another, by the law's decree, close comrades all. No one of them sets apart from the herd or this or that as his [peculiar] friend. Even so, crowding close together, the wolves come in search of food, and the wild asses, shaggy-haired, are joined to their like, now those. The law of the deep is the self-same law : on a lonely strand Proteus counts in herds the sea-calves. The lowly sparrow always has some one with whom to spend his days, gladly, with whom to fly gladly about all the heaps of spelt, visiting again, late, his own shelter : but if chance has done this mate to death—mayhap a kite by its curved beak has brought to it its fate, or perchance a ditcher has laid it low with his shaft—, straightway the sparrow, flying from the spot, seeks another to be his comrade. But we mortals are a rugged race, a race harried by accursed fates, alien one to another in soul, and discordant in spirit : hardly does a man find out of a thousand one—only one—that matches himself, or, if fortune, no longer harsh, at last vouchsafes one to our prayers, him some day, in an hour wherein one expects it not, steals from us, leaving us loss, everlasting, on into the [endless] ages.

> *Go home, unpastured, my lambs :*
> *Your master has no leisure now.*

Appendix II.

Alas! what vagrant wandering drove me to go to stranger shores, across the skyey ridges, and the snow-laden Alps? Was there anything worth its cost in the sight of buried Rome?—[would there have been], even if she were as splendid as in the days when Tityrus went to see her, leaving the while his sheep and his countryside—, anything worth so much that for it I could be without *you*, my sweet, sweet comrade, could set between you and me so many deep seas, so many mountains, so many forests, so many crags, so many sounding streams? Ah! I might at least have been privileged to touch for the last time your hand, and your dear eyes, decently composed as you died in peace, and to say, 'Fare you well, fare you well! Remember me, as you shall take your way to the stars.'

> *Go home, unpastured, my lambs:*
> *Your master has no leisure now.*

And yet I shall never regret that I kept you in mind, shepherds of Tuscany, youths busied with the Muses, for there dwells Charis, there Lepos abides. You too, Damon, were a Tuscan, from the ancient city of Lucumo: thence you derive your lineage. Oh, how wondrous great was I, when, stretched at ease by the prattlings of the cool Arno, in its poplar grove, where the grass was softest, I could pluck now violets, now the tips of the myrtles, and could hear Menalcas vying with Lycidas! I too ventured [then] to contend, and, methinks, I did not much displease, for I have in my possession even now the gifts you, one and all, gave me—baskets of rush, baskets of wicker, and the waxen fastenings of hemlock. Nay, more, Dati and Francini made my name known to the beeches: well known were they both for their songs, and for their studies, and both were of the blood of the Lydians [Tuscans].

> *Go home, unpastured, my lambs:*
> *Your master has no leisure now.*

Such strains the dewy moon used to dictate to me—glad was I in those days—, while by myself I was penning my dainty kids within the hurdles. Ah! How many times I said, even when the black ashes possessed you, 'Damon is singing now, or else he is setting nets 'gainst the hares; now he is intertwining osiers to serve his varied needs'. And what then I, with complaisant mind, hoped would come to pass, I lightly forestalled in my prayers, and I portrayed it as already present. 'What, ho, good sir! [I said to you, Damon], 'you're doing naught? Unless, perchance, something holds you back, are we off, and are we reclining a while in the tuneful shade, at the waters of the Colnus [the River Colne], or where the acres of Cassibelaunus [lie]? You will run through, for me, your healing potions, your herbs, the hellebore, and the lowly crocus, and the leaf of the hyacinth, all the herbs that yonder marsh possesses, and the arts, too, of the healers.' Alas! perish the herbs, perish, too, the arts of the healers, the plants, since they profited not at all him who was their master. I myself too— my pipe was sounding forth some lofty strain, I know not what—another day is come, the day following the eleventh night—I myself, as it chanced, had set my lips to pipes of hemlock, pipes that were new: none the less, bursting their joinings, they leaped asunder, and could brook no longer the weighty strains. I misdoubt that I am over-swollen with pride. Still I will tell the tale. Yield, ye woods.   [

> *Go home, unpastured, my lambs:*
> *Your master has no leisure now.*

I myself shall sing of Dardan ships [making their way] through Rutupian [Kentish] waters, and of the realm, in days of old, of Imogene, daughter of Pandrasus; I shall sing of Brennus and Arviragus, captains [both], and of ancient Belinus, too, and of the settlers from Armorica subject at last to Britons' laws. Next I shall sing of Igraine, mother- [to-be, through fateful trickery, of Arthur, I shall sing of lying features, of the taking of the arms of Gorloïs, guile, all, of Merlin. O, if only life shall endure for me, you, my Pan's pipe, will hang, far away [from me] on an aged pine, utterly forgot by me, or else, transmuted, you will, [with the aid of native Muses, sound forth a truly British strain. Why, pray, [speak I thus]? One man may not, one man may not hope [to achieve] all things [i.e. to win fame by working in Latin and in English both]. It is recompense in plenty, and high glory, too, for me (even though I be unknown to endless time, and utterly without glory from the world without, should the yellow-tressed Usa [the Ouse], and [he that drinks the Alanus [the River Alan], and Abra [the Humber], crowded with whirling eddies, and every grove of Treanta [the Trent], and my beloved Thames, before all others, and the Tamura [The Tamar], swart with metals, and the Orcades in the furthermost billows learn my songs.

> *Go home, unpastured, my lambs:*
> *Your master has no leisure now.*

All these [plans and dreams] I was guarding jealously for you, [Damon, under the pliant bark of the laurel, these, and more as well, and the cups, too, that were given to me by Manso, by Manso, not the least glory of the Chalcidian [Cumaean, Italian] strand, cups two in number, wondrous creations of skill, given to me by Manso, himself a marvel. He had graven them round with a double theme. In the midst are the billows of the Red Sea, and fragrance-bearing spring, [the long shores of Araby, and forests dripping with balsam. Among the trees is Phœnix, bird divine, without its like on earth, gleaming darkly with parti-coloured wings, watching Aurora as she rises from the glassy billows. Elsewhere are the sky, spreading without end, and [mighty Olympus. Here—who would think it?—is Love, too, with his quiver painted amidst a cloud, Love with his gleaming armoury, his torches, and his darts touched with the colour of bronze. Not trivial souls and the ignoble hearts of the rabble does he smite thence [from the cloud, or, perhaps, with these weapons]: but, rolling his flaming eyes, he scatters his shafts, always straight upward, through the [ɪ heavenly spheres, and never looks with glance askant to ply downward blows. Through such strokes holy minds are set ablaze, and shapes of the gods themselves.

You, too, have a place among the gods—no elusive hope beguiles me, Damon: you, too, surely have a place among them, for to what other place would your sweet and holy candour have made her way, whither your snow-white manhood? It is not right, in heaven's eyes, to seek *you* within Lethæan Orcus. Tears fit not *you*: so I will weep no more. Go, get ye gone afar, tears. Damon dwells now in the pure ether, Damon the pure possesses the ether, with his foot he has dashed aside the rainbow. Amid the souls of the heroes, and amid gods that live for ever he is quaffing ethereal draughts, and is drinking joys with holy lips.

Now that you have received your due rights in heaven, stand by me, at my right hand, graciously give me your favour, by whatsoever name you are called, whether you are to be my Damon, or with friendlier feeling you hear 'Diodati', that name divine by which all they that dwell in the skies are to know you, though the woods will still call you Damon.

Because the crimson flush of modesty, and youth without stain were your pleasure, because you ne'er tasted the joys of the marriage couch, see! virginal honours are reserved for you. With your bright head encircled by a radiant crown, and carrying the gladsome shade of the broad-leaved palm, you will consummate, eternally, immortal nuptials, where there is singing, where the lyre revels madly, mingled with choirs beatific, and festal orgies run riot, in bacchante fashion, with the thyrsus of Zion.

X.

Jan. 23. 1646.

To *John Rouse*, Librarian of the University of Oxford.

[Latin on p. 169.]

About a book of poems that had been lost. The librarian was asking that the book should be sent to him anew, that he might place it with others of my books in the general library.

Strophe 1.

Twin books, rejoicing in a single robe [i.e. binding], bright, it may be, with double leaves of laurel [i.e. with two title-pages], and with neatness [of contents] not overlaboured, neatness that a boyish hand bestowed on you, an earnest, zealous hand, but as yet no sure poet's hand, while that poet, wandering where he would, frolicked now in the green places, still untainted of the people [i.e. had not yet taken part

Appendix II.

in matters political], and, far from the beaten tracks, gave free course to his native lute, or, presently, in like manner with a Daunian quill struck out for them that were about him a song brought from far-off lands, the while he scarce touched the ground with his foot,

Antistrophe 1.

Who filched you, tiny book, who filched you by guile from your brothers, when, sent from the city, because a learned friend made ceaseless entreaties, you were pressing along the glorious path towards the cradle of Father Thames's dark-blue stream, where are the limpid fonts of Aonia's daughters, and the holy Bacchic dances, known to all the world as the sky revolves through the immeasurable cycles of time, aye, destined to be famous into endless ages?

Strophe 2.

My one prayer is that some god, or some one born of a god, pitying [the worth that our race had in ancient times—if only we have rendered atonement in full measure for our sins of earlier days, for our ease made degenerate by soft luxury—, may some god, I say, sweep away the godless uprisings of fellow-citizens [against citizens], and, by his holy power, bring back once more life-giving pursuits, and the Muses, [now without their proper seats, banished, now, from wellnigh every nook and corner of the land of England's sons, and may that god stab through and through, with darts from Apollo's quiver, the birds that [threaten us with loathly talons, and may he drive away Phineus's pestilent brood far, far away from the streams of Pegasus.

Antistrophe 2.

Little book, though by the lying faith of the messenger, or, if you will, by his drowsy negligence, you have strayed, once, from the company of your brothers—it may be that some grot keeps you, or [some hiding-place, where, perchance, you are rubbed by the vile, horny hand of some tasteless huckster—, rejoice and be exceeding glad! A new hope is gleaming upon you, a hope that you can escape the deeps of Lethe, and mount, by the oarage of your wings, to the courts [of Jove on high.

Strophe 3.

For Rouse desires you to be his own peculiar property, and he complains that, though you were promised to him, you are wanting to the fair number, and he begs that you shall come to him, to Rouse, to whose careful keeping the glorious memorials of men have been [assigned. He would fain have given you too a place in the holy penetralia o'er which he presides, faithful warder of works that never die, custodian of a treasure more glorious than that o'er which Ion presided, [famous child of Erechtheus's daughter, in the richly laden temple of the god that was his sire [Apollo], golden tripods, and gifts to Delphi, treasures of Ion, son of Actæan [Attic] Creusa.

Appendix II.

Antistrophe 3.

Therefore you shall go to view the lovely groves of the Muses; you shall go again to the house divine wherein Phœbus dwells in the Vale of Oxford, holding less dear Delos and the twin-cleft peak of Parnassus. You shall go in honour, after you too, having won a peerless destiny, shall, prevailed on by the entreaties of an auspicious friend, quit my side. There you will be read among the lofty names of authors, age-old beacons and true glories alike of the Grecian and the Latin race.

Epode.

You, it seems at last, were not empty, idle things, toils of mine, whatever my barren intellect poured forth. I am bidding you now, late though it be, to hope for a calm and quiet rest, a rest that shall be done with envy, I bid you hope for the blest abodes that kindly Hermes and the skilful guardianship of Rouse will vouchsafe you, abodes into which the wanton tongue of the rabble will not make its way, from which the throngs of worthless readers will speed afar. But our latest children's children, and an age of sounder minds will, mayhap, from hearts untainted, apply juster judgements to all things. Then, when envy and malice shall be buried, if we deserve aught, the sound minds of after days will know it, thanks to Rouse's favour.

The ode consists of three strophes, as many antistrophes, and finally, one epode as a close. Though the strophes and the antistrophes do not correspond either in the number of verses, or exactly everywhere with fixed, unvarying cola, nevertheless we have divided them in this fashion, being concerned that they may be read conveniently rather than that they may be chanted after the fashion of the ancient measures.

Otherwise, it had been more proper, perhaps, to call this sort of writing 'monostrophic'. The metres are, in part, κατὰ σχέσιν, i.e. in correlation, responsive, in part ἀπολελυμένα, i.e. free from such restraint of correlation. The Phalæcian verses twice admit a spondee in the third foot. Catullus [in such verses] admits a spondee at will in the second foot.

A READER'S GUIDE
TO MILTON

Compiled by
W. SKEAT
Sometime Scholar of Christ's College

NOTE TO THE READER'S GUIDE.

Owing to the universal element in Milton's knowledge (extending to the utmost limits of the erudition of his time), no really exhaustive glossary to his poems is possible within the limits of the space here available. Every effort, therefore, has been made in the present guide to concentrate mainly upon obscurer words and passages. Only, in 'border-line' cases it has been thought better to include rather than omit.

The subject-matter of the Latin poems has, for the first time, been annotated in a Milton glossary, and a very considerable body of additional material is thus made readily accessible, not only to readers who are Latin scholars, but also to those who are not. As these poems, for the most part, were written during Milton's youth, many of them belonging to his Cambridge University period, they possess unique importance: they provide much material for a re-valuation of Milton's character as a whole, and for a fresh study of the development of his genius.

The references to these Latin poems are distinguished by the abbreviation, **Lat. P.** To meet the difficulties arising from a different arrangement of the Sonnets in modern editions, the references to the Sonnets in the English poems include, in each case, the opening words.   **W. S.**

LIST OF ABBREVIATED TITLES HERE EMPLOYED.

On the Morning of Christ's Nativity	Nat. Od.
The Passion	Pass.
On Time	Time.
Upon the Circumcision	Circ.
At a Solemn Musick	Mus.
An Epitaph on the Marchioness of Winchester	March. Win.
On May morning	May morn.
On Shakspear	Shaks.
On the University Carrier	Univ. Carr.
L'Allegro	L'All.
Il Penseroso	Il Pens.
Sonnets	Sonn.
Sonnets (Italian)	Sonn. Ital.
Arcades	Arc.
Lycidas	Lyc.
A Mask (Comus)	Com.
On the Death of a fair Infant	D. F. I.
At a Vacation Exercise	Vac. Ex.
Translation (Horace)	Trans. Hor.
On the new forcers of Conscience, etc.	Forc. Consc.
A Collection of Passages translated, etc.	Trans.*

(with name of author)

LATIN POEMS:
    (a) Elegies, from first to seventh   El. i, etc.
    (b) Sylvae, from first to tenth, abbreviation of
        M.'s Latin titles as follows :

Sylv. i	Sylv. vi
Sylv. ii	Sylv. vii
Sylv. iii	Sylv. viii
Sylv. iv	Sylv. ix
Sylv. v	Sylv. x

    (c) Epigrams (Bomb. i to v); Leonor. i to 3, etc.,
        Rustic. ; Salm. 1 and 2.

PARADISE LOST	P.L. i to xii
PARADISE REGAINED	P.R. i to iv
SAMSON AGONISTES	S. Ag.

[* References to the translations made by Joseph Washington in 1692, which Mr. John Gawsworth has recently shown to have been included in Mitford's edition by inadvertence, have here been omitted.]

A READER'S GUIDE TO MILTON.

ABADDON : the Pit of Hell (strictly the name of its angel, Rev. ix. 11) ; P.R. iv. 624.

ABARIM : the Mts. of Moab (E. of Jordan), including Nebo and Pisgah ; P.L. i. 408.

ABASSIN : Abyssinian or Ethiopian (the Abyssinians still call their country Itiopia) ; P.L. iv. 280. See also AMARA.

ABBANA : Abana, 'r. of Damascus' (2 Kings v. 12) ; P.L. i. 469.

ABDIEL (lit. 'Servant of God') : a seraph, who rebukes Satan's seditious speech, and (later) brings him to his knees in battle ; P.L. v. 802, 896, vi. 111, 171, 369.

ABRA : uncertain if Humber or Severn (*Columbia Trans.* gives, in brackets, 'Humber') ; Lat. P.-Sylv. ix. 176.

ABSYRTUS : see ÆGIALEUS.

ACADEME : Plato's 'Academy', the site of which was recently rediscovered. (*Journ. Hellenic Studies,* liii, liv) ; P.R. iv. 244, 278 ; Lat. P.–El. vii, *Epilogue* 5 ('Academĭa') ; Sylv. v. 35 ('Academi decus' = Plato).

ACADEMIA (scanned Academĭa) : (*a*) Cambridge ' University ' ; Lat. P.–El. ii. 21–4.
  (*b*) Plato's Academy ; Lat. P.–El. vii, *Epilogue* 5). [See ACADEME, *supra.*]

ACCARON (Vulgate reading) : Ekron (now Akir in Wadi Surar, 5 m. SE. of Ramleh), one of the five chief Philistine cities ; P.L. i. 466 ; Ecron, in S.Ag. 981.

ACHAEMENIAN : ancient royal House of Persia, 521–331 B.C. ; Lat. P.–El. i. 65.

ACHELOUS' DAUGHTER : a title of the Sirens, or water-nymphs (A. being the greatest Gk. river) ; Lat. Epigr. Leonor. iii. 2.

ACHERON : (*a*) a river of Hades ; P.L. ii. 578. Two rivers in Greece and one in S. Italy (Bruttium), so called, were held to be connected with Hades ; cp. Lat. P.–Sylv. ii. 7, 72.
  (*b*) Hades itself ; Com. 604.

ACQUIST, sb. : acquisition ; S.Ag. 1755.

ACROCERAUNIAN (Chain) : the Mountains mentioned formed a Range in Epirus (not, as usual, the Ceraunian Range in the Caucasus) ; Lat. P.–Sylv. iv. 81.

ACTÆON : first k. of Attica ; hence Actæan = ' Attic ' ; Sylv. x. 60.

ADAMANT : see DIAMOND.

ADDREST, prepared ; S.Ag. 729 ; cp. 731.

ADES (i.e. Hades) : P.L. ii. 964.

ADIABENE : the district of Mosul or Mossul (which is the modern city replacing Nineveh) in Assyria proper, formerly part of ancient Parthia ; P.R. iii. 320.

ADMIRE vb. to wonder ; P.L. ii. 677 and numerous other passages.

A Reader's Guide.

ADMIT, vb. to approve (Newton): to commit; P.L. viii. 657.

ADONIS: (*a*) the youthful hunter beloved of Venus; Com. 999; P.L. ix. 440; cp. Lat. P.–El. i. 62; Sylv. iv. 63.
(*b*) the river; P.L. i. 450.

ADRAMELEK: a rebel angel named from the god of Sepharvaim on the Euphrates; P.L. vi. 365.

ADRIA (Hadria): the Adriatic; P.L. i. 520.

ADUST: burnt up, reduced by fire; P.L. xii. 635.

ÆACUS: judge of the Dead; Lat. P.–Sylv. i. 45.

ÆGÆON: a Titan, here the ÆGÆAN personified; Lat. P.-Sylv. iv. 59.

ÆGERIA (i.e. Egeria): Lat. P.–Sylv. vii. 35.

ÆGIALEUS or Ægialus (also known as Absyrtus): brother of Medea, by whom he was murdered; Lat. P.–Sylv. i. 20.

ÆGLE: the name of some musical friend of M. himself and C. Diodati, described by M. as the 'd. of Baucis' (the pious wife of Philemon); Lat. P.–Sylv. ix 89.

ÆMATHIAN: see EMATHIAN

ÆMILIAN ('Way'): this Roman Road, built by M. Æmilius Lepidus, was part of the Flaminian Way, and was continued by Æ. to Placentia (Piacenza). It led to the North, the Appian to the South; P.R. iv. 67–9.

ÆOLIAN charms: songs of Alcaeus and Sappho; P.R. iv. 257.

ÆOLIDES: s. of Æolus, i.e. Cephalus, trad. grands. of Æolus; Lat. P.–El. v. 51. See CEPHALUS.

ÆOLUS: see HIPPOTADES.

ÆSCULAPIUS: Lat. P.–El. ii. 10; Sylv. i. 27–8.

ÆSON: f. of Jason, made young again by Medea (Ov. Met. vii. 162, etc.); Lat. P.–El. ii. 8; Sylv. viii. 75.

ÆTHIOPIANS: Lat. P.–El. v. 31. See ETHIOPE.

ÆTNEAN: Sicilian; Lat. P.–Sylv. i. 46.

ÆTHON, one of the coursers of the Sun; Lat. P.–El. iv. 33.

AFER (the 'African'): WSW. wind; P.L. x. 702.

AFFRONT (= 'confront'): encounter; P.L. i. 391; S.Ag. 531.

AFRICAN, the: (*a*) Hannibal; Sonn. to Sir H. Vane (Vane, young in yeares), 4.
(*b*) Scipio Africanus ('hee sirnam'd of *Africa*'; the ref. here is to his chivalry towards a lady betrothed to a Spaniard (Aluccius)—Livy, xxvi. 50); P.R. ii. 199, iii. 34, 101; P.L. ix. 510.

AGONISTES: combatant.

AGRICAN, K. of Tartary: famous for his (alleged) army of 2,000,000 men and his siege of Albracca in Cathay, undertaken to capture Angelica, d. of Gallaphrone, K. of Cathay; the story is taken from Boiardo's romance of *Orlando Innamorato*, bk. i.; P.R. iii. 338–9; cp. Ariosto, *Orlando Furioso* 3rd ed. (1634), xxxiv. 72, ll. 58, 79. ll. 5–8 Sir J. Harington's translation.

AHAB: Lat. P.–El. iv. 99.

A Reader's Guide.

AIALON : Ajalon (now *Yalo*) ; P.L. xii. 266.

AIR, MIDDLE : see 'MIDDLE AIR'.

ALADULE : greater Armenia—named from Aladules, the last K. of A., slain by the Turks under Selim I ; P.L. x. 435.

ALAN : the R. Allen or Alaun ; Col. Trans. says 'Alan' ; Lat. P.–Sylv. ix. 175.

ALBIONS : the two lands (or peoples) of Britain (E. and Scotland) ; Lat. P.–Sylv. ii. 3.

ALBRACCA : a city in Cathay ; P.L. iii. 339 ; see AGRICAN and CATHANIAN COAST.

ALCAIRO ('Cairo') : used by M. for Memphis. 'Cairo' is an abbreviation of El- or Al-cairo = AL-KAHIRA, the 'victorious' (city) or 'Conqueress' (= Lat. *Augusta*) because built in 968 A.D., when the planet Mars (Ar. *Kahir*) was in the ascendant, by the general of the first Fatimite Sultan of Egypt ; P.L. i. 718.

ALCESTIS : d. of Pelias, who died to redeem her husband Admetus from death, and was brought back from Hades by Heracles ; Sonn. xix. (Methought I saw) 2.

ALCHYMIE ('the sounding') : a trumpet, made of an amalgam of the alchemists called 'alchemy gold' or 'alchemy' ; P.L. ii. 517.

ALCIDES : Hercules, as being s. of Amphitryon, and grandson of Alcæus ; P.L. ii. 542 ; P.R. iv. 565 ; Lat. P.–El. vii. 40 (Hercules) ; Sylv. i. 10, ii. 28 (s. of Amphitryon).

ALCINOUS : K. of the Phæacians, famous in Homer (Od. vii) ; Vac. Ex. 48–52 ; P.L. v. 341, ix. 441 ; Lat. P.–El. iii. 43–4.

ALEIAN FIELD (expld. as the 'Field of Wandering' from Gk. ἄλη) : a tract in Cilicia E. of the r. Sarus in A.M., not far from Tarsus, where Bellerophon is supposed to have fallen from the winged steed, Pegasus—see Hom. Il. vi. 201 ; P.L. vii. 19.

ALEXANDER : (Pellean Conquerour) P.R. ii. 196 ; (s. of Philip) P.R. iii. 32 ; (s. of Olympias and Ammonian Jove) Lat. P.–El. iv. 25–6 ; cp. P.L. ix. 509 ; P.R. iii. 84, iv. 252, etc.

ALGARSIFE : eldest s. of Cambuscan, (q.v.) ; Il Pens. 111.

ALGIERS : one of the five Barbary states in N. Africa ; P.L. xi. 404.

ALLARM'D : prepared for battle (It. '*all' arme*', 'to arms') as in P.L. iv. 985.

ALLEY : an embowered path or walk in a wood ; Com. 311, 990 ; P.L. iv. 626 ; PR. ii. 203.

ALMANSOR : acc. to Masson the famous second Abbasid Caliph of Bagdad (754–5 A.D.) conqueror of N. Africa ; P.L. xi. 403.

ALP : used for any high mountains ; P.L. ii. 620 ; S.A. 628.

ALPHEUS : the chief r. of Peloponnesus, rising in SE. Arcadia, sinks underground more than once in the limestone country, and, rising again, falls into the Ionian sea. Hence the story of his reappearing in Sicily in the fountain of Arethusa, and the symbol of pastoral verse ; Lycidas, 132 ; Arc. 30.

A Reader's Guide.

AMALTHEA : (*a*) Nurse of infant Zeus ; P.R. ii. 356.
  (*b*) one of the names of the m. of Bacchus ; P.L. iv. 278 ; see NYSEIAN ISLE.

AMARA (Amhara) : (whence 'Amharic') Mt. range in Abyssinia, the retreat where the Emperors of Abyssinia educated their sons (cp. Johnson's *Rasselas*) ; P.L. iv. 281.

AMARANT (i.e. AMARANTH) : lit. 'unfading'; the 'immortal' flower of Paradise ; P.L. iii. 352 ; cp. P.L. xi. 78.

AMATHUSIAN : i.e. Cyprian, Aphrodite from the shrine of Aphrodite at Amathus in Cyprus ; Lat. P.-El. vii. 1.

AMAZONIAN VIRGIN : Queen Elizabeth. (Orig. Lat. scans Thermŏdŏontea *sic*; for Thermōdontea, lit. ' Thermodontean Virgin ', Thermōdon being the chief Amazonian river) ; Lat. P.-Sylv. ii. 105 ; cp. P.L. ix. 1111.

AMBIENT : surrounding ; P.L. vi. 481, vii. 89.

AMBITION : lit. ' going round ' to collect votes or get favour (as in Lat.), soliciting or canvassing ; S.A. 247.

AMERCE : to punish ; P.L. i. 609.

AMERICAN : American Indian ; P.L. ix. 1116.

AMICE : the cape and hood worn by Religious Orders ; it was lined with (or made of) grey fur—hence M.'s 'amice gray' of Morning ; P.R. iv. 427 ; Cp. Com. 189 (of Evening).

AMMIRAL : Flagship ; P.L. i. 294.

AMMON : (*a*) the god, see HAMMON.
  (*b*) the Ammonites (collectively) ; Ps. lxxxiii. 25.

AMPHIARAUS, prince of Argos, one of the ' Seven against Thebes '; the earth opening, swallowed him up with his chariot ; Lat. P.-El. vii. 84.

AMPHISBAENA : traditionally, a double snake with head at each end (really a lizard with indistinguishable head and tail) ; in M. a snake ; P.L. x. 524.

AMPHITRITE : wife of Poseidon, hence queen of the sea ; Com. 921.

AMPHITRYON'S SON : i.e. Hercules, stepson of A. ; Lat. P.-Sylv. ii. 28.

AMYMONE : d. of Danaus, beloved of Poseidon ; P.R. ii. 188.

AMYNTORIDES : (s. of Amyntor) = PHŒNIX (*b*), q.v.

ANCHISES, f. of Æneas : see BRUTUS.

ANDROMEDA : the constellation ; P.L. iii. 559 ; see ETHIOPE (QUEEN).

ANGELICA : d. of Gallaphrone, q.v.

ANGOLA (cap. St. Paul) : Loanda, Portuguese E. Africa ; P.L. xi. 401.

ANTIC : (*a*) sb. a performer of ' antics ', a clown or buffoon ; S.Ag. 1325.
  (*b*) antick adj., app. ' antique ', Il. Pens. 158.

ANTIGONUS : K. of Judea ; *not* supported by the R. and captured by the Parthians, as suggested by M. ; the Parthians supported him against his uncle, Hyrcanus (he was eventually captured, and executed, 37 B.C., by the Romans) ; P.R. iii. 367.

ANTIOCHUS : i.e. A. Epiphanes, K. of Syria, 168 B.C. ; P.R. iii. 163.

ANTIOPA : a princess of Thebes, beloved of Zeus, and m. of Amphion ; P.R. ii. 187.

A Reader's Guide.

ANTIPATER : f. of Herod the Great, the wealthy noble of Edom, who became procurator of Judea (47 B.C.) and died by poison, 43 B.C. ; P.R. ii. 423.

ANUBIS (in Eg. hieroglyphs *INPU* or *ANUP*) : the Jackal-god, s. of Set ; local deity of the Necropolis at Abydos ; represented by Gks. and R. as dog-headed. He was guardian of the Scale at the *Psychostasia* or weighing of the heart in Eg. funerary ritual. For the ' dog Anubis' see Nat. Od. 212.

AONIAN MOUNT : i.e. Mount Helicon : one of the chief haunts of the Muses ; P.L. i. 15 ; Lat. P.–El. iv. 29, vi. 17 ; Sylv. i. 32, x. 21 (Aonides = the Muses).

APPAID : satisfied ; P.L. xii. 401.

APPELLANT : challenger ; S.A. 1220.

APPIAN (' Way') : the Roman road built by Appius Claudius leading S. to Brundusium ; P.R. iv. 68.

AQUILO (Gk. Boreas) : the N. Wind ; D.F.I., 8 ; Lat. P.–Sylv. iv. 55.

ARACHOSIA : extreme E. of Parthia (now extending roughly from the NE. part of Baluchistan into Afghanistan) ; P.R. iii. 316.

ARACYNTH : Mt. range placed by late writers between Bœotia and Attica ; Lat. P.–Sylv. ii. 65. [But the true Aracynthus was on the Ætolian coast, 100 m. away from the site here suggested.]

ARAXES : now *Eraskh*, or *Aras*, a r. of Armenia, entering the Caspian ; P.R. iii. 271.

ARBORETS : shrubs or saplings forming underwood or ' bush ' ; P.L. ix. 437.

ARCADY, STAR OF : the Great Bear. The nymph of *Arcady*, Kallisto, beloved by Jupiter, was turned into a she-bear by him to deceive Juno. But she was slain by Juno and set among the stars as Arctos by Jupiter, her son Arcas becoming the lesser Bear ; Com. 341. See CALISTO.

ARCH-CHIMIC SUN : i.e. arch-chemist, or supreme alchemist ; metaph. of the sun, whose influence was held to create gems underground ; see P.L. iii. 609–12.

ARCHILOCHUS (Graius . . . vates) : a Gk. poet very famous for invective ; Lat. P.–Sylv. iii. 20 ; see LYCAMBES.

ARCHIMEDES, the celebrated mathematician and engineer of Syracuse (287–212 B.C.). Sonn. xviii. 7 (Cyriack, whose Grandsire).

ARETHUSE : (i.e. the fountain or spring of Arethusa in the I. of Ortygia at Syracuse, for which see ALPHEUS. Here it suggests Sicily, typifying Greek pastoral verse : Arc. 31 ; Lyc. 85.

ARGESTES : prob. here the NW. wind (WSW., Vitruvius, or WNW., Pliny) ; P.L. x. 699.

ARGOB : a city and district in Bashan, E. of Jordan, the country of Og ; later = Trachonitis ; P.L. i. 398.

ARGUS : cruel hundred-eyed guardian of the heifer Io (= Isis) : P.L. xi. 131 ; Lat. P.–Sylv. ii. 185-8 (Aristorides).

ARIEL (lit. ' Lion of God ') : a rebel angel ; P.L. vi. 371 (perhaps from Isaiah xxix. 1 ; of Jerusalem) cp. Ezra viii. 16.

A Reader's Guide.

ARIES : the constellation ; P.L. x. 329 ; Lat. P.-El. iv. 33 ; cp. P.L. iii. 558.

ARIMASPIAN : traditional one-eyed race of Scythia, E. of the Volga, who stole the gold of the Ural mountains from its guardians, the gryphons, to make ornaments for their hair ; P.L. ii. 945.

ARIOC (perhaps from Dan. ii. 14) : a rebel angel ; P.L. vi. 371.

ARION, the poet : (M.'s compliment to his father) ; Lat. P.-Sylv. vi. 60 *Arionii . . . sis nominis hæres.*)

ARISTORIDES (s. of Aristor) : i.e. ARGUS, q.v.

ARISTOTLE (who bred Great Alexander) ; P.R. iv. 25 ; Lat. P.-El. iv. 25.

ARMADA, defeat of the Spanish : Lat. P.-Sylv. ii. 102-4.

ARMORIC : adj. ' of Brittany ' ; P.L. i. 581 ; Lat. P.-Sylv. ix. 165.

ARNON : r. on N. boundary of Moab, entering the Dead Sea ; P.L. i. 399.

AROER : t. on N. side of the Arnon ; P.L. i. 407-11.

ARREEDE, vb. to advise ; P.L. iv. 962.

ARSACES (i.e. Arsäces) : he revolted against the Seleucids, and founded the Parthian Empire, with a capital at Ctesiphon, about 256 B.C. ; P.R. iii. 295. See CTESIPHON.

ARSENAL, SHOOK THE : M. is paraphrasing Aristoph. *Acharn.* 530-1 and 539 ; ἐντεῦθεν ὀργῇ Περικλέης Ὀλύμπιος | ἤστραπτ᾽ ἐβρόντα συνεκύκα τὴν Ἑλλάδα | . . . κἀντεῦθεν ἤδη πάταγος ἦν τῶν ἀσπίδων. App. he is generalizing too (as usual) and is thinking of the entire course of these wars ; 'resistless eloquence' referring to Athenian oratory as a whole (with special recollection of Pericles, ' thundering and lightening ', and Demosthenes). The defeats of Artaxerxes by the Greeks took place in the latter half of the 5th c. B.C., the speeches of Demosthenes against Philip belong to the latter part of the 4th. I have to thank Mr. A. J. Hughes for pointing out that the ἐκκλησία was sometimes held in the Piræus (in the theatre on the NW. slope of Munichia) ; Dem. *De fals. Leg.* 67 ἠκκλησιάζετε . . . ἐν τῷ Πειραιεῖ. 'Shook the Arsenal' is a paraphrase of l. 539 ; M. must certainly have read of the famous *armamentarium* in the Piræus, built by the architect Philo, where ' 1000 ships could lie ', though this was not built till the last quarter of that century ; P.R. iv. 267-71.

ARTAXATA : ancient capital of Armenia, on the Araxes ; P.R. iii. 292.

ARTFUL : artistic, skilful, beautiful ; Com. 494 (artfull) ; Sonn. xvii. (Lawrence, etc.) artful ; cp. P.R. iv. 33.

ARTHUR, K. (UTHER'S SON, M.'s proposed subject for Epic) : see P.L. i. 580 ; Lat. P.-Sylv. viii. 81-2, ix. 166-8 ; cp. P.R. ii. 360 ; Pr. Wks. *Hist. of Brit.*, etc.

ARTIST (' the Tuscan ') : Galileo (q.v.) ; P.L. i. 288.

ARVIRAGUS : Lat. P.-Sylv. ix. 164. See BRENNUS.

ASCALONITE : inhabitant of Ascalon (Ashkelon, Askelon) ; S.Ag. 138.

ASHTAROTH : (*a*) the Hebrew equivalent of ASTARTE, the Phœnician Moon-goddess (q.v.) ; Nat. Od. 200 ; P.R. iii. 417. (*b*) spelt Astoreth, identified with the rebel angels ; P.L. i. 438.

ASMODEUS : (*a*) a lustful angel of the Incubus type mentioned in the Bk. of

A Reader's Guide.

Tobit, iii. 8, 17. After destroying seven husbands of Sarah, d. of Raguel, was driven off by Tobias, s. of Tobit, who by advice of Raphael burnt the heart and liver of a fish to expel him, and drove him to Egypt; P.L. iv. 168.

(b) identified by M. with one of the fallen angels; Asmodai, P.R. ii. 151; or Asmadai, P.L. vi. 365.

ASOPUS : here prob. the Bœotian A. entering the Eubœan Sea; Lat. P.-Sylv. ii. 66.

ASPECTS (astrol.). See Trine, Square, Sextile, Conjunction, Opposition, and Synod.

ASPHALTICK POOL : the Dead Sea ; P.L. i. 411.

ASPHALTUS : pitch ; P.L. i. 729.

ASPRAMONT : a t. 6 m. N. of Nice, famous in medieval romances ; P.L. i. 583.

ASSASSINATE, vb. : to wound by treachery ; S.A. 1109.

ASSYRIAN, ad. : (a) Assyrian Mount, i.e. Niphates (q.v.) ; P.L. iv. 126.
  (b) A. Priest ; Lat. P.-Sylv. v. 29. See BEROSSUS.
  (c) A. Flood, the Euphrates river ; P.R. iii. 436.
  (d) A. Queen, Ishtar, the Assyrian Venus ; Com. 1002.
  (e) A. Garden, i.e. Eden (q.v.) ; P.L. iv. 285.
  (f) A. Army, El. iv. 144.

ASTARTE, ASTORETH : Ishtar, the great Love-goddess of Mesopotamia and Phoenicia, goddess of the Moon and Evening Star, identified with Aphrodite or Venus : P.L. i. 438, 439, etc.

ASTRACAN (Astrakhan): t. of Russia (at mouth of Volga); P.L. x. 432.

ASTRÆA : (a) personified as the 'star-bright' maiden (Virgo Justissima), goddess of Justice ; Lat. P.-El. iv. 81.
  (b) the constellation Virgo 'Astrea' ; P.L. iv. 998.

ATABALIPA (the Spanish form of Atahualpa) : last Inca Emperor of Peru, famed for his wealth ; P.L. xi. 409 ; cp. Lat. P.-Sylv. vi. 94.

ATHENIAN DAMSEL : Oreithyia, a princess of Athens, d. of K. Erectheus ; straying beyond the Ilissus she was carried off by *Boreas*, who came from his cave in Thrace ; D.F.I. 9.

ATLANTEAN ('shoulders') : powerful as those of Atlas, supporter of the firmament ; P.L. ii. 306 ; Lat. P.-Sylv. v. 24, vi. 40.

ATLANTICK : (a) 'sisters'; the seven daughters of Atlas, who, raised to heaven, became the Pleiads; P.L. x. 674 ; cp. Pleiades P.L. vii. 374.
  (b) A. Stone : called *giallo antico* ; Numidian marble quarried near Mt. Atlas ; P.R. iv. 115. See Blakeney (notes).

ATLAS' GRANDSON : Hermes, whose mother Maia was d. of A. ; Lat. P.-Sylv. viii. 72.

ATREUS' SON : here Agamemnon ; Lat. P.-El. ii. 16.

ATROPATIA (or ATROPATENE) : N. Media, extending to the Caspian, and S. of the Araxes ; P.R. iii. 319.

ATROPOS : properly not a Fury, but one of the three Fates who bore the shears, and cut the thread of life (March. Win. 28) ; M. substitutes Persephone for Atropos in Lat. P.-Sylv. i. 37.

A Reader's Guide.

ATTRITE (of the air): converted or reduced to fire by friction; P.L. x. 1073.

ATTICK BOY: Cephalus, beloved of Eos (Aurora), who gave him the unerring spear with which he unwittingly slew his wife Procris; Il Pens. 124; he was grandson of Æolus (Æolides); cp. Lat. P.-El. iii. 67, v. 51, vii. 38.

AURAN: (Hauran) part of Bashan, on the E. frontier of Palestine; P.L. iv. 211.

AUSONIAN: Italian (poet. for Italy); P.L. i. 739; Lat. P.-El. i. 70; Sylv. ii. 49, x. 7.

AUSTER: the S. wind; Lat. P.-El. iv. 36.

AUSTRIAN WEALTH: i.e. of the Emperor; Lat. P.-Sylv. vi. 94.

AUTUMNAL STARS: Stars such as Sirius, in the autumn, were believed to bring much mischief to men; P.R. iv. 619.

AVERNUS (now *Lago d'Averno*) near Cumæ and Baiæ: trad. entrance to Hades; hence Hades; Lat. P.-El. ii. 17.

AZAZEL: the name of one of the rebel angels, app. from Levit. xvi. 8 (A.V. marg.). Acc. to A.V. 'the scapegoat', but acc. to Newton 'brave in retreat' (either sense would suit M.'s purpose as a name for Satan's Standard-bearer); P.L. i. 534.

AZOTUS: Ashdod (now *Esdud*): anciently the chief seat of the worship of Dagon; P.L. i. 464. ASDOD also occurs; S.Ag. 981.

AZZA: Gaza (now *Azzah*) once the capital city of Philistia; S.Ag. 147; (Gaza) S.Ag. 98.

BAALIM: the collective title for all the rebel angels named after those Mesopotamian and Palestinian gods who were named after the chief Babylonian (Semitic) god Belu (lit. Lord) the god of Babylon. His female counterpart was Ishtar, whence Astarte or Ashtaroth (a collective name as well); P.L. i. 422. See BABEL.

BABEL ('Tower of'): early Semitic name of the Great Tower of Babylon. the city whose name in the Babylonian tongue meant the 'Gate of God' (*Bab ili = Bab El*) being named after the chief Bab. god, *Marduk*, whose title was *Belu* or *Bel*. A modern excavator (Koldewey) has discovered the foundations of the tower and has shown that the tower was 'no dream', but an amazingly lofty and solid rectangular tower of brick compacted with bitumen in several successive terraces of respectively diminishing proportions; the total height of these should apparently have reached an altitude of approximately 300 ft. Such towers, called ZIKKURAT (or 'ZIGGURAT') i.e. mountain peaks, were built on (to their chief Temples only) by the early Sumerian conquerors or settlers in Babylon, app. in substitution for the actual mountain tops on which, they held, their chief gods should in preference be worshipped. From these, through the Arab minaret, was derived the 'Spire'. A second Tower stood, and still stands, more than 150 ft. high near Babylon at Borsippa, left incomplete by the king who began it; it was completed by Neb. II. Some, like that at Ur, also had cultivated plants or trees on their terraces, recalling Nebuchadnezzar's 'Hanging Gardens' at Babylon which became one of the Seven Wonders of the World; P.L. i. 694. Cp. P.L. iii. 466, 468.

A Reader's Guide.

BAAL-ZEBUB : the name under which Baal was worshipped by the Philistines (at Ecron) ; S.Ag. 1231. For Bëëlzebub see P.L. i. 81, 271, ii. 299, 378.

BACTRA (now *Balkh*) in Afghan Turkistan : a great city of Bactria, or Bactriana, and part of the Persian Empire. It was destroyed by Ghengis Khan in A.D. 1220 ; P.L. x. 433 ; P.R. iii. 285.

BALEARIC 'WHALES', i.e. Islands : Lat. P. Sylv. iv. 59.

BANKS, benches : S.Ag. 1610.

BATES ('at noone') : if we may judge by S.Ag. 1538, M. certainly meant 'baits', i.e. 'takes refreshment', the allusion being explained by his just having reached the opening line of the *Twelfth* Book ; this then would be the inward significance of the line : 'As one who in his journey, bates at noon' : (i.e. Twelve o'clock) ; P.L. xii. 1.

BALSARA : Bassora, or Basra, on the Pers. Gulf ; P.R. iii. 321.

BARCA : an inland town of Cyrenaica, founded by a Graeco-Libyan colony, mostly seceders from Cyrene, *c.* 554 B.C. Destroyed by the Persian satrap of Egypt, Aryandes, in 510 B.C. ; P.L. ii. 904.

BARRICADO, vb. : to barricade or bar off ; P.L. viii. 241.

BARONI, LEONORA : the subject of three of M's Lat. Epigrams. Princess Leonora of Este, here mentioned as beloved of Tasso, was the first of these two Leonoras ; the second was Leonora Baroni of Naples, whose singing was so deeply admired at Rome by Milton. See NAPLES.

BASE : a short skirt or 'jupon', worn by knights on horseback ; P.L. ix. 36.

BATTEL : army ; P.L. vi. 202.

BAUK (i.e. BAULK) your eares : to miss, or spare ; this line, when first drafted, had a reference to the lawyer Prynne, whose ears were cropped by order of the Star-Chamber. Forc. Consc. 17.

BAYONA'S HOLD : a fortified post on the Galician Coast of Spain ; Lyc. 162.

BEAR : to outwatch the Bear meant to sit up all night, since the Bear never sets. Il Pens. 87. Cp. also Lat. P.-Sylv. viii. 28 (gelida . . . sub Arcto). See CYNOSURE and CALISTO.

BEARTH : what the Earth *bears*, or yields ; i.e. her produce (often misprinted *birth*) : I have not, however, found this form in the *Oxford Dictionary*. P.L. ix. 624.

BËËLZEBUB. See BAAL-ZEBUB.

BELGIA : an irregular form of Lat. *Belgium*, used in the early seventeenth century. Lat. P.-El. iii. 12.

BELIAL : the rebel angel who 'came last' (P.L. i. 490), was one of the chiefest among the rebel angels ; it was not a personal name, but indicated the principle of evil (utter worthlessness) ; almost equiv. to antichrist (2 Cor. vi. 15).

BELINUS : one of the chief leaders of the Gauls in their march on Rome ; Lat. P.-Sylv. ix. 164 ; cp. M.'s *Hist. Brit.* (*Pr. Wks.*) v. 179. See BRENNUS.

BELLEROPHON : v. ALEIAN FIELD.

BELLERUS : see FABLE OF BELLERUS.

A Reader's Guide.

BELLONA : Roman war-goddess ; P.L. ii. 922 ; (Enyo = Gk. 'Ἐννώ) cp. Lat. P.–El. iv. 75.

BELUS (i.e. Bel or Baal) : chief god of Babylon, after whom the name of the city (*Babilu*) was called. His early Babylonian title was BELU, ' Lord ', since he was held to be ' Lord ' of all the gods ; P.L. i. 720 ; Lat. P.–Sylv. v. 31. See BABEL.

BEROSUS or BEROSSUS (the ' Assyrian priest ') : priest of Bel at Babylon in third cent. B.C. He wrote a history (mostly lost) in Gk. from the temple archives, describing Babylonia and giving a list of kings down to Cyrus ; Lat. P.–Sylv. v. 29.

BION : the famous Gk. pastoral poet of Smyrna, who fl. about 280 B.C. and died by poison in Sicily, where he had gone to live ; Lat. P.–Sylv. ix. 2.

BISERTA : a city of Tunis well known in medieval romance : P.L. i. 585.

BIZANCE : Byzantium, the name of Constantinople before Constantine made it his capital, and called it after his name ; P.L. xi. 395.

BLACK-MOOR SEA : The Moorish or Morocco Sea ; P.R. iv. 72.

BLEAR : blurring the sight, Com. 155.

BOCCHUS : K. of Gætulia in N. Africa (Mauretania) ; he was father-in-law of Jugurtha ; P.R. iv. 72.

BOLT : vb. tr. either (*a*) (metaph.) = ' boult ', to sift or refine to subtlety, Com. 760 or (*b*) to shoot forth as an arrow ; S.Ag. 1696.

BOND INVIOLABLE (between England and Scotland) : the personal union (*not* Treaty) of the two crowns in King James ; Lat. P.–Sylv. ii. 3.

BONNET : a cap such as was at one time worn by men ; Lyc. 104.

BOÖTES : the constellation ; Lat. P.–El. v. 35 ; Sylv. iii. 51 (Boötis sarraca = Boötes' Wain) ; viii. 36-7.

BOSKY : bushy, Com. 313 ; cp. imbos[k]t in S.Ag. 1700.

BOTCH, sb. : a boil ; P.L. xii. 180.

BOUT, sb. : a bend or ' turn ' ; L'All. 139.

BOY, ATTICK : see ATTICK.

BRENNUS : Bran (or ' Brian '), one of the chief (Sennonian) Gaulish Leaders in the March on Rome which he took in 390 B.C. : Lat. P.–Sylv. ix. 164.

BRIARIOS : the Titan, was the 3rd s. of Uranus (Heaven), of whom Homer (Il. i. 403) says that men called him Ægæon, but the blessed gods called him Briareus. A giant with 50 heads and 100 arms, in older trad. he fought for Zeus against the Titans ; P.L. i. 199 ; Lat. P.–Sylv. iv. 59, where he is named Ægæon.

BRIGANDINE : a coat of mail ; S.Ag. 1120.

BRINDED : more or less broadly striped ; Com. 443 ; P.L. vii. 466.

BRITAIN, BRITISH : P.L. i. 581 ; P.R. iv. 77 ; Sonn. xviii. 2 (Cyriack, whose grandsire) ; cp. Com. 27-9. Also cp. Lat. P.–El. i. 71-84, iv. 87-96 ; Epigr. Bomb. i. 1, iii. 5 ; Sylv. ii. 3 (regna Albionum), 31-4, 95-6, 169, 202, iii. 9-10, viii. 30-48, 84, ix. 161-78, x. 8-10. See also ENGLAND, ENGLISH, and under TROY and BRUTUS.

BROMIUS : the ' roaring ' (wine-god), a name of Bacchus ; Lat. P.–Sylv. ii. 64-5.

A Reader's Guide.

BROWN: see IMBROWN.

BRUTUS (in M.'s projected Epic of Britain): great-grandson of Æneas of Troy, legendary ancestor of the Britons; cp. the lines from *Hist. Brit.*, 7. See also under BRITAIN.

BUDGE, adj.: used of the lambskin or goatskin fur of 'doctors'' hoods, hence—*Fur-hooded* doctors of the Stoic sect; Com. 707.

BULLION DROSS: scum thrown up in founding by the (impure) boiling metal; P.L. i. 704.

BUSIRIS: acc. to Gk. tradition, a K. of Egypt notorious for persecuting foreigners; taken by Raleigh (*Hist. of the World*) for the first oppressor of the Israelites; but M. uses it of the Pharaoh who chased (but was not drowned in chasing) the Israelites. Busiris is also the name of a town in the Delta, now Abousir; P.L. i. 307.

BUSKIN (*a*) a high boot (silver buskind); Arc. 33.
(*b*) the high thick-soled boot of Gk. tragedians; Il Pens. 102.

BUXOM: (*a*) yielding (of the air); P.L. ii. 842, v. 270.
(*b*) (bucksom) lithe and lively; L'All. 24.

CADMEAN: see ECHIONIAN.

CADMEAN: Theban. In orig. Lat. text *Echionio*, Echion being one of the five surviving 'Sparti' who had grown up from the dragon's teeth 'sown' by Cadmus, whom he helped to build Thebes; Lat. P.–Sylv. ii. 65.

CAECIAS: the NE. wind (strictly NE. by E.); P.L. x. 699.

CALABRIA: Calabria is the SW. projection of Italy, app. by extension made to include Bruttium, once famous (acc. to Ovid and others) for the copper mines of Tĕmĕsĕ (Temesaeo ex aere); P.L. ii. 661; cp. Lat. P.–Sylv. ii. 207.

CALCHAS: wisest of the Greek seers at Troy; Lat. P.–El. vi. 69.

CALEDONIAN DYE: i.e. woad; Lat. P.–Sylv. viii. 48.

CALES (in Campania): famous for its wines; P.R. iv. 117.

CALISTO (Callisto): an Arcadian nymph, d. of Lycaon, huntress in Artemis' train, beloved by Zeus, who changed her into a she-bear to deceive Hera, and then into the Great Bear, her s. Arcas becoming the little Bear; P.R. ii. 186. See ARCADY, STAR OF.

CAMBALU (properly Can-baluc or 'City of the Khan'): the former capital of Cathay and residence of the Mongol Emperors; now Pekin, but supposed in M.'s time to be a different city; P.L. xi. 388; see CATHAIAN COAST and PAQUIN.

CAMBALL: (*a*) the younger s. of CAMBUSCAN, q.v.
(*b*) app. a second person of the same name, in love with, and ultimately married to, Canace; Il Pens. 111–12.

CAMBRIDGE: Univ. Carr. i. 8; Sonn. xi. (A book was writ); see also CAME or CAMUS, CIRRHA, HELICON, and ACADEMIA.

CAMBUSCAN: (better Cámbŭscán, i.e. Chingis, Jinghis, Genghis, or Ghengis Khan; i.e. the 'Great' Khan), who had two sons, Camball and Algarsife, and was the subject of Chaucer's *Squire's Tale* (note that in all the Chaucer MSS. the name is given as Cambynskan); Il Pens. 110.

(621)

A Reader's Guide.

CAME (March. Winch. 59) : the Cam ; also CAMUS (Lyc. 103 and Lat. P.– El. i. 11, 89).

CAN (i.e. Kaan, Khan, and 'Cham') : title of the Mongol Emperors of China ; P.L. xi. 388. See also CAMBALU.

CANACE : d. of Cambúscan, eventually wedded not to the s. of Cambúscan, but to another 'Camball' ; Il. Pens. 112. See CAMBALL.

CANDAOR (Candahar or Kandahar) : A city of N. Parthia, now capital of the Province of K. in Afghanistan, 318 m. SW. of Cabul ; P.R. iii. 316.

CANON LAWS : used by M. in irony as an eccles. term ; Com. 808.

CANOPIE : the shadow of the earth cast by the Sun from day to day ; P.L. iii. 556.

CANIE, adj. : made of 'cane' (so-called), but really of bamboo ; P.L. iii. 439.

CAPARISON : a rich cloth covering (for saddle or harness) ; P.L. ix. 35.

CAPHTOR, sons of : i.e. the Philistines ; S.Ag. 1713.

CAPITOL : the temple, not the Hill ; P.R. iv. 47.

CAPITOLINE JOVE : trad. f. of Scipio Africanus ; P.L. ix. 508.

'CARPATHIAN WISARD' : Proteus, the infallible seer, who dwelt in the I. of Carpäthus, between Crete and Rhodes ; Com. 872.

CASBEEN (Casveen or Kasvin) a city in the Elburz Mts., NW. of Teheran, in what was once greater Media ; P.L. x. 436.

CASELLA : an old musician friend of Dante, whom D. describes (Purg. ii. 10) as singing at his request, in Purgatory, the second *Canzone* of his *Convito* ; Sonn. xiii. (Harry, whose tuneful) 12–14.

CASIUS, Mt. : (now *Elkas*, or *Katieh*) the summit of a lofty range of sandstone Hills on the NE. border of Egypt, just S. of the 'SERBONIAN' L. q.v. On its W. flank was the Tomb of Pompey. P.L. ii. 593.

CASPIAN TIGER : C. was the N. part of Media ; Lat. P.–Sylv. ii. 20.

CASSIBELAUNUS : Cassivellaunus, whose head-quarters were (as recent excavations have shown) in the Lea valley, Wheathamstead, some 5–6 m. away from the spot where Verulamium came to be built, in the neighbourhood of St. Albans though still not far from the r. Colne. Lat. P.–Sylv. ix. 149.

CASTALIA's 'WINE' : there were two springs, so called, (*a*) at Delphi, issuing from the fissure between the two cliffs (Phædriades). It should be remembered that the better tradition involved the bathing of the head (and hair) in the Castalian Spring. Cp. Hor. III. iv. 61 explaining Lat. P.–El. iv. 32 ; cp. El. v. 9.
    (*b*) the Spring near Apollo's Grove at Daphne near Antioch (where in the time of Seleucus I the tree into which ('root-bound') Daphne was transformed was still actually shown) ; P.L. iv. 274.

CATAPHRACT (Gk. καταφράκτης) : 'all-armed', horse and man ; S.Ag. 1619.

CATHAIAN COAST : (*Areopagitica*, Cataio) correctly explained as China. But in M.'s time often supposed to be a separate country N. of China (in NE. Siberia ?), with Cambaluc as its capital, and Pekin as the capital of China proper. Actually, however, Cambaluc (q.v.) was Pekin ; cp. P.L. x. 293, xi. 388 (Paquin), 390.

A Reader's Guide.

Causey: causeway; P.L. x. 415.

Cecropian: ancient Athenian (from Cecrops, the first K. of Attica): Lat. P.–Sylv. ix. 56.

Cephalus: beloved by Eos (Dawn), who gave him a never-erring spear, with which he accidentally slew his wife (Procris); Lat. P.–El. iii. 67, vii. 38 (Cydonius . . . Venator).

Cerastes (Gk. κεράστης): a horned serpent; P.L. x. 525.

Ceraunian Range: see Acroceraunian.

Cerberus: Lat. P.–El. vi. 58. See also Erebus.

Ceres' Fields: cornfields; Lat. P.–Sylv. ii. 32; cp. P.L. iv. 981 ('a field of Ceres').

Chaeronea: a city in Boeotia, where the liberties of Greece were destroyed by the victory of Philip of Macedon over the Gk. states in 338 B.C.; Sonn. x. 7 (Daughter to that good Earl).

Chalcidian: Neapolitan, because Naples was traditionally founded by a colony from Chalcis in Euboea: Lat. P.–Sylv. ix. 182; Epigr. *Leonor.* iii. 4. Col. Trans. says from Cumae.

Chalybean temper'd: the Chalybes were famous iron-workers of Scythia; S.Ag. 133.

Cham (i.e. Ham): identified by M. with the 'Lybian Jove' (Ammon) as well as with the Gk. Zeus (Ζεὺς Ἄμμων), the Roman 'Jupiter Ammon', and Egyptian 'Amun' or 'Amun-Ra'; P.L. iv. 276, ix. 508. See Nyseian Isle and cp. Lybic Hammon; Nat. Od. 203.

Champain: flat, level country; P.L. iv. 134, vi. 2; P.R. iii. 257.

Chaonian Woman, the: Olympias (the 'Epirot', the Chaonians being a people of Epirus); Lat. P.–El. iv. 26. See Olympias.

Charlemain: P.L. i. 586; Charlemane P.R. iii. 343. See Fontarabbia.

Charm: Song (esp. used of the songs of birds); P.L. iv. 642, 651.

Charybdis: the Sicilian Whirlpool; Com. 259; P.L. ii. 1020.

Chaump (i.e. Champ), vb.: P.L. iv. 859.

Chebar Flood (now the Khabur): a tributary of the Euphrates. Pass. 37. For 'the Prophet' see Eliah.

Cheek, Sir John: first Professor of Greek at Camb. Univ.; Sonn. xi. (A Book was writ).

Chelmer: identified with the r. in Essex, flowing into Blackwater Bay; Lat. P.–Sylv. ix. 90 (Idumanii . . . fluenti).

Chemos (i.e. Chemosh): see Peor.

Chersonese 'the golden' (P.L. xi. 392); or Chersoness (P.R. iv. 74): the Peninsula of Malacca or Malay Peninsula; see Ophir.

Chester: visited by Charles Diodati, who may have practised there; Lat. P.–El. i. 3. See Diodati.

Cherubim: the names of the Cherubs, as given by M., are usually of biblical origin though not the actual names of Cherubs in the Bible; in several cases the names are chosen with reference to the tasks they have to perform; see Zephon, Ithuriel, Zophiel. M. uses Cherub in the Biblical sense, characteristic of the order being fullness of Knowledge, and Contemplation ; Il Pens. 54.

CHIMERA : (*a*) the three-fold monster, compounded of lion, goat, and serpent, slain by Bellerophon mounted on Pegasus ; see BELLEROPHON. (*b*) other such compound monsters ; Com. 517 ; P.L. ii. 628.

CHIOS : C. wine was one of the costliest Gk. wines as the Caecuban (not here given) of the Roman ; P.R. iv. 118.

CHIRON : the wisest of all the Centaurs, became tutor to Achilles. As s. of Kronos and Philyra, is called Philyreius heros ; Lat. P.-El. iv. 27 ; cp. Sylv. i. 25, viii. 60.

CHLORIS : (*a*) a name of Flora ; Lat. P.-El. iii. 44, iv. 35.
  (*b*) the name given by M. to some mutual friend of himself and Diodati described as living near the r. Chelmer ; Lat. P.-Sylv. ix. 90.

CHOASPES (now the *Kherkah*) : a r. of the ancient prov. of Susiana, rising in the Luristan Mts. and flowing, after passing Susa, into the Tigris ; the 'drink of none but Kings' was an idea perhaps from Athenæus ; Herod. (i. 188) only says, the K. 'drank no other.' P.R. iii. 288.

CIMBRIC CLUB : here = Danish c. ; Lat. P.-El. iv. 16.

CIMMERIAN : of a distant race mentioned in the Odyssey as living ' beyond the ocean-stream, unblest by the rays of Helios '. Though they were later identified with a race of the Black Sea Region (whence ' Crimea ') the original legend persisted, as of a people living in perpetual darkness ; L'All. 10, cp. Lat. P.-Sylv. ii. 60.

CIPRES (lawn) : Il. Pens. 35 ; also CIPRESS (bud) March. Winch. 22, see CYPRESS.

CIRCE : Com. 50, 153, 253, 522 ; P.L. ix. 522. Called (*a*) Persean priestess of Phoebus in M.'s Lat. Poems, as being d. of Phoebus and Perseis ; also (*b*) according to post-Homeric tradition, mother of Telegonus. See (*a*) Lat. P.-El. i. 87, vi. 73 ; and (*b*) Sylv. i. 18-19.

CIRRHA (used poetically, by Pindar and others, as the equivalent of Delphi) : here, in compliment to Cambridge ; Lat. P.-Sylv. i. 31. See also HELICON.

CITHÆRON : a lofty mountain-range between Attica and Megara (and Bœotia) ; Lat. P.-Sylv. ii. 67.

CITTRON (' tables ') : tables of citron wood from Mount Atlas (where such trees are still grown) ; it was considered as valuable as gold by the Romans, and cost fabulous sums ; P.R. iv. 115.

' CLEAVING MISCHIEF ' : Dalila is so called because she ' cleaves ' to Samson as the poisoned shirt of Nessus (under his armour and next to his skin) to Hercules ; S.Ag. 1039.

CLEOMBROTUS : a young student of philosophy, from Ambracia in Epirus. On reading Plato's discourse in the *Phaedo*, on the immortality of the soul, he leapt into the sea, to enjoy the delights of Elysium ; P.L. iii. 473.

CLINIADES : s. of Clinias, i.e. Alcibiades ; Lat. P.-El. iv. 24.

CLIO : acc. to one tradition the m. of Orpheus, which probably explains why she was mentioned as his own source of inspiration by M. ; Lat. P.-El. iv. 31 ; Sylv. vi. 14.

A Reader's Guide.

CLYMENE : beloved by Helios or Apollo, and m. of Phaethon ; P.R. ii. 186.

CNIDOS: a centre of pilgrimage in ancient Greece, because of the great statue of Venus (Aphrodite) by Praxiteles, which stood in her temple there ; Lat. P.–El. i. 83.

COARSE: sb. a dead body ; D.F.I. 30. See CORPS.

COCYTUS : the ' r. of lamentation' one of the rivers of Hades ; P.L. ii. 579.

COLD-KIND (' embrace') : a close embrace in which the coldness of ice took the place of warmth ; D.F.I. 20.

COLCHIS : woman of C., i.e. MEDEA, q.v.

COLKITTO : see MACDONNELL.

COLNE WATERS : the Colne, flowing past St. Albans at London Colney (Verulamium being long regarded as the head-quarters of Cassivellaunus) joins the Thames near Coln-brook, not far from Horton, M.'s own home ; Lat. P.–Sylv. ix. 149. See CASSIBELAUNUS.

COLUMBUS : P.L. ix. 1116.

COLURES : two great imaginary circles drawn from the poles intersecting at right-angles on the celestial sphere, and passing through the solstitial and equinoctial points (of the ecliptic) ; P.L. ix. 66.

COMMERCE, vb. : to hold intercourse with ; Il Pens. 39.

COMUS : (Gk. κῶμος) ' revelry ' ; the name of the wicked Magician in M.'s ' Mask', which was later called after him.

CONCENT : concord ; variant reading of 2nd ed. and MSS. ; Mus. 6.

CONCLAVE : used by M. in irony, as an ecclesiastical term ; P.L. i. 795.

CONGLOBE, vb. : to gather into a sphere ; P.L. vii. 239.

CONJUR'D : sworn to act together (as conspirators) ; P.L. ii. 693.

CONNATURAL : innate, sharing the same nature ; P.L. x. 246, xi. 526.

CONNIVE, vb. : to ' wink at' or shut the eyes to what is happening ; S.Ag. 466.

CONVINCE, vb. to convert ; P.R. iii. 3.

CONSISTORY : here used ironically by M. as an ecclesiastical term ; P.R. i. 42.

CORALLI : a savage race of the Lower Danube region, who repeatedly raided Ovid's place of exile at Tomis (q.v.) on the Black Sea ; Lat. P.–El. vi. 19.

CORINEUS' DAUGHTER : C. was trad. a Cornish giant ; Sylv. viii. 46.

CORONIS' SON : Æsculapius, reputed s. of Apollo and Coronis ; Lat. P.–El. ii. 10. Coronis was slain by Apollo in a fit of jealousy, but when her body was being cremated, Apollo saved his son from the flames ; Lat. P.–Sylv. i. 28.

CORPS : here used of a quasi-living body ; P.L. x. 601.

CORSE : see COARSE.

CORUS (or Caurus) : the NW. wind ; Lat. P.–Sylv. iv. 53.

COTYTTO (or Cotys) : a Thracian goddess of the Phrygian (highly secret licentious) type, worshipped with nocturnal rites ; Com. 129.

COUCH'D (' well-couch'd ') : ready and waiting to spring (metaph.) ; P.R. i. 97.

A Reader's Guide.

CRANK: a fantastic phrase ; L'All. 27.

'CREMONA'S TRUMP' : the *Christiad*, a Latin poem, on the life of Christ, by Marco Girolamo Vida, of Cremona ; Pass. 26.

CREON, K. OF THEBES, who surrendered the Kingdom, after Laius's death, to Oedipus. Creon's tyranny caused the death of his own son ; Lat. P.-El. i. 46.

CRETAN HUNTER : the Cretans were very famous bowmen : Cretan here lit. 'Cydonian' hunter (in orig. Lat. text 'Cўdŏnĭus, *sic* for Cўdōnĭus) : Cydon, or Cydonis, being a town in Crete whence the 'Quince' is named; Lat. P.-El. vii. 37.

CREUSA: m. of Ion by Apollo, who brought his son to Delphi, to guard the Delphic Treasure ; Lat. P.-Sylv. x. 56-60.

CRONIAN SEA : a name given to the Arctic Ocean (usually called *Mare Concretum*, or Frozen Sea) by Pliny ; P.L. x. 290. Here Sin and Death, flying into Chaos and driving all before them 'in shoals' to Hell-mouth, are compared to two opposite winds from North and South, choking the NE. passage with icebergs.

CROW-TOE ('the tufted') : either a wild hyacinth or, as usually supposed, the 'crow-flower'; Lyc. 143.

CTESIPHON (or TESIPHON) : nr. Seleucia, a winter-palace of the Parthian Kings but sacked by Saracens A.D. 637; the spelling is Tesiphon in P.R. iii. 292 ; Ctesiphon, P.R. iii. 300.

'CUBIC' phalanx (mil.) : usually taken as 'in square' formation, but may also be cubical, as the Saints are marching aloft in air; P.L. vi. 399.

CUPID'S SHAFTS : (*a*) golden, to kindle love, and (*b*) leaden to repel or divert it. For (*a*) see P.L. iv. 763 ; cp. Lat. P.-El. vii. 47 ; cp. Spicula tincta 'pyropo'; Sylv. ix. 192.

CURIUS (DENTATUS) : Roman Consul, who refused the Samnite bribes, and kept no booty for himself in the R. wars ; P.R. ii. 446.

CUSCO (i.e. CUZCO) : a town in the Peruvian Andes, ancient capital of the Inca Empire ; P.L. xi. 408.

CYBELE (= Rhea): great Mother goddess of A. Minor (Phrygia) usually represented with a high turretted headdress, Arc. 21; Lat. P.-El. v. 126.

CYCLADES : it should be noted that Samos was not one of the Cyclades ; probably M. used the name for the Gk. Islands generally ; P.L. v. 264.

CYCLE : a celestial sphere ; P.L. viii. 84 ; see SPHEAR.

CYDONIAN (Lat. P.-El. vii. 37) : see CRETAN HUNTER.

CYLLENE: a lofty Mt. in NE. Arcadia, traditionally famous as the birthplace of Hermes ; Arc. 98. Cp. Lat. P.-El. ii. 13 (*Cyllenius = Hermes*).

CYNOSURE (lit. Hound's-tail): (*a*) the Gk. name for the Lesser Bear (with the Polestar) ; the Greeks steered by the Great Bear (star of Arcady), the Phœnicians by the Lesser Bear ; hence the phrase 'Tyrian (i.e. Phœnician) Cynosure'; Com. 342. See ARCADY, STAR OF.
(*b*) an object of universal attraction ; L'All. 80.

A Reader's Guide.

CYNTHIAN, THE : named from Mount Cynthus in Delos, birthplace (*a*) of Apollo (Lat. P.–Sylv. viii. 55) and (*b*) Artemis (Lat. P.–El. v. 46).

CYPRESS: of Cyprus (*a*) Cypress lawn (a black gauze or 'crape'); Il. Pens. 35.

   (*b*) cypress bud (an emblem of mourning) : March. Winch. 22.

   (*c*) cypress sprays or boughs worn as an emblem by Silvanus ; Lat. P.–El. v. 121.

CYPRIS : the Cyprian, i.e. Venus or Aphrodite, whose shrine there was famous; Lat. P.–El. iii. 20, vii. 48. See AMATHUS.

CYRENE : see BARCA.

CYRIACK SKINNER : M.'s pupil and lawyer friend and (at one time) neighbour and amanuensis ; Sonn. xviii. 1 (Cyriack, whose grandsire). Sonn. to Mr. C. S. upon his blindness (Cyriack, this three years).

CYTHEREA : a name of Venus, probably from the I. of Cythera (now *Cerigo*), near the spot where she was said to have risen from the sea foam, and where one of her chief shrines existed ; P.L. ix. 19 ; Lat. P.–El. v. 112.

DAGON : (*a*) god of Ashdod (Azotus) P.L. i. 463 ; (*b*) used by M. for the name of a rebel angel ; P.L. i. 462.

DAMON (Charles Diodati) : see DIODATI, and EPITAPHIUM DAMONIS.

DAMSEL, ATTICK : see ATHENIAN DAMSEL.

DAPHNE ('grove of, by Orontes') : see CASTALIA'S SPRING (*b*).

DAPHNIS : a Sicilian hero, inventor of bucolic poetry, named from the laurel grove (Daphne = laurel) in which his mother placed him at birth. Pan taught him to play the flute, and a nymph who loved him made him swear to love none other, on penalty of blindness. Forgetting this, he was struck blind, or (some say) changed to a stone ; Lat. P.–Sylv. ix. 1.

DARDANIAN (i.e. Trojan) SHIPS : see TROY.

DARWEN, r. in Lancs. (entering the Ribble near Preston) : scene of the three days' battle of Preston at which Cromwell routed the invading army of Scots under the Duke of Hamilton, in 1648 (Cromwell's letter to Speaker Lenthall describes the battle for 'the Darwen bridge') ; Sonn. xvi. 7 (Cromwell our cheif).

DATI, CARLO : one of M.'s friends during his Italian tour, and later one of his correspondents ; Lat. P.–Sylv. ix. 137.

DAUNIAN QUILL : app. 'countrified quill'—Daunia being part of Apulia remote from Rome : Lat. P.–Sylv. x. 10.

DAY-STAR : here the Sun ; Lyc. 168.

DEBEL, vb. : to conquer ; P.R. iv. 605.

DEE, the r. of Chester : see DEVA, and WISARD.

DEFEND : forbid ; P.L. xi. 86, xii. 207 ; P.R. ii. 370.

DEIOPE : Deiopeia, the fairest of the seven beautiful nymphs in Juno's train ; Lat. P.–Sylv. vii. 4.

DELIAN, THE : (*a*) Apollo, as b. in Delos ; Lat. P.–El. v. 13, 14.

  (*b*) ARTEMIS (the Moon-goddess) ; Lat. P.–Sylv. iv. 49.

DELOS : one of the Cyclades in the Ægæan ; P.L. v. 265; birth-place of Apollo ; P.L. x. 296.

DELOS : for the mission of the three Hyperborean maidens, held by M. to have been Britons, see Herod. iv. 35 ; cp. Lat. P.–Silv. viii. 45.

DELPHOS, STEEP OF : Delphos was s. of Poseidon and Melantho (some say, of Apollo and Celæno) ; he founded Delphi (hence 'Steep of Delphos ') ; Nat. Od. 168 ; Lat. P.–Sylv. x. 58–60.

DEMODOCUS : famous blind Bard at the Court of King Alcinous, who sang of the gods while Ulysses feasted (Od. viii) ; Vac. Ex. 48 ; cp. Lat. P.–Sylv. vi. 44-9.

DEMOGORGON : a formless Shape of Horror, or Power of Evil, not worshipped, but invoked as the climax of Terror. As ruler of the Fates he is jointly enthroned, in P.L., with the Ruler of Chaos ; P.L. ii. 965.

DEPRAVE, vb. : depreciate ; P.L. vi. 174.

DERIVE : to turn aside ; P.L. x. 77.

DESCRY : to reveal ; Com. 171.

DETERMIN'D : p.p. terminated, brought to an end ; P.L. ii. 330 ; determine, P.L. vi. 318, xi. 227 ; S.Ag. 843.

DEVA : the Dee, the r. of Chester ; Vac. Ex. 98 ; Lyc. 55 ; Lat. P.–El. i. 3. See also WISARD.

DIAMOND, ROCK OF : some think 'diamond' here = 'adamant ; P.L. vi. 364 ; but taken in the usual sense of the gem, the vigour of the conception is worthier of M. And cp. P.L. v. 759 ; Com. 881 ; Ital. Sonn. vi. 8 (d'intero diamante).

DICTAEAN : CRETAN (from Mt. Dicte in Crete, birthplace of Zeus) ; P.L. x. 584.

DIMENTIONLESS : non-material (lacking the 'dimensions' of matter) ; P.L. xi. 17.

DIODATI, CHARLES : M.'s closest friend, ed. with him at St. Paul's School, then went to Oxford (Trin. Coll. 1621, M.A. 1628), studied medicine, practised (perhaps near Chester), d. Aug. 27, 1638, during M.'s absence abroad ; Lat. P.–El. i, vi ; Sylv. ix. (Epitaphium Damonis) ; Ital. Sonn. iv.

DIOMEDE : the bravest Gk. at Troy next to Achilles ; he even wounded Aphrodite and Ares ; Lat. P.–El. vii ; Epil. 10.

DIPSAS : a snake whose bite caused an unendurable agony of mortal thirst ; P.L. x. 526.

DIRCÆAN (PENTHEUS) : Theban P. (because Dirce was queen of Thebes) ; Lat. Epigr. (Leon.) ii. 7. See also TIRESIAS.

DIRE-LOOKING (in active sense) : shedding evil influence ; Arc. 52.

DIS : the Rom. god of Hades = Gk. Pluto, who aided his brothers Jupiter and Neptune against Saturn and the Titans ; P.L. iv. 270 ; Lat. P.–Sylv. iv. 31.

DISASTROUS : 'foreboding' used as in astrology ; 'ill-starred ' ; P.L. i. 597.

DISMAL : in its astrological sense of 'unlucky day', as applied to events ;

Vac. Ex. 68 ; P.L. ii. 572; P.R. i. 101 ; S.Ag. 1519 ; Nat. Od. 210 (dismall).

DISPLODE, vb. : explode ; P.L. vi. 605.

DIVAN : a Council of Oriental, or Turkish, sort, used here ironically ; P.L. x. 457 ; cp. P.L. i. 764 (champions . . . at the Soldan's chair).

DIVIDUAL : (a) separable or rather separated from others ; P.L. xii. 85.
(b) shared with others ; P.L. vii. 382 ; cp. Lat P.–Sylv. vi. 66.

DIVULGE, vb. : proclaim ; P.R. iii. 62.

DODONA : the oracle of Zeus in Epirus ; P.L. i. 518.

DORIC : pastoral ; Lyc. 189; cp. Dorian, P.L. iv. 257.

DORIS : queen of Nereus ; Lat. P.–El. iv. 7.

DOTHAN (still called *Dothan*), *c*. 4 m. SW. of Jenin and 10 m. N. of Samaria, scene of the vision of the chariots of fire about Elisha when he was threatened by the Syrians (2 Kings vi. 17) ; P.L. xi. 217.

DOUBLE-FOUNTED : the r. Jordan had two sources, often popularly called the Dan and the Jor! P.L. xii. 144.

DOWNIE GOLD : i.e. Golden Down ; P.L. v. 282.

DRAFF : dregs, or refuse ; P.L. x. 630 ; S.Ag. 574.

DRIFT : intention ; P.R. iii. 4 ; Sonn. to Sr. H. V. (Vane, young in yeares), 6.

DROP SERENE (Lat. *gutta serena*) : amaurosis, given by M. as a possible cause of his blindness, alternatively with 'dim suffusion' (i.e. cataract). But it was more probably glaucoma. For this passage see P.L. iii. 25.

DROWSIE FRIGHTED : the Cambridge MSS. read 'drowsy-flighted' ; but the reading 'drowsie-frighted' follows the 1645 and 1673 edns. ; Com. 553.

DRUIDS : the priests, prophets, and instructors of the Britons ; Lyc. 53 ; Lat. P.–Sylv. v. 41-3.

DRYOPE : a name given by M. to some mutual friend of himself and Diodati ; Lat. P.–Sylv. ix. 88.

DRYOPES : a primitive people of Greece, at first settled in the neighbourhood of Mt. Œta. Their king, Theiodamas, was traditionally the father of HYLAS, q.v.

DULICHIUM (MAN OF) : Ulysses, perhaps here so called by Milton because he assumed Dulichium to be part of Cephallenia ; Lat. P.–El. vi. 72.

DUN : the river Don (Yorks.) ; Vac. Ex. 92.

DUNBAR FIELD : the 'Roundhead' victory of 3 Sept. 1650 ; Sonn. to Cromwell, 8 (Cromwell, our cheif).

EARL : (a) 'an Earl's heir' ; i.e. of Thomas Darcy, Earl Rivers ; March. Winch. 3.
(b) 'that good Earl' : James Ley, Lord High Treasurer, 1624, first Earl of Marlboro', 1626 ; Lord President of the Council, 1628. Sonn. x. 1 (Daughter to that good Earl).

ECBATAN (P.L. xi. 393) : Ecbatana (P.R. iii. 286) : a capital c. of ancient Media, and summer residence of the Persian kings ; captured by Cyrus.

A Reader's Guide.

ECHIONIAN ARACYNTH : i.e. 'Theban' (or Cadmean) Aracynth, Echion being one of the five survivors of the Sparti, or 'sown men', who had grown up from the dragon's teeth, which Cadmus, founder of Thebes, had sown ; Lat. P.–Sylv. ii. 65.

EDEN : the name is not that of the Garden (as often popularly supposed), but of the Land of Eden where the Garden was planted 'Eastward in Eden' (Gen. ii. 8). This Land, part of the great Mesopotamian plain, was called 'Edin' by the early Sumerian settlers, in whose language 'Edin' actually meant 'the plain'. Of unexampled fertility, its grain was described by ancient writers as producing 100 to 300 seeds for each grain sown, with several crops within the year. As part of the 'Fertile Crescent' it also produced palms or fruit-trees that grew wild (cp. Gen. ii. 9) ; aboriginal wheat still grows wild on Mt. Hermon near Damascus. See esp. P.L. iv. 132, 210–14, etc.

EDWARD : K. Edward VI ; Sonn. xi. 14 ('A Book was writ').

EDWARDS (Rev. Thomas) : M.'s 'shallow Edwards' ; a well-known Presbyterian preacher and author of *Gangræna* (1645) in which M.'s Divorce pamphlets were attacked. Forc. of Consc. 12.

'EEL ISLAND' : Ely ; Lat. P.–Sylv. iii. 13–14 (insulâ ... nomen Anguillæ, etc.).

EGLANTINE : not, as sometimes explained, sweet-briar (mentioned already in the preceding line), but prob. a kind of 'dog-rose' ; called by some rosa eglantaria ; others think woodbine or honeysuckle (because 'twisted '), but 'eglantine ' is named from its thorns ; L'All. 48.

EL DORADO : supposed, in M.'s time, to be a city (Raleigh's legendary 'golden city of Manoa'), but the Spanish phrase 'el dorado' (sc. hombre) shows that it really was the *Inca* (Peruvian Emperor), who once a year sprinkled himself all over with gold dust, app. to represent the sun god, and bathed in one of the sacred Lakes (e.g. Titicaca or Guatabita) ; jars for such gold dust being in the Brit. Museum ; P.L. xi. 411.

ELEALE (or *Elealeh*, now *El-aal* or *El'al*) : a t. of the Reubenites, 1 m. from Heshbon, in Moab ; P.L. i. 411.

ELECTRA'S POET : Euripides, author of the Tragedy so called ; Sonn. viii. 13 (Captain or Colonel).

ELEMENTS : in addition to the four usually reckoned, Plato and Aristotle suggest a fifth (the 'quintessence', ether) from which, it was thought, the stars and heavens were made ; P.L. iii. 715.

ELEUSIS : see TRIPTOLEMUS.

ELIAH, the Prophet (P.R. i. 353, ii. 19) : Elijah (P.R. ii. 268, 277) ; Lat. P.–El. iv. 97–100 ; Sylv. iii. 49–50 ; Epigr. *Bomb.* i. 6-8. And see 2 Kings ii. 11, the scene of which M. places on the Chebar, Pass 36.

ELIS' (i.e. ELEAN) DUST : Olympian (O. being in Elis) ; Lat. P.–El. vi. 26.

ELIXIR (Ar. *al ikthīr*) : the Philosophers' Stone ; an essence thought to turn baser metals into gold and to prolong life ; P.L. iii. 607.

ELLOPS (Gk. ἔλλοψ, 'mute ' or 'dumb') : orig. used of fishes, then of serpents—in M. a serpent ; P.L. x. 525.

ELOQUENT : see OLD MAN ELOQUENT.

A Reader's Guide.

ELY, PRELATE or BISHOP OF: Lat. Memorial verses on, see Sylv. iii. (*In Ob. Praesulis Eliensis*).

EMATHIAN: Macedonian, from part of Macedonia so called; P.R. iii. 290; Sonn. viii. 10 (Captain or Colonel); (Æmathiâ) Lat. P.–Sylv. i. 12.

EMATHIAN CITY: Philippi; Lat. P.–El. iv. 102.

EMBOST (for Emboskt): surrounded with woods: S.Ag. 1700; cp. bosky, Com. 313.

EMIMS (double pl., from EMIM): a giant race of Moab; S.Ag. 1080.

EMPEDOCLES: b. at Agrigentum in Sicily in the fifth century B.C. Was the poet, physician, and philosopher who established the four elements; his throwing himself into the crater of Etna is traditional; P.L. iii. 471–2.

EMPYREAL: heavenly, celestial; P.L. ii. 430, *et pass.*

EMPYREAN: heaven; P.L. ii. 771 *et pass.*

ENDORST: loaded on the back (of elephants); P.R. iii. 329.

ENDYMION'S Goddess: the Moon; Lat. P.–El. i. 78.

ENFOLDED: enclosed one within the other; Arc. 64. See SPHEAR.

ENGIN, TWO-HANDED: there are two main divisions of opinion in regard to this crucial passage: (*a*) that it refers to a sword, and (*b*) that it is an axe. For the first view it is held that the 'engin' may be the two-handed sword of Christ such as that described in Rev. i. 16; cp. ch. ii. 12 and ii. 16. Even the words 'at the door' might be an unconscious echo of Christ's words as given in Rev. iii. 20, 'Behold I stand at the door', etc.; for the general threat to false teachers see 2 Pet. ii. Alternatively the sword is believed to be that of the archangel Michael; for supporting passages see P.L. ii. 294–5, and vi. 250–3, and especially vi. 317–18: 'one stroke ... That might determine and not need repeat': the exact equivalent of 'Stands ready to strike once, and strike no more'. Those who believe that an axe is intended point to the subsequent execution of Laud, though Laud was not in fact beheaded till eight years after the writing of *Lycidas*. Mr. Tillyard suggests (*Milton* 385) that the 'engin' may be 'the iron rod of Christ's anger', quoting Milton's pamphlet *Of Reformation in England* (Bohn ii. 412). But Mr. Visiak has pointed out to me that a passage in the very same pamphlet does in fact actually mention the axe in this connexion; the relevant part is here given from Mitford's edition. Milton is asking whether 'mischiefe' can ever be 'neerer hand' than when 'Bishops shall openly affirme that, No *Bishop*, no King? a trimme Paradox, and that yee may know where they have beene a begging for it, I will fetch you the Twin-brother to it out of the Jesuites Cell; they feeling the Axe of Gods reformation hewing at the old and hollow trunk of Papacie, and finding the Spaniard their surest friend ... have invented this super-politick Aphorisme, as one termes it, One Pope, and one King.' A third view, that the instrument of which M. was thinking may have been a battery engine, is based upon the passage in Ezekiel xxvi. 9: 'he shall set engines of war against thy walls, and with his axes he shall break down thy towers.' But this view does not seem to be widely supported (and even here the axe is mentioned).

A Reader's Guide.

ENGLAND, ENGLISH: Sonn. x. 2 (Daughter to that); Sonn. xiii. 2 (Harry whose tuneful); El. iii. 4; Sylv. ii. 2–6 ,122, 127–8, 197, viii. 27–34, 84, ix. 3, x. 31–2. See also THAMES, LONDON, BRUTUS, BRITAIN, TROY.

ENORMOUS: beyond all knowledge or experience; P.L. v. 297.

ENYO, i.e. BELLONA: Roman war-goddess (Gk. Ἐνυώ); Lat. P.–El. iv. 75.

EPICYCLE: a small circle revolving round a centre on the circumference of a great circle or 'cycle'; P.L. viii. 84.

EPIDAURUS: (the 'God in E.' i.e. Æsculapius) of whose cult E. on the Saronic gulf, in Argolis (now *Pidavro*), was the chief centre; P.L. ix. 507; Lat. P.–Sylv. i. 27, 28.

EPEIROT, THE FEIRCE: Pyrrhus, K. of Epirus; Sonn. to Sr. H. V. the younger (Vane young in yeares) 4.

EPITAPHIUM DAMONIS: In 1933 Dr. Leicester Bradner identified as M.'s a copy of this poem entered in the B.M. catalogue as 'Damon'. No other copy of this edition is known, nor is any other edition recorded. It appears, therefore, to be the actual *Editio Princeps, c.* 1639–40. See *Brit. Mus. Quarterly* (vol. vii) 1932–3, No. 2, p. 42. No doubt, a copy privately printed for M. himself.

EQUINOCTIAL: (*a*) applied by M. to the terrestrial equator; P.L. ix. 64; cp. Æquinoctial ii. 637.
  (*b*) the celestial equator; (Equinoctial Rode) P.L. x. 672.

ERATO: goddess of love-poetry; Lat. P.–El. vi. 51.

ERCOCO (now *Arkoko* or *Arkeeko*): northern port of Abyssinia, on the Red Sea; P.L. xi. 398.

ERE, compar. adv.: earlier; P.L. iv. 10: 'erst' is the superlative.

EREBUS: in classic myth husband of Night; but M. substitutes Cerberus in L'All. 2; cp. however Lat. P.–Sylv. ii. 69 and iii. 33 (Mors . . . Erebove patre creta).

ERECTED: high-souled, exalted, sublime; P.L. i. 679; P.R. iii. 27.

ERECHTHEUS: f. of Creusa, and grandf. of Ion. See CREUSA.

EREMITE, GLORIOUS: i.e. Jesus Christ; P.R. i. 8.

ERRONEOUS: wandering, straying; P.L. vii. 20.

ERUPTION: the escape of the Rebel Angels from Hell; P.L. i. 656, viii. 235.

ERYMANTH (i.e. Erymanthus): a lofty range on the borders of Arcadia, Achaia, and Elis; Arc. 100.

ESHTAOL: a c. of Judah, allotted to Dan, near which Samson (b. at Zora) was buried; S.Ag. 181.

ESTOTILAND: in seventeenth century, a vast tract of country between Baffin's and Hudson's Bays, in N. America; P.L. x. 686.

ETERNITY (personified): Lat. P.–Sylv. v. 4.

ETHAM (or ETAM, now *Beit 'Atub*): an isolated Rock-mass beside which was Samson's 'retirement'; S.Ag. 253.

ETHIOPE (QUEEN): Cassiopeia, who boasted of the beauty of her d. Andromeda. (M. says of her own); Il Pens. 19.

ETHIOPIAN (Sea): M. here means the Indian Ocean (as in classical usage), though in his days it also often meant the Sea off W. and SW. Africa (the South Atlantic); P.L. ii. 641.

EUAN: a name of Bacchus: Lat. P.-El. vi. 23.

EUBOIC ('Sea'): between the I. of Euboea and the Gk. mainland; P.L. ii. 546.

EUPHRASIE: formerly much used as an eye specific, bearing, according to the doctrine of signatures, an eye-like mark; P.L. xi. 414.

EUPHRATES: P.L. i. 420, xii. 114; P.R. iii. 272, 384.

EUPHROSYNE, one of the three Graces 'with two sister graces more', viz. Aglaia and Thalia; L'All. 12.

EUROTAS: chief r. of Laconia, also, acc. to some accounts, the name of the father of Hyacinthus; D.F.I. 25.

EURUS: the SE. wind (but often used for the E.); Lat. P.-El. iv. 39; Sylv. ix. 60.

EURYNOME ('Wide-ruling'), wife of Ophion, one of the oldest of the Titans, with whom she ruled Olympus, till they were conquered by Kronos and Rhea; P.L. x. 581.

EURYBATES: Ulysses' herald at Troy; Lat. P.-El. ii. 15.

EURYPYLUS: see MACHAON.

EVANDER: trad. founder of the early settlement at Pallantium, afterwards included in Rome; Lat. P.-Sylv. vii. 28.

EVINCE, vb. tr.: conquer; P.R. iv. 235.

EXORBITANT: 'out of orbit' (astron.); hence 'extravagant, irregular'; P.L. iii. 177.

EXPATIATE, vb. intr.: to walk abroad, 'take the air'; P.L. i. 774.

EXPLODE: to hoot or 'hiss off' (the stage); to chase away; P.L. xi. 665.

EXTENUATE, vb.: to make less (Lat. *tenuis*), 'make light of', underrate, disparage; P.L. x. 645; S.Ag. 767.

FABLE OF BELLERUS: i.e. 'fabled Bellerus'; the name being taken by M. from Bellerium (Belerium in Diodorus), i.e. the 'Land's End', Bellerus suggesting one of the Cornish giants; Lyc. 160.

FABLE: of the Countryman and his Master: see Lat. P., *Apologus de Rustico et Hero.*

FABRICIUS: the heroic antagonist of Pyrrhus; P.R. v. 446.

FADOM: M.'s spelling of fathom; P.L. ii. 934.

FAIRFAX: Thomas, third Lord Fairfax (1612–71), contemporary of M.'s at Cambridge (at St. John's), later Commander-in-Chief of the forces of the Parlt. in the Civil War; Sonn. On the Lord Gen. F. 1 (Fairfax whose name).

FAME: (a) personified; Arc. 8, 41; Sonn. to H. Lawes (Harry whose tuneful) 12 (of Dante); Lyc. 70–84.
   (b) for M.'s 'Tower of Fame' see Lat. P.-Sylv. ii. 171–93; cp. ib. 204–10.
   (c) in sense of rumour, report; Lat. P.-El. iv. 71; Sylv. iii. 7–8.

FAUN: one of a class of semi-divine beings haunting the countryside; Lyc. 34.

FAUNUS (P.L. iv. 708); or FAWN (P.R. ii. 191): the god of the countryside (esp. of shepherds and farms); cp. Lat. P.–Sylv. vii. 27, ix. 32.

FAVONIUS: Sonn. xvii. (Lawrence of vertuous) 6; Lat. P.–El. iii. 47.

FAVOURITE, the (of Tiberius): i.e. Sejanus; P.R. iv. 95.

FEATURE: in special sense of a 'Shape': P.L. x. 279.

FENCE: skill in 'parrying' questions; Com. 791.

FENEL (i.e. FENNEL): attractive to serpents, as helping them to shed their skins and to clear their sight; P.L. ix. 581.

FET: fetched; P.R. ii. 401.

FEZ: one of the five Barbary States in N. Africa; P.L. xi. 403.

FIERY ROD, HEAV'NS: the sun's rays; S.Ag. 549.

FIGTREE ('not that . . . for Fruit renown'd): Pliny (Nat. Hist. xi. 5), followed by Gerard, confuses the banyan-tree of India (*ficus indica*), whose leaves are quite small, with the banana (*Musa Paradaisica*), whose leaves are quite as large as here described. It may be added that (perhaps owing to some such confusion) small bananas are still called 'figs' by Barbadians in the B.W.I.; note that the phrase 'broad as Amazonian targe' exactly translates Pliny's phrase; P.L. ix. 1101.

FIRST MOV'D, THAT: the *Primum Mobile*. See SPHEAR.

FLAMIN: one of the orders of R. priests each serving one special god (e.g. Jupiter, Mars, Quirinus; hence 'each peculiar power'); Nat. Od. 194.

FLEDGE, adj.: fledged or full-feathered; P.L. vii. 420; cp. P.L. iii. 627.

FLEECIE STARR: Aries; P.L. iii. 558; cp. Lat. P.–El. iv. 33-4.

FLORA: (in Lat. text Chloris): Lat. P.–El. iii. 43-4, cp. iv. 35; P.L. v. 16; P.R. ii. 365.

FOIL: a leaf of metal placed at the back of a gem to set it off, Lyc. 79.

FONTARABBIA (now Fuentarabbia): a frontier fortress of Spain, S. of Biarritz on the B. of Biscay. F. is about 40 miles from Roncesvalles, the scene of the defeat of the rearguard of Charlemagne's army when the Gascons or Basques joined the Saracens in attacking the Franks in 778 A.D. Charles himself was not slain, as this passage suggests, but d. and was buried at Aix in 814; P.L. i. 587.

FORGERY: fabrication; S.Ag. 131.

FRANCINI: one of M.'s friends during his Italian tour, and one of his correspondents afterwards; Lat. P.–Sylv. ix. 137.

FRANCISCUS: either St. Francis Xavier or (more probably), Francis of Assisi; Lat. P.–Sylv. ii. 86.

FREAKT WITH JEAT (or 'jet'): because broadly splashed with black as pansies are (a finely imaginative phrase), not spotted or 'freckled', as sometimes inadequately explained; Lyc. 144.

FREQUENT: thronged or crowded; P.L. i. 797, *et pass.*

FRET, sb.: (*a*) a small crosspiece of wood or other material, set transversely on the finger-board of a guitar or lute, to guide the fingering; P.L. vii. 597.
(*b*) fretted; i.e. adorned with 'fret-work' designs of trellis character; P.L. i. 717.

A Reader's Guide.

Friars lanthorn : properly 'Jack o' lantern' or 'Will o' the wisp', here invented with ironic allusion to the reputed character of the Friars (L'All. 104), whom M. had satirized as an undergraduate at Cambridge ; Lat. P.–Sylv. ii. 58.

Friers ('White, Black, and Grey') ; P.L. iii. 474–5.
  (*a*) the White Friars were the Carmelites (so called from Mt. Carmel, where they were first established) ; they wear a white garb.
  (*b*) the Black Friars (so called from their black garb) were the Dominicans ; they were founded by St. Dominic of Spain.
  (*c*) the Grey Friars (who are garbed in grey) are the Franciscans, and were founded by St. Francis of Assisi. In Lat. P.–Sylv. ii. 81–2, M. speaks of their gown as being ashen grey (*Cineracea*).
  (*d*) The fourth order, Augustinians, or 'Austin' Friars, is omitted by M.

Frizl'd : curled or 'crisped' (of foliage) ; P.L. vii. 323.

Frontispice : the principal front or pediment of a building designed in the classical tradition ; P.L. iii. 506.

Frore : frozen ; P.L. ii. 595.

Frounc't : with crimped or 'fluffed' hair ; Il P. 123.

Fulgent : shining, gleaming ; P.L. x. 449.

Fulmin'd, vb. : thundered (metaph.) ; this refers to Demosthenes and Pericles ; P.R. iv. 270. See **Arsenal.**

Furniture : tilting equipment ; P.L. ix. 34.

Fusil : molten, or cast in moulds ; P.L. xi. 573.

Gabriel : 'hero of God', one of the chief warrior angels, though inferior to Michael, q.v. ; P.L. iv. 549, *et pass.*

Gadarene : see **Gergessa.**

Gadez : see **Gadire.**

Gadire (1st ed. **Gadier** from Gk. Γάδειρα—in the orig. Phœnician *Gadir*) = L. castrum (S.Ag. 716) or Gadez (P.R. iv. 77) ; Cadiz in Spain.

Galasp : app. (George) Gillespie, a Scottish Presbyterian representative at Westminster ; Sonn. xi. 9 (A Book was writ).

Galaxie : Galileo hoped that with a sufficiently powerful telescope the stars of the Galaxy might be resolved ; P.L. vii. 579 ; Lat. P.–El. i. 58 ; Sylv. iii. 60. See next entry.

Galileo : G. (P.L. i. 288, v. 262) taking the *idea* of a telescope from Lippershey, the Dutch optician, re-invented it for himself, and in 1609 applied it to astronomy, discovering the spotted and uneven surface of the moon (P.L. v. 262, 419, viii. 145 ; and esp. P.L. i. 291) ; the 'moons' or satellites of Jupiter and Saturn (P.L. viii. 149) ; the crescent form of Venus in or near conjunction (P.L. vii. 366), and the stars of the Galaxy (that 'Milkie way: . . . pouderd with stars' ; P.L. vii. 579–81). These passages are clearly among the fruits of M.'s friendship with G. See **Galaxie.**

Gallaphrone, K. of Cathay, and father of Angelica. See **Agrican** ; P.R. iii. 340.

A Reader's Guide.

GALLUS : the Roman poet, and friend of Ovid, Virgil, etc. ; Lat. P.–Sylv. viii. 4.

GANYMED (i.e. Ganymede) : P.R. ii. 353 : cp. Lat. P.–El. vii. 21-2, where he is called the Sigeian (i.e. Trojan) youth.

GELONI : a race of Asiatic Sarmatia E. of the Don (Tanais) ; Lat. P.–Sylv. iv. 54.

GERGESSA ('fishy', in Lat. Piscosae . . . Gergessae) : Gadara ; Lat. P.–El. iv. 103-4.

GERYONS SONS : Spaniards (named ironically from Geryon, an early but monstrous, perhaps deformed, K. of Erythīa, usually identified with Gadiz in Spain) ; P.L. xi. 410.

GINN : short for ENGIN : a snare ; S.Ag. 933.

GIVES : i.e. gyves, here ankle-fetters ; S.Ag. 1093.

GLAUCUS SPELL : this Glaucus was a fisherman of Anthedon in Boeotia, who became immortal through eating part of the divine herb sown by Kronos ; a clever diver, he became a sea deity ; Com. 874.

GLIBB'D, vb. tr. : made glib or fluent ; P.R. i. 375.

GOBLIN, DRUDGING : Robin Goodfellow ; L'All. 105.

GORDIAN : this famous 'knot' was the 'inextricable' fastening of tree-bark fibre, used by Gordius, the Phrygian K., for binding the yoke of his chariot to the chariot-pole when he dedicated it to the gods in their temple ; Vac. Ex. 90 ; P.L. iv. 348 (metaph. of the Serpent).

GORDON : either (a) George, Lord Gordon, e. s. of the Marquis of Huntley, or (b) his brother, Charles Gordon, Viscount Aboyne ; both of whom were among the chief supporters of Montrose ; Sonn. xi. 8 (A Book was writ).

GORLOIS : see IGRAINE.

GOSHEN, SOJOURNERS OF : the Israelites ; P.L. i. 309.

GRAIN : scarlet dye ; P.L. v. 285 ; xi. 242.

GRAY-FLY : the trumpet-fly or 'breeze' (a great pest to cattle) ; Lyc. 28.

GREEK, THE : Ulysses ; P.L. ix. 19.

'GREEN' CAPE : Cape Verd ; P.L. viii. 631.

GRIDE : to cut with a grating sound ; P.L. vi. 329.

GRINDE ('the air') : to reduce or convert the air by friction into fire ; P.L. x. 1072.

GRIS-AMBER-STEAM'D : steamed with 'amber-gris' ; P.R. ii. 344.

GROTTESQUE : irregularly, or strangely and picturesquely shaped (like a grotto) ; whence 'grotesque' ; P.L. iv. 136.

GRUNSEL (or 'grundsel', i.e. 'ground-sill') edge : the door-sill ; P.L. i. 460.

GRYFON : a GRYPHON or GRIFFIN. These were eagle-headed winged lions, fabled guardians of the gold in the Rhipæan (or Ural) Mountains, the country lying between the lands of the Hyperboreans and the one-eyed Arimaspians, who had been first to discover how to steal this gold, with which they adorned their hair ; P.L. ii. 943.

A Reader's Guide.

GUENDOLEN : here the daughter of Corineüs (the Cornish giant) and wife of Locrine, q.v. ; Com. 830.

'GUNPOWDER PLOT' : see Four Lat. Epigrams (with one on the invention of gun-powder). And cp. the 'November Verses' (*In quintum Novembris*).

GURGE : a whirlpool ; P.L. xii. 41.

GYVES : see GIVES.

HABERGEON : a coat of chain-mail or plate worn as armour ; S.Ag. 1120.

HABOR (now *Kabur*) : trib. of the Euphrates ('in Habor' = in the land of H.) ; P.R. iii. 376.

HÆMONY : M.'s name for a magical plant, prob. so called from the ancient association of Hæmonia or Thessaly with magic ; Com. 638 ; cp. Lat. P.-El. ii. 7.

HÆMUS (the *Balkhan*) : Mount. range betw. Thrace and Mœsia ; Lat. P.-Sylv. iv. 29-30.

HALF-MOON (mil.) : an ancient battle-formation, in the shape of a crescent with backward-pointing horns ; P.R. iii. 309.

HAMMON : identified by M. with Zeus Ammon in Gk., and with Jupiter Ammon in Latin ; as worshipped especially in N. Africa—as well as with Cham and with the Ram-headed god Amun-Ra of Egypt (hence 'Libyc Hammon shrinks his horn', he being a ram-headed god himself). For identification see Nat. Od. 203 ; P.L. iv. 276-7, cp. ix. 508-9.

HARAN (HARRAN or CHARRAN ; Lat. CARRHÆ) (scene of the defeat of Crassus by the Parthians, 53 B.C.) : the town at which Abraham settled on leaving Ur. In the cuneiform Assyrian inscriptions Harran or Harranu means the 'Road' ; an Arab village in this district is still called *Harran* ; P.L. xii. 130-1.

HARAPHA : the name was app. suggested to M. by 'Rapha' (f. of Goliath) in the O.T. (cp. (for similar names) 1 Chron. viii. 37 ; 2 Sam. xxi. 16, 18, 20, A.V. (marg.), etc.) ; S.Ag. 1068, 1079.

HARNEST : armoured ; Nat. Od. 244 ; P L. vi. 202.

HARPYIES (HARPIES) : see PHINEUS. HARPY-FOOTED : with taloned feet like the Harpies ; P.L. ii. 596 ; P.R. ii. 403.

HARRY (LAWES) : the famous musician and friend of M., to whom M. owed the production of *Comus* ; Sonn. xiii (Harry whose tuneful).

HEALTH (L. Salus) : personified as sister of Hebe ; Lat. P.-Sylv. vii. 23-4.

HEARS (March. of Winch. 58), or HERSE (Lyc. 151) : a triangular frame (L. *hirpex*, 'harrow'), for lights esp. for the Tenebræ service (*hercia ad tenebras*) in Holy Week ; the triangular framework cover for a bier, with lights at ends ; hence the bier itself.

HEBRUS (now *Maritza*) the chief R. of Thrace, rising in Rhodope ; Lyc. 63 ; cp. P.L. vii. 34-8.

HECAËRGE : see DELOS.

HECAT' (abbr. of Hecatë) : the Moon-goddess, called tri-form or 'triple', from her three phases ('crescent', 'full', and 'waning'). She was held to be a great enchantress ; Com. 135, (Hecate) 535 ; Lat. P.–Sylv. i. 17, iii. 56–8.

HECATOMPYLOS (city of the 'hundred gates' or 'pylons') : the capital c. of Elam, later of central Parthia, which became chief residence of the Parthian Kings under the Arsacidæ ; P.R. iii. 287. [Other cities, e.g. Thebes in Upper Egypt, were similarly named—Thebes from the pylons of its temples.]

HELICON : here means 'our *new* Helicon', i.e. the University of Cambridge as a seat of the Muses ; see March. Winch. 56, 59 ; Lat. P.–Sylv. i. 32 ; and see Tillyard, *Milt. Priv. Corr. and Prol.*, p. 123, etc.

HERCULES' FRIEND : not yet certainly identified (Hylas having been mentioned earlier) ; Lat. P.–El. vii. 40. Most likely Telamon.

HERMES : (*a*) 'volatil', in sense of 'quicksilver' or 'Mercury' ; P.L. iii. 603.

  (*b*) HERMES the god, thrice-great. HERMES identified by the Gks. with the Eg. god Tahuti (usually known as Thoth), who was the divine scribe of the Eg. gods (and hence the Eg. god of knowledge) came to be regarded as the composer of the forty-two 'Hermetic' books (so called) ; the work of philosophers of the Neo-platonic school in the fourth century A.D. Hence the books of Hermes 'thrice great' (Gk. τρισμέγιστος) came to be held as an encyclopaedic medieval authority on philosophy, alchemy, and the Black Art or Magic ; Il Pens. 88 ; Lat. P.–Sylv. v. 33. [Recently translated by the late Walter Scott and published as *Hermetica* (4 vols.), O.U.P. 1924–36.]

HERARCHIE : i.e. hierarchies, referring to the nine celestial orders (three hierarchies each of three orders or quires) ; P.L. i. 737 ; (Hierarchies) P.L. v. 591, vii. 192 ; cp. Forc. Consc. 7.

HERMIONE : Harmonia, wife of Cadmus ; P.L. ix. 506.

HEROD : s. of Antipater, q.v. Appointed K. of Judea by Mark Antony ; P.R. ii. 424.

HERODOTUS : the life of Homer, formerly attributed to him, is not now so regarded ; Lat. P.–Sylv. viii. 22–3.

HESEBON (Heshbon) : P.L. i. 408.

HESPERIA : a name given by the Gks. to Italy (as being W. of Greece) ; and then by the Romans to Spain and Portugal (as being W. of Italy). See P.L. i. 520 ; Lat. P.–El. v. 82 ; Sylv. ii. 102 (of Spain) and El. iii. 46 (of Portugal).

HESPERIAN GARDENS : i.e. of the Hesperides ; P.L. iii. 568 (Hesperean), viii. 632 ; cp. (Hesperian) Com. 393 ; P.L. iv. 250 ; ('Hesperides') P.R. ii. 357.

HESPERUS : (*a*) the Evening Star ; P.L. iv. 605, ix. 49 ; Lat. P.–El. iii. 32 ; cp. Sylv. iv. 45–7. And see Galileo.

  (*b*) father of the Hesperides, who guarded the golden apples ; Com. 982.

HILL (the Opprobrious) : see OPPROBRIOUS.

HILL (of Scandal) : see SCANDAL.

HIMERA : (*a*) Lat. Himerides ; i.e. Nymphs, or Muses of Himera, prob. the *northern* r. of that name in Sicily (there are two so called) ; Lat. P.–Sylv. ix. 1.

A Reader's Guide.

(b) Himĕra or Hemĕra: was the name of 'Prince Memnon's sister'; Il Pens. 18.

HINGES: cardinal points (L. cardines); P.R. iv. 415.

HIPPOGRIF: a creature with the forepart of a griffin, and the hindpart of a horse; taken by M. from Ariosto's *Orlando Furioso*; P.R. iv. 542.

HIPPOTADES: s. of Hippotas, i.e. Æolus, the god of the winds; Lyc. 96; cp. Lat. P.–El. iv. 6, v. 51. For the cave in which Æolus bound the winds see also P.R. iv. 44.

HISPAHAN (Ispahan or *Isfahan*, anciently *Aspadana*): c. on the r. Zayendeh; it became the capital city of Persia, the t. of Shah Abbas, flourishing still in the seventeenth century, though now decayed; P.L. xi. 394.

HOLOCAUST: a burnt-offering offered whole; S.Ag. 1702.

HOMER (MELESIGENES): so called from the Meles, a r. of Smyrna; P.R. iv. 259; also MAEONIDES, i.e. son of Mæon, or from Mæonia (Lydia); P.L. iii. 35; cp. Lat. P.–El. i. 23, vi. 71; Silv. viii. 23. See also HERODOTUS.

HOOK: i.e. the shepherd's crook; Lyc. 120; Com. 872.

HOOKED CHARIOT: doubtless in ref. to the (reputed) scythed chariot-wheels of the Britons, a view now questioned; Nat. Od. 56–7.

HORNED FLOUD: the flood with its main stream divided into two channels. So Ovid calls the Nile 'Seven-horned' (from its seven branches or mouths) and river gods were called by the Romans 'bull-horned' (*tauri-formis*), from their divided channels; P.L. xi. 827.

HORONAIM: a c. of Moab; P.L. i. 409.

HOSTING, sb.: a warlike encounter; P.L. vi. 93.

HOURS, THE: i.e. the Seasons, daughters of Jove and Themis; Lat. P.–Sylv. iii. 39–40.

HUDDLING: hurrying; Com. 495.

HULL, vb.: to drift with the current (of a vessel at sea); P.L. xi. 836.

HUMOURS (doctrine of the four): formerly held to be blood, choler, phlegm, and black bile (melancholy); S.Ag. 600.

HYACINTH (HYACINTHUS): the comely youth of the classical legend; D.F.I. 23–8; Lat. P.–Sylv. iv. 63.

HYALINE: the 'glassy sea' of Rev. iv. 6, xv. 2; see P.L. vii. 619.

HYAS: one of the Hyades, a family of nymphs trad. raised to the stars (with the Pleiades) to reward them for their sisterly love shown at the death of their brother; M. here applies the name to some unknown mutual friend of himself and Diodati; Lat. P.–Sylv. ix. 87.

HYDASPES (Sanskr. *Vitasta*) now the r. *Jhelum* or *Jelum*, one of the chief rivers of the Punjaub; P.L. iii. 436.

HYDRA: the many-headed snake slain by Hercules at Lerna at the SW. end of the Argive plain; Com. 605; P.L. ii. 628; Sonn. On the Lord General Fairfax, 7; Lat. P.–Sylv. i. 26 (where the Lat. text has *echidnae*, usually a viper or adder, but the same word is used by Ovid for the hydra).

HYDRUS: a sea-snake; P.L. x. 525.

HYLAS: s. of Theiodamas, k. of the Dryopes, famous for his comeliness; a companion of Hercules in the Argo, he was carried under water by a nymph in Asia Minor and drowned ; P.R. ii. 353 ; Lat. P.-El. vii. 24 ; Sylv. ix. 1.

HYMENÆUS : (the Hymenæan) the marriage song in ancient Rome, from Hymen, god of marriage ; Lat. P.-El. v. 105, 106.

HYPERBOREAN : northern (applied by M. to Britain) ; Lat. P.-Sylv. ii. 95, viii. 26.

HYPERION, CHARIOT OF : in allusion to the trad. of Phaethon ; Lat. P.-Sylv. vi. 99, 100.

HYRCANIA : a prov. of Parthia, separated by the Oxus from Margiana and bounded on the N. by the Caspian ; P.R. iii. 317.

HYRCANUS : i.e. H. II, the uncle of Antigonus and grandf. of Mariamne. He was High Priest (78 B.C.), a prince who was last but one of the royal House of the Maccabees, Asmonean dynasty. Though carried away by the Parthians, and mutilated, his ears being cropped by Antigonus, he returned to Jerusalem, and lived there under Herod till 40 B.C., when Herod executed him ; P.R. iii. 367.

IAPETUS (the Titan) : f. of Prometheus, identified by M. with Japhet, held by the Gks. to have been through Deucalion (s. of Prometheus), the ancestor of mankind ; P.L. iv. 717 ; Lat. P.-Sylv. i. 4 ; Epigr. Bomb. v.

IBERIA : (a) Spain and Portugal ; Com. 60 ; P.R. ii. 200 ; Lat. P.-Sylv. ii. 103, 126. See also HESPERIA.
   (b) a province of ancient Parthia, lying N. of Armenia, between the Black Sea and the Caspian, roughly equivalent to the modern Georgia, or Grusia (in Russia). Hence 'dark Iberian dales' ; P.R. iii. 318.

IBIS : Ovid's poem of bitter invective against a (to us) unknown enemy ; Lat. P.-Sylv. iii. 18 ; cp. ARCHILOCHUS.

ICARIUS' DAUGHTER : Penelope ; Lat. P.-El. iv. 56 (Icaris).

IDA, MOUNT : (a) in Crete, trad. the birthplace of Zeus ; Il Pens. 29 ; P.L. i. 515 : Lat. P.-El. v. 61-2.
   (b) in Mysia (Asia Minor) S. boundary of the Troad. Mt. Alexandria near Antandrus, which is a part of the range of Ida, is mentioned by ancient writers (Strabo, etc.) as having been the actual scene of the judgement of Paris ; P.L. v. 382.

IDOL : in special sense of 'mock image', 'simulacrum' ; P.L. vi. 101.

IDOLISMS : personal prejudices ; P.R. iv. 234.

IDOLIST : idolater ; S.Ag. 453.

IDUMANIAN STREAM : see CHELMER.

IGRAINE (Lat. IÖGERNE) : widow of Gorlois, beloved of Uther ; Lat. P.-Sylv. ix. 166.

IMAUS, Mt. : (Sanskr. Himava 'snowy') the name of this system of mountain ranges in Central Asia was applied at first by the Gk. geographers to the Hindu Kush and Himalayas, and later employed app. for the Bolor Range between China and Turkistan (Ptolemy places it much too far to the East) ; P.L. iii. 431.

IMBROWN, vb. M. uses 'brown' for 'dusky' shades, esp. those of evening ; cp. Il Pens. 134 ('shadows brown') ; cp. P.L. ix. 1087-8 (umbrage...

A Reader's Guide.

'brown as evening'); P.R. ii. 293 (alleys brown). Here 'when late eve imbrowns' (*al imbrunir di sera*); Ital. Sonn. ii. 1.

IMOGEN (INOGENIA): d. of K. Pandrasus; Lat. P.-Silv. ix. 163.

IMP: (*a*) sb. an evil spirit; P.L. ix. 89.
(*b*) impe, vb. to graft a sound feather in place of a broken one (hawking term); Sonn. On the lord general F. (Fairfax whose name), 8.

IMPALE: to surround, enclose (as with a palisade); P.L. ii. 647, vi. 553.

IMPERTINENCE: irrelevance; P.L. viii. 195.

IMPERVIOUS: impenetrable; P.L. x. 254.

IMPLICIT (of bushes): entangled, interwoven (as in Lat.); P.L. vii. 323.

IMPRESES, sb. pl. (Ital. *impresa*): devices on shields; P.L. ix. 35.

INCENTIVE (reed): reed for 'kindling' (used of the 'match' for firing cannon); P.L. vi. 519.

INCOMPOS'D: discomposed; P.L. ii. 989.

INCORPORATE: dwelling together in one body (cp. Rom. vii. 20); P.L. x. 816; cp. S.A. 161.

INCUBUS: see ASMODEUS.

INDECENT: ungraceful, unbecoming; P.L. vi. 601.

INDENTED: with short sharp (zigzag) turns (of the banks of a river or the track of a serpent, etc.); Vac. Ex. 94; P.L. ix. 496.

INDITE: to describe in writing; P.L. ix. 27.

INDIVIDUAL: indivisible, inseparable, distinctive. Time, 12; P.L. iv. 486, etc.

INDUCE: to bring on; P.L. vi. 407.

INDULGENCE: formal remission of penalty for sin, after absolution; P.L. iii. 492.

INDUSTRIOUS: zealous (for a particular object); P.L. ii. 116.

INFAM'D, INFAMOUS: defam'd, notorious; P.L. ix. 707.

INFANTRY: of a body of foot-soldiers, e.g. of the Dwarfs ('that small infantry') in their war with the Cranes (prob. with play on the word 'infantry'); P.L. i. 575.

INFINITE, sb. (*a*) Illimitable; P.L. iii. 273 (of God).
(*b*) void and formless, of Chaos; P.L. ii. 405.

INFLUENCE: the good or evil force believed to emanate from the stars, as 'cosmic rays' from space; Nat. Od. 71; L'All. 122; Com. 336; P.L. ii. 1034, etc.

INFRINGE, vb. tr.: to break up or shatter; P.R. i. 62.

INLAND: the interior of Hell; P.L. x. 423.

INSCRIB'D WITH WOE: The sedge of the Cam, when dry, shows markings like a palm-leaf MS. (or like the legendary marks of the hyacinth); Lyc. 105.

INSENSATE: devoid of understanding; P.L. vi. 787; S.Ag. 1885.

INSINUATE: to progress sinuously or in curves (of a serpent, etc.); P.L. iv. 348.

INSIST: persist; S.Ag. 913.

INSPHEAR : to 'translate' or raise to a celestial sphere ; Com. 3 ; cp. unsphear, Il Pens. 88. And see SPHEAR.

INSTILL'D : poured in drop by drop ; P.L. xi. 416.

INSTINCT, p.p. : impelled ; P.L. ii. 937, vi. 752.

INSTRUCT, p.p. : instructed, taught ; P.R. i. 439 ; cp. Pass 48 ; S.Ag. 757.

INSUPPORTABLY : irresistibly ; S.Ag. 136.

INTEND : to occupy one's-self ; P.L. ii. 457.

INTENSE, p.p. : strained to the uttermost, taut (opposed to 'remiss', i.e. slackened, as of a violin string) ; P.L. viii. 387.

INTERLUNAR CAVE : M. imagines the Moon to retire into a cavern during the intervals between the Old Moon and the New ; S.Ag. 89.

INTERMINABLE : the 'Illimitable' or 'Infinite', i.e. God ; S.Ag. 307.

INTERNAL : mental, spiritual ; S.Ag. 1334, 1686.

INTERVEIND : (of a country, intersected by rivers, like the veinings of a leaf) ; P.R. iii. 257.

INTERVOLV'D : with linked, or interlocked, revolutions ; P.L. v. 623 ; cp. Lat. P.–Sylv. iv. 38.

INVERT : to reverse the purpose (e.g. of a deed) ; Com. 682.

INVEST : to clothe as with a garment (e.g. night 'invests' the sea) ; P.L. i. 208.

INVIOLABLE : (*a*) inviolate ; P.L. iv. 843.
  (*b*) unyielding, hence safe (from violence) ; P.L. vi. 398.

INVISIBLE : 'the invisible glory of Him that made them' app. means (by hypallage) the 'glory of the Invisible' (i.e. God) ; P.L. i. 369.

INVOLVE : (*a*) to entwine or entangle ; P.L. vii. 483.
  (*b*) to envelop ; P.R. i. 41, etc.

Io (identified with Eg. goddess Isis) : the Argive Princess who was beloved by Zeus and so cruelly treated by Argus (servator inique juvencæ), appointed by Hera to watch her ; Lat. P.–Sylv. ii. 185–6.

ION : see CREUSA.

IRASSA : t. and district of N. Africa (in Lybia not far from Cyrene) ; acc. to M. the scene of the conflict between Hercules and Antæus, described by Pindar. But Pindar tells how Alexidamus won the d. of a *later* Antæus in marriage. M. has 'confused the two'—Blakeney, notes (more probably, *more suo*, was 'fusing' them) ; P.R. iv. 564. [The name 'Irassa' is from Pindar, *Pyth.* ix. 106, but should be spelt *Irasa*.]

IRIS : (*a*) the rainbow goddess ; Com. 83, 992 ; P.L. xi. 244 ; Lat. P.–El. iii. 41.
  (*b*) the plant ; P.L. iv. 698.

IRRESOLUTE : undecided, 'irr. of thoughts revolv'd ', unable to decide between all the plans considered ; P.L. ix. 87.

IRRIGUOUS : well-watered ; P.L. iv. 255.

ISIS : (*a*) the Eg. goddess, wife of Osiris ; P.L. i. 478 ; Nat. Od. 212 ; cp. Lat. P.–Sylv. v. 34.
  (*b*) Io, q.v. *supra*.

A Reader's Guide.

ISMENIAN (i.e. 'Theban') steep: the Theban acropolis overlooking the r. Ismenus; called the Hill or Rock of the Sphinx (Mt. Phicium), as being the Rock from which she flung herself when her riddle was guessed by Œdipus; P.R. iv. 575.

ITHURIEL (lit. 'Search of God'): the cherub who, finding Satan disguised in Eden 'squat like a Toad, close at the eare of Eve', pricks him with his spear, forcing him to return to his own shape; P.L. iv. 788. 810–14.

ITS: Nat. Od. 106; P.L. i. 254, iv. 813. M. almost invariably uses 'his' or 'her', e.g. of plants (March. Winch. 37, 43); Ital. Sonn. ii. 5.

IVY: sacred to Bacchus; Lat.P.–El. vi. 15, 16.

JACULATION: the act of throwing or hurling; P.L. vi. 605.

JANUS: the R. god with two faces, looking opposite ways; hence a 'double Janus' would have four faces; P.L. xi. 129.

JAPHET: see IAPETUS.

JASON: see MEDEA.

JAUNT: a short journey; P.R. iv. 402.

JAVAN: s. of Japhet; rightly identified by M. with Ion, ancestor of the Ionians, and hence of the Greek race; P.L. i. 508; S.Ag. 716.

JESUS: (a) the Gk. septuagint form of Joshua as a type of Christ; P.L. xii. 310.
    (b) elsewhere, Christ himself.

JOCOND: blithe and gay; L'All., 94.

JONSON, BEN: L'All. 132.

JOVE: identified by M. (a) with Heb. Jehovah.
    (b) with N. African or Lybian Ammon (or Cham).
    (c) with Zeus Ammon, Jupiter Ammon, and Eg. Amun-Ra. See HAMMON.

JUBILY: joyful acclaim; Mus., 9; P.L. iv. 348 (Jubilee), vi. 884 (Jubilie); cp. vii. 564.

JULEP (from Pers. word for 'rose water'): a sweet drink or potion; Com. 672.

JULIUS (CÆSAR): weeps at Alexander's tomb; P.R. iii. 41.

JUNKET: Ital. cream cheese in rush basket; L'All. 102.

JUNO'S SON: Vulcan (= Hephaistos); Lat. P.–El. vii. 81 (proles Junonia); Sylv. iv. 23. See VULCAN.

JUST MAID: see ASTREA.

JUSTLING ROCKS: the Symplegades, at the mouth of the Black Sea. The Argo and her crew, by the advice of Phineus the sage, and Hera's aid, passed through in safety, and thenceforth they were fixed and motionless; P.L. ii. 1018.

KEYES (of St. Peter): Lyc. 110; Com. 13; P.L. iii. 484–5; cp. Lat. P.– Sylv. ii. 101; (*Apostolicæ custodia clavis*) cp. Dante Purg. c. ix. 109–10.

KIRIATHAIM: a c. in Moab; S.Ag. 1081.

KSAR (abbn. of Kaisar, i.e. 'Czar' or 'Tsar'): see 'the Russian Ksar In Mosco'; P.L. xi. 394.

A Reader's Guide.

LADON: a Gk. r. in Arcadia, flowing into the Alpheus; Arcad. 97.

LANCELOT (the knight of Arthur): P.R. ii. 361. See also ARTHUR, KING.

LANTHORN: (lantern) see FRIARS LANTHORN.

LANTSKIP (M.'s usual spelling): landscape. M. is said to have borrowed the word from the great Dutch landscape painters; L'All. 70.

LAPLAND: one of the chief reputed homes of witchcraft and sorcery; P.L. ii. 665.

LAPSE (in sense of a flowing current): P.L. viii. 263; cp. Lat. P.-El. iii. 22; Sylv. x. 23.

LARS: household (tutelary) ancestral spirits worshipped in ancient Rome; Nat. Od. 191; Lat. P.-El. iv. 126.

LAUREAT: adorned or furnished with laurels; Lyc. 151; Sonn. to Cromwell, 9 (Cromwell, our cheif).

LAVER: a vessel for bathing; Com. 838; cp. S.A. 1727.

LAVINIA: d. of Latinus, betrothed to Turnus, but later perfidiously married to Æneas (of the cause of that war); P.L. ix. 17.

LAWES, H.: see HARRY (Lawes).

LAWN (cipres): black gauze or crape—'cypress' (named from 'Cyprus') cloth and 'lawn' (named from Laon), usually distinguished, are here identified; Il Pens. 35.

LAWN: a cleared space in the woods, a glade; also used of pasture land; Nat. Od. 85; L'All. 71; Lyc. 25; Com. 568, 965; P.L. iv. 252.

LAWRENCE: s. of Henry Lawrence, Lord President of Cromwell's State Council; Sonn. xvii. 1 (Lawrence of virtuous).

LAXE ('inhabit laxe'): dwell at ease, or 'at large'; P.L. vii. 162.

LEARN'D OF GREEKS (MOST): SOCRATES, q.v.

LEMURES: spectres of the departed in ancient Rome, spirits of evil; Nat. Od. 191.

LEONORA: see BARONI.

LESBIAN SONGS: airs like those of Sappho, Alcæus, or Arion; Lat. P.-Sylv. vii. 22; cp. Lyc. 63.

LEUCOTHEA: (a) identified with Ino, wife of Athamas, who became a sea-goddess when drowned; Com. 875.

 (b) id. with the Roman goddess Matuta or goddess of Dawn; P.L. xi. 135.

LEVANT, LEVANTINE: the Rising, or 'Dawn' (E.) wind; P.L. x. 704. See PONENT.

LEWDLY-PAMPER'D: basely indulged; Com. 770.

LIBBARD: used in sixteenth century for leopard; P.L. vii. 467.

LIBECCHIO: the SW. wind; P.L. x. 706.

LIBITINA: an ancient R. goddess of the charnel-house; hence a death-goddess; Lat. P.-El. iii. 4.

LIBRA: the constellation of Libra (the Scales); P.L. iii. 558, iv. 997–1001; cp. Lat. P.-Sylv. iv. 33-5.

LICHAS: the attendant of Hercules who brought him the poisoned robe,

A Reader's Guide.

was thrown into the sea by H.; he was changed into the *Lichadian Islands*; P.L. ii. 545.

LICKERISH : seductive ; Com. 700.

LIGEA : a sea-nymph (as in Georg. iv. 336) ; Com. 880. (Lewis and Short give Ligea as a wood-nymph, or Dryad.) See SIRENS.

LIMBEC : an alembic (Ar. *al anbiq*) ; P.L. iii. 605.

LIMBER FANS : pliant wings ; P.L. vii. 476.

LIMBO (*limbus fatuorum*) : Milton's idea of this region as one of the extramundane regions to which all vain and foolish persons and things were consigned, pending the Last Day's arrival, seems to partake of the popular ideas ; acc. to the Schoolmen it was a definite region next to Hell, to which the souls of unbaptized infants went ; P.L. iii. 495.

LIMITARIE CHERUBE : app. ch. of the frontiersmen or 'marches' (and of nothing else, as in the Tennysonian 'Lords of waste marches' cp. Lat. *milites limitanei*). Satan's sneering allusion to the 'hallow'd limits' mentioned in the speech of Gabriel ; P.L. iv. 971.

LINEAMENTS : outlines (not merely of the countenance but of the body also) ; P.L. v. 278.

LINUS : a bard of Argos or (as in M.) of Thebes, untimely slain ; his tomb was claimed by Argos, Thebes, and Chalcis in Eubœa ; Lat. P.-El. vi. 68.

LISTED : (*a*) broadly striped ; P.L. xi. 862.
(*b*) used of an enclosed space, roped off like a ring, or enclosed with 'lists', as for a tournament ; S.Ag. 1087.

LITTER : a horse-litter, suspended between two horses at front and back, such as that used for Qu. Henrietta Maria, wife of Charles I, at her entry into London ; cp. Com. 554.

LOCRIAN BLADE : Locri (Epizephyrii), now *Motta di Burzano*, colonized by Locrians from Greece, was in Bruttium, a well-known mining district, which may help to explain M.'s use of the word ; Lat. P.-Sylv. i. 16.

LODGE : a shelter of boughs ; cp. P.L. iv. 720, v. 377 ; the small rustic cottage of the keeper of the wood ; Com. 346.

LOFTS : the middle stratum of the atmosphere, Vac. Ex. 42 ; see 'MIDDLE AIR'.

LOGRES : the Midlands, or main part of England E. of the Severn (called Loegria in M.'s P. Wks.) ; as dist. from Lyones or Cornwall ; P.R. ii. 360.

LONDON : Lat. P.-El. i. 9, 73-4, 86-8, vii. 51 ; Sylv. vii. 9, x. 15.

LOXO : Lat. P.-Sylv. viii. 46. See DELOS.

LUCIFER : (*a*) Satan, as in Isa. xiv. 12 ; P.L. v. 757, vii. 131, x. 425 ; cp. P.L. v. 655 ('his former name') ; and P.R. i. 294 (metaph.).
(*b*) the Morning Star ; Nat. Od. 74. Note—that when W. of the Sun, Venus rises as the Morning Star, or Lucifer, when E. of the Sun, as Vesper or Hesperus ; cp. Lat. P.-Sylv. iv. 45.

LUCRINE BAY : now the Gulf of Pozzuoli, near Naples, famous for oysters ; P.R. ii. 347.

LUCUMO ('city of the ') : Lucca (owing to the traditional derivation of its

A Reader's Guide.

name from its supposed founder, a Lucumo or Etruscan noble) : from this city came Diodati's family ; **Lat. P.**–Sylv. ix. 128.

LUZ (' Hazel-trees') : the older name of the settlement at Bethel ; P.L. iii. 513.

LYÆUS : a name of Bacchus as banisher of care ; **Lat. P.**–El. vi. 21 ; –Sylv. vi. 43.

LYCAMBES and his d. NEOBÚLÉ, being lampooned by Archilochus for rejecting his suit, slew themselves ; **Lat. P.**–Sylv. iii. 21–2.

LYCÆUS (now *Dioforti*) : a range of Mts. in SW. Arcadia, the resort of Pan and the Nymphs ; Arc. 98.

LYCAONIAN . . . BOÖTES : Lycaon, K. of Arcadia, and f. of Callisto (q.v.) was trad. turned by Jupiter into a wolf. Callisto his daughter, being changed into the Bear, was hence called Lycaonius Arctos, or 'Lycaonian' Arctos ; M. uses it of the constellation before the Great Bear (Arcturus or Boötes) ; **Lat. P.**–El. v. 35.

LYCEUM : the schools where Aristotle taught outside Athens—not inside the walls, as here ; P.R. iv. 253.

LYNX : the OUNCE, q.v.

LYONES : in Camden, a tract of land now lost in the sea, between the Scillies and Cornwall, perhaps here put for Cornwall, but alternatively held to be Brittany, or Armorica, whence Sir Tristram came ; P.R. ii. 360.

MAB : the Fairy Queen ; L'All. 102.

MACDONNEL (or Macdonald) : prob. Alexander Macdonald the younger, one of the chief officers on the royal side under Montrose ; the members of this family being called MacCollkittok or 'descendants of Colin the Lame' ; Sonn. xi. 9 (A Book was writ).

MACHABEUS : Judas Maccabeus ; P.R. iii. 165.

MACHAON : surgeon of the Gks. in the Trojan war ; his death by the spear of Eurypylus is later tradition ; **Lat. P.**–Sylv. i. 23–4.

MACHÆRUS : a stronghold of the Kings of Ar. Petraea in the time of Herod, situated in S. Peraea, E. of the Dead Sea—the Baptist's prison. It was reckoned by Pliny as second in strength after Jerusalem ; P.R. ii. 22.

MÆNALUS : a Mt. of Arcadia, especially sacred to Pan (the god of Mænalus) ; he was often trad. heard here playing on his pipes ; Arc. 102 ; **Lat. P.**–El. v. 125.

MÆONIDES : one of the names given to Homer, either because he was said to be Mæonian (i.e. Lydian) by birth, or because Mæon was said to be his father's name ; P.L. iii. 35. See HOMER.

MÆOTIS, THE POOLE : Sea of Azov ; P.L. ix. 78. See TAURIC POOL.

MAGNETIC : sb., P.R. ii. 168, the loadstone ; adj., P.L. iii. 583.

MAHANAIM : E. of Jordan, S. of the Jabbok, on the boundaries of Gad and Manasseh ; P.L. xi. 214.

MAIA : d. of Atlas, and m. of Hermes ; P.L. v. 285 ; cp. **Lat. P.**–Sylv. viii. 72 (Atlantis . . . nepos = Hermes).

A Reader's Guide.

MAID ('that Just') : see ASTREA.

MAIN, THE: the universe; P.R. iv. 457.

MAMMON: ('Wealth', in Syriac) the name of one of the chief rebel angels; P.L. i. 678, ii. 228, 291.

MANACLES: in special sense of ankle-fetters; S.Ag. 1309; cp. GIVES.

MANTLE, HAIRY: perhaps referring to the 'river-sponge' of the Cam; Lyc. 104.

MANTLING: raising both wings to meet each other, cloak-fashion (of a swan); P.L. vii. 439; cp. P.L. v. 279.

MANURING (i.e. 'manœuvring'): in older use of 'manual labour'; P.L. iv. 628, xi. 28.

MANSO: Gio. Battista, Marquis of Villa, friend of Tasso, patron of poets, who befriended M. on his Italian tour. M.'s Lat. poem addressed to; see Sylv. viii (*Ad Mansum*).

MARASMUS: consumption (the 'wasting' sickness); P.L. xi. 487.

MARBLE: transparent, pure, glistening (of the air); P.L. iii. 564.

MAREOTICK WATERS (now *Birket el Maryût*): the Lacus Mareotis in the NW. of the Nile Delta; here if correct put for Egypt (and Africa?) generally; Col. Trans. gives 'Mæotick'; Lat P.-Sylv. ii. 171.

MARGARET ('honour'd'): Lady M. Ley, d. of James Ley; see EARL (*b*) Sonn. x. 14 (Daughter to that good Earl).

MARGIANA (now roughly Khorassan): named from its chief river Margus (now the Murg Roab or Murgav), in Merv district of Russ. Cent. Asia; P.R. iii. 317.

MARINI: Ital. poet, composer of an immensely long poem on the 'amours of the Assyrian gods'; Lat. P.-Sylv. viii. 9, 51.

MARLE SOIL: perhaps attributed by M. to Hell because of its frequently rich brown and consequently 'burnt' appearance; P.L. i. 296.

MAROCCO (Arab. *Marrakush*): one of the five Barbary states in N. Africa; P.L. i. 584, xi. 404.

MARSHAL'D, p.p.: at a medieval feast the Marshal superintended the seating and serving of the guests; hence 'marshal' = 'master of the ceremonies'; P.L. ix. 37.

MASSY PROOF: the general sense is of *tried* and as it were of guaranteed solidity; Il Pens. 158.

MAURUSIAN: Moorish (of Mt. Atlas in Morocco); see ATLAS.

MEANDER (i.e. Mæander, now the r. Mendereh) which rises near Celænæ in Phrygia; it was famed for its windings, and is much haunted by wild swans; Com. 232.

MEATH: mead; P. v. 345.

MEDAL: metal; P. . 592.

MEDEA: d. of Æetes, k. of Colchis (whence she is called 'the Colchian'; Lat. P.-El. iv. 10) and sister of Absyrtus (also called Ægialeus; see Sylv. i. 20); when deserted by Jason for Glauce, she poisoned her rival, murdered her two children by Jason, and fled from her husband to Athens in a chariot drawn by winged dragons; Lat. P.-El. iv. 10.

A Reader's Guide.

MEGÆRA : 'snakie locks that curld'; one of the grim Eumenides, or Furies, whose 'snakie locks' (P.L. x. 560) are described by Æschylus.

MELANCHOLY: see HUMOURS.

MELES, MELESIGENES : see HOMER.

MELIBÆAN : Melibæa in Thessaly was famed for its purple dyes ; P.L. xi. 242.

MELIND (Melinda) : a seaport and t. in the N. prov. of Zanzibar ; P.L. x. 399.

MEMNON : Prince of Ethiopia ; the comely s. of Tithonus (the founder of Susa) and Eos, and brother of the beautiful Himera or Hemera. He was famed as the builder of Susa's citadel, and was said to have been slain at Troy ; Il Pens. 18 ; P.L. x. 308 ; Lat. P.–Sylv. ii. 133-6. [M. at first spoke of him as the founder of Nineveh ; Lat. P.–El. i. 67.]

MEMPHIS : referred to as great Alcairo ; P.L. i. 718. See ALCAIRO.

MERIDIAN TOWRE : noonday height (of the Sun) ; P.L. iv. 30, 58.

MERLIN : the famous seer and magician at Arthur's Court ; Lat. P.–Sylv. ix. 168.

MEROE ('Nilotic Isle') : in upper Nubia, or Ethiopia, far south of Syene and under the equator. Though described as an island by old geographers, it was really an irregular space between confluent rivers ; P.R. iv. 70-71.

MESSAGE : messenger ; S.Ag. 635.

MICHAEL : the archangel ; leader-in-chief of the warrior angels ; P.L. ii. 294, and numerous other passages.

MICROSCOPE (AERIE) : Satan is using the air as the means for refracting and magnifying the distant view, and implies that he has given the air these special properties ; P.R. iv. 57.

MIDDLE AIR : this was the 'middle region' of the atmosphere in late medieval theory ; indescribably cold, and full of vapours, where rain and hail and snow were born ; D.F.I. 16 ; Nat. Od. 164 ; P.L. i. 516 ; P.R. i. 39, ii. 117 ; Lat. P.–Sylv. ii. 12 ; Vac. Ex. 41-2 ; cp. P.L. ii. 718, vi. 314, 536 ; P.R. i. 39 ; P.L. iv. 940.

MILKY WAY : see GALAXIE.

MILTON, JOHN (father of J. M.) : Lat. poem addressed to ; see Sylv. vi (*Ad Patrem*).

MIMICS (misprinted *mimirs* in 1st ed.) : players, actors ; S.Ag. 1325.

MINCING, ad. : daintily-stepping ; Com. 964.

MINCIUS (now *Mincio*) : a tributary of the r. Po, which it joins near Mantua. As Virgil dwelt on its banks, it here typifies Roman pastoral verse ; Lyc. 86.

MINIMS (from the Lat.) : minute humans, pygmies, or dwarfs—perhaps survivors of some primitive race (the word is said to be still used in Cornwall) ; P.L. vii. 482.

MISSIVE : missile ; P.L. vi. 519.

MITER'D (i.e. mitred). Masson noted that M. allowed to the Apostle what he ridiculed in English bishops. But it was spiritual wickedness, not spiritual goodness, in high places that M. attacked. He had no

A Reader's Guide.

hatred of kings *qua* kings, but as tyrants (Blakeney, P.R. ii. 463 n.), and he had a strong friend among the Roman cardinals; Lyc. 112.

MODIN ('and her suburbs'): the original home of the Maccabees near Bethhoron; P.R. iii. 170.

MOGUL ('great'): this title, which means 'Great Mongol', came to be used of the Mongol Empire in India, established by Akbar at Agra (the court being afterwards transferred to Lahore); P.L. xi. 391.

MOLOCH: (*a*) the chief god of the Ammonites (from Malik = King): Nat. Od. 205.
 (*b*) one of the rebel angels: P.L. i. 392, 417, etc.).

MOLY: the magical herb of Homer (Od. iv. 219-29); Com. 636; cp. Lat. P.-El. i. 88.

MOMBAZA (Mombasa): Island and t. N. of Zanzibar; P.L. xi. 399.

MONTALBAN: a castle in Quercu, a subdivision of Guienne in Languedoc (France), famous in romance for the deeds of its owner, the Knight Renaud, or Rinaldo; P.L. i. 583.

MOONS, ATTENDANT: satellites (app. a reference to the discovery by Galileo of the satellites of Jupiter and Saturn); P.L. viii. 149.

MOOR ATLAS: i.e. Moorish A. (Lat. *Maurusius Atlas*), because situate in Morocco; Lat. P.-Sylv. vi. 40.

MOPSUS: s. of Apollo and Manto (d. of Tiresias), a famous seer, who out-did even Calchas in prophecy, hence described as astrologer-diviner by M., who applies the name to a friend; Lat. P.-Sylv. ix. 76.

MOREH ('PLAINE OF'): near Shechem; P.L. xii. 137; cp. 'oak of', Gen. xii. 6, R.V.

MOROCCO: see MAROCCO.

MORRICE: i.e. Morris or Moorish; hence 'morris-dance'; also called the 'Morisco'; (metaph.) Com. 116.

MORUS (Lat. Epigr. *De Moro*): attribution of this Epigram to Milton him-self seems doubtful.

MOSCO: v. KSAR.

MOTEZUME (so in 1st ed.): nearer to the native Aztec form of the name (Mo-teuczoma, Verity) than the Spanish Montezuma: the famous Emperor of Mexico conquered by Cortez; P.L. xi. 407.

MOULD: in M. means (*a*) soil; P.L. vi. 473.
 (*b*) substance or essence; Nat. Od. 138; Arc. 73; Com. 17, 244, etc.

MOUNTAIN, TH'OFFENSIVE: the S. summit of Olivet, profaned by Solomon, who built 'high places' there for the gods of his many wives; P.L. i. 443.

MOUST, sb.: must; unfermented grape-juice; P.L. v. 345; P.R. iv. 16.

MOZAMBIC (Mozambique): a Portuguese Prov. in E. Africa, opp. Mada-gascar; P.L. iv. 161.

MULCIBER: see VULCAN.

MUSÆUS: trad. a great early Gk. poet, contemporary with Orpheus; Il. Pens. 104.

MUSES, the nine: see 'NINEFOLD DEITY'.

A Reader's Guide.

MYCALE: the composer of the Life of Homer who was 'born at the foot of lofty M.' was, of course, Herodotus: but this Life is not now attributed to him; Lat. P.-Sylv. viii. 22, 23.

MYRMIDONS: an Achaean race of Phthiotis in Thessaly, of whom Achilles was King; Lat. P.- El. iv. 28 (Myrmidonum regi).

MYRRHINE: cups or vases made of *murra*, either some kind of mined stone, as in Pliny—Blakeney suggests 'fluor spar'—or glass imitations of it such as the Polychrome Roman glass of which specimens found in Britain are in the B.M. (*milleofiri* glass is also suggested; but myrrhine does not appear to be *millefiori*, and identification is still uncertain). Cp. Stuart Jones, *Compan. Rom. Hist.*, O.U.P. 1912, p. 442; P.R. iv. 119.

MYSTERIOUSLY, symbolically: 'each stair mysteriously was meant', i.e. had a mystic meaning; cp. Dante's account of the three steps in Purgatory (white, burnt (black), and 'porphyry'; Purg. c. ix. 68-92; P.L. iii. 516.

NAIADES: nymphs of rivers or springs; Com. 254; P.R. ii. 355; cp. Lat. P. Epigr. *Leonor.* iii.

NAMANCOS: a stronghold of Spain, in Galicia, near Cape Finisterre; Lyc. 162.

NAPLES: (a) called 'Chalcidic' in Lat. P. because trad. a colony from Chalcis in Euboea; Lat. P.-Sylv. ix. 182; Epigr. *Leonor.* iii.
(b) Sometimes called after Parthenope, the Siren, trad. buried there; cp. Com. 879; Lat. P.-Epigr. *Leonor.* iii.

NAPHTHA: fluid asphaltus (mineral or 'rock'-oil); P.L. i. 729.

NARCISSUS (legend of); Com. 237; Lat. P.-Sylv. iv. 61.

NASO: Ovid, q.v.

NAVIL: central point; Com. 520.

NEBAIOTH: Ishmael's first-born s., but put here for Ishmael himself; his descendants settled in Mt. Seir and Petra (the 'rose-red city') and later became allies of the Jews; P.R. ii. 309.

NECESSITY: i.e. Destiny (or Fate) personified; Arc. 69; cp. P.L. vii. 172; S.A. 1666.

NECTAR: a divine liquid of which (a) heavenly beings drink, and (b) in which they bathe. (a) See Vac. Ex. 39; P.L. iv. 240, v. 428, 633, ix. 838; (b) D.F.I. 49; Lyc. 175; Com. 838, etc.

NEGUS: the Emperor of Abyssinia; P.L. xi. 397.

NEOBOLE or NEOBULE: see LYCAMBES.

NEPENTHES: the magical, care-dispelling drink in Homer (Od. iv. 219-21, etc.); Com. 675.

NEPTUNE'S SON: Albion, or Alebion; Lat. P.-Sylv. ii. 27 (Neptunia proles).

NEPTUNE'S SONS: the people of Britain; Lat. P.-Sylv. iii. 10 (populos Neptuno satos).

NEREUS: god of the Ægæan Sea (E. Mediterranean)—the Nereids were his 50 beautiful daughters; Lat. P.-Sylv. iv. 27.

NICE: over-particular or fastidious; Com. 139.

(650)

A Reader's Guide.

NIGHTINGALE : see Com. 234 (metaph.), 566; P.L. iv. 602, 771, v. 40 (Nightingal), vii. 435; and cp. Sonn. i. with Lat. P.–El. v. 25.

NIGHT-RAVEN (νυκτικόραξ) : a raven in poetic usage only, neither ravens nor crows being night-birds. It is now identified (see Sir D'Arcy Thompson, *Gloss. of Gk. Birds*, new ed. s.v., and Liddell and Scott, 1936) as the long-eared owl; L'All. 7.

NIGHT-STEEDS : prob. the steeds of Night's car ; others say night-hags (or night-mares?); Nat. Od. 236; cp. P.L. ii. 662.

NIMROD : the 'mighty hunter' but not, as in M., the builder of Babel ; P.L. xii. 44.

NINEVEE : Nineveh, confused by M. at first with Susa, e.g. in Lat. P.–El. i. 66. See NINUS. M. takes Jonah iii. 3 to mean the compass of the city '*within her wall*', but the passage only says 'an exceedingly great city of three days' journey', probably including all her suburbs—cp. 'greater than Babylon' (Strabo) ; of 60 m. circumference (Diodorus) ; P.R. iii. 275.

NINUS : trad. founder of Nineveh, the city of Ninus (but the Assyrian name, Ninuwa, or Ninua, is more probably connected with the word for 'Fish' as it is written in cuneiform, with the 'fish' character) ; P.R. iii. 275 ; Lat. P.–El. i. 66; Sylv. v. 30.

NIPHATES : 'the Assyrian Mount' (Niphates—10,000 ft.—is explained as meaning 'Snow' mountain). Part of the Taurus range in Armenia, W. of Lake Van, on the Assyrian border; P.L. iii. 742.

NISIBIS (now *Nisibin*) : a famous t. of NE. Mesopotamia on the Tigris, flourishing down to the Parthian Period, when it was taken, lost, and retaken by Rome ; P.R. iii. 291.

NISROC : one of the chief rebel angels ; the name is taken from 2 Kings xix. 37.

NITRE : saltpetre. Hence nitrous powder : gunpowder; P.L. iv. 815, vi. 512; cp. P.L. ii. 937; Lat. P.–Sylv. ii. 120. See also Epigrams; cp. SULPHUROUS.

NOCENT : harmful ; P.L. ix. 186.

NORUMBEGA : in seventeenth-century maps a tract of S. and SE. Canada, at that time including the states of N. York and Maine; P.L. x. 696.

NOTUS : the SW. wind ; P.L. x. 702.

NOVEMBER VERSES (*In Quintum Novembris*) : In a letter of 1647 to C. Dati, M. himself apologizes to his correspondent for the harshness of his expressions about the Pope, and begs Dati to intercede with his other Italian friends on the ground that he is only asking for such licence as had always been given to Dante, Petrarch (and even to Milton himself during his Italian visit).

NYSEIAN ISLE : this island of *Nysa* (whence the name *Dionysus*) is described as 'girt by the river Triton', and was situate off the coast of Lybia, near Tunis ; in tradition, it was the Island where Amalthea's 'florid son' (Bacchus) grew up, being hidden by Hammon (or Ammon), the 'Lybian Jove', from the jealous eyes of Rhea. This account, which explains the whole passage, is from Diodorus Siculus, iii. 67; P.L. iv. 275. See also HAMMON (AMMON).

A Reader's Guide.

OB : the r. Obi in W. Siberia ; P.L. ix. 78.

OBLIGE : to make liable to penalty ; to 'render guilty'; P.L. ix. 980.

OBNOXIOUS : liable, exposed to harm or injury ; S.Ag. 106 ; P.L. ix. 170, 1094.

OBSEQUIOUS : (a) complaisant, but perhaps with root sense of following in the train, as night after day ; P.L. vi. 10 ; cp. vi. 783 ; S.Ag. 1732.

(b) compliant ; P.L. viii. 509.

OBVIOUS : lying or being in the way (as in Lat.) ; P.L. vi. 69.

OCCASION : personified ; P.R. iii. 173.

ODRYSIAN : Thracian ; Lat. P.-El. iv. 78.

ŒALIA (1st ed. reading for OECHALIA) : a t. in Thessaly ; P.L. ii. 542.

ŒDIPUS, NIGHT OF, i.e. total blindness ; Lat. P. Sylv. iv. 3.

ŒTA, Mt. (now *Katavothra*) : mountain-range in Central Greece between Ætolia and Thessaly, the t. of Trachis being situated on part of it ; P.L. ii. 545 ; cp. Lat. P.-Sylv. i. 12, viii. 66. (*Trachinia rupes.*)

OFFENSIVE MOUNTAIN : see MOUNTAIN OFFENSIVE.

OFFICIATE : to supply ; P.L. viii. 22.

OFFICIOUS : ministering, obliging ; P.L. ii. 102.

OGYGIAN : Theban. Ogygia is a poetical name for the country of Thebes. Lat. P.-El. vi. 68.

OLD MAN ELOQUENT : Isocrates (the orator), said to have expired on hearing of Philip's victory over the Athenians (338 B.C.) ; Sonn. x. (title in Camb. MSS., To Lady M. Ley) 7-8 (Daughter to that good Earl).

OLIVE, the (as a symbol of peace) : Nat. Od. 47 ; P.L. xi. 856 ; Lat. P.-El. iv. 79 ; Sylv. ii. 15.

OLIVE-GROVE of Academe : see ACADEME.

OLYMPIAS : wife of Philip II of Macedon., and m. of Alexander (traditionally by Zeus) ; P.L. ix. 509 ; Lat. P.-El. iv. 26. (Chaonis alma.) See CHAONIAN.

OMNIFIC : all-creating ; P.L. vii. 217.

OOSE : prob. the Oxfordshire Ouse, flowing ultimately into the Wash ; Vac. Ex. 92 ; Lat. P.-Sylv. ix. 175 ('Usa').

OPHION : one of the oldest of the Titans, the first, with Eurynome, to rule Olympus, before the time of Kronos (Saturn) ; P.L. x. 581.

OPHIR : one of the chief trad. sites of Mt. Ophir was the mountain near Malacca in the Malay Peninsula (anciently called the 'Golden Cherso-nese'). M. evidently had doubts, since he speaks of 'Sofala thought Ophir' (the southernmost prov. of Zanzibar). There can be little doubt, however, that Solomon's Ophir was really in Southern Arabia ; P.L. xi. 392, 400 ; P.R. iv. 74.

OPHIUCHUS (in Gk. lit. 'Serpent-holder') : a constellation next to, but quite distinct from Serpens ; P.L. ii. 708. See SERPENT.

OPHIUSA : the 'I. of Serpents' (the 'Colubraria' of the Romans) now For-mentera, one of the Balearic Isles ; P.L. x. 528.

OPPORTUNE : liable or exposed (to injury or harm) ; P.L. ix. 481.

A Reader's Guide.

OPPROBRIOUS HILL: (the Mt. of Olives, because of the temple to Moloch built there by Solomon); P.L. i. 403. Also called ' Hill of Scandal' and ' Offensive Mountain ', q.v.

OPPOSITE: two planets are said to be in opposition (or ' opposite ') when separated by 180° (or half the zodiac) a fatal omen (astrol.); P.L. vi. 314, x. 659, etc. And cp. P.L. ii. 803.

OPS: wife of Saturn; id. with Rhea or Cybele; P.L. x. 584; cp. Lat. P.–El. v. 62 (Idæam . . . Opim).

ORBICULAR: spherical; P.L. x. 381, cp. iii. 718.

ORC: a grampus or whale? P.L. xi. 835.

ORCADES: see ORKNEYS.

ORCUS: the god of the lower world = Pluto; P.L. ii. 964; cp. Lat. P.–El. vii. 83; Sylv. vi. 118, viii. 18, ix. 201.

ORE: in sense of 'gold'; Lyc. 170.

OREAD: a mountain nymph; P.L. ix. 387; cp. Lat. P.–El. v. 127.

ORGAN (M.'s favourite instrument); Nat. Od. 130; Il Pens. 161; P.L. i. 708, vii. 596, xi. 556.

ORIGINALS (adj. for sub.): originators; P.L. ii. 375.

ORIENT: in earlier sense of 'rising'; P.L. ii. 399, iv. 644, vi. 524.

ORION: the constellation; P.L. i. 305; Lat. P.–El. vii. 39; Sylv. iii. 54, vi. 39.

ORKNEYS (' Orcades '); Lat. P.–Sylv. ix. 178.

ORMUS (or HORMUZ): formerly ARMUZA, a great mart for pearls and gems (on an island near the opening of the Persian Gulf). Taken by D'Albuquerque in 1507, it flourished greatly till taken by Shah Abbas, 1662; P.L. ii. 2.

ORONTES (now Nahr' el 'Asi): the frontier stream of N. Syria, emptying itself into the Gulf of Issus; P.L. iv. 273, ix. 80.

ORPHEUS, ORPHEAN: one of M.'s favourite Bards; L'All. 145; Il Pens. of 105; Lyc. 58; P.L. iii. 17; cp. Lat. P.–El. vi. 69–70; Sylv. vi. 52–3.

ORUS (properly HORUS from Eg. Her or Hor): (a) the hawk-headed sun-god of Egypt, s. of Osiris and Isis; Nat. Od. 212.

(b) the name used by M. for one of the rebel angels; P.L. i. 478.

OSIRIS: (a) husband of Isis and f. of Horus (Orus). Trad. the earliest introducer of agriculture and viticulture into Egypt. Became chief agricultural god, and hence chief god of the Dead, Eg. mummies being moulded in his image. The Bull Apis (Eg. Hapi) was one of his manifestations, or theophanies; (Nat. Od. 213) different bull-theophanies (Apis, Mnevis, Bouchis) appearing in different Eg. cities. See also Lat. P.–Sylv. v. 31.

(b) Osiris, Isis, Orus, and their train, names used by M. for rebel angels; P.L. i. 478.

OSSA (ATHOS or PELION piled on O.); Lat. P.–Sylv. ii. 174.

OUGHLY-HEADED (' monsters '): understood to be a fanciful spelling of ugly-headed, and commonly so corrected by modern editors; is it possible that M. may have followed some variant spelling of 'ouphe' which is found in use, with oaf, auf, or alf for ' Elf ' (in which case it would signify 'oaf-headed' or 'elf-headed')? It seems best in any case to keep the spelling 'oughly' as here; Com. 695.

OUNCE, the lynx; Com. 71; P.L. iv. 344, vii. 466; cp. Lat. P.–Sylv. viii. 69.

OUSE. See OOSE.

OUTLANDISH: foreign, hence extravagant (of flatteries); P.R. iv. 125.

OUTLAST, vb. to outlive; D.F.I. 3.

OUTLIVE: to survive; Pass. 7; P.L. xi. 538.

OUTRAGEOUS: excessively violent, with unrestrained fury; P.L. ii. 485, v. 587, vii. 212, x. 232.

OVERBUILD: to build over, to span; P.L. x. 416.

OVER-EXQUISITE: over-particular, over-careful; Com. 359.

OVERPLY: to exhaust the strength by excessive effort. Sonn. to C. Skinner (Cyrack, this three) 10.

OVID (M.'s early favourite); see Lat. P.–El. i. 21, 69–70; El. vi. 19–20; Sylv. iii. 18.

OXFORD: Lat. P.–Sylv. x. 18–24, 50–60, 61–71.

OXUS: the great r. of Central Asia (now called the *Jihoun* or *Amou*), flowing into the sea of Aral. But 'Samarchand by Oxus', as M. calls it, is about 100 m. from the river; P.L. xi. 389.

PACKING: trickeries; Forc. of Consc. 14.

PAEAN: the 'Healer' (Gk. Παιάν); Lat. P.–Sylv. vii.

PALE (studious Cloysters): if 'pale' is here a noun = an 'enclosed place', like 'cloisters', it is surely redundant. And M.'s habit of placing a noun between two adjectives seems to show it should be adjectival; if so he is thinking of his beloved 'shadows', as in P.R. iv. 243, studious walks and shades; Il Pens. 156.

PALES: protecting god (or goddess?) of farms and flocks; (treated by M. as goddess); P.L. ix. 393; (uncertain which), Lat. P.–Sylv. ix. 32.

PALMER: strictly a pilgrim who brought a palm-leaf home with him; Com. 189. For palm-leaves as emblems of victory see S Ag. 1735; cp. Lat. P.–Sylv. ix. 216.

PALPABLE OBSCURE: darkness that may be felt; P.L. ii. 406; cp. P.L. xii. 188.

PAN: (a) As a type of Christ; Nat. Od. 89.
(b) For the god himself; Arc. 106; Com. 176, 268; P.L. iv. 266, 707; P.R. ii. 190; Lat. P.–El. v. 125; Sylv. ix. 52.

PANDÆMONIUM: the name of Satan's capital; P.L. i. 756, x. 424.

PANDORA: trad. the first woman, created by Hephaistos at the bidding of Zeus, to avenge the theft of fire by Prometheus; P.L. iv. 714.

PANDRASUS: an early (traditional) King of Britain, f. of Imogen (called by M. Inogenia); Lat. P.–Sylv. ix. 163.

PANEAS (Banias): the Gk. name of Dan, named from the cave of Pan at Cesarea Philippi, near the fountains of Jordan; P.L. iii. 535.

A Reader's Guide.

PANIM (P.L. i. 765), paynim (P.R. iii. 343) : Pagan.

PANOPE : a sea-nymph, one of the fifty beautiful daughters of Nereus ; Lyc. 99.

PAPHOS : in Cyprus, one of the chief shrines of Aphrodite ; Lat. P.–El. i. 84, v. 60, vii. 2 ; Sylv. vii. 92.

PAQUIN (for Pekin, now Peiping) : the recent capital of China, before the establishment of the Govt. at Nanking ; P.L. xi. 390. See also CAMBALU.

PARAGOND, p.pt. : parallelled or compared with another person or object ; P.L. x. 426.

PARALLAX : apparent displacement or change of position of an object seen from different-angled view points ; P.R. iv. 40.

PARAMOUNT, sb. : supreme chief (a law term for the head of an estate) ; P.L. ii. 508.

PARANYMPH ; 'Friend of the Bridegroom' (the Gk. word used in St. John iii. 29) ; corresponding to our own phrase 'best-man' ; S.Ag. 1020.

PARLAMENT : Sonn. x. 5 (Daughter to that good Earl) ; ('Parliament') Forc. of Consc. 15.

PARNASSUS : Lat. P.–El. iv. 30, v. 9 ; Sylv. vi. 3, 16, x. 66.

PARTHENOPE : one of the Sirens, trad. d. of Achelous, whose 'tomb' was said to have been at Naples, and after whom N. was sometimes called ; Com. 879. See also Lat. EPIGRAM to Leonora Baroni (3) *Ad Eandem.*

PARTIAL : prejudiced in their own favour ; P.L. ii. 552.

PAUSILIPUM (or PAUSILIPI) : a villa bequeathed by Vedius Pollio to Augustus, from which the famous grotto near Naples was named ; Lat. Epigr. Leonor. iii. 6.

PAYNIM : see PANIM.

PEAL : to assail, or 'din' the ears ; P.L. ii. 920 ; cp. S.Ag. 235, 906.

PECULIAR (adj. for sb.) : exclusive property ; P.L. vii. 368.

PEEL, vb. : to plunder or pillage ; P.R. iv. 136.

PECHORA : see PETSORA.

PEGASEAN (of the winged Horse of the Muses) : hence 'P. Wing' means in M. the vehicle of poetic inspiration ; P.L. vii. 4 ; Lat. P.–Sylv. x. 36.

PELIDES' GHOST (or 'Shadow') : i.e. Patroclus ('Shadow' or ghost of Achilles) ; Lat. P.–Sylv. i. 15.

PELLEAN CONQUEROUR : Alexander (named from his birthplace at Pella, Macedonia) ; P.R. ii. 196.

PELLEAS, PELLENORE : knights of Arthur's 'Round Table' ; P.R. ii. 361.

PELOPS : Il Pens. 99 ; Lat. P.–El. i. 45, 57. (For the story of 'Pelops' line' cp. Æsch. *Agamemnon, Choephori, Eumenides,* Soph. *Electra,* and Eurip. *Electra, Orestes, Iphigenia in Aulide, Iphigenia in Tauris.*)

PELORUS (now *Capo di Faro*) : the NE. cape of Sicily ; P.L. i. 232 ; Lat. P.–Sylv. iv. 56.

PENANCE : penitence ; S.Ag. 738.

PENDANT WORLD : not the Earth but the Universe ; P.L. ii. 1052.

A Reader's Guide.

PENDULOUS: suspended (of the Earth); P.L. iv. 1000; cp. Lat. P.–El. i. 76; Sylv. i. 3.

PENEIS' LAUREL: Laurel of Daphne (d. of the river god Peneus); Lat. P.–El. v. 13, vii. 33.

PENELOPE: (called Icaris = d. of Icarius in Lat. text); Lat. P.–El. iv. 56.

PENNON: a pinion or wing; P.L. ii. 933, vii. 441.

PENNS (i.e. 'pens' or feathers): see SUMM'D.

PENSIONERS: personal attendants or 'body-guard' of a king (mostly old *pensioned* soldiers), like the bodyguard of Henry VIII and that of Queen Elizabeth; Il Pens. 10.

PENTHEUS: the grandson of Cadmus, called Dircæan (i.e. Theban), after Dirce, queen of Thebes; Lat. Epigr. *Leonor.* ii. 7.

PENURIOUS: miserly, parsimonious; Com. 726.

PEOR (more fully Baal-Peor): a god held by some to be identical with Chemosh, the god of licentiousness worshipped by the Moabites; Nat. Od. 197; ('Chemos') P.L. i. 406–12.

PEREA (Peræa): the Gk. name given by the Romans to Transjordania, esp. Moab and Gilead; P.R. ii. 24.

PERIPATETICS: the School of Philosophy founded by Aristotle; P.R. iv. 279.

PERNICIOUS ('with one touch to fire'): baleful or ruinous (here perhaps with some sense of swiftness); P.L. vi. 520.

PERSEPHONE (Gk.): = the Roman PROSERPINA, q.v.

PERSEIS, PRIESTESS OF PHŒBUS: Circe (whose m. was the ocean-nymph Perse). v. CIRCE.

PERSEPOLIS: the Gk. name of the great city that succeeded Pasargadæ as the Persian capital. Later, in the Middle Ages, it was called *Istakhar*, now *Takht-i-Jamshid* (or *Chil-Minar*); i.e. Throne of Jamshid, or the Forty Pillars, no doubt from the surviving pillars of the Palace; P.R. iii. 284.

PERSIA (Achaemenian dynasty): Lat. P.–El. i. 65.

PERU, WEALTH OF: i.e. of the INCA; Lat. P.–Sylv. vi. 94; see ATABALIPA and EL DORADO.

PEST, PESTILENCE: the Plague; (metaph. of Death) P.L. ii. 735; cp. Lat. P.–El. iii. 3–15 (Cladis . . . Libitina); cp. ('pestilence') D.F.I. 68; P.L. ii. 711; P.R. iii. 412.

PETRIFIC: petrifying; P.L. x. 294.

PETSORA: PECHORA (Petzora, in M.'s *History of Mosco*); a r. flowing into a gulf of the same name on the Arctic Ocean, in the extreme NE. of Russia: P.L. x. 292.

PHAETHON: borrowing his f. Helios' chariot, he crashed earthwards, and was slain by Zeus to save earth from disaster; Lat. P.–El. v. 92; Sylv. iv. 25, vi. 98–100.

PHARAOH'S DAUGHTER: see 1 Kings iii. 1. She was the Egyptian princess (cp. Song of Sol. vii. 1) whom Solomon married; P.L. ix. 442.

PHERES' SON: i.e. Admetus; Lat. P.–Sylv. 57 (Pheretiades).

A Reader's Guide.

'PHENICIAN': the 'Phœnician' colour, i.e. purple; Lat. P.-El. v. 108. See SARRA, and TYRIAN.

PHILOSOPHER : in sense of alchemist ; P.L. iii. 601.

PHILYREIAN HERO : the Centaur Chiron, who was the s. of Kronos and Philyra. See CHIRON.

PHINEUS: the king of Thrace, old, blind, and a seer, who was tormented by the Harpies ; P.L. iii. 36; Lat. P.-Sylv. x. 35.

PHLEGETON : one of the rs. of Hades ; P.L. ii. 580 ; cp. Lat. P.-Sylv. ii. 74.

PHLEGRA (now Kassándra) : former name of the Isthmus of Pallene (the westernmost of three headlands) in Macedonia, where the ancient conflict between the giants and the gods is said to have taken place ; P.L. i. 577.

PHŒBUS' PRIESTESSES : Lat. P.-Sylv. vi. 25 (Phœbades).

PHŒNIX : (a) the beautiful solitary Arabian bird that was believed, after completing each fifth century, to immolate itself and rise from its own ashes—being, acc. to the Rabbis, the only bird that did not eat of the forbidden fruit, and therefore remained immortal ; P.L. v. 272 ; S.Ag. 1699-1707; cp. Lat. P.-Sylv. ix. 187-9.
  (b) the s. of Amyntor, who became tutor of Achilles ; Lat. P.-El. iv. 28 (Amyntorides).

PIEMONT, ON THE LATE MASSACHER IN : this massacre, by the Duke of Savoy, took place in 1655 ; Sonn. xv (Avenge O Lord).

PIERIAN SOURCE (or SPRING) : the sacred spring or abode of the Muses at the foot of Mt. Olympus in Thessaly, whose associations were later transferred to HELICON, q.v. ; Lat. P.-El. iv. 31 ; Sylv. vi. 1 ; Epigr. Leonor. ii. ; cp. Lyc. 15-16.

PIGMEAN RACE : i.e. the Pygmies or race of African Dwarfs ; P.L. i. 780.

PINACLE : (of the Temple) not what is now so called, but the crowning point of the lofty columnar 'Porch' overlooking the Tyropœon Valley, reminiscent of its Mesopotamian origin, in form between the square ramps of the Babel Tower and the minaret ; P.R. iv. 549.

PINDARUS (PINDAR) : Sonn. viii. 11 (Captain or Colonel); P.R. iv. 257 (' Dorian lyric odes '); Lat. P.-El. vi. 21-6.

PIN-FOLD : a pound, for confining or impounding ' strays ', here metaph. of the world ; Com. 7.

PIONER : pioneer ; P.L. i. 676 ; P.R. iii. 330.

PIRENE : see PYRENE.

PLANTER, THE SOVRAN : in reference to God ; P.L. iv. 691 ; cp. Ital. Sonn. ii. (*Qual in colle*) 13-14.

PLATAN : a plane-tree ; P.L. iv. 478.

PLATO : Il Pens. 89 ; P.L. iii. 472 ; P.R. iv. 245 ; cp. Lat. P.-El. vii. (Epil.) (Academia) ; Silv. v. 35, etc.

PLAUSIBLE : genuinely deserving of applause ; P.R. iii. 393.

PLEIADES : the group of stars into which the daughters of Atlas were said to have been changed (hence called the ' Atlantick Sisters ')—to be found in the constellation Taurus ; P.L. vii. 374 ; cp. P.L. x. 674.

A Reader's Guide.

PLËIONE : M. of the Pleiades by Atlas ; one of the Pleiades (Maia) becoming m. of Hermes ; **Lat. P.**–Sylv. v. 27.

PLOUGH : the constellation ; **Lat. P.**–El. v. 35 (plaustrum cœleste), the ' Wain '.

PLUTO, or Hades : god of the Infernal Regions (the name means ' wealth ') ; for his various names see L'All. 149 ; Il Pens. 107 ; P.L. x. 444 ; **Lat. P.**–El. ii. 17, iii. 16, v. 66, vi, 75 ; Sylv. ii. 7, etc., iii. 33. [Acc. to Plato, Hades was called Pluto ' for euphony '.]

PLY : (*a*) to hasten ; P.L. ii. 642, 954.
(*b*) to apply oneself ; Com. 750 ; P.L. ix. 201.

POISE : (*a*) give weight to ; P.L. ii. 905.
(*b*) balance ; Com. 410 ; P.L. v. 579.

POLITIC, POLITICIAN : intriguing ; P.R. iii. 400 ; S.Ag. 1195.

POLLUTE, p.p. : polluted ; Nat. Od. 41.

POMONA : goddess of fruit ; P.L. v. 378 ; ix. 393, 394.

POMP : a magnificent procession or train ; P.L. vii. 564.

POMPEY'S COLUMNS, or PORTICO : a fashionable resort at Rome ; **Lat. P.**–El. i. 69.

PONENT (wind) : wind of the sunset ; opp. to Levant ; P.L. x. 704.

PONTIFICAL : bridge-building, with veiled religious allusion ; P.L. x. 313.

PONTIFICE : a bridge ; P.L. x. 348.

PORT : (*a*) ' Ivorie Port ', i.e. gate ; P.L. iv. 778.
(*b*) to port arms : to carry aslope in both hands, pointing across the left shoulder (mil.) ; P.L. iv. 980 (with ported spears).

PORTUMNUS or Portunus : R. god of Harbours, who had a temple at Ostia, and was identified with Palæmon or Melicertes ; **Lat. P.**–Sylv. vii. 41.

POURLIEU (P.L. ii. 833), purlieu (P.L. iv. 404) : the precincts or outskirts of a palace, a forest, etc.

PREAMBLE : prelude ; P.L. iii. 367.

PRECINCTS : confines (of light) ; P.L. iii. 88.

PRESBYTER : see PRIEST.

PRETENDED : stretched, spread before screen-wise (as Lat.) ; P.L. x. 872.

PRETOR : a civil officer, equivalent to Mayor or Magistrate, at Rome ; P.R. iv. 63.

PREVENIENT : forestalling ; P.L. xi. 3.

PREVENT : to forestall ; Nat. Od. 24.

PRIEST : abbreviation of Presbyter (Gk. πρεσβύτερος) ; Forc. Consc. 20.

PRIME WHEEL OF CREATION : see SPHEAR.

PRINCIPALITIES : the seventh order of heavenly beings, here of the rebel angels ; P.L. vi. 447 ; x. 186.

PROCINCT : in p., i.e. in prompt readiness ; P.L. vi. 19 (cp. SUCCINCT, q.v.).

PRODIGIOUS : monstrous, unnatural ; P.L. ii. 625, xii. 683.

PROEM : preface ; P.L. ix. 549.

PROLIFIC : fertilizing, generative ; P.L. vii. 280.

A Reader's Guide.

PROMETHEUS : **Lat. P.**-Sylv. vi. 20 ; Lat. Epigr. *Bombard.* v.

PROSERPIN, PROSERPINA : P.L. iv. 269, ix. 396, etc. ; cp. **Lat. P.**-El. ii. 17 (sepulchrorum reginâ), v. 65-6 ; Sylv. i. 37, 46.

PROSPECTIVE GLASS : glass by which the future can be forecast ; Vac. Ex. 71.

PROTEUS : the infallible seer and sea-shepherd, who tended the flocks of Poseidon, i.e. the sea-calves, or seals ; **Lat. P.**-El. iii. 26 ; Sylv. ix. 99-100. See also CARPATHIAN WISARD.

PROWEST : most valiant ; P.R. iii. 342.

PSYCHE (the soul) : beloved by and wedded to Eros. (M. uses Plato's story to suggest that there is love in Heaven—i.e. spiritual love) ; Com. 1003-11 ; cp. **Lat. P.**-Sylv. ix. 191, etc.

PUNCTUAL SPOT : a spot the size of a mere point in comparison ; P.L. viii. 23.

PUNIE : (lit. later-born, Fr. *puis-né*, hence inferior) ; P.L. ii. 367.

PURCHASE : (*a*) prey or quarry (hunting term) ; P.L. x. 579 ; Com. 607. (*b*) to gain) ; P.L. x. 500.

PURFL'D : decorated with a coloured border (e.g. with blue and white, gold and pearl, etc.) ; fig. of the rainbow ; Com. 995.

PYRAMIDS : P.L. v. 755 ; On Shaks. 4.

PYRENE (M.'s spelling of Pirene) : the spring in the citadel of Corinth, said to have been caused by the stroke of Pegasus' hoof, hence sacred to the Muses ; **Lat. P.**-El. v. 10.

PYTHON : the famous serpent slain by the sun-god, whence Apollo's name of 'Pythian' ; P.L. x. 530, 531 ; **Lat. P.**-El. vii. 31 ; Sylv. vii. 25.

QUADRATE : in 'square' formation ; P.L. vi. 62.

QUADRATURE : M. describes the territory of heaven as being of four-square shape (like the Heavenly Jerusalem of Rev. xxi. 16) ; P.L. x. 351. Earlier (P.L. ii. 1048) he had declared its shape to be uncertain (undetermin'd square or round ').

QUAFF : vb. to drink in (fig.) immortality and joy ; P.L. v. 638 (added in 1674 edn.) ; cp. **Lat. P.**-Sylv. ix. 206.

QUAINT : exquisite, choice, pretty ; Lyc. 139 ; cp. Arc. 47.

QUARRY : (*a*) a squared stone block (as in Latin, cp. Pliny's *saxum quadratum*) ; hence, a stone meant to bear an inscription ; Pass. 46. (*b*) a place for quarrying stone ; P.L. v. 756.

QUARRY : object of pursuit, or chace ; P.L. x. 281.

QUATERNION : 'in quat.' i.e. in fourfold combination ; (of the elements, Air, Earth, Water, Fire) ; P.L. v. 131.

QUILL : a pipe or tube used as a musical instrument ; Lyc. 188.

QUILOA : (or *Kilwa*) Island and t. off E. Africa, a province of Zanzibar ; P.L. xi. 399.

QUINTESSENCE : a fifth 'essence' apart from (or supplementary to) the four elements (in Plato and Aristotle) ; P.L. iii. 716, vii. 244.

QUINTILIAN : M. Fabius, b. in Spain, A.D. 40, the most celebrated of Roman rhetoricians. Sonn. xi (A Book was writ), 11.

QUINTIUS : L. Qu. Cincinnatus, the Dictator ; P.R. ii. 446.

A Reader's Guide.

QUIRE : M.'s spelling of 'choir' (as in the Prayer-book rubrics—'in quires and places where they sing'); Nat. Od. 27, 115; Il Pens. 162 ; (of birds) P.L. iv. 264, etc.

RABBA : the capital of the Ammonite country ; P.L. i. 397.

RAMATH-LECHI : S.Ag. 145.

RAMIEL : ('Exaltation of God') one of the rebel angels (M.'s authority for this name is unknown) ; P.L. vi. 372.

RAMOTH (in Gilead) : P.R. i. 373.

RATHE : old positive form of 'rather' (in the sense of 'soon' or 'early') ; Lyc. 142.

REALTIE : reality ; P.L. vi. 115 (perhaps an error for 'fealtie').

REBECK (Ar. *rĕbab*) a fiddle ; it reached Spain through the Moors ; L'All. 94.

REBUFF : repulsion ; P.L. ii. 936.

RECORDER : a kind of flageolet, with a pitch an octave above the flute, and very soft in tone ; P.L. i. 551.

RECREANT : renegade, apostate ; P.R. iii. 138.

RED SEA : v. SERBONIAN BOG.

REDOUBLE : (*a*) to re-echo ; Sonn. xv (Avenge, O Lord).
(*b*) to repeat ; P.L. ix. 562.
(*c*) to make twice as great ; S.Ag. 923.

REDOUND : (*a*) to be superfluous or excessive ; P.L. v. 438 ; cp. ii. 889.
(*b*) to return or rebound upon ; P.L. iii. 85, vii. 57, x. 739.

REGORGE : to gorge to surfeit ; S.Ag. 167.

REGULUS : M. Atilius R., the heroic R., prisoner of the 1st Punic War. P.R. ii. 446.

REINS : the kidneys ; P.L. vi. 346 ; S.Ag. 609.

RELIQUE : P.L. v. 273, On Shaks., 3 ; cp. P.L. iii. 491 ; cp. Lat. P.–Sylv. ii. 110.

RELUCTANT : forcing violent way through (of flames) ; P.L. vi. 58.

REMARK, vb. : to distinguish ; S.Ag. 1309.

REMEDILES : irreparable Circ. 17 ; ('remediless') P.L. ix. 919, S.Ag. 648.

REPROBATE (Gk. ἀδόκιμος) : used especially in metallurgy of an alloy that will not endure the trial, but shows itself to be adulterate when tested. So in Jer. vi. 30 (A.V.) of 'reprobate silver') ; cp. the description *of the metal workers* in Hell ; P.L. i. 697 ; and cp. P.R. 491 ; S.Ag. 1685. Not in *Oxf. Dic.*

RESONANT : repeating or re-echoing the same notes from part to part (as in a fugue) ; P.L. xi. 559.

RESPIRATION : a refreshing ; P.L. xii. 540.

RETORTED : flung back ; P.L. v. 906, x. 751.

RHEA : (*a*) wife of Saturn, and m. of Jove ; P.L. i. 513.
(*b*) wife of the Libyan 'Jupiter Ammon' ; P.L. iv. 279.

RHENE : the Rhine ; P.L. i. 353.

RHENO : the r. which forms one of the frontiers of Romagna (twice mentioned by Dante ; Inf. xviii. 61 ; Purg. xiv. 95) ; Ital. Sonn. 1. 2.

A Reader's Guide.

RHEUM : rheumatism ; P.L. xi. 485.

RHODOPÉ, Mt. : the W. continuation of the Hæmus range, between Thrace and Macedonia and the source of the Hebrus ; P.L. vii. 35.

RHOMB : (a) an infantry formation in the shape of a diamond (or acute-angled parallelogram) ; P.R. iii. 309 (mil.).
  (b) wheel-like revolution of the heavens (from Gk. ρόμβος, wheel) ; P.L. viii. 134.

RICHBORO' : the Roman Rutupiæ in Kent ; Lat. P.-Sylv. ix. 162.

RIDGES : ranks ; P.L. vi. 236.

RIN'D : spelt by M. as if p.p. from a vb. ' rine ' = rinded (i.e. furnished with a rind or husk) ; P.L. v. 342. See also RINDE.

RIMMON : the storm god, worshipped in Damascus, whose name was taken by M. for one of his rebel angels ; P.L. i. 467.

RINDE : a thick outer coat or skin ; Com. 664, etc. ; cp. RIN'D.

RIVER-DRAGON : a crocodile, used fig. of Pharaoh ; P.L. xii. 191.

RIVERS : probably in allusion to the sons of Sir John Rivers ; Vac. Ex. 91.

ROBUSTIOUS : superlatively vigorous : S.Ag. 569.

ROMULUS : in this passage the ' s. of Mars . . . violent death '. M. seems to allude to the tradition that R. was murdered by the senators (Liv. i. 16) ; the death of Alexander (the reputed s. of Jove) of fever brought on by drink took place in 323 B.C. at Babylon ; P.R. iii. 84.

ROUND TABLE : see ARTHUR, K.

ROUS or ROUSE (JOHN) Librarian of the Bodleian at Oxford : for Lat. poem addressed to, see Sylv. x. 47, 87 (Ad Rousium).

RUBRIC, THE STARRY : fig. of the directions, or prognostications, to be read in the stars ; like the law-headings in red ochre (rubrica) of ancient Rome ; P.R. iv. 393.

' RUSTICATION ' : M.'s brief banishment from Christ's College ; Lat. P .-El. i. 11-24.

RUTHERFORD (1673 ed. ROTHERFORD): Samuel Rutherford, a prominent Divine of M.'s times, Professor of Divinity at St. Andrews and one of the eight Scottish members of the Westminster Assembly ; Forc. Consc. 8.

RUTUPIÆ, SEA OF : i.e. the sea off Richborough, Rutupiæ becoming a Roman port at time of the Roman invasion ; Lat. P.-Sylv. ix. 162.

SABEAN (i.e. SABÆAN) : of the land of Saba or Sheba in SW. Arabia ('Araby the blest ') ; P.L. iv. 162 ; cp. P.R. ii. 363.

SAFFRON : the colour of the marriage robe in ancient Rome ; L'All. 126.

SAGACIOUS : keen-scented (hunting term, used of hounds) ; P.L. x. 281.

SALEM : (a) Salim, near the springs of Ænon on the Jordan—exact position unknown ; P.R. ii. 21.
  (b) Jerusalem ; Pass. 39.

SALMANASSAR : this means—not Shalmaneser IV, as formerly stated, but Shalmaneser V, who besieged, but did not take, Samaria. The city was taken in 722 B.C. by Shar-ukin or Sargon (Is. xx), an Assyrian general,

A Reader's Guide.

who thereupon seized the throne and reigned as Sargon II (721 B.C.), and became the f. of Sennacherib ; P.R. iii. 278.

SALMASIUS : two epigrams (*a*) *In Salm. Hundredam,* (*b*) *In Salmasium.* [S. was the Leyden Professor employed by the Royalist party to reply to M.'s republican pamphlets.]

SALZILLI, G. (Salsillus) : It. poet and man of letters, friend of M. on his It. tour. He extolled M. as above Homer, Virgil, and Tasso, and M. thanked him for this extravagant praise in 'limping iambics' ('*Sca-zontes*'). See Sylv. vii. 17 (*Ad Salsillum*).

SAMARCHAND ('by Oxus') : earlier called Maracanda, a great city of what was once called Sogdiana (q.v.) ; in the thirteenth century it became the capital of Timur i Leng, commonly called Tamurlane, who was buried there. But it is at least 100 m. from the Oxus. Now in Russian Turkestan ; P.L. xi. 389.

SAMOED SHOAR : NE. of Siberia ; P.L. x. 696.

SAMOS : the Island. (Note that Samos is not one of the Cyclades, but M. may be referring to the Gk. islands generally) ; P.L. v. 265.

SAMOS' SAGE : Pythagoras ; Lat. P.-El. vi. 59.

SARMATIANS : the S. of Europe, including a number of vague nomad ethnic groups between the Vistula and the Volga, the Asiatic groups extending to the Caucasus, Astrakhan, Kazan, etc. ; P.R. iv. 78.

SARRA : one of the old names of Tyre ; hence used of the Tyrian purple dye ; P.L. xi. 243.

SAXON : (*a*) of England ; Lat. P.-Sylv. viii. 84.
 (*b*) of Germany ; El. iv. 74.

SCALES OF FATE, THE : Lat. P.-Silv. iv. 34-5 ; cp. P.L. iv. 997, 1014 (with ref. to *Libra*, the constellation ; P.L. x. 676).

SCANDAL, HILL OF : the S. crest of Olivet ; P.L. i. 416 ; see also OPPRO-BRIOUS HILL, and MOUNTAIN OFFENSIVE.

SCIPIO : see AFRICAN.

SCORPION : the constellation ; P.L. iv. 998, x. 328 ; Lat. P.-Sylv. iii. 53.

'SCOTCH WHAT D'YE CALL' : this was the Rev. Robt. Baillie, Prof. of Divinity at Glasgow, and afterwards Principal, a strong critic of M.'s 'Divorce Pamphlets' ; Forc. Consc. 12.

SCRANNEL : shrivelled and thin, harsh, rasping, 'screeching' (still used in northern Eng. dialects ; cp. scrawny, scranky, etc.) ; Lyc. 124.

SCULLES : shoals of fish ; in some southern Eng. dialects, 'shoals' of herrings are 'sculls' ; cp. also the sailor's 'Schools' of fish ; P.L. vii. 402.

SCYLLA : a beautiful maiden beloved by Glaucus ; changed by Circe (who in jealousy of her threw magic herbs into the water where she bathed) into a monster from the waist downwards, ending in the tail of a fish, encircled by barking dogs ; Com. 258, hence metaph. of Sin ; P.L. ii. 795.

SDEIND : disdained (cp. Spenser's 'Sdeigne') ; P.L. iv. 50.

SEA-IDOL : Dagon, the fish-god ('upward man and downward fish') ; P.L. i. 462 ; S.Ag. 13.

A Reader's Guide.

SEAVENTIMES-WEDDED MAID : Sara, in the Book of Tobit ; P.L. v. 223. See ASMODEUS.

SECHEM (i.e. Shechem) : a c. in central Palestine, between Ebal and Gerizim ; P.L. xii. 136.

SECULAR : age-old ; in sense of living for 'ages' (of the Phoenix) ; S.Ag. 1707.

SELEUCIA (the 'Great') : the magnificent city built by Seleucus I (Nicator, d. 280 B.C.) on the W. bank of the Tigris, 20 m. SE. of Baghdad ; he ruled it from Antioch, and it was later eclipsed by Ctesiphon, q.v. ; P.L. iv. 212 ; P.R. iii. 291.

SEMELE : d. of Cadmus, k. of Thebes, and m. of Bacchus. Beloved of Zeus, she was slain when he visited her as Thunder-god, but her child Dionysus (or Bacchus) was saved by Z. She was also called Thyónë ; P.R. ii. 187 ; cp. Lat. P.-El. v. 91, vi. 18.

SENATE : (a) of Rome ; Sonn. to Sr. H. V. the younger, 2 (Vane, young in yeares).
(b) the Seventy Elders ; P.L. xii. 225.

SENESHAL : house-steward ; P.L. ix. 38.

SENIR : properly an ancient Amorite name of Mt. Hermon, but M. app. means some south-easterly range ; P.L. xii. 146.

SENNAAR : the Plain of Shinar ; P.L. iii. 467.

SEPTENTRION (i.e. northern) constellation, the Plough ; P.R. iv. 31 ; the 7 stars near the N. Pole were called 'septentriones' ; cp. Lat. P.-Sylv. viii. 36 (septeno sulcata Trione).

SERAPIS (L. Sĕrăpis = Gk. Sĕrāpis) : the Eg. Usir-Hāpi was the Osirified or 'Underworld' form of the Bull god Hāpi, whose cult, Hellenized by Ptolemy I, spread over the Gk. world ; the most famous Serapeum (T. of Sĕrāpis) being at Alexandria, the lesser at Memphis (Wilcken, Urkunden der Ptolemäerzeit, i. 82, 85) ; P.L. i. 720.

SERBONIAN BOG (Hebr. Yam Suf) : on the coast of Lower Egypt, separated from the sea by a strip of sand (Herod. iii. 5). The idea of the loss of whole armies here is from D. Siculus (i. 30) ; Darius II (Nothus) lost part of his army there on his invasion of Egypt ; P.L. ii. 592. See BUSIRIS. (Note that the words 'Red Sea' do not occur in the Hebrew but in the Gk. LXX translation.)

SERICANA : a vaguely described country, lying WSW. of China ; P.L. iii. 438.

SERPENT : the constellation Serpens ; Lat. P.-Sylv. vi. 38. (Cowper translates Serpens by Ophiuchus, but Serpens is a distinct constellation, of eleven stars, next to it.) See OPHIUCHUS.

SERRALIONA : W. Afr. (mountainous) Colony, with 6 months' rainy season ; P.L. x. 703.

SETIA : an ancient (originally Volscian) city of Latium, which became a Roman colony, and later provided some of the best wine in Italy ; P.R. iv. 117.

SEWER : the Head-servant in charge of the Dishes at a medieval feast ; P.L. ix. 38.

SEXTILE : in astrology the influences of stars or planets were said to be benign or favourable, whenever they were 'in trine', or 'in sextile', i.e. when their rays met indirectly instead of being in direct opposition. Here 'Sextile' means at a distance of 60° (or a sixth of the zodiac) from each other; P.L. x. 659.

SHAKSPEAR : with M.'s lines On S., compare L'All. 133.

SHINAR : see SENNAAR.

SHOALE (of fish): see SCULLE.

SHROUD, sb. : shelter or concealment; Nat. Od. 218; Com. 147.

SIBMA (or Sibmah): a valley in Transjordania, once famous for its vineyards (Is. xvi. 8); P.L. i. 410.

SIBYL : see SYBIL.

SICANIAN = SICILIAN; Lat. P.-El. iv. 5 (' S. prison' = Lipara).

SICILIAN GODDESS ; Persephone ; Lat P.-El. v. 66 ; cp. P.L. iv. 269.

SIDEBOARD (STATELY) : evidently in the earlier (medieval) sense of a shelf or shelves for drinking cups at the side of the hall; a sideboard of state is a court 'cup-board', or shelves, for royal plate. Court cupboards of five shelves (built in tiers) being a privilege reserved for kings, it was thus a royal compliment to Christ ('stately', here meaning royal); P.R. ii. 350.

SIDING : defending or protecting; Com. 212.

SIDON (ACCURSED WOMAN OF) : Jezebel, the fiendish queen of Ahab ; Lat. P.-El. iv. 100.

SIGEIAN YOUTH : 'Ganymed', q.v. 'Sigeian' gets the sense of Trojan from the Sigeian promontory in the Troad; Lat. P.-El. vii. 21.

SILLY : in old sense of innocent, simple, harmless ; Nat. Od. 92.

SILO (SHILOH): t. in Ephraim where the ark was kept, down to the time of Samuel ; S.Ag. 1674.

SILOA'S BROOK : the stream that formed the Pool of Siloam ; P.L. i. 11.

SILVANUS : see SYLVAN.

SINÆAN (KINGS) : i.e. Emperors of China; P.L. xi. 390.

SIRENS : acc. to one account there were three, Parthenope, Ligea, and Leucosia, and three small rocky islets off Cape Misenum in Campania were named as their abode (Æn. v. 864) ; Com. 253, 878; Arc. 63 ; Mus. 1 ; Cp. Lat. P.-El. vi. 74. See SPHEAR.

SIROCCO (from Ar. 'Shark' or 'Sharq'): the E. or SE. wind ; P.L. x. 706.

SITTIM (i.e. *Abel-Sittim* or *Shittim*) in the plains of Moab; P.L. i. 413.

SKIE ROBES : i.e. robes dyed with the hues of the rainbow, perhaps also with some suggestion of their fitness to be worn in heaven ; Com. 83; cp. P.L. v. 285.

SKINNER : see CYRIACK.

SOCK : the light shoe worn by actors in R. Comedy ; L'All. 132.

SOCRATES : Lat. P.-El. iv. 23.

SOFALA ('thought Ophir'): properly pronounced Sofāla, the Saphara of Ptolemy, a district of Mozambique in Portuguese E. Africa ; P.L. xi. 400.

A Reader's Guide.

SOGDIANA (now roughly Turkestan and Bokhara) still called Sogd, the northernmost prov. of Parthia, between the Oxus and Jaxartes; P.R. iii. 302.

SOLSTICES: the two points in the apparent path of the sun when it is furthest (N. or S.) from the Equator; Pass. 6; P.L. x. 656.

'SONS OF GOD': in Christ's teaching confined to those who are willing to accept His Kingdom. Not so SATAN (See Blakeney); P.R. iv. 520.

SOPHI, the Bactrian: i.e. the 'Sāfi' (pron. broadly Sofi), i.e. the 'Elect' Rulers of Persia, a title used during the *Sufawi* dynasty; P.L. x. 433.

SORD: sward; P.L. xi. 433.

SOREC: thought to be Surar, in the neighbourhood of Ekron, the (Philistine) city of Delilah; S.Ag. 229.

SPAN, vb.: app. to 'space out' words in reading, giving full unforced natural stress and value to each syllable; Sonn. xiii. 2 (Harry whose tuneful).

SPECKL'D: spotted as with plague-spots; Nat. Od. 136.

SPECT: (i.e. SPECKED) marked with spots; P.L. ix. 429.

SPECULAR MOUNT: point of observation or 'Look-out' Hill; P.R. iv. 236; cp. P.L. xii. 588.

SPET, vb. tr.: to eject from the mouth; Com. 132.

SPHEAR: the older astronomers, down to Milton's time, still held the theories of Ptolemy, the geographer. The universe consisted of a succession or set of eight hollow globes or 'spheres', revolving round a common centre, and, according to M.'s understanding of Plato, bearing round with them as they revolved the heavenly bodies, affixed to their surface. This view was, however, post-Platonic. The outermost sphere, of some opaque material, was the Prime Mover or Primum Mobile, which gave motion to all the rest. Two more spheres, making ten in all, were added to this system by Alphonsus; D.F.I. 30; Lat. P.–Sylv. iv. 37, etc. It was, indeed, further imagined (by Plato) that nine 'sirens' sat, one in each of the planetary orbits, and that as they all sang together, they provided the 'harmony' or 'music' of the spheres of which so many poets have written; Arc. 64. Aristotle (De Caelo II. ix. 290) denies this, declaring that there is no such 'harmony' and that the 'sphere music' has never been heard. The Diurnal Sphere is the one to which, in later theory, the 'astronomical Universe' or system was attached, and which was believed to rotate around the earth itself once in every twenty-four hours; the ninth or 'crystalline' sphere being sometimes identified with the waters that were above the firmament; P.L. iii. 482, *et pass.*

SPIRES: P.R. iv. 54. Blakeney points out this anachronism, the 'spire' being medieval. But see PINACLE (the form out of which the spire grew).

SPRING: (e.g. of roses) a thicket; P.L. iv. 219.

SPUNGE (sponge), 'worth a spunge': i.e. worth the effort of obliteration (and no more!); P.R. iv. 329.

SQUARE: when two planets are separated by 90° (a quarter of the zodiac), they are said to be 'in square'; P.L. x. 659.

SQUINT, adj. : looking askance ; Com. 413.

STABL'D WOLVES : doubtless wolves that have been captured, and imprisoned in dens (the reason for their howling !) ; Com. 534.

STAGIRA'S SAGE : Aristotle (Stagira being his birthplace) ; Lat. P.–El. iv. 25.

STAKES (to 'fall on iron s.' : the advice is merely cautionary). It is possible M. may have been thinking of the thin wooden or iron spikes planted at the bottom of medieval pitfalls by trappers, to kill the wild beasts that fell into them. But in any case, the phrase is used figuratively of the swords ; Com. 491.

STARR'D : translated to the stars ; Il Pens. 19.

STARVE : to become numb, or die with cold ; P.L. iv. 769.

STAR-YPOINTING : pointing to the stars. On Shaks. 4. [An irregularly formed compound, the 'y' being properly the prefix of the past part.]

STATE : canopy ; hence (a) chair or throne of state, a chair with a canopy or 'dais' (in the older sense) ; P.L. x. 445 ; Arc. 81.
(b) a royal *levée* ; L'All. 60.

STATELY : adj. royal. See SIDEBOARD.

STATIST : statesman ; P.R. iv. 354.

STEAD, sb. : service, assistance ; Com. 611 ; P.R. i. 473.

STEAR (i.e. steer) : Satan 'stearing his zenith' directed the highest part of his flight towards the opening at the top of the sphere through which he had entered ; P.L. x. 328.

STEUART, ADAM : was the 'mere A.S.' of M.'s sonnet because of his pamphlets published in 1644 with those initials only : a conspicuous Presbyterian ; Forc. of Consc. 8.

STOA (from Gk. στοά a Porch) : especially the ' Painted Porch ' (or Stoa) of Athens, really a marble colonnade, famous for its wall-paintings by Polygnotus, and the School where Zeno taught his 'Stoic' philosophy ; P.R. iv. 253.

STOLE : in M. usually a veil (as in Spenser) ; Il Pens. 35.

STOOP, vb. to swoop down upon the quarry (hawking term) ; P.L. xi. 185.

STOPS : the small ventages, or windholes, in a flute by means of which the notes are produced ; Com. 345 ; P.L. xi. 557 ; Lyc. 188 ; P.L. vii. 596. [But in Com. 552 'stop' refers to the cessation of the dance.]

STORIED ; adorned with scenes from sacred story, or church history ; Il Pens. 159.

STUB : the hard root part of a small tree or shrub left standing in the ground when the ground was 'cleared' ; P.R. i. 339.

STUPENDIOUS : in M.'s time, this was the form used in the London dialect— and M. was a Londoner ! see P.L. x. 351 ; S.A. 1627.

SUBDUCT : to take away ; P.L. viii. 536.

SUBLUNAR VAULT : the open expanse of heaven below the moon ; P.L. iv. 777.

SUBMISS : i.e. submissive ; P.L. v. 359, viii. 316, ix. 377 ; P.R. i. 476.

SUBORN : to incite or tempt to evil ; P.L. ix. 361.

A Reader's Guide.

SUCCESS: the issue or 'result' of an enterprise; hence in some cases it even comes to mean ill-fortune or non-success (e.g. in P.L. ii. 9, 123, iv. 932, vi. 161; P.R. iv. 1—elsewhere in a good sense).

SUCCINCT: i.e. girt up; P.L. iii. 643.

SUCCOTH: site near Jordan, not far s. of the confluence of the Jabbok; S.Ag. 278.

SUFFUSION: see DROP SERENE.

SULPHUROUS FIRE: gunpowder; P.L. xi. 654; cp. P.L. vi. 512 (and see NITRE).

SUMMANUS: a R. god scarcely known even to the R.'s themselves. Associated with nocturnal darkness, midnight lightnings, and storm; Lat. P.-Sylv. ii. 23.

SUMLESS: incalculable; P.L. viii. 36.

SUMM'D THIR PENNS: completed the full growth of all their feathers (a hawking term); P.L. vii. 421; cp. P.R. i. 14.

SUPPLANT, vb.: to trip up by the heels, an 'athletic' term; P.L. x. 513.

SURCEASE: to come to a dead stop; P.L. vi. 258; S.Ag. 404.

SUS: (a) a prov. of Morocco (now Tunis); one of the five Barbary States in N. Africa; P.L. xi. 403.
(b) see SUSA.

SUSA (i.e. 'Shushan the Palace', of the Bks. of Esther and Daniel), capital of Susiana; winter residence and Treasury of the Old Persian Kings, situate on the Choaspes (or Eulæus), their 'only Drink'; Herod. i. 88. Founded traditionally by Tithonus, f. of Memnon, Memnon himself building the Acropolis. The site is now identified as that of the modern *Sus*; P.L. x. 308; P.R. iii. 288; Lat. P.-El. i. 66. See MEMNON.

SUSIANA: see SUSA.

SWEDE (the 'Swede'): the allusion is to Chas. X, then at war with Russia and Poland; Sonn. xviii. 8 (Cyriack, whose Grandsire).

SWILL'D: drunken; Com. 178.

SWINDGE, vb.: to lash; Nat. Od. 172.

SWINK'T, p.p.; worn out with toil; Com. 293.

SYBIL: i.e. Sibyl; Vac. Ex. 69; but cp. Lat. P.-Sylv. vi. 25 (Sibyllæ).

SYENE: Aswan or Assouan, long the southernmost outpost of the R. Empire. The midday sun at Syene being vertical, casts no shadow—Pliny (*N.H.*) says that at Meroe (S. of Syene) the sun twice a year 'casts no shadow'; P.R. iv. 70.

SYLVAN: the god Silvanus, the deity of fields and forests (and also of flocks); Il Pens. 134; (Silvan) Com. 268; P.R. ii. 191; P.L. iv. 707 (Silvanus); Lat. P.-El. v. 121 (Sylvanus).

SYMPHONIOUS: harmonious; P.L. vii. 559.

SYNOD: (a) assembly; P.L. ii. 391, vi. 150, xi. 67.
(b) conjunction of planets; P.L. x. 661.

SYRTIS: name of two gulfs on the N. African coast, called the Greater and the Lesser; now called *Cabes* and *Sidra* respectively. Notorious for their quicksands. Hence here, a quicksand; P.L. ii. 939.

A Reader's Guide.

TABLE (the Round T. of King Arthur): Lat. P.–Sylv. viii. 81-2. See ARTHUR.

TAGUS, the r.: Lat. P.–El. iii. 46. See also HESPERIA.

TÆNARIAN GOD: god of TÆNARUM, i.e. Hades from an entrance to H. said to be near Cape Tænarum in Sparta; Lat. P.–El. v. 66; Sylv. i. 5; Epigr. *Bomb.* iv.

TAMAR, the r., between Devon and Cornwall; Lat. P.–Sylv. ix. 178.

TAMMUZ: see THAMUZ.

TAPROBANE: the former name of Ceylon (to which island the Romans sent an embassy in the reign of Claudius); P.R. iv. 75.

TAPSTRY: (i.e. 'tapestried') Halls; Com. 324; cp. Lat. P.–El. vi. 39 (*suspensa tapetia circum*).

TARPEIAN ROCK: the southern summit of the Capitoline Hill (P.R. iv. 49), near which once stood the house of Ovid (hence called *Tarpeia Musa*); Lat. P.–El. i. 69. See OVID.

TARSUS (Ship of): Tarsus is here (since Aesch. and Pindar both describe Typhoeus—here called Typhon—as pent in a Cilician cave) the capital of Cilicia; it had a great harbour, only 12 m. from the city, and a great commerce; P.L. i. 200; S.Ag. 715.

TARTAR, adj. of Tartary, the chief country of Central Asia; Il Pens. 115; P.L. iii. 432, x. 431.

TARTARUS: (placed in Homer below Hades) identified by M. with Hell; P.L. ii. 858, vi. 54; Lat. P.–El. iii. 16, v. 20.

TARTESSUS: identified as Tarshish on the Atlantic coast of Spain (now *El Rocadillo*), W. of Gibraltar. See Comus 97, where M. actually printed 'Tartessus' for 'Atlantick' in his ed. of 1673. See also Lat. P.–El. iii. 33 (Tartessiaco . . . æquore). Cp. El. v. 83 (quid cum Tartesside lympha?).

TASSO, TORQUATO: befriended by Manso, Marquis of Villa; Lat. P.–Sylv. viii. 7, 50; enamoured of Leonora, Princess of Este; Lat. Epigr. Leonor. ii. 1.

TAURIC, adj.: (of Taurica, now the Crimea): e.g. Tauric Pool (L. Mæotis); the sea of Azov; P.R. iv. 79. See also MÆOTIS.

TAURIS: Tabriz, the chief t. of Azerbaijan, the N.W. prov. of Persia; P.L. x. 436.

TEAR, sb.: sometimes taken in the sense of a poetical lament or Elegy; Lyc. 14. [But the simpler sense seems more suitable here.]

TEDDED (of grass) spread out to dry after mowing; P.L. ix. 450.

TEIAN MUSE: i.e. Anacreon; Lat. P.–El. vi. 21-2.

TELAMON'S GREAT-GRANDSON: (T. being f. of Ajax). See CLINIADES, q.v.

TELASSAR (Thelassar): a district of Western Mesopotamia, where the 'sons of Eden' once dwelt; P.L. iv. 214.

TELEGONUS: in late post-Homeric tradn. the s. of Ulysses by Circe; Lat. P.–Sylv. i. 18 (Telegoni parens).

TEMESÆAN BRONZE. See CALABRIA.

A Reader's Guide.

TEMIR : i.e. Timur ('the Tartar'), commonly called Tamerlane (the *Lame* Timur): the Mongul conqueror ; P.L. xi. 389.

TEREDON (Diridotis, now *Dorah*?) : a great city in ancient Babylonia. The site is now identified as Jebel Sanam (on the Euphrates) considerably north of the present mouth of the Euphrates and the Persian Gulf; P.R. iii. 292.

TERF : turf; Lyc. 140; Com. 280 ; P.L. v. 391 ; (terfe) P.L. xi. 324.

TERNATE : Island of the Moluccas, the native region of the clove-tree ; visited by Drake, 1579 ; P.L. ii. 639.

TERRENE : ground, i.e. earth (F. *terrain*) ; P.L. vi. 78.

TETHYS: wife of Oceanus and m. of the ocean-nymphs ; Com. 870; cp. Lat. P.–El. v. 83.

TETRARCH : the R. Governor of the fourth part of a province (Gk. τετράρχης), hence a sub-governor, given as a title to the four rebel angels represented by M. as governors of the 'four Elements', Fire, Air, Flood, Earth ; P.R. iv. 201.

TETRACHORDON : lit. 'Four-stringed' (as of a musical instrument, from Gk. τετράχορδος) the title given by M. to his pamphlet on the 'Four chief places in Scripture' dealing with marriage and its dissolution ; pubd. in 1645 ; Sonn. xi. 1 (A Book was writ).

TEUMESSIAN : from a Mt. near Thebes, famous as a resort for Bacchus and his fox ; Lat. P.–El. vi. 23.

THAME (or Thames) : Vac. Ex. 100 ; cp. Lat. P.–El. i. 9 (Thamesis) ; Sylv. viii. 32, ix. 3, 177, x. 18, 35 (amne Pegaséo).

THAMUZ (THAMMUZ or TAMMUZ) : A Semitic form of the original Sumerian 'Dumuzi'. From the Babylonian Semites the legend of Tammuz passed to the Phœnicians, the Israelites, and the Greeks : the latter, however, substituted for Tammuz the name Adonis, the Babylonian Semitic goddess Ishtar (Astarte of the Phœnicians and Ashtoreth of the Israelites) being identified with Aphrodite and (by the Romans) with Venus. For Thamuz see Nat. Od. 204; elsewhere his name is used for that of one of the rebel angels ; (Thammuz) P.L. i. 446, 452. See also ADONIS.

THAMYRIS : a Thracian seer blinded for challenging the Nine Muses to surpass him in song ; P.L. iii. 35.

THAUMAS' DAUGHTER : Iris, the goddess of the Rainbow; Lat. P.–El. iii. 41.

THEBAN MONSTER : the Sphinx (of Thebes) ; P.R. iv. 572.

THEBEZ : a t. in Ephraim, app. taken by M. for Tisbeh or Thesbeh (1 Kings, xvii. 1), a village in Gilead ; (some, however, read the Jabeshite, 'of Jabesh') ; the birthplace of Elijah ; P.R. ii. 16, 313; cp. Lat. P.–El. iv. 97–100 ; Silv. iii. 49–50. [Note—M. may well have avoided the 'sh' in such names in following the Vulgate (Blakeney, note, p. 111), but Lowell's argument from P.L. vi. 340 fails since it misses the intentional harshness of that line.] See ELIAH.

THEB'S : (*a*) (for Thebes in Egypt) Ægyptian ; P.L. v. 274.
(*b*) THEBS (for Thebes in Greece) ; Il Pens. 99 ; also Theb'in in P.L. i. 578 ; Lat. P.–El. vi. 23, 68 (Teumessus . . . Ogygium).

A Reader's Guide.

THEIODAMAS : f. of HYLAS, q.v.

THEMIS : Goddess of Justice ; Sonn. xviii (Cyriack, whose Grandsire) ; Lat. P.–Sylv. iii. 40.

THERMODON : r. rising in the Amazonian Mounts. (now *Mason Dagh*) in Pontus ; Lat. P.–Sylv. ii. 105. See also AMAZONIAN.

THESSALIAN : of Thessaly as a land of Magic ; Lat. P.–El. ii. 7 (Hæmonio).

THISBITE : (Gk. Θεσβείτης) ; cp. P.R. ii. 16 ; Lat. P.–El. iv. 97–100 ; Sylv. iii. 49–50. See also THEBEZ.

THONE : k. of the c. of Thone in Egypt (Strabo) ; the incident of Polydamna, his wife, is from Homer (Od. iv. 219–29) ; Com. 675. (See Strabo, xvii. 800.)

THRASCIAS : the NNW. wind (or N. by NW. ?) : P.L. x. 700.

THRACIAN BARD : Orpheus ; P.L. vii. 34. Cp. 'Thracian lyre' (l. of Orpheus) ; Lat. P.–El. vi. 37, 38. See ORPHEUS.

THUNDERER, the : i.e. Zeus or Jove, identified by M. with Jehovah ; P.L. ii. 28, vi. 491 ; Lat. P.–Sylv. ii. 204.

THWART : thwarting, i.e. transverse or crosswise ; hence, injurious. Arc. 51.

THYESTEAN BANQUET : the feast at which Atreus served up the murdered bodies of his brother Thyestes' children—a crime against nature so revolting that M. represents the sun in the heavens as similarly shrinking backwards to avoid the sight of Eve's crime (and travelling from W. to E. for a whole day) ; P.L. x. 688.

THYONE. See SEMELE.

TIAR : tiara ; P.L. iii. 625.

TIBER : P.R. iv. 32 ; Lat. P.–Sylv. ii. 52, vii. 36–41.

TIDORE (i.e. TIDOR) : one of the islands of the Malayan Archipelago in the Moluccas close to TERNATE, q.v. ; P.L. ii. 639.

TIGRIS ; P.L. ix. 71.

TIMELY-HAPPY : successful in early life (i.e. in season) ; Sonn. vii. (How soon hath Time), 8.

TIMNA : i.e. Timnath, a Philistine c. of the N. frontier of Judah ; S.Ag. 219, 383, 795 ; cp. 1018.

TINCTURE : absorption (e.g. of the sun's rays) ; P.L. viii. 367.

TINE (whence ' tinder ') : to kindle ; P.L. x. 1075.

TINE : the river Tyne ; Vac. Ex. 98.

TINSEL : an exceedingly fine gauze tissue interwoven with gold or silver threads ; P.L. ix. 36 ; cp. Com. 877.

TIPHŒUS : see TYPHON, TYPHŒUS.

TIRESIAS : the blind soothsayer of Thebes ; P.L. iii. 36 ; Lat. P.–El. vi. 67–8 ; Sylv. v. 25–6 (called Dircean in the Lat. from Dirce, queen of Thebes).

TISHBITE : see THISBITE.

TISSUE : an exceedingly fine cloth enwrought with gold or silver ; P.L. v. 592 ; cp. Nat. Od. 146.

(670)

A Reader's Guide.

TITAN : the eldest of the Titans, Oceanus; here identified with one of the rebel angels; P.L. i. 510.

TITHONUS : beloved by Aurora, the Dawn-goddess, he became immortal, but not unageing ; Lat. P.-El. v. 49-50 ; Sylv. ii. 133 (Tithonia . . . arva ; fields of Tithonus, i.e. the lands of the Eastern sun) : cp. Titho-nian, the, i.e. Aurora ; Lat. P.-Sylv. ii. 133.

TITYRUS : Spenser's and M.'s name for Chaucer ; see Lat. P.-Sylv. viii. 34.

TOBIAS : son of Tobit ; P.L. v. 222.

TOBIT : see ASMODEUS.

TOMIS (or TOMI, now *Tomisvar*) : the place on the Black Sea coast to which Ovid was banished ; Lat. P.-El. i. 22, vi. 19-20 (Corallæis . . . agris).

TOPHET : a site in the Valley of Hinnom, defiled by Moloch-worship, hence abominable ; P.L. i. 404. Also called Gehenna ; P.L. i. 405.

TORQUATO : see TASSO.

TOUR (i.e. 'tower') : a mounting or 'soaring' flight; (hawking term) P.L. xi. 185; cp. ii. 635.

TOWR'D : furnished with towers, turreted (of the headdress of Cybele, etc.) ; Arc. 21 ; cp. Lat. P.-El. i. 65.

TRACHINIAN cliff : named from Trachis of the Malis district in Thessaly, at one time the abode of Hercules ; Lat. P.-Sylv. viii. 66. See OETA.

TRAGEDY (personified) : Il Pens. 97 ; Lat. P.-El. i. 37-40.

TRAINS, sb. : tricks or wiles ; Com. 151 ; S.Ag. 533, 932 (traines) ; P.L. xi. 620.

TRANSVERSE : = THWART, q.v.

TREANTA : see TRENT.

TREBISOND : a great port of the R. Empire on the coast of Pontus, formerly called Trapezus. Surrendered to Muhammad II in 1460, it has ever been since a Turkish town. Once very celebrated in medieval romances ; P.L. 584.

TREMISEN : t. and province, one of the five N. African ('Barbary') states ; corresponding to Algiers ; P.L. xi. 404.

TRENT, THE COUNCIL OF : 1545-63, where the R. Catholic members controlled the assembly ; Forc. of Consc. 14.

TRENT, the r. : Vac. Ex. 93 ; Lat. P.-Sylv. ix. 176.

TREPIDATION : the theory of the oscillations of the 'Starry Sphere' under the Ptolemaic system ; P.L. iii. 483. See SPHEAR.

TRINACRIAN : Sicilian (from Trinacria, an old name of Sicily) ; P.L. ii. 661 ; cp. Lat. P.-Sylv. ii. 36 (Trinacriâ . . . Ætnâ).

TRINE, in : the aspect of two planets, 120° (or one-third of the Zodiac) apart and therefore a 'benign' aspect) ; P.L. x. 659. See SEXTILE.

TRIPLE TYRANT : an allusion to the Triple Crown of the Papacy ; Sonn. xv. 12 (Avenge O Lord) ; Lat. P.-Sylv. ii. 55. (Tricoronifer.)

TRIPLE GODDESS : HECATE, q.v.

TRIPTOLEMUS : s. of Celeus and Metanira, he became a favourite of Demeter, who gave him a chariot with winged dragons and the seeds of wheat.

A Reader's Guide.

In this chariot he rode over earth from Eleusis, introducing the cultivation of wheat; Lat P.-El. iv. 11-12.

TRITON, the River: see NYSEIAN ISLE.

TRIUMPHALS: trophies; P.R. iv. 578.

TROPIC: (*a*) the tropic Crab, i.e. the tropic of Cancer; P.L. x. 675.
(*b*) either tropic: the arctic and antarctic (i.e. Northern and Southern) regions of the sky; P.R. iv. 409.

TROULE, vb. tr.: to 'roll' the tongue, i.e. to speak glibly; P.L. xi. 616.

TROY: in M.'s proposed 'Epic of Britain', Troy, as the mother city of the Britons (descendants of the Trojan Brutus), was to have taken a great place. Hence the many refs. See Il Pens. 100; P.L. ix. 16; Lines from the *Hist. of Brit.* 12; and Lat. P.-El. i. 45, 68, 73, 83, ii. 13-16, ('Sigeius') vii. 21; Sylv. i. 14, etc., ii .2 (Teucrigenas), 30, ix. 162 (for the drama of 'Troy divine', (see PELOPS).

TRUMP ('Cremona's'): the *Christiad*, a poem on Christ by M. G. Vida, a poet of Cremona; Pass. 26.

TRUMPETER (or HERALD) OF THE SEA: i.e. Triton; Lyc. 89; cp. Com. 873; Lat. P.-Sylv. iv. 58. (M.'s usual spelling is 'Harald').

TUB ('the Cynick'): i.e. the tub in which the cynic Diogenes is said to have lived; Com. 708.

TUBE (glaz'd optic): a telescope; P.L. iii. 590.

TURBANT: turban; P.R. iv. 76.

TURCHESTAN: Turkestan; P.L. xi. 396.

TURKIS: turquoise; Com. 894.

TURME: a Roman military expression for a troop of horse, upwards of thirty in number; P.R. iv. 66.

TURNEY: tournament; Il Pens. 118.

TURNUS: K. of Rutulians, who fought against Æneas, because K. Latinus, f. of Lavinia, to whom Turnus was first betrothed, bestowed her upon Æneas instead; P.L. ix. 17.

TUSCAN ARTIST: see Galileo.

TWEED: (the r.) Vac. Ex. 92.

TWIN-BORN PROGENY (Latona's): i.e. Apollo and Artemis, Sonn. xii (I did but prompt).

TWINS, THE SPARTAN: the constellation named after Castor and Pollux, sons of Tyndareus, k. of Sparta; P.L. x. 674.

TWO-HANDED ENGIN: see ENGIN.

TYNE. See TINE.

TYPHON. TYPHŒUS: comparison of the Eng. with the Latin poems shows that M. did distinguish between them just as Hesiod does. Typhœus, a hundred-headed giant, who lived in a cave in Cilicia, was slain by Zeus with a thunderbolt, and buried under Mt. Etna; Typhaon, a fearful monster, was his son. But Typhaon, or rather Typhon, was later identified, as by M., with Set, the Eg. god of evil. For Typhon see Nat. Od. 226; P.L. i. 199; Lat. P.-Sylv. ii. 37 (Tiphœus); cp. P.L. ii. 539.

TYRIAN: Phœnician (esp. of purple dyes); Nat. Od. 204. See also Sarra.

TYRIAN CYNOSURE : see ARCADY, STAR OF.

TYRRHENE SHORE : i.e. the coast of the Tyrrhene (Etruscan) Sea ; Com. 49 ; Lat. P.-Sylv. ii. 108.

ULISSES : Vac. Ex. 50 ; Com. 637 (Ulysses) ; P.L. ii. 1019 ; Lat. P.-El. iv. 56, vi. 72-6 (Dulichium . . . virum).

UMBRAGE : shade or foliage ; P.L. ix. 1087 ; cp. P.L. iv. 257 ; Lat. P.-Sylv. ix. 216 (*umbracula palmæ*).

UNARGU'D : unquestioningly ; P.L. iv. 636.

UNCESSANT : The MS. reading is incessant, but uncessant was printed both in the 1645 and 1673 edns., and is therefore kept here ; Lyc. 64.

UNCIRCUMSCRIB'D : unrestricted ; P.L. vii. 170.

UNCOLOURD skie : of the dull leaden uniform morning heavens, not yet diversified with the many-hued clouds of sunrise ; P.L. v. 189.

UNCOMPOUNDED : elemental ; P.L. i. 425.

UNCONFORM : dissimilar ; P.L. v. 259.

UNCREATE, vb. : to reverse the act of creation, hence to annihilate ; P.L. v. 892 ; ix. 943.

UNCTION : anointing with consecrated oil ; P.L. vi. 709.

UNCTUOUS : oily ; P.L. ix. 635.

UNESSENTIAL : lacking real essence ; P.L. ii. 439.

UNEXEMPT : admitting no exception ; Com. 685.

UNEXPRESSIVE : unutterable ; Lyc. 176.

UNFOUNDED : bottomless, foundationless ; P.L. ii. 829.

UNFUM'D : undistill'd ; P.L. v. 349.

UNHARBOUR'D : shelterless ; Com. 423.

UNHIDE-BOUND : 'undistended' (not enlarged, as is usual after food)—Death being gaunt with famine ; P.L. x. 601.

UNISON : sung by a single voice, a solo ; P.L. vii. 599.

UNIVERSE, MANS LESS : because man himself is a microcosm ; P.R. iv. 459.

UNJOINTED : disconnected ; S.Ag. 177.

UNLAID : unexorcised ; Com. 434.

UNLIGHTSOM : devoid of light ; P.L. vii. 355.

UNMINDED : unnoticed ; P.L. x. 352.

UNOBNOXIOUS : unliable or unexposed (to) ; P.L. vi. 404.

UNORIGINAL (used of Night) : without origin or beginning ; hence existent from the first ; P.L. x. 477.

UNPREDICT : to revoke (or reverse) a prediction ; P.R. iii. 395.

UNPRINCIPL'D : ungrounded in principles ; Com. 367.

UNREPROV'D : without fear of blame, blameless ; P.L. iv. 493 ; cp. unreproved pleasures ; L'All. 40.

UNSHOWR'D (grass) : unwatered (because of the absence of rain in Egypt) ; Nat. Od. 215.

A Reader's Guide.

UNSPHEAR : Il Pens. 88. See INSPHEAR.

UNSUCCEEDED : without successor ; P.L. v. 818.

UNVALU'D : inestimable. On Shaks., 11.

UNWEETING : i.e. unwitting ; D.F.I. 28 *et pass.*

UPIS : see DELOS.

UP-LIFT : p.pt., P.L. i. 193 ; (elsewhere uplifted).

UR ('of the Chaldees') : formerly considered to be Urfa on the Upper Euphrates (about 400 miles from its true position) ; now proved by excavation to have been one of the earliest great capital Sumerian cities in Southern Babylonia (the scene of the epoch-making discoveries of Sir L. Woolley) ; when built, it stood on the Euphrates, but is now a few miles off in the desert ; P.L. xii. 130.

URANIA : not the ancient Gk. muse of Astronomy, but of divine inspiration ; the heavenly Muse ; P.L. i. 6-16, vii. 1-31.

URCHIN : adj. elvish, mischievous ; Com 845.

URIEL : the archangel (as Regent of the Sun ; P.L. iii. 690, ix. 60) ; see P.L. iii. 648.

USA : see OUSE.

UTENSILS : (implements of war) ; P.R. iii. 335.

UTHER (Pendragon) : see ARTHUR, and see also TROY.

UZZEAN JOB : Job of the land of Uz ; the latter was probably part of the wide tract of open country extending eastward between Jordan and the Arabian desert – Blakeney ; P.R. i. 369.

UZZIEL : ' Strength of God ' one of the cherubim named by M. ; P.L. iv. 782. See CHERUBIM.

VAGARIES : wild or extravagant actions or attitudes ; P.L. vi. 614.

VALDARNO (i.e. Val d'Arno) : the valley of the Arno near Florence ; P.L. i. 290.

VALLOMBROSA (the Leafy Vale) : sit. about 18 m. E. of Florence ; visited by M., who is said to have played the organ at the monastery ; P.L. i. 303.

VANE, Sir H. (the 'younger') : b. 1612, he became Governor of Massachusetts in 1636–7, and Treasurer of the Navy under Charles I. Later he became one of the leaders of the Independents and Republicans (M.'s party), who were implacably opposed to King Charles, and one of the prominent members of the Long Parlt. He was executed at the Restoration in 1662 ; Sonn. to Sr. H. V. (Vane, young in yeares).

VANNES : wings ; P.L. ii. 927 ; (vans) P.R. iv. 583.

VANT-BRASS (i.e. ' Vambrace ') : armour for the fore-arm ; S.Ag. 1121.

VARIOUS-MEASUR'D : with a variety of metres ; P.R. iv. 256.

VARNISH : ' make-up ' ; P.R. iv. 344 ; cp. P.L. ii. 485 ; S.Ag. 901.

VENUS : L'All. 14 ; Com. 124 ; P.R. ii. 214 ; Lat. P.-El. i. 82, v. 103-4, 112, vi. 51, vii. 1-2, 48, 63 ; Epil. 10 ; Sylv. iv. 63.

VERDIT : verdict ; S.Ag 324, 1228.

VERGIVIAN : i.e. Irish ; either ' from " Mor-weridh ", for this name the Britons gave it, or else from " Farigi ", by which name the Irishmen

A Reader's Guide.

call it '—Camden's *Ireland* (1637), p. 61. Drayton also uses the name several times in his *Polyolbion* — Lat. P.-El. i. 4.

VERMEIL-TINCTURED : vermilion-tinted ; Com. 752.

VERNANT : i.e. verdant, vernal; P.L. x. 679 ; cp. Lat. P.-El. iii. 45 (vernantes . . . campos).

VERTUMNUS : lover of Pomona, and god of the Change of Seasons and of the Development of flower and fruit ; P.L. ix. 395.

VERULAMIUM : see CASSIBELAUNUS.

VESTA, the R. Hearth-Goddess: M. makes her m. of Melancholy by Saturn ; Il Pens. 23 ; Lat. P.-El. v. 102.

VICE-CHANCELLOR : the 'Medical' V.C., Dr. J. Gostlin, Master of Caius, Memorial verses on ; see Sylv. i (*In ob. Procan. medici*).

VILLATIC : 'Farmyard' (used of fowl, Pliny, N. Hist. xxiii. 17); S.Ag. 1695).

VINTAGE TIME : P.R. iv. 15.

VIOL : a six-stringed somewhat large instrument of the violin type played with a bow. Now disused ; the name survives as a general term in phrases such as tenor-viol, bass-viol, etc. ; Pass. 28.

VIRGIL : see Mincius, Lyc. 86, and cp. Lat. P.-(Maro) El. i. 24.

VIRGIN, THAT JUST : see ASTRAEA.

VISCOUNT SAVAGE: March. Winch. 3.

VISOR'D (FALSHOOD) : masked deceit ; Com. 698.

VOLANT (lit. 'flying') : of light, quick, nimble touch ; P.L. xi. 557.

VOLATIL : winged, hence passing off or evaporating into air, used of Hermes or Mercury, with play on the word, Hermes being the winged God ; P.L. iii. 603.

VOLUBIL : rolling, revolving ; P.L. iv. 594.

VOLUMINOUS, THE STARS : i.e. reading of the stars, by volumes or single characters ; P.R. iv. 384 ; Starry rubric, ib. 393.

VOTARIST : votary ; Com. 189.

VOUTSAFE : M.'s spelling of vouchsafe (prob. to avoid the awkward sound 'chs'; but still said to be sometimes pronounced as M. spelt it) ; P.L. xi. 170, *et pass.*

VULCAN (or MULCIBER) : Com. 655 ; P.L. i. 740 ; Lat. P.-(proles Junonia) El. vii. 81, 82 ; Sylv. iv. 23-4, vii. 2.

WANDERING STARS : i.e. the Planets ; Lat. P.-Sylv. iii. 59 (erraticorum syderum . . . ordines).

WARDROP (i.e. wardrobe) : fig. of the 'attire' of flowers ; Lyc. 47 ; cp. WARDROPE, fig. of the 'trimings' of words and phrases ; Vac. Ex. 18.

WARRANTED : safeguarded ; Com. 327.

WAY (STREAMING) : see GALAXIE.

WEDGE (mil.) : a troop-formation of infantry in the shape of half a rhomb (q.v.) hence an acute-angled triangle, with the angle in front ; cp. P.R. iii. 309.

A Reader's Guide.

WHILEARE: a little while since; Circ. 10.

WHILOME: once on a time, formerly; D.F.I. 24.

WHIST: hushed; Nat. Od. 64.

WHITE THORN: the hawthorn; Lyc. 48.

WICKET: a small side-gate; P.L. iii. 484.

WIDE-ENCROACHING: i.e. trespassing, used of Eve—probably to 'set off' the description of Eurynome ('wide-governing'); P.L. x. 581.

WINCHESTER: (a) Bp. of: Lat. P.-El. iii. 53.
(b) Marquis of: i.e. J. Paulet, fifth Marquis; March. Win. 2.

WINDS, CAVE OF THE: see HIPPOTADES.

WINE-PRESS: P.R. iv. 16.

WINNOW: to beat the air with wings; P.L. v. 270.

WINTONIAN PRELATE: the Bp. of Winchester; Lat. P.-El. iii. 53 (præsul Wintonius).

WISARD (used of the Dee): because it was thought to foretell the future by its encroachments now on English, now on Welsh territory; Lyc. 55.

WISARD, a 'Wise Man': (a) of the Magi (Star-led Wisards) Nat. Od. 23).
(b) of Proteus; Com. 872.
(c) the chief magician in Comus; Com. 571.

WITCHES (of Lapland); P.L. ii. 655.

WOLF ('unless some w. prevent my sight'): the R. believed that if a wolf, on meeting a man, saw him first, the man would be stricken dumb; Lat. P.-Sylv. ix. 27.

WOLVES (used of false clergy); Lyc. 128; P.L. xii. 508; Sonn. to Cromwell, 14 (Cromwell our cheif); Lat. P.-Sylv. ix. 41.

WONNS, vb.: i.e. dwells; P.L. vii. 457.

WOODS (the 'Arabian woods'): strictly, there was but a solitary tree wherein the Phœnix nested; S.Ag. 1700.

WORSTER (battle of) in 1651 (Worsters laureat wreath); Sonn. to Cromwell 9 (Cromwell our cheif).

WORM: the Serpent; P.L. ix. 1068.

WRENCH, vb.: to pervert, or wrest (the law); Sonn. xviii. 4 (Cyriack whose Grandsire).

XERXES: k. of Persia (scourges the Hellespont); P.L. x. 311.

YOUNG, THOS.: Lat. poem addressed to; see Lat. P.-El. iv.

YOUNGEST TEEMED STAR: latest-appearing (of the Star of Bethlehem); Nat. Od. 240.

ZEPHON (lit. 'Searcher'); name of one of the cherubim; P.L. iv. 781, etc.

ZOPHIEL (lit. 'Spy' or 'Scout' of God): a cherub; P.L. vi. 535.

ZORA: a town situated a little s. of ESHTAOL, q.v.

INDEX OF FIRST LINES.

A Book was writ of late call'd *Tetrachordon*, 82.
Adhuc madentes rore squalebant genæ, 150.
A little onward lend thy guiding hand, 509.
All night the dreadless Angel unpursu'd, 295.
Altera Torquatum cepit Leonora Poëtam, 141.
Ἀμαθεῖ γεγράφθαι χειρὶ τήνδε μὲν εἰκόνα, 158.
Among the holy Mountains high, 108.
Angelus unicuique suus (sic credite gentes), 140.
Answer me when I call, 91.
As one who in his journey bates at Noone, 432.
Avenge O Lord thy slaughter'd Saints, whose bones, 84.

Back Shepherds, back, anough your play, 73.
Because you have thrown of your Prelate Lord, 86.
Before the starry threshold of *Joves* Court, 49.
Be not thou silent now at length, 101.
Bless'd is the man who hath not walk'd astray, 89.
Blest pair of *Sirens*, pledges of Heav'ns joy, 15.

Captain or Colonel, or Knight in Arms, 32.
Cede Meles, cedat depressa Mincius urna, 117.
Credula quid liquidam Sirena Neapoli jactas, 141.
Cromwell, our cheif of men, who through a cloud, 88.
Cum simul in regem nuper satrapasque Britannos, 139.
Curre per immensum subitò mea littera pontum, 127.
Cyriack, this three years day these eys, though clear, 89.
Cyriack, whose Grandsire on the Royal Bench, 85.

Daughter to that good Earl, once President, 32.
Descend from Heav'n *Urania*, by that name, 318.
Dicite sacrorum præsides nemorum deæ, 153.
Diodati, e te'l dirò con maraviglia, 30.
Donna leggiadra il cui bel nome honora, 29.

Ere-while of Musick, and Ethereal mirth, 12.
Ergimi all' Etra ò Clio, 118.

Fairfax, whose name in armes through Europe rings, 87.
Fly envious *Time*, till thou run out thy race, 14.

Gaudete scombri, et quicquid est piscium salo, 142.
Gemelle cultu simplici gaudens liber, 169.
Giovane piano, e semplicetto amante, 31.
God in the great assembly stands, 101.
Græcia Mæonidem, jactet sibi Roma Maronem, 118.

Hail holy light, ofspring of Heav'n first-born, 227.
Hail native Language, that by sinews weak, 79.

Index of First Lines.

Hæc quoque Manse tuæ meditantur carmina laudi, 160.
Harry whose tuneful and well measur'd Song, 83.
Hence loathed Melancholy, 20.
Hence vain deluding joyes, 24.
Here lies old *Hobson,* Death hath broke his girt, 19.
Here lieth one who did most truly prove, 19.
Heu quàm perpetuis erroribus acta fatiscit, 151.
High on a Throne of Royal State, which far, 201.
Himerides nymphæ (nam vos & Daphnin & Hylan, 163.
How lovely are thy dwellings fair, 103.
How soon hath Time the suttle theef of youth, 31.

I did but prompt the age to quit their cloggs, 83.
In se perpetuo Tempus revolubile gyro, 130.
Ἰσραὴλ ὅτε παῖδες, ὅτ' ἀγλαὰ φῦλ' Ἰακώβου, 157.
It was the Winter wilde, 2.
I who e're while the happy Garden sung, 451.

Jam pius extremâ veniens Jäcobus ab arcto, 144.
Japetionidem laudavit cæca vetustas, 140.
Jehovah to my words give ear, 92.

Lady that in the prime of earliest youth, 32.
Lawrence of vertuous Father vertuous Son, 85.
Let us with a gladsom mind, 9
Look Nymphs, and Shepherds look, 33.
Lord God that dost me save and keep, 108.
Lord how many are my foes, 90.
Lord in thine anger do not reprehend me, 93.
Lord my God to thee I flie, 94.

Mean while the new-baptiz'd, who yet remain'd, 464.
Meanwhile the hainous and despightfull act, 382.
Methought I saw my late espoused Saint, 86.
Mitto tibi sanam non pleno ventre salutem, 134.
Mæstus eram, & tacitus nullo comitante sedebam, 125.

No more of talk where God or Angel Guest, 351.
Nondum blanda tuas leges Amathusia noram, 136.
Now morn her rosie steps in th' Eastern Clime, 272.
Now the bright morning Star, Dayes harbinger, 18.
Nunc mea Pierios cupiam per pectora fontes, 154.
Nymphs and Shepherds dance no more, 36.

Ὦ ἄνα εἰ ὀλέσῃς με τὸν ἔννομον, οὐδέ τιν' ἀνδρῶν, 158.
O fairest flower no sooner blown but blasted, 76.
Of Mans First Disobedience, and the Fruit, 181.
O for that warning voice, which he who saw, 247.
O Jehovah our Lord how wondrous great, 96.
O Musa gressum quæ volens trahis claudum, 158.
O Nightingale, that on yon bloomy Spray, 28.
O're the smooth enameld green, 35.

(678)

Index of First Lines.

Parere fati discite legibus, 143.
Per certo i bei vostr' occhi, Donna mia, 30.
Perplex'd and troubl'd at his bad success, 487.
Purgatorem animæ derisit Jäcobus ignem, 140.

Qual in colle aspro, al imbrunir di sera, 29.
Quem modò Roma suis devoverat impia diris, 140.
Qui legis Amissam Paradisum, grandia magni, 177.
Quis expedivit Salmasio suam Hundredam, 142.

Ridonsi donne e giovani amorosi, 30.
Rusticus ex Malo sapidissima poma quotannis, 142.

Sabrina fair, 70.
Siccine tentasti cælo donâsse Jäcobum, 139.
So spake the Son of God, and Satan stood, 476.
Sweet Echo, sweetest Nymph that liv'st unseen, 55.

Tandem, chare, tuæ mihi pervenere tabellæ, 122.
Te, qui conspicuus baculo fulgente solebas, 124.
The Angel ended, and in *Adams* Eare, 334.
The Star that bids the Shepherd fold, 51.
This is the Month and this the happy morn, 1
This rich Marble doth enterr, 16.
Thou Shepherd that dost Israel keep, 97.
Thus they in lowliest plight repentant stood, 409.
Thy gracious ear, O Lord, encline, 106.
Thy Land to favour graciously, 104.
To God our strength sing loud, and clear, 99.

Ut mens, forma, decor, facies, mos, si pietas sic, 117.

Vane, young in yeares, but in sage counsell old, 88.

What needs my *Shakspear* for his honour'd Bones, 18.
What slender Youth bedew'd with liquid odours, 82.
When Faith and Love which parted from thee never, 84.
When I beheld the Poet blind, yet bold, 178.
When I consider how my light is spent, 85.
When the blest seed of *Terah's* faithfull Son, 9.
Why do the Gentiles tumult, and the Nations, 90.

Ye flaming Powers, and winged Warriours bright, 14.
Yet once more, O ye Laurels, and once more, 38.

PRINTED IN
GREAT BRITAIN
AT THE
UNIVERSITY PRESS
OXFORD
BY
JOHN JOHNSON
PRINTER
TO THE
UNIVERSITY